H A

CANCÚN & COZUMEL

Gary Chandler & Liza Prado with Beth Kohn

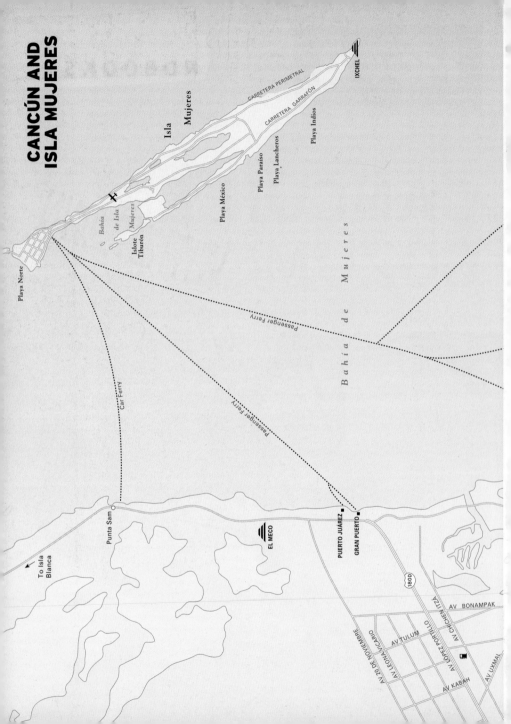

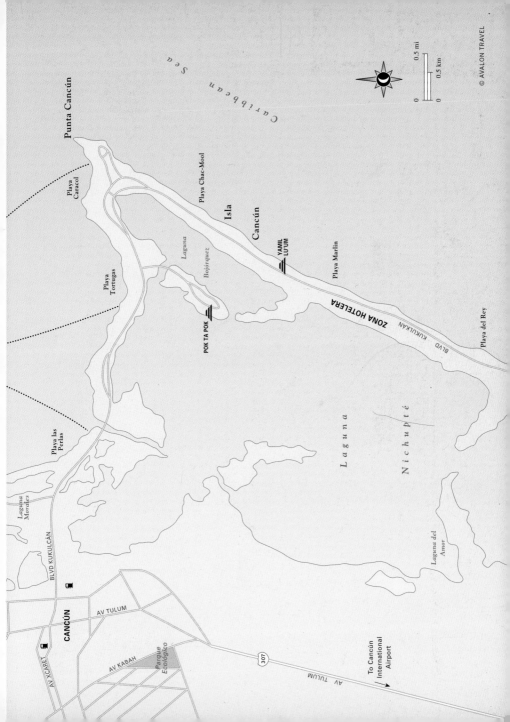

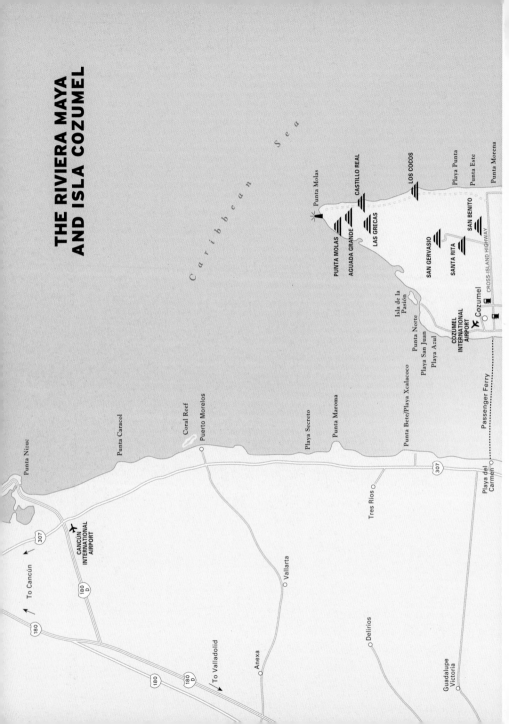

THE RIVIERA MAYA
AND ISLA COZUMEL

Caribbean Sea

Punta Molas
PUNTA MOLAS
AGUADA GRANDE
CASTILLO REAL
LAS GRECAS
LOS COCOS
Playa Punta
Punta Este
Punta Morena
SAN GERVASIO
SANTA RITA
SAN BENITO
CROSS-ISLAND HIGHWAY
Isla de la Pasión
Punta Norte
Playa San Juan
Playa Azul
Cozumel
COZUMEL INTERNATIONAL AIRPORT
Passenger Ferry

Punta Nizuc
To Cancún
CANCÚN INTERNATIONAL AIRPORT
307
Punta Caracol
Coral Reef
Puerto Morelos
Playa Secreto
Punta Maroma
Punta Bete/Playa Xcalacoco
307
Playa del Carmen
Tres Ríos
Vallarta
Delirios
Anexa
To Valladolid
Guadalupe Victoria
180
180 D
180
180 D
180 D

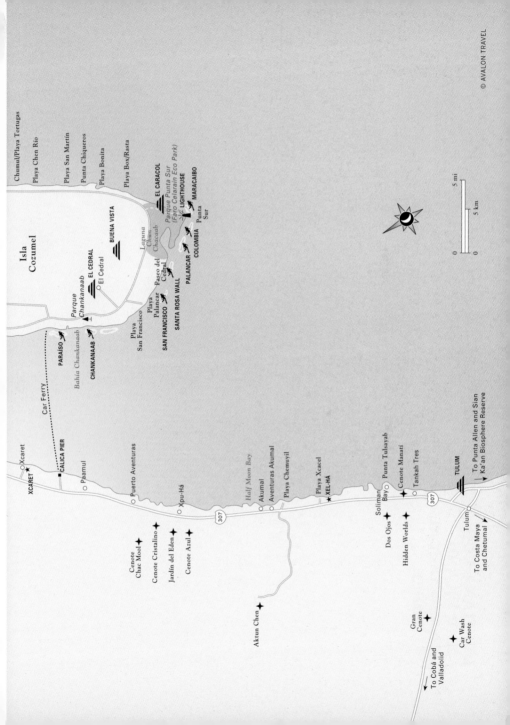

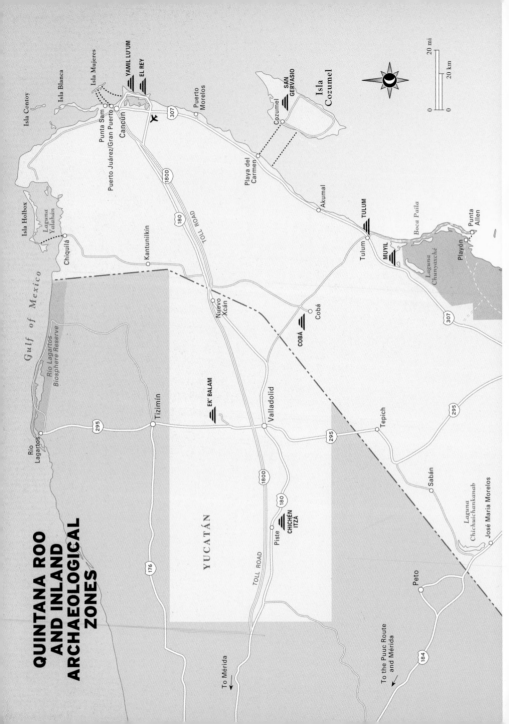

QUINTANA ROO AND INLAND ARCHAEOLOGICAL ZONES

Gulf of Mexico

YUCATÁN

Isla Contoy
Isla Blanca
Isla Mujeres
Isla Holbox

Punta Sam
YAMIL LU'UM
EL REY
Puerto Juárez/Gran Puerto
Cancún
Puerto Morelos
307

Laguna Yalahau
Chiquilá
Kantunilkin

SAN GERVASIO
Cozumel
Isla Cozumel

Playa del Carmen
Akumal

180D
180
TOLL ROAD

TULUM
Tulum
MUYIL
Boca Paila
Punta Allen
Playón
Laguna Chunyaxché

Nuevo Xcán
Cobá
COBÁ

Río Lagartos
Biosphere Reserve

295
Tizimín

EK' BALAM

Valladolid
295
Tepich

295
Sabán

Laguna Chichankanab
José María Morelos

Río Lagartos
176

180D
TOLL ROAD
Piste
CHICHÉN ITZÁ
180

Laguna Chichancanab
Peto

To Mérida

To the Puuc Route and Mérida
184

20 mi
20 km

307

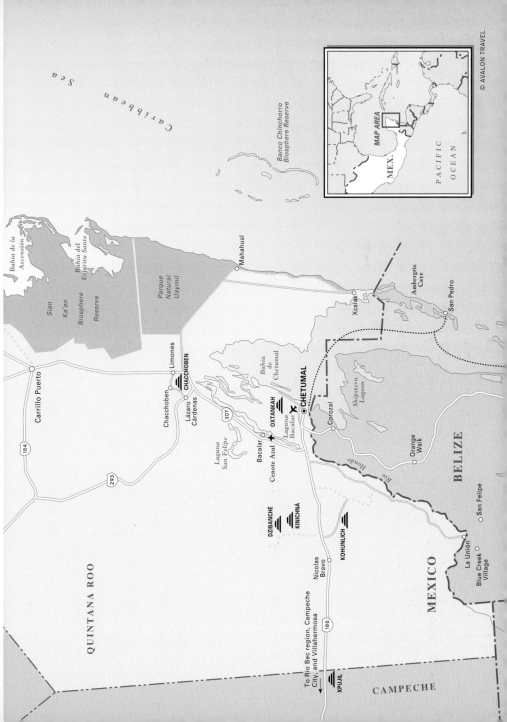

Contents

DISCOVER
Cancún & Cozumel

Cancún and Cozumel are places that deserve—and defy—the myriad descriptions given them. The name Cancún evokes images of white-sand beaches, turquoise seas, and raucous nightclubs. Isla Cozumel is no less mythical, at least among divers, with its pristine coral reef and abundant sealife. The secret is definitely out on the Riviera Maya, the long coastline south of Cancún, with resorts of all sizes and favorite getaways like Tulum and Playa del Carmen. But farther south, the Costa Maya remains relatively undeveloped, while the inland archaeological sites, which range from packed to practically empty, never fail to impress.

Some people dismiss Cancún and Cozumel for being overcommercialized and "Americanized." True, there are places saturated with American stores and chain restaurants (and actual Americans), where you hear as much English as Spanish. But you may be surprised to learn how culturally rich those cities, and the whole region, really are. Just minutes from Cancún's famous hotel zone is the lively downtown area, where you can sip pinot grigio at a wine bar, listen to live music, or eat tacos in a park without another tourist in sight. Likewise, just a couple of blocks from Cozumel's touristy main drag is a friendly island community

where kids play soccer in the street and old men play dominoes in the afternoon sun. There are large parts of Cozumel that have no roads or power lines, with miles of deserted beach where you hear nothing but the birds and the surf.

Equally unexpected are the area's numerous natural and ecological attractions. You can dive and snorkel in the longest underground river system in the world, kayak through mangrove forests and freshwater lagoons, and even go snorkeling with whale sharks, 10-ton behemoths that congregate near Isla Holbox every summer. At Cobá archaeological site, you can climb the second-highest Maya pyramid, *and* see parrots and toucans, *and* bike from temple to temple on wide forest paths, all in the same visit.

So what sort of trip will it be? Sunbathing by the pool, diving the coral reefs, snorkeling with whale sharks, or exploring the Maya ruins? With luck, you'll do a little of each, and more. In the process, you may discover that Cancún, Cozumel, and the Riviera Maya are much more than they seem. They are places to love, laugh at, be surprised by, and above all, to experience and explore.

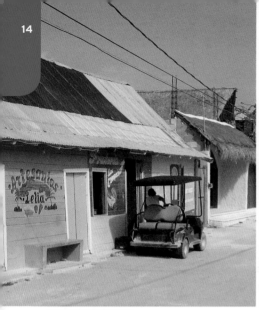

rush hour on Isla Holbox

Isla Mujeres, the easternmost point in Mexico

Planning Your Trip

Where to Go

Cancún

Cancún has two parts: The Zona Hotelera (Hotel Zone) has Cancún's top resorts and nightclubs, plus miles of beautiful beaches. But if you don't mind hopping a bus to the beach, downtown has cheaper food and lodging, plus some unexpectedly cool bars and cafés. Most travelers visit Isla Mujeres, a sliver of an island offshore from Cancún, as a day trip, but nice hotels and a mellow ambience make it a tempting place to stay. Isla Holbox is even smaller, with sand roads and virtually no cars. The beaches aren't glorious, but the tranquility is sublime.

Isla Cozumel

Cozumel's pristine coral reefs and crystalline water attract divers the world over; fewer people realize the island also has a scenic national park, numerous beach clubs, a tournament golf course, even an important Maya ruin. Beat the cruise ship crowds by heading to the east side's isolated beaches and dramatic surf. Most people arrive by ferry—it's just a half-hour ride from Playa

IF YOU HAVE...

- **A WEEKEND:** Visit Cancún
- **ONE WEEK:** Add Isla Mujeres, Isla Cozumel, or Inland Archaeological Zones
- **TEN DAYS:** Add the Riviera Maya or Tulum
- **TWO WEEKS:** Add Isla Holbox or the Costa Maya

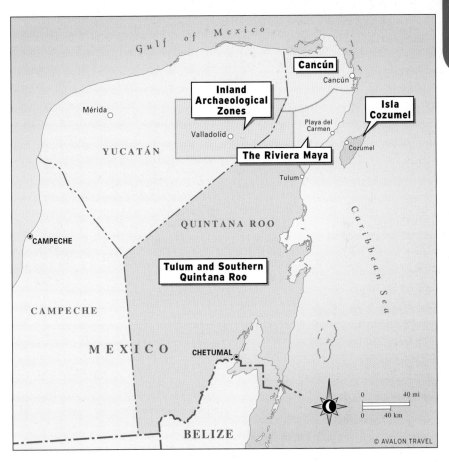

Cancún

Inland Archaeological Zones

Mérida

Valladolid

YUCATÁN

Playa del Carmen

The Riviera Maya

Isla Cozumel

Cozumel

Tulum

Gulf of Mexico

QUINTANA ROO

CAMPECHE

Tulum and Southern Quintana Roo

CAMPECHE

MEXICO

CHETUMAL

Caribbean Sea

BELIZE

0   40 mi

0   40 km

© AVALON TRAVEL

del Carmen—but there's also an airport with international arrivals.

The Riviera Maya

Stretching 130 kilometers (81 miles) from Cancún to Tulum, the Riviera Maya has megaresorts and boutique bed-and-breakfasts, busy cities and quiet villages, great reef diving and amazing cenotes (freshwater sinkholes). Playa del Carmen has the area's largest selection of hotels, food, nightlife, and services; try Puerto Morelos and Akumal for something a bit smaller, or isolated clusters of beachfront hotels like Tankah Tres for even more R&R.

Tulum and Southern Quintana Roo

Tulum is justly famous for its stunning beaches, eco-chic bungalows, and namesake Maya ruin, with a dramatic view of the Caribbean. Directly south is the pristine Sian Ka'an Biosphere Reserve and beyond that the isolated beach towns of the Costa Maya. There's a lovely freshwater lagoon, Laguna Bacalar, a short distance from Chetumal, the busy state capital and gateway to Belize.

Inland Archaeological Zones

Several fascinating Maya ruins are within

easy reach of Cancún and the Riviera Maya. Chichén Itzá is one of the most impressive and recognizable of all Maya ruins, and just two hours from Cancún. Even closer, Ek' Balam is small but has a spectacular stucco frieze and relatively few visitors. An hour from Tulum is Cobá, boasting the second-tallest Maya pyramid and a lovely forest setting teeming with birds.

When to Go

Considering weather, prices, and crowds, the best times to visit the Yucatán Peninsula are from late November to mid-December, and from mid-January to early May. You'll avoid the intense heat from June to August, the rain (and possible hurricanes) in September and October, and the crowds and high prices around the winter holidays.

The big caveats with those periods are spring break (March/April) and Semana Santa (the week before Easter), when American and Canadian students, and then Mexican tourists, turn out in force and prices spike temporarily.

Be aware that certain attractions are only available (or recommendable) during specific months, whether snorkeling with whale sharks (June-September) or visiting Chichén Itzá on the spring equinox. Even many year-round activities like sportfishing, kiteboarding, and bird-watching are better or worse according to the season.

Before You Go

Passports and Visas

American travelers are now required to have a valid passport to travel to and from Mexico. Tourist visas are issued upon entry; you technically are allowed up to 180 days, but agents often issue just 30 or 60 days. If you want to stay longer, request the time when you present your passport. To extend your visa, visit the immigration office in Cancún.

Vaccinations

No special vaccines are required for travel to the Yucatán Peninsula, but it's a good idea to be up-to-date on the standard travel immunizations, including hepatitis A, MMR (measles-mumps-rubella), tetanus-diphtheria, and typhoid.

Transportation

Cancún International Airport (CUN) is far and away the most common and convenient entry point to the region. A handful of flights go directly to Cozumel or Chetumal, and there are plans (but nothing more) for a new airport outside Tulum; there also is an airport near Chichén Itzá, but it is used exclusively for charter flights. An excellent network of buses, shuttles, and ferries covers the entire region, though a rental car makes a world of difference in more remote areas.

What to Take

Bring to Cancún and Cozumel what you would to any beach destination: light cotton clothing, hat, sunscreen, sunglasses, flip-flops, etc. Beach buffs should bring two or even three swimsuits, plus snorkel gear if you've got it. Water shoes come in handy wherever the beach is rocky, while tennis shoes and bug repellent are musts for the Maya ruins. Finally, it's always smart to bring an extra pair of glasses or contacts, prescription medications, birth control, and a travel clock. If you do leave anything behind, no worries—there's a Walmart in all the major cities.

The Best of Cancún and the Riviera Maya

There is *a lot* to do in Cancún, Cozumel, and the Riviera Maya, so this itinerary packs a lot into a little time. We always suggest starting on the beach—it's a vacation, after all. Spend the middle days exploring, first down the coast to Puerto Morelos and Playa del Carmen, and then inland to Maya ruins like Chichén Itzá and Ek' Balam; consider renting a car for these days. Returning to the coast, you can catch a ferry to Isla Cozumel or Isla Mujeres for some snorkeling and island time. Then it's back to Cancún for one last day on the beach (or enjoying underwater art), and you're done!

Day 1

Arrive in Cancún. If you're staying in the Zona Hotelera, head straight to the beach after you check in—the beautiful beach will be a welcome sight after hours on a plane. If you're staying downtown, you can either hop on a bus to the beach or stroll around Parque Las Palapas. In the evening, head to dinner at one of Cancún's fabulous open-air eateries.

Day 2

Spend the morning on the beach or by the pool. In the Zona Hotelera, you're just steps away from either. Those staying downtown can take a bus to one of the public beach areas—Playa Delfines has a bus stop right in front, and El Rey, a Maya ruin, is across the boulevard when you need a change of scenery. After a day in the sun, unwind some more at one of the Zona Hotelera's outdoor lounge bars, or head downtown to catch some jazz.

Day 3

Spend a day exploring the Riviera Maya. A rental car makes life easier, but it's certainly doable by bus or taxi. Playa del Carmen and Akumal make for interesting exploring and

You can't beat Cancún's Zona Hotelera for great beaches and even better views.

Calzada de los Frailes is Valladolid's most scenic colonial street.

could easily take up your entire day; if you like snorkeling, consider going to Puerto Morelos, Laguna Yal-Ku, or Cenote Manatí.

Day 4

Leave bright and early to get to the Maya ruins of Chichén Itzá before the crowds do. Spend the morning there, followed by lunch in the colonial city of Valladolid. From there, go swimming in nearby cenotes, or visit Ek' Balam, a much smaller ruin. Both Valladolid and Ek' Balam have good lodging options, if you want to turn this into an overnight trip.

Day 5

Spend this day on either Isla Mujeres or Isla Cozumel, both easy to reach by ferry. Divers can plan on enjoying a tank or two, especially at Cozumel. If you prefer snorkeling, trips can be booked at dive shops or on the ferry pier of either island. Or just chill out on the beach—Playa Norte in Isla Mujeres is a sure bet, and the windswept eastern side of Cozumel is a great option for beachcombing. Either way, definitely think about renting a car or golf cart, which allow you time and flexibility to explore either island beyond their central areas.

Day 6

Back in Cancún, this is your last full day. If you're up for it, book a snorkeling tour or visit the Museo Maya de Cancún, an excellent new archaeological museum at the southern end of the Zona Hotelera. Otherwise, sit back, relax, and enjoy the pool and beach—it's been a busy week!

a reclining *chac-mool* figure flanked by serpents, at Chichén Itzá

Rich sealife and warm crystal-clear water make the Riviera Maya a great place for snorkeling.

The Best of Isla Cozumel

Isla Cozumel is Mexico's third largest island, with much to offer the curious traveler, from Maya ruins to deserted beaches. Cozumel's claim to fame is its diving and snorkeling, and this tour allots plenty of bubble time. If you prefer to stay on dry land, there's still plenty to do and see in Cozumel, although you also could just take the ferry to Playa del Carmen to explore the mainland for a day or two.

Day 1

Fly straight to Cozumel. There are numerous daily flights, including a few nonstops from the United States. (This saves you the time and expense of taking a bus or taxi to Playa del Carmen, then a ferry across to Cozumel.) Your first order of business is to book a day or two of diving or snorkeling. If you don't have your own snorkeling equipment, arrange an extended rental at any of the dive shops in town. Spend the balance of your day on the beach, whether at your hotel or at one of the beach clubs on the west side of the island.

Day 2

Revel in Isla Cozumel's richest resource: its marine park and pristine coral reef. Palancar Reef is a good warm-up site, with a shallow profile and mild current. In the evening, enjoy dinner and a stroll around the central plaza.

Day 3

Rent a car and spend a day exploring the island. San Gervasio archaeological zone, in the middle of the island, is a good place to start. Continue on to Cozumel's barely developed east side for lunch on a deserted beach while watching the waves crash ashore. Plan on returning to town in time for a night dive—an incredible experience.

Maya Ruins Within Reach

Chichén Itzá, the Yucatán's most famous ruin

Besides its incredible beaches and world-class resorts, Mexico's Caribbean coast is also home to (or within easy reach of) numerous ancient Maya ruins, including some of the most important archaeological sites in the country and the continent. A visit to one or more is well worth a day off the sand, even for committed beach hounds. (And at least one site—Tulum—has historical value *and* a pretty little beach. Sweet!)

- **Chichén Itzá,** with its iconic pyramid and massive ball court, was voted one of the New Seven Wonders of the World. Scores of tours head there from Cancún, but getting to the site early—by bus or rental car—lets you beat the crowds and enjoy this fascinating site at your own pace.

- **Ek' Balam** boasts one of the best-preserved stucco friezes in the Maya world and an all-embracing view from atop its main pyramid. A nearby cenote is great for cooling off.

- **Cobá** has an even better view from its main pyramid—at 42 meters (138 feet) high, it's the second tallest in the Yucatán Peninsula. Nestled in a forest near several small lakes, it's also a good place to spot birds and butterflies.

- **Tulum** is the subject of innumerable postcards, perched on a bluff overlooking the turquoise Caribbean Sea. Like Chichén Itzá, it's far more rewarding to skip the tour and make your way to Tulum early to enjoy the site before the throngs arrive.

- **Kohunlich,** in southern Quintana Roo, is the most remote of the ruins listed here and is best known for a series of imposing stucco masks. Nearby is a unique luxury resort with guided trips in the surrounding forest and river areas.

- **San Gervasio** is Isla Cozumel's main archaeological site, with several modest temples connected by forest paths. Dedicated to the goddess of fertility, San Gervasio was an important pilgrimage site for ancient Maya women.

- **El Rey** and **Yamil Lu'um** are two small ruins right in Cancún's Zona Hotelera. El Rey is larger and better preserved, and is also home to hundreds of iguanas—almost as interesting to see as the structures themselves.

Day 4

Spend the day at one of Cozumel's ecoparks, either Parque Punta Sur (Faro Celarain Eco Park) or Chankanaab, if you feel like more creature comforts. Take your snorkeling gear and a towel—both are great places to get in the water.

Best Beaches

If you love beaches, you've come to the right place. Remember that beaches in Mexico are public; hotels can "claim" an area by setting out guest-only lounge chairs, but you are free to lay out your towel and umbrella wherever there's space.

Cancún

Cancún's beaches are in the Zona Hotelera and are famous for their deep, powdery white sand. Along the Zona Hotelera are numerous public access points, so people staying elsewhere don't have to pass through hotels to get to the beach. Be aware that the surf can be quite heavy at times.

- Playa Gaviota Azul is centrally located and has parasailing and other beach activities. The high-rise hotels behind it cast cooling shadows over the beach in the afternoon.

- Playa Delfines is at the southern end of the strip and the only beach not backed by hotels. It has the largest waves of Cancún's beaches—you may even see a few surfers—and there's a small Maya archaeological site just across the road.

- Playa Marlin is near Plaza Kukulcán mall, which has numerous restaurants, shops, and even a kids club if you need a break from the sun (or each other).

Isla Mujeres

Isla Mujeres's best beaches are located at the northern tip of the island. Unlike Cancún, the beaches here have virtually no surf, making them ideal for families traveling with small children.

- Playa Norte has soft white sand and water so shallow and calm you have to wade out nearly 100 meters (328 feet) before it's deep enough to swim. Beach gear can be rented, and there are several oceanfront restaurants.

- Playa Sol is around the corner from Playa Norte and is also quite beautiful. Larger and nearer to the ferry pier than Playa Norte, it can get crowded with day-trippers from Cancún.

Isla Cozumel

Cozumel is better known for its diving than its beaches, but there are a few spots where you can catch some rays. The island's west side has calm seas and several public beach clubs, while the east side has scenic windswept beaches and heavy surf.

- Playa Palancar is the most low-key of the west-side beaches, with a well-maintained beach area and a restaurant serving tasty meals.

- Playa San Francisco is another fine west-side beach, with a string of large beach clubs. It's good if you want a bit more action than the scene at Playa Palancar.

- Playa Chen Río is one of several beaches on the east side, but is the only one protected from the waves so you can swim. It can get crowded on weekends, but it's wide, so a quiet spot always can be found. A lone restaurant serves pricey meals—do like the locals do and bring your own eats.

- Isla de la Pasión is a private island off Cozumel's north coast, and the only practical way to get there is by package tour. But the beach is gorgeous—Corona actually filmed one of its commercials there—and the open bar and open buffet make it a worthwhile splurge.

Isla Holbox

Isla Holbox's scenic main beach, Playa Norte, extends several miles and is backed by a low coastal forest.

- The sand and water at Playa Norte aren't as classically idyllic as, say, Tulum, but are still lovely and striking in a Robinson Crusoe-type way. Plus, a long sandbar has emerged just offshore; covered in an inch or two of water, it's perfect for wading and cooling off. (Here's hoping it sticks around for a while!)

The Riviera Maya

If you're staying at a resort in the Riviera Maya, you're likely to have a great patch of sand just steps away. But there are plenty of great ones accessible to all travelers.

- In Playa del Carmen, Playa Tukán is a long swath of blond sand with medium surf. Two beach clubs here rent chairs and umbrellas, and offer meal service and even small swimming pools. There's also plenty of open sand, if you'd rather just lay out a towel.

- South of Playa del Carmen, Xpu-Há is easy to miss but rewards those who find it with a broad white-sand beach and mellow surf. There are fewer services here than elsewhere—and fewer people, too—but a couple of hotels and restaurants make Xpu-Há a great beach getaway.

- Farther south, the town of Akumal has a long curving public beach with great snorkeling. Hotel guests can use beach chairs; others should bring a towel and umbrella of their own.

- For maximum isolation, Playa Xcacel has a small parking lot, simple restroom area, and over a mile of gorgeous white

a perfect spot on a perfect beach: Playa Norte, on Isla Mujeres

Palm trees are a good substitute for umbrellas on Tulum's lovely beaches.

A Family Affair

Playa Norte, on Isla Mujeres, is ideal for children, with virtually no waves.

Cancún and the Riviera Maya are excellent family destinations, with plenty to see and do for kids and parents, and good hotels and restaurants to help take the stress out of traveling en masse. Here are some recommended spots:

CANCÚN

Isla Mujeres: Super-calm water, a turtle farm, an ecopark plus a ferry ride there and back–what's not to love?

Parque Las Palapas: Downtown Cancún's main plaza, where kids can run around and munch on chocolate-filled churros.

El Rey Archaeological Zone: Hundreds of beefy iguanas make this a fun stop for kids, even if they're lukewarm about piles of old rocks. (Hint: The iguanas love bananas!)

Shopping Malls: Easy places to cool off and recharge, whether at the Interactive Aquarium or movie theater in La Isla mall, or the kids club at Plaza Kukulcán.

COZUMEL

Playa Chen Río: This protected ocean beach on Cozumel's east side is deserted midweek and busy with local families on weekends.

Parque Punta Sur (Reserva Ecológica Faro Celarain): A scenic natural reserve with a nice beach and fantastic snorkeling, plus a maritime museum and a lighthouse you can climb.

THE RIVIERA MAYA

Xcaret: This huge ecopark is an all-day excursion, with snorkeling, tubing, an aquarium, and a fun evening show.

Croco Cun Zoo: Charming little zoo near Puerto Morelos where you can see, pet, and even hold animals (including babies).

Hidden Worlds Cenotes Park: Great cenote snorkeling for all ages, plus a zipline.

INLAND ARCHAEOLOGICAL ZONES

Chichén Itzá: Impressive ruins with several family-friendly hotels nearby. The Ik Kil cenote just east of town is a sure hit.

Valladolid: Charming midsize city, with three impressive cenotes nearby for swimming.

Cobá: Renting bikes or bicycle taxis makes visiting these ruins especially fun for kids, while the thick forest provides cool shade and a chance to spot birds and insects.

Punta Laguna Monkey Reserve: A great family outing, where you'll spot not only spider and howler monkeys, but a slew of birds, tropical vegetation, and more.

sand. (There's a small freshwater cenote, too.) Located between Xel-Há ecopark and Chemuyil community, Xcacel is a sea turtle nesting ground, so it's off-limits to construction. Good for turtles—and beach lovers, too!

Tulum and Southern Quintana Roo

Many people consider Tulum's beaches to be the best of Mexico's Caribbean coast. It's hard to disagree with white sand, gentle azure surf, and a backing of palm trees and bungalow-style hotels. Southern Quintana Roo doesn't have much to offer the hard-core beachgoer, though the fishing, kayaking, snorkeling, and diving are all stellar.

• Tulum's northern beaches are easier to reach if you're not staying at one of the hotels, with several public access points and affordable restaurants and beach clubs.

• Tulum's southern beaches are truly stunning, plucked from a postcard. Hotel guests have easy access, though nonguests can park just south of Punta Piedra and walk down the shore. Bring your own supplies or plan to eat at one of the small hotel restaurants.

Under the Sea

For all its terrestrial wonders, the Yucatán Peninsula's underwater treasures are no less compelling, including the world's longest underground river system, the second-longest coral reef, and the Northern Hemisphere's largest coral atoll. Isla Cozumel, fringed by pristine coral reefs and remarkably clear water, is one of the world's top diving and snorkeling destinations. But you need not leave the mainland to appreciate the Yucatán's underwater realm—eerily beautiful cenotes and healthy coral reefs all along the Caribbean coast offer fantastic views and unforgettable experiences, and can be enjoyed either on an organized tour or on your own.

Playa del Carmen is the starting point for each of these under-the-sea adventures, both for its central location and its large selection of dive shops and other services. Puerto Morelos, Akumal, and Tulum make good bases, too. You'll need to rent a car (available in each of the above towns, but most convenient to rent from the Cancún airport) plus snorkel gear if you didn't bring your own.

Bear in mind that you should not dive within 24 hours of your flight home.

The Riviera Maya and Tulum

DAY 1

Spend a day snorkeling or diving on the ocean reef. Puerto Morelos and Akumal are especially good for both, but you can't go wrong anywhere along the coast. Snorkeling or diving on the reef is a good way to tune up for cenote trips, coming up tomorrow. Estuary zones like Laguna Yal-Ku in Akumal and Cenote Manatí in Tankah Tres make for nice exploring, too.

DAY 2

A day for journeying into the abyss—the Riviera Maya's famous cenotes. Cenote parks like Dos Ojos and Hidden Worlds are good one-stop destinations for divers and snorkelers of all levels. Otherwise, grab your snorkel gear, or sign up for a guided dive trip, for a day of cenote-hopping. Great stops include Siete Bocas and Lucerno Verde on the Ruta de los Cenotes, just south of Puerto Morelos; Jardín del Edén and Cenote Cristalino, both on Highway 307 across from Xpu-Há; and the string of cenotes west of Tulum including Car Wash and Gran Cenote.

Cenote Hopping

The Yucatán Peninsula has hundreds of cenotes, from simple pools to spectacular caverns like Cenote Choo-Ha outside Cobá.

All along the coast and well inland are dozens of cenotes—pools of shimmering blue water fed by a vast underground freshwater river system. Some look like large ponds, others are deep sinkholes, others occupy gaping caverns or have dramatic rock formations. Many cenotes are open to the public, and their cool clear water is perfect for swimming, snorkeling, and scuba diving. Facilities range from simple restrooms and snorkel rental to full-service "cenote parks" with guided tours. Some favorites include:

THE RIVIERA MAYA

Ruta de los Cenotes: Sure, some spots along the "Cenote Route" are tourist traps, but others are sublime, like Siete Bocas, a huge eerie cavern filled with shimmering water, and Lucerno Verde, a gorgeous open-air pool filled with freshwater turtles and fish.

Jardín del Edén: The best and biggest of a cluster of cenotes near Playa Xpu-Há, with a large cavern that forms a dramatic overhang.

Cenote Cristalino: Next to Jardín del Edén, Cristalino also has an overhanging cliff but a smaller swimming area.

Cenote Manatí: Near Tankah Tres, this is actually a series of connected cenotes and lagoons that wind inland through a tangled scrub forest.

NEAR TULUM

Dos Ojos and Hidden Worlds: Side-by-side cenote parks with rentals, guides, and spectacular caverns.

Gran Cenote: Lovely cavern with natural arches and stalactite formations; east of Tulum on the road to Cobá.

Car Wash: Just past Gran Cenote, this innocuous-looking cenote has stunning rock formations below the surface.

INLAND AREAS

Cenote X'Canché: A pretty 12-meter-deep (39-foot) cenote, a kilometer (0.6 mile) down a forest path from Ek' Balam ruins.

Cenote Choo-Ha: One of four dramatic cenotes near Cobá, with a high domed ceiling and iridescent blue water.

Cenote Ik Kil: Just three kilometers (1.9 miles) from Chichén Itzá, this huge deep cenote can be crowded but is impressive all the same.

Cenote Yokdzonot: Also nearby Chichén Itzá, this little-known gem is all the more rewarding for being operated by a cooperative of enterprising local women.

Isla Cozumel

DAY 1

Take the ferry to Isla Cozumel and arrange snorkeling or diving trips for the following two days. Spend the rest of the day relaxing on the beach and snorkeling from shore. Good spots for both include Parque Punta Sur (Faro Celarain Eco Park), Parque Nacional Chankanaab, and Playa Azul. In the evening, having dinner and take a stroll around the central plaza.

DAY 2

Go on a snorkel or dive trip. Ask about taking your surface interval (or mid-snorkel break) at Playa Palancar, a gorgeous west-side beach with a low-key beach club.

DAY 3

Cozumel's reef diving and snorkeling are well worth a second day.

La Costa Maya

DAY 1

From Playa del Carmen, head south to Mahahual or Xcalak, two small towns near the Belize border. Sign up for diving and snorkeling trips, then spend the rest of the day on the beach—both towns have fantastic snorkeling and diving right from the shore, including at night.

DAY 2

A trip to Banco Chinchorro makes for a long day (just getting there takes 2-3 hours by boat), but this massive and pristine coral atoll has spectacular diving and snorkeling and is well worth the time and expense.

DAY 3

Treat yourself to an easy day of diving or snorkeling at the nearby reef, just minutes by boat from the shore. You'll be done early enough to enjoy beer and fish tacos on the beach, or even to drive back to Tulum or Playa del Carmen.

Sea turtles in Mexico are protected, monitored, and assisted by a variety of NGOs and government initiatives.

Into the Wild

one of the long-armed, long-tailed residents of Punta Laguna Spider Monkey Reserve

Cancún and the Caribbean coast may be best known for white-sand beaches and deluxe resorts, but they also have many excellent areas and opportunities to spot wildlife, especially birds. When you need a break from the sun and surf, here are some places to get back in touch with nature:

- **Sian Ka'an Biosphere Reserve:** This sprawling coastal reserve south of Tulum is home to an astounding array of wildlife, including dolphins, howler monkeys, crocodiles, sea turtles, and hundreds of bird species. Harder to spot, but still there, are manatees, tapirs, and even jaguars.

- **Isla Holbox:** Come here to snorkel with whale sharks, gentle giants that congregate just offshore between June and September. Later, book a kayak or motorboat tour to visit the island's bird-rich lagoons.

- **Isla Cozumel:** Cozumel's protected coral reef system teems with sponges, sea turtles, rays, eels, and countless tropical fish. Divers can get up close and personal, but even snorkelers get an eyeful in these pristine waters.

- **Punta Laguna Spider Monkey Reserve:** This small reserve north of Cobá is home to several families of rambunctious *monos arañas* (spider monkeys). A small lagoon has canoes to go looking for crocodiles.

- **Akumal:** Yucatec Maya for "Place of the Turtle," Akumal is the center for turtle preservation along the Riviera Maya. A local organization welcomes visitors on nighttime excursions to find and protect sea turtle nests (May-July) and to release hatchlings back to the sea (August-October).

Seven Days of Ecoadventure

Lazing on a beach or contemplating museum displays is all right, but some travelers crave a little more action. The Yucatán has plenty to offer active travelers, including scuba diving, kiteboarding, fly-fishing, kayaking, and bird-watching. This tour covers it all, with add-on days for Isla Holbox, a windswept island north of Cancún where you can snorkel with whale sharks.

Day 1

Start your ecoadventure by snorkeling or diving the Riviera Maya's stunning coral reef: There are great tours and shore options in Akumal and Puerto Morelos, and of course Cozumel.

Day 2

You've gotten your feet wet, and now it's time for some cenote-hopping, either on your own or as part of a cenote diving or snorkeling tour. Visit one-stop cenote parks like Dos Ojos or Hidden Worlds, or create your own adventure along the Ruta de Cenotes.

Day 3

Spend a day above water, either stand-up paddleboarding or kayaking. Both are challenging but fairly easy to master, and especially rewarding in the Riviera Maya's warm clear water. Playa del Carmen is a convenient place to do both, but Tulum and Cozumel are great alternatives and have good kiteboarding, too.

Day 4

Heading south, spend a day kayaking, swimming, bird-watching, and animal-spotting in Sian Ka'an Biosphere Reserve, the spectacular nature reserve south of Tulum. End the day by relaxing on Tulum's gorgeous beaches—no shame in that!

Day 5

Promise yourself you'll try something you've never done before: There's sportfishing in

The Yucatán offers great opportunities for active travelers, including kayaking, snorkeling, and diving.

Best Restaurants

The Yucatán Peninsula's food scene ranges from hole-in-the-wall taco joints to ultra-gourmet restaurants, and from traditional Maya fare to international cuisine. Some of our favorites, in no particular order, include:

- **Quesadillas Tierra del Sol** (Downtown Cancún): Delicious street grub served hot and fresh right on Cancún's busy downtown plaza.

- **Kinta** (Cozumel): Hip restaurant-bar serving modern Mexican creations and outstanding cocktails.

- **John Gray's Kitchen** (Puerto Morelos): You can trace the growth of haute cuisine in the Riviera Maya to this innocuous restaurant in little Puerto Morelos, with an ever-changing international menu.

- **La Cueva del Chango** (Playa del Carmen): Leafy restaurant serving innovative comfort food at the far north end of town is a perennial favorite for locals and visitors alike.

- **Qubano** (Isla Mujeres): Best sandwich in the Yucatán Peninsula—just ask the droves of people who visit this homey eatery.

- **Azafrán** (Tulum Pueblo): One of the best breakfasts around, featuring super-fresh ingredients and friendly service.

- **El Tábano** (Tulum's Zona Hotelera): For all the scenic meals to be had on Tulum's beachfront, the tastiest are at this no-frills open-air eatery on the other side of the road.

- **Leaky Palapa** (Xcalak): Funky little restaurant in this out-of-the-way Costa Maya town.

Xcalak, skydiving and scenic flights out of Playa del Carmen, and zip-lining over cenotes at Hidden Worlds or Lucerno Verde.

Day 6

If you're visiting between June and September, plan a trip to Isla Holbox, on the peninsula's northeastern tip. You get there via the small town of Chiquilá, where you can leave your rental car and catch a ferry to Holbox. Take an afternoon kayak tour of the mangroves, where there's great bird-watching.

Day 7

Go snorkeling with whale sharks, with a stop for snorkeling on the reef on the way back. Enjoy a late lunch on Holbox's central plaza, then take the ferry back to Chiquilá.

Romantic Tulum Getaway

Although a number of places in and around Cancún have the makings of a romantic getaway—picturesque beaches, elegant restaurants, relaxing spas, and cozy accommodations—we picked our favorite for this itinerary: Tulum. The beaches are spectacular, and the *cabaña*-style hotels exude a quiet charm like nowhere else. Many offer professional massages and other spa treatments, while others specialize in gourmet dining.

Day 1

Fly into Cancún, and make your way by bus or taxi to Tulum. Settle into your beachside bungalow, complete with a hanging bed,

Tulum is the only Maya ruin with its very own white sand beach—don't forget your swimsuit!

mosquito net, and candles. If you want something a little more upscale, consider staying in a suite at one of the chic high-end hotels. Spend the remainder of the day on the beach. In the evening, head to Mezzanine or La Zebra for drinks, followed by dinner at Posada Margherita.

Day 2

Visit the Tulum ruins in the morning before the crowds arrive. Bring your swimsuits to enjoy the small beach there. Afterward, walk to gorgeous Playa Paraíso, just south of the ruins. Eat lunch at the beachfront restaurant and, if you're up for it, take a private kiteboarding lesson together here with Extreme Control. For something a little mellower, head down the road for a drop-in yoga class at Yoga Shala Tulum instead.

Day 3

Choose between taking an organized eco-tour in the Sian Ka'an Biosphere Reserve, cenote hopping (four cenotes on the road to Cobá are just minutes away), or just beachcombing on Tulum's southern beaches. If you are at a high-end hotel, book a beachside dinner for two—complete with a personalized menu—before starting your day. Also consider reserving a couples massage for your last day at the Maya Spa Wellness Center.

Day 4

Have breakfast brought to your room, and enjoy lingering over it in bed. Spend your last full day on the beach, for maximum relaxation. And don't forget to go to your massages!

CANCÚN

Cancún is a big, beautiful, contradictory place. For many people, it has all the makings of the ultimate vacation destination: five-star hotels, thick white sand, impossibly blue waters, and a night-life that never stops. Others chafe at Cancún for seeming more American than Mexican, a place where you need never speak a word of Spanish, never eat at a restaurant you couldn't find at

© GARY CHANDLER

Highlights

LOOK FOR **(** TO FIND RECOMMENDED SIGHTS, ACTIVITIES, DINING, AND LODGING.

(Playa Delfines: Located at the far southern end of the Zona Hotelera, this is one of few spots without highrise resorts gobbling up beach space with their chairs and blocking the afternoon sun, and it has a refreshing mix of foreign and local visitors (page 41).

(Cancún Nightlife: You don't have to be on spring break to enjoy Cancún's nightclubs—but it helps! If the all-night-every-nightclub scene isn't for you, head downtown for wine bars, jazz clubs, and cafés featuring local guitarists (page 41).

(Museo Subacuático de Arte: This remarkable "museum" features hundreds of statues of people of all ages and walks of life, standing on the ocean floor in 12-40 feet of crystal-clear water. The statues are made of material designed to promote coral growth, so they'll only get more interesting as time passes (page 69).

(Isla Contoy: Go island hopping on this popular day trip from Isla Mujeres. A morning boat ride is followed by snorkeling on a rich coral reef, hiking and bird-watching on Contoy's protected shores, chilling out in the sun, and digging into a fresh fish barbecue on the beach (page 70).

(Playa Norte: Surfers need not apply—Isla Mujeres's best beach has virtually no waves, just soft white sand lapped by glassy turquoise water. Relax under a palm tree or nosh on ceviche at a beachfront restaurant. Playa Norte is great for families, couples, and single sun worshippers (page 72).

(Whale Shark Feeding Grounds: Just because they weigh 10 tons and are longer than a Winnebago doesn't make whale sharks bad snorkeling partners. Get goggles-to-gills with the world's biggest fish in these krill-rich waters between June and September (page 86).

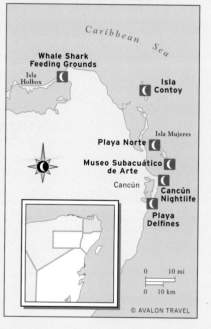

a mall back home, and never convert your dollars into pesos.

Both perspectives are true, but one-sided. It's hard not to cringe at those loud tourists who don't bother to explore—or even care about—any part of Mexico beyond their beach chairs. Yet those who pooh-pooh Cancún are also selling the city short. Cancún is a working, breathing city that's vital to Mexico's economy and imbued with a fascinating history and plenty of "real" Mexican culture for those willing to seek it out. And contrary to impressions, Cancún has accommodations and services for visitors of all budgets and tastes.

Why not take advantage of both sides of Cancún? The resorts, beaches, and nightclubs will blow your mind—don't miss them! But be sure not to overlook Cancún's more subtle side, too, from live music in a bohemian downtown café to munching on *elote* (corn on

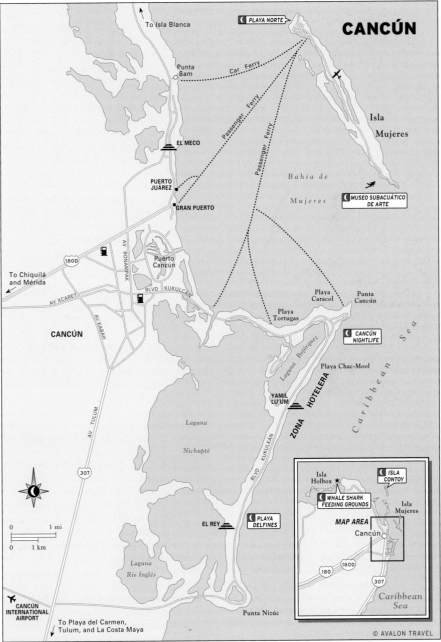

CANCÚN

To Isla Blanca

PLAYA NORTE

Punta Sam

Car Ferry

Passenger Ferry

Passenger Ferry

Isla Mujeres

EL MECO

PUERTO JUÁREZ

GRAN PUERTO

Bahía de

Mujeres

MUSEO SUBACUÁTICO DE ARTE

180D

AV BONAMPAK

Puerto Cancún

To Chiquilá and Mérida

AV XCARET

BLVD KUKULCÁN

AV KABAH

CANCÚN

AV TULUM

Laguna Bojórquez

Playa Caracol

Punta Cancún

Playa Tortugas

CANCÚN NIGHTLIFE

Sea

Caribbean

Playa Chac-Mool

YAMIL LU'UM

ZONA HOTELERA

BLVD KUKULCÁN

Laguna

Nichupté

307

N

0   1 mi

0   1 km

Laguna
Río Inglés

EL REY

PLAYA DELFINES

Isla Holbox

ISLA CONTOY

WHALE SHARK FEEDING GROUNDS

Isla Mujeres

MAP AREA

Cancún

180   180D

307

Caribbean Sea

CANCÚN INTERNATIONAL AIRPORT

To Playa del Carmen, Tulum, and La Costa Maya

Punta Nizúc

© AVALON TRAVEL

the cob) sold from a cart in the city's pleasant central square.

And when you need to, just get away. A 15-minute ferry ride delivers you to the slow-paced island of Isla Mujeres, a sliver of sand surrounded by breathtaking blue waters. Farther north and even more laid-back is Isla Holbox; no cars, no banks, no post office—it's a world away from Cancún yet reachable in a morning.

HISTORY

Cancún is a new city in a new state. In the 1960s, the Mexican government set out to create the next Acapulco, and surveyors selected a swampy sandbar on the Caribbean coast as the country's most promising tourist town. Not everyone was convinced: the area was a true backwater—not even a state yet—with no infrastructure and few roads in or out. But Mexico's planners forged onward, paving roads, building bridges, installing electrical lines. Thousands of mangroves were torn out, sadly, to expand the beaches and make room for hotels. Today's downtown Cancún started out as a small mainland fishing village that grew rapidly with the influx of workers; it serves much the same purpose today, though now has an economy and dynamic unto itself, including banks, real estate, multinational companies, and more. Cancún officially "opened" in 1974, the same year the territory was elevated to statehood. (The state was named after army general Andrés Quintana Roo and is pronounced keen-TA-nah Roh.) Today, it is one of the top beach destinations in the world and draws nearly 25 percent of all the foreign travelers in Mexico.

PLANNING YOUR TIME

A week will do just fine in Cancún, allowing time enough to get your tan on plus take a day trip or two, such as to Isla Mujeres or one of the nearby Maya ruins. Ten days gives you time to explore deeper and farther, turning a day trip to Isla Mujeres or the Maya ruins into an overnighter, or venturing north to the remote island of Isla Holbox. Isla Mujeres and

Isla Holbox are small but wonderfully relaxing; if either is your main destination, budget three or four days to experience them fully, but don't be surprised if you end up staying longer.

You don't *need* to rent a car to enjoy Cancún, Isla Mujeres, and Isla Holbox, especially if you don't plan on moving around much; all can be navigated easily by bus, ferry, taxi, and foot. That said, having a car makes many excursions easier, quicker, and more fun, especially if you've got kids in tow. Rather than booking a crowded and expensive tour to, say, Chichén Itzá, you can drive there yourself, arriving before the big groups and then hitting a second ruin or an out-of-the-way cenote on the way home. With the price of rental cars surprisingly low, and well-marked roads and highways, it's certainly worth considering.

ORIENTATION

Cancún's Zona Hotelera lies on a narrow white-sand island in the shape of a number 7. The 7's short upper arm leads directly into downtown Cancún, while the longer one (13 kilometers/8 miles) connects to the mainland near the airport. The elbow of the 7 is Punta Cancún—this is the fast-beating heart of the Zona Hotelera's nightlife, including all the major nightclubs, plus several resorts, hotels, restaurants, and shopping malls. The rest of the resorts and several more malls, restaurants, and water sports agencies are spread along the two arms, especially the southern one. The far southern tip of the 7 is called Punta Nizúc and has a few hotels, plus Cancún's largest archaeological site (El Rey). Busy Boulevard Kukulcán runs the entire length of the 7, and most addresses in the Zona Hotelera are simply a kilometer marker. Finally, the huge lagoon that's enclosed by the mainland and the Zona Hotelera is called Laguna Nichupté, and is a popular spot for fishing, waterskiing, and boating.

Downtown Cancún is on the mainland and is divided into numbered *super manzanas* (square blocks, or SM for short). Avenida Tulum is downtown's main thoroughfare; west of Avenida Tulum is Parque Las Palapas (downtown's central plaza), and beyond that Avenida Yaxchilán. Most of downtown Cancún's hotels, restaurants, and music venues are on or around Parque Las Palapas and Avenida Yaxchilán, primarily in SMs 22-25.

Sights

ARCHAEOLOGICAL ZONES

Cancún has three notable archaeological sites, two in the Zona Hotelera and a third north of town, near the Isla Mujeres ferry. None compare in size or wow factor to the Yucatán Peninsula's major sites, but they are still worth visiting, and the Zona Hotelera ones can be easily combined with a day at the beach.

El Rey Archaeological Zone

At the southern end of the Zona Hotelera, across from Playa Delfines, **Ruínas El Rey** (Blvd. Kukulcán Km. 17.5, 8am-5pm daily, US$3.50) consists of several platforms, two plazas, and a small temple and pyramid, all arranged along an ancient 500-meter (1,640-foot) roadway. The ruins get their name (Ruins of the King) from a skeleton found during excavation and believed to be that of, what else, a king. The ruins date from the late Post-Classic period (AD 1200-1400); signage is available in English and Spanish. Last visitors are admitted at 4:30pm.

The ruins are home to literally hundreds of iguanas, some quite beefy, which makes a visit here all the more interesting.

Yamil Lu'um Archaeological Zone

Lodged between Park Royal Pirámides and the Westin Lagunamar, **Yamil Lu'um** (Blvd. Kukulcán Km. 12.5, 8am-5pm daily, free) consists of two small temples built between AD 1200 and 1550: **Templo del Alacrán** (Temple of the Scorpion) and **Templo de la Huella** (Temple of the Handprint); unfortunately neither the scorpion nor the handprint that gave the temples their names is visible anymore. The temples were built on Cancún's highest point, suggesting they were used as watchtowers or navigational aids. The ruins can be reached through the Park Royal (nonguests may need to ask permission) and are visible from the beach at Playa Marlin.

El Meco Archaeological Zone

Archaeologists think **El Meco** (Av. López Portillo s/n, 8am-3pm daily, US$4) was a major gateway to and from Isla Mujeres—fitting considering it's located just north of the modern-day ferry terminal at Puerto Juárez. The ancient city seems to have thrived in its role as a port town, building the tallest pyramid along this part of the coast before collapsing abruptly around AD 600. It was reoccupied four or five centuries later, probably as an outpost for the powerful Chichén Itzá kingdom. The site is smaller than El Rey, in the Zona Hotelera, but the structures are more substantial.

MUSEUMS
Museo Maya de Cancún

Housed in a gorgeous new building at the southern end of Zona Hotelera, **Museo Maya de Cancún** (Blvd. Kukulcán Km. 16.5, tel. 998/885-3842, 9am-6pm daily, US$5) displays hundreds of Maya artifacts in bright airy display rooms, including new discoveries and others that have never been displayed before. Two permanent exhibition rooms are dedicated to finds from Quintana Roo and the greater Maya world, respectively, while a third room hosts temporary displays. Many of the displays lack English translations, though that will likely be fixed over time. Note that only Mexican pesos are accepted.

Museo Pelopidas

Museo Pelopidas (La Isla Shopping Village, Blvd. Kukulcán Km. 12.5, tel. 998/146-5151, www.museopelopidas.com, 10am-10pm daily,

CANCÚN

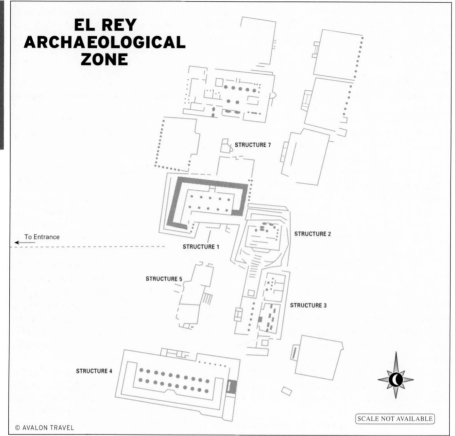

EL REY ARCHAEOLOGICAL ZONE

STRUCTURE 7

To Entrance

STRUCTURE 1

STRUCTURE 2

STRUCTURE 5

STRUCTURE 3

STRUCTURE 4

SCALE NOT AVAILABLE

© AVALON TRAVEL

free) is a large, sleek, somewhat gimmicky, yet mildly interesting art gallery on the 2nd floor of a Zona Hotelera mall. Check out the "New Originals": a roomful of high-quality hand-painted imitations of masterworks by Klimt, Picasso, and others, which bear slight but deliberate alterations to distinguish them from forgeries. Half-hour guided tours are offered in English and Spanish at 11am, 1pm, 4pm, and 6pm.

PARQUE LAS PALAPAS

Parque Las Palapas is a classic Mexican plaza, mostly, where locals congregate most nights and tourists have a chance to enjoy

Cancún's quotidian side. The plaza doesn't have the grand cathedral and government buildings typical of Mexico's older colonial cities—remember Cancún isn't even 50 years old—but it's still a place for adults to gossip with friends, for teenagers and couples to circle about, and for youngsters to chase balls and ride electric cars in the spacious central square. Dozens of stands and street carts sell *nieve* (ice cream), *elote* (corn on the cob, also available in a cup, served with chile and mayo), and knickknacks of all sorts. The music and neon lights can be a bit much, but just as often there's an interesting performance scheduled for the plaza's huge palapa-roofed stage, whether live music or traditional dance. Along the edges of the main park are smaller squares, some used for art expositions, others favored by young bohos for plucking guitars and engaging in the occasional drum circle.

Beaches

ZONA HOTELERA BEACHES

Cancún's beaches are back! A series of severe hurricanes had left the famous shoreline rocky and sloped for a few years, and everyone wondered if the beaches would ever recover. But thanks to emergency efforts by the government (including the dredging of thousands of tons of sand) and the gradual blessings of Mother Nature, Cancún's beaches are as wide and glorious as ever—in some places, even better than before. Will they last? Hard to say. Currents and sand are always shifting, and there's simply no way to know how a particular storm—or even an overall increase in the number and strength of storms, as most scientists predict—will affect Cancún's beaches. Only time will tell, so enjoy then while you can!

Be aware that the surf along the Zona Hotelera's long, east-facing arm can be heavy, and drownings and near-drownings do occur. There are lifeguards near all public access points, and colored flags (Green is Safe, Yellow is Caution, Red is Closed) for reference. But nothing is more important than common sense: Don't swim if the conditions (or your own condition) aren't suitable. The beaches along the short, north-facing leg are much calmer. For really calm waters head to Isla Mujeres, where there are no waves and the water in places is only waist deep more than 75 meters (250 feet) from shore. The Laguna Nichupté is not recommended for swimming because of pollution and crocodiles.

Playa Caracol

Playa Caracol (Blvd. Kukulcán Km. 8.5) has a small stretch of beach right at the public access point, but it's not too pleasant and often very crowded. The beach is much better just east of there, in front of the Fiesta Americana Coral Beach, but you have to cut through the hotel to get there and the hotel lounge chairs take up most of the beach.

Playa Gaviota Azul

The pathway to **Playa Gaviota Azul** (Blvd. Kukulcán Km. 10), a huge, beautiful beach, is between The City nightclub and Forum by the Sea mall, and it extends well north and south of there (merging with Playa Chac Mool just to the south) with plenty of room to set up a towel and umbrella. Parking can be tricky here—better to arrive by bus or taxi—but you've got plenty of eating and shopping options, if you need a break from the sun. The City operates a beach club called **Cabana Beach** (Blvd. Kukulcán Km. 10, tel. 998/848-8385, http://cabanabeach.mx, 9am-5pm daily, US$10 pp), which is open to the public and has raised wooden beach beds with flowing linen curtains, full bar and restaurant service, swimming pool, and DJ. It can definitely be a scene, but that's pretty much the point.

Playa Marlín

Playa Marlín (Blvd. Kukulcán Km. 12.5) is a clean, attractive beach—narrower and steeper than it was before Hurricane Wilma, but still a nice spot. Look for the access point between Plaza Kukulcán mall and the police and fire station; there's plenty of parking on the dirt road parallel to the beach, and the mall has restaurants and a kids club just a few steps away.

Playa Ballenas

Playa Ballenas (Blvd. Kukulcán Km. 14.5) is a long, pretty beach, with an access path between the Hard Rock and Secrets resorts. There is no food or drink service on the beach, but look for

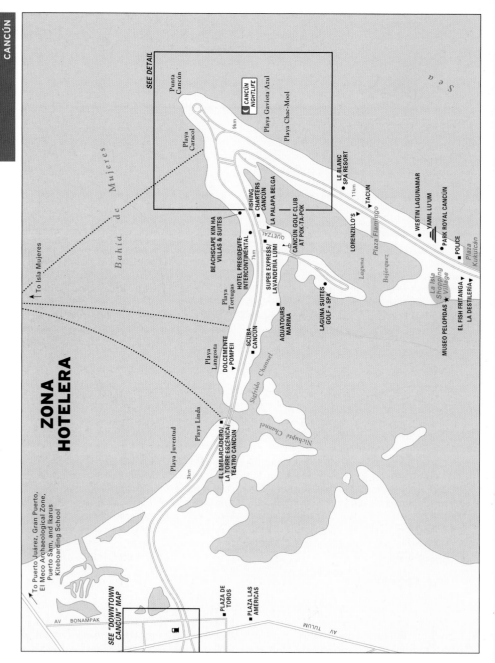

ZONA HOTELERA

SEE DETAIL

CANCÚN NIGHTLIFE

Punta Cancún

Playa Caracol

Playa Gaviota Azul

Playa Chac-Mool

9km

Sea

Bahia de Mujeres

To Isla Mujeres

LE BLANC SPA RESORT

WESTIN LAGUNAMAR

YAMIL LU'UM

PARK ROYAL CANCÚN

POLICE

11km

TACUN

Plaza Flamingo

Plaza Kukulcán

LORENZILLO'S

La Isla Shopping Village

FISHING CHARTERS CANCÚN

LA PALAPA BELGA

BEACHSCAPE KIN HA VILLAS & SUITES

QUETZAL

CANCÚN GOLF CLUB AT POK-TA-POK

HOTEL PRESIDENTE INTERCONTINENTAL

7km

SUPER EXPRESS/ LAVANDERIA LUMI

Laguna

Bojórquez

EL FISH FRITANGA

LA DESTILERÍA

MUSEO PELOPIDAS

Playa Tortugas

LAGUNA SUITES GOLF + SPA

AQUATOURS MARINA

SCUBA CANCÚN

Playa Langosta

DOLCEMENTE POMPEII

Sigfrido Channel

Playa Linda

EL EMBARCADERO/ LA TORRE ESCÉNICA/ TEATRO CANCÚN

Nichupté Channel

Playa Juventud

3km

To Puerto Juárez, Gran Puerto, El Meco Archaeological Zone, Puerto Sam, and Ikarus Kiteboarding School

AV BONAMPAK

SEE "DOWNTOWN CANCÚN" MAP

PLAZA DE TOROS

PLAZA LAS AMÉRICAS

AV TULUM

CANCÚN

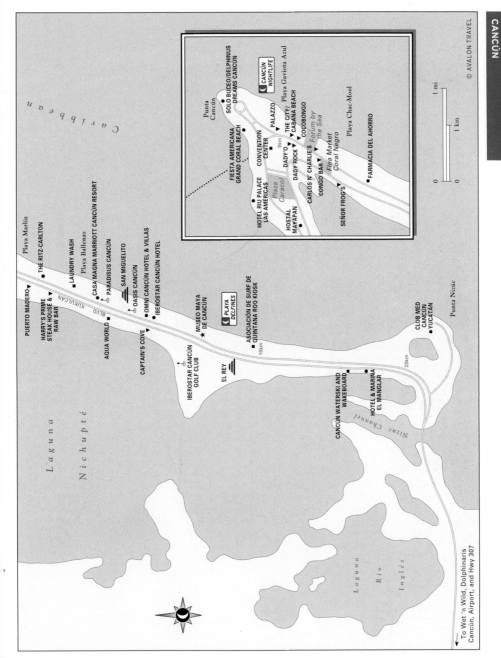

© AVALON TRAVEL

Caribbean

Punta Cancún

SOLO BUCEO/DELPHINUS DREAMS CANCÚN

CANCÚN NIGHTLIFE

Playa Gaviota Azul

PALAZZO

THE CITY
CABANA BEACH

FIESTA AMERICANA GRAND CORAL BEACH

CONVENTION CENTER

DADY'O

COCOBONGO

Forum by the Sea

Playa Chac-Mool

9km

DADY ROCK

CARLOS N' CHARLIE'S

CONGO BAR

Flea Market

Coral Negro

Plaza Caracol

HOTEL RIU PALACE LAS AMÉRICAS

SEÑOR FROG'S

FARMACIA DEL AHORRO

HOSTAL MAYAPAN

0   1 mi

0   1 km

Laguna Nichupté

Playa Marlín

THE RITZ-CARLTON

LAUNDRY WASH

Playa Ballenas

CASA MAGNA MARRIOTT CANCÚN RESORT

PARADISUS CANCÚN

PUERTO MADERO

HARRY'S PRIME STEAK HOUSE & RAW BAR

BLVD KUKULCÁN

SAN MIGUELITO

OASIS CANCÚN

OMNI CANCÚN HOTEL & VILLAS

IBEROSTAR CANCÚN HOTEL

AQUA WORLD

MUSEO MAYA DE CANCÚN

PLAYA DELFINES

ASOCIACIÓN DE SURF DE QUINTANA ROO KIOSK

18km

CAPTAIN'S COVE

IBEROSTAR CANCÚN GOLF CLUB

EL REY

20km

Punta Nizúc

CLUB MED CANCÚN

YUCATÁN

CANCÚN WATERSKI AND WAKEBOARD

HOTEL & MARINA EL MANGLAR

Nizúc Channel

Laguna Río Inglés

To Wet 'n Wild, Dolphinaris Cancún, Airport, and Hwy 307

Beach Access

© GARY CHANDLER

Look for these signs in the Zona Hotelera for public access to the beach.

There is a notion that the high-rise hotels have monopolized Cancún's best beaches, but this is only partly true. While most hotels *do* front prime real estate, all beach areas in Mexico are public (except for military zones). Hotels cannot, by law, prohibit you or anyone else from lying out on a towel and enjoying the sun and water. Many high-end hotels subvert this by making it difficult or uncomfortable for nonguests to use "their" beaches: Very few maintain exterior paths, and others spread guest-only beach chairs over the best parts. (In the hotels' defense, they also typically do a good job of keeping their areas clear of trash and seaweed, which can mar otherwise beautiful beaches.) If your hotel has a nice beach area, you're all set. If not, you can just walk through a hotel lobby to the beach—as a foreigner, you are very unlikely to be stopped. (Sadly, locals are likely to be nabbed if they do the same thing.) But even that is unnecessary: The city maintains several public access points marked with prominent blue and white signs along Boulevard Kukulcán. The area right around the access point is often crowded, but you can walk a couple hundred meters in either direction to have more breathing room. One public access point—Playa Delfines, at the southern end of the Hotel Zone—has no nearby hotels and is used by a refreshing mix of Mexican and foreign beachgoers.

© GARY CHANDLER

beach scene along Cancún's Zona Hotelera

a few small shops selling water and snacks on the frontage road rear the public access point.

(Playa Delfines

Located at the far southern end of the Zona Hotelera, **Playa Delfines** (Blvd. Kukulcán Km. 17.5) is situated at the bottom of a bluff, so you can't see it from the road. But once parked, or off the bus, you're treated to a panoramic view of the beach and ocean, unobstructed by hotels.

There are a handful of fixed wooden umbrellas and plenty of open sand if you brought your own. Perhaps best of all is the mix of people you'll find here: independent travelers, local families, even some surfers if the swell is high. (Speaking of which, take care swimming as the waves and tide can be strong here.) The beach is across the road from the El Rey ruins, which makes a nice side trip. The bus stops directly in front; there is no food or drink service.

Entertainment and Events

Cancún is justly famous for its raucous nightclubs, pulsing with lights and music and packed with revelers of all ages every night of the week. The club scene is especially manic during spring break, July, August, Christmas, and New Year's, but you can count on finding a party no matter when you visit. And those with quieter tastes will be happy to learn there's more to Cancún's nightlife than clubs, including a nice mix of small music venues, lounge bars, theaters, and cinemas.

(NIGHTLIFE

Cancún's most popular nightclubs are within walking distance of each other in the **Zona Hotelera,** at Punta Cancún. The Zona Hotelera also has some great lounge bars. Downtown, meanwhile, has nightclubs specializing in Latin

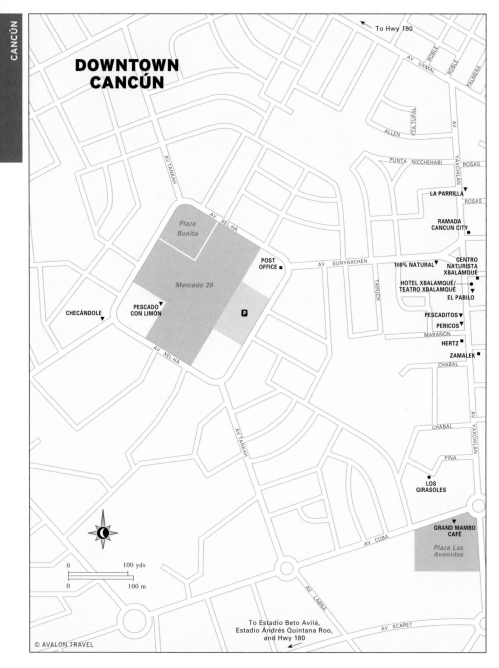

DOWNTOWN
CANCÚN

To Hwy 180

AV UXMAL
ROBLE
ROBLE
PALMERA

PTA TUPAL
AV
ALLEN

AV TANKAH

PUNTA NICCHEHABI
YAXCHILAN
ROSAS

LA PARRILLA
ROSAS

Plaza
Bonita

AV XEL-HA

RAMADA
CANCUN CITY

POST
OFFICE ■

AV SUNYAXCHEN

CENTRO
100% NATURAL ▼ NATURISTA
XBALAMQUÉ

HOTEL XBALAMQUÉ/
TEATRO XBALAMQUÉ
EL PABILO

TAHUCH

Mercado 28

CHECÁNDOLE ▼

PESCADO ▼
CON LIMÓN

P

PESCADITOS ▼
PERICOS ▼
MARAÑON
HERTZ ■

ZAMALEK ■

AV XEL-HA

CHABAL

CHABAL

AV TANKAH

AV XEL-HA

YAXCHILAN

PIÑA

LOS
GIRASOLES

0   100 yds

0   100 m

GRAND MAMBO ▼
CAFÉ

Plaza Las
Avenidas

AV COBA

AV LABNA

To Estadio Beto Avilá,
Estadio Andrés Quintana Roo,
and Hwy 180

AV XCARET

© AVALON TRAVEL

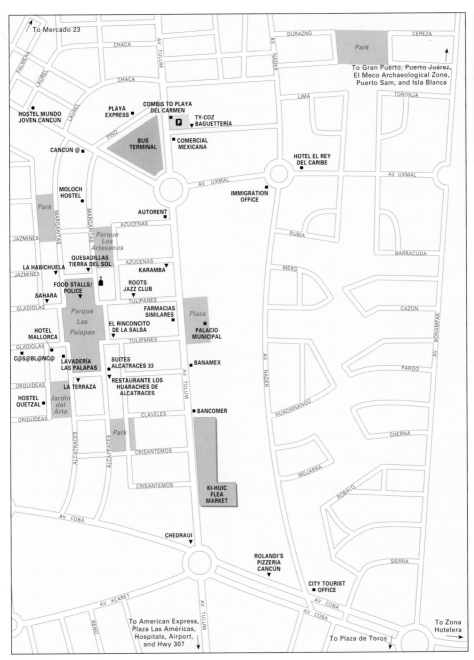

music, and the city's best live music, theater, and movies.

Cuncrawl (www.cuncrawl.com, US$79 pp) does fun guided bar/club crawls in the heart of Cancún, hitting three different clubs (they vary by night) with VIP entrance and seating, open bar, and available transport to/from your resort (US$10 pp).

Nightclubs
ZONA HOTELERA
Nightclubs in the Zona Hotelera charge US$40-50 admission with open bar included. The clubs open every day, from around 10pm until 4am or later. Special events, like ladies night or bikini parties, vary by the day, club, and season; check the clubs' websites or Facebook pages for the latest info and deals, or ask the concierge at your hotel.

CocoBongo (Blvd. Kukulcán Km. 9, tel. 998/883-5061, www.cocobongo.com.mx, 10pm-4am daily, US$40 with open bar) is a spectacular club featuring live rock and salsa bands, flying acrobats, and Beyoncé, Madonna, and Guns n' Roses impersonators. Movie clips are also projected onto huge screens.

The City (Blvd. Kukulcán Km. 9, tel. 998/848-8380, www.thecitycancun.com) is a megaclub with four levels and a total capacity of 4,000 (and allegedly the world's biggest disco ball). Be sure to take a whirl on the movable dance floor, which descends from the 3rd floor to the center of the club below.

Dady-O (Blvd. Kukulcán Km 9.5, tel. 998/883-3333, www.dadyo.com.mx) is, well, the daddy of Cancún's nightclubs, with seven different "environments," including laser shows, swimsuit contests, and theme parties on several different levels.

Next door, **Dady Rock** (Blvd. Kukulcán Km 9.5, tel. 998/883-3333, www.dadyrock.com.mx) is technically a restaurant and bar, so it opens as early as 6pm and doesn't have a dance floor. Nevertheless, driving rock music, sometimes live, soon has partiers dancing every place possible, including on tables and the bar.

Palazzo (Blvd. Kukulcán Km 9, tel. 998/848-8380, http://palazzodisco.com)

took over the building occupied by the late great Bulldog Café, which closed in 2012. Fortunately, the Palazzo (which is owned by the same company as The City and has a sister location in Playa del Carmen) has continued the Bulldog's tradition of booking big-name live acts and drawing raucous crowds. The interior has been totally refurbished, with a sleek Vegas-like look and a VIP section.

DOWNTOWN
Downtown clubs can be just as packed as those in the Zona Hotelera, but offer something different (and don't open every day). There are two great spots for salsa and other Latin music and dancing, and at least one gay and gay-friendly club. Cover is much cheaper, but you pay for drinks.

Grand Mambo Café (Plaza Monarca, aka Plaza Hong Kong, 2nd Floor, Av. Xcaret at Av. Tulum, tel. 998/884-4536, 10pm-4am Wed.-Sun., US$5) is Cancún's biggest Latin music club, and popular with locals, tourists, and expats alike. Live music doesn't start until midnight, but the crowds arrive earlier than that, spinning to salsa, cumbia, merengue, and more.

El Rinconcito de la Salsa (Av. Tulipanes 3, tel. 998/187-5349, 10pm-4am Fri.-Sun., US$5) is a smallish salsa club with a great location, just a half block off Parque Las Palapas. It's operated by the same person who ran Azucar, a former and much-missed salsa club in the Zona Hotelera. Live music starts at midnight.

Karamba (Av. Tulum at Calle Azucenas, tel. 998/884-0032, 10:30pm-6am Tues.-Sun.) is mostly gay, but not exclusively, with frequent drag shows and theme parties. There's a fun mix of men, women, and cross-dressers. Look for the fabulous zebra facade.

Bars and Live Music
Several of the major nightclubs in the Zona Hotelera feature live rock music and even big-name concerts, most notably Palazzo and Dady Rock, while the lounges and bars tend toward DJs or recorded music. Downtown, you'll find smaller venues featuring more intimate live music, whether jazz, solo guitarists, or trios.

© GARY CHANDLER

For clubs and nightlife, you've come to the right place.

ZONA HOTELERA

Congo Bar (Blvd. Kukulcán Km. 9.5) is about as lively as a bar can get without being called a club. Music is upbeat and drinks are plentiful. A congo line inevitably forms at some point (or points) and usually heads out the door and onto the street for a quick spin.

Old standbys **Carlos n' Charlie's** (Forum by the Sea, Blvd. Kukulcán Km. 9, tel. 998/883-4468, www.carlosandcharlies.com) and **Señor Frog's** (Blvd. Kukulcán Km. 9.5, tel. 998/883-1092, www.senorfrogs.com) both open at noon for meals and stay open until 3am for drinking, dancing, and general mayhem.

For a more mellow scene, pop down to your hotel's **lobby bar** to socialize with other guests.

DOWNTOWN

◖ **Roots Jazz Club** (Tulipanes 26, tel. 998/884-2437, www.rootsjazzclub.com, 7pm-2am Thur.-Sat.) is arguably the best live music venue in town, the go-to spot for live jazz, funk, and flamenco, both traditional and contemporary, for over two decades. Music starts at

around 10pm, but it's worth getting there early for dinner and a good seat near the small stage. A cover (US$3-6) sometimes applies.

El Pabilo (Hotel Xbalamqué, Av. Yaxchilán 31, tel. 998/892-4553, 6pm-midnight Tues.-Sun.) is a small, artsy café with great live music on the weekends, including Cuban, fusion jazz, classical guitar, and flamenco. Music usually starts around 9pm; a moderate cover (US$5-9) is sometimes charged.

On the southern end of Parque Las Palapas, **La Terraza** (Alcatraces 29, tel. 998/126-0131, 6pm-1am Tues.-Sat.) is a pleasant open-air wine bar that books live guitar soloists most nights starting at 9pm.

THE ARTS

THEATER

Teatro Cancún (El Embarcadero, Blvd. Kukulcán Km. 4, tel. 998/849-5580, www.teatrodecancun.com.mx, ticket office on ground level 9am-9pm Mon.-Sat.) stages shows of all sorts, from music and dance to comedy and theater, both amateur and professional, mostly in Spanish. Ticket prices vary, but average US$5-30.

Teatro Xbalamqué (Hotel Xbalamqué, Av. Yaxchilán 31, tel. 998/892-4553) stages experimental and one-act theatre performances in a small space inside the hotel of the same name; when we last visited, *Dracula Has AIDS* was playing. Most shows are in Spanish; check at reception for showtimes.

Cinema

Cancún has two convenient movieplexes, one in the Zona Hotelera and one downtown, both offering the latest American and Mexican releases. Most Hollywood movies are subtitled, but be aware that those made for kids, and even teenagers, are likely to be dubbed. Look for "DOB" (for *doblado,* or "dubbed") or "SUB" for (*subtitulada,* or "subtitled") to be sure. Ticket prices average around US$6; early shows may be discounted, but two-for-one Wednesdays are a thing of the past, unfortunately.

In the Zona Hotelera there's **Cinemark** at La Isla mall (Blvd. Kukulcán Km. 12.5, tel. 998/883-5604), while downtown has

Cinépolis at Plaza Las Américas (Av. Tulum at Av. Sayil, tel. 998/884-0403). For a real treat, try **Cinépolis VIP,** which has reclining leather seats and wait service, with a menu that includes sushi, gourmet baguettes, cappuccinos, and cocktails (oh yeah, and popcorn and soda). Same location but tickets are sold at a separate window, costing around US$8.

FESTIVALS AND EVENTS

Puerto Vallarta and Acapulco have long been Mexico's top destinations for gay travelers, but organizers of the **Cancún International Gay Festival** are working to put Cancún on the list. Inaugurated in 1995 and typically held in May, the festival includes beach parties, sunset cruises, city tours, and more.

Since 2001 the **Concurso Municipal de Artesanías,** a citywide handicraft competition, has been held annually in Cancún's Palacio Municipal. In addition to showcasing the city's best artisans, many participants also sell their work just in front of the building. Look for the large white tents—and the crowds—on Avenida Tulum in early August.

Shopping

Cancún has five major malls, a handful of open-air markets, and hundreds of independent shops, so you can buy just about anything. Most mall and independent shops accept credit cards, but plan on paying cash at the markets.

OPEN-AIR MARKETS

Mercado 28 (Av. Sunyaxchen at Av. Xel-Há, 9am-8pm daily) is a large open-air market featuring a wide variety of Mexican handicrafts: ceramics from Tonalá, silver from Taxco, hammocks from Mérida, *alebrijes* (wooden creatures) from Oaxaca, handwoven shirts from Chiapas. You'll also find a fair share of T-shirts, key chains, coconut monkeys, and the like. A handful of restaurants in the center of the market offer traditional Mexican fare.

Adjacent to Mercado 28, **Plaza Bonita** (Av. Sunyaxchen at Av. Xel-Há, 9am-8pm daily) is a multilevel shopping center built to look like a colonial village—bright courtyards, fountains, greenery, and all. Folk art here is a bit more expensive than that in the market next door, but the quality is usually better.

On weekend evenings, stroll through **Parque Las Palapas** and **Parque Los Artesanos,** both great spots to pick up local handicrafts, Chiapanecan clothing, bohemian jewelry, and art.

MALLS

A recent renovation has transformed **Plaza Caracol** (Blvd. Kukulcán Km. 8.5, www.caracolplaza.com, 8am-10pm daily) from its former

Plaza Kukulcán is one of several large modern malls in Cancún's Zona Hotelera and downtown area.

jungle-themed family restaurant), a great steak house, and various mid- to high-end shops offering everything from T-shirts to expensive jewelry. There are cheaper food options—and a spectacular view of the beach and ocean—on the 3rd floor.

A mostly outdoor shopping center, **La Isla Shopping Village** (Blvd. Kukulcán Km. 12.5, www.laislacancun.com.mx, 10am-10pm daily) is the most pleasant of the Zona Hotelera malls. It is set around an artificial river, with wide shady passageways, a nice variety of shops, and an excellent food court, including crepes, tacos, Italian, and more. A newer enclosed section called El Palacio Boutique houses various luxury shops. La Isla is also home to the popular Interactive Aquarium and has a five-screen movie theater.

Plaza Kukulcán (Blvd. Kukulcán Km. 12.5, www.kukulcanplaza.com, 9am-11pm daily) is the Zona Hotelera's swankiest mall, with a section called Luxury Avenue selling fine watches, jewelry, clothing, and more from brands like Cartier and Mont Blanc. The main mall area has some usual suspects like Sunglass Island and MixUp music store, plus a supervised children's play area called **Kukulkids** (2nd Fl., tel. 998/885-3405, noon-9pm daily), if you want some quality shopping time without the kiddos; socks are required, and children can be no taller than 1.3 meters (51 inches).

You don't have to go to the Zona Hotelera for your mall fix. **Plaza Las Américas** (Av. Tulum at Av. Sayil, 9am-10pm daily) stretches almost a block and includes dozens of mid- to upscale shops, an arcade, and two movie theaters. **Plaza Las Avenidas** (Av. Cobá at Av. Tulum, 9am-10pm daily) has similar offerings.

desultory state into a genuinely pleasant place to shop. It's the best mall in the Zona Hotelera for any beach essentials you left at home, with good brands and decent prices on bathing suits, flip-flops, sunglasses, sunscreen, etc. You can also grab a cup of Starbucks and good cheap grub at several small eateries.

Forum by the Sea (Blvd. Kukulcán Km. 9, www.forumbythesea.com.mx, 10am-11:30pm daily) is a horseshoe-shaped mall with three floors opening onto the airy main lobby. It's home to Hard Rock Café—hence the huge guitar out front—the Rainforest Café (a

Sports and Recreation

While relaxing by the pool or on the beach is more than enough sports and recreation for many of Cancún's visitors—and who can blame them?—there *are* a number of options for those looking for a bit more action. From golf and fishing to scuba diving and kiteboarding (and a whole bunch of things in between), Cancún has something for everyone.

BEACH ACTIVITIES

Parasailing (*paracaídas* in Spanish) can be booked as a traditional one-person ride (with takeoff from the shore) or a two-person ride, in which you can take off from the boat or the water. Prices and duration are fairly uniform: US$50-60 per person for a 10- to 12-minute ride. Look for independent operators on the beach, especially on Playa Ballenas (Blvd. Kukulcán Km. 14.5), Playa Chac-Mool (Blvd. Kukulcán Km. 10), and Playa Delfines (Blvd. Kukulcán Km. 17.5). Or sign up at Solo Buceo (Dreams Cancún Hotel, Blvd. Kukulkán Km. 9.5, tel. 998/883-3979, www.solobuceo.com, 9am-4:30pm daily) or Aqua World (Blvd. Kukulcán Km. 15.2, tel. 998/848-8327, www. aquaworld.com.mx, 7am-8pm daily).

Wave Runners are rented on the same beaches where parasailing is pitched. Prices average US$50 for 30 minutes; one or two people can ride at a time.

SNORKELING AND SCUBA DIVING

Cancún doesn't compare to Cozumel, Isla Mujeres, or really anywhere along the Riviera Maya for snorkeling and diving. Its coral and other sealife is less plentiful and far less healthy, making for rather dull excursions. If you're really hankering for some bubbly, we recommend booking a trip with a shop in Isla Mujeres or Puerto Morelos, both easy to reach from Cancún. (Cozumel is harder to do as a day trip, requiring a ferry to and from Playa del Carmen.) Or consider arranging a snorkeling or diving trip in a cenote, the otherworldly freshwater caves that dot the coast south of Cancún.

Snorkeling

For the best open-water snorkeling, book a trip with one of the dive shops listed below. All offer guided snorkeling trips in addition to diving, and are invariably better than the "jungle trips" hawked around Cancún, even for beginners. **Cenotes** also make for fascinating snorkeling, and many dive shops arrange tours there, too. No previous experience is required.

Scuba Diving

A number of shops offer fun dives as well as certification courses at all levels. Hotels with their own dive shop may offer special rates to guests, but not necessarily.

Solo Buceo (Dreams Cancún Hotel, Blvd. Kukulkán Km. 9.5, tel. 998/883-3979, www. solobuceo.com, 9am-4:30pm daily) is a friendly shop with a strong reputation for service. Two-tank reef dives run US$77, while two-tank Cozumel or cenote trips cost US$145, including lunch; prices include all gear except a wetsuit (US$10, recommended for cenote trips). Open-water certification classes (US$420, 3-4 days) can also be arranged. Despite its name, Solo Buceo offers more than "only diving," including snorkeling, parasailing, deep-sea fishing, and wave runner rentals.

Scuba Cancún (Blvd. Kukulcán Km. 5, tel. 998/849-7508, www.scubacancun.com.mx, 7am-8pm daily) was founded in 1980 and is still run by the same family. It offers the standard selection of dives, including one-tank (US$54), two-tank (US$68), and two-tank cavern and Cozumel dives (US$155, including lunch); all prices include equipment. Snorkel trips are offered in Cancún (US$29), Cozumel (US$105), and nearby cenotes (US$85). Trips can sometimes get crowded—ask about the size of your group before you book.

Aqua World (Blvd. Kukulcán Km. 15.2,

tel. 998/848-8300, toll-free U.S./Can. tel. 877/730-4054, www.aquaworld.com.mx, 7am-8pm daily) is Cancún's biggest, most commercialized water sports outfit, of which scuba diving is only a small part. Come here if you're looking for activities for the whole family, divers and nondivers alike, all in one spot. Otherwise, head to smaller shops for more personal attention.

KITEBOARDING

Ikarus Kiteboarding School (tel. 984/803-3490, www.kiteboardmexico.com) is based in Playa del Carmen but opened a kiteboarding camp at Isla Blanca, a huge saltwater lagoon north of Cancún. Conditions for learning to kiteboard don't get much better than this: steady wind, kilometers of flat water with few boats or other obstacles, and water never more than waist deep. Private classes are US$67-83 per hour, while groups are US$55-65 per hour per person (3 hours minimum). Simple lodging also is offered at Ikarus's camp (US$8.50 pp hammock, US$8.50 pp tent, US$50 s/d).

WATERSKIING, WAKEBOARDING, AND SURFING

Cancún Waterski and Wakeboard (Marina Manglar, Blvd. Kukulcán Km. 19.8, cell. tel. 998/874-4816, www.waterskicancun.com, by appointment only) has three slalom courses and a number of ski sites at the southern end of Laguna Nichupté. Free skiing and wakeboarding costs US$220 per hour, while the slalom courses are US$60 for 15 minutes.

Though the waves aren't huge, Playa Delfines is as good as it gets for surfers in Cancún. The **Asociación de Surf de Quintana Roo** (Quintana Roo Surf Association, Blvd. Kukulcán Km. 13, cell. tel. 998/118-2466, www.surfcancunmex.com, 8am-6pm daily) occasionally mans a kiosk there, offering surf classes and rentals.

SPORTFISHING

More than a dozen species of sport fish ply the waters off Cancún, including blue and white marlin, blackfin tuna, barracuda, dolphin

© GARY CHANDLER

Small kiosks along the beach offer parasailing and other activities.

dorado, wahoo, grouper, and more. **Fishing Charters Cancún** (Blvd. Kukulcán Km. 7.5, tel. 998/883-2517, U.S. tel. 954/283-8621, www.fishingcharterscancun.com, 6:30am-9pm daily) offers four- to eight-hour trips on its fleet of custom fishing boats (US$450-850). Individual anglers also can sign up for "shared" trips (US$125-135, 4-6 hours). All trips include captain, mates, gear, bait, tackle, drinks, and, in some cases, lunch. Fly-fishing trips also can be arranged.

SWIMMING WITH DOLPHINS

Located within Wet n' Wild water park, **Dolphinaris Cancún** (Blvd. Kukulcán Km. 25, tel. 998/881-3030, toll-free Mex. tel. 800/365-7446, www.dolphinaris.com) offers dolphin interaction programs that include "fin shaking" and receiving a "kiss" (US$79, 1 hour), as well as swimming with and getting a foot push from them (US$119, 1 hour). For those toying with the idea of working with dolphins, visitors also can help out as Trainers for the Day (US$199, 8 hours).

Delphinus Dreams Cancún (Dreams Cancún Resort, Blvd. Kukulcán Km. 7.5, tel. 998/206-3304, toll-free Mex. tel. 800/335-3461, www.delphinus.com.mx) offers similar dolphin interaction programs in a group setting (US$99-149, 1 hour), as a couple (US$399, 1 hour) and one-on-one (US$499, 1 hour). Trainer for the Day programs are offered too (US$199, 8 hours). Check the website for online deals.

Interactive Aquarium (La Isla Shopping Village, Blvd. Kukulcán Km. 12.5, tel. 998/883-0411, www.aquariumcancun.com.mx, 10am-6pm daily, US$10) has a disappointingly small display of fish and other sea creatures, but its raison d'être are the interactive dolphin and shark exhibits. Like other dolphin programs, activities range from receiving a "kiss" and getting a "foot push" (US$85-135, 30-55 minutes) to a Trainer for the Day program (US$250, 8 hours). Shark "interactions" involve climbing into an acrylic booth and being lowered into the aquarium's huge shark tank to get a close-up look at bull, brown, and nurse sharks (US$30 pp, 30 minutes).

ECOPARKS AND WATER PARKS
Ecoparks

Despite the deluge of advertising you'll see for Xcaret, Xel-Há, Xplor, and Parque Garrafón, none are actually in Cancún. Parque Garrafón is the closest, situated on the southern end of Isla Mujeres. The others are 60-90 minutes south of Cancún, nearer to Playa del Carmen and Tulum. You can buy tickets at the gates, though most people buy them at their hotels or through a travel agency in Cancún so bus transportation is included in the cost; discounted park tickets also are popular giveaways for taking part in a time-share presentation.

Water Parks

Also known as Parque Nizúc, **Wet n' Wild** (Blvd. Kukulcán Km. 25, tel. 998/193-2000, www.wetnwildcancun.com, 9:30am-5pm daily, US$49 adult all-inclusive, US$43 child all-inclusive) is a small but classic water park with a handful of twisting slippery slides, high-speed water toboggans, and family-size inner tubing. It's a great way to cool off, especially if you're traveling with kids (or want to channel your own inner five-year-old). The all-inclusive plan includes all rides, meals, and drinks though, oddly enough, not the inner tubes. BYO towel too. The park is also home to **Dolphinaris Cancún** (Blvd. Kukulcán Km. 25, tel. 998/881-3030, toll-free Mex. tel. 800/365-7446, www.dolphinaris.com, US$79-199), a dolphin interaction program.

GOLF

The **Iberostar Cancún Golf Club** (Blvd. Kukulcán Km. 17, tel. 998/881-8016, www.iberostargolfresorts.com/cancun, US$179/79 public/hotel guests, US$105/45 public/guests after 1pm) is considered one of the finer courses in the region. This 18-hole par-72 course hugs Laguna Nichupté and boasts a great view of the Maya ruins El Rey from the 16th hole. Alligators also are rumored to be in one of the water hazards, so consider leaving those water-bound balls behind.

The **Cancún Golf Club at Pok-ta-Pok** (Blvd.

CANCÚN

© H.W. PRADO

Cancún and the Riviera Maya boast some of the country's finest golf courses.

Kukulcán Km. 7.5, tel. 998/883-1230, www.cancungolfclub.com) is an 18-hole championship golf course designed by Robert Trent Jones Jr. It winds its way along the Caribbean and Laguna Nichupté and features its own Maya ruin near the 12th hole, discovered when the course was built. Greens fees are US$175 and drop to US$125 after 1pm. Rates include a shared golf cart. Some Zona Hotelera hotels offer discounts—ask your concierge for details.

If you feel like a short round of golf and don't want to shell out the big bucks, there are two par-3 courses in the Zona Hotelera open to the public: **Paradisus Cancún** (Blvd. Kukulcán Km. 16.5, tel. 998/881-1100, www.melia.com, 7am-1pm last tee-off, US$35 greens fees, US$8 club rentals) and **Oasis Cancún** (Blvd. Kukulcán Km. 16, tel. 998/885-0867, 8am-2:30pm last tee-off, US$17.50 greens fees including clubs).

You'll find two Jack Nicklaus courses at **Moon Palace Golf & Spa Resort** (Hwy. 307 Km. 340, tel. 998/881-6100, www.palaceresorts.com/golf, US$289 for 18 holes, US$178 for 9 holes, just 15 minutes south of the Zona

Hotelera. It has three nine-hole courses spanning nearly 11,000 yards. Greens fees include a shared golf cart, snacks, and drinks; from 2:30pm until closing at 6pm, greens fees are US$178 for as many holes as you can play. There's also a driving range, a green-side bunker, and putting and chipping greens. Club rentals are US$50.

SPECTATOR SPORTS
Bullfights
Cancún's **Plaza de Toros** (Av. Bonampak at Av. Sayil, tel. 998/884-8372, US$34, children under 12 free) hosts a bullfight every Wednesday at 3:30pm. Bullfights here differ from traditional *corridas* (runnings) in that only four bulls are fought (versus five or six) and a mini-*charrería* (rodeo) is performed. Advance tickets are sold at most travel agencies in Cancún.

Baseball
Baseball (*béisbol* in Spanish) is huge in Mexico, particularly in the north, where there are as many baseball diamonds as soccer fields. While

still not having the pull in the Yucatán as it does elsewhere, it is a sport on the rise. The local team, **Tigres de Quintana Roo** (Quintana Roo Tigers, www.tigresqr.com), is one of the 16 teams that make up Mexico's professional baseball league, the Liga Mexicana de Béisbol (www.lmb.com.mx). You can catch a game March-September at the **Estadio Beto Ávila** (Av. Xcaret s/n, behind Walmart, US$3-10).

Soccer

Arriving in Cancún from Mexico City in 2007, **Atlante** (www.club-atlante.com) is the city's first professional *fútbol* team. And arrive they did: Atlante won the Mexican League's championship and the Apertura 2007 Championship, both in their first year in residence. The following season Atlante won the 2008-09 CONCACAF Champions League, earning it a spot in the 2009 FIFA Club World Cup, where the team placed fourth. The team plays at the **Estadio Andrés Quintana Roo** (Av. Mayapán s/n, US$15-50), west of the baseball stadium, August-May.

SPAS AND GYMS

Many hotels and resorts have spas, but the following are some of the finest, and are open to the public. Reservations are strongly encouraged.

Le Blanc Spa (Le Blanc Spa Resort, Blvd. Kukulcán Km. 10, tel. 998/881-4740, toll-free U.S. tel. 877/325-1538, www.leblancsparesort.com, 9am-8pm) is considered by many to be Cancún's best spa, and is a big reason Le Blanc Spa Resort as a whole gets such great reviews. The resort is adults-only, so the spa caters to couples, from joint massages and treatments to the Golden Spa Suite, a spa-within-a-spa.

Spas don't get much better, or bigger, than the new 40,000-square-foot **Gem Spa** (Fiesta Americana Grand Coral Beach, Blvd. Kukulcán Km. 9.5, tel. 998/881-3200, www.coralbeachcancunhotel.com) at the Fiesta Americana. There are dozens of available treatments, all said to be inspired by the precious stones of the Maya, Asian/South Pacific, and Baltic regions.

Obsidian, amber, amethyst, even diamond dust are used to sooth and smooth your body and mind. Be aware the spa charges US$85 just to get in—ouch.

Downtown, the well-regarded **Centro Naturista Xbalamqué** (Hotel Xbalamqué, Av. Yaxchilán 31, tel. 998/887-7853, www.xbalamque.com, 9am-8pm Mon.-Sat., by appointment only on Sun.) offers a full line of massages, facials, and body wraps, plus Reiki, crystal therapy, and *temescal* treatments. The spa's entrance is on Calle Jazmines, around the corner from the main hotel entrance. Prices are very reasonable, most ranging US$30-50.

TOURS
Jungle Tour

It sure *looks* like it would be fun to drive a wave runner or speedboat across the lagoon to a national marine park to snorkel. Unfortunately, the rules—Stay in line! Don't go too fast! Don't pass!—keep the boat part pretty tame, and there are few birds in the mangroves. The snorkeling also is disappointing, with dozens of tourists swarming a small section of coral reef. We don't recommend this sort of trip, but dozens of agencies will gladly take your money (US$60-75 pp, 2.5 hours).

Aerial Tours and Views

AeroSaab (Playa Del Carmen Airport, 20 Av. Sur near Calle 1, tel. 998/865-4225, www.aerosaab.com) offers scenic full-day tours from Cancún—Chichén Itzá, Isla Holbox, Mérida, Uxmal—and as far as Palenque, with time to visit the area. Trips are in four- or five-seat Cessna airplanes and run US$118-787 per person, plus airport fees. Most trips require a minimum of two people.

If you prefer to stay (somewhat) grounded, board **La Torre Escénica** (Scenic Tower, El Embarcadero, Blvd. Kukulcán Km. 4.2, tel. 998/849-7777, 9am-9pm daily, US$9.50 adult, US$5 child 5-11), an 80-meter (262.5-foot) tower with a rotating passenger cabin, affording a beautiful 10-minute view of this part of the coastline. A brief history of the region also is played over the audio system.

Accommodations

Cancún has scores of hotels, varying from backpacker hostels to ultra-high-end resorts. They're also divided by their location: the Zona Hotelera or downtown. The Zona Hotelera has spectacular views, easy access to swimming pools and the beaches, and excellent restaurants, but prices are higher and you won't get much "authentic" interaction with local people. Downtown Cancún has a variety of food, shopping, and services (from Walmart to laundries) at generally lower prices, but staying downtown also means driving or taking a bus to the beach and not having access to hotel pools and amenities.

ZONA HOTELERA
Under US$100
The Zona Hotelera's one and only youth hostel, **Hostal Mayapan** (Plaza Caracol, Blvd. Kukulcán Km. 8.5, tel. 998/883-3227, www. hostalmayapan.com, US$20-22 dorm with a/c, US$62 d with a/c) occupies, of all things, a defunct mall, complete with escalators and faux Maya artwork. The upside is you're within walking distance of the clubs and some nice beaches. The downside is, well, everything else: marginally clean linens and restrooms, ambivalent staff, paltry breakfast, no real common area, and air-conditioning that's on only intermittently. Private rooms aren't worth the extra cost.

US$100-150
Located on Laguna Nichupté, **Hotel & Marina El Manglar** (Blvd. Kukulcán Km. 19.8, tel. 998/885-1808, www.villasmanglar.com, US$120 s/d with a/c) has simple and spacious rooms, each with cable TV, air-conditioning, a king-size bed, and two couches that double as twin beds. There's a well-maintained pool on-site, and beach access across the street. Popular with people who enjoy diving, fishing, water skiing and wake boarding, with tours and instruction available on-site.

Located alongside the Pok-Ta-Pok golf course, **Laguna Suites Golf + Spa** (Paseo Pok-Ta-Pok No. 3, tel. 998/891-5252, toll-free U.S./Can. tel. 866/760-1843, www.lagunasuites. com.mx, US$122/280 European plan/all-inclusive for two adults and two kids) has just 47 suites, allowing for genuinely personalized service with none of the hub-bub of a large beachfront resort. There's a small pool and a chic *palapa* lounge, plus free hourly shuttles to two nearby sister resorts—the Royal Sunset and Ocean Spa—where you can enjoy the pool, beach, restaurants and other amenities like any other guest. A great option if you don't mind a little resort hopping.

An excellent value, **Beachscape Kin Ha Villas & Suites** (Blvd. Kukulcán Km. 8.5, tel. 998/891-5400, toll-free U.S./Can. tel. 866/340-9082, www.beachscape.com.mx, US$146 s/d, US$196-619 suite) is a comfortable, low-key resort on a beautiful and spacious beach on the upper arm of the Zona Hotelera. The resort's one-, two-, and three-bedroom suites have fully equipped kitchens, living and dining areas, and ocean-view terraces; there also are a handful of standard hotel rooms. In addition to that huge beach, the property has a large (and rather plain) pool, restaurant-bar, and children's play area. Though lacking the style and ambience of Cancún's top resorts, Beachscape Kin Ha can hardly be beat for location and value. Coin-op laundry, an exercise room, and Wi-Fi (reception area only) is available.

US$150-300
Part of the Royal Resorts company, **Royal Cancún** (Blvd. Kukulcán Km. 4.5, toll-free U.S. tel. 888/838-7941, toll-free Mex. tel. 01-800/888-7744, US$200-250 villas for 4-6 pax with a/c) is a small resort that's especially well-suited for families and small groups on a budget. Units here are well maintained, though dated, and have two bedrooms and a full kitchen. The resort doesn't have an all-inclusive

option; while this is somewhat less convenient, shopping and cooking for yourself is significantly less expensive (and then you don't guilty going off-site for a special meal or two). The resort's also on the short, north-facing part of the Zona Hotelera, with virtually no waves—a big difference from east-facing beaches, and a relief for parents with young kids.

CasaMagna Marriott Cancún Resort (Blvd. Kukulcán Km. 14.8, tel. 998/881-2000, toll-free U.S./Can. tel. 888/236-2427, www.marriott.com, US$249-299 s/d with a/c, US$329 suite with a/c) has over 400 rooms, all with private terraces and amenities like flat-screen TVs and wireless Internet. Guests can choose from eight eateries including an Argentinean steak house, a sushi restaurant, and a Thai restaurant. There's also a full-service spa, illuminated tennis courts, and a gym with separate men's and women's saunas. The hotel's main drawback is the pool—it's well maintained but small for the size and caliber of the resort; fortunately, it's just steps from the Caribbean.

Over US$300

❪❪ Fiesta Americana Grand Coral Beach (Blvd. Kukulcán Km. 9.5, tel. 998/881-3200, www.coralbeachcancunhotel.com, US$310-410 junior suite with a/c, US$580-680 master suite with a/c) is an elegant hotel offering spacious and comfortable suites, all with spectacular ocean-view balconies. It features a series of infinity pools, lush and manicured gardens, and one of the calmest beaches of the Zona Hotelera. The hotel has six restaurants and cafés, a huge luxurious spa, a kids club, and activities ranging from Spanish lessons to golf.

The Ritz-Carlton (Blvd. Kukulcán Km. 13.9, tel. 998/881-0808, www.ritzcarlton.com, US$359-409 s/d with a/c, US$579 suite with a/c) is unparalleled in its elegance. Fine art, chandeliers, and marble floors greet you the moment the white-gloved porter opens the door. All rooms have stunning ocean views and boast features like goose down comforters, espresso machines, downpour showerheads,

and twice-daily housekeeping. Other high-end features of the resort include a full-service spa and gym, tennis courts, the Culinary Center (a gorgeous kitchen where guests can take cooking classes), and, of course, a well-maintained beach. The only hiccups are the unremarkable pools—nice enough but nothing special—an odd oversight given the luxuriousness of the rest of the hotel.

All-Inclusive Resorts

Hotel Riu Palace Las Américas (Blvd. Kukulcán Km. 8.5, tel. 998/881-4300, www.riu.com, US$139-171 pp) is a Victorian-style hotel with 350-plus suites that, while not as elegant as the common areas, are quite nice nonetheless. Each has a separate sitting area, a minibar that's restocked daily, and standard amenities like satellite TV and in-room safe; most rooms also have ocean views. Beds are ultrafirm—ask for a foam topper if that's an issue. Outside of the rooms, the beach is narrow but well maintained; there are also two infinity pools, endless water activities, six restaurants, and five bars.

Located at the southernmost tip of the Zona Hotelera, **Club Med Cancún Yucatán** (Blvd. Kukulcán Km. 20.6, tel. 998/881-8200, toll-free U.S. tel. 888/932-2582, www.clubmed.com, US$380 d all-inclusive) is a secluded resort with a huge offering of activities—from wakeboarding and waterskiing to flying trapeze and salsa dancing. If you've got kids, the Mini Club keeps the little ones happy and busy all day long with activities like tennis lessons and tie-dyeing. There also are three good restaurants and a handful of bars—enough variety to keep most guests happy.

A luxurious adults-only resort, **❪❪ Le Blanc Spa Resort** (Blvd. Kukulcán Km. 10, tel. 998/881-4740, toll-free U.S. tel. 877/325-1538, www.leblancsparesort.com, US$694-730 s/d with a/c, US$789-884 suite with a/c) offers all the amenities a vacationing couple could want: infinity pools, à la carte gourmet restaurants, a fully equipped gym and spa, Pilates and yoga classes, bars and lounges, and yards and yards of white-sand beach. The guest rooms are minimalist chic, all with views of the Caribbean or the lagoon. Each has a double whirlpool tub, marble bathroom with double showerheads, flat-screen TVs, even a pillow menu. Best of all, there is a butler assigned to each floor to ensure that every guest's needs are met—from unpacking bags and running a bubble bath to delivering the morning paper.

DOWNTOWN
Under US$50
A huge mural marks the entrance of (**Hostel Quetzal** (Jardín del Arte, Orquídeas 10, tel. 998/883-9821, www.hostelquetzal.com, US$19-21 pp dorm, US$46/54 pp s/d), a dance studio turned hostel. An artsy place, it's got bright and airy rooms, all with air-conditioning, plus a verdant garden and a rooftop lounge with views of downtown Cancún. A spiral staircase leads to the dorm, which is spacious and colorful. Private rooms are scattered around, all with terraces and plenty of natural light. All guests enjoy a full breakfast and family-style dinner as part of the rate. Wi-Fi is available.

Hostel Mundo Joven Cancun (Av. Uxmal 25, tel. 998/898-2104, www.mundojovenhostels.com, US$12 dorm with fan, US$14 dorm with a/c, US$36 d with shared bath, US$45 with private bath) is a sleek affair with cool minimalist decor inside and out. Dorms are airy and bright, with outlets inside the lockers, so you can charge your devices without worrying they'll get swiped. Private rooms are equally stylish, and there's a rooftop lounge with a bar, Jacuzzi, and nice views. Continental breakfast, kitchen access, and computers and Wi-Fi are all included.

Welcoming of all ages, **Moloch Hostel** (Margaritas 54, tel. 998/884-6918, www.moloch.com.mx, US$15 dorm, US$26/40 s/d with shared bath, US$32/48 s/d with private bath) is a laid-back and super-clean hostel with mini-split air conditioners in all the rooms, including the dorms, and an inviting kidney-shaped pool in back. Dorms are a bit cramped but the beds are good; private rooms are larger and would even work for families. There's a

fully equipped kitchen for all to use, as well as continental breakfast, a TV lounge, and free computers. All that, and it's just a block from the bus station and the park.

Located on a leafy residential street, **Los Girasoles** (Piña 20, tel. 998/887-3990, www.losgirasolescancun.com.mx, US$33/37 s/d one bed with a/c and kitchenette, US$41 s/d two beds with a/c and kitchenette) offers 18 spotless and colorful rooms with kitchenettes. Rooms are sunny and have heavy wood and ironwork furnishings; the TVs and air-conditioning are rather old, but still functional, and there's Wi-Fi throughout. Family owned and operated, the hotel's friendly service and quiet locale make up for being a bit removed from the center.

US$50-100
Bougainvillea and a gurgling fountain welcome you to (**Hotel El Rey del Caribe** (Av. Uxmal at Nader, tel. 998/884-2028, www.reycaribe.com, US$75 s with a/c and kitchenette, US$85 d with a/c and kitchenette), an ecofriendly hotel two blocks east of the bus terminal. Rooms are clean and comfortable (those in the newer section are more spacious, with lovely wood floors), but it's the verdant tropical garden with hammocks, pool, and an outdoor dining area that really sets El Rey apart—you might even forget for a moment you're in the city. The hotel employs solar heating, rainwater recovery, and organic waste composting. Breakfast is included in the rate.

(**Hotel Mallorca** (Calle Gladiolas at Av. Alcatraces, tel. 998/884-4285, http://mallorcahotalandsuites.com, US$66 d with a/c, US$100 suite with a/c and kitchenette) has large comfortable rooms, friendly service, and a perfect location, just a half block from Parque Las Palapas. Rooms combine warm colors and wood furniture with modern amenities, like glass showers and mini-split air conditioners. A rooftop lounge, still in the works when we visited, has superb views of the park and city. All in all, it's a great new addition to downtown.

Suites Alcatraces 33 (Calle Alcatraces

33, tel. 998/887-5579, www.suitesalca-traces33.com, US$60-95 d with a/c and Wi-Fi) is an attractive and well-located condo-hotel overlooking Parque Las Palapas. The high, narrow building has tidy, moderately sized rooms with king-size beds, flat-screen TVs, and views of the park. A plunge pool—though awkwardly positioned at the entrance—is a plus.

You can't miss **Hotel Xbalamqué Resort & Spa** (Av. Yaxchilán 31, cell. tel. 998/193-2720, www.xbalamque.com, US$88 s/d with a/c, US$111 suite) with its grand Maya-theme facade and the halls and stairways are covered in murals depicting important Maya leaders and notable cities in ancient times. Excellent service, a small pool, artsy café, and in-house spa all make this a fine choice. The rooms, however, are weirdly out-of-date, with cottage cheese stucco and old-school TVs and air conditioners. If that doesn't bother you, Xbalamqué is a good option.

The **Ramada Cancun City** (Av. Yaxchilán at Calle Jazmines, tel. 998/881-7870, www.ramada.com, US$65) is cool and sleek, yet affordable and centrally located. Rooms have stark white interiors accented by rust and brown furniture, with basin sinks and flat-screen TVs for a modern touch. Noise from nearby clubs can be a problem, and maintenance and service can be uneven. Still, it's a favorite among business travelers and would suit travelers looking for a reliable, modern downtown hotel. There's a small pool and fitness room, and guests can take advantage of free transport and discounted entrance at **Cabana Beach** (http://cabana-beach.mx), a hip beach club at Playa Chac-Mool in the Zona Hotelera.

Food

Cancún has dozens of excellent restaurants—from Cajun to Japanese, and from Argentinean steak houses to vegetarian. The finest restaurants are in the Zona Hotelera, mostly in the high-end resorts and along the west (lagoon) side of Boulevard Kukulcán. Be aware that eating out in the Zona Hotelera can be shockingly expensive, especially for dishes like lobster and imported steaks. There are a handful of Zona Hotelera gems, with great food at lower prices, and of course plenty of fast-food restaurants like McDonald's and Subway. For something more authentic but still affordable, downtown Cancún is the place to go. Parque Las Palapas and the surrounding streets have restaurants for all tastes and budgets, from fine dining to tasty street food, plus a number of great little cafés and sandwich shops.

ZONA HOTELERA
Mexican
La Destilería (Blvd. Kukulcán Km. 12.5, tel. 998/885-1086, www.ladestileria.com.mx/cancun, 1pm-midnight daily, US$12-30) serves a variety of decent Mexican dishes, including cilantro fish fillet and *molcajete,* a hearty stew served in a traditional stone bowl. Despite the name, tequila isn't actually distilled here—like champagne, it can only be produced in certain parts of Mexico—but you can choose from over a hundred varieties and even take a tequila "tour" (1pm-5pm daily, 30 minutes, US$7) to learn how it's made. Dinner, appetizers, and drinks can add up to a hefty outlay here, but it's worth the expense. Live mariachi music 8pm-9pm daily; reservations are recommended.

Easy to miss, **Tacun** (Blvd. Kukulcán Km. 11.5, tel. 998/593-3638, 11am-10pm daily, US$5-10) is a roadside taco joint at heart, and one of the few places in the Zona Hotelera to get good, genuine Mexican food at reasonable prices. Try a taco sampler platter with shrimp, beef, chicken, and *al pastor* tacos, served piping hot with a variety of fresh salsas. The staff and ambience are friendly, and it's located across the street from Margaritaville and the Flamingo Mall.

a perfect plate of *huevos rancheros,* a classic Mexican breakfast

Seafood

A hidden gem in the Zona Hotelera, **❰ El Fish Fritanga** (aka Pescadillas, Blvd. Kukulcán Km. 12.7, tel. 998/840-6216, 7am-11pm daily, US$3-12) offers tasty homestyle seafood at great prices. If you're stumped, try the *pescadillas* or grilled nurse shark tacos, both house classics. The restaurant faces the lagoon and is below street level, making it easy to miss—look for a small parking lot under a bright Domino's Pizza sign.

Classy but unassuming, **Captain's Cove** (Blvd. Kukulcán Km. 16.5, tel. 998/885-0016, www.captainscoverestaurant.com, noon-11pm Tues.-Sat., 8am-11pm Sun., US$15-39) has a lovely lagoon-side location and excellent seafood, including fresh lobster, stuffed crab, and octopus and shrimp risotto. For a memorable dinner, call ahead to reserve a table on the patio at around sunset. It's located across from the Royal Mayan and Omni resorts.

The nautical-themed **Lorenzillo's** (Blvd. Kukulcán Km. 10.5, tel. 998/883-1254, www. lorenzillos.com.mx, 1pm-12:30am daily, US$18-45) is known as one of the best lobster houses in town. Live lobster is kept in an adapted rowboat tank at the entrance—select the one you want, weigh it on an old-time scale, and before you know it, dinner's on. Seating is indoors under a *palapa* roof or outdoors on the narrow patio overlooking the lagoon.

Italian

With a view of Isla Mujeres, **❰ Dolcemente Pompeii** (Pez Volador 7 at Blvd. Kukulcán Km. 5.5, tel. 998/849-4006, noon-midnight Tues.-Sun., US$8-25) serves up hearty Italian dishes like salmon lasagna, fettuccine with grilled jumbo shrimp, and pizza. Be sure to leave room for the homemade gelato, too. There's live music on weekends.

La Madonna (La Isla Shopping Village, Blvd. Kukulcán Km. 12.5, tel. 998/883-2222, noon-midnight daily, US$15-42) is in a mall, yes, but the larger than life decor and surprisingly good food make that fact easy to forget. A huge modern replica of the *Mona Lisa* peers over an ornate dining room, where the menu includes veal, lamb, shrimp fettuccine, risotto, and more. The bar specializes in martinis, with over 150 variations to choose from.

Steak Houses

Puerto Madero (Marina Barracuda, Blvd. Kukulcán Km. 14, tel. 998/885-2829, www. puertomaderocancun.com, 1pm-1am daily, US$15-65) is a longtime favorite serving carefully prepared meats in huge Argentinean-style portions. Choose a table in the warehouse-style dining room (an homage to the Puerto Madero shipyard in Argentina) or on the open-air patio with views of the lagoon. The menu includes salads, pastas, and excellent seafood, in addition to the many cuts of beef, some of which serve two. Prices are high, but not outrageously so, and you're sure to leave full.

Harry's Prime Steak House & Raw Bar (Blvd. Kukulcán Km. 14.2, tel. 998/840-6550, www.harrys.com.mx, 1pm-1am daily, US$25-100) specializes in best-of-the-best beef, expertly prepared (some cuts are dry-aged for up to four weeks) and cooked in blazing hot broilers. There's also a long menu of sashimi, oysters, ceviche, tartar, and other seafood dishes, plus salad and excellent wine and cocktails. The prices are sky-high, but it's a memorable and worthwhile splurge for steak-lovers.

Other Specialties

Hidden in a small hotel near the Pok-ta-Pok golf course, **La Palapa Belga** (Hotel Imperial Laguna, Calle Quetzal 13, tel. 998/883-5454, www.palapabelga.com, 2pm-11pm Mon.-Sat., US$14-28) has been serving fine French-Belgian cuisine for almost two decades. It's worth searching out both for its views across the lagoon to the Zona Hotelera and its delicious food like duck confit, steak tartare, and "Pot of mussels marinière." Reservations are recommended on weekends.

For a change of pace, **Elefanta** and **Thai Lounge** (La Isla Shopping Village, Blvd. Kukulcán Km. 12.5, tel. 998/176-8070, www. elefanta.com.mx and www.thai.com.mx, noon-midnight daily, US$15-42) are sister restaurants serving quality Indian and Thai food, respectively. The ambience at both is quite nice, despite being in a mall; the Thai Lounge, in particular, has private cabanas on stilts overlooking the lagoon and stays open late as a bar-lounge.

Groceries

Numerous small markets along Boulevard Kukulcán sell chips, water, sunscreen, and other beach basics. For a more complete grocery, head to **Super Express** (Plaza Quetzal, just west of Hotel Presidente-Intercontinental, Blvd. Kukulcán Km. 8, tel. 998/883-3654, 8am-11pm daily), which has canned food, meats, produce, and more.

DOWNTOWN
Mexican

On the southeast corner of Parque Las Palapas, **Restaurante Los Huaraches de Alcatraces** (Alcatraces 31, tel. 998/884-3918, 8am-6:30pm Tues.-Sun., US$3-8) is a classic Mexican cafeteria serving traditional dishes like garlic-baked fish or chicken in homemade *mole.* All dishes come with a choice of two sides, such as veggie or beans. For something a little different, try one of the pre-Hispanic options, such as quesadillas made with blue-corn tortillas.

Combine Disneyland and the Mexican Revolution and you might get **Pericos** (Av. Yaxchilán 61, tel. 998/884-3152, www.pericos. com.mx, noon-midnight daily, US$14-25), a classic Cancún family restaurant. *Bandito* waiters sport crisscrossed ammo belts, the bar has saddles instead of stools, and kids may get a rubber chicken on their plates as a joke. Low-key it is not, but Pericos has a solid reputation for serving good grilled meats and seafood in a fun, boisterous atmosphere. Live marimba and mariachi starts at 7:30pm.

Checándole (Av. Xpuhil at Av. Xel-Há, tel. 998/884-7147, noon-10pm Mon.-Sat., US$5-12) serves up tasty Mexican dishes—tacos, enchiladas, *tortas,* fajitas—in a fast-food-type setting. The set lunch (*menú del día*) costs US$5.

Quesadillas Tierra del Sol (Margaritas near Tulipanes, 8am-midnight daily, US$2-4) has a new name and new owners, but the food and location, right on Parque Las Palapas, are great as ever. Hefty quesadillas (and *sopes, panuchos,* and *salbutes*) come with Oaxacan cheese and your choice of stuffing, from chorizo to *nopales* (cactus). Two will satisfy a decent appetite, four could push you over the edge. Fresh, fruity *aguas* help wash it down. Order at the register and they'll call your number.

On the north end of Parque Las Palapas is a set of **food stalls** (8am-midnight daily, US$1.50-4) selling cheap Mexican and Yucatecan eats—tacos, quesadillas, tostadas, and *salbutes*. It's perfect if you're looking for some good street food or are on a tight budget.

Pescaditos (Av. Yaxchilán 59, noon-midnight daily, US$3-10) is the sort of restaurant you expect to see on the beach, complete with reggae music, a handful of tables, and a sign made from an old surfboard. And like the best beach shacks, Pescaditos will wow you with simple tasty meals, especially the seafood. The ceviche, beer-battered shrimp, and fish tacos and quesadillas are all outstanding, and very well priced. Wash it down with a frosty beer or homemade *limonada.*

Italian

Rolandi's Pizzeria Cancún (Av. Cobá 12, tel. 998/884-4047, www.rolandirestaurants.com, noon-12:30am daily, US$10-24) is an institution, with sister pizzerias in Isla Mujeres, Playa del Carmen, and Cozumel. The food here—and at all of them—is consistently good; choose among thin-crust pizzas, calzones, and great homemade pastas. Pocket bread, warm and inflated, and a dish of olive oil comes with every order. Sit on the veranda, which has trellises draped in ivy that block out street noise.

Other Specialties

One of downtown's finest restaurants, **La Habichuela** (Parque Las Palapas, Calle Margaritas 25, tel. 998/884-3158, www.lahabichuela.com, noon-midnight daily, US$15-42) has been serving excellent Caribbean and Yucatecan dishes in its elegant park-side location since 1977. The seafood is especially good—try the giant shrimp in tamarind sauce or *cocobichuela,* the house specialty, with lobster and shrimp in a sweet curry. For dessert, the Maya coffee flambé is a treat.

Sahara (Calle Gladiolas 12, tel. 998/898-2222, 1pm-11pm Tues.-Sat., 1pm-8pm Sun., US$5-12) prepares authentic Lebanese food like hummus, falafel, and tabbouleh in a casual setting. A huge buffet, featuring the entire menu plus some extras, is served on Sunday only. Fun extras include hookah "hookups" (US$12.50) or having your coffee grounds read (US$12.50, including the coffee). Belly dancers perform on Wednesday starting at 9pm.

La Parrilla (Av. Yaxchilán 51, tel. 998/287-8119, www.laparrilla.com.mx, noon-2am daily, US$8.50-30) is one of the most popular of the restaurant-bars on this busy street, grilling a variety of delicious beef fillets, plus shrimp and lobster brochettes, chicken, fajitas, and tacos—the fiery spit in front is for *taquitos al pastor,* a Mexican classic. The breezy street-side eating area is comfortable and casual—good for families. There also is live mariachi music every night starting at 8pm.

Pescado Con Limón (Mercado 28, tel. 998/887-2436, 11:30am-7:30pm daily, US$6-12) may be short on ambience—plastic tables and chairs facing the Mercado 28 parking lot—but the seafood is as fresh and good as it comes, an open secret among locals and expats. For a sure thing, try a shrimp dish or one of the fried-fish platters.

Light Fare

El Pabilo (Hotel Xbalamqué, Av. Yaxchilán 31, tel. 998/892-4553, 5pm-1am daily, US$3.50-8) is a classy but unassuming café serving up excellent coffee drinks and light meals. The space also serves as an art gallery, with rotating exhibits, and a multilingual bookstore. It is a great place to listen to live music, too—every night but Sunday, you can hear genres ranging from *bohemia cubana* to fusion jazz. Music starts at 9:30pm.

Get a tasty baguette sandwich at █ **Ty-Coz Baguettería** (Av. Tulum at Av. Uxmal, tel. 998/884-6060, 8am-10pm Mon.-Sat.), a cozy eatery tucked behind the Comercial Mexicana supermarket opposite the bus terminal. Popular with local professionals and students, the menu includes French- and German-inspired baguette sandwiches and *cuernos* (croissants). Most are US$3-5, but you can always order the *económica* baguette with ham, salami, and cheese for just US$1.25.

100% Natural (Av. Sunyaxchén at Av. Yaxchilán, tel. 998/884-0102, www.100natural.com.mx, 7am-11pm daily, US$6-12) is a popular and tasty vegetarian restaurant chain, with a large menu that includes salads, veggie and faux-meat sandwiches, and freshly squeezed juices. The ambience can be somewhat sterile—the potted plants and filtered light help—but it's a welcome alternative for non-meat-eaters, locals and tourists alike.

Groceries

Chedraui (Blvd. Kukulcán at Av. Tulum) and **Comercial Mexicana** (Av. Tulum at Av. Uxmal) are huge supermarkets with everything from produce and in-house bakeries to pharmacies and beach supplies. Both are open 7am-11pm daily and have ATMs just inside their doors.

Just a couple of blocks from the bus station, **Mercado 23** (Calles Ciricote and Cedro, three blocks north of Av. Uxmal via Calle Palmeras, 6am-6pm daily) has stands of fresh fruits and vegetables, and none of the touristy trinkets that Mercado 28 has. The selection is somewhat limited, but the produce is the freshest around.

DINNER CRUISES

For couples, the **Lobster Dinner Cruise** (Aquatours Marina, Blvd. Kukulcán Km. 6.5, toll-free Mex. tel. 800/727-5391, toll-free U.S. tel. 866/393-5158, www.thelobsterdinner.com, US$89 dinner with open bar, no children under 14, departs at 5pm, 5:30pm, 8pm, and 8:30pm nightly) offers a change of pace, serving three-course dinners aboard a Spanish-style galleon. The ship cruises the Laguna Nichupté for 2.5 hours, accompanied by live jazz. An additional dock fee applies (US$6 pp).

If you've got kids, the **Galleon of Captain Hook** (Terminal Maritima Puerto Juárez, tel. 998/849-4451, toll-free Mex. tel. 800/010-4665, www.capitanhook.com, US$82-92 dinner with open bar, children under 12 free, departs at 7pm nightly, 3.5 hours) offers dinner plus a costumed crew, tales of pirate conquest, and even a "disco party" on the deck while cruising the open sea. An additional dock fee applies (US$10 pp). The boat leaves from Puerto Juárez north of Cancún; hotel pickup is available for an extra fee.

Information and Services

TOURIST INFORMATION

Downtown, the **City Tourist Office** (Av. Nader at Av. Cobá, tel. 998/887-3379, www.turismo.cancun.gob.mx, 9am-4pm Mon.-Fri.) is a bustling office with staffers who happily provide information on city and regional sights. A kiosk just outside of the office has brochures and maps. English is spoken.

Note: Be aware that booths with Tourist Information signs along Avenida Tulum and Boulevard Kukulcán are in fact operated by **time-share companies,** offering free tours and other goodies in exchange for attending a sales presentation.

There are also several publications that are worth picking up: *Cancún Tips* (www.

cancuntips.com.mx) is a free tourist magazine with general information about Cancún and nearby sights; both **Restaurante Menu Mapa** and **Map@migo** (www.mapapocket-cancun.com) have maps, restaurant menus, reviews, and discount coupons; and **Agenda Cultural** has listings of Cancún's upcoming cultural events, exhibitions, and workshops. This last one can be hard to find—ask at the tourist office.

EMERGENCY SERVICES

There are several recommended private hospitals within a few blocks of each other in downtown Cancún. All have emergency rooms and English-speaking doctors and are open 24 hours daily: **Hospitén Cancún** (Av. Bonampak s/n, south of Av. Nichupté, tel. 998/881-3700, www.hospiten.com), **AmeriMed Hospital** (Av. Bonampak at Av. Nichupté, behind Las Américas mall, tel. 998/881-3400, www.amerimedcancun.com), and **Hospital Galenia** (Av. Tulum at Av. Nizuc, tel. 998/891-5200, www.hospitalgalenia.com).

For meds in the Zona Hotelera, try any of the malls or head to **Farmacia del Ahorro** (Blvd. Kukulcán Km. 9.5, tel. 998/892-7291, 24 hours). Downtown, **Farmacias Similares** (Av. Tulum near Calle Crisantemos, tel. 998/898-0190, 24 hours) is a reliable national chain.

The **police department, fire station,** and **ambulance** all can be reached by dialing toll-free 060 or 066 any time. In the Zona Hotelera, all three are located in the same building next to Plaza Kukulcán (Blvd. Kukulcán Km. 12.5). Downtown, the main police station (Av. Xcaret at Av. Kabah, tel. 998/884-1913, 24 hours) faces the Carrefour supermarket, and there's a small office on Parque Las Palapas, near the food stalls, which is usually open 24 hours.

MONEY

You'll have no problem accessing or exchanging your money in Cancún. ATMs are ubiquitous, including at all the shopping malls, and give the best exchange rate. Many resorts will exchange dollars and euros, or simply accept them directly as payment. Ditto for many tour operators and even restaurants, especially in the Zona Hotelera. The exchange rate may be awful, however.

If you need an actual bank, head to **Plaza Caracol** (Blvd. Kukulcán Km. 8.5), where you'll find Bancomer, HSBC, and Banamex; or **Plaza Kukulcán** (Blvd. Kukulcán Km. 12.5), where there's a Banco Serfín. All have ATMs that accept foreign cards and are open roughly 9am-4pm Monday-Friday.

Downtown, the best-located banks are on Avenida Tulum between Avenida Cobá and Avenida Uxmal: **Bancomer** (Av. Tulum 20, 8:30am-4pm Mon.-Fri., 10am-2pm Sat.) and **Banamex** (Av. Tulum 19, 9am-4pm Mon.-Fri., 10am-2pm Sat.).

American Express (Av. Tulum 208 at Calle Agua, tel. 998/881-4000, 9am-5pm Mon.-Fri., 9am-1pm Sat.) offers money exchange and other services to cardholding travelers. There's also an AmEx kiosk in La Isla Shopping Village (9am-10pm daily).

MEDIA AND COMMUNICATIONS
Post Office

The **post office** (Av. Sunyaxchen at Av. Xel-Há, tel. 998/834-1418, 8am-6pm Mon.-Fri., 8am-1pm Sat.) is located in front of Mercado 28. There is no post office in the Zona Hotelera, though your hotel may mail postcards for you.

Internet and Telephone

Most hostels, hotels, and resorts now offer Wi-Fi service, whether for free or at a small cost, and many have computers available for those without a laptop or mobile device of their own. Malls, restaurants, and even the Mexican government is following suit: Most Mexican cities, Cancún among them, have public Wi-Fi in their main plazas. If all else fails, you can get online at local cybercafés, scattered throughout downtown and in the main Zona Hotelera malls. Most have Skype-enabled computers, but also offer direct-dial national and international calls for US$0.20-0.40 per minute.

In the Zona Hotelera, Internet cafés are located at **Plaza Kukulcán** (Blvd. Kukulcán Km. 12.5, 10am-10pm daily, US$8.50/hour) and at **Forum by the Sea** (Blvd. Kukulcán Km. 9, 10am-10pm Mon.-Sat., US$7/hour).

Downtown is far cheaper, including at **Cancún @** (Av. Uxmal 22-D, tel. 998/892-3484, 8am-midnight daily), located near the bus station, with air-conditioning, friendly service, and fast Internet connections for around US$1 per hour.

Just off Parque Las Palapas, **C@s@bl@nc@** (Gladiolas near Alcatraces, 10am-midnight daily) charges the same but is sometimes closed unexpectedly.

Newspapers

There are a handful of newspapers for local and regional news: In Spanish, **Novedades de Quintana Roo** (www.sipse.com/novedades) is the state's oldest newspaper, centrist in coverage, with a good classified section; **¡Por Esto!** (www.poresto.net) is a left-of-center paper with Quintana Roo and Yucatán versions; and **Diario de Yucatán** (www.yucatan.com.mx) is more conservative and covers the entire region. The Cancún version of the **Miami Herald Tribune** is a good English-language alternative.

IMMIGRATION

Cancún's **immigration office** (Av. Nader at Av. Uxmal, tel. 998/884-1749 or 998/881-3560, 8am-1pm Mon.-Fri.) is an efficient, welcoming office—worlds better than the one in Playa del Carmen.

LAUNDRY AND STORAGE

Downtown, **Lavandería Las Palapas** (Parque Las Palapas, Alcatraces near Gladiolas, 7am-10pm Mon.-Sat.) will do your laundry for US$4.25 per three kilos (6.6 pounds), or you can do it yourself for US$1.25 per wash or dry. A block away, **Zamalek** (Gladiolas near Av. Yaxchilán, 8:30am-8pm Mon.-Fri., 10am-6pm Sat.) is slightly cheaper at US$3.25 per three kilos. Both offer two-hour rush service for 50 percent extra.

In the Zona Hotelera, **Lavandería Lumi** (Plaza Quetzal, Blvd. Kukulcán Km. 7.4, tel. 998/883-3874, 8am-8pm Mon.-Sat., 9am-5pm Sun.) will wash, dry, and fold your dirty clothes for US$10 for four kilos (8.8 pounds); rush service is available for double price, while pickup/drop-off service costs an additional US$8.50.

Another Zona Hotelera option is **Laundry Wash** (Blvd. Kukulcán Km. 14.5, no phone, 8am-7pm Mon.-Fri., 8am-3pm Sat.), which charges US$8.50 per three kilos (6.6 pounds) for 24-hour service or US$12 per three kilos for express service and has hotel drop-off. It's located on the access road behind Secret resort, near Playa Ballenas.

On the 1st floor of the bus station, **Guarda Equipaje** (tel. 998/884-4352, ext. 2851, 6am-9:30pm daily) will store luggage for US$0.50-1.20 per hour, depending on the size, or a flat US$8.50 per day.

Storage lockers (US$7 per 24 hours) also can be rented in Terminal 3 at Cancún's International Airport; they are big enough to hold carry-on bags only. Look for the lockers as you exit Customs.

Getting There and Around

GETTING THERE
Air
The **Cancún International Airport** (CUN, tel. 998/848-7200, www.cancun-airport.com) is 20 kilometers (12.4 miles) south of Cancún. Most international flights arrive and depart from the airport's Terminal 3, which also has airline, taxi, bus, and car rental desks, as well as ATMs. In general, Terminal 2 is used for domestic flights with some overflow international flights; Terminal 1 is reserved for charter flights. A free shuttle ferries travelers between Terminal 2 and 3 only.

Bus
Buses leave Cancún's clean and modern **bus terminal** (Av. Tulum at Av. Uxmal) for destinations in the Yucatán Peninsula and throughout the interior of Mexico.

Combi
Combis, public shuttle vans, run between

Flying to Cancún

The following airlines serve **Cancún International Airport** (CUN, Carr. Cancun-Chetumal Km. 22, tel. 998/848-7200, www.cancun-airport.com):

- **Aeroméxico** (Av. Cobá at Av. Bonampak, tel. 998/287-1860, airport tel. 998/193-1866, toll-free Mex. tel. 800/021-4000, toll-free U.S. tel. 800/237-6639, www.aeromexico.com)

- **Air Canada** (airport tel. 998/886-0883, toll-free Mex. tel. 800/719-2827, toll-free U.S./Can. tel. 888/247-2262, www.aircanada.com)

- **American Airlines** (airport tel. 998/886-0086, toll-free Mex. tel. 800/904-6000, toll-free U.S./Can. tel. 800/433-7300, www.aa.com)

- **Continental** (airport tel. 998/886-0006, toll-free Mex. tel. 800/900-5000, toll-free U.S./Can. tel. 800/864-8331, www.continental.com)

- **Copa Airlines** (airport tel. 998/886-0652, toll-free Mex. tel. 800/265-2672, toll-free U.S. tel. 800/359-2672, www.copaair.com)

- **Cubana de Aviación** (Av. Tulum 232, tel. 998/887-7210, airport tel. 998/886-0355, www.cubana.cu)

- **Delta** (airport tel. 998/886-0668, toll-free Mex. tel. 800/123-4710, toll-free U.S. tel. 800/221-1212, www.delta.com)

- **Frontier Airlines** (toll-free U.S. tel. 800/432-1359, www.frontierairlines.com)

- **InterJet** (Plaza Hollywood, Av. Cobá at Av. Xcaret, tel. 998/892-0278, toll-free Mex. tel. 800/011-2345, toll-free U.S. tel. 866/285-9525, www.interjet.com.mx)

- **Lan** (airport tel. 998/886-0360, toll-free Mex. tel. 800/123-1619, toll-free U.S. tel. 866/435-9526, www.lan.com)

- **Lufthansa** (airport tel. 998/886-0122, toll-free U.S. tel. 800/645-3880, www.lufthansa.com)

- **Spirit Airlines** (Retorno Jazmines at Av. Yaxchilán, tel. 998/886-0708, airport tel. 998/887-1862, toll-free Mex./U.S./Can. tel. 800/772-7117, www.spiritair.com)

- **United Airlines** (toll-free Mex. tel. 800/900-5000, toll-free U.S./Can. tel. 800/864-8331, www.united.com)

- **US Airways** (airport tel. 998/886-0373, toll-free Mex. tel. 800/843-3000, toll-free U.S. tel. 800/428-4322, www.usairways.com)

CANCÚN BUS SCHEDULE

Cancún's **bus station** (tel. 800/702-8000) is located downtown at Avenidas Tulum and Uxmal. Departures listed below include both first- and second-class service; in many cases, second-class buses take significantly longer for only marginal savings.

DESTINATION	PRICE	DURATION	SCHEDULE
Campeche City	US$32-38	7-8 hrs	11 departures 7:45 am-11:30 pm
Cancún Int'l Airport	US$4.50	25 mins	every 30 mins 7:30 am-8 pm; and 9:15 pm and 10 pm
Chetumal	US$17.25-25.25	5-6 hrs	every 30-90 mins 4 am-midnight
Chichén Itzá	US$10.25-17	3.5-4.5 hrs	4 departures 5 am-1 pm or take any Pisté bus
Chiquilá	US$6	3 hrs	6 departures 4:30 am-2:15 pm
Mahahual	US$31	5.5 hrs	3:15 pm
Mérida	US$24.50-41	4 hrs	every 30-60 mins 5:15 am-11:59 pm
Mexico City	US$127-149	24-26 hrs	6 departures 10 am-8 pm

Cancún and Playa del Carmen. They queue up directly across Avenida Tulum from the bus terminal, near the Comercial Mexicana, and depart every 10-15 minutes 24 hours a day (US$2.75, one hour). For slightly more, **Playa Express** has larger, air-conditioned shuttles, departing on roughly the same schedule from the parking lot in front of the bus terminal (US$3, 50 minutes). Both services make stops along the way, including Puerto Morelos (US$2-2.50, 30 minutes).

GETTING AROUND
To and from the Airport
Cancún's airport is served by taxi, shuttle, and bus. The authorized airport taxi service, **Yellow Transfers** (toll-free Mex. tel. 01-800/021-8087, www.yellowtransfers.

com), has two booths inside the airport and another at the exit, and has taxi and shuttle service, including luxury class and for the disabled, anywhere on the coast. Fares are fixed and prominently displayed at the airport and online (where rates are sometimes discounted). Rates to the Zona Hotelera vary by distance, but private taxis and shuttles run US$48-80 (4-8 pax), while shared shuttles are US$12-16. To downtown, it's US$64 private and US$12 shared. Yellow Transfers offers round-trip service at a discount, or you can hire an ordinary taxi; you'll end up paying roughly the same. Service down the coast includes Playa del Carmen (US$95/35 private/shared) and Tulum (US$164/53).

   ADO has a ticket counter right outside the airport; bear right as you leave the main doors.

DESTINATION	PRICE	DURATION	SCHEDULE
Palenque	US$57-68	12 hrs	6 departures 3:45pm-8:30pm
Pisté	US$10.25-17	4 hrs	every 30-60 mins 7am-11:45pm
Playa del Carmen	US$2.75-4.75	1 hr	every 15-30 mins 4am-11:59pm
Puerto Morelos	US$1.85-2.25	40 mins	every 15-30 mins 4am-11:30pm
Río Lagartos	–	–	no direct service; connect through Tizimín
Tizimín	US$8.75	3-4 hrs	6 departures 3:30am-6:30pm
Tulum	US$6.75-8.75	2.5 hrs	every 60-90 mins 4am-11:59pm
Valladolid	US$8-12.50	2-3 hrs	every 15-60 mins 3am-11:45pm
Xpujil	US$21.25-33.50	7-8 hrs	6 departures 4am-6:30pm

Comfortable, air-conditioned buses leave every half hour for downtown Cancún (8:15am-11pm daily, US$4.25, 25 minutes) and every 40 minutes for Playa del Carmen (10am-10:15pm daily, US$10.50, 1 hour); the latter stops in Puerto Morelos (US$6, 25 minutes) along the way. For Tulum (US$14.50, 2 hours), there are direct buses at 2:10pm, 7:45pm and 8:45pm; otherwise take any bus to Playa del Carmen and transfer. ADO's airport buses do not enter Cancún's Zona Hotelera, however.

Bus

Frequent buses (US$0.75) run between downtown Cancún and the Zona Hotelera—you'll rarely have to wait more than five minutes for one to pass. The buses are red and have "R-1," "Hoteles," or "Zona Hotelera" painted on the front, and stop along Avenida Tulum, the bus station, and near most major hotels, beaches, and ferry ports.

Taxi

You'll have no trouble finding a taxi around town or in the Zona Hotelera—they are everywhere tourists are. Before getting into one, however, make sure to agree upon a price—meters are not used, and drivers sometimes overcharge. As of this writing, the rate around downtown is US$1.75, from downtown to the Isla Mujeres ferries US$4.25, and from downtown to the Zona Hotelera US$7-17, depending on the destination. Rates within the Zona Hotelera jump dramatically and depend on how far you're going. Ask your concierge for specific rates, but expect to pay US$5-20.

Car

Although you won't need a car to visit Cancún proper, renting one is a great way to visit the nearest archaeological sites (i.e., Tulum, Cobá, Ek' Balam, and Chichén Itzá) without being part of a huge tour group. A rental also makes exploring the Riviera Maya a little easier, though buses cover that route fairly well. Driving in the Cancún area is relatively pain free—unexpected speed bumps and impatient bus drivers are the biggest concern.

Most international car rental companies, and a few local ones, have offices at the airport (some are right at the terminal, others in a purpose-built rental center few miles away) as well as in select resorts and at offices downtown and in the Zona Hotelera. Various sizes and types of vehicle are available, from SUVs to Volkswagen bugs (optimistically dubbed VW sedans); prices with insurance and taxes start at around US$40 a day. The best rates are online with the international companies; you also can sometimes get discounted rates by spending half a day in a time-share presentation. Commonly used companies include:

- **Thrifty** (Cancún Airport, tel. 998/886-0333; Hotel Presidente InterContinental, Blvd. Kukulcán Km. 7.5, tel. 998/848-8700, www.thrifty.com)

- **Avis** (Cancún Airport, tel. 998/883-0221; La Isla Shopping Village, Blvd. Kukulcán Km. 12.5, tel. 998/176-8030, www.avis.com)

- **National** (Cancún Airport, tel. 998/881-8760; La Isla Shopping Village, Blvd. Kukulcán Km. 12.5, tel. 998/176-8117, www.nationalcar.com)

- **Hertz** (Cancún Airport, tel. 998/887-0142; Av. Yaxchilán 27, tel. 998/882-1524, www.hertz.com)

- **America Car Rental** (Cancún Airport, tel. 998/253-6100; Flamingo Plaza, Blvd. Kukulcán Km. 11.5, tel. 998/883-0160, www.america-carrental.com)

- **Avicar** (Cancún Airport, tel. 998/887-0142, toll-free Mex. tel. 800/282-7875, toll-free U.S./Can. tel. 888/903-2666, www.avicar.com.mx)

- **AutoRent** (Av. Tulum at Calle Azucenas, tel. 998/887-0709)

Parking lots in the Zona Hotelera are in the shopping centers: La Isla Shopping Village, Forum by the Sea, Plaza Kukulcán, and Plaza Caracol. Rates are typically US$1.50 for the first hour and US$0.50 for each additional hour. Downtown, it's easiest—and relatively safe—to park on the street or in the public lots around Parque Las Palapas.

Travel Agencies

Most travelers handle their travel and hotel bookings online, but there are scores of travel agencies in Cancún for anyone who finds a need for their service—look especially on Avenidas Tulum and Uxmal. Worth noting is **American Express** (Av. Tulum 208 at Calle Agua, tel. 998/881-4000, 9am-6pm Mon.-Fri., 9am-1pm Sat.), which has special services for cardholders.

DRIVING DISTANCES FROM CANCÚN

LOCATION	DISTANCE	LOCATION	DISTANCE
Airport	20 km (12.5 mi)	Playa del Carmen	68 km (42.5 mi)
Akumal	105 km (65 mi)	Puerto Aventuras	87 km (54 mi)
Bacalar	320 km (199 mi)	Puerto Morelos	36 km (22.5 mi)
Campeche	487 km (302.5 mi)	Punta Allen	182 km (114km)
Chetumal	382 km (237.5 mi)	Tulum	130 km (81 mi)
Chichén Itzá	178 km (110.5 mi)	Valladolid	158 km (98 mi)
Cobá	173 km (107.5 mi)	Xcalak	411 km (255.5 mi)
Izamal	266 km (166 mi)	Xcaret	74 km (46 mi)
Mahahual	351 km (218 mi)	Xel-Há	122 km (76 mi)
Mérida	320 km (199 mi)	Xpu-Há	101 km (63 mi)
Paamul	82 km (51 mi)	Xpujil	501 km (311 mi)

Isla Mujeres

Just eight kilometers (5 miles) long and no more than a quarter mile wide, Isla Mujeres is a sliver of land fringed by white-sand beaches amid the wide turquoise sea. It actually was one of the first places in the Mexican Caribbean to have hotels and other tourist developments, but attention quickly shifted to Isla Cozumel and then Cancún proper. It may have been a blessing in disguise: As those areas exploded, rushing to build high-rise hotels and ports for cruise ships, Isla Mujeres developed more slowly, attracting backpackers and bohemians while remaining pretty much what it always was—a quiet, picturesque fishing community.

Of course, even slow change adds up, and today Isla Mujeres is a well-established tourist destination. Thousands of day-trippers come from Cancún to shop, eat, and relax on the island's calm beaches. While still popular with backpackers, Isla Mujeres now also attracts midrange and upscale travelers with an ever-expanding selection of boutique hotels and bed-and-breakfasts.

Despite higher hotel prices and T-shirt shops, golf carts, and pushy tour operators, Isla Mujeres remains at its core a mellow tropical island with a friendly and laid-back population. Passersby greet one another, people stroll in the middle of the street, and many businesses close for long lunches. Add to that beautiful beaches and numerous options for snorkeling, biking, and other outdoor excursions, and it's no wonder so many visitors find themselves extending (and re-extending) their time here.

HISTORY

The precise origin of the name Isla Mujeres (Island of Women) is unknown, though not

ISLA MUJERES

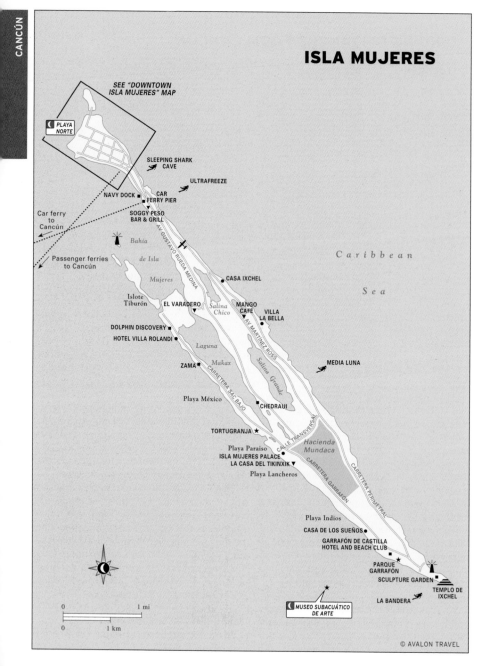

SEE "DOWNTOWN
ISLA MUJERES" MAP

PLAYA NORTE

SLEEPING SHARK CAVE

ULTRAFREEZE

NAVY DOCK

CAR FERRY PIER

Car ferry to Cancún

SOGGY PESO BAR & GRILL

Bahía

AV GUSTAVO RUEDA MEDINA

Passenger ferries to Cancún

de Isla

Mujeres

CASA IXCHEL

C a r i b b e a n

Islote Tiburón

EL VARADERO

Salina Chico

MANGO CAFÉ

VILLA LA BELLA

S e a

DOLPHIN DISCOVERY

HOTEL VILLA ROLANDI

Laguna

AV MARTINEZ ROSS

ZAMA

Makax

CARRETERA SAC BAJO

Salina Grande

MEDIA LUNA

Playa México

CHEDRAUI

TORTUGRANJA

CALLE TRANSVERSAL

Hacienda Mundaca

Playa Paraíso
ISLA MUJERES PALACE
LA CASA DEL TIKINXIK

CARRETERA GARRAFÓN

CARRETERA PERIMETRAL

Playa Lancheros

Playa Indios

CASA DE LOS SUEÑOS
GARRAFÓN DE CASTILLA
HOTEL AND BEACH CLUB

PARQUE GARRAFÓN

SCULPTURE GARDEN

TEMPLO DE IXCHEL

LA BANDERA

MUSEO SUBACUÁTICO DE ARTE

0   1 mi

0   1 km

© AVALON TRAVEL

for lack of theories. Some say the name comes from the days of pirates trolling the Caribbean; they allegedly kept their female captives on Isla Mujeres while they ransacked boats sailing along the coast. Another more likely story is that the island served as a stopover (or secondary site) for Maya pilgrims on their way to Isla Cozumel to worship Ixchel, the female goddess of fertility. When Spanish explorers landed here, they reportedly found a large number of female-shaped clay idols and named the island after them.

ORIENTATION

The town of Isla Mujeres (known as the *centro,* or center) is at the far northwestern tip of the island; at just eight blocks long and five blocks deep, it is very walkable. This is where most of the hotels, restaurants, shops, and services are. There is no main street per se, although Avenida Hidalgo intersects with the town *zócalo* (central plaza) and has a bustling pedestrian-only section. Avenida Rueda Medina is the busy street that runs along the south side of the *centro* past the ferry piers and continues all the way to the island's other end, becoming Carretera Punta Sur at Parque Garrafón (and therefore also known as Carretera Garrafón). The road that runs along the north side of the island is Avenida Martínez Ross as it leaves the downtown area, becoming Carretera Perimetral partway down the island.

SIGHTS
Hacienda Mundaca
A sad dilapidated estate, **Hacienda Mundaca** (Av. Rueda Medina at Carr. Garrafón Km. 3.5, no phone, 9am-5pm daily, US$1.75) is not interesting enough to visit, but is just historical enough that tourism folks (including guidebook authors) can't just ignore it. It was built by a 19th-century retired slave trader, Antonio Mundaca, to woo a local woman; when she rejected his advances, Mundaca went crazy, holing up in the estate while it crumbled around him . . . and that's pretty much where things stand today.

Tortugranja

A modest sea turtle sanctuary on the island's southwestern shore, **Tortugranja** (Carr. Sac Bajo 5, tel. 998/888-0507, 9am-5pm daily, US$2.50) makes for an interesting stop on your golf-cart tour of the island. The one-room cement structure contains several enclosures with sea turtles of different ages and species. The tank of just-hatched *tortuguitas* is always a hit; please respect the rules (and huge signs) and refrain from touching or picking them up. During the nesting season (May-October), one section of sand is fenced off, and eggs collected from nests are transplanted here for protection. Small aquariums along the walls contain sea anemones, sea horses, and the deadly rockfish, among others.

Between July and November, travelers may be able to accompany the center's workers to look for fresh sea turtle nests on the island's eastern shore and relocate eggs to protected areas, and, until October and November, help release hatchlings into the sea. Both activities take place in the evening several nights a week but are not formal tours. Those interested should inquire at the center, and having basic Spanish (and possibly your own vehicle) will make participating much easier. There's no charge, but a tip is customary.

◖ Museo Subacuático de Arte
Underwater sculpture is nothing new, but there's never been a project as ambitious—or as gorgeous, frankly—as the **Subaquatic Museum of Art** (MUSA, www.asociados-nauticoscancun.com). British sculptor Jason de Caires Taylor created hundreds of life-size statues of everyday people—garbage men, pregnant women, wizened tribal leaders, and more—and sank them in 12-40 feet of crystalline water near Manchones reef. Striking for their lifelike quality, the figures were made from special cement that will promote coral and other sealife, eventually forming an artificial reef system. Diving is the best way to enjoy the statues, though snorkelers can manage a decent look, too; most dive shops offer both options.

Templo de Ixchel and Sculpture Garden

At the far southern tip of the island, a crumbling Maya temple stands on a cliff overlooking the sea. Its original function is unknown: The location suggests it was an observation post or even an astronomical observatory, but most experts believe it was related to Ixchel, the Maya goddess of the moon, fertility, weaving, and childbirth, possibly as a secondary pilgrimage site after Isla Cozumel. Whatever its history, the temple was abandoned long before Francisco Hernández de Córdoba first reported their existence in 1517.

The temple alone isn't too exciting, as time and weather have all but destroyed it. But a visit here also includes stopping in a tiny museum, climbing a renovated lighthouse, and pondering a dozen or so multicolored modern sculptures lining the path to the ruins. And just past the ruins, the trail continues to the very tip of the island—the easternmost point of Mexico, in fact—before looping back along the craggy waterfront to the entrance. It's a decent side trip, with some fine photo ops along the way.

Admission to the Ixchel ruins is included in the ticket price to Parque Garrafón; all others must pay US$3 (10am-5pm daily).

🄲 Isla Contoy

Peeking out of a crystal-clear sea and dotted with saltwater lagoons, mangrove trees, and coconut palms, Isla Contoy is home to over 150 species of birds, including herons, brown pelicans, frigates, and cormorants, and is a preferred nesting ground for three different species of endangered sea turtles. The island was decreed a national park in 1998, and its only structures are a three-story viewing tower, a visitors center, and a small museum; a few trails allow for appreciating the otherwise pristine island environment. Just 24 kilometers (14 miles) north of Isla Mujeres, Isla Contoy is a popular and rewarding outing for nature buffs and average day-trippers alike.

Various tour operators on Isla Mujeres offer the same basic trip for a standard price (US$65, including the US$5 park entrance fee): Depart

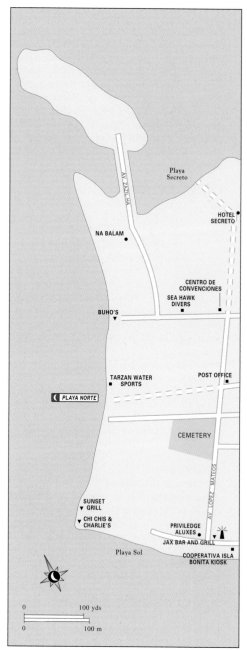

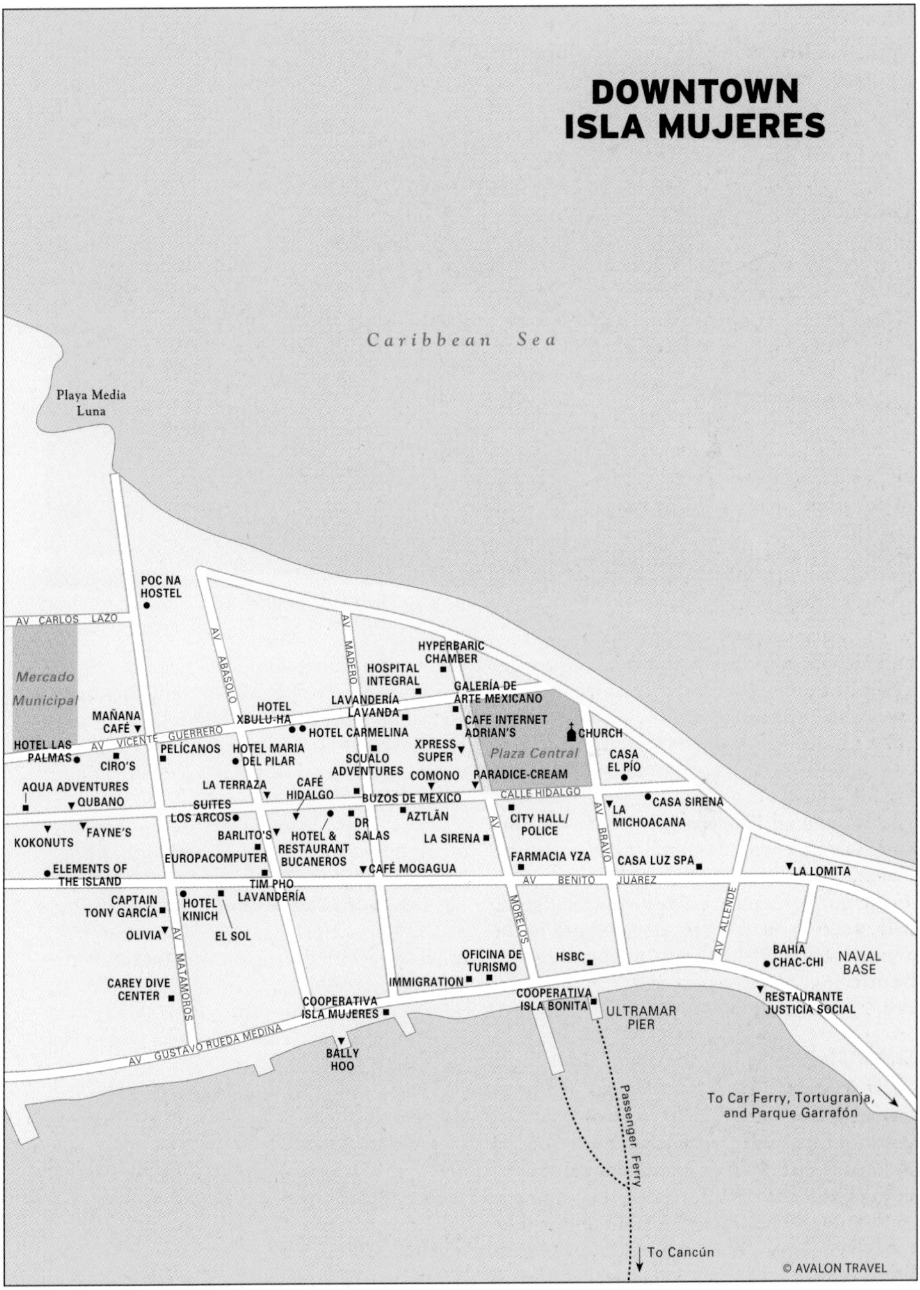

CANCÚN

DOWNTOWN
ISLA MUJERES

Caribbean Sea

Playa Media
Luna

POC NA
HOSTEL

AV CARLOS LAZO

AV ABASOLO

AV MADERO

Mercado
Municipal

HYPERBARIC
CHAMBER

HOSPITAL
INTEGRAL

GALERÍA DE
ARTE MEXICANO

MAÑANA
CAFÉ

HOTEL
XBULU-HA

LAVANDERÍA
LAVANDA

AV VICENTE GUERRERO

CAFE INTERNET
ADRIAN'S

CHURCH

HOTEL LAS
PALMAS

PELÍCANOS

HOTEL CARMELINA

HOTEL MARIA
DEL PILAR

CIRO'S

SCUALO
ADVENTURES

XPRESS
SUPER

Plaza Central

CASA
EL PÍO

AQUA ADVENTURES

LA TERRAZA

CAFÉ
HIDALGO

COMONO

PARADICE-CREAM

QUBANO

SUITES

LOS ARCOS

BUZOS DE MEXICO

CALLE HIDALGO

AV BRAVO

LA
MICHOACANA

CASA SIRENA

KOKONUTS

FAYNE'S

BARLITO'S

AZTLÁN

DR
SALAS

LA SIRENA

CITY HALL/
POLICE

AV

EUROPACOMPUTER

HOTEL &
RESTAURANT
BUCANEROS

FARMACIA YZA

CASA LUZ SPA

ELEMENTS OF
THE ISLAND

CAFÉ MOGAGUA

AV BENITO JUAREZ

LA LOMITA

CAPTAIN
TONY GARCÍA

TIM PHO

HOTEL
KINICH

LAVANDERÍA

AV MATAMOROS

MORELOS

OLIVIA

EL SOL

BAHÍA
CHAC-CHI

NAVAL
BASE

CAREY DIVE
CENTER

OFICINA DE
TURISMO

HSBC

AV ALLENDE

RESTAURANTE
JUSTICIA SOCIAL

IMMIGRATION

COOPERATIVA
ISLA MUJERES

COOPERATIVA
ISLA BONITA

ULTRAMAR
PIER

AV GUSTAVO RUEDA MEDINA

BALLY
HOO

Passenger Ferry

To Car Ferry, Tortugranja,
and Parque Garrafón

To Cancún

© AVALON TRAVEL

© LIZA PRADO

Brown pelicans are one of dozens of species of birds you'll see on Isla Contoy.

around 9:15am with a 30- to 45-minute stop for snorkeling along the way, then three hours to explore the island or just relax, including lunch on the beach (typically freshly grilled fish or chicken). Boats head back around 3pm, reaching Isla Mujeres at 4pm.

Recommended operators include **Captain Tony García** (Av. Matamoros near Av. Benito Juárez, tel. 998/877-0229, captaintonys@hotmail.com), a friendly English-speaking guide with over 20 years' experience whose house doubles as his office, and **Cooperativa Isla Bonita** (Av. Madero pier, cell. tel. 998/134-6103, 9am-5pm daily).

BEACHES
◖ Playa Norte

Playa Norte (North Beach) is a long undulating strip of sand on the northern edge of Isla Mujeres. Its fine white sands descend ever so slowly into a gorgeous turquoise sea—you can wade almost a hundred yards out and still be only waist deep. The long shallow shelf means Playa Norte has virtually no waves, adding to the beach's tranquility. It's a favorite spot for visitors of all ages: couples sunning themselves and sipping margaritas, backpackers on colorful beach towels, kids frolicking in the calm water, and older travelers relaxing under huge umbrellas.

You can rent beach chairs and umbrellas at a number of spots along Playa Norte, including **Buho's** (end of Av. Carlos Lazo, US$12.50/day for 2); **Chi Chis & Charlie's** (southwestern end of Playa Norte, US$12.50/day first row, others free with purchase); and **Tarzan Water Sports** (end of Av. Guerrero at Playa Norte, tel. 998/877-0679, 9am-sunset daily, US$10/day for 2), where there also are lockers, restrooms, and free Wi-Fi.

Tarzan also rents snorkel gear (US$10/day), single and double kayaks (US$15-20/hour), Hobie Cats (US$45/hour), and stand-up paddleboards (US$12.50/hour) and can arrange snorkel tours (US$25 pp, 2 hours).

Playa Sol

Around the corner, Playa Sol is also lovely,

CANCÚN

© GARY CHANDLER

Isla Mujeres's peaceful Playa Norte

with deeper water and a wider beach than Playa Norte's. One end of the beach has long been packed with fishing boats, while the other end has recently been cordoned off for use by guests at a nearby resort. That said, there's still a large section in the middle where you can stretch out a towel. **Cooperativa Isla Bonita** (cell. tel. 998/134-6103) operates a small kiosk there with lounge chairs and umbrellas for rent.

Other Beaches

Zama (Carr. Sac Bajo s/n, tel. 998/877-0739, www.zamabeach.com, 10am-6pm daily) is a small beach club on the island's calm southwest shore that's gotten popular as a wedding spot, if that gives you an idea of how pretty it is. You can relax in a comfy beach-bed on the large clean beach or in a hammock in the shady garden. The sand is a bit thin and there's sea grass in the shallows, but you can swim comfortably from the long pier or in one of the two appealing midsize pools. The tidy open-air restaurant is reasonably priced and has everything from burritos to shrimp dishes, plus a kids menu

(US$5-20). There's no admission or minimum consumption, but they charge US$8.50 to use the lounge chairs.

ENTERTAINMENT AND EVENTS

Isla Mujeres's nightlife ranges from laid-back lounges to nightclubs, and from beach bars to sports bars. Fortunately, the town is small enough that you can wander about until you find the scene that suits you best.

Bars

At the north end of Playa Norte, **Buho's** (end of Av. Carlos Lazo, no phone, 11am-10:30pm daily) is a classic beachfront watering hole, with swings instead of bar stools, shells and buoys as decoration, and hammocks and lounge chairs within easy reach.

Soggy Peso Bar & Grill (Av. Gustavo Rueda Medina, tel. 998/274-0050, http://soggypeso. net, 9am-8:30pm daily) is a favorite for daytime drinkin' Americans, open early and closed not long after sunset (the view of which, by the way, is terrific here). The vibe is casual and jocular, and every day there's a different special from the kitchen: Hot Wings Wednesdays, Cheeseburgers in Paradise Thursdays, BBQ Sunday, etc. It's located south of the center, on the waterfront.

Live Music

La Terraza (Av Hidalgo at Av. Abasolo, tel. 998/236-3879 or 998/877-0528, 5pm-midnight daily) has great live salsa, cumbia, and other Latin dance music most nights after 10pm. Drinks here are excellent and the food isn't bad, but it's the music and lively atmosphere that will draw you in, night after night.

Fayne's (Hidalgo 12, tel. 998/877-0528, 5pm-midnight daily, no cover) features live nightly music, mostly Caribbean but with a smattering of rock and reggae acts as well. The high *palapa* roof and spacious bar area make it equally suited for dancing or just chilling out; you can even order dinner here, from pasta to seafood. Thursday-Sunday are the busiest nights, often with two bands starting as early as 6pm; otherwise, things get hopping around 10pm.

Down the street, the tiki-bar-themed **Kokonuts** (Av. Hidalgo near Av. López Mateos, tel. 998/125-1772, 7pm-3am daily, no cover) features cover bands, from salsa to Johnny Cash.

JAX Bar and Grill (Av. López Mateos at Av. Rueda Medina, tel. 998/877-1254, www.jaxsportfishing.com/bar.asp, 8am-11pm daily, no cover) has catered to Isla's yacht crews and visiting Joe Six-Packs for years, with utilitarian breakfasts and burgers during the day and live country blues and classic rock bands playing nightly during the high season (9pm-11pm). JAX is closed in September.

SHOPPING

It's easy to be put off by the onslaught of kitschy souvenirs and cheap T-shirts that greet you as soon as you step off the ferry. But fear not: Isla Mujeres has a number of genuinely good specialty stores, especially for Mexican *artesanía,* if you keep your eyes open.

A jewel in a street of T-shirt shops, **Aztlán** (Av. Hidalgo at Av. Madero, tel. 998/887-0419, 9am-9pm Mon.-Sat.) sells gorgeous Mexican masks and folk art from every corner of the country. The owners, transplants from Mexico City, also make popular religious art that fills one section of the shop.

Galería de Arte Mexicano (Parque Central, Av. Guerrero 3, tel. 998/877-1272, 9:30am-9pm Mon.-Sat., 9:30am-5pm Sun.) has fine Talavera pottery as well as an extensive selection of silver jewelry. The prices are somewhat higher here than elsewhere, but so is the quality.

La Sirena (Av. Morelos near Av. Hidalgo, tel. 998/877-0223, 10am-6pm Mon.-Sat.) is a tiny shop that's jam-packed with high-quality folk art from all over Mexico: textiles from Chiapas, masks from Guerrero, skeleton art from Mexico City, and *alebrijes* (wooden creatures) from Oaxaca. The prices are somewhat inflated, but bargaining is welcome.

Mañana Café (Av. Matamoros at Av. Guerrero, tel. 998/877-0555, 8am-4pm Mon.-Sat.) has long housed Isla Mujeres's best foreign-language bookstore. You can buy, sell, and trade everything from beach trash to Maya history; there are titles in English, German, Hebrew, and Spanish.

SPORTS AND RECREATION
Scuba Diving

Beginner divers will appreciate the still water and vibrant sealife on Isla Mujeres's western side, while the east side presents more challenging options for advanced divers, with deeper water (up to 40 meters/131 feet), more varied terrain, and even a couple of shipwrecks. Favorite sites include La Bandera (a reef dive), Media Luna (a drift dive), Ultrafreeze (a shipwreck, in notoriously chilly water), and the famous Sleeping Shark Cave—a deep cave known to attract sharks, where they fall into a strangely lethargic and nonaggressive state. Explanations for this last phenomenon vary: Salinity of the water, low carbon dioxide, and underwater currents are some theories. Unfortunately, overfishing (and overdiving)

CANCÚN

has disrupted the slumber party, and there's only a 50-50 chance, at best, of seeing sharks on any given day. September seems to be the best month, but you just never know.

Isla Mujeres's dive shops charge fairly uniform rates: US$65-80 for two tanks; gear and marine park admission is sometimes included, otherwise they cost US$10-18 per day. The Sleeping Shark Cave and deep dives run a little higher, and most shops offer multi-dive specials. Open-water certification courses cost around US$365, including equipment and materials.

Aqua Adventures (Av. Juárez at Calle Morelos, tel. 998/236-4316, www.diveislamujeres.com, 9am-9pm Mon.-Sat.) goes the extra mile to provide friendly, professional service.

Sea Hawk Divers (Av. Carlos Lazo at Av. López Mateos, tel. 998/877-1233, www.islamujeres.net/seahawkdivers, 9am-8pm daily) is a recommended dive shop owned and run by island local Ariel Barandica. Sea Hawk has a half-dozen comfortable rooms and studios attached to the dive shop, which it can include as part of a diving package.

Buzos de Mexico (Av. Madero at Hidalgo, tel. 998/877-1117, www.buzosdemexico.com, 8am-8pm daily) is a newer dive shop with a youthful vibe.

Scualo Adventures (Av. Madero at Guerrero, tel. 998/877-0607, www.scualoadventures.com, 8:30am-8pm daily) is another reliable option.

Carey Dive Center (Av. Matamoros near Av. Rueda Medina, tel. 998/877-0763, www.careydivecenter.com, 8am-8pm daily) is a recommended dive shop that enjoys lots of repeat customers.

Snorkeling

Isla Mujeres's western side has calm water and extensive coral reefs that make for excellent snorkeling, though relatively few spots are accessible from the shore. Snorkeling tours can be booked at **dive shops** or with one of the local cooperatives—**Cooperativa Isla Bonita** (UltraMar Pier, cell. tel. 998/134-6103) and **Cooperativa Isla Mujeres** (aka Cooperativa

Isla Contoy, end of Av. Madero, tel. 998/877-1363)—or from booths on Playa Norte and at the ferry pier. Most operators take snorkelers to El Farito (The Lighthouse) and other spots near the northern end of the island, where the coral is decent but quite trafficked; afternoons are less busy. Dive shops are more likely to take you to less-visited spots.

You can also arrange to snorkel at MUSA, the remarkable underwater sculpture park near Manchones reef, at the southern end of the island. Dive shops and other operators charge around US$40 per person for a trip combining MUSA and one other spot.

Yet another option is to take a trip to **Isla Contoy** (US$65 pp), which includes snorkeling on Ixlanche reef in addition to exploring the island. Boats depart Isla Mujeres around 9:15am and return at 4pm.

And you can snorkel on your own at **Garrafón de Castilla Hotel and Beach Club** (Carr. Punta Sur Km. 6, tel. 998/877-0107, 9am-5pm daily, US$4.25), at the southern tip of the island. The club itself is pretty desultory, but you can explore over 300 meters (894 feet) of coral reef, including the part used by its much-hyped neighbor, Parque Garrafón. Snorkel gear rents for US$6, and lockers and towels can be rented for around US$2.

Whale Shark Tours

Snorkeling with whale sharks, the world's largest fish, is an experience you won't soon forget. These gentle giants congregate along the northeastern tip of the Yucatán Peninsula from mid-May to mid-September and typically measure 6-7.5 meters (20-25 feet) and weigh more than 10 tons. (They're known to grow upwards of 18 meters, or nearly 60 feet, though such behemoths are rare here.) From Isla Mujeres, whale shark tours leave around 8am for a 60- to 90-minute boat ride northwest past Isla Contoy toward Isla Holbox (where such tours first became popular). Once in the feeding grounds, you'll see the huge sharks trolling along the surface, feeding on krill. The boat is maneuvered nearby the shark, and a guide plus two guests slip overboard and swim alongside. The sharks are surprisingly fast, despite their languid appearance, and you have to kick hard to keep up and get a good look at their sleek spotted bodies and massive gaping mouths. The smaller your group, the more chances you'll have to get into the water, though most people welcome the short breathers between turns. Rules also require that boats not linger with any one shark more than 30 minutes; in all, each guest can expect to have two to four chances to jump in.

Two local cooperatives handle most whale shark tours, charging around US$110 per person: **Cooperativa Isla Bonita** (UltraMar Pier, cell. tel. 998/134-6103, 9am-5pm daily) and **Cooperativa Isla Mujeres** (aka Cooperativa Isla Contoy, end of Av. Madero, tel. 998/877-1363, 9am-5pm daily). Most **dive shops** in Isla Mujeres also offer whale shark tours, charging around US$125 per person. Always confirm the departures times, how long the tour will last, and whether lunch and water are provided.

Swimming with Dolphins

Dolphin Discovery (end of Carr. Sac Bajo, tel. 998/849-4748, toll-free Mex. tel. 800/713-8862, www.dolphindiscovery.com, US$79-169) offers various dolphin interaction programs on the island's calm western shore, as well as ones with manatees and sea lions. Parque Garrafón, a nearby sister park with snorkeling, ziplines, and more, has packages combining Dolphin Discovery programs and admission to Garrafón, a good option if you'd like to make a day of it. Most visitors come from Cancún on Dolphin Discovery's private ferry (included in the price), though no transport is provided for guests staying on Isla Mujeres. Reservations are required.

Ecoparks

Built on a bluff at the southern end of Isla Mujeres, **Parque Garrafón** (Carr. Garrafón Km. 6, tel. 998/849-4748, www.garrafon.com, 10am-5pm daily, US$85-175 adult all-inclusive, US$65-115 child all-inclusive) is a combo ecopark and water park. There's snorkeling, kayaking, ziplining, an interactive dolphin program (conducted at Dolphin Discovery, a

nearby sister park), and, of course, just relaxing on the beach or by the pool. Ferry service to and from Cancún is included, as well as admission to Templo de Ixchel, a tiny Maya ruin nearby. However, if you're staying in Isla Mujeres, transportation to and from the park is *not* included.

Sportfishing

Cooperativa Isla Bonita (UltraMar Pier, cell. tel. 998/134-6103, 9am-5pm daily) and **Cooperativa Isla Mujeres** (aka Cooperativa Isla Contoy, end of Av. Madero, tel. 998/877-1363, 9am-5pm daily) both offer *pesca deportiva* (sportfishing). Boats typically carry up to six people for the same price, and prices include nonalcoholic drinks, sandwiches, and bait. Two trips are usually available, depending on the season: Pesca Mediana (US$50 per hour, 3-4 hours minimum) focuses on midsize fish, including snapper, grouper, and barracuda; and Pesca Mayor (US$250 for 4 hours, US$600 for 8 hours) goes after large catch such as marlin and sailfish. Reserve directly at the pier. **Sea Hawk Divers** (Av. Carlos Lazo at Av. López Mateos, tel. 998/877-1233, www.isla-mujeres.net/seahawkdivers, 9am-10pm daily) offers comparable services for half-day shore and deep-sea fishing trips (US$350).

JAX Sportfishing (JAX Bar and Grill, Av. López Mateos at Av. Rueda Medina, tel. 998/877-1254, www.jaxsportfishing.com, US$950) has an experienced English-speaking captain and offers all-day charters for a maximum of four anglers, ensuring highly personalized service.

Spas

Hotel Villa Rolandi (Carr. Sac Bajo 15-16, tel. 998/999-2000, www.villarolandi.com, 9am-8:30pm daily) has a full-service spa that specializes in using the positive energy and elements of the ocean. A full line of massages, body treatments, and facials is offered.

In downtown Isla, **Casa Luz Spa** (Av. Juárez btwn Calles Bravo and Allende, tel. 998/202-0081, casaluz_280@yahoo.com.mx, 7am-8pm Mon.-Sat.) has a loyal following among locals and repeat visitors thanks to the skill and personalized service of its founder. Massages, facials, and body treatments include first-rate products, yet remain quite affordable. Some treatments are available at your hotel.

Yoga

Yoga classes are offered at two hotels on Isla: **Elements of the Island** (Av. Juárez btwn Avs. López Mateos and Matamoros, cell. tel. 998/274-0098 or 998/117-8651, www. elementsoftheisland.com, 9am Mon.-Fri., US$10) and **Na Balam** (Calle Zazil-Ha No. 118, tel. 998/881-4770, www.nabalam.com, 9am, 11am, and 6pm daily, US$12). At either place, ask about monthly rates if you plan to stay awhile.

ACCOMMODATIONS

Isla Mujeres has a wide variety of lodging options, from youth hostels to upscale boutique hotels. Most budget and midrange places are in the *centro,* while higher-end resorts occupy secluded areas farther down the island (which may mean you'll need to rent a golf cart to get around).

Under US$50

Isla Mujeres's longtime backpacker haven, **Poc Na Hostel** (Av. Matamoros near Av. Lazo, tel. 998/877-0090, www.pocna.com, US$6.25 pp camping, US$10-13 pp dorm, US$14.50 pp dorm with a/c, US$25 s/d with shared bath, US$30 d with private bath, US$25-35.50 with private bath and a/c) is a busy labyrinth of rooms, courtyards, and common areas, just steps from the island's best beach. Dorm rooms have 4-9 bunks each and are priced by the thickness of the mattress (thin, thinner, and thinnest); private rooms have cement floors and whitewashed walls. There's foosball, table tennis, and TV in the various common areas, plus a dining room with basic food service. The hostel hosts live music most nights and organizes frequent events—from volleyball tournaments to Isla Contoy excursions. The drawbacks are no kitchen access and a serious risk

of never leaving. Visa and MasterCard are accepted.

Hotel Maria del Pilar (Calle Abasolo 15, tel. 998/877-0071, US$22-26 d) is a small, well-located hotel with simple but tidy rooms, most with TV, air-conditioning, and minifridge, plus Wi-Fi and shared kitchen for all. It's a fine choice for budget travelers who want some of the conveniences of a hostel without the scene.

Hotel Carmelina (Av. Guerrero 4, tel. 998/877-0006, US$29 s/d with a/c) is a reliable budget choice. It has a slightly residential-motel feel (the family who runs it lives on the ground floor, and another room houses a manicure shop), but the rooms are clean, albeit small, with hot water, TV, and air-conditioning. Larger double and triple rooms are available (US$47.50-55).

US$50-100

A charming place and outstanding value, **Casa El Pío** (Av. Hidalgo near Av. Bravo, tel. 998/229-2799, www.casaelpio.com, US$65-72 s/d with a/c) is a four-room boutique-ish hotel with cool minimalist decor accented with artsy touches and splashes of color. Rooms are spacious and comfortably equipped with good beds, separate seating areas, balconies (two with ocean view), and Wi-Fi; each also has a minifridge, coffeemaker, and a cutting board for light food preparation. There's also a small mosaic-tile plunge pool for cooling off after a day at the beach. Adults only; reservations are highly recommended.

Hotel Kinich (Av. Juárez near Av. Matamoros, tel. 998/877-0791, www.islamujereskinich.com, US$62-72 s/d, US$109 suite) is a great find in downtown Isla: Rooms are simple but elegant with warm wood furnishings, muted colors, and Mexican wall art from Guadalajara. All rooms have quiet air-conditioning, cable TV, and Wi-Fi, and more than half of them also have king-size beds. Two gorgeous suites occupy the top floor—modern one-bedroom apartments with state-of-the-art kitchens, outdoor Jacuzzis, and views of town. The only downer is that the hotel occupies a four-story building with no elevator, but, hey, at least you'll get your workouts in. **Hotel Xbulu-Ha** (Av. Guerrero btwn Avs. Abasolo and Madero, tel. 998/877-1783, www. islamujeres.biz, US$46-57 s/d, US$58-70 suite with kitchenette and a/c) offers bright and airy rooms with modern amenities like cable TV, mini-split air conditioners, and safety deposit boxes. The beds are double sized—something to consider if you plan on sharing. Suites are larger versions of the standard rooms, with fully equipped kitchenettes and king-size beds. Wi-Fi and beach supplies (towels, chairs, and coolers) are included in the rate. The hotel is located just one block from the Caribbean.

Hotel Las Palmas (Av. Guerrero near Av. López Mateos, cell. tel. 998/236-5803, www. laspalmasonisla.com, US$80 s/d with a/c, US$90 s/d with a/c and kitchenette, US$100 penthouse) is a homey hotel run by a friendly mother-daughter team from Canada. Rooms are small but tastefully decorated, with creature comforts like good water pressure, pillow-top beds, even full-length mirrors. There's lots of common space for relaxing and socializing, including a rooftop lounge with hammocks, shared kitchen, and a plunge pool. Most guests enjoy the camaraderie, but those seeking seclusion may find it overly hostel-like. (It doesn't help that most rooms open right onto the common areas.) There's a five-night minimum in high season.

Seemingly out of place on this boho island is **Bahía Chac-Chi** (Av. Rueda Medina near Av. Allende, tel. 998/877-1797, www.bahiachac-chi.com, US$107 bay view, US$93 pool view, including continental breakfast), a sleek hotel that oozes cool, with gleaming white floors, minimalist decor, and original fine art. Rooms themselves have all the amenities of a high-end hotel—plasma TVs, central air-conditioning, thick beds, hydromassage showers—plus balconies with incredible ocean views. An inviting pool is tucked into an interior courtyard. The only thing missing is the beach, and that's just a five-minute walk away. Service is excellent.

© GARY CHANDLER

B&Bs and boutique hotels are a nice way to enjoy Isla Mujeres's tranquil island atmosphere.

Elements of the Island (Av. Juárez btwn Avs. López Mateos and Matamoros, cell. tel. 998/274-0098 or 998/117-8651, www.elementsoftheisland.com, US$85 s/d with a/c) has three lovely studio apartments, each with fine wood furnishings, flowing white curtains, and bursts of color. All rooms have king-size beds and basic kitchenettes, plus Wi-Fi and TVs with DVD players. Guests pass through a leafy courtyard with a gurgling fountain to access the rooms, which are behind the hotel's highly recommended restaurant. Common spaces include a hot tub and hammock area as well as a rooftop yoga studio. Kind and attentive owners provide excellent service.

Simple and well located, **Suites Los Arcos** (Av. Hidalgo near Av. Abasolo, tel. 998/877-1343, US$70-80 s/d with a/c) has large, colorful rooms with gleaming bathrooms and heavy wood furnishings. All have a small fridge, microwave, and coffeemaker, plus TV, air conditioner, and Wi-Fi. Four of the 12 rooms have balconies—two overlook the pedestrian walkway and are great for people-watching (but can be noisy), while the others face the opposite direction and are huge and sunny.

Hotel & Restaurant Bucaneros (Calle Hidalgo near Av. Madero, tel. 998/877-1228, toll-free Mex. tel. 800/227-4765, www.bucaneros.com, US$45-55 s/d with a/c, US$62-80 s/d with a/c and kitchenette) has 16 nicely appointed rooms, all with modern bathrooms, air-conditioning, and Wi-Fi, plus continental breakfast. The budget rooms are quite small, though not uncomfortable, while larger ones have a kitchenette (hot plate, minifridge, and toaster) and in some cases a balcony and separate dining area. The location couldn't be more central, but it can be noisy at night.

US$100-200

A colonial-style home turned boutique inn, **◖ Casa Sirena** (Av. Hidalgo near Av. Bravo, no phone, www.sirena.com.mx, US$125-155 s/d with a/c) has just six rooms, all sumptuously appointed with teak furnishings, Tiffany lamps, stone-tiled bathrooms, and

extras like iPod docks and laptop-size safes; some rooms also boast beautiful Talavera tile floors. A full Mexican breakfast—*huevos divorciados, enfrijoladas,* chicken enchiladas—is served daily (except Sunday) on the small, leafy patio. Every evening, guests also enjoy a happy hour with the gregarious owner, who serves up potent cocktails on the rooftop terrace. Other features include two plunge pools (one with Venetian glass tiles), a sundeck with almost 360-degree views of the Caribbean, and Wi-Fi. Online reservations are required; adults only.

The boutique **Casa IxChel** (Av. Martínez Ross at Carr. Perimetral, tel. 998/888-0107, www.casaixchelisla.com, US$64-181 s/d with a/c, US$208 one-bdrm apt with a/c, US$353 three-bdrm apt with a/c) has just 10 rooms, all with names like Grace, Karma, and Serenity. Standard rooms are tiny, suites have a bit more breathing room, and you can actually unpack your bags in the apartments. But even in the small quarters, each room has a deep bathtub, luxurious beds, and classy decor; the apartments have fully equipped kitchens, too. There are great ocean views from the pool and patio area, though it's too rough and rocky for swimming here. A top-floor restaurant serves mostly Italian, American, and seafood dishes. Children over 12 only, except during Easter, Christmas, and summer, when all ages are welcome.

The adults-only **Villa La Bella** (Carr. Perimetral, tel. 998/888-0342, www.villalabella.com, US$135 s/d with a/c, US$175 suite, US$195 honeymoon suite with a/c) is run by an amiable American couple who give warm, personalized service to all their guests. There are just six units: three bright pool-front rooms with whimsical decor, two 2nd-floor *palapa*-roofed units with hanging beds (but no air-conditioning), and a colorful honeymoon suite with fantastic ocean views from its two terraces. There also is a well-maintained pool on-site. A gourmet breakfast is included (except Monday) and served in the eclectic open-air lounge, where you can also score great cocktails and ice-cold beer.

Over US$200

Hotel Secreto (Sección Rocas 11, tel. 998/877-1039, www.hotelsecreto.com, US$225-300 s/d with a/c) is classy glass and stucco hotel that's good for couples who want a quiet getaway without having to go down island. The beach here isn't swimmable (Playa Norte is a short walk away), but there are gorgeous views from the rooms and the hotel's long, narrow infinity pool. Rooms have native stone floors, plasma TVs, iPod docks, pillow-top mattresses, and huge private balconies. Upkeep can be lacking, but not egregiously. Continental breakfast is included, and there's a small gym.

C Hotel Villa Rolandi (Carr. Sac Bajo 15-16, tel. 998/999-2000, www.villarolandi.com, US$307-389 s/d with a/c) is a Mediterranean-style hotel on Isla's calm southwestern shore. *Romance* is the buzz word here, with two-person showers, steam baths, and private terraces with whirlpool tubs; ask for a room on the 2nd and 3rd floor for the most privacy. Continental breakfast at the hotel's excellent oceanfront restaurant is included. The concierge can organize personalized excursions around the island, though the hotel's elevated pools, private beach, and first-rate spa are good reasons to stay put. Complimentary yacht service to and from Cancún's Playa Linda is included, too. Note that it's for children over age 13 only.

Casa de los Sueños (Carr. Garrafón, tel. 998/888-0370, www.casasuenos.com, US$275-375 d, US$550 presidential suite) is a gorgeous boutique hotel with just 10 immaculate rooms and personalized service. Located on a bluff at the southern end of the island, the hotel has gorgeous views, including from the large infinity pool. There's no beach, unfortunately, but a large pier does well for swimming, sunbathing, and spa treatments, while the hotel's excellent restaurant-bar is on the water's edge. Bikes, kayaks, and snorkel gear are available for exploring.

All-Inclusive

Privilege Aluxes (Av Lopez Mateos at Gustavo Rueda Medina, tel. 998/848-8470, www.privilegehotels.com, US$120-250 d) is a newish resort with both all-inclusive and B&B options. The beach club is lovely and a highlight for most travelers, despite having to walk across the street to get there. The hotel's pool is sleek and clean (though oddly chilly), and rooms large and comfortable.

Isla Mujeres Palace (Carr. Sac Bajo, tel. 998/999-2020, www.palaceresorts.com, US$260-450 s/d with a/c) is an upscale, couples-only all-inclusive resort with just 62 rooms and an exclusive getaway vibe. Suites have king-size beds and muted modern decor. There's only one restaurant, but it's a good one, with international cuisine and even a dress code. The beach and pool areas are lovely, though noise from neighboring beach clubs can be annoying.

Apartments and Private Homes

If you feel like lingering for a while in Isla Mujeres—and who doesn't?—consider booking an apartment or private home. There are a surprising number available, both in town and down island, running the gamut in size and price, and available by the week or month. Check out the options at agencies like Lost Oasis (www.lostoasis.net) and Isla Beckons (www.islabeckons.com), which specialize in Isla Mujeres, or at Vacation Rentals by Owner (www.vrbo.com).

FOOD

Seafood is the specialty in Isla Mujeres, even more so than in Cancún. In fact, much of the lobster and fish served on the Riviera Maya is caught near Isla Mujeres, so it stands to reason that it's freshest here.

Mexican and Seafood

Run and supplied by the fishermen's co-op, **Restaurante Justicia Social** (Av. Rueda Medina near Av. Allende, cell. tel. 998/230-4803, 11am-8pm Mon.-Fri., 10am-8pm Sat.-Sun., US$6-12) serves up some of the freshest seafood on the island. Octopus, shrimp, oysters, conch, and all sorts of fish fillets are served on the patio overlooking the Caribbean or in the simple dining room. *Tikinxik* (TEEK-in-cheek), a whole grilled fish prepared using a spicy red sauce that's derived from pre-Hispanic Maya cuisine, is offered weekends only; delivery is available daily.

Bally Hoo (Av. Rueda Medina near Av. Abasolo, no phone, 7:30am-11pm daily, US$3.50-10) may be stuck behind a gas station and a slew of moored boats, but the Baja-style breaded fish tacos are to die for, and well worth any necessary searching. The fish and chips are great, too, and if you've got an appetite, the fish fillet or shrimp dishes are filling. Cold beers (US$1.50) and margaritas (US$3) are the perfect accompaniment.

La Lomita (Av. Juárez near Av. Allende, tel. 998/826-6335, 9am-6pm Mon.-Sat., US$4.25-6), a brightly painted restaurant frequented by locals, offers tasty Mexican fare. *Comida corrida*—a two-course lunch special with drink—is offered daily and often includes chiles rellenos, tacos, and stews. Ceviche, grilled whole fish, and other seafood meals also are featured at reasonable prices.

Mercado Municipal (Av. Guerrero at Av. Matamoros, 6am-4pm daily) also has a handful of simple eateries that serve cheap meals.

On Playa Lancheros, **La Casa del Tikinxik** (tel. 998/274-0018, 11am-7pm daily, US$6-10) is a classic Mexican beach restaurant, with metal tables, cold beer, and finger-licking dishes that make the long wait worth it. Be sure to try the specialty, *pescado tikinxik.*

Other Specialties

Upscale but homey, **Olivia** (Av. Matamoros btwn Calle Juárez and Av. Rueda Medina, tel. 998/877-1765, www.olivia-isla-mujeres.com, 5pm-9:30pm Tues.-Sat., US$8-18) serves up the best Mediterranean cuisine on the island. Owned by an Israeli couple who pooled their families' recipes and opened shop, the menu is a phenomenal amalgam of specialties from Morocco, Greece, Bulgaria, and Turkey. Seating is either in the *palapa*-roofed dining room or in the lush garden courtyard. Reservations are recommended, and it's cash only.

A casual chic eatery, **CoMoNo** (Av. Hidalgo btwn Avs. Madero and Morelos, no phone, 2pm-11pm Mon.-Sat., US$8-15) offers a wide range of foods—tapas, falafel, shrimp tempura, Argentinean chorizo, and more—plus sandwiches, great salads, and even hookahs with flavored tobacco. Upstairs, there's a cool lounge bar where you can catch live music and occasional movies. Seating is indoors and out.

Qubano (Av. Hidalgo btwn Avs. Matamoros and Mateos, cell. tel. 998/214-2118, noon-5pm Mon.-Fri., US$3-6) is a colorful little place offering up a tasty selection of Cuban sandwiches, burgers, and salads. Favorites include the Tostón (plantain slices stuffed with chicken, pork, or *picadillo*), the Cuban (grilled ham, pork, and cheese), and the goat-cheese-stuffed burger. Snag one of the four tables, enjoy a Cuban coffee while you wait, or take your eats to go.

In a clapboard house facing the lagoon, with fishing boats crowded up next to it, **El Varadero** (no phone, noon-10pm Tues.-Sun., US$7-14) doesn't really evoke the famous white-sand beach east of Havana that it's named for, but good food—and even better mojitos—have a way of trumping geography. Dig into classic Cuban fare while sitting at aluminum tables on an outdoor patio decorated with shipping buoys. Find it at the mouth of Laguna Makax, near Puerto Isla Mujeres.

Whether it's the prime location, cheerful yellow exterior, or the allure of freshly made cinnamon rolls, **Barlito's** (Av. Hidalgo at Av. Abasolo, 8am-3pm Tues.-Sat., US$2-10) is a perennial gathering spot in the center of town. Huge salads, tasty sandwiches, and oh-so-decadent sweets can be eaten in or taken out.

On Playa Norte in front of Nautibeach condos, **Sunset Grill** (Av. Rueda Medina, tel. 998/877-0785, www.sunsetgrill.com.mx, 8am-10pm daily, US$9-21) offers a great view with mellow beats on one of the best beaches on the island. Beachside chairs and umbrellas are also available for the day if you order from the menu. Food is standard but good, including grilled fish, ceviche, hamburgers, and specials like rib eye and barbecue ribs.

Cafés

Located partway down the island, **◖ Mango Café** (Carr. Perimentral at Calle Payo Obispo, tel. 998/274-0118, 8am-3pm and 4pm-10pm daily, US$4-12) has a cheerful bohemian exterior that practically begs a closer look. You'll be glad you do: Dishes like coconut French toast and eggs Benedict with chaya and portabella mushrooms, plus drinks like ginger lemonade and bottomless organic coffee make this small eatery an island favorite—and that's just breakfast!

Day and night, **Café Hidalgo** (Av. Hidalgo near Av. Abasolo, no phone, 8am-10:30pm Tues.-Sun., US$2.50-5) serves up first-rate crepes stuffed with everything from Nutella to *huitlacoche* (corn fungus). Egg dishes and baguettes also figure prominently for those looking for a bit more heft. Sit at one of the handful of tables on the pedestrian walkway—a great place to linger while watching the beachgoers (and window shoppers) walk by.

Café Mogagua (Av. Madero at Av. Juárez, tel. 998/877-1799, 7am-midnight daily, US$7-12) is a chic but laid-back open-air café with a wide range of eats, from a simple sandwich to a full-on seafood meal. Judging from the comfy lounge chairs aimed at the sun, it's a good bet no one would bat an eye if you just hunkered down with a paperback novel and an espresso.

Mañana (Av. Matamoros at Av. Guerrero, 8am-4pm Mon.-Sat., US$4-8) offers an eclectic menu with everything from kabobs and falafel to cheeseburgers and schnitzel. Great breakfast options include bagels, omelets, fruit, and granola. Half the dining area houses a bookstore, which, along with the good food and cheerful decor, makes for a natural travelers' hub.

Specializing in organic products, **Elements of the Island Café** (Av. Juárez btwn López Mateos and Matamoros, tel. 998/274-0098, www.elementsoftheisland.com, 7:30am-1pm daily except Wed., US$4-8) serves up hearty and healthy meals. Breakfasts are especially popular, with homemade bread and marmalade, and cappuccinos to die for.

Sweets

La Michoacana (Av. Bravo at Av. Hidalgo, 9am-10pm daily, US$1-2.50) offers homemade *aguas, paletas,* and *helados* (juices, popsicles, and ice cream). Choose from seasonal fruits including passion fruit, watermelon, pineapple, and mamey. Of course, chocolate- and vanilla-flavored treats are available, too.

Try **ParadICE-CREAM** (Av. Hidalgo at Av. Morelos, 9:30am-midnight daily, US$2.50-6.50) for terrific handmade gelato.

Groceries

There's a new **Chedraui** (7am-8pm daily) about halfway down the island, across from the baseball diamond. To get there, simply follow Avenida Gustavo Rueda Medina; the supermarket will be on your right, just before a sharp bend known as "devil's curve."

Xpress Super (Av. Morelos, 7am-10pm daily) is the island's longtime local grocery store, facing the central plaza.

Mercado Municipal (Av. Guerrero at Av. Matamoros, 6am-4pm daily) has a good selection of fresh fruits and vegetables, and is a fun experience to boot.

INFORMATION AND SERVICES
Tourist Information

The **Oficina de Turismo** (Av. Rueda Medina 130, tel. 998/877-0307, www.islamujeres.gob. mx, 9am-4pm daily) sometimes has maps and useful information.

The English-language website **www. islamujeres.info** has concise and accessible descriptions of various aspects of Isla Mujeres, including activities, tours, taxis, ferry schedules, and history, plus a Q&A section frequented by longtime expats.

Soul de Isla Mujeres (www.souldeisla.com) also has information and recommendations about Isla Mujeres, from restaurants to wedding planners.

Also try **www.isla-mujeres.net** for information about visiting Isla.

Can-Do Isla Mujeres (www.cancunmap.

com, US$10) is a fantastic professional-quality color map of Isla Mujeres. It is extremely detailed, including annotated listings of almost every restaurant, hotel, and point of interest on the island. It is available at a handful of Isla's restaurants and hotels, and also can be ordered online.

Emergency Services

General practitioner **Dr. Antonio E. Salas** (Av. Hidalgo 18-D, tel. 998/877-0021, 24-hour tel. 998/877-0477, drsalas@cancun.com.mx, 9am-3pm and 4pm-9pm daily) is highly recommended by islanders. He speaks fluent English and basic German.

If you need immediate assistance, **Hospital Integral Isla Mujeres** (Av. Guerrero 7, tel. 998/877-0117, 24 hours) is equipped to handle walk-in consultations, simple surgeries, and basic emergencies. In case of a serious injury or illness, patients are taken to a Cancún hospital.

For diving-related injuries, Isla Mujeres's primary **hyperbaric chamber** (tel. 998/877-0819, 9am-4pm daily), or *cámera hiberbárica* in Spanish, is on the pedestrian-only extension of Avenida Morelos, just north of the *zócalo*.

Farmacia YZA (Av. Benito Juárez at Calle Morelos, no phone, 24 hours) has sunscreen, bug repellent, and toiletries in addition to medications.

The **police station** (tel. 998/877-0082, 24 hours) is on the central plaza.

Money

HSBC has a bank and ATMs across from the UltraMar pier (Av. Rueda Medina btwn Avs. Madero and Morelos, tel. 998/877-0005, 9am-6pm Mon.-Fri., 9am-3pm Sat.) and an ATM only at Xpress Super grocery store on the central plaza.

Media and Communications

Like many cities in Mexico now, Isla Mujeres has **free public Wi-Fi** in the central plaza, available to anyone with a computer or mobile device. Most hotels offer Wi-Fi to guests, too.

There are numerous Internet cafés around town, including **Europacomputer** (Av. Abasolo near Av. Hidalgo, tel. 998/877-1724, 9am-10pm Mon.-Sat., 4pm-9pm Sun, US$1.75/hour) and **Café Internet Adrian's** (9am-10pm daily, US$1.75/hour Internet, US$0.35/minute international calls), facing the central plaza.

The **post office** (Av. Guerrero at Av. López Mateos, tel. 998/877-0085) is open 8am-4pm Monday-Saturday.

Immigration

The **immigration office** (Av. Rueda Medina near Av. Morelos, tel. 998/877-0189, 8am-6pm Mon.-Fri., 9am-6pm Sat.-Sun.) issues tourist cards to those arriving by boat from another country; for all other matters, including visa extensions, visitors should go to Cancún.

Laundry

Lavandería Lavanda (Av. Vicente Guerrero near Av. Madero, no phone, 7am-9pm Mon.-Sat., 7am-3pm Sun.) will wash, dry, and fold for US$1 per kilo, with a minimum of three kilos (6.6 pounds).

Tim Pho Lavandería (Av. Juárez at Abasolo, no phone, 8am-8pm Mon.-Sat., 8am-2pm Sun.) offers same-day service with a two-hour wait. Loads cost US$5.50 per four kilos (8.8 pounds).

GETTING THERE

A number of ferries ply the turquoise waters of the Bahía de Mujeres (Bay of Women) between Isla Mujeres and various mainland ports in and around Cancún. There is no direct ferry service from Isla Cozumel, however, and despite having an airstrip, no regular air service either.

Passenger Ferries

Passenger-only ferries leave for Isla Mujeres from Cancún in the Zona Hotelera and from Puerto Juárez, about three kilometers (1.9 miles) north of downtown Cancún. If you are just visiting for the day, reconfirm the return times and remember that service to the Zona Hotelera ends earlier than service to Puerto Juárez.

Ferries to Isla Mujeres

Various passenger ferries (and also a car ferry) leave for Isla Mujeres from Cancún every day. Those leaving from the Zona Hotelera are more expensive and take longer but may be more convenient. In case you've got a car, there's also a vehicle ferry. **Note:** During the high season, additional departures are occasionally offered.

ZONA HOTELERA
El Embarcadero
UltraMar (Blvd. Kukulcán Km. 4, tel. 998/881-5890, www.granpuerto.com.mx, US$11/17 one-way/round-trip, 30 minutes). **Departure:** 9am, 10:30am, noon, 1:30pm, 2:30pm, and 4:30pm. **Return:** 9:30am, 11am, 12:30pm, 2pm, 4pm, and 5:30pm.

Playa Tortugas
UltraMar (Blvd. Kukulcán Km. 7, tel. 998/881-5890, www.granpuerto.com.mx, US$11/17 one-way/round-trip, 30 minutes).

Departure: hourly 9am-5pm. **Return:** hourly 9:30am-5:30pm.

Playa Caracol
UltraMar (Blvd. Kukulcán Km. 9.5, tel. 998/881-5890, www.granpuerto.com.mx, US$11/17 one-way/round-trip, 30 zzzminutes). **Departure:** 10:10am, 11:40am, 1:10pm, and 4:50pm. **Return:** 9:30am, 11am, 12:30pm, and 4pm.

DOWNTOWN
To get to either of the passenger ferries in downtown Cancún, take the red R-1 bus (US$0.75) on Boulevard Kukulcán or Avenida Tulum; continue past the downtown bus terminal and north out of the city. **Gran Puerto** is easily located by its tall observation tower. (Be aware that you may be approached by people dressed in UltraMar uniforms who are in fact selling time-shares here.) **Puerto Juárez** is two blocks past Gran Puerto. It's the original

Car Ferries

A vehicle ferry operates from Punta Sam, about eight kilometers (5 miles) north of Cancún past Puerto Juárez.

GETTING AROUND

Isla Mujeres is a small and mostly flat island. In town you can easily walk everywhere. Buses and taxis are available for exploring farther afield, but definitely consider renting a golf cart, moped, or bike for more flexibility and independence.

Bus

There are two bus lines on Isla Mujeres (US$0.35), running the same route but in opposite directions, from downtown to Playa Lancheros and back. They stop in local neighborhoods, but do not reach the far southern tip. Theoretically the buses run every 30 minutes, but be prepared to wait longer than that. There

are some official stops, but you can just flag one down wherever you see it.

Taxi

Isla Mujeres has many more taxis than seem necessary—in town, it feels more likely that you'd be hit by a taxi than you'd have trouble finding one. Out of town, you shouldn't have to wait too long for a taxi to pass, either, and Parque Garrafón, Dolphin Discovery, and Playa Lancheros all have fixed taxi stands. From downtown, rates are US$1-3 around town (including the beaches) and US$3-7 elsewhere on the island. Official rates are posted wherever taxis line up, including Parque Garrafón, Punta Sur, and downtown. Taxis are per trip, not per person, and drivers may pick up other passengers headed the same direction. You can also hire a taxi to give you a private driving tour of the island for US$12.50 per hour. **Note:** Taxi fares double after dark.

Isla Mujeres ferry pier, but the boats and waiting area are older. The vehicle ferry at **Punta Sam** is located on Avenida López Portillo, about five kilometers (3 miles) north of Gran Puerto. On Isla Mujeres, the car ferry pier is a few hundred meters south of the passenger piers, past the naval dock.

Gran Puerto
UltraMar (Av. López Portillo s/n, tel. 998/881-5890, www.granpuerto.com.mx, US$6 each way, 15 minutes) boats feature comfy seats in an air-conditioned cabin and an open-air deck, with televisions playing a short promotional program on Isla Mujeres. **Departure:** every 30 minutes 5am-8:30pm, then hourly 9:30pm-11:30pm. **Return:** every 30 minutes 5:30am-9pm, then hourly 9:30pm-midnight.

Puerto Juárez
Transportes Marítimos Magaña (Av. López Portillo s/n, tel. 998/877-0618, US$6 each way,

15 minutes). **Departure:** every 30 minutes 6:30am-8:30pm, then 11:30pm and 12:30am. **Return:** every 30 minutes 6am-8pm, then hourly 9pm-11pm.

Punta Sam (Vehicle Ferry)
The lumbering vehicle ferry to Isla Mujeres is run by **Marítima Isla Mujeres** (Av. López Portillo s/n, tel. 998/877-0065, www.maritimaislamujeres.com, 45-60 minutes). Rates are according to vehicle: US$21.50 for cars, US$28.50 for SUVs and vans, US$7.25 for motorcycles or mopeds, US$6.85 for bicycles. Rates include the driver only—each additional passenger costs US$3. Arrive about an hour early to get in line; tickets go on sale 30 minutes prior to departure. **Departure:** 7:15am, 11am, 2:45pm, 5:30pm, and 8:15pm Mon.-Sat. and 9:15am, 1:30pm, 5:30pm, and 8:15pm Sun. **Return:** 6am, 9:30am, 12:45pm, 4:15pm, and 7:15pm Mon.-Sat. and 8am, noon, 4:15pm, and 7:15pm Sun.

Golf Cart, Moped, and Bicycle Rental

Most rental operations on the island share the same fixed rates: golf carts US$15 per hour, US$46 per day (store hours), and US$54 for 24 hours; mopeds US$8.50 per hour, US$21 per day, US$29 for 24 hours; and bicycles (including helmet and lock) US$2.50 per hour, US$10 per day, US$12.50 for 24 hours.

Note: Isla Mujeres has a regular occurrence of serious accidents involving tourists driving mopeds. Riding double is a major culprit: Mopeds are much harder to control with two people riding instead of one. Poor roads and wet and windy conditions are also dangerous, not to mention unpredictable. Better to rent a bike or golf cart, or at least separate mopeds.

Agencies right at the ferry pier sometimes charge slightly more than those a few blocks away. Solid choices include **Ciro's** (Av. Guerrero near Av. Matamoros, tel. 998/877-0568, 8:30am-5pm daily), **El Sol** (Av. Juárez btwn Avs. Abasolo and Matamoros, tel. 998/877-0791, 9am-5pm daily), and **Pelícanos** (Av. Matamoros near Av. Guerrero, cell. tel. 998/223-1365, 7am-5pm daily).

Isla Mujeres Golf Cart Rentals (www.islamujeresgolfcartrentals.com) is a convenient new service that makes renting a golf cart easy. Rates are slightly higher than you'd pay normally, but you can reserve and pay online, the cart can be delivered to your hotel, and someone even comes by every day or two to fill the gas tank. Four- and six-seat carts are available; discounts for longer rentals.

Isla Holbox

At the northeastern tip of Quintana Roo, where the Caribbean Sea mingles with the Gulf of Mexico, and completely within the Yum Balam reserve, Isla Holbox (hole-BOASH) is one of the last reasonably obscure islands along the Yucatán Peninsula. The town of Holbox is a fishing village with sand roads, golf carts instead of cars, no cell phone service, no hospital, and no post office. (There *is* one ATM on the 2nd floor of the town hall, though it's often empty.) Instead, you'll find brightly painted homes, *palapa*-roofed hotels, and a handful of Italian and Spanish expats who have opened bed-and-breakfasts and small restaurants. The water here is emerald—not the clear turquoise of Cancún and Tulum—and while the sand is thinner, the beach is loaded with seashells and is no less scenic. Holbox is becoming well known as a place to snorkel with behemoth but harmless whale sharks—present from June to September—and also has great opportunities for bird-watching, kayaking, and sportfishing. Above all, Holbox offers a sense of peace and tranquility that is increasingly hard to find on Mexico's Caribbean coast, and the feeling of a place as yet untouched by big business.

HISTORY

Indigenous Maya inhabited Holbox for centuries but abandoned the island more than 300 years before the first Europeans arrived. The name of the island and town is a matter of some dispute. Some say *holbox* is derived from a Maya term meaning "black water" and is a reference to the island's natural springs, whose dark depths make the water appear black. A more popular, albeit fantastical, story is that the pirate Francisco de Molas buried a treasure on the island and cut off the head of his African bodyguard so that his ghost would watch over the spot for eternity. De Molas was promptly killed by a snakebite, but the disembodied head of his bodyguard has appeared occasionally to islanders, trying to divulge the treasure's location but succeeding only in scaring everyone away. By this latter account, the island originally would have been called *poolbox* (black head), and was altered later by European settlers.

Storms are serious business on this low, flat island, which is regularly buffeted by tropical conflagrations. In fact, the town was originally located farther west but was destroyed by a hurricane and rebuilt in its current location about 150 years ago. *Nortes* are fall and winter storms that sweep down the Gulf coast bringing rain and turbid seas. *Maja'che* is the Maya name for sudden winds that can knock over trees; they are most common in April and May. In major storms, the whole island is evacuated.

SIGHTS

◖ Whale Shark Feeding Grounds

From June to September, large numbers of whale sharks—the world's largest fish, typically measuring 6-7.5 meters (20-25 feet) and weighing more than 10 tons—congregate in shallow waters about 16 kilometers (10 miles) east of Holbox village. Despite their size, the sharks are completely harmless, eating plankton, krill, and other tiny organisms, much like baleen whales. Snorkeling with whale sharks is a unique and (to some) nerve-wracking experience. The captain pulls the boat alongside a shark—at Holbox they tend to feed on the surface—and two guests and a guide slip into the water with life jackets, masks, snorkels, and fins. The water tends to be murky (it's all the sealife in the water that attracts the sharks in the first place), and the sharks are surprisingly fast. Still, you get a good view of these enormous, gentle animals, with their tiny eyes, bizarre shovel mouths, and dark spotted skin. It's best to be on a small tour—since you go in two by two, you'll get more time in the water. Tours cost around US$85-140 per person, last 4-6 hours, and typically include snorkel gear, a life preserver, a box lunch, and nonalcoholic

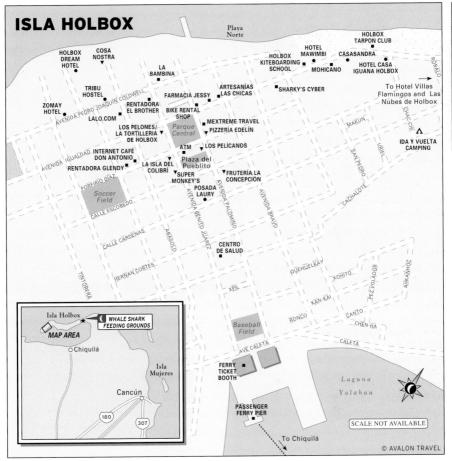

beverages. Some trips also include a stop on the way back for snorkeling or to visit the island's inland lagoons and mangrove forest.

Playa Norte

Playa Norte is Holbox's scenic main beach, extending eastward along the island's long, north-facing shore; it is broad and flat, with white sand, and dotted with stands of tangled dune grass. The number of homes and hotels along the beach grows every year—most have lounge chairs available to guests, but there's less and less open space for everyone else to lay out a

towel. That said, Playa Norte is still great for beachcombing and shell collecting, and sunbathing if you walk far enough down. Better yet, spring for a hotel on the beach.

Isla Pájaros

Located in Yalahau Lagoon, Isla Pájaros (Bird Island) is a wildlife sanctuary and the permanent home to some 150 species of birds, including frigate birds, white ibis, double-crested cormorants, roseate spoonbills, and boat-billed herons. In addition, between May and September up to 40,000 flamingos nest

© LIZA PRADO

Snorkel with whale sharks, the biggest fish in the world, from Isla Holbox.

on Holbox before their long winter migration to South America. Environmental restrictions mean you can't simply wander on Isla Pájaros, but two observation towers and walkways make spotting birds easy. Most tour operators offer bird-watching trips here (US$45 pp), usually by *lancha* (motorboat), though kayak tours also can be arranged.

Yalahau Spring

Said to have been used by pirates to fill their water barrels, Yalahau Spring is an *ojo de agua* (natural spring) on the edge of the mainland. Today, it is a picturesque swimming hole complete with a large *palapa,* picnic area, and pier. A trip here typically is combined with a stop to Isla Pájaros.

Isla de la Pasión

Just 15 minutes from town by boat, Isla de la Pasión is a tiny deserted island just 50 meters (164 feet) wide. It's known for its white-sand beach and beautiful emerald waters—perfect for a relaxing day at the beach. There are trees and a large *palapa* for shade. Be sure to bring plenty of water and snacks—there are no services on the island.

CINEMA

Holbox's long-suffering cinephiles can finally rejoice: The island's first **movie theater** (Plaza del Pueblito, Av. Benito Juárez near Porfirio Díaz, no phone, US$2.75) opened in 2011 in Plaza del Pueblito, a small commercial center just off the main square. It may diminish the deserted-island feel somewhat, but locals certainly appreciate not having to trek to Cancún for the latest *Twilight* flick.

FESTIVALS AND EVENTS
Festival de San Telmo

Most of Holbox's residents live by fishing, and the island has over 400 fishing boats and numerous fishing cooperatives. It's no surprise, then, that San Telmo, the patron saint of fishermen, is celebrated here with fervor. The party lasts for two weeks in mid-April, with food stands, live performances, and special events, including a popular sportfishing tournament. The festival ends on April 19 when fishermen and their families participate in a huge boat procession followed by general revelry in the decked-out main square.

Festival de La Virgen de Fatima
In mid-May, Holbox celebrates the Virgin of Fatima, the community's official patron saint. Held just a month after the San Telmo blow-out, this festival is more austere, with religious processions and more folksy music and other performances. That said, it's still a party.

Environmental Week
What started as an effort to educate children about the environment has turned into an annual island-wide event known as "Environmental Week." The first week of July is dedicated to environmental education and action, still focused on schoolkids, but involving parents and even visitors. Tourists can join the students in one of the week's biggest events: picking up trash from the beach.

SHOPPING
Holbox isn't exactly a shopper's paradise, but there is a **string of boutiques** along Avenida

Bug Patrol

Isla Holbox's famous whale sharks may weigh 10 tons and have mouths that measure five feet across, but it's the island's itty-bitty residents that pack the meanest bite. Mosquitoes, sand flies, and *tábanos* (horseflies) can be fierce, particularly in the summer and after heavy rains. Bring bug repellent and use it liberally, day and night. Another tip: Always dry off and re-apply repellent immediately after swimming—horseflies love skin that's moist, especially with seawater.

Igualdad (just east of the central plaza) selling everything from handcrafted jewelry to whale shark magnets. Among them, **Artesanías Las Chicas** (tel. 984/875-2430, 9am-3pm and 6pm-10pm Tues.-Sun.) stands out for its high-end folk art, mostly from central and southern Mexico. It's a bit pricey, but the items are unique.

If you're into shells, **Lalo.com** (Av. Abasolo near Av. Pedro Joaquín Coldwell, tel. 984/875-2118) is jam-packed with beautifully polished *conchas* from around the world. The owner, *maestro* Lalo, lives below the shop—just ring his bell, and he'll open up the shop.

Malls and movies have come to Holbox—well, make that "mall" and "movie," but it's a milestone all the same. Inaugurated in 2011, **Plaza del Pueblito** (Av. Benito Juárez near Porfirio Díaz) is a small commercial center located just off the central plaza, with boutiques, eateries, and the island's one and only movie theater, a one-screen affair showing reasonably recent Hollywood films (US$2.75).

SPORTS AND RECREATION
There is a lot to do on Holbox, and various excursions can be arranged through your hotel, local tour operators, or done on your own. Most of Holbox's tour operators offer the full gamut of excursions, at comparable prices. Recommended outfits include **Posada Mawimbi** (Av. Igualdad on the beach, tel. 984/875-2003, www.mawimbi.net) and **Mextreme Travel** (central plaza, Av. Palomino s/n, tel. 984/875-2358, www.mextreme-travel.com, 8am-11pm daily).

Snorkeling
Besides swimming with whale sharks, the best place to snorkel on Isla Holbox is **Cabo Catoche,** a coral reef in about 2-4 meters (6.5-13 feet) of water at the far eastern end of the island. The water isn't as clear as in Isla Mujeres or Cancún, but the reef here is more pristine and the animal life more abundant, including stingrays, moray eels, nurse sharks, sea stars, conch, and myriad fish. Because it is so

far from town, tour operators usually prefer to combine it with another outing, such as an island tour or a whale shark excursion.

Wind Sports

Holbox's steady winds and shallow, nearly waveless coastal waters make it ideal for wind sports, particularly kiteboarding and windsurfing. The strongest winds are from September to March, while July and August tend to have lighter, novice-friendly breezes.

Gabriel Olmos Aguirre (aka Gabo) is a popular and accomplished instructor offering courses at all levels through his outfit, **Holbox Kiteboarding School** (Hotel Casa Las Tortugas, Av. Igualdad s/n, cell. tel. 984/144-2227, www.holboxkiteboarding.com), and in association with shops elsewhere in the Riviera Maya. Instruction prices, including gear, range US$50-65 per hour (private lessons) to US$40-45 per hour (group lessons); nine-hour courses also are offered for US$500 (private) and US$360 (group). Wakeboarding classes are offered on those days the wind dies down (US$60-75/hour).

Another one-man shop, **Mohicano** (Av. Igualdad s/n, cell. tel. 984/115-9090, babyshark6977@hotmail.com) is based out of a beach cabana near Casa Sandra. Kiteboarding rates range US$70-80 per hour (private lessons) and US$48-60 per hour (group lessons). Windsurfing (US$70 for 2 hours) and sailing (US$80 for 90 minutes) lessons also are offered. Rentals for all three sports can be arranged, too.

Kayaking

Kayaking is a great way to see the interior lagoons of the island, and especially for spotting birds. A fun and challenging option is to hire a golf-cart taxi to drive you and your boat—balanced on the back—to the main inlet where you can put in. From there it's possible to wend through the lagoons to the other side of the island, then paddle along the shore to the main ferry dock, passing Isla Pájaros along the way. Several shops and hotels rent kayaks (US$8-12/

hour), while **Andrés Limón** (tel. 984/875-2220, kayak_holbox@hotmail.com) is a popular private guide.

Bird-Watching

Holbox has more than 30 species of birds, including herons, white and brown pelicans, double-crested cormorants, roseate spoonbills, and greater flamingos (the brightest pink of the five flamingo species). Most hotels can arrange a standard bird-watching excursion (approximately US$45 pp, 3-4 hours, minimum 4 people), which generally includes taking a motorboat or kayaks through the mangroves to Isla Pájaros and the flamingo nesting grounds. More specialized bird-watchers may want to contact **Juan Rico Santana** (tel. 984/875-2021)—he leads many of the hotel trips, but he can arrange separate, more focused trips that are tailored to your interests.

Fishing

Holbox is an excellent spot for **sportfishing,** yet it's still relatively unknown. A deep-sea fishing excursion costs US$250-450, depending on how long you go out. A coastal fishing tour with a local fisherman, going after smaller and more plentiful catch, lasts 4-5 hours and costs around US$100. Local tour operators, and most hotels, can help you organize either trip.

Holbox also has great **fly-fishing,** with 100-plus-pound giant tarpons cruising the coastal waters, and smaller juveniles plying the interior lagoons, along with snook and jack. **Holbox Tarpon Club** (tel. 984/875-2144, www.holboxtarponclub.com) offers personalized tours, running US$400 per boat (8 hours, lunch included, maximum 2 anglers per boat).

Baseball

Holbox has an amateur baseball team, known simply as **Selección Holbox** (Team Holbox). The season lasts all summer, and games against visiting teams are held most Sundays at noon at the baseball "stadium" on Avenida Benito Juárez, a few blocks from the pier. It's a popular outing for island families, who typically bring

© LIZA PRADO

Head to Isla Holbox for long walks on the beach and plenty of peace and quiet.

tostadas and huge bowls of homemade ceviche to go with the cold beer and soda on sale in the stands. Admission is US$1-2; bring a hat as there is little shade.

ACCOMMODATIONS

For most travelers, Holbox's most appealing accommodations are its beachfront bungalows; they vary in style, amenities, and price, but all offer simple rest and relaxation in a peaceful seaside setting. Alternatively, hotels in town offer comfortable rooms at more accessible rates, and you're still just a short distance from the beach. Be aware that rates may rise during whale shark season (mid-May to mid-September).

Under US$50

Holbox's best budget choice is ◖**Tribu Hostel** (Av. Pedro Joaquín Coldwell s/n, tel. 984/875-2507, www.tribuhostel.com, US$9.25-10.50 pp dorm, US$26-30.50 s/d). Set in two-story *palapa*-roofed buildings with polished wood

floors, each room is named after one of the world's tribes—Maori, Huli, Woodabe, etc.—and is decorated accordingly. Dorms have 3-5 bunks apiece, fans, en suite bathrooms, and private balconies. Sheets and big lockers (BYO lock) are included in the rate. Private rooms are similarly outfitted but smaller. Common areas are first-rate, too: a fully equipped kitchen, an outdoor dining room, a rooftop lounge with lots of hammocks and stellar views, a bar with swings for seats and a flat-screen TV, and even a screening room with a small library of movies. Wi-Fi, laundry, and kayak rentals are also available.

Located on a quiet residential street, **Posada Laury** (Calle Cardenas near Av. Palomino, tel. 984/875-2133, US$42 s/d with a/c) offers stark rooms with unexpected creature comforts: air-conditioning, cable TV, and minifridge, plus hot water and decent beds, too. It's a great deal, especially considering it's just two blocks from the central plaza.

If you're willing to slather yourself with bug

repellent, **Ida y Vuelta Camping** (Calle Plutarco Elias Calles btwn Róbalo and Chacchi, tel. 984/875-2358, www.holboxhostel.com, US$8 pp hammock, US$8 pp camping, US$9 pp dorm, US$30 s/d bungalow with shared bath, US$35 s/d *cabaña,* US$55 house) has a good range of options—from hammock and tent sites to fully equipped houses. The most popular choices are the garden bungalows, which have sand floors, screened windows, and shared bathrooms, and the *cabañas*—wood plank cabins on stilts, each with two basic rooms with private bathrooms. All guests have access to a fully equipped kitchen, colorfully tiled bathrooms with 24/7 hot water, and free Wi-Fi.

US$50-100

Hotel Casa Iguana Holbox (Av. Igualdad s/n, tel. 984/875-2469, www.hotelcasaiguanaholbox.com, US$70-92 s/d garden view, US$121 ocean view) offers simple rooms with painted cement floors and Talavera-tiled bathrooms. Deluxe rooms are bigger and feature handcrafted wood furnishings and private terraces facing the beach; most have air-conditioning, but there's a discount if you don't use it. Outdoors, there are plenty of lounge chairs and *palapa* shades on the beach, and town is just a few minutes' walk away.

US$100-200

Hotel Villas Flamingos (Av. Igualdad s/n, tel. 984/875-2167, www.villasflamingos.com, US$139-146 s/d with a/c, US$227-263 suite with a/c) is one of the nicest places to stay on the beach. Units are modern with boho flair: conch shell showerheads, coconut lamps, bamboo accents, and gorgeous mosaic tile bathrooms. All rooms have air-conditioning and ocean views (some partial, some dramatically expansive), and most have *palapa* roofs. There is a well-tended pool just feet from the ocean, as well as a high-end restaurant/bar.

Hotel Mawimbi (Av. Igualdad s/n, tel. 984/875-2003, www.mawimbi.net, US$90-125 s/d with a/c, US$115-145 s/d with a/c and kitchenette, US$165 suite with a/c) offers modern rooms and comfortable bungalows with a touch of boho flair. Guatemalan bedspreads, colorful tiles, and shell accents all lend an artistic touch, while quiet air-conditioning and free Wi-Fi keep you cool and connected. The shady garden has plenty of lounge chairs and hammocks, and is just steps from one of the best-kept stretches of beach. The low-key Italian owners maintain a friendly, welcoming atmosphere and offer recommended island excursions. There also is a good restaurant on-site, El Barquito, where a complimentary continental breakfast is served.

Holbox Dream Hotel (Av. Pedro Joaquín Coldwell s/n, tel. 984/875-2433, www.holboxdream.com, US$95 s/d with a/c, US$125 deluxe s/d with a/c, US$139 studio) is a refreshingly normal alternative to the deserted-isle getaways that make up most of Holbox's accommodations. Standard rooms are comfortable and modern, with air-conditioning, good mattresses, stone basin sinks, and balconies with partial ocean views; deluxe rooms are bigger, with minifridges, security boxes, and better views. There's free Wi-Fi in all the rooms. The hotel also has a well-maintained stretch of beach and a small pool that's inviting although squeezed between the reception and the guest rooms—a minor drawback to an otherwise excellent choice.

Zomay Hotel (Av. Pedro Joaquín Coldwell s/n, tel. 984/875-2090, www.zomayholbox.com, US$80 s/d with a/c, US$90-140 s/d with kitchenette, US$160-180 s/d with kitchenette and a/c, US$220 apartment with a/c) has bungalows and apartments, some with kitchenettes or lofts, each featuring homey decor and a small patio or veranda looking onto the large palm-shaded garden or the beachfront. Zomay is about five blocks west of the central plaza and a bit farther to the best swimming and beach areas, but bike rentals are available. There's Wi-Fi in the reception area, too.

Over US$200

⟨ **CasaSandra** (Calle Igualdad s/n, tel. 984/875-2171, www.casasandra.com,

US$250-417 s/d with a/c, US$612 suite) is one of Holbox's most exclusive resorts, though it still maintains the welcoming feel of a home. The main building looks like a Swiss ski lodge (it houses ocean-view rooms, the library, and a restaurant), but it also has a handful of smaller *palapa*-roofed buildings, more in style with their island neighbors. Rooms vary from shabby chic to tropical safari in decor and have features like claw-foot tubs and original art. Outside, guests can relax on the well-tended beach or by the large pool. A full breakfast is included in the rate.

Las Nubes de Holbox (Paseo Kuka s/n, tel. 984/875-2300, www.lasnubesdeholbox.com, US$300-450 s/d with a/c) is an upscale resort with *palapa*-roofed bungalows and modern hotel suites that are undeniably lovely but lacking the boho spirit of the island. Nevertheless, it is a comfortable place, with a waterfront restaurant, an inviting pool, and a well-tended beachfront. Continental breakfast is included in the rate, as are use of bicycles and kayaks.

FOOD

There are only a handful of restaurants on Isla Holbox, so anyone staying more than a day or two could easily sample them all. It wouldn't even take much effort, as virtually all face the central plaza or are less than a block off it. A quick stroll around the plaza lets you whet your appetite while sizing up the options.

Restaurants

Los Pelones (central plaza, Av. Benito Juárez btwn Avs. Porfirio Díaz and Igualdad, no phone, 6:30pm-11pm daily, US$6-21) is a small 2nd-floor restaurant overlooking the central plaza. It features mostly Italian dishes, including great handmade pasta. Grab a table on the balcony for the best view and sea breeze.

Cosa Nostra (Hotel La Palapa, Av. Morelos at the beach, tel. 984/803-3018, 7:30am-10pm daily, US$8-25) may have a long list of pizzas, but it's much more than a simple pizza joint.

This is first-class Italian cuisine, featuring handmade sausage, perfect pasta, and expertly prepared seafood, including whole lobster and octopus salad. (And, yes, the pizza's good, too.) Breakfasts are less successful, but dinner is a worthwhile splurge. You'll find a strong wine list and excellent service here. Beachfront seating has nice views but can be buggy—bring repellent.

◖ **La Tortilleria de Holbox** (central plaza, tel. 984/875-2443, 7am-4pm daily, US$3-7) is a breakfast favorite in a central location, with great fresh-brewed coffee to go along with omelets, yogurt and fresh fruit, and more—all with friendly service. For lunch, the Spanish tortilla feeds two and is to die for.

Pizzería Edelín (central plaza, Av. Palomino at Av. Porfirio Díaz, tel. 984/875-2024, 11am-midnight daily, US$5-17) manages to stay busy even in the low season, serving decent thin-crust pizza—try the lobster or olive-and-caper ones for a treat—plus a smattering of fish, pasta, and Mexican dishes. The ovens can really heat up the place, so nab a table on the porch for the breeze.

A colorful clapboard house, **La Isla del Colibrí** (central plaza, Av. Benito Juárez at Av. Porfirio Díaz, no phone, 8am-1pm and 6pm-11pm daily, US$4-9) is a decent breakfast place offering fresh fruit juices and big *licuados,* egg dishes, and Mexican classics. It's open for lunch and dinner, too, but there are better places for those meals.

Groceries

Supplies ebb and flow in Isla Holbox, so you might have to go to more than one store to find everything you're looking for.

Super Monkey's (Av. Benito Juárez near Calle Escobedo, 6:30am-11pm daily) has canned and packaged food, bug repellent, sunscreen, and toiletries.

The best selection of fruits and vegetables on the island typically is at **Frutería La Concepción** (Calle Escobedo near Av. Palomino, 7am-6pm daily). You'll also find eggs, honey, and spices.

INFORMATION AND SERVICES

While Holbox is making it onto more travelers' radars, there still is no bank (though there is one ATM) and no post office. Also, note that hours of operation on the island are decidedly flexible—"open all day" usually means "closed for a couple of hours in the middle of the day for lunch."

Emergency Services

Holbox's **Centro de Salud** (Av. Benito Juárez btwn Oceano Atlántico and Adolfo López Mateos, tel. 998/875-2406, 8am-2pm and 4pm-8pm Mon.-Sat., until 6pm Sun.) offers basic health services and occasionally runs out of medicine. For more advanced medical attention, head to Cancún or Mérida; in emergencies, you may be able to charter a small plane.

Farmacia Jessy (Av. Igualdad near Av. Bravo, no phone, 9am-10pm daily) usually has a moderate selection of medications and basic toiletries.

Money

There is **no bank** on Isla Holbox, but there is one **Bancomer ATM** on the 2nd floor of the *Alcaldía* (City Hall, central plaza, Av. Porfirio Díaz s/n); it often runs out of money, though, so plan accordingly.

Though some hotels, restaurants, and tour operators accept credit cards, don't count on using plastic; be sure to **bring enough cash** for the length of your stay (plus an extra day or two, in case you decide to extend your visit).

Media and Communications

Sharky's Cyber (Av. Igualdad near Av. Bravo, 10am-11pm daily, US$1.25/hour) has Skype-ready computers, though it can sometimes be overrun by kids playing video games. Another option is **Internet Café Don Antonio** (corner of Avs. Porfirio Díaz and Morelos, 9am-11pm daily), which charges US$1.50 per hour.

Laundry

If your hotel doesn't offer laundry service (many

do), a number of local women wash clothes in their homes, charging around US$5 for three kilos (6.6 pounds). Look for signs around town or ask at your hotel for a recommendation.

GETTING THERE
Car, Ferry, Bus, and Taxi

To get to Holbox, you first need to get to the small coastal village of Chiquilá. There are direct buses from Cancún and Mérida. If you're driving, take old Highway 180 (not the *autopista*) to El Ideal, about 100 kilometers (62 miles) west of Cancún. Turn north onto Highway 5 and follow that about 140 kilometers (87 miles) to Chiquilá, passing though the town of Kantunilkín. (There are shortcuts from both Mérida and Cancún, but they follow smaller, less-maintained roads.) You'll have to leave your car in Chiquilá. Several families run small overnight parking operations, charging around US$4 per day; ask about weekly rates.

Ferries operated by **9 Hermanos** (tel. 984/875-2010) leave Chiquilá for Isla Holbox (US$6.75, 25 minutes) at 6am, 8am, 10am, and 11am, noon, and 1pm, 2pm, 4pm, 5pm, 7pm, and 9:30pm. Returning boats leave Holbox at 5am, 7am, 9am, 10am, and 11am, noon, and 1pm, 3pm, 4pm, 6pm, and 8pm. Going to Holbox, it's a good idea to get to the dock a half hour early, as the boat occasionally leaves ahead of schedule. Private boatmen make the trip in either direction for approximately US$30-40 for up to six people; ask at the dock. **Note:** Private boats are prohibited from ferrying passengers to/from Holbox after dark.

From Chiquilá, **second-class buses** to Cancún (US$7, 3.5 hours) leave the dock parking area at 5:30am and 7:30am and 1:30pm; all wait for the ferry arriving from Holbox. To Mérida, there's just one bus at 5:30am (US$12.50, 7 hours).

Taxis also often are available at the dock to take travelers door-to-door to Cancún (US$65-85), Cancún International Airport (US$90), Playa del Carmen (US$100), and Valladolid

the ferry to Isla Holbox

(US$43); be sure to agree upon a price before you step into the car.

If you get stuck in Chiquilá, the **Hotel Puerta del Sol** (tel. 984/267-1004, US$27 s/d with fan, US$33 s/d with a/c) is your only option, located a short distance back down the main road from the dock. Rooms here are very simple but have TV and private bath. If you can swing it, opt for a room with air-conditioning—they are newer and considerably nicer than the fan rooms. There also is a string of basic restaurants, most with a focus on seafood, facing the dock.

Air

If you've got the money and the stomach for itty-bitty planes, **AeroSaab** (tel. 998/865-4225, www.aerosaab.com) offers a full-day tour to Isla Holbox departing from Cancún, Playa del Carmen, or Cozumel. Using Cessna airplanes, the trip begins with a scenic one-hour flight up the coast to Holbox, followed by a tour of Isla Pájaros and Yalahau Spring,

lunch, and a chance to explore the village and beach (US$296-373 pp, minimum 4 people). Overnight trips and/or whale shark excursions also can be arranged.

GETTING AROUND

Holbox is very easy to get around on foot. Even the farthest hotels are no more than a half hour's walk from town, and it's very safe day or night. The only time you may really need a lift is when you're lugging your bags between the pier and your hotel.

Taxi

Golf carts serve as the island's taxis (some are even painted in yellow-and-black checkers). A ride from the pier into town is US$1.50-2.50 per person or US$3-5 to the hotels farther down the beach. They are almost always parked on the plaza, or your hotel can call one.

Golf Cart

Though you really don't need a golf cart to get

around Holbox, you may enjoy the convenience of one. Rates, though not cheap, are relatively uniform: US$10 per hour, US$60 for 12 hours, and US$68 for 24 hours.

Recommended outfits include **Rentadora Glendy** (Av. Porfirio Díaz at Av. Morelos, tel. 984/875-2093, 7am-11pm daily) and **Rentadora El Brother** (Av. Benito Juárez at Av. Igualdad, tel. 998/875-2018, 8am-10pm daily).

Bicycle

Other than walking, the easiest—and most affordable—way of getting around town is by bike. A **no-name bike rental shop** (Av. Igualdad near Av. Palomino, no phone) rents bikes for US$8.50 per day; weekly rates are negotiable. The small eatery **Tortilleria de Holbox** (central plaza, tel. 984/875-2443, 7am-4pm daily) also rents bikes.

ISLA COZUMEL

All around Isla Cozumel, the Caribbean Sea glitters a hundred shades of blue. Beneath the waves, pristine coral reefs make for spectacular diving and snorkeling, the island's number-one draw. San Miguel de Cozumel—usually just called Cozumel, since it's the only city on the island—is where the ferries from Playa del Carmen land. It's also where cruise ships, as many as 30 per

© LIZA PRADO

Highlights

LOOK FOR ◖ TO FIND RECOMMENDED SIGHTS, ACTIVITIES, DINING, AND LODGING.

◖ **Santa Rosa Wall:** Sit back and enjoy the ride at one of Cozumel's marquee dive sites. A strong current whisks you past a long wall, mottled with stony overhangs and gaping caves, and home to massive sea fans, translucent sponges, and tropical fish of every size and color (page 103).

◖ **Palancar:** With five sections spread over nearly five kilometers (3 miles), this massive dive site has something for everyone. Snorkelers can check out Palancar Shallows, while divers can explore the winding ravines and natural arches of Palancar Horseshoe. No matter where you go, you'll enjoy rich coral and vibrant sealife (page 106).

◖ **San Gervasio:** Smack dab in the middle of the island, Cozumel's best and biggest Maya ruin is thought to be dedicated to Ixchel, the goddess of fertility; in ancient times, it attracted women from all over the Yucatán seeking her favor (page 106).

◖ **Playa Chen Río:** Heavy surf makes most of Cozumel's east side unswimmable, except here, where a rocky arm forms a calm natural pool. Come midweek to have it all to yourself, or on a Sunday to *convivir* (literally, share life) with local families (page 110).

◖ **Parque Punta Sur (Faro Celarain Eco Park):** Snorkel the colorful ocean reef, or stay

above water on the long curving beaches of this scenic nature reserve. There's also a small maritime museum, a Maya ruin, and a lighthouse you can climb for a birds-eye view of the gorgeous surroundings (page 121).

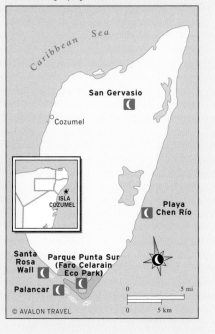

week in the high season, arrive; it's then that the waterfront promenade becomes a human river, flowing slowly down a channel of jewelry stores, souvenir shops, and open-air restaurants.

Just a few blocks from the promenade, another Cozumel emerges—a small, friendly community where old folks sit at their windows and dogs sleep in the streets. In spring, masses of orange *framboyán* (poinciana) flowers bloom on shade trees in the plaza, and festivals and religious celebrations are widely attended.

Cozumel's interior—including an important Maya ruin—and its eastern shore are yet another world, lacking even power lines and telephone cables. Heavy surf makes much of the eastern shore too dangerous for swimming, but you easily can spend a day beachcombing or relaxing on the unmanicured beaches and lunching at small restaurants overlooking the sea.

As Mexico's third largest island, it shouldn't be surprising to discover that it's so multifaceted. But it's hard not to marvel at how stark the differences are. Come for the diving and

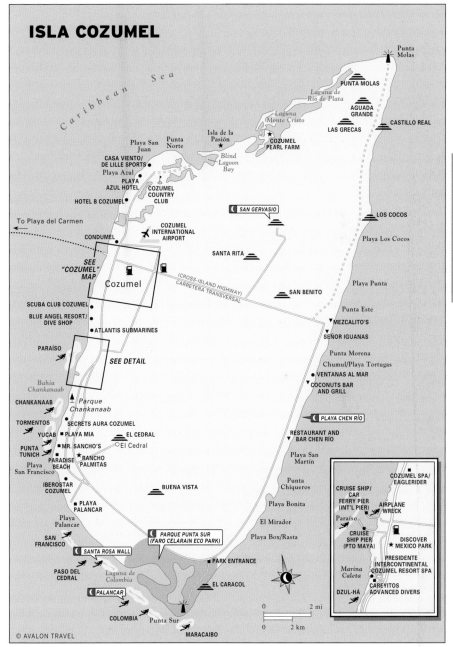

ISLA COZUMEL

ISLA COZUMEL

snorkeling, but leave time to experience a side of Cozumel you may not have expected.

HISTORY

Cozumel has been inhabited since 300 BC and was one of three major Maya pilgrimage sites in the region (the others were Chichén Itzá and Izamal in Yucatán state). The name is derived from the island's Maya name, *Cuzamil* (Land of Swallows). The height of its pre-Hispanic occupation was AD 1250-1500, when Putún people (also known as the Chontol or Itzás, the same group who built Chichén Itzá's most famous structures) dominated the region as seafaring merchants. Capitan Don Juan de Grijalva arrived on the island in 1518 and dubbed it Isla de Santa Cruz, marking the beginning of the brutal dislocation of the native people by Spanish explorers and conquistadors. It eventually was overrun by British and Dutch pirates who used it as a base of operations. By the mid-1800s, however, the island was virtually uninhabited. The henequen, chicle, and coconut-oil booms attracted a new wave of people to the Quintana Roo territory (it didn't become a state until 1974), and Cozumel slowly rebounded, this time with a mostly Mexican mestizo population.

Cozumel benefitted mightily from the worldwide popularity of Jacques Cousteau's early underwater films (which were not filmed there, contrary to legend, but inspired others that were) and later, of course, the establishment of Cancún in the 1970s.

PLANNING YOUR TIME

Don't let the cruise ship hubbub on Avenida Rafael Melgar turn you off from the town altogether. Besides the fact that most of the hotels, dive shops, banks, and other services are here, the town itself has much to offer, including a pleasant central plaza and a great museum. Budget a day or two to rent a car and explore the rest of the island, including the beach clubs, Maya ruins, family-friendly ecoparks, and the wild beaches and deserted coastline of Cozumel's eastern side.

ORIENTATION

The town of San Miguel de Cozumel (aka "Downtown Cozumel") is located on the west side of the island. The main passenger ferry lands here, across from the central plaza.

Avenida Benito Juárez is one of the main streets in Downtown Cozumel, beginning at the central plaza, crossing town, and becoming the Carretera Transversal (Cross-Island Highway). The highway passes the turnoff to the San Gervasio ruins before intersecting with the coastal road. The coastal road follows Cozumel's eastern shore, which is dotted with a few beach clubs and restaurants. Rounding the southern tip, the road heads north along the west shore before becoming Avenida Rafael Melgar and returning to the central plaza. Continuing north, the road passes turnoffs to the airport and a country club before turning to dirt and eventually dead-ending.

Sights

PARQUE BENITO JUÁREZ

Cozumel's central plaza is surprisingly peaceful considering the mass of humanity that disembarks at the ferry pier directly across the street and from cruise ship ports just down the road. Few foreign visitors take time to linger in the park itself, which has wood benches, tree-filled planters, a boxy clock tower, and busts of late Mexican president

Benito Juárez and General Andrés Quintana Roo. The city municipal building, occupying most of the plaza's east side, was beautifully restored in 2005, with an airy commercial center on the ground floor and civic offices above. And though the central plaza is smack in the middle of Cozumel's tourist corridor, it is still a place local families come to stroll about, especially weekends, when live bands play in the central gazebo, and balloon and cotton candy vendors do a brisk trade.

MUSEO DE LA ISLA DE COZUMEL

The town's small but excellent museum, **Museo de la Isla de Cozumel** (Av. Rafael Melgar at Calle 6, tel. 987/872-1434, 9am-5pm Mon.-Sat., 9am-4pm Sun., US$3, free child 8 and under), is on the waterfront in what was once a turn-of-the-20th-century hotel. Well-composed exhibits in English and Spanish describe the island's wildlife, coral reefs, and the fascinating, sometimes tortured, history of human presence here, from the Maya pilgrims who came to worship the fertility goddess to present-day survivors of devastating hurricanes. The museum also has a small bookstore and a library. For a good photo-op head to the terrace, which has a great view of the main drag, ferry pier, and—on a clear day—Playa del Carmen.

COZUMEL PEARL FARM

Located on a remote private island on Cozumel's northern shore, the **Cozumel Pearl Farm** (cell. tel. 984/114-9604, www.cozumel-pearlfarm.com, US$110 pp) is a new and fun place to spend a day and learn about these unique nature-made jewels. The six-hour trip includes touring the farm's facilities to learn how and why pearls form, and how they are farmed and harvested, then snorkeling around the underwater installations. A beach barbecue is included, plus time for relaxing in hammocks and "power snorkeling"—snorkeling while being tugged by a boat. Service is friendly and professional, and transportation is included.

DISCOVER MEXICO PARK

Discover Mexico Park (Carr. Costera Sur Km. 5.5, 8am-4pm Mon.-Sat., US$20 adult, US$10 child) boasts hundreds of enthusiastic reviews from visitors, but we're hard pressed to understand the appeal. Exhibits include a video on Mexican history, scale-models of various iconic Mexican structures (the cathedral in Mexico City, the pyramid at Chichén Itzá, etc.), a gallery of Mexican folk art, and, of course, plenty

of opportunities for eating, drinking, and shopping. The center's tour guides are peppy and well informed, and Mexican art never fails to impress, but the overall experience is too gimmicky to be truly satisfying.

CORAL REEFS

Cozumel's coral reef—and the world-class diving and snorkeling it provides—is the main reason people come to the island. The reef was designated a national marine reserve more than two decades ago, and the waters have thrived under the park's rigorous protection and clean-up programs. In 2005, Hurricane Wilma took a major toll on the reef, snapping off coral and sponges with its powerful surge and leaving other sections smothered under a thick layer of sand and debris. But hurricanes are nothing new to Cozumel or its coral, and reports of vast damage to the reef were greatly exaggerated. Cozumel's underwater treasure remains very much alive, supporting a plethora of creatures, its seascapes as stunning as ever. Dozens of dive and snorkeling sites encircle the island, and the 1,000-meter-deep (3,281-foot) channel between Cozumel and the mainland still provides spectacular drift and wall dives. Here is a list of some of the most popular dives, though by no means all the worthwhile ones.

Airplane Wreck

A 40-passenger Convair airliner lies on Cozumel's seabed, about 65 meters (213 feet) from the shore near El Cid hotel. Sunk in 1977 for the Mexican movie production of *Survive II,* the plane has been broken into pieces and strewn about the site by years of storms. The site itself is relatively flat, though with parrot fish, damselfish, and a host of sea fans and small coral heads, there's plenty to see. With depth ranges of 3-15 meters (10-49 feet), this is a good site for snorkelers.

Paraíso

Just south of the international pier, and about 200 meters (656 feet) from shore, lies Paraíso, an impressive three-lane coral ridge. Medium-size coral—mostly brain and star—attract

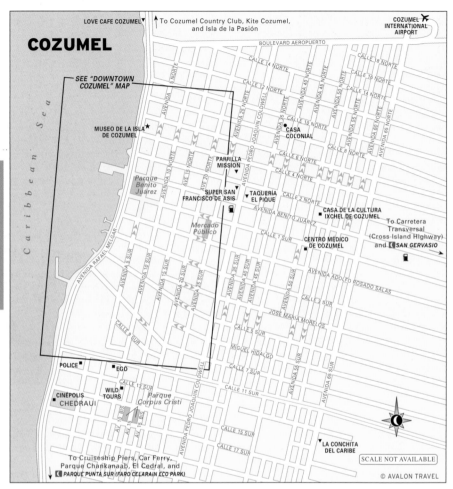

sergeant majors, angelfish, grunts, squirrel fish, and snappers. This site also is popular for night dives because of its proximity to hotels, which means less time on the boat. Depth ranges 5-13 meters (16-43 feet). Snorkeling is decent near the shore, but be very careful of boat traffic.

Dzul-Há (aka The Money Bar)

Located off the old coastal road (Km. 6.5), Dzul-Há is one of the best spots for DIY snorkeling, with small coral heads and sea fans

that support a colorful array of fish like blue tangs, parrot fish, and queen angels. Steps lead into the ocean, where depths range 3-10 meters (10-33 feet). You can rent snorkel gear on-site for US$14, including the marine park fee (US$2).

Tormentos

At this site divers can see about 60 coral heads, each decorated with an assortment of sea fans, brain and whip corals, and sponges. Invertebrates like to hide out in the host of

ISLA COZUMEL

© 123RF.COM

Cozumel's central plaza is a nice place to take a stroll, day or night.

crevices—look for flamingo tongue shells, arrow crabs, and black crinoids. Lobster like the scene, too—keep your eyes peeled for them, especially at the north end of the site. Depth ranges 5-15 meters (16-49 feet). The site is popular with photographers.

Yucab

A perfect drift dive, Yucab has archways, overhangs, and large coral heads—some as tall as three meters (10 feet)—that are alive with an incredible array of creatures: Lobsters, octopus, scorpionfish, banded coral shrimp, and butterfly fish can almost always be found here. Videographers typically have a field day. Depth ranges 5-15 meters (16-49 feet).

Punta Tunich

Punta Tunich usually has a 1.5-knot current, which makes it an excellent drift dive. The site itself has a white-sand bottom with a gentle downward slope that ends in a drop-off. Along the way, the reef is dotted with finger coral and elephant ear sponges. Divers regularly encounter eagle rays, barracuda, sea horses, bar jacks, and parrot fish. The depth ranges 5-18 meters (16-59 feet).

◖ Santa Rosa Wall

With a sensational drop-off that begins at 22 meters (72 feet), this spectacular site is known for its tunnels, caves, and stony overhangs. Teeming with sealife, it's home to translucent sponges, mammoth sea fans, file clams, horse-eyed jacks, fairy basslets, gray angelfish, and black groupers. Strong currents make this a good drift dive, especially for experienced divers. Depth ranges 5-27 meters (16-89 feet).

Paso del Cedral

A strip reef lined with small corals like disk and cactus, this site attracts large schools of fish like blue-striped grunts and snapper—perfect for dramatic photographs. Southern stingrays often are seen gliding over the sandy areas just inside the reef. Depths range 10-20 meters (33-66 feet).

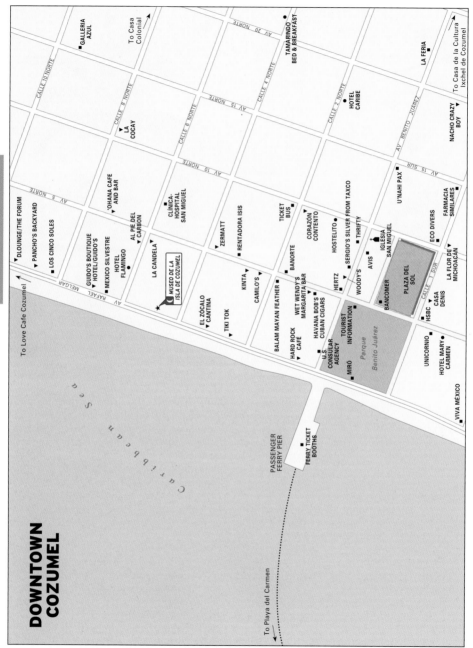

ISLA COZUMEL

DOWNTOWN
COZUMEL

Caribbean Sea

To Playa del Carmen

PASSENGER FERRY PIER

FERRY TICKET BOOTHS

To Love Cafe Cozumel

AV. RAFAEL MELGAR

AV. 5 NORTE

CALLE 10 NORTE

GALLERIA AZUL

To Casa Colonial

AV. 20 NORTE

TAMARINDO BED & BREAKFAST

AV. 15 NORTE

LA FERIA

CALLE X NORTE

To Casa de la Cultura
Ixchel de Cozumel

CALLE 2 NORTE

HOTEL CARIBE

AV. BENITO JUAREZ

NACHO CRAZY BOY

CALLE 8 NORTE

LA COCAY

CALLE 6 NORTE

AV. 15 SUR

AV. 10 NORTE

'OHANA CAFE AND BAR

CLINICA-HOSPITAL SAN MIGUEL

FARMACIA SIMILARES

U'NAHI PAX

DLOUNGE/THE FORUM

PANCHO'S BACKYARD

LOS CINCO SOLES

GUIDO'S BOUTIQUE
HOTEL/GUIDO'S

MEXICO SILVESTRE

AL PIE DEL CARBON

ZERMATT

RENTADORA ISIS

TICKET BUS

CORAZÓN CONTENTO

ECO DIVERS

HOTEL FLAMINGO

LA CANDELA

MUSEO DE LA ISLA DE COZUMEL

BANORTE

HOSTELITO

THRIFTY

SERGIO'S SILVER FROM TAXCO

IGLESIA SAN MIGUEL

LA FLOR DE MICHOACÁN

KINTA

CAMILO'S

HERTZ

WOODY'S

AVIS

PLAZA DEL SOL

CALLE 1 SUR

EL ZOCALO CANTINA

TIKI TOK

BALAM MAYAN FEATHER

WET WENDY'S MARGARITA BAR

HAVANA BOB'S CUBAN CIGARS

BANCOMER

CASA DENIS

HARD ROCK CAFÉ

U.S. CONSULAR AGENCY

TOURIST INFORMATION

Parque
Benito Juárez

HSBC

MIRÓ

UNICORNIO

HOTEL MARY CARMEN

VIVA MEXICO

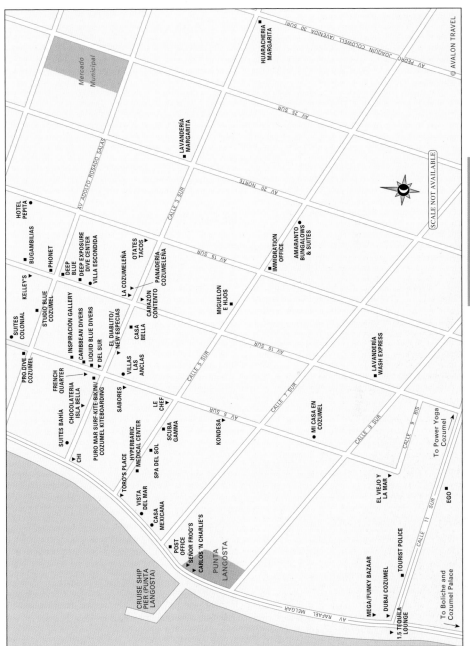

ISLA COZUMEL

SCALE NOT AVAILABLE

Mercado Municipal

AV PEDRO JOAQUIN COLDWELL (AVENIDA 30 SUR)

HUARACHERIA MARGARITA

AV 25 SUR

LAVANDERIA MARGARITA

CALLE 3 SUR

AV 20 NORTE

AV ADOLFO ROSADO SALAS

HOTEL PEPITA

BUGAMBILIAS

PHONET

DEEP BLUE
DEEP EXPOSURE DIVE CENTER
VILLA ESCONDIDA

LA COZUMELEÑA

OTATES TACOS

PANADERIA COZUMELEÑA

AV 15 SUR

IMMIGRATION OFFICE

AMARANTO BUNGALOWS & SUITES

KELLEY'S

STUDIO BLUE COZUMEL

INSPIRACION GALLERY

CARIBBEAN DIVERS

LIQUID BLUE DIVERS

DEL SUR

EL DIABLITO/
NEW ESPECIAS

CASA BELLA

CARAZON CONTENTO

MIGUELON E HIJOS

SUITES COLONIAL

PRO DIVE COZUMEL

VILLAS LAS ANCLAS

CALLE 5 SUR

AV 10 SUR

LAVANDERIA WASH EXPRESS

FRENCH QUARTER

CHOCOLATERIA ISLA BELLA

SABORES

LE CHEF

CALLE 7 SUR

SUITES BAHIA

PURO MAR SURF-KITE-BIKINI/
COZUMEL KITEBOARDING

SCUBA GAMMA

KONDESA

AV 5 SUR

MI CASA EN COZUMEL

CALLE 9 SUR

CHI

HYPERBARIC MEDICAL CENTER

SPA DEL SOL

CALLE 9 BIS

To Power Yoga Cozumel

TORO'S PLACE

VISTA DEL MAR

CASA MEXICANA

EL VIEJO Y LA MAR

CALLE 11 SUR

EGO

To Boliche and Cozumel Palace

CRUISE SHIP PIER (PUNTA LANGOSTA)

POST OFFICE

SEÑOR FROG'S

CARLOS 'N CHARLIE'S

PUNTA LANGOSTA

MEGA/FUNKY BAZAAR

DUBAI COZUMEL

TOURIST POLICE

1.5 TEQUILA LOUNGE

AV RAFAEL MELGAR

◖ Palancar

This spectacular five-kilometer-long (3.1-mile) dive spot is actually made up of five different sites—Shallows, Garden, Horseshoe, Caves, and Bricks. It is known for its series of enormous coral buttresses. Some drop off dramatically into winding ravines, deep canyons, and passageways; others have become archways and tunnels with formations 15 meters (49 feet) tall. The most popular site here is Palancar Horseshoe, which is made up of a horseshoe-shaped series of coral heads at the top of a drop-off. All the sites, however, are teeming with reef life. Palancar ranges in depth 5-40 meters (16-131 feet).

Colombia

An enormous coral buttress, Colombia boasts tall coral pillars separated by passageways, channels, and ravines. Divers enjoy drifting past huge sponges, anemones, and swaying sea fans. Larger creatures—sea turtles, groupers, nurse sharks, and southern stingrays—are commonly seen here. The site is recommended for experienced divers. Depths range 5-40 meters (16-131 feet).

Maracaibo

At the island's southern tip, Maracaibo is a deep buttress reef interspersed with tunnels, caves, and vertical walls. It is known for its immense coral formations as well as for the possibility of spotting large animals—sharks (black tip and nurse) as well as turtles and eagle rays. A deep-drift dive, this site is recommended for advanced divers only. Depths range 30-40 meters (98-131 feet).

ARCHAEOLOGICAL ZONES

Isla Cozumel played a deeply significant role in the Maya world as an important port of trade and, more importantly, as one of three major destinations of religious pilgrimages (the others were Izamal and Chichén Itzá, both in Yucatán state). The island's primary site—known as San Gervasio today—was dedicated to Ixchel, the Maya goddess of fertility as well as of the moon, childbirth, medicine, and weaving.

Archaeologists believe that every Maya woman was expected, at least once in her lifetime, to journey to Cozumel to make offerings to Ixchel for fertility—her own, and that of her family's fields. Cozumel's draw was powerful, as inscriptions there refer to places and events hundreds of miles away.

Over 30 archaeological sites have been discovered on the island, though only four are easily accessible, and only the largest—San Gervasio—can properly be called a tourist attraction. San Gervasio is certainly not as glorious as ruins found on the mainland, but it's worth a visit all the same.

◖ San Gervasio

The area around **San Gervasio** (Cross-Island Hwy. Km. 7.5, www.cozumelparks.org.mx, 8am-4pm daily, US$8) was populated as early as AD 200 and remained so after the general Maya collapse (AD 800-900) and well into the Spanish conquest. In fact, archaeologists excavating the ruins found a crypt containing 50 skeletons along with numerous Spanish beads; the bodies are thought to be those of 16th-century Maya who died from diseases brought by the conquistadors.

Today's visitors will find a modest ruin, whose small square buildings with short doors are typical of those found elsewhere on the island. This style, known as *oratorio,* almost certainly developed in response to climatic imperatives: Anything built here needed to withstand the hurricanes that have pummeled Cozumel for millennia.

San Gervasio has three building groups that are accessible to the public—Las Manitas, Plaza Central, and Murciélagos; all are connected by trails that follow the same ancient causeways used by the city's original inhabitants. A fourth building group—El Ramonal—is not yet open to the public.

Entering the site, you'll come first to the building group named after the structure **Las Manitas** (Little Hands), for the red handprints still visible on one of its walls. This structure is thought to have been the home of one of San Gervasio's kings, Ah Huneb Itza, and the inner

© H.W. PRADO

San Gervasio is Cozumel's most accessible Maya ruin.

temple was likely a personal sanctuary. Just east of the Las Manitas building is **Chi Chan Nah;** consisting of two rooms, it is the smallest structure in San Gervasio. The exact purpose of this building is unknown, though it is theorized that it was used for rituals.

Bearing left, the trail leads to the **Plaza Central,** a large courtyard surrounded by nine low structures in various states of decay; it is believed that the structures were made taller with wood extensions. The Plaza Central served as the seat of power in San Gervasio's latest era, from AD 1200 onward. At the northwest side of the Plaza Central is the somewhat precarious-looking **El Arco** (The Arch), which served as an entrance to this section of the city.

At 0.5 kilometer (0.3 mile) from the Plaza Central is the **Murciélagos** (Bats) building group, containing the site's largest and most important structure: Ka'na Nah (Tall House). Also dating to San Gervasio's later era, this was the temple of the goddess Ixchel, and in its heyday would have been covered in stucco and painted red, blue, green, and black.

Finally, on the northeastern edge of San Gervasio rests **Nohoch Nah** (Big House), a boxy but serene temple. With an interior altar, the temple might have been used by religious pilgrims to make an offering upon entering or leaving San Gervasio. It was originally covered in stucco and painted a multitude of colors.

Guides can be hired at the visitors center for a fixed rate: US$20 for a one-hour tour in Spanish, English, French, or German. Prices are per group, which can include up to four people. Tips are customary and are not included in the price.

El Cedral

El Cedral is the "other town" on Cozumel, a sleepy village south of San Miguel that's home to a small historic church and modest Maya structure of the same name. It's got a pleasant central plaza, and tour operators, including horseback riding guides, often bring visitors here to visit the church and temple, and to peruse the souvenir stands normally set up here. Once a year, El Cedral hosts one of Cozumel's largest festivals, a 10-day blowout celebration of the Catholic holy cross.

Although overshadowed by San Miguel today, El Cedral is actually the older settlement. It was here that a group of 18 families of indigenous Christian converts fled in 1847 to escape persecution by fellow Maya during the War of the Castes. They came bearing a small wooden cross known as *Santa Cruz de Sabán* (Holy Cross of Sabán) and founded their church and village alongside a Maya temple that they discovered just inland from their landing site. The group was led by Casimiro Cárdenas, whose descendants still serve as caretakers, or *mayordomos,* of the temple and church; there's a statue of Don Casimiro in the central plaza.

El Cedral is famous for its Fiesta de la Santa Cruz (Festival of the Holy Cross), which begins in late April and culminates on May 3. The celebration includes food, music, dance, performances, rodeo, and fireworks aplenty, and even some traditions of distant Maya origin. The party is open to everyone, including tourists, and makes for a fun and fascinating outing if your visit happens to coincide with it.

A well-marked turnoff just south of Playa San Francisco leads 5 kilometers (3.1 miles) to the village. El Cedral's **Maya ruin** (8am-5pm daily, free) is small and underwhelming, though it still bears a few traces of the original paint and stucco. The church is directly adjacent and contains the original wooden cross borne by El Cedral's founders.

El Caracol

Located inside **Parque Punta Sur** (Carr. Costera Sur Km. 27, tel. 987/872-0914, http://cozumelparks.gob.mx, 9am-5pm daily, US$10 adult, US$5 child over 8), El Caracol is a small, conch-shaped structure that dates to AD 1200. It's believed to have been a lighthouse where Maya used smoke and flames to lead boats to safety. Small openings at the top of the structure also acted as whistles to alert Maya to approaching tropical storms and hurricanes. Admission to the reserve includes access to this small site.

Castillo Real

Castillo Real is a partially excavated site with a temple, two chambers, and a lookout tower. It is believed to have been a Maya watchtower to protect against approaching enemies. It's located on the remote northeastern corner of the island, along the sand road leading to Punta Molas. The road is quite treacherous, such that even ATVs and motorcycles can have trouble making it. Ask at the tourist office for the latest before making any plans to head up there.

Beaches and Beach Clubs

Cozumel isn't famous for its beaches, but it is not without a few beautiful stretches of sand. The best beaches are on the protected southwestern coast, with soft white sand and calm azure waters. The best stretches are occupied by large beach clubs, which have conveniences like lounge chairs, umbrellas, restrooms, restaurants, and water sports; a few even have swimming pools. Most beach clubs charge either a cover or a minimum consumption, but neither is exorbitant. The clubs cater to cruise shippers and range from peaceful and low-key to boisterous and loud. Independent travelers are perfectly welcome too, of course.

Beaches on Cozumel's east side are wild and picturesque, with virtually no development beyond a few small restaurants. The surf can be fierce here, though a few sheltered areas have good swimming and are popular with locals. The municipal government has been steadily improving the road on the east side, including adding signs, stairways, and parking, but it remains a far different experience than the westside beach clubs.

NORTHWESTERN COZUMEL
Isla de la Pasión

One of Cozumel's loveliest beaches is **Isla de la Pasión** (no phone, www.isla-pasion.com, US$65 adult, US$40 child), a privately owned island and beach club just off Cozumel's north shore. Although aimed squarely at cruise ship passengers, anyone can sign up for a package tour, which includes a buffet, open bar, and free beach activities. The beach is gorgeous—one of Corona's commercials was filmed here—and the island is covered, oddly, with wispy pine trees. (Scientists believe their seeds were washed or blown from the Atlantic coast of the United States.) The price is a bit steep, but the main bummer is you only get four hours at the beach.

It's possible, though not easy, to visit Isla de la Pasión on your own; the beach itself is public, after all, and you can stay as long as you like. From the northern end of Avenida Rafael Melgar, a dirt road continues 5 kilometers (3.1 miles) past a water treatment plant to the port at Bahia Ciega. (The road isn't bad, but drive carefully, as your vehicle's insurance is probably void here.) At the port, ask around for a fisherman to take you across (around US$10, 20 minutes). Be sure to arrange a time for him to return, and cross your fingers he's got a good memory; otherwise, you'll be left begging a ride with a tour group. Bring food, water, and an umbrella—you won't be allowed to use the beach club facilities, but there's plenty of beach to lay out a towel. If you do book a tour, you can save US$20 per person by getting to the port yourself.

SOUTHWESTERN COZUMEL

The majority of beach clubs are clustered on Playa San Francisco, a three-kilometer (1.9-mile) stretch of white-sand beach that begins just south of the Aura Cozumel all-inclusive resort. Another beach, Playa Palancar, is farther south, near the tip of the island, and has a beach club of the same name.

Paradise Beach

Paradise Beach (Carr. Costera Sur Km. 14.5, tel. 987/872-6177, www.paradise-beach-cozumel.com, 9am-sunset daily, US$10 minimum consumption) has a gorgeous pool and a spacious picture-perfect beach, dotted with palm trees. Oddly, they charge US$2 for beach chairs and US$12 for use of the water sports gear, like kayaks, trampoline floats, paddleboards, and snorkel gear. Nevertheless, it's a lovely and not-too-raucous place to spend a day at the beach.

Playa Mia

Playa Mia (Carr. Costera Sur Km. 14.25, 987/564-0960, www.playa mia.com, 9am-6pm daily, US$40 with open bar, US$52 with open bar, buffet, towel, and snorkel gear) is big, busy, and energetic without being crass or obnoxious, like other clubs. The beach is decent, though often very crowded, and there's an excellent beach-side pool. The restaurant-buffet area is cool and pleasant, thanks to a high-peaked tent à la the Denver airport. And there's certainly no shortage of activities: volleyball, table tennis, a kids' play structure, massage, snorkeling, parasailing, catamaran rides, water trampoline, even a huge inflatable "iceberg," and more.

Mr. Sancho's

All-inclusives can make life easy, even when you're just going to the beach. **Mr. Sancho's** (Carr. Costera Sur Km. 15, 987/871-9174, www.mrsanchos.com, 9am-6pm daily, US$50 adult, US$45 teen, US$35 child) has a good Mexican restaurant, fairly mellow ambience, and plenty of extras, from snorkeling to massage. The beach is a bit narrow, meaning the lounge chairs are squeezed pretty tight, but it's a lovely spot all the same, and a great option for a no-brainer beach day.

Playa Palancar

With a calm atmosphere to match the calm turquoise waters, **Playa Palancar** (Km. 19.5, no phone, 8am-5pm daily, no cover or minimum consumption) is just the place to relax in a hammock under a palm tree or dig into a long book while digging your toes into the thick white sand. Playa Palancar has gotten busier over the years, now with music and even parasailing, but it's still the mellowest of Cozumel's main beach clubs. And there happens to be great diving and snorkeling at nearby Palancar and Columbia reefs; an on-site dive shop offers fun dives (US$65/90 one/two tanks) and guided snorkeling trips (US$35-45, 60-90 minutes), with daily departures at 9am, noon, and 2pm. Snorkel gear can be rented separately (US$10), but there's not much to see close to shore. A *palapa*-roofed restaurant serves classic Mexican seafood and a wide range of drinks (US$5-16). The club is 750 meters (0.5 mile) off the main road.

SOUTHEASTERN COZUMEL

On the east side of the island, you'll find a wild and windswept coastline dotted with beaches facing the open ocean. The surf here can be quite rough, and only a few beaches are safe for swimming.

Parque Punta Sur (Faro Celarain Eco Park)

As the name suggests, Punta Sur covers Cozumel's southern point, but the entrance is on the east side and the ambience and appeal is certainly akin to that of the eastern beaches. Officially called Faro Celarain Eco Park, **Parque Punta Sur** (Carr. Costera Sur Km. 27, tel. 987/872-0914, http://cozumelparks. gob.mx, 9am-5pm daily, US$10 adult, US$5 child over 8) is an important natural reserve that happens to have a fine beach and outstanding snorkeling. Because it faces south, the surf tends to be light. There's a small eatery, plus restrooms, a changing area, and a kiosk renting snorkel gear.

Playa Box (Playa Rasta)

Playa Box (pronounced Boash, Yucatec Maya for head) is better known as Playa Rasta for the two Jamaica-themed bars that occupy it. It's just past Punta Sur, where the road turns north along Cozumel's eastern shore. It's a rocky stretch of coastline with only a few sandy inlets and the two restaurants blasting reggae at each other. It's not really the best place to spend the day—unless you like rambling on rocks and have a serious craving for jerk chicken.

El Mirador

Spanish for The Lookout, this is the best place to appreciate Isla Cozumel's dramatic ironshore formations, including a natural arch and exposed huge bulges of the black jagged stone. Ironshore is formed when waves, wind, and especially microscopic organisms erode the ancient limestone cap that underlies much of the island. Be very careful walking on the ironshore; flip-flops are not recommended considering how sharp and slippery it can be.

Playa Bonita and Punta Chiqueros

Playa Bonita is another picturesque curve of sand with plenty of room to lay out a towel and soak in the sun. Heavy surf usually makes swimming here inadvisable, but it's definitely dramatic. The northern end of the beach is Punta Chiqueros, where a small **beach restaurant** (no phone, 10am-5pm daily) serves hamburgers, fresh fish, and other standards at decent prices.

Playa San Martín

A wooden stairway leads from the road down to the beach at this long, scenic, windswept beach. There are a handful of permanent *palapa* umbrellas near the stairway that are popular with couples and families, but otherwise you're likely to have the beach virtually to yourself.

◖ Playa Chen Río

The best place to swim on the east side of the island is **Playa Chen Río** (1 kilometer/0.6 mile south of Coconuts Bar), where a rocky spit blocks the waves, forming a huge natural pool, and lifeguards are on duty on weekends. Quiet during the week, it's lively and bustling most Sundays, when local families turn out in force. **Restaurant and Bar Chen Río** (no phone, 11am-6pm daily, US$12-26) is located here, but the prices are quite high, so it's not uncommon to see families with coolers and baskets and even small grills.

Chumul (Playa Tortugas)

About six kilometers (3.7 miles) south of the

© LIZA PRADO

A naturally protected pool makes Playa Chen Río the best swimming and family beach on Isla Cozumel's east side.

Carretera Transversal intersection is Chumul, also known as Playa Tortugas, a broad beautiful beach on the north side of the Ventanas al Mar hotel. The scenic windswept beach is good for surfing—and has nesting turtles May-November—but it is often too rough for swimming or snorkeling. Still, it makes a good place to watch the wild and crashing waves anytime.

A few steps away is **Coconuts Bar and Grill** (no phone, 10am-sunset daily, US$6-14). Set on a dramatic palm-studded bluff—the only piece of elevated land on the island, in fact—the tables are arranged for diners to enjoy the fabulous views of the beach below and the Caribbean beyond. Classic beach fare is served—ceviche, tacos, nachos—and plenty of cold beer. There's rum punch and live music daily between 2pm and 3pm.

Punta Morena

This scenic and little-used stretch of beach has a small restaurant with restrooms. Like elsewhere on the eastern shore, swimming here can be hazardous because of heavy surf and rocky outcrops, but it's still a nice place to relax or search for shells on the beach.

Mezcalito's and Señor Iguanas

These two low-key restaurants—**Mezcalito's** (no phone, www.mezcalitos.com, 9am-sunset daily) and **Señor Iguanas** (no phone, 8am-6pm Mon.-Sat., 9am-6pm Sun.)—are located side-by-side, right where the Carretera Transversal hits the coast. Longtime Cozumel institutions, they have similar menus (ceviche, fried fish, hamburgers, US$7-15), drinks (beer, margaritas, and tequila shots, US$2.50-5), and services (beachside chairs, hammocks, and *palapas,* free if you buy something from the restaurant). Boogie boards also are available for rent at Señor Iguanas (US$5 for 2 hours)—a lot of fun if you can handle the rough surf.

NORTHEASTERN COZUMEL

Cozumel's northeastern shoulder is its long lost coast, the wildest and least-visited part of the

Sea Turtles of the Yucatán

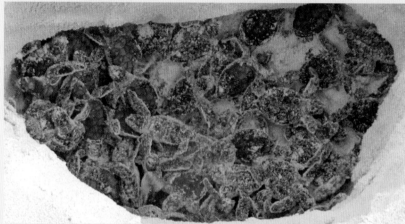

© LIZA PRADO

Visiting in the summer or fall, you can sometimes see sea turtle hatchlings emerging from their nests.

All eight of the world's sea turtle species are endangered, thanks to a combination of antiquated fishing practices, habitat destruction, and a taste for turtle products. Four turtle species–hawksbill, Kemp's ridley, green, and loggerhead–nest on the shores of the Yucatán Peninsula, and until recently, were a common supplement to the regional diet. Turtles make easy prey, especially females clambering on shore to lay eggs. They are killed for their meat, fat, and eggs, which are eaten or saved for medicinal purposes, as well as for their shells, which are used to make jewelry, combs, and other crafts.

Various environmental organizations collaborate with the Mexican government to protect sea turtles and their habitats; they maintain strict surveillance of known nesting beaches to stop poaching and have developed breeding programs, too. This, in combination with laws that prohibit the capture and trade of sea turtles or their products, has tremendously increased awareness about their protection.

On Isla Cozumel, travelers can volunteer to monitor nests and to release hatchlings into the sea. Nesting season runs May-September, and during that period volunteers join biologists on nighttime walks of Cozumel's beaches, locating and marking new nests, and moving vulnerable eggs to protected hatcheries. From July to November, volunteers release hatchings, typically at sundown, by encouraging the tiny turtles to move toward the water (without touching them) and scaring off birds in search of an easy meal.

Dirección Municipal de Ecología y Medio Ambiente (Calle 11 at Av. 65, tel. 987/872-5795) monitors Cozumel's sea turtles and manages volunteer opportunities. It maintains a **visitors center** (9:30am-2pm and 3:30pm-5:30pm daily May-Nov. only) in a small trailer, usually parked on the roadside near Playa San Martín on the eastern side of the island. Inside are a handful of aquariums, Plexiglas-enclosed nests, and more; stop by for information on upcoming beach walks and hatchling releases, or just to learn more about these endangered creatures. Donations are appreciated. Spanish is useful but not required.

Similar volunteer opportunities also are available in Akumal at the **Centro Ecológico Akumal** (CEA, tel. 984/875-9095, www.ceakumal.org) as well as on Isla Mujeres at **Tortugranja** (Carr. Sac Bajo 5, tel. 998/888-0507).

island. The 25-kilometer (15.5-mile) stretch from the Carretera Transversal north to Punta Molas includes coastal dunes, scrub forest, and deserted beaches, plus the ancient Maya site of **Castillo Real** at around the 22-kilometer (14-mile) mark. This untended coast also is the final resting spot of a shockingly large amount of trash and jetsam, an ugly reminder of civilization in the one place on the island it ought to be easy to forget.

The road itself is a challenge—four-wheel drive is essential to avoid becoming mired in deep sand—and hurricanes and other storms can render it impassable. The area also is at the center of a bitter, on-again off-again land dispute and is occasionally closed without warning.

If you do go, be aware that there are no facilities whatsoever, or any other people most of the time. If you plan to camp, take plenty of water and food, a flashlight, extra batteries, bug repellent, and a mosquito net. Remember, too, that most car insurance policies (including all policies sold by rental agencies on the island, regardless of the vehicle) specifically exclude this and other dirt roads from coverage.

Entertainment and Events

NIGHTLIFE

Most of the partying on Cozumel happens during daylight hours, when cruise ships disgorge thousands of tourists eager to stretch their legs and see some new faces. Beach clubs can get raucous, and many bars in town are open before lunch. Still, there are enough locals, expats, and overnight visitors to support a growing cadre of lounges and nightclubs. Most places don't charge a cover; if they do, it's on select nights, like when there's a live band.

Nightclubs

Tiki Tok (Av. Rafael Melgar btwn Calles 2 and 4, tel. 987/869-8119, www.tikitokcozumel. com, 9am-2am Mon.-Wed., 10am-4am Thurs.-Sun., no cover) sports a hodgepodge of beach-isle decor, from Polynesian lamps to Jamaican carved masks and figures. The plastic tables and chairs are a killjoy, but the upstairs beach patio, complete with sandy floor and nice sea views, is a nice touch. A live salsa band gets the crowd moving Friday and Saturday nights, starting at around 10:30pm.

El Zócalo Cantina (Av. Rafael Melgar btwn Calles 2 and 4, tel. 987/869-1213, 7pm-4am Wed.-Sun.) is an eclectic 2nd-floor cantina with long high tables, music and dancing most nights (live salsa 11pm-2am Fri.-Sat.), and frequent special events, from major sports games

projected on a huge screen to surprise happy hours where everyone drinks for free.

Love Cafe Cozumel (Av. Rafael Melgar at Blvd. Aeropuerto, tel. 987/107-1252, 10am-midnight daily) is a large open-air *palapa* with wood floors and killer views, especially at sunset. It's best known as a place to enjoy live reggae; at the time of research, a hot local band was packing the place Wednesday-Sunday, with a DJ most other nights. Fridays are all-you-can-drink for US$8.

Dubai Cozumel (Av. Rafael Melgar at Calle 11, tel. 987/119-9691, 10pm-5am Thurs.-Sun.) is a traditional nightclub playing a variety of music, from techno to Mexican ballads, with breaks in between for karaoke.

Bars and Lounges

El Diablito (Calle 3 Sur btwn Avs. 5 and 10, tel. 987/869-7947, 6pm-2am daily except Wed.) is a fun, trendy bar that shares a building with New Especias Italian restaurant. The bar is on the bottom floor, with red and black decor befitting its name (Spanish for Little Devil). The stairway leading to the restaurant is painted with puffy clouds, and the bar food sent down, like paninis and fritattas, is indeed heavenly. Out front are tables and a mural featuring Mick Jagger on a chopper.

Wet Wendy's Margarita Bar (Av. 5 Norte

ISLA COZUMEL

btwn Av. Benito Juárez and Calle 2, tel. 987/872-4970, 10am-11pm Mon.-Thurs., 10am-midnight Fri.-Sat.) is your classic expat island bar, with usual features like Monday Night Football, giant bacon burgers, and a jocular atmosphere. But it's famous for its huge handcrafted margaritas: potent creations that look more like sundaes than cocktails and range from mango and strawberry to avocado and cucumber-jalapeño.

1.5 Tequila Lounge (Av. Rafael Melgar at Calle 11, tel. 987/872-1537, 9pm-5am Thurs.-Sat.) is a modern lounge bar overlooking the ocean. It has low couches and chairs, outdoor decks, and house music playing in the background. Specialty shooters are the way to go, though the premium martinis pack a punch. Ladies night is on Thursday.

The world's smallest **Hard Rock Café** (Av. Rafael Melgar near Av. Benito Juárez, tel. 987/872-5271, www.hardrock.com, 10am-1am daily) has ocean views during the day and live music starting at 10pm Friday and Saturday. The food is unremarkable—stick to drinks— and if you're still collecting them, T-shirts are sold at the boutique up front.

For a spring break atmosphere all day (and all year) long, head to the Punta Langosta shopping center, where **Carlos 'n Charlie's** (Av. Rafael Melgar at Calle 9, tel. 987/869-1647, www.carlosandcharlies.com/cozumel, 10am-1:30am Mon.-Fri., 11am-1:30am Sat., 5pm-1:30am Sun.) and **Señor Frog's** (Av. Rafael Melgar at Calle 9, tel. 987/869-1658, www.senorfrogs.com, 10am-1am Mon.-Fri., 10am-4am Sat.) make driving beats, drink specials, and dancing on tables the norm.

THE ARTS
Cultural and Music Performances
Every Sunday evening, the city hosts an **open-air concert** in the central plaza. Locals and expats come out to enjoy the show—put on a clean T-shirt and your nicest flip-flops, and you'll fit right in. Concerts typically last two hours, beginning at 7pm in the summer, 8pm in the winter. Simple food stands selling homemade flan, churros, and other local goodies set up around the park these nights, too.

Casa de la Cultura Ixchel de Cozumel (Av. 50 btwn Av. Benito Juárez and Calle 2 Norte, tel. 987/872-1471, www.casadelaculturaixchel. blogspot.com, 9am-5pm Mon.-Fri.) hosts free concerts, movies, and art exhibits year-round. If you'll be on the island for an extended (or permanent) stay, a variety of classes—dance, art, music, drama, creative writing—also are offered, with a wide selection for children.

Cinema
You can catch relatively recent releases at **Cinépolis** (Av. Rafael Melgar btwn Calles 15 and 17, tel. 987/869-0799, www.cinepolis.com. mx, US$5.25 adult, US$4.25 child, US$3.25 before 3pm and all day Wed.), which is located in the Chedraui shopping center.

FESTIVALS AND EVENTS
Carnaval
Cozumel is one of the few places in Mexico where Carnaval is celebrated with vigor. Held in February, the one-night celebration centers around a parade of floats and dance troupes, all decked out in colorful dress, masks, and glitter. Entire families come to participate and watch. Spectators dance and cheer in the streets as the floats go by, and many join the moving dance party that follows the floats with the largest speakers. Eventually the parade ends up in the center of town, where more music, dancing, and partying continue late into the night.

Festival de El Cedral
Residents of the village of El Cedral celebrate their namesake festival beginning in late April and culminating on May 3, the Day of the Holy Cross. Traditionally, the festival entails daily prayer sessions and ends with a dance called the Baile de las Cabezas de Cochino (Dance of the Pigs' Heads). The festival, started by a survivor of the Caste War to honor the power of the cross, has morphed over the years into a somewhat more secular affair, with rodeos, dancing, music, and general revelry.

Rodeo de Lanchas Mexicanas

Every May, Cozumel hosts a popular sportfishing tournament known affectionately as the Mexican Boat Rodeo. Anglers from all over Mexico participate—including nearly 200 boats—and international anglers are welcome as long as they register their boats in Mexico. The tournament is timed to coincide with the arrival of big game to Cozumel's waters; tuna, dorado, marlin, and sailfish are often among the fish caught.

Fiesta de San Miguel Arcángel

You'd be forgiven for not knowing that the main town on Cozumel is officially called San Miguel. Hardly anyone, local or tourist, calls it that, preferring just Cozumel instead. One story, among many, is that the city got its name when construction workers unearthed a centuries-old statue of the winged saint on September 29, the very day Saint Michael the Archangel is traditionally celebrated. San Miguel was designated the town's patron saint, and every year September 29 is marked with a citywide celebration, including special masses and religious processions, a rodeo, food stands, music, and general revelry, mostly in and around the central square and San Miguel church.

Ironman Cozumel

Ironman Cozumel (www.ironmancozumel.com) is the only qualifying event in the Ironman series to be held in Mexico, featuring a course that's as beautiful as it is grueling. The swim (3.8 kilometers/2.4 miles) is certainly the most distinctly *cozumeleño* part, starting and ending at Chankanaab National Park, with gorgeous underwater vistas, and scuba divers and sea creatures observing from below. The bike ride (180 kilometers/112 miles) entails three laps around the island, with lovely sea views but crosswinds strong enough to topple unwitting racers. The run is oddly uninspired, three laps between downtown and the airport, although the sunsets there are spectacular (and you've got until midnight to finish). Ironman Cozumel is usually held in late November and attracts around 2,500 triathletes from around the world.

Shopping

Shopping in Cozumel is aimed straight at cruise ship passengers—and it's no wonder, since they tend to spend a lot of money quickly. Avenida Rafael Melgar is where most of the action is, with a succession of marble-floored shops blasting air-conditioning to entice sweaty passersby in for a refreshing look around. For better prices and more variety, head inland a block or two.

AVENIDA MELGAR

Populated with a mix of high-end jewelry shops and souvenir chain stores, Avenida Melgar has the highest prices in town for items that, on the whole, can be found back home. None of the shops are open to bargaining—at least when there is a cruise ship in port—so if you're looking for a deal, head inland a couple of blocks. In fact, unless you find something you absolutely can't live without, you're uniformly better off shopping elsewhere on the island.

The one exception to this general rule is **Los Cinco Soles** (Av. Rafael Melgar at Calle 8, tel. 987/872-9004, www.loscincosoles.com, 9am-8pm Mon.-Sat., 11am-5pm Sun.). A labyrinth of rooms at the northern end of Avenida Melgar, it's filled with high-end Mexican folk art from every state in the country: pre-Columbian replicas, *barro negro* pottery, colorful *rebozos* (shawls), hand-carved furniture, silver jewelry, handmade wood toys, alabaster sculptures, wool rugs, and more. The prices are higher than others in town but it's reflected in the quality. It's definitely worth a stop, if even

ISLA COZUMEL

© LIZA PRADO

Cozumel has shops for all budgets.

just to admire the artisanship. There's a smaller satellite shop at the Punta Langosta mall, too (Av. Rafael Melgar btwn Calles 7 and 11, no phone, 9am-8pm Mon.-Sat., 11am-5pm Sun.).

CENTRAL PLAZA AND BEYOND

Though pricey, **Pro Dive Cozumel** (Calle Rosado Salas at Av. 5, tel. 987/872-4123, 9am-9pm Mon.-Sat., 1pm-9pm Sun.) has a great selection of snorkel and dive equipment—perfect if you've forgotten your mask or lost a fin.

If you're looking for beachwear and gear, check out **Puro Mar Surf-Kite-Bikini** (Av. 5 Sur at Calle 3, tel. 987/872-4483, 9am-9pm Mon.-Sat.). A small shop, it's jam-packed with everything from bikinis and swim trunks to kiting and surfing gear.

Casa Bella (Calle 3 btwn Avs. 5 and 10, no phone, 9am-6pm Mon.-Sat.) sells beautiful household items created by artisans from around the country. Items include pewter trays, talavera pottery, and whimsically painted mirrors.

Located on a quiet residential street, **Galeria Azul** (Av. 15 btwn Calles 8 and 10 Norte, tel. 987/869-0963, www.cozumelglassart.com, 11am-7pm Mon.-Fri.) sells works of art by locals, including expat owner Greg Dietrich. Beautiful handblown glasswork, wood carvings, and paintings on silk dominate the gallery, but there also is poster art and tinwork.

For more local art, check out the small shop **Miguelon e Hijos** (Calle 5 Sur btwn Avs. 10 and 15, 987/872-5549, 9am-6pm Mon.-Sat.), which specializes in conch shells with intricately carved portraits and ancient Maya tableaus. It's not exactly everyone's taste, but the craftsmanship is remarkable.

Whether or not you play an instrument, **U'nahi Pax** (Av. Juárez at Av. 15, 987/872-5269, 9am-6pm Mon.-Sat.), Maya for The House of Music, is a great little shop jam-packed with a variety of handcrafted instruments from over 37 countries—you'll find everything from drums and rain sticks to flutes and guitars.

Bugambilias (Av. 10 Sur btwn Calles Rosado Salas and 1, tel. 987/872-6282,

9am-6pm Mon.-Sat.) sells traditional handmade linens and clothing, most incorporating embroidery and lace. The quality is excellent, and prices range from moderate to high.

SHOPPING CENTERS

Punta Langosta (Av. Rafael Melgar btwn Calles 7 and 11, 9am-8pm daily) is Cozumel's swankiest shopping center. The ultramodern open-air building is home to high-end clothing boutiques, air-conditioned jewelry stores, and fancy ice cream shops. It's a good place to window shop, especially if you want to buy a memento but aren't sure exactly what you'd like.

Located in a yellow building on the east side of the main plaza, **Plaza del Sol** (Av. 5 Norte btwn Av. Benito Juárez and Calle 1, 9am-8pm Mon.-Sat., 11am-5pm Sun.) houses a labyrinth of small souvenir shops selling everything from bad T-shirts to quality silver jewelry. You'll have to poke around a bit to find items worth buying, but a little perseverance will go a long way, especially if you're on a tight budget.

Sports and Recreation

SCUBA DIVING

Cozumel is one the world's best (and best known) places to scuba dive and snorkel, so it's no surprise that the island is home to dozens of dive shops—more than 100 at last count. Virtually all offer diving, snorkeling, and all levels of certification courses; there are a handful of dive "resorts," too, which offer packages that include lodging, diving, gear, and sometimes food.

Rates can vary considerably from shop to shop, and season to season, so be sure to clarify all the details up front. For most of the year, a two-tank fun dive costs US$72-90, plus US$12-35 per day if you need gear. Low-season rates can be significantly lower, and often include gear rental. PADI open-water certification courses (3-4 days) generally cost US$415-535, including all equipment and materials. Most shops also offer advanced courses, Nitrox and night diving, and multi-dive packages. All divers also must pay US$2 per day for marine park admission and to support Cozumel's hyperbaric chambers and marine ambulance; ask if the fees are included in a shop's rates or charged separately.

Dive Shops

Cozumel's diver safety record is good, and there are many competent outfits in addition to those listed here. Consider this list a starting point, to be augmented by the recommendations of trusted fellow divers, travelers, locals, and expats. Most important, go with a shop you feel comfortable with, not just the cheapest, the cheeriest, or the most convenient. Dive shops are generally open 8am-8pm daily, closing during those business hours only if no one's around to run the shop during a dive trip.

- **Blue Angel Dive Shop** (Carr. Costera Sur Km. 2.2, tel. 987/872-1631, www.blueangel-resort.com)

- **Careyitos Advanced Divers** (Marina Caleta, tel. 987/872-1578, www.advanced-divers.com)

- **Caribbean Divers** (Av. 5 at Calle 3 Sur, tel. 987/872-1145, www.caribbeandiverscozumel.com)

- **Deep Blue** (Calle Rosado Salas at Av. 10 Sur, tel. 987/872-5653, www.deepbluecozumel.com)

- **Deep Exposure Dive Center** (Av. 10 Sur btwn Calles 3 Sur and Rosado Salas, tel. 987/872-3621, toll-free U.S. tel. 866/670-2736, www.deepexposuredivecenter.com)

- **Eco Divers** (Av. 10 at Calle 1 Sur, tel.

How to Choose a Dive Shop

There are close to 100 dive shops on Isla Cozumel, and scores more at Isla Mujeres, Playa del Carmen, Cancún, Tulum, and elsewhere. Choosing just one—and then placing all your underwater faith into its hands—can be daunting.

Safety should be your number-one concern in choosing a shop. Fortunately, the standards in Cozumel and the Riviera Maya are almost universally first-rate, and accidents are rare. But that's not a reason to be complacent. For example, don't dive with a shop that doesn't ask to see your certification card or logbook—if they didn't ask you, they probably didn't ask anyone else, and ill-trained divers are as dangerous to others in the group as they are to themselves.

Equipment is another crucial issue. You should ask to inspect the shop's equipment, and the dive shop should be quick to comply. Although few casual divers are trained to evaluate gear, a good dive shop will appreciate your concern and be happy to put you at ease. If the staff is reluctant to show you the gear, either they aren't too proud of it or they don't see clients as equal partners in dive safety—both red flags.

Of course, the most important equipment is not what's on the rack but what you actually use. On the day of your dive, get to the shop early so you have time to **double-check your gear.** Old equipment is not necessarily bad equipment, but you should ask for a different BCD, wetsuit, or regulator if the condition of the one assigned to you makes you uneasy. Learn how to check the O-ring (the small rubber ring that forms the seal between the tank and the regulator), and do so before every dive. You also should attach your regulator and open the valve, to listen for any hissing between the regulator and the tank, or in the primary and backup mouthpieces. If you hear any, ask the dive master to check it and, if need be, change the regulator. Arriving early lets you do all this before getting on the boat—ideally before leaving the shop—so you can swap gear if necessary.

Feeling comfortable and free to ask questions or raise concerns (of any sort at any time) is a crucial factor in safe diving. That's where a dive shop's **personality** comes in. Every dive shop has its own culture or style, and different divers will feel more comfortable in different shops. Spend some time talking to people at a couple of different dive shops before signing up. Try to meet the person who will be leading your particular dive—you may have to come in the afternoon when that day's trip returns. Chances are one of the shops or dive masters will click with you.

Finally, there are some specific questions you should ask about a shop's practices. Has their air been tested and certified? Do they carry radios and oxygen? Does the captain always stay with the boat? How many people will be going on your dive? How advanced are they? How many dive masters or instructors will there be? And how experienced are they? Above all, be vocal and proactive about your safety, and remember *there are no stupid questions*.

And, of course, have fun!

987/872-5628, www.cozumel-diving.net/ecodivers)

- **Liquid Blue Divers** (no storefront, tel. 987/869-7794, www.liquidbluedivers.com)

- **Scuba Gamma** (Calle 5 near Av. 5 Sur, tel. 987/878-4257, www.scubagamma.net)

- **Scuba Tony** (no storefront, tel. 987/869-8268, U.S. tel. 303/519-4410, www.scubatony.com)

- **Studio Blue Cozumel** (Calle Rosado Salas btwn Avs. 5 and 10 Sur, tel. 987/872-4414, toll-free U.S. tel. 866/341-1090, www.studioblue.com.mx)

SNORKELING

Snorkelers have plenty of options in Cozumel, from cheap-and-easy snorkeling tours to renting gear and exploring on your own, right from shore.

Most dive shops offer snorkeling as well as diving, usually visiting 2-3 sites for a half hour each (US$50-70 pp). Snorkelers often go out with a group of divers and either snorkel in the same general location or go to a nearby site while the divers are underwater. This can mean some extra downtime as divers get in and out of the water, but the advantage is that you typically go to better and less-crowded sites.

For a quick and easy snorkeling tour, stop by one of the booths that flank the ferry pier. These trips are somewhat less expensive (though with larger groups) and can be booked right as you disembark from the ferry. Most offer two tours daily at around 11am and 2pm; some use a glass-bottom boat for extra pizzazz. The standard trip (US$45, including equipment) lasts 2-3 hours, visiting two or three sites, spending 30-45 minutes snorkeling at each one. Among many operators vying for your business are **Kuzamil Snorkeling Tours**

Dive Insurance

Although diving and snorkeling accidents are relatively rare on Cozumel, especially among beginning divers, you might consider purchasing secondary accident and/or trip insurance through the **Divers Alert Network** (DAN, toll-free U.S. tel. 800/446-2671, 24-hour emergency Mex. tel. 919/684-9111, accepts collect calls, www.diversalertnetwork.org), a highly regarded, international, nonprofit medical organization dedicated to the health and safety of snorkelers and recreational divers. Dive accident plans cost just US$30-75 per year, including medical and decompression coverage and limited trip and lost equipment coverage. More complete trip insurance—not a bad idea in hurricane country—and life and disability coverage are also available. To be eligible for insurance, you must be a member of DAN (US$35 per year).

(tel. 987/111-9333), **Dive Cozumel 1** (tel. 987/869-2591), and **Amazing Cozumel Tours** (no phone).

There are several terrific snorkeling spots near town and just offshore where you don't need a boat or a guide at all. Cozumel's boat drivers are careful about steering clear of snorkelers, but even so, do not swim too far from shore, look up and around frequently, and stay out of obvious boat lanes. If you plan to do a lot of snorkeling, especially outside of established snorkeling areas, consider bringing or buying an inflatable personal buoy. Designed for snorkelers, they are brightly colored and have a string you attach to your ankle or to a small anchor weight, alerting boat drivers of your presence. Also be aware of the current, which typically runs south to north and can be quite strong.

KITEBOARDING

Kiteboarding has quickly and thoroughly morphed from a novelty act to one of the most popular beach sports worldwide. Cozumel is no exception, with a dedicated cadre of kiteboarders and a growing number of options for travelers who want to learn or practice the sport.

De Lille Sports (formerly Kite Cozumel, Casa Viento, Carr. Costera Norte Km. 7, tel. 987/103-6711, www.delillesports.com) is operated by Cozumel native Raul de Lille, a former Olympic-level windsurfer and now one of Mexico's top kiters and instructors. (He now also offers stand-up paddling, hence the change of name.) Raul doesn't come cheap, but he's an outstanding instructor, not least for his calm demeanor and excellent English. Private lessons are US$125 per hour or US$500 per day. An intensive three-day introductory kiteboarding course includes 15 hours of instruction and costs US$900 per student (maximum 2 students per instructor); it also can be broken into modules depending on your time and previous experience. Kiteboarding rentals are US$150 per day for a full kit. For experienced kiters, de Lille offers clinics on kite control, tricks, and other specialties, plus adventuresome tours like downwinding the entire island. De Lille Sports

© LIZA PRADO

Cozumel is one of the Riviera Maya's best places for kiteboarding.

operates out of the Casa Viento (www.casaviento.net), a great hotel north of the center and a short walk from the beach.

Another locally run option is **Cozumel Kiteboarding** (Av. 5 Sur at Calle 3, tel. 987/876-1558, www.cozumelkiteboarding.com). Headquartered downtown in the Puro Mar Surf-Kite-Bikini shop, it offers kiting excursions around the island (4 hours, US$250 for 1 to 2 people), including to the little-visited northern lagoons: Río de Plata, Monte Cristo, and Blind Bary. Kiteboarding instruction for beginners and more experienced students also is offered.

STAND-UP PADDLING

Stand-up paddling (or "SUPing") is the sport du jour in Cozumel and around the world, and for good reason: It's fun and easy to learn (yet challenging to master), and is a unique way to experience Cozumel's rich coastline and extraordinarily clear waters. The glassy waters on Cozumel's western shore are perfect for the sport, which involves standing upright on an oversized surfboard-like board and using a long paddle to cruise around. Fitness buffs appreciate the full-core workout SUPing provides, while the elevated perspective allows you to see surprisingly well into the surrounding water—significantly better than in a kayak, in fact. It's not uncommon to see fish, rays, even sea turtles and dolphins swimming below and around you. Numerous resorts have SUP boards available for guests, and a handful of agencies offer instruction, rentals, and tours.

De Lille Sports (Casa Viento, Carr. Costera Norte Km. 7, tel. 987/103-6711, www.delillesports.com) is operated by windsurfing and kiteboarding legend (and Cozumel native) Raul de Lille, but he's big on SUPing too, even designing his own line of boards. The sports complement each other well: If there's not enough wind for kiting, it's probably perfect for SUPing, and vice versa. The agency offers private and group lessons, plus tours in remote areas of the island. SUP instruction runs US$75 per student (2-3 hours, maximum 8 students), while high-quality SUP rentals are US$25 per hour or US$85 per day.

KAYAKING

Cozumel's calm, clear waters make it a nice place to kayak. Most **all-inclusive resorts** and some **beach clubs** have a handful of kayaks available for guests to use (free to $10/hour). If you plan to swim or snorkel along the way—a great way to enjoy little-visited spots on the reef—be sure the kayak has a small anchor to prevent it from floating away.

SPORTFISHING

Cozumel boasts good deep-sea fishing year-round. It's one of few places anglers can go for the grand slam of billfishing: hooking into a blue marlin, a white marlin, a sailfish, and a swordfish all in a single day. It's also got plentiful tuna, barracuda, dorado, wahoo, grouper, and shark.

Albatros Charters (tel. 987/872-7904, toll-free U.S. tel. 888/333-4643, www.albatroscharters.com, US$420-450 for 4 hours,

US$500-575 for 6 hours, US$575-650 for 8 hours) has a variety of boats, each able to carry a maximum of six anglers. Trips include hotel pickup and drop-off, beer and soda, snacks, bait, and gear.

Other recommended outfits include **Aquarius Travel** (tel. 987/869-1096, toll-free U.S. tel. 800/371-2924, www.aquariusflatsfishing.com) and **Wahoo Tours** (tel. 987/869-8560, toll-free U.S./Can. tel. 866/645-8977, www.wahootours.com).

ECOPARKS AND WATER PARKS

◖ Parque Punta Sur (Faro Celarain Eco Park)

Better known as Parque Punta Sur, **Faro Celarain Eco Park** (Carr. Costera Sur Km. 27, tel. 987/872-0914, http://cozumelparks.gob.mx, 9am-5pm daily, US$10 adult, US$5 child over 8) is a massive natural reserve on the southern tip of Cozumel. The park spans thousands of acres of coastal dunes, beaches, mangroves, and wetlands, and extends well

© LIZA PRADO

the road into Parque Punta Sur, a large natural reserve with excellent beaches and snorkeling out into the ocean, including large areas of coral reef. It's home to a vast array of land and sea creatures, including 30 types of seabirds and some huge crocodiles that live in the park's large inland lagoons. There's a small Maya ruin known as El Caracol, which dates to AD 1200 and is believed to have been used for navigation, plus the park's famous lighthouse (which you can climb for great views) and a small but rewarding maritime museum. At the park's long, lovely beach—about a kilometer past the lighthouse—there are beach chairs, restrooms, a small eatery, and a shop to rent snorkel gear (US$10) and kayaks. The snorkeling here is outstanding, including sea fan "forests" that wave gently in the current.

Most visitors visit on package tours, but it's perfectly easy to visit independently; there's even a separate area away from the volleyball nets and buffet lines for people arriving on their own. You'll need a car—there used to be shuttle service into the park, but no longer—and you should arrive no later than 1pm in order to take full advantage of all the park has to offer.

Parque Chankanaab

Some 9 kilometers (5.6 miles) south of town, **Parque Chankanaab** (Carr. Costera Sur Km. 9, tel. 987/872-0914, http://cozumelparks.gob.mx, 8am-5pm daily, US$21 adult, US$14 child under 12) is a national park that operates mainly as a beach club and water park; that is to say, more Xcaret than Punta Sur. A visit here includes sunbathing by the pool, snorkeling in the ocean, relaxing in a hammock, and watching the sea lion and dolphin shows (included in the ticket price). **Dolphin Discovery** (toll-free Mex. tel. 800/727-5391, www.dolphindiscovery.com) has a facility within the park, with various interactive programs with dolphins, as well as manatees and sea lions, for an additional fee. Reserve in advance or right upon arrival, as they fill up fast. Chankanaab also has a fully equipped dive shop on-site, plus two thatch-roofed restaurants, a handful of gift shops, lockers, and restrooms. Chankanaab may be

a bit commercialized for independent travelers—consider Punta Sur instead—but it's a great option for families looking for an easy all-day option.

GOLF

Jack Nicklaus designed the par-72 championship course at **Cozumel Country Club** (Carr. Costera Norte Km 6.5, tel. 987/872-9570, www.cozumelcountryclub.com.mx, 6:30am-6pm daily), located at the far end of the northern hotel zone. Greens fees are US$169 until 12:30pm, when they drop to US$105. Carts are required and included in the rate. In addition to the slightly rolling, moderately challenging course, the club has a driving range, putting and chipping areas, overnight bag storage, a retail shop, and lessons from PGA golf pros. Book online for a discount.

SPAS AND GYMS

Cozumel Spa (Condos El Palmar, Carr. Costera Sur Km. 3.8, tel. 987/872-6615, www.cozumelspa.com) gets high marks from visitors and locals alike. A wide range of services includes massages for singles or couples (US$50-140), facials (US$50), and specialty treatments like aromatherapy, cold stone massage, and chocolate body wraps (US$50-100).

The most modern gym on the island, **EGO** (Calle 11 at Av. 5, tel. 987/872-4897, 5am-11pm Mon.-Fri., 6am-6pm Sat.) is a full-service facility complete with free weights, weight machines, cardio machines (plus personal trainers to help), and a slew of classes including Pilates, yoga, spinning, and kickboxing. Monthly membership is US$55, while visitors pay US$8 for the day. All that, plus the air-conditioning can't be beat!

TOURS
Horseback Riding

Located on the inland side of the highway across from Nachi-Cocom beach club, **Rancho Palmitas** (Carr. Costera Sur Km. 16, cell. tel. 987/119-1012, 8am-4pm daily) offers two horseback tours. A 2.5- to 3-hour tour (US$40 pp) includes stops at a cavern with a cenote, the archaeological site of El Cedral, and a few un-excavated Maya ruins. A shorter 1.5-hour tour (US$35 pp) leads to the cavern only. Call to set up a tour or just drop in—the last excursion leaves at 3pm.

ATV Excursions

Though catering to cruise ship passengers, **Wild Tours** (Av. 10 Bis btwn Calles 13 and 15, tel. 987/872-5876, toll-free U.S./Can. tel. 888/497-4283, www.wild-tours.com, 9am-7pm Mon.-Fri., 9am-2pm Sat.-Sun.) offers ATV excursions to everyone. Tours include off-roading through the jungle, vis-iting isolated Maya ruins, and snorkeling at Chankanaab reef (US$70-80 adult, US$110 child with adult, 4 hours; US$58-65 adult, US$90 child with adult, 2 hours). Tours

leave from a staging area in front of Carlos 'n Charlie's in Punta Langosta.

Submarine Tour

Atlantis Submarines (Carr. Costera Km. 4, tel. 987/872-4354, www.atlantissubmarines.com, US$99 adult, US$59 child) offers 40-minute underwater excursions near Chankanaab eco-park. The subs have oversized portholes with low seats in a long row down the center. Staff members describe what you're seeing outside. The sub dives as deep as 120 feet; you're sure to see plenty of fish and coral formations, and, if you're really lucky, a shark or sea turtle. It's pretty pricey considering how short the actual tour is, but it's a memorable way for young-sters and nondivers to admire Cozumel's ma-rine riches.

ISLA COZUMEL

Accommodations

DOWNTOWN COZUMEL
Under US$50

Just one block from the central plaza, **Hostelito** (Av. 10 btwn Av. Benito Juárez and Calle 2 Norte, cell. tel. 987/869-8157, www.hostelco-zumel.com, US$12.50 dorm, US$37.50-55 s/d with a/c) is a stylish hostel—Cozumel's only hostel, in fact—with a large coed dorm packed with bunks, lockers, and fans. Groups of four or more should ask about the air-conditioned dorm with private bathroom—at US$12.50 per head, they're a steal. Private doubles have air-conditioning, minifridge, and TV—they were being renovated when we passed through, so ought to be in nice condition. A fully equipped rooftop kitchen is available for all to use, as is a great lounge and solarium with hammocks for just kicking back. There's free Wi-Fi, too.

Hotel Pepita (Av. 15 Sur btwn Calles 1 and Rosado Salas, tel. 987/872-0098, US$35 s/d with a/c) is a good value for traveler 'tweens: post-hostel but pre-B&B. The friendly owners keep the rooms very clean, though some of the beds are saggy, and the decor could use some serious updating. All have air-conditioning,

ceiling fan, cable TV, minifridge, and two dou-ble beds. There's also fresh coffee every morn-ing in the long inner courtyard.

Hotel Caribe (Calle 2 Norte btwn Avs 15 and 20, tel. 987/872-0325, US$46-54 s/d with a/c) has a small, appealing pool in a leafy cen-tral garden—a rare and welcome feature in the ranks of budget hotels. Rooms are plain but clean, with one, two, or three beds, okay bath-rooms, and old-school air conditioners. Service can be ambivalent, but you can't argue with the value.

Hotel Mary Carmen (Av. 5 Sur btwn Calles 1 and Rosado Salas, tel. 987/872-0581, US$33 s/d with a/c) is a simple but reliable budget hotel, with a great location to make up for so-so rooms. Rooms have cute decor and are reasonably clean, though the air condition-ers and bathrooms are showing their age. The owners are friendly, and you can't beat being on the pedestrian walkway just a half block from the square.

US$50-100

◀ **Mi Casa en Cozumel** (Av. 5 btwn Calles 7

and 9, tel. 987/872-6200, www.micasaencozumel.com, US$45-70 s/d, US$160 penthouse) is a terrific boutique hotel and an architectural gem—the curves of the spiral staircase and interior walls are counterbalanced by triangular patios and angled nooks occupied by whirlpool tubs. All nine units have contemporary Mexican decor, most have a minifridge and cable TV, and a few have kitchenettes. Complimentary continental breakfast is served in a cozy ground-floor dining area. Several units have air-conditioning, while the others were designed for natural ventilation and are quite comfortable with fans only. The split-level penthouse is stunning, with full kitchen, outdoor hot tub, front and rear patios, and great views. The hotel's lofty structure is equally impressive, but could be difficult for guests who have trouble climbing stairs. Weekly rates are available.

⏺ Tamarindo Bed and Breakfast (Calle 4 btwn Avs. 20 and 25 Norte, tel. 987/872-6190 or 987/112-4111, www.tamarindobedandbreakfast.com, US$45-51 s/d with fan, US$57 s/d with a/c and minifridge, US$62 suite with a/c and kitchenette) is a pleasant B&B owned by a friendly French expatriate who lives on-site. The hotel has seven units bordering a large, leafy garden. Each room is different from the other, from two boxy but comfortable hotel rooms to a whimsical *palapa* bungalow with boho flair. All have cable TV and Wi-Fi. Full breakfast is included for rooms without a kitchenette, and there's a small communal kitchen. Rinse tanks and storage facilities are provided for guests with dive gear, too. The same owner also rents three **apartments and bungalows** (US$69-79 s/d) known as Tamarindo II; located south of the center a few blocks from the water, they've got one or two bedrooms, air-conditioning, kitchen, cable TV, Wi-Fi, and a small pool. Reservations are highly recommended.

Amaranto Bungalows & Suites (Calle 5 btwn Avs. 15 and 20 Sur, cell. tel. 987/106-6220, www.amarantobedandbreakfast.com, US$59 s/d bungalow with a/c, US$65 s/d suite, US$75 s/d suite with a/c) offers seclusion and privacy, while still within easy walking distance from downtown. The shining stars of the place are the suites, in a three-story tower, each with a sitting area and 360-degree views; the lower unit has air-conditioning, high ceilings, and a modern feel, while the upper one has a *palapa* roof that offers a birds-eye view. There also are three thatch-roofed bungalows with modern bathrooms and beachy decor. All the rooms have king-size beds, minifridges, microwaves, cable TV, and security boxes. There is a plunge pool on-site—perfect for cooling off after a day in the sun—and Wi-Fi in the lobby. Breakfast is included during high season, too. Amaranto doesn't have a full-time attendant, so it's best to reserve in advance.

Hotel Flamingo (Calle 6 btwn Avs. Rafael Melgar and 5 Norte, tel. 987/872-1264, toll-free U.S. tel. 800/806-1601, www.hotelflamingo.com, US$79-91 s/d with a/c, US$195 penthouse) offers classy, well-priced rooms with modern furnishings, mosaic tile bathrooms, and colorful Guatemalan decor, all in a quiet north-of-center location. Rooms have mini-split air-conditioners, electronic safes, and cable TV. Three common areas provide lots of extra outdoor space for guests—a rooftop solarium with lounge chairs and Jacuzzi, a shady midlevel area with hammocks, and a garden courtyard with tables and chairs. Wi-Fi is available in the lobby and bar areas. Families and groups should consider the penthouse, a two-bedroom apartment with full-size kitchen, private Jacuzzi, even a rooftop grill. Book in advance to get full breakfast at no charge.

Located in the heart of San Miguel, **Villa Escondida** (Av. 10 Sur btwn Calles 3 Sur and Rosado Salas, tel. 987/120-1225, www.villaescondidacozumel.com, US$90 s/d with a/c) is an adults-only B&B with just four guest rooms. Each is modern—if a bit sparse—in style, with comfortable beds and spacious bathrooms. All look onto a well-tended garden complete with an inviting swimming pool, lounge chairs, and hammocks. A full-size breakfast—from pancakes to *chilaquiles*—is served on the hotel terrace. Complimentary bicycles and snorkeling gear also are available to guests.

ISLA COZUMEL

words of wisdom at Hotel B Cozumel

Vista del Mar (Av. Rafael Melgar btwn Calles 5 and 7 Sur, tel. 987/872-0545, toll-free U.S./Can. tel. 888/309-9988, www.hotelvistadelmar.com, US$78-90 s/d with a/c) is a charming hotel in the middle of a string of tacky souvenir shops. Rooms have muted earth tones, high-end decor, inlaid stone walls, and balconies (some with spectacular views of the Caribbean). All have cable TV, minifridges, safety deposit boxes, robes—even turndown service. The hotel's patio also has lots of comfy lounge chairs as well as a hot tub with a mosaic-tile floor—a great space to hang if you don't mind the view of the kitsch below. Continental breakfast, delivered to your room, is included.

Suites Bahía (Calle 3 btwn Avs. Rafael Melgar and 5 Sur, tel. 987/872-9090, toll-free Mex. tel. 800/277-2639, toll-free U.S. tel. 877/228-6747, www.suitesbahia.com, US$67-92 s/d with a/c) and **Suites Colonial** (Av. 5 Sur btwn Calles 1 and Rosado Salas, 987/872-0506, same toll-free tels., www.suitescolonial.com, US$59 s/d with a/c, US$67 suite with a/c) are sister hotels, renting unremarkable but functional and well-priced rooms. The Colonial is more central, right on the pedestrian walkway, with slightly newer rooms and full kitchenettes. For a bit higher rate, rooms at the Bahía are larger and brighter (especially the ocean-view ones), and still have minifridges and microwave ovens. Neither hotel will win any awards for charm, but units are clean and reasonably comfortable, and include air-conditioning, cable TV, Wi-Fi, and (perhaps best of all) buffet breakfast at upscale Casa Mexicana hotel, a third sister in the family.

Over US$100

Villa Las Anclas (Av. 5 Sur btwn Calles 3 and 5, tel. 987/872-5476, www.hotelvillalasanclas.com, US$110 s/d with a/c) is a great option for those who want a little home away from home. Seven pleasantly decorated apartments open onto a leafy, private garden, each with a fully equipped kitchen, a living room, and a loft master bedroom accessed by spiral stairs. Using the sofas as beds, the apartments can accommodate up to four people while still not feeling overcrowded. All units also have air-conditioning and Wi-Fi. New owners have brought some welcome updates—a fresh coat of paint, newer TVs and appliances, and a reception area and dive shop in front—while the friendly vibe and great value remain the same.

Guido's Boutique Hotel (Av Rafael Melgar btwn Calles 6 and 8 Norte, tel. 987/872-0946, www.guidosboutiquehotel.com, US$110-130) is less a hotel and more do-it-yourself apartments, but the location, amenities, and price make Guido's an outstanding option. Masters have king beds, while juniors have queens; all are spacious, with full-size kitchens, stylish decor, and satellite TV and Wi-Fi. Each has a small balcony overlooking the street and ocean—traffic can get noisy but the views are priceless. The hotel is located just north of the center, above Guido's Restaurant, one of the island's best. There's no formal reception, so reserve ahead.

Casa Mexicana (Av. Rafael Melgar btwn Calles 5 and 7, toll-free Mex. tel. 800/277-2639, toll-free U.S. tel. 877/228-6747, www.casamexicanacozumel.com, US$90-110 s/d with a/c) is a modern beauty with a soaring interior courtyard and gorgeous views of the Caribbean from the ocean-side rooms, including cruise ships gliding in and out of port. Rooms are attractive and bright, though less inspired than the building itself, with good beds, quiet air conditioners, and updated bathrooms. There is a small infinity pool overlooking the water on one end of the spacious lobby; it's a little strange to be taking a dip in view of desk staff and inquiring guests, but still quite nice. Rates include buffet breakfast in an impressive open-air dining room.

A long walk from town but worth every step, **Casa Colonial** (Av. 35 btwn Calles 8 and 10, toll-free U.S./Can. tel. 866/437-1320, www.cozumelrentalvillas.com, US$1,075/week with a/c) has four fully equipped Mexican-style villas. All are two stories with two bedrooms, 2.5 bathrooms, a living room, a dining room, a modern kitchen, 32-inch hi-def TV, Wi-Fi, even a washer and dryer. And unlike many longer-term rentals, you still get daily maid service and complimentary concierge service. All villas face a lush courtyard with a large pool and hot tub. Dive rinse tanks are available, too.

NORTHWESTERN COZUMEL US$100-150

Located just minutes from some of Cozumel's best kiteboarding spots, the aptly named **Casa Viento** (House of Wind, Country Club Estates, tel. 987/869-8220, www.casaviento.net, US$110-190 s/d with a/c) has comfortable rooms and cheerful *mi casa es su casa* service from the live-in owners. Choose between large standard rooms, one- and two-bedroom suites with kitchen, and a honeymoon suite with cupola and great ocean views; all rooms have air-conditioning and Wi-Fi, and look onto a welcoming pool. If you're interested in kiting, Casa Viento also is home base for De Lille Sports, a kiting school and tour operator run by legendary Mexican kiteboarder Raul de Lille.

Condumel (Zona Hotelera Norte Km. 1.5, tel. 987/872-0892, www.condumel.com, US$120-142 for up to 4 people) is an old-school but very agreeable oceanfront condo complex, located a 15-minute walk from downtown. Spacious one-bedroom apartments have king-size beds, Wi-Fi, fully equipped kitchens, and daily maid service. Oversized sliding-glass doors offer awesome views of the Caribbean and incoming airplanes. The coast here is ironshore, so there's just a small patch of sand; steps and a ladder make swimming and snorkeling easy.

Over US$150

Playa Azul Hotel (Zona Hotelera Norte Km. 4, tel. 987/869-5160, www.playa-azul.com, US$165 s/d) caters mostly to golfers—guests pay no greens fees at Cozumel Country Club—but has packages for divers and honeymooners as well. Medium-size rooms and more spacious suites all have fairly modern furnishings, large bathrooms, and excellent ocean views, and include full breakfast. The pool is clean and attractive, but the beach (already small) can get crowded with day-trippers.

Oozing cool, ◖ **Hotel B Cozumel** (Zona Hotelera Norte Km. 2.5, tel. 987/872-0300, www.hotelbcozumel.com, US$216 s/d) is a boutique hotel that combines midcentury aesthetic with traditional Mexican decor. Rooms have clean lines, lots of natural light, and feature gorgeous Mexican folk art. All have a balcony or patio and the amenities you'd expect—silent air-conditioning, cable TV, and Wi-Fi. Most have ocean views, too. Outdoors, there's a breezy gourmet restaurant, a great half-moon pool, plus lots of sandy areas with hammocks and beach chairs. The only thing missing is a beach. The waterfront has lots of ironshore, so the hotel has done its best to create plenty of entry points to the water.

SOUTHWESTERN COZUMEL
Under US$150
A laid-back dive resort, **Blue Angel Resort** (Carr. Sur Km. 2.2, tel. 987/872-0819, www.blueangelresort.com, US$110 s/d) provides all the amenities a diver could want: a reputable dive shop, reliable boats, an on-site dock, and drying racks and lockers for gear. The rooms themselves are modern but basic; all have great ocean views. There's also an open-air restaurant, a well-tended pool, and plenty of shady places to sit back and relax. The only thing really missing is a beach. If you can live with that, this a perfect place to stay awhile.

Scuba Club Cozumel (Carr. Sur Km. 1.5, tel. 987/872-0853, toll-free U.S. tel. 800/847-5708, www.scubaclubcozumel.com, US$130 pp all-inclusive) is an old-school dive hotel with great packages, an on-site dock, and drying racks for your gear. Rooms are basic—clean and bare bones (good beds and a balcony yes, cable TV and Wi-Fi no). There's a small pool and a sandy area on the water, too. Meals are typically included in the rate and are served in a bustling dining room with plastic tables and chairs. Not exactly a tropical getaway but perfect if you'll be underwater most of the time anyway.

Over US$150
◖ **Presidente InterContinental Cozumel Resort Spa** (Carr. Sur Km. 6.5, tel. 987/ 872-9500, toll-free U.S. tel. 800/327-0200, www.intercontinentalcozumel. com, US$218-415 s/d with a/c, US$1,080-2,250 suite) may well be the best resort in Cozumel, with sleek sophisticated rooms that have high-end amenities as well as niceties like twice-daily maid service and turndown service. While the views are of either garden or ocean, all roads lead to a mellow and welcoming pool scene and a great beach—despite the ironshore—thick white sand and calm, turquoise waters with plenty of access points for snorkelers and shore divers. A well-regarded dive shop, two lighted tennis courts, three restaurants, and a full-service spa round out this elegant hotel.

Iberostar Cozumel (Carr. Sur Km. 17.8, tel. 987/872-9900, toll-free U.S. tel. 888/923-2722, www.iberostar.com, US$200-450 s/d all-inclusive) is a basic all-inclusive with well-kempt, lush grounds. It's a good option if you're traveling on a budget but want a resort experience. The rooms, for instance, are located in two-story bungalows but have dated decor. The beach is wide but has lots of rocky areas—great for snorkeling, not so great for wading (bring water shoes). The food is fine for a long weekend—there's an extensive buffet and snack bar plus two reservations-only restaurants (dinner only). Service is consistently good too, and the activity offerings include water aerobics and yoga. There's also an on-site dive and snorkel shop. All in all, this is a good value if you find an online deal. If it's rack rates only, head elsewhere.

The adults-only **Secrets Aura Cozumel** (Carr. Sur Km. 12.9, toll-free Mex. tel. 800/546-7445, toll-free U.S. tel. 800/413-3886, www.secretsresorts.com, US$243-305 pp all-inclusive) is a small all-inclusive resort sitting on a lush oceanfront property. It has features like à la carte dining (no buffets here) and top-shelf drinks, and modern, spacious rooms. If you can swing it budget-wise, opt for a "swim-up" room, which provides direct access to one of the resort's winding pools through the room's patio door (as in open the door and step right in).

ISLA COZUMEL

SOUTHEASTERN COZUMEL

The only hotel on the east side of the island, **Ventanas al Mar** (south end of Playa Tortugas, cell. tel. 987/105-2684, www.ventanasalmar.com.mx, US$94-104 s/d, US$164-184 s/d suite) has 12 large rooms and two suites, all with high ceilings and private patios or decks, many with marvelous ocean views. The interiors lack the detailing and upkeep you'd expect at this price but suit the hotel's isolated feel. All have kitchenettes with microwaves; some have minifridges. There's no air-conditioning, as the hotel runs almost entirely on wind and solar power. Fortunately, the constant sea breeze keeps rooms cool. There's a popular restaurant and beach club next door, but you'll probably want a car, as the east side has no ATM, grocery stores, or other services. Or you can embrace the isolation: Many guests spend a week or more without going to town at all. Rates include full breakfast.

Food

Cozumel's food scene is steadily improving, with an ever-increasing variety and quality of restaurants. Like most islands, it has terrific seafood, always served fresh, from gourmet restaurants with executive chefs to simple eateries operated by local fisherman's cooperatives. (You may be surprised to learn, though, that much of the catch actually comes from around Isla Mujeres because the waters around Cozumel are protected). The island's popularity with Americans, especially hungry divers, means you'll never want for steak, pizza, or big breakfasts, but there's a growing number of fine international options, including Italian, Argentinean, and, of course, Mexican.

MEXICAN AND YUCATECAN

C Kinta (Av. 5 btwn Calle 2 and 4 Norte, tel. 987/869-0544, www.kintacozumel.com, 5:30pm-11pm Tues.-Sun., US$10-17) is a chic restaurant serving gourmet Mexican dishes and out-of-sight cocktails. Seating is indoors in a modern, welcoming space or outdoors in a leafy tropical garden. The menu includes such specialties as the chile relleno, a poblano chile stuffed with ratatouille and Chihuahua cheese, and *kamarón adobado,* grilled shrimp marinated in achiote with caramelized pineapple salsa. Be sure to try the tamarindo martini—unforgettable! Reservations are recommended.

C Parrilla Mission (Av. 30 btwn Calles 2 and 4, tel. 987/872-3581, www.parrillamission.

com, 7am-11pm daily, US$3-14) specializes in tacos, served on delicious handmade corn tortillas and heaped with fresh grilled steak, chicken, or everyone's favorite, *al pastor* (spicy grilled pork). A self-serve "sides bar" includes not just salsa, cilantro, and lime, but Spanish rice, beans, and grilled onions as well. The rest of the menu is pretty outstanding too, including mole, chiles rellenos, and fajitas, all very reasonably priced. This place is a favorite among locals and a highlight for tourists willing to venture beyond the main downtown area.

The breezy *palapa*-roofed **La Candela** (Av. 5 at Calle 6 Norte, tel. 987/878-4471, 8am-11:30pm Mon.-Sat., US$3-14) offers an extensive lineup of Mexican and traditional Yucatecan dishes in a cafeteria-style setting. Check out what's steaming behind the glass window cases, find a seat, then place your order with your waiter. Lunch specials typically include soup or pasta, a main dish, and a drink (US$5-6).

For some local flavor, **Sabores** (Av. 5 btwn Calles 3 and 5, no phone, noon-4pm Mon.-Sat., US$5-13) is a great family-run restaurant operated out of a bright yellow house. Lunch specials, known across Mexico as *comida corrida,* run US$4-8 and come with soup, fruit drink, and your choice among a selection of traditional main dishes. Dine in the converted living room or under the shade trees in the backyard.

Pancho's Backyard (Av. Rafael Melgar 27 btwn Avs. 8 and 10 Norte, tel. 987/872-2141, www.panchosbackyard.com, 10am-11pm Mon.-Sat., 6pm-11pm Sun., US$11-24) is Mexico epitomized: gurgling fountains, colonial-style decor, live marimba during the lunch hour, and Mexican haute cuisine, including *camarones a la naranja* (orange shrimp flambéed in tequila) and chiles rellenos (peppers stuffed with meat, bananas, and walnuts). Though popular with cruise ship travelers, this perennial favorite is big enough that it never feels crowded.

Otates Tacos (Av. 15 btwn Calles Rosado Salas and 3, no phone, noon-11pm daily, US$2-6) is a bustling taco joint serving authentic Mexican grub at nearly street-cart prices. Tacos are just the beginning, served piping hot on tiny corn tortillas; the quesadillas, *tortas* (Mexican-style sandwiches), and *pozole* (pork and hominy soup) are all terrific, and the guacamole is rave-worthy. Service is fast and friendly, with menus in Spanish and English.

Taquería El Pique (Av. Pedro Joaquín Coldwell btwn Av. Benito Juárez and Calle 2, 7pm-midnight daily, US$2-5) is a classic taco joint serving pint-size tacos, chunky guacamole, gooey *queso fundido* (melted cheese for dipping), and more. It's a locals' favorite, though a small stream of expats and tourists make their way here too.

La Cozumeleña (Av. 10 Sur at Calle 3, 7am-3pm daily) is popular with local families and professionals, serving classic dishes in a quiet air-conditioned dining area. For breakfast, try *chilaquiles* (fried tortilla strips, scrambled eggs, and chicken doused in green or red salsa) or eggs with chaya. Lunch specials include a main dish, like fish tacos or baked chicken, and a drink. There's a bakery next door too, for fresh breads and pastries.

Corazón Contento (Av. 10 Sur at Calle 3, 7am-3pm daily) has a peaceful and welcoming ambience befitting its name (Contented Heart), while the stenciled walls and colorful tile floors are reminiscent of Mérida. Service is friendly, with great bottomless coffee and simple breakfast and lunch specials. Watch out: The bread basket is charged per item, and the chocolate-filled croissants are almost impossible to resist!

SEAFOOD

◖ **El Viejo y La Mar** (Av. 5 Sur btwn Calles 9 and 9 Bis, no phone, noon-8pm daily, US$5-15) is a low-key eatery run by a local fisherman's cooperative, so the fish is especially fresh and well-priced. Whole fried fish is US$9 per kilo (2.2 pounds); a half kilo makes for a hefty meal. There are a dozen different ceviche and cocktail options, and just as many fillets. Eat in the large open-air dining area, or order to go if it's near closing time.

Camilo's (Av. 5 btwn Calles 2 and 4, tel. 987/872-6161, 11am-9pm daily, US$8-16) is a small place offering an abundance of fresh seafood: ceviche, shrimp cocktail, lobster tail, fried fish, grilled fish—you name it, they've probably got it. It's popular with locals, and travelers are beginning to trickle in now, too.

A family-run restaurant, **La Conchita del Caribe** (Av. 65 btwn Calles 13 and 15, tel. 987/872-5888, www.laconchitadelcaribe.com, 11:30am-7:30pm daily, US$9-16) is another locals' favorite, in a spacious location. When ordering whole fish—the house specialty, served grilled or fried—you'll be asked to pick the fish you want out of a cooler by the counter and will be charged according to size. And whether you order fish, shrimp, or other seafood, it was almost certainly swimming earlier in the day. This is a great off-the-tourist-path option; takeout is also available.

OTHER SPECIALTIES

La Cocay (Calle 8 btwn Avs. 10 and 15, tel. 987/872-5533, www.lacocay.com, 5:30pm-11pm Mon.-Sat., US$15-22) offers Mediterranean cuisine with flair. The menu changes seasonally, but expect to see dishes like fish of the day with cilantro herb mojo and blue-cheese-filled phyllo dough rolls with black cherry sauce. Seating is in a candlelit dining room or on the breezy garden patio—perfect for a special night out.

Al Pie del Carbon (Calle 6 at Av. 5, cell. tel. 987/101-2599, 3pm-11pm Tues.-Sun.,

Fish tacos are a Riviera Maya staple: simple, classic, delicious.

© LIZA PRADO

US$8-16) is a popular Argentinean steak house serving up excellent cuts of beef, plus tasty salads and sides, and a decent wine list. Steaks are grilled over an open flame and can be enjoyed in the restaurant's air-conditioned dining room or open-air patio. The empanadas, another Argentinean classic, make great appetizers.

Founded in 1978 and passed from father to daughter, **Guido's** (Av. Rafael Melgar btwn Calles 6 and 8, tel. 987/872-0946, www.guidoscozumel.com, 11am-11pm Mon.-Sat., 2:30pm-9:30pm Sun., US$13-17) is a bit pricey but worth every peso, serving unique Italian-ish dishes like brick-oven baked lasagna, homemade pastas, memorable seafood dishes (like prosciutto-wrapped sea scallops), and excellent sangria and desserts. The leafy courtyard setting makes a meal here all the more worthwhile.

Cruise ship crew members beeline to **Chi** (above Pizza Hut, Calle 3 at Av. Rafael Melgar, tel. 987/869-8156, www.chicozumel.com, 9:30am-midnight Mon.-Wed., 9:30am-2am

Thurs.-Sat., noon-midnight Sun., US$8-15) for its gorgeous ocean views and extensive pan-Asian menu, including Chinese, Thai, Japanese, and Filipino dishes. The sushi is mediocre (ham nigiri?) but the rest is quite tasty, and a nice change of culinary pace.

Not content to rest on its laurels, **New Especias** (Calle 3 btwn Avs. 5 and 10, tel. 987/869-7947, 6pm-11pm daily except Wed., US$6-18) has a new look, new menu, and new location—sort of. The restaurant occupies just the 2nd floor of the building now, including a narrow patio with street views and a breezy dining area in the rear. That makes room for a lively new bar downstairs, with the idea that guests will migrate from one to the other, and even to the bistro tables set up on the sidewalk in front. The menu, once an eclectic mix of Argentinian, Thai, and Jamaican, is now strictly Italian—and quite good at that.

Del Sur (corner of Av 5 Sur and Calle 3, tel. 987/871-5744, 5pm-11pm Mon-Sat, US$2-21) serves crispy Argentinian empanadas and hearty steak (plus seafood, chicken, and salads) in a homey and attractive dining room. Order a couple of empanadas as a starter, or several for a full meal; either way, they go great with a cold beer. If you're ordering from the grill, ask for a recommendation from the restaurant's excellent wine list. There's live tango on Fridays.

SWEETS
At **Zermatt** (Av. 5 Norte at Calle 4, tel. 987/872-1384, 7am-8:30pm Mon.-Sat., 7am-noon Sun., US$1-2.50) you may have to jostle with locals for a crack at the island's best fresh breads, pastries, and other traditional Mexican baked goods.

Nacho Crazy Boy (Av. 20 Sur btwn Av. Benito Juárez and Calle 1, 8am-11pm Mon.-Sat., 10am-2pm Sun., US$2) serves outstanding juices and smoothies right from the patio of the owner's modest house. Fruits fresh from the market are squeezed and blended on the spot by Nacho Crazy Boy himself, an earnest and interesting guy who makes time for conversation with customers.

La Flor de Michoacán (Calle 1 near Av. 10, 9am-11pm daily, US$1-2) serves cool treats, including *aguas* (fruit drinks), *nieves* (ice cream), and *paletas* (popsicles).

GROCERIES
Whatever groceries you need, you'll find them and more at **MEGA** (Av. Rafael Melgar at Calle 11, tel. 987/872-3658, 7:30am-11pm daily), the island's largest supermarket.

Super San Francisco de Asis (Av. Pedro Joaquín Coldwell btwn Av. Benito Juárez and Calle 2, 7:30am-11pm daily) is another large supermarket.

For a traditional market experience, Cozumel's **Mercado Municipal** (Av. 25 btwn Calles 1 and Rosado Salas, 7am-3pm daily) has stalls brimming with colorful produce, freshly butchered chickens, eggs, cheese, spices, and more, all at reasonable prices.

Information and Services

TOURIST INFORMATION
The city tourist office has three **information booths** (8am-7pm Mon.-Sat., 9am-2pm Sun.)—in the central plaza, at the international pier, and at Puerta Maya pier. English is spoken at all locations.

The *Free Blue Guide to Cozumel* has good maps and listings for a range of services, from restaurants to dive shops. Look for the booklet as you get off the ferry.

There are numerous websites with news, tips, maps, special deals, discussion groups, and other information about Cozumel, including www.thisiscozumel.com, www.cozumelinsider.com, www.cozumelmycozumel.com, www.cozumeltoday.com, http://everythingcozumel.com, and even www.cruiseportinsider.com.

EMERGENCY SERVICES
Centro Médico de Cozumel (CMC, Calle 1A Sur at Av. 50, tel. 987/872-9400, www.centromedicodecozumel.com.mx, 24 hours) accepts many foreign insurance plans, though the prices tend to be high.

A good alternative is the **Clínica-Hospital San Miguel** (Calle 6 Norte btwn Avs. 5 and 10, tel. 987/872-0103, 24 hours), offering general medical services.

Cozumel's **Hyperbaric Medical Center** (Calle 5 btwn Avs. Rafael Melgar and 5 Sur, tel. 987/872-1430, office hours 10am-5pm daily, nurse and doctor on-call 24 hours) specializes in diver-related medical treatment, though nondiving ailments also are treated.

For meds, try **Farmacia Similares** (Calle 1 Sur at Av. 15 Norte, tel. 987/869-2440, 9am-10pm Mon.-Sat., 9am-2pm Sun.). Mexico now requires a prescription for many antibiotics; this pharmacy has an on-site *consultorio* (doctor's office), open roughly the same hours.

The **tourist police** (Calle 11 Sur near Av. Rafael Melgar, 8am-11pm daily) are stationed in a kiosk near Punta Langosta, though officers often can be found patrolling the central plaza.

The **police station** (Palacio Municipal, Calle 13 btwn Avs. 5 and Rafael Melgar, tel. 987/872-0092, 24 hours) can be reached toll-free at 066.

MONEY

Accessing your money is not difficult in Cozumel, especially near the central plaza. **HSBC** (Av. 5 Sur at Calle 1, 9am-6pm Mon.-Fri., 9am-3pm Sat.), **Bancomer** (Av. 5 Sur btwn Av. Juárez and Calle 1, 8:30am-4pm Mon.-Fri.), and **Banorte** (Av. 5 Norte btwn Av. Juárez and Calle 2, 9am-5pm Mon.-Fri., 9am-2pm Sat.) all have ATMs and exchange foreign cash.

MEDIA AND COMMUNICATIONS

Cozumel's **post office** (Av. Rafael Melgar at Calle 7, 9am-5pm Mon.-Fri., 9am-1pm Sat.) is next to Punta Langosta shopping center.

There are myriad Internet cafés where you can get online, make international phone calls, burn photos to CDs, and more. **Phonet** (Calle

Rosado Salas at Av. 10, 8am-11pm daily) is a quiet, reliable place charging US$0.85 per hour for Internet use and US$0.35 per minute for calls to the United States and Canada.

IMMIGRATION AND CONSULATES

The **immigration office** (Av. 15 Sur at Calle 5, tel. 987/872-0071) is open 9am-1pm Monday-Friday. There are immigration agents at the airport, too (7pm-9pm daily).

The **U.S. Consular Agency** (Plaza Villamar, central plaza, tel. 987/872-4574, usgov@cozumel.net) is open noon-2pm Monday-Friday. Look for it on the 2nd floor toward the back.

LAUNDRY

Lavandería Margarita (Av. 20 btwn Calle 3 and Av. Rosado Salas, no phone, 7am-9pm Mon.-Sat., 8am-4pm Sun.) charges US$7.75-10 per load to wash and dry, up to 8 kilos (17.5 pounds).

Lavandería Wash Express (Av. 10 btwn Calles 7 and 9, no phone, 7:30am-9pm Mon.-Sat., 8am-3pm Sun.) charges US$1.25 per kilo; drop off early for same-day service.

Getting There and Around

GETTING THERE
Air
Cozumel International Airport (CZM, tel. 987/872-2081, www.asur.com.mx) is approximately three kilometers (1.9 miles) from downtown. The airport has an ATM in the departures area, AmEx currency exchange at arrivals, and a few magazine stands and duty-free shops. The **airport taxi cooperative** (tel. 987/872-1323) provides private and shared transport to the center and to resorts along the western coast. Prices vary by destination. Private taxis are US$11-21 per person, while shared transport costs US$5-8 per person and utilizes 10-person shuttles or Suburbans;

departures are every 5-20 minutes. A taxi stand near the exit sells tickets and has prices prominently displayed.

Bus
Ticket Bus (Calle 2 at Av 10 Sur, tel. 987/869-2553, 8am-9pm Mon.-Sat., 10am-8pm Sun.) sells tickets for ADO buses leaving from Playa del Carmen at no extra charge, a handy service for when you're ready to move on.

Ferry
Passenger ferries to Playa del Carmen (US$13 each way, 30 minutes) leave from the passenger ferry pier across from the central plaza.

Flying to Cozumel

The following airlines service **Cozumel International Airport** (CZM, tel. 987/872-2081, www.asur.com.mx):

- **Air Canada** (toll-free Mex. tel. 800/719-2827, toll-free U.S./Can. tel. 888/247-2262, www.aircanada.com)
- **American Airlines** (toll-free Mex. tel. 800/904-6000, toll-free U.S./Can. tel. 800/433-7300, www.aa.com)
- **Continental** (airport tel. 987/872-0847, toll-free Mex. tel. 800/900-5000, toll-free U.S./Can. tel. 800/864-8331, www.continental.com)
- **Delta** (toll-free Mex. tel. 800/123-4710, toll-free U.S. tel. 800/221-1212, www.delta.com)
- **Frontier Airlines** (toll-free U.S. tel. 800/432-1359, www.frontierairlines.com)
- **United Airlines** (toll-free Mex. tel. 800/900-5000, toll-free U.S./Can. tel. 800/864-8331, www.united.com)
- **US Airways** (toll-free Mex. tel. 800/843-3000, toll-free U.S. tel. 800/428-4322, www.usairways.com)

UltraMar (www.granpuerto.com.mx) and **Mexico Water Jets** (www.mexicowaterjets.com.mx) alternate departures and charge the same amount, though UltraMar's boats are newer. Their ticket booths are opposite each other partway down the pier, with the time of the next departure displayed prominently. The ticket seller may try to sell you a round-trip ticket, but there's no savings in doing so; better to buy a *sencilla* (one-way ticket) and wait to see which company's ferry is departing when you're ready to return. Between the two companies, there are ferries every 1-2 hours on the hour 6am-9pm daily.

Car ferries operated by **Transcaribe** (tel. 987/872-7688 or 987/872-7671 in Cozumel, www.transcaribe.net) depart the international pier in Cozumel for the Calica dock south of Playa del Carmen at 6am, 11am, 4pm, and 8:30pm Monday-Saturday and at 8am and 8pm on Sunday. Returning ferries leave Calica at 4am, 8am, 1:30pm, and 6pm Monday; 1:30 and 6pm Tuesday and Friday; 8am, 1:30pm, and 6pm Wednesday, Thursday, and Saturday; and 6am and 6pm on Sunday. The trip takes about an hour and 15 minutes and costs US$60 for a passenger car including driver, and US$5.50 per additional passenger. Reservations are available online, by phone, or at the pier, and are strongly recommended.

GETTING AROUND

In town, you can easily walk anywhere you like. However, the powerful taxi union has succeeded in quashing any and all efforts to start public bus service out of town and around the island. It is a shame, really, since it would be so easy and convenient to have a fleet of buses making loops around the island, or even just up and down the western shore. Until that changes (don't hold your breath), you'll need a car, moped, or bike to explore the rest of the island on your own.

Bicycle

A bike can be handy for getting to beach clubs and snorkel sites outside of town. Traffic on Avenida Rafael Melgar can be heavy south of town, but once clear of that, the roadway is relatively unhurried. **Rentadora Isis** (Av. 5 Norte btwn Calles 2 and 4, tel. 987/872-3367, www.rentadoraisis.com.mx, 8am-6:30pm daily) rents bikes—including helmet and lock—for US$10 per day.

Taxi

Taxis are everywhere—you can easily flag one down on Avenida Rafael Melgar, near the main passenger pier, and around the plaza. If you want to be picked up at a specific place and time, call the **taxi union office** (Calle 2 btwn

ISLA COZUMEL

© LIZA PRADO

Passenger ferries from Playa del Carmen arrive at Cozumel's sleek new ferry dock, located opposite the central plaza.

Avs. 5 and 10, tel. 987/872-0041, 24 hours daily). Cabs typically charge US$3.25 around town and US$5.75 from the center to the airport, for up to four people. For hotels and beach clubs on the western shore south of town, you'll pay US$5 to US$20, depending on the distance. Fares to the east side are a bit more, US$12.50-30, while San Gervasio and Punta Sur cost US$50-60. A trip around the island runs US$85. Most taxi stands have the current fares prominently displayed; always agree on a price before getting into a taxi.

Car and Moped Rental

Renting a car is a nice way to get out of downtown and see the rest of the island. It is virtually impossible to get lost, and you can visit all the main spots in a day or two.

If you do decide to rent some wheels, go to the agency yourself—do not allow one of the friendly guys at the pier to lead you there. They are *comisionistas,* freelancers who earn hefty commissions for bringing tourists to particular

shops, which then pass the cost on to you. Shop owners go along begrudgingly; if they decline the "service," the same freelancers will actively steer future tourists away from the shop, saying it's closed, burned down, fresh out of cars—you get the idea.

Excluding commissions, rental cars in Cozumel start at around US$40-50 for a compact car, including insurance and taxes. Mopeds rent for around US$25 per day. Be aware that scooters account for the majority of accidents here, as speed bumps, potholes, and windy conditions can upend even experienced drivers; having a second person on the back is even more dangerous. Also remember that unpaved roads are not covered by most rental car insurance plans.

Rentadora Isis (Av. 5 Norte btwn Calles 2 and 4, tel. 987/872-3367, www.rentadoraisis. com.mx, 8am-6:30pm daily) consistently has the island's best rates, and friendly service to boot; their Internet specials often are good, too. Another good local option is **Sol y Mar** (Calle

2 near Av. 5 Norte, tel. 987/869-0545, 8am-7pm daily).

International companies have newer fleets, and often have good rates if you book online. Try **Thrifty** (Av. Juárez at Av. 10 Norte, tel. 987/869-8090; at airport 987/869-2957; www.thrifty.com), **Avis** (Av. Juárez at Av. 5 Norte, tel. 987/872-1923; at airport 987/872-0099; www.avis.com), or **Hertz** (Av. Juárez at Av. 5 Norte, tel. 999/911-8040; at airport 987/869-8184; www.hertz.com).

Motorcycle Rental

To explore the island in style, head to **Eaglerider** (Palmar Plaza, Carr. Costera Sur Km. 3.8, U.S. toll-free tel. 888/879-7873, tel. 987/857-0106, www.eaglerider.com, US$159-199/day), which rents several types of Harley-Davidson motorcycles, from Sportsters to Road Kings and Electra Glides.

Highways and Road Conditions

The distance around the island—on paved roads, and including the northwestern arm that dead-ends after Cozumel Country Club—is approximately 93 kilometers (58 miles). Driving without stopping, it takes a little under two hours to circumnavigate the island. If doing this, consider going counterclockwise so there's nothing between your vehicle and the ocean, especially on the east side. Biking around the island is possible but challenging, given the strong crosswinds.

Cozumel has three **PEMEX gas stations** (7am-midnight daily). Two are in town on Avenida Benito Juárez (at Avs. Pedro Joaquin Coldwell and 75), and the third is four kilometers (2.5 miles) south of town on the Carretera Costera Sur, across from Puerta Maya, the main cruise ship pier.

Note: Most streets are one-way in town; if you're driving, be aware that *avenidas* (avenues) run north-south and have the right-of-way over *calles* (streets), which run east-west. Once you leave town, there is a single road that circles the entire island.

ISLA COZUMEL

THE RIVIERA MAYA

Cancún may be the name everyone recognizes, but for many people—especially repeat visitors—the best of Mexico's Caribbean coast is the Riviera Maya. Stretching more than 130 kilometers (81 miles) south from Cancún to Tulum, the Riviera Maya is home to fast-growing cities like Playa del Carmen, low-key towns like Puerto Morelos, and tiny beachfront settlements like Tankah

Highlights

◖ **Puerto Morelos's Coral Reef:** Skip the tourist-trap snorkeling trips in Cancún and Playa del Carmen and go snorkeling where the reef is still healthy, the water uncrowded, and the price unbeatable. Book a tour with a local dive shop or the long-operating fisherman's cooperative (page 140).

◖ **Playa del Carmen's Quinta Avenida:** Ever growing yet still walkable, Playa's 5th Avenue has block after block of tempting restaurants, hipster boutiques, and lively bars. The ferry and bus terminals are at the busy southern end, while the northern end is cooler and quieter, with a distinctive European flair (page 149).

◖ **Playa del Carmen's Beaches and Beach Clubs:** Playa's beaches are among the Riviera Maya's most beautiful, and its beach clubs make them some of the most enjoyable, too. Of Playa's many great beaches, **Playa Tukán** takes the cake: ankle deep white sand, mild surf, two beach clubs (one mellow, one hoppin'), yet plenty of open sand for those who just want to lay out a towel and relax (page 149).

◖ **Xcaret:** The Riviera Maya's elaborate eco-parks are a hit with parents looking for a safe, active, friendly place to take the kids. Xcaret is the most ambitious of them all, with tubing and snorkeling, an aquarium and animal enclosures, an orchid greenhouse, and an end-of-the-day extravaganza (page 153).

◖ **Laguna Yal-Ku:** A long elbow of water fed by freshwater cenotes and flowing into the sea, this Akumal-area lagoon is a snorkeler favorite for its colorful fish and jumble of underwa-

ter rocks. Curious bronze statues dot the rocky shore, and parking and changing areas make visiting here a cinch (page 174).

◖ **Playa Xcacel:** Just off the highway down an easy-to-miss sand road, this glorious stretch of white-sand beach has nary a beach bed or banana boat in sight. The secret? It's a sea-turtle nesting area protected from development–at least for now (page 182).

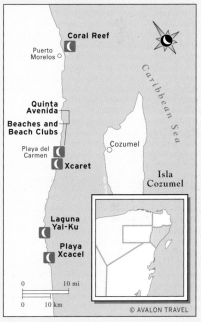

THE RIVIERA MAYA

Tres. It boasts megaresorts and tiny bed-and-breakfasts, and is flanked by the world's longest underground river on one side and the world's second-longest coral reef on the other. And, of course, the Riviera Maya has the same spectacular beaches Cancún is famous for.

There's plenty to see and do, much of it do-it-yourself: go snorkeling in freshwater cenotes and lagoons, help release newly hatched sea turtles into the sea, explore little-visited Maya ruins, or spend the day at a family-friendly eco-park. For party hounds, Cancún still has a lock on over-the-top nightspots, though Playa del Carmen now has several of its own, and there

THE RIVIERA MAYA

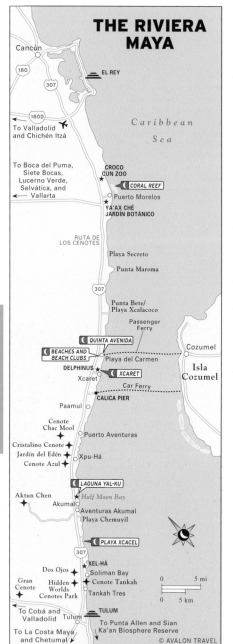

are plenty of lounge bars, beach clubs, and resort nightclubs where visitors can kick back or cut loose.

PLANNING YOUR TIME

You'll probably want to pick a home base (or two) for your time here and make day trips from there. Playa del Carmen is the area's only real city, with all the expected urban amenities, including nightlife. (It's also the gateway to Isla Cozumel.) Puerto Morelos and Akumal are smaller but still have a decent selection of hotels and restaurants. If isolation is more important than convenience, the Riviera Maya has some secret getaways, like Xpu-Há and Tankah Tres. If you've got a week or more, consider spending half your time in the northern section—around Playa del Carmen, for example—and then move farther south, to enjoy Akumal, Tankah Tres, and even Tulum.

A rental car isn't absolutely necessary but will certainly make exploring the Riviera Maya a lot easier. Cheap public shuttles zip up and down the coast, but they only stop along the highway, which in most places is about a kilometer (0.6 mile) from the ocean. That leaves you to make the hot dusty walk up and down the access roads, especially in more rural areas where taxis are uncommon.

Puerto Morelos

Puerto Morelos has largely escaped the mega-development that has swept up and down the Riviera Maya, despite being squeezed between the booming cities of Cancún and Playa del Carmen. It remains, for the most part, a quiet seaside town. Yes, the town fills up with tourists in the high season—and more and more condos and resorts are cropping up—but it is still a place where a substantial part of the local population lives by fishing, where life revolves around the central plaza, and where kids and dogs romp in the streets.

The beach in Puerto Morelos has improved significantly in the last few years, and more and more travelers are spending lazy afternoons in the sun and sand. But Puerto Morelos is best known for the reef system just offshore. Local residents fought tirelessly (and successfully) to have a large section in front of town designated a national reserve, and as a result the snorkeling and diving are superb. A town cooperative and several local dive shops offer tours of various sorts, most highly recommended and quite affordable. Puerto Morelos also is gaining popularity as a destination for yoga and meditation groups—no surprise given its serene atmosphere—and a growing number of hotels and resorts cater to that market.

Be aware that the low season here is *very* low, and many businesses close in May, September, and/or October.

SIGHTS AND BEACHES
Playa Principal
Puerto Morelos improved its beachfront area considerably, with leafy arbors and

THE RIVIERA MAYA

© LIZA PRADO

Puerto Morelos's main pier is the jumping-off place for affordable and rewarding snorkeling trips to the nearby reef.

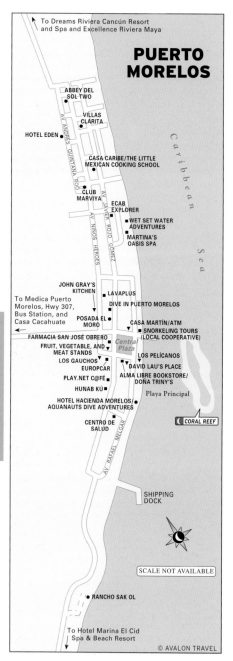

palm-shaded benches. The beach itself, however, lacks the creamy white sand found elsewhere in the Riviera Maya, and the same regulations that protect the town's famous coral reef also prevent the removal of sea grass in the shallow areas. Fishing boats also moor on the beach, though there's still plenty of room to lay out a towel. A good beach option is **Club de Playa Los Pelícanos** (central plaza, 9am-3pm Mon.-Sat.), which has lounge chairs, umbrellas, and kayaks. It's located off one corner of the main plaza, in front of the restaurant of the same name.

Coral Reef

Puerto Morelos's top attraction is snorkeling on the reef. Directly in front of the village, around 500 meters (0.3 mile) offshore, the reef here takes on gargantuan dimensions—up to 30 meters (99 feet) wide. Winding passages and large caverns alive with fish and sea flora make for great exploring. And since it's a marine reserve, and fishing and motor traffic are limited, the reef is more pristine here than almost any place along the Riviera. A **local cooperative** (central plaza, Av. Rafaél Melgar s/n, no phone, 9am-3pm Mon.-Sat., US$25 pp for 2 hours) offers guided tours of the reef, with boats leaving every 30 minutes—or sooner, if there are four snorkelers—from the municipal pier.

The Central Plaza

Puerto Morelos's peaceful central plaza has always been a highlight of the town, but a face-lift has made it even more appealing. New paint, better landscaping, and an improved play structure for kids make it a great place to while away the early evening hours, especially for families. Locals and visitors alike mingle on shaded benches and in the bleachers facing the basketball court. Many of Puerto Morelos's best restaurants face the plaza or are just a block away, so you're sure to pass by more than once. On Sunday, a small *tianguis* (flea market) is held here, and you can have fun browsing through someone else's old treasures.

Ruta de los Cenotes

Marked by an enormous mustard-yellow arch on Highway 307, the "Cenote Route" is one of the newest developments along the Riviera Maya, and a sign, for better or worse, that the megaresorts are finally starting to appreciate cenotes. The route is simply a paved road, which begins just south of Puerto Morelos and extends nearly 20 kilometers (12.4 miles) into the scrub forest, passing several cenotes along the way. The most popular stops, at least for tour groups, are cenotes like **Boca del Puma** and **Selvática,** which also have ATV tours, ziplines, paintball—you get the picture. But the route also has some true gems: gorgeous and remote cenotes, undeveloped and all but overlooked by the package tours, and well worth the drive to reach them.

Independent travelers will particularly enjoy **Siete Bocas** (Carr. Pto. Morelos-Vallarta Km. 16, no phone, 8am-4pm daily, US$10 including life vest), so named for its seven openings (or "mouths"). Three openings have steep stairways leading straight into the cool, clear water; the other four allow sunlight into the underground chamber, lighting up the water dramatically, especially around midday. Inside, you can swim or float through the cave, with its spectacular stalagmites and stalactites, often with no one else around (BYO snorkel gear). Most visitors stay only a short time, but camping is permitted on-site (US$16 pp), just a few meters from the cenote.

Just down the road from Siete Bocas is **Lucerno Verde** (Carr. Pto. Morelos-Vallarta Km. 17, cell. tel. 998/224-3731, 8am-5pm daily, US$5 including life vest), an open-air cenote surrounded by huge tropical trees. Completely different from its neighbor but no less dramatic, Lucerno Verde is like an enormous swimming hole with clear turquoise water and seemingly no bottom. There's a zipline as well as a thick safety line stretching across the cenote. Look for the freshwater turtles that make their home here. Camping is permitted here, too (US$10 pp).

Croco Cun Zoo

A charming little tropical petting zoo, **Croco Cun Zoo** (Hwy. 307, tel. 998/850-3719, www.crococunzoo.com, 9am-5pm daily, US$26 adult, US$16 child 6-12, free 5 and under) is located five kilometers (3.1 miles) north of the Puerto Morelos turnoff. Seventy-five-minute guided tours, offered in English or Spanish, bring visitors up close and personal to all sorts of local creatures. You can feed spider monkeys, walk through a crocodile enclosure, and hold boas, iguanas, and baby crocs. Well managed and reasonably affordable, Croco Cun is a hit for youngsters and adults alike.

Ya'ax Ché Jardín Botánico

Just south of the Puerto Morelos turnoff, a sprawling peaceful botanical garden, **Ya'ax Ché Jardín Botánico** (Hwy. 307 Km. 320, tel. 998/206-9233, www.ecosur.mx, 8am-4pm daily Nov.-Apr., 9am-5pm daily May-Oct., US$8.50 adult, US$4.25 child), has three kilometers (1.9 miles) of trails winding through diverse habitat, from tropical forest to mangrove swamp. In addition to hundreds of marked plants, there are remains of a Maya ruin and a re-creation of a modern Maya home. Monkeys can be sometimes spotted in the afternoon. Wear long sleeves and pants, and plenty of bug repellent.

SHOPPING

A so-called **Mayan Jungle Market** (Calle 2, Zona Urbana, tel. 998/208-9148, 9:30am-2pm Sun., Dec.-Easter only) is held at Casa Cacahuate bed-and-breakfast in the residential part of Puerto Morelos, on the other side of the highway. This cheerful family-friendly event is facilitated by the nonprofit founded by the bed-and-breakfast's owners. The market includes a variety of handicrafts produced by local women, as well as tasty food and drink. A traditional Maya dance is held at 11:30am.

The artisan's market of **Hunab Kú** (Av. Javier Rojo Gómez s/n, 9am-8pm daily) may be your best bet for finding handicrafts in Puerto Morelos. Here you'll find a bunch of stands with colorful blankets, ceramics, hammocks,

Cenotes: Then and Now

One of the Yucatán Peninsula's most intriguing features is its cenotes, freshwater sinkholes, sometimes hundreds of meters deep and filled with crystalline freshwater that is fed by underground rivers. Cenotes owe their formation to the massive meteorite that hit the Yucatán Peninsula 65 million years ago. The impact shattered the peninsula's thick limestone cap like a stone hitting a car windshield, and in the millions of years that followed, rainwater seeped into the cracks, carving huge underground caverns and hundreds of kilometers of channels out of the highly soluble limestone. Cenotes are former caverns whose roofs collapsed—caveins are extremely rare today, however—and together the channels form the world's longest underground river system.

Cenotes were sacred to Maya, who relied on them for water and viewed them as apertures to the underworld. (The name is derived from the Yucatec Maya word *dz'onot*.) Sacrificial victims were sometimes thrown into their eerie depths, along with finely worked stone and clay items, and archaeologists have learned a great deal about early Maya rituals by dredging cenotes near archaeological sites, most notably Chi-

chén Itzá. Indeed, the name Chichén Itzá means Well of the Itzá, undoubtedly a reference to the ancient city's dramatic cenote.

Today the peninsula's cenotes attract worshippers of a different sort: snorkelers and scuba divers. The unbelievably clear water—100-meter (328-foot) visibility in places—is complemented by what other inland and underground diving environments (like lakes and flooded mines) lack: stunning stalactites and stalagmites. During early ice ages, water drained from the cenotes, giving time for the slow-growing features to form. When the climate warmed, the cenotes filled with water once again, their depths now forested with dramatic stone spires, pillars, and columns.

Divers with open-water certification can dive in the cenotes. Though "full-cave" diving requires advanced training, most cenote tours are actually "cavern" dives, meaning you are always within 40 meters (130 feet) of an air pocket. It's a good idea to take some openwater dives before your first cenote tour—buoyancy control is especially important in cenotes, and you'll be contending with different weights and finning technique.

masks, jipi hats, shell art—pretty much anything you'll see sold up and down the coast.

One of the best bookstores on the peninsula, **Alma Libre Bookstore** (central plaza, tel. 998/251-1206, www.almalibrebooks.com, 10:30am-1:30pm and 3pm-8pm daily, closed June to mid-Nov.) has a whopping 20,000 titles, new and used, ranging from "beach trash to Plato," in the words of the friendly Canadian owners. There's Maya culture, Mexican cooking, ecology, mysteries, guidebooks, maps, and more, and not just in English but Spanish, French, German, Dutch, Italian, and others. The store's website is an outstanding resource for everything Puerto Morelos.

SPORTS AND RECREATION
Snorkeling
Puerto Morelos is justly famous for its

snorkeling, with a protected stretch of coral reef running very near shore. A **local cooperative** (central plaza, Av. Rafaél Melgar s/n, no phone, 9am-3pm Mon.-Sat.) offers excellent and affordable guided tours, visiting two spots on the reef for 45 minutes apiece, and using boats with sunshades. Prices are fixed: US$25 per person, including equipment, park fees, and a bottle of water. Boats leave every 30 minutes from the municipal pier; if there are fewer than three people, you'll have to wait up to 30 minutes (but no more) for additional passengers to come. Sign up at the cooperative's kiosk at the northeast corner of the plaza; late morning is the best time to go, as the sun is high but the afternoon winds haven't started. The **dive shops** in town also offer snorkeling tours to the town reef and beyond, for similar prices.

Caution: *Do not swim to the reef* from

anywhere along the beach. Although it's close enough for strong swimmers to reach, boats use the channel between the reef and the shore, and tourists have been struck and killed in the past.

Scuba Diving

Puerto Morelos has over two dozen dive sites within a 15-minute boat ride, virtually all in protected marine reserve waters. Add to that the nearby cenotes, plus night and wreck diving, and divers have plenty to keep them happy and interested. The dive shops in town—there were three at last count—tend to have small groups and offer a full range of fun dives and certification courses. Prices are fairly uniform—US$60-80 for one tank, US$75-100 for two tanks, and US$400 for open-water certification. Be sure to ask about any extra fees, like equipment, taxes, and marine park fee. Shop hours are irregular, and reservations are strongly recommended.

Dive In Puerto Morelos (Av. Javier Rojo Gómez 14, tel. 998/206-9084, www.diveinpuertomorelos.com) is run by a friendly American dive instructor who emphasizes safety and small groups.

Wet Set Water Adventures (Hotel Ojo de Agua, Av. Javier Rojo Gómez s/n, tel. 998/871-0198, www.wetset.com, 8am-2pm daily) is one of the longest-running dive shops around, offering top-to-bottom service and extensive area expertise.

Aquanauts Dive Adventures (Hacienda Morelos, Av. Rafael Melgar 5, tel. 998/206-9365 or 984/138-8463, www.aquanautsdiveadventures.com) is another long-operating dive shop.

Sportfishing

The dive shops in Puerto Morelos also offer fishing trips, whether trolling for barracuda or marlin, or dropping a line for "dinner fish" like grouper or snapper. **Wet Set Water Adventures** (Hotel Ojo de Agua, Av. Javier Rojo Gómez s/n, tel. 998/871-0198, www.wetset.com) has been taking visitors fishing for many years; a **local cooperative** (central plaza, Av. Rafaél Melgar s/n, no phone, 9am-3pm

Mon.-Sat.) does the same. Both charge around US$50-60 per hour.

Tours

ECAB Explorer (cell. tel. 998/123-5062, www.ecabexplorer.com) is a small but reliable tour operator run by a longtime Puerto Morelos resident (and former purveyor of fine shrimp tacos). Tours include not only the main destinations—Cobá, Ek' Balam, Sian Ka'an, etc.—but also interesting add-ons, from bird-watching to visits with a local family. Groups are small and rates reasonable considering the tours' length and depth: around US$70-100 adult, with discounts for children and groups. Check the website for scheduled outings or to arrange a private tour.

Spas

The **Ixchel Jungle Spa** (Casa Cacahuate, Calle 2, Zona Urbana, tel. 998/208-9148, www.mayaecho.com, 10am-3:30pm Tues.-Sat., Sun. by appointment only) is one of several community projects undertaken by Maya Echo, a nonprofit founded by the owners of Casa Cacahuate B&B. Local women provide professional massage and traditional Maya treatments for far less than at ordinary spas. Treat yourself to one of various available treatments, from a four-handed full-body massage (US$80, 1 hour) to a chocolate body wrap and massage (US$60, 1 hour). Group massage or *temascal* (traditional Maya sweat lodge) also can be arranged with advance notice. A cab ride from Puerto Morelos's central plaza runs about US$5.

Martina's Oasis Spa (Calle Rojo Gómez 7, tel. 998/213-4595, www.martinasoasis.com, by appointment only) draws on the considerable skills of its owner, Martina, a licensed massage therapist with an uncanny ability to zero in on the precise source of discomfort and know just how to alleviate it. Prices are reasonable: US$40-85 for facials, mani-pedis, etc., and US$65-165 for one- and two-hour massages, including Swedish, Thai, deep tissue, and hot stone, and in combination with other treatments. You can go to her spa or she can come to your hotel.

Cooking Classes

The Little Mexican Cooking School (Casa Caribe, Calle Rojo Gómez 768, tel. 998/251-8060, www.thelittlemexicancookingschool. com, 10am-3:30pm Tues.-Fri. and some Sat., US$110 pp, including complimentary recipe book and apron) offers a fun and unique introduction to Mexican cuisine. Smallish classes (12 maximum) begin with a light breakfast and a discussion of Mexican food and ingredients, followed by demonstrations and hands-on practice of 7-8 recipes, from pumpkin seed salsa to chicken mole. Class ends with a luncheon from the dishes you helped create. Cooking and lodging packages are available.

ACCOMMODATIONS

Under US$50

A 10-minute walk from the center, **Hotel Edén** (Av. Andrés Quintana Roo near Calle Lázaro Cardenas, tel. 998/871-0450, www.puerto-moroseden.com, US$47.50 studio with a/c and kitchenette) is rather more austere than its name might suggest, but is a fine budget option all the same. Spacious studios have cable TV, Wi-Fi, clean hot-water bathrooms, and small but well-equipped kitchenettes. Weekly (US$400) and monthly (US$850) rates are also available.

Casa Cacahuate (Calle 2, Zona Urbana, tel. 998/208-9148, www.mayaecho.com, US$30 s, US$50 d, breakfast included) is a bed-and-breakfast located in Puerto Morelos's residential area on the inland side of the highway, offering a rare opportunity to experience the nontouristed side of the Riviera Maya. Homey even by bed-and-breakfast standards, the house has two tidy guest rooms upstairs and the personable owners below, with a large lush garden space. The owners maintain close ties with the community and host a popular crafts market and Jungle Spa on-site. The beach and central plaza are a bit of a hike—and that's the main drawback to staying here—but taxis are plentiful and inexpensive.

US$50-100

Posada El Moro (Av. Javier Rojo Gómez near central plaza, tel. 998/871-0159, www.posadaelmoro.com, US$65 s/d, US$70-85 s/d with a/c and TV, US$95 suite with a/c, TV, and kitchenette) is a homey hotel with spacious units, most with polished cement floors and lots of natural light. There's Wi-Fi throughout most of the hotel, plus a pleasant little pool surrounded by hammocks and lounge chairs toward the back. Continental breakfast is included in the rate, and weekly rates also are available.

Rancho Sak Ol (1 kilometer/0.6 mile south of the central plaza, tel. 998/871-0181, www.ranchosakol.com, US$89 s/d with a/c, US$99 s/d, US$139 suite, 2-night minimum) is a relaxing *palapa* hideaway located a 15-minute walk south of town. Rooms have hanging beds and private patios with hammocks. A buffet breakfast is included in the rate, and guests can use the well-stocked community kitchen. The beach here is just okay—very clean, with good snorkeling offshore, but boxed in by the cargo ferry on one side and a condo complex on the other. Still, there's enough breathing room so as not to spoil Rancho Sak Ol's quiet, isolated feel. The resort is for adults and teens only, except during the school holidays, when children over the age of three are welcome. The use of snorkel equipment and bicycles also is included in the rate.

US$100-200

A perfect place if you're planning a longer stay, **Abbey del Sol Two** (Av. Niños Héroes s/n, tel. 998/871-0127, U.S. tel. 651/690-3937, www.abbeydelsol.com, US$60 s/d with a/c, US$105-155 apartments with a/c) offers nicely appointed units with king-size beds, balconies or private courtyards, and fully equipped kitchens (all except one). There's a small pool in the leafy garden and a rooftop patio with *palapa*-shaded hammocks. Complimentary use of bicycles also is included. If it's booked, check the website for availability in its other properties around town.

Villas Clarita (Av. Niños Héroes near Calle Benito Juárez, tel. 998/871-0042, Can. tel. 250/244-1754, www.villasclaritamexico.com, US$120-150 with a/c) has eight comfortable

© LIZA PRADO

Puerto Morelos is known for its yoga retreats and small hotels, like Posada El Moro near the center of town.

apartments that open onto two courtyards: One has a large pool with lots of lounge chairs and tables, the other has an open-air yoga studio and shady garden. Most of the apartments have a hacienda-like feel and feature heavy wood Mexican furnishings. (The better ones open onto the garden courtyard, though families may like having an apartment right next to the pool.) All have full kitchen, air-conditioning, cable TV, Wi-Fi, purified water, and even daily maid service. Breakfast is included in the rate, too.

Occupying a converted hacienda-style mansion, **Casa Caribe** (Av. Javier Rojo Gómez near Calle Lázaro Cardenas, tel. 998/251-8060, U.S. tel. 512/410-8146, www.casacaribepuertomorelos.com, US$121.50 s/d with or without a/c) has a new owner and fresh new look and ambience. Four bright 2nd-floor rooms have whitewashed walls, colorful paintings, and large glass doors opening onto private ocean-view terraces. They don't have air-conditioning, but between the ceiling fan and ocean breezes, you really don't

miss it. (A fifth room on the ground floor does have air-conditioning.) Casa Caribe is home to The Little Mexican Cooking School, so naturally the rates include a full delicious breakfast, served in the hotel's interior patio-garden. Hotel/cooking class packages can be arranged; beach gear is available free of charge.

Club Marviya (Av. Niños Héroes near Calle Lázaro Cardenas, tel. 998/871-0049, Can. tel. 450/492-9094, www.marviya.com, US$775 per week) is a quiet hotel with tidy one-bedroom apartments, each decorated slightly differently but all with air-conditioning, kitchenettes, and cable TV. They open onto a leafy courtyard with a nice pool—a welcome feature on a hot day. Look for deep discounts in the off-season, too.

On the main beach, **Hotel Hacienda Morelos** (Av. Rafaél Melgar 5, tel. 998/871-0448, toll-free Mex. tel. 800/227-6366, www.haciendamorelos.com, US$85 s/d with a/c) is a big rambling hotel with spacious rooms, most with ocean views, good beds, tile floors, and quiet air-conditioning. There's also a small pool overlooking the beach. Decor is pretty minimal and the whole place is rather dated, but the views, location, and the rate make this an attractive option. A longtime dive shop is on-site, which is convenient if you plan to dive a lot.

Over US$200

Dreams Riviera Cancún Resort and Spa (Hwy. 307 Km. 324, tel. 998/872-9200, toll-free U.S. tel. 866/237-3267, www.dreamsresorts.com, US$216-242 s with a/c, US$332-383 d with a/c, US$465-1,620 suite) is a bustling all-inclusive resort north of downtown Puerto Morelos. Aesthetically, it has a South Pacific feel with airy rooms that feature tropical woods and bamboo accents. The amenities are high-end and luxurious. Outside there are lots of pools and a long wide beach with plenty of places to relax (no need to get up at 6am to save a spot!). Nine restaurants round out the resort nicely, providing enough options to keep most people happy during their stay.

Located south of town, **Hotel Marina El Cid Spa & Beach Resort** (Blvd. El Cid Unidad 15, tel. 998/872-8999, toll-free U.S. tel. 888/733-7308, www.elcid.com, US$181 s with a/c, US$232 d with a/c, US$206-306 suite, US$268-350 one-bedroom apartment) is Puerto Morelos's first all-inclusive resort—a milestone that didn't please everyone in this tightly knit town. The resort gets high marks from families though, with a kids club, waterslide, and manageable size, though the beach is smallish and sometimes littered with coral fragments. There is a full-service spa on-site—including beachfront massage tables—as well as a great gym with floor-to-ceiling windows facing the Caribbean. Rooms have modern, tasteful decor and lots of natural light; larger units have two full bathrooms, kitchen, and en suite hot tubs.

The adults-only **Excellence Riviera Maya** (Hwy. 307 Km. 324, toll-free U.S. tel. 866/540-2585, www.excellence-resorts.com, US$257-299 s with a/c, US$342-426 d with a/c) is a rambling resort located north of town. The size can be overwhelming, but it gets

points for the number of options it provides: eight restaurants, six pools, an expansive beach area, a sports center, and an entertainment complex. The rooms themselves are modern and comfortable, with king-size beds, Jacuzzis, and private patios or balconies. This is a great choice if you're traveling with a group—given the number of options here, there's something for almost everyone.

FOOD

Who knows how it happened, but modest little Puerto Morelos is home to an amazing array of restaurants and eateries, from cheerful holes-in-the-wall to international cuisine that draws diners all the way from Cancún and Playa del Carmen.

Mexican and Seafood

Doña Triny's (central plaza, no phone, 8am-11pm daily, US$4-9) serves home-style Mexican and Yucatecan standards like enchiladas, huaraches, and chiles rellenos, plus some adopted dishes like stuffed portobello mushrooms; most dishes can be adjusted for vegetarians on request, too.

Los Pelícanos (central plaza, tel. 998/871-0014, 8am-11pm daily, US$7-20) has a wraparound patio overlooking the plaza and the ocean—perfect for an afternoon beer or margarita. Food here can be a bit uneven, but with so many anglers in town, it's hard to go wrong with shrimp, octopus, or fish, all served fresh in a half dozen different ways.

Asian

David Lau's Place (central plaza, tel. 998/251-2531, www.davidlaus.com, 3pm-11pm Tues.-Sat., 1pm-9pm Sun., US$8-15) was opened by the chef of the much-loved but now-closed Puerto Morelos restaurant Hola Asia and also serves terrific Asian-inspired dishes, plus a handful of select Italian dishes. Meals are made to order and are served in a colorful dining room; portions tend toward enormous.

Other Specialties

C John Gray's Kitchen (Av. Niños Héroes

s/n, tel. 998/871-0665, 2pm-10pm Mon.-Sat., US$12-30) is the mother restaurant of John Gray's Place in Playa del Carmen, and without question it is the finest restaurant in Puerto Morelos. The menu changes every day, though a few perennial favorites are almost always available, like mac n' cheese with jumbo shrimp and white truffle oil as well as pan-roasted duck breast with chipotle, honey, and tequila. Fine cuts of meat, inventive sauces, and fresh pastas and vegetables are a given. Occupying a boxy building two blocks from the plaza, the dining room is elegant and understated.

There's great homemade pizza and pasta at **Los Gauchos** (Calle Tulum, cell. tel. 998/166-5879, www.losgauchosdelpuerto.com, 11am-11pm Wed.-Sun., US$5-15), but don't leave without trying the empanadas: a classic Argentinean snack made of puffy, crispy fried dough stuffed with cheese or other goodies. At just US$1.50-2.50 apiece, a plate of five or six and a couple of sodas make a great cheap meal for two.

Groceries
Casa Martín (central plaza, 6:30am-10pm daily) has a fairly large selection of canned foods, pastas, snacks, and drinks; there's also a small produce section near the back.

Every Wednesday, **fruit, vegetable, and meat stands** (Calle Tulum near Av. Javier Rojo Gómez, 7am-2pm) set up a half block from the central plaza. Prices are by the kilo.

INFORMATION AND SERVICES
Although this town sees a good number of tourists, the services remain somewhat sparse.

Emergency Services
Médica Puerto Morelos (Calle Ignacio López Rayón; tel. 998/251-1478 or 998/201-2456, 24 hours) is the small but well-equipped medical office of Dr. Víctor Ballestros, a young, serious Mexico City-trained surgeon and general practitioner. Look for signs leading to his office along the access road, near the highway. English is spoken.

Centro de Salud (no phone, 8am-2pm and 4pm-6pm daily) is south of the plaza, on an unmarked connector street between Avenidas Javier Rojo Gómez and Rafaél Melgar.

Farmacia San José Obrero (central plaza, Av. Javier Rojo Gómez, tel. 998/871-0053, 8am-2pm and 4pm-10pm daily) is a mom-and-pop pharmacy selling basic meds and toiletries.

Money
There is no bank in Puerto Morelos, but there are two **ATMs**—an HSBC one, in front of the grocery store, and a Santander ATM on the northwest corner of the central plaza.

Media and Communications
Play.net C@fé (Av. Javier Rojo Gómez s/n, no phone, 9am-10pm daily, US$1.75/hour) is located just off the central plaza. And like many Mexican towns, there's **free Wi-Fi** (24 hours) in the central plaza.

Laundry
The bustling **LavaPlus** (Av. Niños Héroes s/n, cell. tel. 998/198-4850, 8am-7pm daily) charges US$1 per kilo (2.2 pounds). For service in five hours, the rate jumps to US$1.35 per kilo. Coin-operated machines are also available.

GETTING THERE AND AROUND
Puerto Morelos is almost exactly halfway between Cancún (36 kilometers/22 miles, 40 minutes driving) and Playa del Carmen (35 kilometers/21 miles, 35 minutes). The Cancún airport is closer, just 18 kilometers (11 miles, 20 minutes) north of Puerto Morelos. A rental car isn't really necessary around town, but makes exploring the Riviera Maya beyond Puerto Morelos significantly easier.

Europcar (Calle Tulum near Av. Javier Rojo Gómez, tel. 998/206-9372, www.europcar.com.mx, 8am-6pm daily) has a small office just off the main plaza, making it the most convenient option for renting a car. Otherwise, Cancún airport has a large number of agencies, and you can often find excellent deals online.

Bus

ADO buses pass the Puerto Morelos turn-off on Highway 307 but do not enter town. The northbound stop is right at the turnoff, while the southbound bus stop is across the highway and a block south. Headed north to Cancún (US$2, 45 minutes) or south to Playa del Carmen (US$2, 35 minutes), second-class buses and *combis* (shared vans) pass every 10-15 minutes 5:30am-10pm daily, and less frequently throughout the night. A handful continue to Tulum, but it may be quicker to go to Playa and transfer. Buses to the Cancún airport (US$5.50, 25 minutes) pass roughly every 30-60 minutes 7:55am-8:45pm daily. Buy your ticket a day in advance, as buses often fill in Playa del Carmen.

Taxi

Taxis line up day and night at the taxi stand on the northwest corner of the central plaza. Prices are fixed and prominently displayed on a signboard at the taxi stand. A ride to the highway costs around US$2.

PUNTA BETE AND PLAYA XCALACOCO

It used to be that the only way to find Punta Bete and its main beach, Playa Xcalacoco, was to look for the big Cristal water plant. That's still the best landmark, but a flurry of new construction, and renovation of existing locations, has prompted hoteliers to finally add signs along the highway as well. The beach here is decent—the sand is clean but coarse, and the shoreline rocky in places—but the snorkeling is good, and the isolation has always been a big plus. It's still a quiet place, but all the new development—including a huge condo complex—may mark a new chapter for this long-overlooked stretch of beach.

Accommodations

◖ **Hotel Petit Lafitte** (Hwy. 307 Km. 296, tel. 984/877-4000, www.petitlafitte.com,

US$162-237 s with a/c, US$184-263 d with a/c, US$189-307 s bungalow with a/c, US$219-307 d bungalow with a/c) offers the comfort of a full-scale hotel on this isolated stretch of beach, including a large pool, plenty of lounge space, and a well-maintained beach area with *palapas* and hammocks. Accommodations are either in the main building, where all the rooms have at least partial ocean views, or in spacious beachfront bungalows. All accommodations have one or two beds, cable TV, air-conditioning, minibar, and Wi-Fi. Rates include a full breakfast and dinner.

Owned by a Mexican-Swiss couple, **Coco's Cabañas** (Hwy. 307 Km. 296, tel. 998/874-7056, www.cocoscabanas.com, US$65-95 s/d with a/c, US$105 suite) has a handful of charming *palapa*-roofed bungalows on a small garden plot. The *cabañas* are comfortable and attractive, with large paintings and artful stonework, plus patios with hammocks. There's a heart-shaped pool next to the open-air restaurant and bar, and the beach is just 30 meters (100 feet) away. Breakfast is included in the rate.

Food

Coco's Cabañas (Hwy. 307 Km. 296, tel. 998/874-7056, www.cocoscabanas.com, 8:30am-8pm daily, US$6-18) has a small outdoor bar and restaurant that specializes in wood-oven pizzas, though there are lots of seafood dishes as well. It's a bit pricey for the location, but then again you don't often see prosciutto, arugula, and Brie pizza around here.

Getting There and Around

From the highway, follow the access road two kilometers (1.2 miles) until it forks at the Tides Riviera Maya resort. Bear left to reach the listed hotels and beach.

There is no taxi stand in this tiny community; when guests need one, hotels call cabs from Playa del Carmen or Puerto Morelos. A ride to the airport costs around US$45, to Playa del Carmen US$10.

Playa del Carmen

Playa del Carmen (or Playa for short) has long been a favorite among travelers looking for an alternative to Cancún, a place where boutique hotels and lounge bars outnumber glitzy high-rises and all-night clubs. There also are more opportunities for tourists and locals to interact in Playa, and it's easier to find "authentic" Mexican outlets, especially compared to Cancún's Zona Hotelera. And while Cancún is an American playground, Playa attracts mostly Europeans, especially Italians.

But Playa is no longer the small seaside town many remember. Its population has exploded in recent years, with tourist and residential development stretching farther and farther up the coast every year. The main tourist strip, Quinta Avenida (5th Avenue) is still mostly pedestrian, but walking from end to end is no longer the casual jaunt it once was; a bike path along 10 Avenida is a smart and welcome addition. And while lounge bars and beach clubs are still the mainstay of Playa's nightlife, the opening of Coco Bongo Playa, an offshoot of the famous Cancún nightclub, has fanned fears of an impending "Cancunification" of Playa del Carmen.

Playa still has plenty of small hotels, cool bars, offbeat shops, and funky charm, and remains a genuine alternative to Cancún. It's got stellar beaches, and the atmosphere remains decidedly mellow, even with all the changes. Playa's location also makes it a convenient base from which to explore the rest of the Riviera Maya and Yucatán Peninsula, whether snorkeling in cenotes, diving on Isla Cozumel, or visiting inland Maya ruins.

SIGHTS AND BEACHES
Quinta Avenida

Playa's main pedestrian and commercial drag is Quinta Avenida, or 5th Avenue, which stretches more than 20 blocks from the ferry dock northward. Pronounced KEEN-ta av-en-EE-da, you may see it written as 5 Avenida or

5a Avenida, which is akin to "5th" in English. The southern section, especially near the ferry dock, is packed with typical tourist traps: souvenir shops, chain restaurants, etc. North of Calle 10 or Calle 12, and even farther past Avenida Constituyentes, the atmosphere is somewhat cooler and mellower, with more bistros, coffee shops, and high-end boutiques. The north-south division is less stark than it used to be, with some nice spots opening in the former and plenty of kitsch in the latter. You'll probably walk the length of Quinta Avenida once or twice, and everyone seems to find his or her favorite part. There are excellent beaches virtually the entire length.

Beaches and Beach Clubs

Playa del Carmen is blessed with gorgeous beaches stretching from the resort enclave of Playacar, south of town, all the way north past the last development. The sand is thick and white, and in places dozens of yards wide, with clear aquamarine water and mild surf. It's a change from several years ago, when a series of large storms and shifting currents left many beach areas thin and rocky. Online forums are a good way to get the latest info, but for the time being, Playa's *playas* are spectacular.

All along the beach are numerous beach clubs where, for a small fee or for simply ordering something from the menu, you can make use of the lounge chairs, umbrellas, restrooms, even swimming pools and changing rooms. If beach clubs aren't your thing, there are several convenient beaches to lay out your own towel and umbrella.

BEACH CLUBS
Playa Tukán (end of Calle 28) has two popular beach clubs. **Mamita's Beach Club** (end of Calle 28, tel. 984/803-2867, www.mamitasbeachclub.com, 8am-6pm daily) is one of Playa's best-known beach clubs, with thumping music and a lively atmosphere. It's the

THE RIVIERA MAYA

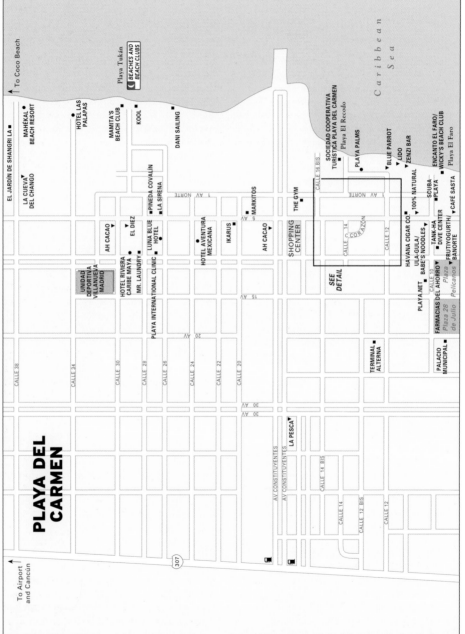

PLAYA DEL CARMEN

To Coco Beach

To Airport and Cancún

Caribbean Sea

Playa Tukán

BEACHES AND BEACH CLUBS

Playa El Recodo

Playa El Faro

EL JARDIN DE SHANGRI LA

MAHEKAL BEACH RESORT

LA CUEVA DEL CHANGO

HOTEL LAS PALAPAS

MAMITA'S BEACH CLUB

KOOL

DANI SAILING

SOCIEDAD COOPERATIVA TURISTICA PLAYA DEL CARMEN

PLAYA PALMS

BLUE PARROT

LIDO

ZENZI BAR

ENCANTO EL FARO/ WICKY'S BEACH CLUB

100% NATURAL

SCUBA PLAYA

CAFÉ SASTA

PINEDA COVALÍN

LA SIRENA

AH CACAO

EL DIEZ

LUNA BLUE HOTEL

MARKITOS

THE GYM

IKARUS

AH CACAO

HOTEL AVENTURA MEXICANA

HOTEL RIVIERA CARIBE MAYA

MR. LAUNDRY

PLAYA INTERNATIONAL CLINIC

UNIDAD DEPORTIVA VILLANUEVA MADRID

SHOPPING CENTER

SEE DETAIL

HAVANA CIGAR CO.

ULA-GULA/ BABE'S NOODLES

TANK-HA DIVE CENTER

FRUTIYOGURTH/ BANORTE

PLAYA.NET

FARMACIAS DEL AHORRO

Plaza Pelicanos

Plaza 28 de Julio

PALACIO MUNICIPAL

TERMINAL ALTERNA

LA PESCA

CALLE 16 BIS

1 AV NORTE

1 AV NORTE

5 AV

CALLE C. 14

C. CORAZON

CALLE 12

CALLE 10

15 AV

20 AV

30 AV

30 AV

AV CONSTITUYENTES

AV CONSTITUYENTES

CALLE 38

CALLE 34

CALLE 30

CALLE 28

CALLE 26

CALLE 24

CALLE 22

CALLE 20

CALLE 14 BIS

CALLE 14

CALLE 12 BIS

CALLE 12

307

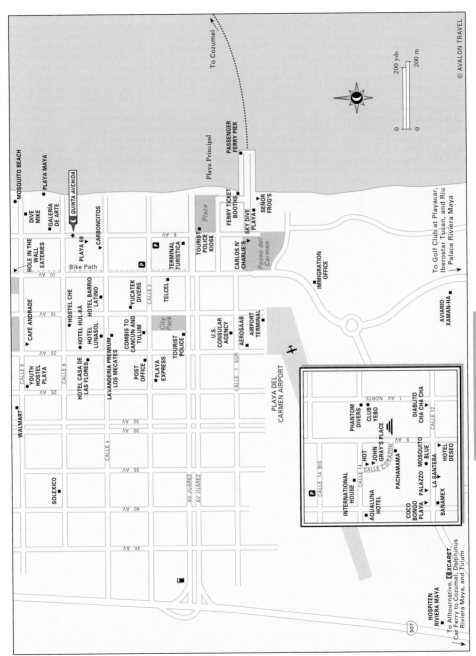

THE RIVIERA MAYA

© LIZA PRADO

Playa's pedestrian-only Quinta Avenida (5th Avenue) has it all, from fine dining and boho shops to open-air bars and tourist traps.

one place in Playa where topless sunbathing is permitted and common. Just down the beach is **Kool** (end of Calle 28, tel. 984/803-1961, www.koolbeachclub.com.mx, 8am-6pm daily), which is more laid-back and good for a slightly older crowd and families with young children. Both have food service, restrooms, changing areas and lockers, and similar prices: around US$2.50 apiece for chairs and umbrellas, US$15-25 for beach beds and large *palapas;* and US$5-15 for snacks and drinks. Both also have small swimming pools; it's free at Kool, while Mamita's asks for a US$12.50 per person minimum consumption.

Playa El Recodo is the little-used name for the stretch of sand stretching south of the pier at Avenue Constituyentes to Playa's historic lighthouse. The northernmost section, adjacent to the pier, is used to moor fishing boats and is unusable for swimming and sunbathing, but the rest is gorgeous and benefits from relatively little foot traffic. **Lido** (btwn Calle 10 and 12, tel. 984/803-1090, 8am-5:30pm daily,

minimum consumption US$12.50, chairs free, beach beds US$8) has cheery lime-green umbrellas and faces an equally smile-inducing beach. The food service here is surprisingly refined, unlike the Plain Jane fare served up at most beach clubs. Next door, **Zenzi Bar** (btwn Calle 10 and 12, 8am-2am daily, minimum consumption US$17 pp) is primarily a restaurant-bar known for its variety of live music, but also has umbrellas and beach beds for rent. Nearby are beach booths offering massages, snorkeling trips, catamaran rides, and more.

Playa El Faro, named for the large lighthouse (or *faro*) at one end, is a lovely beach that's convenient to just about everywhere. **Wicky's Beach Club** (at Calle 10, tel. 984/873-3541, www.wickysplayadelcarmen.com, 7am-midnight daily, US$12.50 pp minimum consumption) is an upscale, welcoming spot with beach chairs, a shaded patio with chairs and tables, and a large indoor restaurant area. Food and drinks are excellent, though service can be aloof. Nearby operators can arrange snorkel

© GARY CHANDLER

Another day comes to an end at Playa Tukán.

tours, Jet Skis, and more. Alas, the very enticing swimming pool is for condo guests only.

BEACHES

If beach clubs aren't your thing, there are plenty of spots to claim your own patch of sand. The best are **Playa Tukán** (end of Calle 28) and **Playa El Faro** (btwn Calles 8 and 16); while both have beach clubs, they also boast long lovely stretches of open sand and are popular with independent travelers and locals. Note that Playa Tukán is popular with Europeans, and topless sunbathing is not uncommon. Another option, if you don't mind the walk (or taxi or bike ride), is **Coco Beach;** located between Calles 38 and 46, it's ideal for laying out on your towel, listening to the waves, and chilling out. And just north of there is **Chunzubul Reef,** one of Playa's best spots for snorkeling.

◖ Xcaret

Just five kilometers (3.1 miles) south of Playa, **Xcaret** (Hwy. 307 Km. 282, tel. 998/883-0470, www.xcaret.com.mx, 8:30am-9:30pm daily, US$79/39.50 adult/child, US$139/69.50 adult/child including transportation and buffet) is a mega-ecopark offering water activities like snorkeling in underground rivers and swimming with dolphins and sharks; up-close animal viewing areas including jaguar and puma islands, a butterfly pavilion, and an aquarium; a phenomenal folk art museum that's brimming with *artesanía* from around Mexico; and spectacular shows, like a Maya ball game, regional dances, and music performances. Xcaret is thoroughly touristy and prepackaged, yes, but also surprisingly well done and a worthwhile day trip, especially for families. There are numerous packages and prices, including combo visits with sister parks **Xplor** and **Xel-Há;** be sure you know what you're getting (and not getting) when you book. Discounts are available for booking online.

Aviario Xaman Ha

A short distance inside the Playacar entrance off 10 Avenida, the small bird sanctuary **Aviario Xaman Ha** (Paseo Xaman Ha s/n, tel.

© H.W. PRADO

Traditional Maya costumes and dancing are part of the end-of-the-day extravaganza at Xcaret.

984/873-0593, 9am-5pm daily, US$22 adult, child under 12 free) is home, or a stopover, for more than 60 species of tropical birds, including toucans, flamingos, cormorants, and parrots. Some birds are in enclosures, but many are not, and a stone path meanders through the leafy grounds. It's a pleasant place to spend an hour, though the admission price is ridiculously inflated. If you do go, be sure to bring bug repellent.

ENTERTAINMENT

Playa del Carmen's nightlife has long been dominated by bars and lounges, as if deliberately leaving the raucous clubs and discotheques to Cancún. While that's still mostly the case, Playa is definitely getting rowdier, with several major nightclubs and the increasingly boisterous cluster of club-like bars at the corner of 1 Avenida and Calle 12. Note the large signs prohibiting open containers in the streets; although many bars are clustered together, finish your drink before heading to the next.

Lounges and Bars

With retro tables and armchairs, low beats, and even lower lights, **Diablito Cha Cha Cha** (1 Av. at Calle 12, tel. 984/803-4506, www. diablitochachacha.com, 7pm-3am daily) is certainly one of the most stylish of the bars in this up-and-coming area. Order anything under the sun from the bar, and munch on unlikely Mexican-Japanese fusion snacks and meals.

At sunset, the 2nd-floor patio at **Hotel Deseo** (5 Av. at Calle 12, tel. 984/879-3620, www.hoteldeseo.com, 5pm-2am daily) transforms into a sleek lounge, with DJs spinning urban beats and a reliable crowd of local and foreign hipsters. A candlelit stone stairway leads from the street to the open-air terrace, where a long swimming pool is surrounded by queen-size cushions and billowing curtains. There's food service until midnight, and the pool-side bar stirs up creative cocktails.

One of Playa's only gay clubs, **Club 69** (off 5 Av. between Calles 4 and 6, tel. 984/876-9466, 9pm-4am daily) doesn't get interesting until after 1am, and sometimes later. There are regular drag shows and exotic dancers, and, of course, music and dancing. Drinks are so-so and the place could use a good scrub, but it's not bad considering Playa's thin pickings for gay travelers. The entrance is easy to miss—look for the 7-Eleven mini-mart on the west side of Quinta Avenida, then follow the rainbow sign down an alley.

A Playa institution for nearly 30 years, the **Blue Parrot** (Calle 12 at the beach, tel. 984/206-3350, www.blueparrot.com, 8pm-2am daily, free before 10pm, US$8.50 after 10pm) has sand floors, swing bar seats, a candlelit *palapa* lounge, and a small dance floor, all within earshot of the crashing waves. DJs play everything from old-school rock to underground electronica; scantily clad fire dancers perform nightly at 11pm.

A **cluster of small bars** (5pm-midnight daily) on 5 Avenida between Calles 26 and 30 make it an area to wander over to after dinner. Among several worth checking out are **La Fe, Rufino, Santa Remedio,** the Brazilian-style **La Choperia,** and **La Casa del Hábano,** a cigar shop by day and cocktails and hookah joint at night.

Nightclubs
Coco Bongo Playa (Av. 10 at Calle 12, tel. 984/803-5939, www.cocobongo.com.mx, 10:30pm-4:30am Mon.-Sat., US$50-60 including open bar) is a satellite of the famous nightclub in Cancún. Like the original, Coco Bongo Playa features a slew of celebrity impersonations, from Kiss to Beyoncé, plus acrobats, light shows, and multiple DJs to keep everyone dancing. The space here is fairly small, but the crowds can be huge and boisterous—tons of fun, assuming you're not claustrophobic. At last check, Tuesday was Ladies Night; check Facebook for current promos, and with your hotel concierge about VIP tickets and party-hopper tours; shows begin at 11:30pm.

There are two more clubs nearby, which either benefit from or are overshadowed by the crowds amassing outside Coco Bongo.

Directly next door to Coco Bongo is another Cancún offshoot, **Palazzo** (Av. 10 at Calle 12, tel. 984/803-0730, www.palazzodisco.com, 10pm-5am daily, US$30-50), a sister club to The City and Palazzo Cancún in the Zona Hotelera. It offers a somewhat more traditional techno nightclub scene, while aiming to inject old-school glamour through its decor and image. Across the street, **La Santera** (Av. 10 at Calle 12, tel. 984/803-2856, http://lasantera.com, 10pm-3:30am daily, US$20-25) is going for an edgier ambience and has a host of "resident DJs."

And, of course, you can always find a party at **Señor Frog's** (ferry pier, tel. 984/803-3498, 9am-3am daily) and **Carlos n' Charlie's** (Paseo del Carmen, southern end of 5 Av., tel. 984/803-3498, 10am-1am daily), both near the Cozumel ferry pier. These bars are a fixture in Mexican beach towns and are famous for their yard-long drinks, dancing on the tables, and nonstop parties.

SHOPPING
Playa del Carmen offers some of the best shopping on the Riviera Maya, and Quinta Avenida is where it's at.

Artesanía
There are numerous souvenir shops along Quinta Avenida, from small to gargantuan, open all day every day. For something more unique, try the following stores.

La Sirena (5 Av. at Calle 26, tel. 984/803-3422, lasirenaplayadelcarmen@hotmail.com, 9am-10pm daily) is a boutique specializing in Mexican folk art. Italian shop owner Patrizia personally selects the exceptional pieces—whimsical skeleton art, colonial statuettes of La Virgen de Guadalupe, tin-framed mirrors, bright shawls—and you're sure to find something you can't resist.

Jam-packed with high-end Mexican folk art, **Pachamama** (Calle Corazón near 5 Av., tel. 984/803-3355, 9am-11pm daily) is a sure thing if you're willing to drop a load of pesos. Skeleton art and hipster clothes from Mexico City figure prominently.

THE RIVIERA MAYA

Specialty Items

Pineda Covalín (5 Av. between Calle 26 and 28, www.pinedacovalin.com, 10am-11pm daily) has gorgeous high-end accessories, including purses, scarves, and wallets, made from silk and other fabrics printed with traditional Mexican and indigenous images. This is the largest Pineda Covalín store in the Riviera Maya, with smaller displays in Cancún and many Mexican airports.

Opening onto a leafy courtyard, **Galería de Arte** (5 Av. near Calle 6, no phone, 10am-10pm daily) is a collection of about a dozen galleries featuring modern art paintings, sculptures, and wood carvings. Items are by no means cheap, but can be quite special.

For cigars, stop by **Havana Cigar Co.** (5 Av. btwn Calles 10 and 12, tel. 984/803-1047, 9am-11pm daily). Cuban and Mexican *puros* are sold individually (US$5-15) or by the box (US$55-450).

Shopping Centers

At the southern end of Quinta Avenida, **Paseo del Carmen** (10am-10pm daily) is a shady outdoor shopping center with high-end clothing boutiques, jewelry stores, art galleries, and restaurants. Its series of modern fountains make it an especially pleasant place to window-shop or enjoy a nice lunch after a morning at the beach. A **large multi-story shopping center** on Quinta Avenida just south of Avenida Constituyentes was near completion at the time of research.

SPORTS AND RECREATION

Scuba Diving

Playa del Carmen has decent offshore diving—virtually all drift dives, thanks to prevailing currents—and relatively easy access to Cozumel and inland cenotes. It's a logical base if you want a taste of all three, plus the convenience of being in a major town. However, if diving is the main reason you came, consider basing yourself on Cozumel itself, or closer to the cenotes, such as at Akumal or Tulum. This will save you the time, money, and effort of going back and forth.

Diving prices in Playa del Carmen are reasonable, and fairly uniform from shop to shop. Two-tank reef dives cost US$75-90, Cozumel trips run US$85-100, cenote trips are around US$120, and open-water certification courses run US$400-425. Gear is included in the courses but may be charged separately for fun dives (US$15-20/day). Most shops do not include the price of taking the ferry to Cozumel (US$24 round-trip), and additional fees, like marine park and cenote admissions, may also apply.

Tank-Ha Dive Center (Calle 10 btwn 5 and 10 Avs., tel. 984/873-0302, www.tankha.com, 8am-10pm daily) is one of the longest-operating shops in Playa and a PADI Gold Palm resort and instructor training facility.

Dive Mike (Calle 8 btwn 5 Av. and the beach, tel. 984/803-1228, www.divemike.com, 7am-9pm daily) is a very friendly, professional, and reasonably priced shop. Check out its excellent website for additional info and pictures.

Phantom Divers (1 Av. Norte at Calle 14, tel. 984/879-3988, www.phantomdivers.com, 8am-8pm Mon.-Sat., 8am-7pm Sun.) is one of a handful of locally owned dive shops offering lower-than-average prices. Cash only.

Yucatek Divers (15 Av. btwn Calles 2 and 4, tel. 984/803-1363, www.yucatek-divers.com, 7:30am-5pm daily) is a longtime shop with instruction available in several languages. Notably, all fun dives are led by instructors.

Scuba Playa (Calle 10 btwn 1 and 5 Avs., tel. 984/803-3123, www.scubaplaya.com, 8am-8pm daily) specializes in small groups and offers a six-dive package that includes two tanks apiece in Cozumel, the cenotes, and the reef.

Snorkeling

In Playa itself it's best to go snorkeling with a boat tour, since the snorkeling off the beach isn't too rewarding. There are also numerous cenotes near Playa that make for unique snorkeling, including several you can visit on your own.

Most of Playa's dive shops offer guided snorkeling tours to excellent sites. Ocean trips cost US$30-50, while cenote trips are

US$50-75, all gear included. Be sure to clarify how many reefs or cenotes you'll be visiting and for how long. A wetsuit is strongly recommended, even if it means paying extra to rent one. Cenotes can be quite cold, while sunburn is a serious concern in the open ocean; wetsuits protect against both, as well as against accidental scrapes and cuts.

Dani Sailing (Kool Beach Club, end of Calle 28, cell. tel. 984/155-2015, http://danisailing. com, 9am-5pm daily) offers fun catamaran trips with an hour spent sailing and another hour snorkeling. Or rent snorkel gear and a kayak or stand-up paddleboard (US$15-20/ hour) and find a spot of your own. Instruction is available. Look for the small shop where Calle 28 hits the beach.

Sociedad Cooperativa Turística Playa del Carmen (Playa El Recodo, end of Calle 14, no tel., 7am-6pm daily) is a local fisherman's cooperative offering snorkeling tours from a kiosk on the beach (US$30/50 pp for one/two sites).

Wind Sports

Kiteboarding, sailboarding, and sailing have grown in popularity along the Caribbean, a trickle-down effect from the world-famous wind belt on the Gulf coast northwest of here. You can catch at least some breeze almost any time of the year, but the strongest, most consistent winds blow November-March.

Ikarus (5 Av. and Calle 20, tel. 984/803-3490, www.kiteboardmexico.com, 9am-10pm daily) is a full-service kiteboarding retail shop and school. Classes are typically conducted at Isla Blanca, in the massive flat-water Chacmochuch Lagoon north of Cancún, which is ideal for kiting but nearly two hours by car or bus from Playa del Carmen. Transport from Cancún is included in the high season, and simple lodging is offered at Isla Blanca (US$10 pp tent, US$50 s/d). Private classes are US$95 per hour or US$450 for six hours, while groups are US$70 per hour per person (maximum 3 to a group) or US$350 for six hours. Equipment is included for students or can be rented separately (US$95/day). Classes are mainly held November-May, when the conditions are best.

Dani Sailing (Kool Beach Club, end of Calle 28, cell. tel. 984/155-2015, http://danisailing. com, 9am-5pm daily) offers catamaran rentals and tours, with or without snorkeling, as well as kiteboarding rentals and instruction. Prices vary.

Stand-Up Paddling and Kayaking

Stand Up Paddle Playa del Carmen (cell. tel. 984/168-0387, www.suppdc.com) in a one-man operation offering hour-long lessons for US$65 (US$50 pp for 2 people) at the beach nearest you, with an hour's free rental afterward to practice your skills. There's no fixed storefront so reservations are recommended; otherwise, look for SUP gear near the pier at Avenida Constituyentes or near Fusion beach bar (end of Calle 6). Rental gear is available (US$20/ hour, US$65/day).

Do-it-all beach sports outfit **Dani Sailing** (Kool Beach Club, end of Calle 28, cell. tel. 984/155-2015, http://danisailing.com, 9am-5pm daily) rents kayaks (US$15/hour single, US$20/hour double) and stand-up paddleboards (US$20/hour). Hour-long instructional courses (US$20) are available for anyone new to "SUPing."

Swimming with Dolphins

With swimming pens set up in the ocean, **Delphinus Riviera Maya** (Hwy. 307 Km. 282, toll-free Mex. tel. 800/335-3461, toll-free U.S./ Can. tel. 888/526-2230, www.delphinus.com. mx, US$109-499) is about as good as it gets for performing dolphins. There are various packages, from 30-minute group interactions to hour-long one-on-one encounters. Check the website for complete descriptions, photos, and a 15 percent discount for booking online. Prices are a bit higher at Delphinus Riviera Maya, mainly because round-trip transportation is included. Ticket prices also include a locker, towel, and goggles.

Sportfishing

Playa de Carmen has excellent sportfishing and bottom fishing, with plentiful wahoo, dorado, mackerel, snapper, barracuda, and—especially

April-June—sailfish and marlin. Trips depend mostly on the size and power of the boat that's used, but a four- to five-hour trip for 1-6 people usually costs US$200-250, including tackle and drinks. Many dive shops offer tours, as does **Sociedad Cooperativa Turística Playa del Carmen** (Playa El Recodo, end of Calle 14, no tel., 7am-6pm daily).

Golf

The **Golf Club at Playacar** (Paseo Xaman-Há opposite Hotel Viva Azteca, tel. 998/193-2010, www.palace-resorts.com, 6am-sundown daily) is a challenging 7,144-yard championship course designed by Robert Van Hagge and located in Playacar, the upscale hotel and residential development south of Playa del Carmen proper. Greens fees are US$180 per adult, US$120 after 2pm, and US$80 child under 17 (accompanied by adult), including cart, snacks, and drinks; free hotel pickup is included for full-price rounds. Reserve at least a day in advance November-January.

Skydiving

Gleaming white beaches and brilliant turquoise seas make the Riviera Maya a spectacular place for skydiving. If you're up for it, **Sky Dive Playa** (Plaza Marina, just south of the ferry dock, tel. 984/873-0192, www.skydive.com.mx, 9am-4pm Mon.-Sat.) has been throwing travelers out of planes at 10,000 feet since 1996. You freefall for 4,500 feet—about 45 seconds—then the chute opens for a seven- to eight-minute ride down to a soft landing on the beach. Tandem dives (you and an instructor, US$250) are scheduled every hour; walk-ups are accepted, but reservations are highly recommended. For an additional US$150, cameramen also can be booked to freefall alongside you to record your jump.

Tours

Alltournative (Hwy. 307 Km 287, tel. 984/803-9999, toll-free Mex. tel. 800/466-2848, toll-free U.S. tel. 877/437-4990, toll-free Canada and other countries tel. 877/432-1569, www.alltournative.com, 9am-7pm daily,

US$119-129 adult, US$79-99 child under 12) offers a variety of full-day conservation-minded tours, including a combination of activities like canoeing, ziplines, off-road bicycling, caving, and snorkeling, plus visits to the Tulum or Cobá archaeological zone—even to a small Maya village. Guides speak English, Italian, French, German, Dutch, and Spanish, and there are several informational kiosks on Quinta Avenida.

AeroSaab (Playa del Carmen Airport, 20 Av. Sur near Calle 1, tel. 998/865-4225, www.aerosaab.com) offers stunning panoramic flights of Playa del Carmen and the Riviera Maya (US$183-1,013, 4-6 passengers, 15 minutes-2 hours), as well as scenic full-day tours to places like Chichén Itzá, Isla Holbox, and Mérida/Uxmal (US$296-520 pp). Trips are in four- to six-seat Cessna airplanes and typically require a minimum of 2-4 people.

Spas and Gyms

El Jardín de Shangri La (Calle 38 at Calle Flamingo, tel. 984/801-1295, www.jardindeshangrila.com, 7am-9pm Mon.-Sat., noon-5pm Sun., US$15 per class, multi-class packages available) is a large jungly plot with a *palapa*-roofed area for yoga and meditation classes. It also hosts "community meditation" on Friday (voluntary donation) and "tribal yoga" with drumming on Saturday (US$20). Check online for the class schedule and upcoming workshops and events.

The Gym (Av. 1 near Calle 16 Bis, tel. 984/873-2098, www.thegymplaya.com, 6am-10pm Mon.-Fri., 7am-7pm Sat., 8am-5pm Sun.) is a modern facility offering state-of-the-art equipment and a host of classes, including yoga, Pilates, spinning, and martial arts. There are personal trainers on-site, too. Day passes are US$15; multiday and monthly passes also are available.

You can get a **massage on the beach** at various locations, including at a large no-name spa on Playa El Recodo (entrance at end of Calle 14, no tel., 7am-6pm daily, US$18 for 70 minutes).

The well-tended **Unidad Deportiva**

Villanueva Madrid (10 Av. near Calle 30, 6am-10:30pm daily) is Playa del Carmen's public sporting facility, with a gym, tennis and basketball courts, track, and soccer field. All have night lighting and are open to the public free of charge, but you need to bring your own gear.

ACCOMMODATIONS

Playa del Carmen has a huge selection and variety of accommodations, from youth hostels to swanky resorts to condos and long-term rentals. Most all-inclusives are located in Playacar, just south of town.

Under US$50

Youth Hostel Playa (Calle 8 near 25 Av., tel. 984/803-3277, www.hostelplaya.com, US$12 dorm, US$26/40 d/t with shared bath) has long been one of Playa del Carmen's best hostels, despite being somewhat removed from downtown and the beach. The dorm rooms are narrow but clean and have thick, comfortable mattresses, individual fans, mosquito nets, and free lockers. The private rooms are spotless, although light sleepers may be bothered by street noise. There's a clean, well-equipped kitchen and free PCs and Wi-Fi. Best of all is the hostel's enormous common area, which is perfect for eating, playing cards, reading, watching TV, or just kicking back.

Hostel Che (Calle 6 btwn 15 and 20 Avs., 984/147-1741, www.hostelche.com.mx, US$8.25-13.50 dorm with a/c, US$25 d with a/c and shared bath, US$50 quad with a/c and private bath) is a cool new hostel, with a lively atmosphere and reasonably comfortable accommodations. The higher-priced dorms are worth the investment, and there's a nice terrace with a full bar and music and activity into the wee hours. It's a good option if you're looking to meet people and have fun, less so if you're an early sleeper. There's also kitchen access, free breakfast, and Wi-Fi.

US$50-100

Tucked into a quiet leafy courtyard, **Club Yebo** (Av. 1 at Calle 14, tel. 984/803-3966, toll-free Mex. tel. 800/681-9510, toll-free U.S./Can. tel. 888/676-4431, www.clubyebo.com, US$45 s/d bungalow, US$69 studio with a/c, US$95 one-bedroom apartment with a/c, US$115 two-bedroom with a/c) is a small hotel offering tasteful studios and apartments with modern furnishings and fully equipped kitchens. All have quiet air-conditioning, cable TV, Wi-Fi, and daily maid service. Common areas include a small pool and two *palapa* lounges with hammocks. The only downside is if you need front desk assistance after hours, you must go down the street to its sister establishment, Playa Palms Hotel.

Hotel Hul-Kú (20 Av. btwn Calles 4 and 6, tel. 984/873-0021, www.hotelhulku.com, US$61-71 s/d with a/c) is a clean, well-located alternative that won't break the bank. Rooms are plain but well maintained and perfectly comfortable, all with TV, Wi-Fi, and air-conditioning—some with basic kitchenettes. There's even a crystal-clean swimming pool, set in the hotel's shady courtyard.

◖ **Hotel Casa de las Flores** (20 Av. btwn Calles 4 and 6, tel. 984/873-2898, www.hotelcasadelasflores.com, US$90-100 s/d with a/c) offers a cheerful hacienda-esque exterior that gives way to a leafy courtyard and garden, with a small stone-paved pool and rooms arranged on two levels in back. All units have comfortable beds and warm artful decor; the "plus" rooms have king-size beds, flat-screen TVs, and more space and light, and are well worth the higher rate.

Hotel Barrio Latino (Calle 4 btwn 10 and 15 Avs., tel. 984/873-2384, www.hotelbarriolatino.com, US$69 with a/c) offers charming rooms with mosaic-tile bathrooms, stone-inlaid floors, and private balconies. A complimentary continental breakfast is served in a leafy courtyard with a *palapa*-roofed lounge—a good place to write postcards or play cards. Wireless Internet access and most international phone calls are also included in the rate.

Hotel Riviera Caribe Maya (10 Av. at Calle 30, tel. 984/873-1193, www.hotelriviera-maya.com, US$60 s/d-130 s/d with a/c) offers bright rooms with hand-carved Mexican furnishings and modern amenities like mini air

THE RIVIERA MAYA

conditioners, cable TV, in-room phones, and minifridges. Many have patios or balconies that look out onto the hotel's small inviting pool, which is tucked into a pleasant courtyard. The more expensive rooms are located in a newer building and are larger, with wood-floor balconies and deluxe features like king-size beds and Jacuzzi tubs. Continental breakfast and Wi-Fi (lobby only) are included in all the rates.

US$100-150

Hotel LunaSol (Calle 4 btwn 15 and 20 Avs., tel. 984/873-3933, www.lunasolhotel.com, US$80-110 s/d with a/c) offers 16 comfortable rooms, all with private balconies or terraces, on spacious leafy grounds. The rooms are a bit sparse but have nice tile bathrooms, minifridges, and flat-screen TVs; 2nd-floor rooms have higher ceilings and better light. Though well located for eating out, the hotel has a fully equipped outdoor kitchen if you'd rather stay in, plus a sparkling swimming pool and Jacuzzi.

Hotel Aventura Mexicana (Calle 24 btwn 5 and 10 Avs., tel. 984/873-1876, www.aventuramexicana.com, US$118-132 s/d with a/c, US$144 deluxe s/d with a/c) has two sections: The newer adults-only area has deluxe rooms with muted colors, elegant furnishings, and a nicely manicured garden and pool. The older section isn't dumpy, but has plainer decor and a long thin pool squeezed in the center of the courtyard; it's also slightly cheaper and open to families. Guests give both areas top marks, though, making it a versatile option.

An adults-only hotel, **☾ Luna Blue Hotel** (Calle 26 btwn 5 and 10 Avs., tel. 984/873-0990, www.lunabluehotel.com, US$80-110 s/d with a/c) is a leafy oasis, and an excellent value, just off busy Quinta Avenida. Rooms are tidy and cool, with pithy travel-related quotes stenciled on the wall, and range from standard hotel rooms to suites with balconies and kitchens. A pleasant garden has colorful Adirondack chairs and a sunken pool, all beneath a canopy of tropical trees. The friendly American owners also provide Wi-Fi, beach club passes, purified water, and morning coffee and muffins.

Aqualuna Hotel (Av. 10 at Calle 14, tel. 984/873-1965 or 984/803-3018, www.aqualunahtl.com, US$85-125 s/d with a/c) is an intimate hotel with Mediterranean style. Units are simple and airy, with curving whitewashed walls, blue accents, and original art from Jalisco, plus upscale amenities like flat-screen TVs; all open onto a leafy, winding courtyard. Guests enjoy beach access and pool access at sister establishments. The hotel is gay friendly.

US$150-200

Playa Palms (Av. 1 Bis near Calle 14, tel. 984/803-3908, toll-free Mex. tel. 800/681-9510, toll-free U.S./Can. tel. 888/676-4431, www.playapalms.com, US$180-235 s/d with a/c, US$185 suite with a/c) is a classy beachfront hotel, with airy and colorful rooms, most with kitchenettes and fine ocean views. A thin pool winds through the hotel's leafy interior courtyard; it's picturesque though not really practical for actually swimming in. Likewise, the beach area is comfortable, but fishing boats moored there can make it hard to enjoy the water. Still, the location and amenities made this a popular option. Rooms have Wi-Fi and iPod docks.

Playa Maya (on the beach btwn Calles 6 and 8, tel. 984/803-2022, www.playa-maya.com, US$150-210 s/d with a/c, US$180 suite with a/c and kitchenette) is one of the few small hotels in Playa with direct beach access. All 20 rooms are modern and comfortable, including some with kitchen, balcony, and ocean views. There are a tiny pool, Jacuzzi, and sundeck, located somewhat awkwardly at the entrance. The beach is lovely and relaxing, though, with lounge chairs, shaded tables, and food and drink service. Note that even the entrance faces the beach, so you may need a porter to help carry bags across the sand. There's a four- to five-night minimum, depending on the season.

Over US$200

With gorgeous gardens and one of the best beachfronts in Playa, **Hotel Las Palapas** (Calle 34 btwn 5 Av. and the beach, tel.

984/873-4260, www.laspalapas.com, US$235-315 s/d with a/c) makes the most of its somewhat removed location. There are 75 rooms in one- and two-story thatched-roof bungalows, either garden or ocean view. All units are peaceful, if a bit dated (they're slowly being renovated), with comfortable beds and large patios with hammocks. There's a pool, spa, dive shop, and, of course, beach chairs and umbrellas on that beautiful beach. Rates are a tad inflated, and noise from a beach club down the way can be a bit annoying, but it's still a lovely choice. A full buffet breakfast is included.

Mosquito Blue (5 Av. btwn Calles 12 and 14, tel. 984/873-1245, toll-free Mex. tel. 800/999-6666, toll-free U.S. tel. 866/547-8756, toll-free Can. tel. 866/940-5518, www.mosquitoblue.com, US$200-385 s/d with a/c) boasts lush interior courtyards with two amoeba-shaped pools, an impressive *palapa*-roofed lounge, and striking fine art throughout. Rooms, though somewhat cramped, are beautifully appointed and have high-end amenities: digital safes, minibars, Egyptian linens, cable TV, and Wi-Fi. Its sister hotel, **Mosquito Beach** (Calle 8 at the beach, same tels., www.mosquitobeachhotel.com), has a similar style and rates but is located on the beach. It's adults only for both; deep discounts are available when booking online.

Mahékal Beach Resort (Calle 38 near 5 Av., tel. 984/873-0579, toll-free Mex. tel. 800/836-8942, toll-free U.S. tel. 877/235-4452, www.mahekalplaya.com, US$279-494 s/d with a/c, US$520 casita with a/c, including breakfast and dinner) is a huge yet tranquil resort, divided into three sections: upscale oceanfront units, adults-only garden-view units, and a family area with garden- and ocean-view rooms. All units feature private terraces, air-conditioning, and safe-deposit box, but purposefully do not have TV, phone, or Wi-Fi in the rooms. Some of the rooms have been renovated, but others are a bit dated, as are some common areas. The resort's beach, though, is gorgeous—a good thing since that's where you're sure to end up most days.

All-Inclusive Resorts

Most of Playa del Carmen's all-inclusives are in Playacar, an upscale hotel and residential development south of town.

Iberostar Tucan (Av. Xaman-Ha, tel. 984/877-2000, www.iberostar.com, US$260-450 d all-inclusive) has a spacious lobby-entryway and wide attractive beach with palm trees, beach chairs, and mild surf. Separating the lobby and the beach is a broad patch of healthy coastal forest, where you can spot monkeys, parrots, and other native creatures in the treetops. After so many sterile and manicured resorts, the Tucan makes for a welcome change of scenery. The pool is huge and near the beach. Rooms occupy large buildings along the property's edges and are clean and comfortable, though plain. Junior suites have sea views.

Riu Palace Riviera Maya (Av. Xaman-Ha, tel. 984/877-2290, www.riu.com, US$260-575 d all-inclusive) is one of six all-inclusive Riu resorts clustered together in Playacar and the most upscale, though each resort in the group has its own appeal. The Palace Riviera Maya has an old-world look, with a soaring marble-floored lobby, ornate ironwork, and Renaissance-style paintings and artwork. Suites feature additional sitting areas, understated colors and decor, top-shelf liquors, and modern bathrooms, including hydromassage tubs. The beach and pool areas are spacious and appealing, and there are well-supplied gym and spa areas. Nightlife here can be a bit sedentary, but the advantage of the Palace category is that you have access to the other more lively Riu resorts, like the Tequila or Yucatán.

Rental Properties

Playacar has scores of houses for rent, of all sizes and styles. Prices vary considerably, but expect to pay a premium for ocean views and during peak seasons. A number of property-management companies rent houses, including **Playacar Vacation Rentals** (Calle 10 s/n, tel. 984/873-0418, toll-free U.S. tel. 866/862-7164, www.playacarvacationrentals.com) and **Playa Beach Properties & Rentals** (Plaza Antigua, Calle 10 s/n, tel. 984/873-2952, U.S.

tel. 205/332-3458, www.playabeachrentals. com). Both offices are south of Avenida Juárez near the Playacar entrance.

Encanto El Faro (beachfront at Calle 12, www.vrbo.com, US$180-350 with a/c and kitchen) is one of very few accommodations in Playa proper with a swimming pool facing the beach. It's a lovely pool, too: large, sparkling clean, and encircled by dark-wood walkways and lounge chairs, with a children's area as well. The lodging itself is less successful: One-, two-, and three-bedroom condos have full kitchens and partial ocean views, but can be rather dark. Condos here are individually owned, so it's worth doing your homework before booking; VRBO and TripAdvisor are good places to start. The all-inclusive plan is not worth the price.

FOOD

Playa del Carmen has restaurants and eateries for all tastes and budgets. Those on Quinta Avenida are pricier, of course, many for good reason, others less so. Cheaper eats tend to be off the main drag.

Mexican

◖ **La Cueva del Chango** (Calle 38 near 5 Av., cell. tel. 984/147-0271, www.lacuevadelchango.com, 8am-11pm Mon.-Sat., 8am-2pm Sun., US$5-15) means The Cave of the Monkey, but there's nothing dim or primitive about it: The covered dining area has lighthearted decor (and a back patio ensconced in leafy vegetation), while the menu features crepes, empanadas, and innovative items like eggs with polenta and *chaya*. It's often packed with Playa's upper crust, though the prices make it accessible to all.

Carboncitos (Calle 4 btwn Avs. 5 and 10, tel. 984/873-1382, 7:30am-11pm daily, US$5-15) is a traveler favorite in Playa, serving terrific Mexican food (and some things you may be missing from home, like fresh salads) in a friendly and welcoming setting. Prices and portions are reasonable by Playa standards, and the restaurant gets the little things right, like tasty guacamole and homemade salsas.

Frutiyogurth (Plaza Pelícanos, Av. 10 near Calle 10, tel. 984/803-2516, www.frutiyogurth.com.mx, 8:30am-10:30pm daily, US$3-7) is bustling little eatery, serving classic Mexican *tortas* (sandwiches) piled high with fillings like chipotle chicken and *milanesa* (chicken-fried steak), plus a monster selection of fresh juices and smoothies.

An old-school Mexican coffee shop that's popular with locals, **Café Andrade** (Calle 8 near 20 Av., tel. 998/846-8257, 7am-11pm daily, US$2-5) serves up mean breakfast and dinner plates with tacos, *chilaquiles,* mole, enchiladas—you name it, they've probably got it. Lunch specials include soup, a main dish, dessert, and a half pitcher of fresh juice for just six bucks.

Seafood

Unassuming and refreshingly untouristy, **La Pesca** (30 Av. near Av. Constituyentes, no phone, noon-10pm daily, US$5-15) specializes in super-fresh seafood, including hefty fish and shrimp plates, tasty ceviche, and great fish tacos. It's a bit of a hike from the center and has a view of a supermarket parking lot, but it is a tasty way to get off Quinta Avenida.

Ula-Gula (5 Av. at Calle 10, 2nd Fl., tel. 984/879-3727, 4:30pm-midnight daily, US$9-25) serves outstanding gourmet meals in an appealing dining area overlooking Quinta Avenida. The seafood is the real standout here, whether appetizers like tuna with wasabi and soy sauce, or the fish of the day prepared with a parsley Gorgonzola sauce. For dessert, try the chocolate fondant—a small chocolate cake filled with rich chocolate syrup and accompanied by ice cream.

On a fun, busy block at the north end of Playa, **El Diez** (5 Av. at Calle 30, tel. 984/803-5418, 1pm-midnight daily, US$10-25) is an Argentinean steak house, borrowing the nickname of Argentina's larger-than-life footballer, Diego Maradona. The specialties here are grilled meats and fresh seafood, but the long menu also includes items like burgers, salads, and empanadas. Service can be a bit slow, but the large outdoor dining area is perfect for enjoying the goings-on.

Other Specialties

John Gray's Place (Calle Corazón near Calle 14, tel. 984/803-3689, www.johngrayrestaurantgroup.com, 1pm-5pm and 6pm-11pm Mon.-Sat., US$15-30) is an offshoot of the original John Gray's Kitchen in Puerto Morelos, widely considered one of the best restaurants on the Riviera Maya. The kid lives up to expectations, expertly fusing gourmet American cuisine with flavors from around the world, like tuna carpaccio with wasabi cream and sweet soy sauce, or spicy crab cakes with cilantro-leek fondue.

Although occasionally missing the mark, old-timer **Babe's Noodles and Bar** (Calle 10 btwn 5 Av. and 10 Av., tel. 984/803-0056, www.babesnoodlesandbar.com, 1pm-11pm Mon.-Sat., US$6-14) still serves up delicious Thai-fusion meals in a hip bistro setting. Dishes come in half and full orders. Don't miss a chance at ordering the *limonmenta,* an awesome lime-mint slushie. It's not a huge place, so you may have to wait for a table during high season, or if you prefer, head down the street to its like-named sister restaurant (5 Av. btwn Calles 28 and 30), which has the same menu and hours.

100% Natural (5 Av. btwn Calles 10 and 12, tel. 984/873-2242, 7am-11pm daily, US$6-12) serves mostly vegetarian dishes and a large selection of fresh fruit juices. Service can be hit or miss, but the food is fresh and well prepared. Tables are scattered through a leafy garden area and covered patio—great for taking a break from the sun.

If you're looking for cheap eats, check out the string of **hole-in-the-wall eateries** (Av. 10 btwn Calles 8 and 10, US$1.25-4) across the street from Plaza Pelícanos. Here you'll have your choice of tacos, *tortas* (Mexican-style sandwiches), crepes, pizza by the slice, and smoothie stands, all at decent prices. Most are open 9am-10pm daily.

Cafés and Bakeries

Two doors down from Starbucks, **Café Sasta** (5 Av. btwn Calles 8 and 10, tel. 984/873-3030, 7am-11pm daily, US$1.50-5) is putting up the good fight, with old-time charm and a tempting display of muffins, scones, cupcakes, and cheesecake to go along with the full coffee menu. Seating is available indoors and outdoors.

Chocolate lovers will melt over **Ah Cacao** (5 Av. at Av. Constituyentes, tel. 984/803-5748, www.ahcacao.com, 7:15am-11:30pm daily, US$2-5), a chocolate café where every item on the menu—from coffees to cakes—is homemade from the finest of beans. A sister shop (Calle 30 near 5 Av., tel. 984/879-4179, 7am-11:30pm daily) is located up the street from Playa Tukán.

You'll smell **Hot** (Calle Corazón at Calle 14, tel. 984/879-4520, www.thehotbakingcompany.com, 7am-10pm daily, US$4.50-10) a block away—this café bakes fresh breads and pastries all day. Most people end up staying for more than just a brownie, though—the menu full of sandwiches prepared on whole-wheat or sunflower-seed bread is almost impossible to resist. The shady outdoor eating area is a great place to enjoy a leisurely breakfast, too.

Groceries

Walmart (Calle 8 btwn Avs. 20 and 25, toll-free Mex. tel. 800/710-6352, 7am-midnight daily) is located right behind city hall—how's that for a metaphor?—with everything from clothes, shoes, and snorkel gear to groceries, prepared food, and a full pharmacy. Liquor sales end at 11pm.

INFORMATION AND SERVICES

Tourist Information

There is no tourist information office in Playa, but the **tourist police** have a kiosk on the plaza (5 Av. at Av. Juárez, 24 hours), which often is stocked with brochures and maps.

Quinta (www.allrivieramaya.com) and *Sac-Be* (www.sac-be.com) are free monthly magazines that usually offer a handful of useful articles, listings, and events calendars.

Emergency Services

Hospiten Riviera Maya (Hwy. 307 s/n, tel.

984/803-1002, www.hospiten.com, 24 hours) is a private hospital offering modern, high-quality medical service at reasonable rates. Many of the doctors have U.S. training and speak English, and are accustomed to treating foreign visitors and expats. It is located along the east side of the highway on the southern side of Playa.

Playa also has a hyperbaric chamber, operated by **Playa International Clinic** (10 Av. at Calle 28 Norte, tel. 984/803-1215, emergency tel. 984/873-1365, 9am-8pm Mon.-Fri., 9am-2pm and 5pm-7pm Sat.).

For emergency **ambulance service,** call 065 from any phone.

Prescriptions are required for many antibiotics now, unlike years past. **Farmacias del Ahorro** (10 Av. at Calle 10, toll-free Mex. tel. 800/711-2222, 9am-10pm daily) has a full pharmacy on the 1st floor and a **free walk-in clinic** on the 2nd floor, where a doctor can write prescriptions after a short interview or exam; the clinic is closed 3pm-5pm and weekends.

The **tourist police** (tel. 984/877-3340, or 060 from any pay phone) have an office on Avenida Juárez and 15 Avenida, and informational kiosks along Quinta Avenida, theoretically operating 24 hours a day.

Money
Banamex (Calle 12 at 10 Av., 9am-4pm Mon.-Fri.) and **Banorte** (Plaza Pelícanos, 10 Av. btwn Calles 8 and 10, 9am-6pm Mon.-Fri., 10am-2pm Sat.) are full-service banks with ATMs and foreign exchange. There also are several freestanding **ATMs** around town.

Media and Communications
The **post office** (Calle 2 at Av. 20, 9am-4pm Mon.-Fri., 9am-noon Sat.) is easy to miss—look for the dilapidated building near the *combi* terminal.

Internet cafés have gone from ubiquitous to nearly obsolete, thanks to the proliferation of mobile devices and the availability of free Wi-Fi at most hotels. Among the remaining locations include **Playa.Net** (Calle 10 near 10 Av.,

9am-3pm and 4pm-10pm Mon.-Sat., US$1.25/hour), **Telcel** (10 Av. btwn Av. Juárez and Calle 2, 9am-10pm Mon.-Sat., US$1/hour), and the overpriced **Markitos** (5 Av. at Calle 20, 9am-11pm daily, US$3.25/hour).

Immigration and Consulates
Playa del Carmen's **immigration office** (Plaza Antigua mall, 2nd Fl., Calle 10 s/n, tel. 998/881-3560, 9am-1pm Mon.-Fri.) is located on the road to Playacar. Avoid using it, however, as the one in Cancún is more efficient. A tourist visa extension, or *prórroga,* can take a week or more in Playa and involves considerable documentation; in Cancún, the same process is simplified and takes as little as two hours.

The **U.S. Consular Agency** (Calle 1 btwn Avs. 15 and 20, tel. 984/873-0303, playausca@gmail.com) is open 10am-1pm Monday, Wednesday, and Friday.

Laundry and Storage
At the north end of town, **Mr. Laundry** (10 Av. btwn Calles 28 and 30, 7am-10pm Mon.-Sat., 8am-5pm Sun.) charges US$1-1.75 per kilo with a two-kilo (4.4-pound) minimum. **Lavandería Premium Los Mecates** (Calle 4 near 20 Av., 8am-9pm Mon.-Sat.) charges US$0.80-1.25 per kilo and has a three-kilo (6.6-pound) minimum. At both places, the lower rate is for one- to two-day service, the higher is for express.

Luggage storage is available at both bus stations. **Guarda Plus** (6am-10pm daily) charges US$0.50-1.25 per hour depending on the size of the bag, or US$8.25 per day.

Language and Instruction
Playa del Carmen is becoming a popular place to study Spanish, with several schools, plenty of options for cultural and historical excursions, and, of course, great beaches and nightlife.

Solexico (Calles 6 btwn 35 and 40 Avs., tel. 984/873-0755, www.solexico.com) is a highly recommended school with a welcoming campus and reputation for professionalism. Classes are offered one-on-one or in groups no larger than five, and for 15, 20, 25, or 40 hours per week

(US$190-625/week). All levels of courses are offered, including instruction geared toward professionals who have regular contact with Spanish speakers. Students can stay with local families (US$180-245/week), at the school's 10-room student residence (US$225-280/week), or arrange for hotel and condo rentals. Ask about volunteer opportunities.

International House (Calle 14 btwn 5 Av. and 10 Av., tel. 984/803-3388, www.ihrivieramaya.com, 7am-9pm Mon.-Fri., 9am-1pm Sat.) occupies a pretty and peaceful colonial home, with a large classroom, garden, and café on-site. Group classes (US$220/week) meet 20 hours per week with a maximum of eight students, though typically just 3-4, and can be paired with instruction in things like diving, Mexican cooking, and Latin dancing. Private and two-person classes are also available, as well as custom courses for medical professionals, teachers, and other groups. Family stays can be arranged for US$210-245 per week, with breakfast or half board, while a variety of furnished apartments and student rooms, single and shared, with or without meals, run US$160-595 per week.

GETTING THERE

Air

Playa del Carmen has a small airport a few blocks from the ferry pier, but it's used for private and charter flights only. Commercial service is available at Cancún's international airport.

Bus

Playa del Carmen has two bus stations: **Terminal Turística** (aka Terminal Riviera, 5 Av. and Av. Juárez) is in the center of town and has frequent second-class service to destinations along the coast, including Cancún, Tulum, and everything in between; and **Terminal Alterna** (Calle 20 btwn Calles 12 and 12 Bis) has first-class and deluxe service to interior destinations such as Mérida, Campeche, and beyond. There is some overlap, and you can buy tickets for any destination at either station, so always double-check from which station your bus departs.

Combi

Combis (shuttle vans) are an easy way to get up and down the Riviera Maya. In Playa, northbound *combis* line up on Calle 2 near 20 Avenida, with service 24 hours a day (every 10 minutes until 11pm, then every 30 minutes). For slightly more, **Playa Express** has larger, air-conditioned shuttles, departing from a lot on Calle 2 between 20 and 25 Avenidas 5:15am-11:15pm daily. The final destination of both services is Cancún's main bus terminal (US$3, 50 minutes), but you can be dropped off anywhere along the highway, including Puerto Morelos (US$2.50, 30 minutes). *Combis* do not enter Cancún's Zona Hotelera, but you can catch a bus there from outside the terminal.

South from Playa del Carmen, ordinary *combis* leave from the same corner around the clock, going as far as the Tulum bus station (US$3.50, 1 hour), passing the turnoffs for Puerto Aventuras (US$2, 10 minutes), Xpu-Há (US$2.50, 20 minutes), Akumal (US$2.50, 25 minutes), Hidden Worlds (US$3.50, 40 minutes), Tankah Tres (US$3, 45 minutes), and Tulum Ruins (US$3, 50 minutes). To return, flag down a *combi* anywhere along the highway.

Car

If you are driving to Playa del Carmen, look for the two main access roads to the beach—Avenida Constituyentes on the north end of town and Avenida Benito Juárez on the south. Playacar has its own entrance from the highway but can also be reached by turning south on Calle 10 off Avenida Juárez.

Ferry

Passenger ferries to Cozumel (US$13 each way, 30 minutes) leave from the pier at the end of Calle 1 Sur. **UltraMar** (www.gran-puerto.com.mx) and **Mexico Water Jets** (www.mexicowaterjets.com.mx) alternate departures and charge the same amount, though UltraMar's boats are newer. Their ticket booths are side by side at the foot of the pier, with the time of the next departure displayed prominently. The ticket seller will try to sell you a round-trip ticket, but there's

PLAYA DEL CARMEN BUS SCHEDULES

Terminal Turística (5 Av. and Av. Juárez, tel. 984/873-0109, ext. 2501, toll-free Mex. tel. 800/702-8000) is located near the ferry dock and has frequent service north to Cancún and south to Tulum, and most locations in between. Long-distance buses use the Terminal Alterna.

Most Tulum-bound buses stop at the turnoffs for destinations along the way, including **Paamul** (US$1.25-3.50, 15 minutes), **Puerto Aventuras** (US$1.50-3.50, 20 minutes), **Xpu-Há** (US$2-4, 25 minutes), **Akumal** (US$2.50-4.50, 30 minutes), **Xel-Há** (US$3-5, 30 minutes), and **Hidden Worlds** and **Dos Ojos** (both US$3-5, 40 minutes).

Most Chetumal-bound buses stop at **Carrillo Puerto** (US$6.75-9.50, 2-2.5 hours) and **Bacalar** (US$13.50-18.25, 4.5 hours).

Most Cancún-bound buses stop at **Puerto Morelos** (US$2-5.50, 35 minutes), but *not* the airport or Cancún's Zona Hotelera.

DESTINATION	PRICE	DURATION	SCHEDULE
Cancún	US$2.75-8	1 hr	every 15-30 mins 12:30am-11:59pm
Cancún Int'l Airport	US$10	1 hr	every 30-60 mins 5am-8pm
Chetumal	US$16-21	4.5 hrs	every 60-90 mins 4:10am-11:30pm
Tulum	US$3.25-5.50	1 hr	every 15-30 mins 1am-11:40pm
Xcaret (main entrance)	US$0.85-4	25 mins	every 30-60 mins 6:10am-11:30pm

no disadvantage to buying a *sencilla* (one-way ticket) and waiting to see which ferry has the next departure when you're ready to return. Between the two companies, there are ferries every 1-2 hours on the hour 7am-10pm daily.

Car ferries operated by **Transcaribe** (tel. 987/872-7688 or 987/872-7671 in Cozumel, www.transcaribe.net) depart from the Calica dock south of Playa at 4am, 8am, 1:30pm, and 6pm Monday; 1:30 and 6pm Tuesday and Friday; 8am, 1:30pm, and 6pm Wednesday, Thursday, and Saturday; and 6am and 6pm on Sunday. Returning from Cozumel, the ferry leaves from the international pier at 6am, 11am, 4pm, and 8:30pm Monday-Saturday and at 8am and 8pm on Sunday. The trip takes about an hour and 15 minutes and costs US$60 for a passenger car including driver, and US$5.50 per additional passenger. Reservations are available online, by phone, or at the pier, and are strongly recommended.

GETTING AROUND

Playa del Carmen is a walking town, although the steady northward expansion is challenging that description. The commercial part of Quinta Avenida now stretches over 40 blocks and keeps getting longer. Cabs are a good option, especially if you have luggage.

Taxi

Taxis around town cost US$2-5, or a bit more if you use a taxi stand or have your hotel summon one. All taxi drivers carry a *tarifário*—an

Terminal Alterna (Calle 20 btwn Calles 12 and 12 Bis, tel. 984/803-0944, toll-free Mex. tel. 800/702-8000) departures include:

DESTINATION	PRICE	DURATION	SCHEDULE
Campeche	US$42.25-44.50	6.5-8 hrs	10am, 11:30am, 4:40pm, 8pm
Chichén Itzá	US$10.75-22.50	4 hrs	6:10am, 7:30am, and 8am
Cobá	US$6-7.75	2 hrs	every 30-90 mins 6:10am-5:50pm
Mérida	US$28-34	4.5-5.5 hrs	every 60-90 mins 4am-11:59pm
Palenque	US$52.25-62.50	12 hrs	take San Cristóbal bus
San Cristóbal (Chiapas)	US$66.50-79	17-19 hrs	5:15pm, 6:45pm, 7:15pm, and 9:55pm
Valladolid	US$9-12.50	2.5 hrs	every 30-60 mins 6am-6:30pm, plus 4am

THE RIVIERA MAYA

official fare schedule—which you can ask to see if you think you're getting taken for a ride (so to speak). Prices do change every year or two, so ask at your hotel what the current rate is, and always be sure to agree on the fare with the driver before setting off.

Car

Playa has myriad car rental agencies, and prices can vary considerably. Major agencies like Hertz, National, Avis, and Executive are the most reliable and often have great deals if you reserve online.

Parking in Playa in the high season can be a challenge, especially south of Avenida Constituyentes. Many hotels have secure parking; there are also parking lots around town, including on Calle 2 at 10 Avenida (8am-10pm daily) and at Calle 14-bis and 10 Avenida (8am-10pm daily), charging around US$1 per hour or US$9 per day.

PAAMUL

What started out as an unassuming trailer park on a beautiful stretch of beach has now become a seaside community all its own. Located about 20 kilometers (12.4 miles) south of Playa del Carmen, Paamul has everything from RVs with elaborate wood and *palapa* structures over them to hotel rooms, a restaurant, and even a dive shop.

Beach

Paamul stretches over a wide curving beach. It's

clean and classically pretty with white sand and turquoise water—perfect for swimming and exploring. Watch your step on the south end of the beach, as its waters harbor prickly sea urchin—consider wearing water shoes.

Snorkeling and Scuba Diving
Scuba-Mex (Hwy. 307 Km. 85, tel. 984/807-7866, toll-free U.S. tel. 888/871-6255, www.scubamex.com, 8am-5pm daily) is a full-service shop offering fun dives, dive packages, and dive courses at rock bottom prices. If you're just interested in snorkeling off the beach, the shop also rents snorkel gear.

Accommodations
Sitting alone on a gorgeous bay is 🌊 **Paamul Hotel & Cabañas** (Hwy. 307 Km. 85, tel. 984/875-1050, U.S. tel. 615/597-0888, www.paamul.com, US$12.50 pp tent, US$45 s/d RVs, US$85 s/d *cabañas,* US$100 s/d with a/c, US$125 s/d with a/c and kitchenette). From elegant hotel rooms to simple camp sites, it appeals to travelers of all budgets. The hotel rooms are simple and elegant with features like minifridges and microwaves, quiet air-conditioning, and gorgeous ocean views from private terraces. The tent and trailer spaces are just steps from the Caribbean and have electricity and running water, and share clean hot-water bathrooms. The *cabañas,* unfortunately, miss the mark. Though tempting in a rustic sort of way, they are so ill-maintained, they're not worth the cost. Nevertheless, once you factor in the on-site restaurant and dive shop, this place is a rare find.

Food
Open-air, modern, and with a great view of the Caribbean, the **Reefs of Paamul Restaurant and Bar** (Hwy. 307 Km. 85, tel. 984/875-1050, 8am-8pm daily, US$5-16) serves up classic Mexican dishes along with a variety of international meals. There's something for everyone, which makes it an easy choice. (Good thing, since it's the only restaurant in Paamul.)

For groceries, the very mini **Mini Super Paa Mul** (7am-8pm Mon.-Sat., 7am-2pm Sun.) sells basic foodstuffs. It's located at the highway turnoff to Paamul.

Information and Services
There are no health, banking, Internet, postal, or laundry services in Paamul. The closest town for a full range of services is Playa del Carmen, 20 kilometers (12.4 miles) north.

Puerto Aventuras

Puerto Aventuras is an odd conglomeration of condos, summer homes, and hotels, organized around a large marina, including a swim-with-dolphins area. It's more than a resort but not really a town. Whatever you call it, Puerto Aventuras's huge signs and gated entrance are impossible to miss, located a few minutes north of Akumal on Highway 307.

SIGHTS
Museo Sub-Acuático CEDAM
Short for Conservation, Ecology, Diving, Archaeology, and Museums, CEDAM runs the very worthwhile **Museo Sub-Acuático CEDAM** (Bldg. F, no phone, 9am-1pm and 2:30pm-5:30pm Mon.-Sat., donation requested), displaying a wide variety of items: Maya offerings that were dredged from the peninsula's cenotes, artifacts recovered from nearby colonial shipwrecks, early diving equipment, and photos of open-water and cenote explorations, some from the halcyon days of diving when *jeans* were the preferred getup.

SPORTS AND RECREATION
Snorkeling and Scuba Diving
Some 25 dive sites lie within a 10-minute boat ride from the marina, each boasting rich coral, abundant sealife, and interesting features, like

CEDAM and the Riviera Maya

In 1948, a small group of Mexican divers—active frogmen during World War II—created a nonprofit organization called Club de Exploración y Deporte Acuáticos de México (Exploration and Aquatic Sports Club of Mexico, or CEDAM). Their mission was to promote ocean conservation and educate others about its treasures and resources.

In 1958, the group set about salvaging the *Mantanceros*, a Spanish galleon that foundered offshore in 1741. It set up camp in present-day Akumal, then just an uninhabited beach owned by a man named Argimiro Arguelles. Arguelles leased CEDAM an old work boat for their project, the SS *Cozumel*, and worked as its captain.

It was this relationship that sealed Akumal's—and arguably, the Riviera Maya's—destiny. During a relaxed evening around the campfire, Arguelles sold Pablo Bush Romero, one of CEDAM's founders, the bay of Akumal and thousands of acres of coconut palms north and south of it. For the next 12 years, CEDAM continued its work in the rustic and beautiful place—replacing their tents with sturdy *palapa* huts, and using the creaky SS *Cozumel* to carry divers to work sites along the coast.

It wasn't long before the idea of promoting tourism on Mexico's forgotten Caribbean coast arose. In 1968, the group—which had changed the words behind its initials to Conservation, Ecology, Diving, Archaeology, and Museums—donated 5,000 acres of land to the government, including the Cove of Xel-Há, to create a national park. The aim was to open the isolated area to tourists and, in so doing, create jobs for local residents. CEDAM also provided housing, food, electricity, running water, a school for the children, and a first-aid station with a trained nurse.

Still based in Akumal, CEDAM has grown into an important scientific and conservation organization. The group plays an active role in the archaeological exploration of cenotes, among other things, and hosts regular symposiums and seminars. A small but worthwhile museum in Puerto Aventuras—Museo Sub-Acuático CEDAM (Bldg. F, no phone, 9am-1pm and 2:30pm-5:30pm Mon.-Sat., donation requested)—displays some of the fascinating items the group has recovered in the region's waters over the years.

pillars and swim-throughs, found up and down the coast.

Aquanauts (Bldg. A, tel. 984/873-5041, toll-free U.S. tel. 877/623-2491, www.aquanauts-online.com, 8am-5pm daily) is a full-service shop that enjoys lots of repeat guests. The shop offers the full range of dives and courses, including reef dives (US$49/one tank, US$94/two tanks), cenote dives (US$130/two tanks) and all levels of certification courses. The shop also offers snorkel tours, including one with a stop at Tulum ruins (US$45-90). Reservations are recommended, especially during the high season.

Swimming with Dolphins

Dolphin Discovery (Marina, tel. 984/873-5078, toll-free U.S. tel. 866/393-5158, www.dolphindiscovery.com, 9am-5pm daily) offers several dolphin encounter activities; prices vary according to the duration and degree of interaction (US$79-139 adult, US$79 child). The center also has manatee and sea-lion programs that can be taken in combination with dolphin activities. Programs start at 9am, 11:30am, 1:30pm, and 3:30pm daily; free round-trip shuttle service is available from area hotels.

Sportfishing

Capt. Rick's Sportfishing Center (past Omni Puerto Aventuras hotel, tel. 984/873-5195, toll-free U.S. tel. 888/449-3562, www.fishyucatan.com, office 8am-7pm daily) offers customized fishing trips, both trolling and deep-sea fishing, utilizing a fleet of 10 boats, including a 56-foot yacht with room for up to 15 people. You can also arrange time for visiting a deserted beach or Maya ruin, snorkeling on the reef, or just cruising by upscale homes and

THE RIVIERA MAYA

THE RIVIERA MAYA

© H.W. PRADO

Dolphin encounter programs include a variety of activities, from petting the animals to swimming with them.

hotels. Rates are for half day (US$390-650), three-quarter day (US$560-825), and full day (US$690-1,050).

Sailing

Fat Cat (Bldg. E, tel. 984/873-5899, toll-free Mex. tel. 800/724-5464, www.fatcatsail.com, 8:30am-5pm Mon.-Sat.) offers a spacious custom-designed catamaran used for half-day excursions (US$95 adult, US$59 child 5-12) that include sailing north toward Bahía Ihna, or south toward Xpu-Há—both with good snorkeling in shallow and protected waters.

Golf

Puerto Aventuras Club de Golf (across from Bldg. B, tel. 984/873-5109, www.puertoaventuras.com/golf.html, 7:30am-dusk daily, US$88) offers a nine-hole, par-36 golf course right in town. The course, designed in 1991 by Tom Lehman, is flat but has two par 5s over a total 2,961 yards (3,255 championship).

ACCOMMODATIONS

The road into town bumps right into **Omni Puerto Aventuras Hotel Beach Resort** (tel. 984/875-1950, www.omnihotels.com, US$189-219 s/d with a/c), a small upscale resort with the marina on one side and a fine, palm-shaded beach on the other. There are just 30 rooms, all reasonably spacious and attractive, with colorful regional decor and private patio and hot tub; ocean-view rooms are particularly nice. The resort's small size and low-key atmosphere make it easy to meet other guests, and nighttime typically finds everyone around the main hot tub/beach bar overlooking the ocean.

Casa del Agua (Punta Matzoma 21, tel. 984/873-5184, www.casadelagua.com, US$500 s/d with a/c) is a beacon of class and charm amid the plastic commercialism of Puerto Aventuras. What looks like a private home is actually a boutique hotel with a handful of spacious suites. Each has elegant decor, a king-size bed, and luxurious bathrooms and amenities. There is a small sunny pool and private beach as well as complimentary kayaks and snorkeling gear. Daily maid service and the availability of a private chef are included in the rate. There's a seven-night minimum during the high season, three-night minimum the rest of the year.

FOOD

A short stroll around Puerto Aventuras's marina takes you past pretty much every restaurant in town, including Mexican, Italian, Mediterranean, and American options.

Latitude 20 (across from Dreams Puerto Aventuras Resort, Caleta Xel-ha, tel. 984/128-2933, www.restaurantlatitude20.com, 12:30pm-9:30pm daily, US$5-15) is a popular place serving up simple Caribbean dishes, including lots of seafood. There's live jazz on Tuesday and Saturday nights and happy hour every night 3pm-7pm. Cash only.

Specializing in crepes and smoothies, **Tesoros Café & Curio Shop** (Edif. C, no phone, 8am-8pm, US$4-7) offers a great change of pace, food-wise—or at least a substantial afternoon snack. After eating, browse the curio shop, which has a wide selection of Mexican folk art.

Though it has a limited menu, **Ristorante Massimo** (Bldg. C, tel. 984/873-5418, 3pm-10pm daily, US$9-25) prepares what it does incredibly well. The pastas are freshly made and a variety of sauces makes it tough to choose just one. Nab a table facing the marina if you want to catch the dolphins jumping out of the water.

Café Olé International (Bldg. A, tel. 984/873-5125, 8am-10pm daily, US$5-25) has an extensive menu with something for just about everyone. It's best known, though, for its filet mignon and homemade desserts.

If you're cooking for yourself or just want some fresh fruit, check out the outdoor **fruit and vegetable market** (8:30am-3pm), which is held every Wednesday and Saturday next to the town's kiosk.

Located conveniently across from the Omni hotel, **Super Akumal** (7am-10pm Mon.-Sat., 7am-8pm Sun.) is the local market. Be aware that you can't buy alcohol before 10am or after 9pm Monday-Saturday, nor after 2pm on Sunday. For serious shopping—and better prices—head to the mega store **Chedraui** (tel. 984/802-8773, 7am-8pm daily), located directly across Highway 307 from the Puerto Aventuras entrance.

INFORMATION AND SERVICES
Tourist Information

Despite the numbers of travelers who come to Puerto Aventuras, there is no tourist information office. Nevertheless, the town website—**www.puertoaventuras.com**—is a good resource.

Emergency Services

There is one pharmacy in town: **First Aid Pharmacy** (Bldg. A, tel. 984/873-5305, 8am-10pm daily, or by telephone 24 hours).

Money

Puerto Aventuras doesn't have a bank, but there's a **Banamex ATM** next to Capt. Rick's Sportsfishing Center and a **Santander ATM** near the entrance of Museo CEDAM. Both are accessible 24 hours.

Media and Communications

The **post office** (11am-2:30pm Mon.-Sat.) is in a large kiosk a short distance from the golf club entrance.

The coffee and brownies are great at **Café-C@fé** (Bldg. E, tel. 984/873-5728, 7am-10pm Mon.-Fri., 8am-10pm Sat.-Sun.), where you can get online for US$5 per hour or for much less with a prepaid 5- or 10-hour package. Wi-Fi is free if you buy something to eat or drink.

Laundry

Opposite the post office, **Mikamale Mami** (9am-7pm daily) charges US$1.50 per kilo (2.2 pounds) for next-day pickup, or US$2.25 per kilo for same-day service, both with a three-kilo (6.6-pound) minimum.

GETTING THERE AND AROUND

Arriving by public transportation, you can take a *combi* from Cancún, Playa del Carmen, or Tulum. Let the driver know where you're going, and he'll drop you off on the side of the highway. From there, it's 500 meters (0.3 mile) into town. Arriving by car, you'll pass through a large control gate, but no one who looks like a tourist is stopped.

In Puerto Aventuras, you can walk just about everywhere, as virtually all shops and services are centered around the marina.

Xpu-Há

This long, picturesque beach has clusters of development on either end and practically nothing in between. It seems only a matter of time before the owners of this enviable stretch of sand give their blessing to a megaresort, but for now it's a gorgeous and peaceful spot where you could easily while away the whole day, or several.

SPORTS AND RECREATION
Beach Clubs

La Playa Xpu-Há (Hwy. 307 Km. 265, tel. 984/106-0024, www.laplayaxpuha.com, 10am-6pm daily) is a bustling club that offers a slew of classic beach activities, including parasailing, fishing, snorkeling, and kayaking, all at standard prices. On weekends and holidays, there's a US$2 per person "toll" at the entrance, charged by the landowner for upkeep of the access road. You get it back, though, as a credit on restaurant bills over US$10.

Just down the beach, **Xpu-Há Bonanza** (Hwy. 307 Km. 265, tel. 984/116-4733, 9am-5pm daily, US$3.25) has a much quieter scene, with umbrellas and lounge chairs on the beach (US$16.50/day umbrella and 2 chairs) and a kiosk to rent snorkel gear, kayaks, and more. There's parking and clean bathrooms but no food or drink; bring your own or plan on paying a visit to La Playa, a short walk down the beach.

Snorkeling

In addition to the ocean reef, there's great snorkeling in the numerous cenotes along the inland side of Highway 307, including a cluster just north of Xpu-Há. They vary in size,

but most are like large ponds, some with high or overhanging limestone walls, and all filled with cool crystalline water—heaven on a hot day. The cenote floor is often a jumble of stone slabs and in places quite deep—some even have gaping underwater caves that descend out of sight. The cenotes near Xpu-Há are not, however, the huge stalactite-laden caverns you may have seen in photos; for those, head south to Hidden Worlds or Dos Ojos cenote parks, both near Tulum.

Cenote Cristalino (Hwy. 307, 2 kilometers/1.2 miles north of Xpu-Há, 8am-6pm daily, US$5, no rental gear available). Much of this half-moon-shaped cenote is shallow and covered in algae, but one section extends under a deep overhanging rock ceiling.

Jardín del Edén (formerly Ponderosa Cenote, Hwy. 307, 1.75 kilometers/1 mile north of Xpu-Há, 8am-5pm Sun.-Fri., US$5 adult, US$3 child, US$4.25 mask and snorkel, US$4.25 life vest) is much larger than most cenotes—almost like a small lake—with a craggy floor that makes for fun snorkeling. At one end, the floor falls away into a deep underwater cave, where you can see divers emerging—or disappearing—into the abyss, their halogen lights piercing the shadows. A six-meter (19.7-foot) cliff is fun to jump off; just be alert for divers who may be coming up. Between cave-diving classes, snorkeling groups, and independent travelers, Jardín del Edén can get busy but is generally big enough to make a stop here worthwhile.

At **Cenote Azul** (Hwy. 307, 1.5 kilometers/0.9 mile north of Xpu-Há, 8am-6pm

© GARY CHANDLER

Snorkel, dive, or just enjoy the sun and water at Jardín del Edén, one of dozens of cenotes along the Riviera Maya.

daily, US$5, US$3.75 mask and snorkel, US$3.75 life vest), a few large pools and a section of overhanging rock are the highlights, and walkways along the edges facilitate getting in and out.

Scuba Diving

Bahía Divers (Hwy. 307 Km 265, tel. 984/120-1546, www.bahiadivers.com) operates out of a small hut a short distance down the beach from La Playa Xpu-Há beach club. It offers the full gamut of ocean and cenote dives, plus certification courses and snorkeling and fishing trips, all with the advantage of small groups (6 divers maximum) and personalized service. They also provide transport to and from your hotel, which is very handy. Ocean dives cost US$85 for two tanks, while cenote diving runs US$110 for two tanks, all including gear. Snorkeling trips are US$25 per person in the ocean (minimum 4 people) or US$50 per person in the cenotes (minimum 2 people).

ACCOMMODATIONS AND FOOD

Xpu-Há Bonanza (Hwy. 307 Km. 265, tel. 984/116-4733, US$12.50 pp camping, US$29 RVs, US$71/79 d/t) is a low-key beachfront spot with room for camping and RVs, plus eight large hotel rooms. The latter have two beds and two hammocks and clean cold-water bathrooms, but they lack natural light. Travelers with tents can set up in the sand under a palm tree and have access to clean-ish shared bathrooms. To get here, look for a narrow dirt road with a small sign, just south of the Catalonia Royal Tulum resort.

Hotel Esencia (Hwy. 307 Km. 265, tel. 984/873-4835, toll-free U.S. tel. 877/528-3490, www.hotelesencia.com, US$650 s/d, US$725-935 suite, US$2,179 two-bedroom cottage with pool) is a luxurious private estate turned resort. It boasts 29 gorgeous units, including classy garden-view rooms (some with private plunge pools), larger ocean-view suites, and stunning split-level cottages with private swimming pools and amenities like surround-sound audio systems and electronic window shades. The beach is just steps away and stretches, virtually untouched, for over a mile. Meal plans are available at the hotel's gourmet restaurant, and there's a full-service spa on-site. Service, as expected, is impeccable.

INFORMATION AND SERVICES

There are no services in Xpu-Há, save what's available to guests at the hotels. For Internet cafes, laundry, ATM, and other services, head to Akumal or Puerto Aventuras.

GETTING THERE AND AROUND

Each of the listings for Xpu-Há has its own access road, marked with large or small signs, and located at or near Kilometer 265 on the main coastal highway (Hwy. 307). Catalonia Royal Tulum resort is the largest and most obvious landmark; the other access roads are within a few hundred yards. La Plaza and Xpu-Há Bonanza, at the southern end of the beach, are the best access points if you're only staying the day, and are located 25 kilometers (15.5 miles) south of Playa.

Akumal

Unreachable by land until the 1960s, Akumal (Yucatec Maya for Place of the Turtle) is a quiet destination community that has developed on two bays, known as Akumal Bay and Half Moon Bay. It's a very agreeable mid-range place with sand roads and dozens of condominiums and rental homes. The beach in town is quite nice, if you don't mind the boats occasionally parked on the sand; the beach at Half Moon Bay is narrow and rocky. Just offshore, a spectacular portion of barrier reef makes for great diving and snorkeling, and protects Akumal's bays from heavy surf.

A short distance south of Akumal proper is **Aventuras Akumal,** another small bayside development. It doesn't have the townlike feel or activity that Akumal does, but two good condo-hotels and a truly gorgeous beach make this a tempting alternative. Aventuras Akumal has a separate access road from the highway, and walking there along the beach takes about 45 minutes.

SIGHTS AND BEACHES
Beaches
Akumal Bay—the one right in front of town—has a long, slow-curving shoreline, with soft sand shaded by palm trees. The water is beautiful and there's great snorkeling, including a good chance at spotting sea turtles. It's a bit rocky underfoot, and you should be aware of boat traffic when swimming or snorkeling. **Half Moon Bay** also can be nice for swimming and snorkeling, but there's no beach to speak of. Water shoes are handy in both areas.

【 Laguna Yal-Ku

At the mouth of an elbow-shaped lagoon at the north end of Akumal, an endless upwelling of underground river water collides with the tireless flow of seawater—the result is a great place to snorkel, teeming with fish and plants adapted to this unique hybrid environment. Once a secret snorkeler's getaway, **Laguna Yal-Ku** (9am-5:30pm daily, US$10 adult, US$6 child 4-12, free 3 and under, US$5 apiece for mask, fins, and life vest, US$2 locker) now has a spot in every guidebook and tour group itinerary—come before 10am or anytime on Sunday for the least traffic. (That, and a shot at snagging a private picnic area [US$20], complete with *palapa* shade, a table, and chairs). Use a T-shirt or wetsuit instead of sunscreen, as even the biodegradable kind can collect on plants and coral. The lagoon is dotted with various

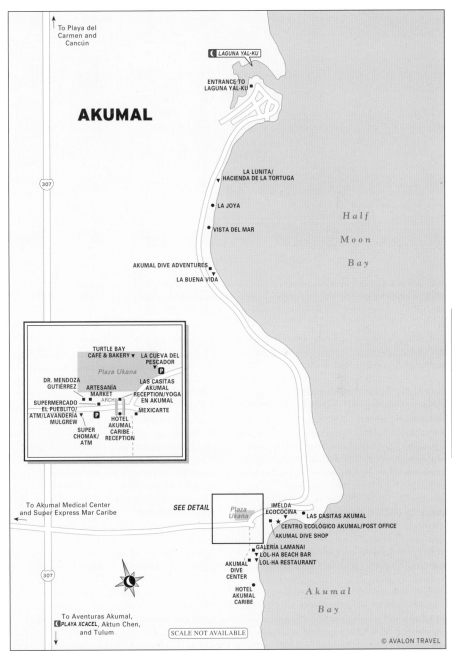

THE RIVIERA MAYA

To Playa del
Carmen and
Cancún

LAGUNA YAL-KU

ENTRANCE TO
LAGUNA YAL-KU

AKUMAL

307

LA LUNITA/
HACIENDA DE LA TORTUGA

LA JOYA

VISTA DEL MAR

AKUMAL DIVE ADVENTURES
LA BUENA VIDA

Half

Moon

Bay

TURTLE BAY
CAFÉ & BAKERY
LA CUEVA DEL
PESCADOR
Plaza Ukana
DR. MENDOZA
GUTIÉRREZ
LAS CASITAS
AKUMAL
RECEPTION/YOGA
EN AKUMAL
ARTESANÍA
MARKET
ARCH
SUPERMERCADO
EL PUEBLITO/
ATM/LAVANDERÍA
MULGREW
MEXICARTE
HOTEL
AKUMAL
CARIBE
RECEPTION
SUPER
CHOMAK/
ATM

To Akumal Medical Center
and Super Express Mar Caribe

SEE DETAIL
Plaza
Ukana
IMELDA
ECOCOCINA
LAS CASITAS AKUMAL
CENTRO ECOLÓGICO AKUMAL/POST OFFICE
AKUMAL DIVE SHOP
GALERÍA LAMANAI
LOL-HA BEACH BAR
LOL-HA RESTAURANT
AKUMAL
DIVE
CENTER
HOTEL
AKUMAL
CARIBE

307

Akumal

Bay

To Aventuras Akumal,
PLAYA XCACEL, Aktun Chen,
and Tulum

SCALE NOT AVAILABLE

© AVALON TRAVEL

THE RIVIERA MAYA

© H.W. PRADO

Sea turtles are a universal favorite among divers and snorkelers, and can even be spotted on boat tours when they come to the surface to breathe.

intriguing bronze sculptures by Mexican artist Alejandro Echeverría.

Centro Ecológico Akumal

Next to Akumal Dive Shop, the **Akumal Ecological Center** (CEA, tel. 984/875-9095, www.ceakumal.org, 9am-1pm and 2pm-6pm Mon.-Fri.) is a nonprofit founded in 1993 to monitor the health of Akumal's ecosystems, particularly related to coral and sea turtles. From May to July, you can join CEA volunteers on nighttime turtle walks, helping move newly laid eggs to protected hatcheries. From August to October, visitors can help release hatchlings into the sea. Both activities are free, but a US$10 donation is appreciated. The center also has free displays and frequent evening lectures on ocean ecology in the high season.

CEA operates long-term volunteer projects on reef monitoring, sea-turtle monitoring, and environmental education projects. Volunteers stay in the center's dorms, with kitchen and

Internet access; minimum age is 21, and some fees are required. See the website for details.

Aktun Chen

Yucatec Maya for Cave with an Underground River, **Aktun Chen** (Hwy. 307 Km. 107, tel. 998/881-9400, www.aktunchen.com, 9am-5pm Mon.-Sat., last tour 1 hour before closing, US$30-97 adult, US$30-58 child) is certainly that, plus a cenote for swimming and snorkeling, and a canopy/zipline route. You can do all three activities, or just the ones that interest you. The cave tour is a walk of about 0.6 kilometer (0.3 mile) amid a breathtaking array of stalactites and stalagmites; at the end is a 12-meter-deep (39-foot) cenote filled with crystalline water. Lighting and a pathway make it accessible to all. You can't swim in that cenote, but there's another nearby, with stairs and platforms for getting in and out. Lastly, the canopy tour is made up of 10 ziplines and two wobbly suspension bridges, covering a full kilometer (0.6 mile). Between activities, check out the park's small "zoo," with spider monkeys, toucans, and more. Admission adds up fast, especially for families, but the experience is memorable.

Tours are offered in English and Spanish and last about 90 minutes. Round-trip transportation is available, or you can go independently—look for the turnoff just across from Aventuras Akumal, and continue three kilometers (1.9 miles) to the entrance. Mosquito repellent and a bottle of water are recommended. You'll encounter the least crowding before 11am and on weekends.

SHOPPING

Mexicarte (tel. 984/875-9115, 9am-9pm daily) is the small, bright-pink shop just inside the arches on your right. The owner hand-selects the best folk art from around the region and country. Prices are high, but so is the quality and artisanship.

Galería Lamanai (tel. 984/875-9055, www.galerialamani.com, 8am-9pm daily) offers similar wares, both in quality and price. The shop is located on the beach near Snack Bar Lol Ha.

There is an open-air *artesanía* **market** behind Playa Ukana, facing the town basketball court. The items are standard Mexican handicrafts, like colorful ceramics from Puebla and textiles from Chiapas.

SPORTS AND RECREATION
Scuba Diving

Some of the Riviera Maya's first scuba divers waded into the waves right here at Akumal Bay, and the area has been special to the sport ever since. Akumal's diving is easy and fun, with a mellow current and moderate depths; few profiles go below 20 meters (66 feet). The reef here is predominantly boulder coral, which isn't as picturesque as other types, but it still teems with tropical fish and plant life.

Founded more than 30 years ago, **Akumal Dive Shop** (tel. 984/875-9032, www.akumaldiveshop.com, 8am-5pm daily) was the first dive shop in the Riviera Maya. Still located on the beach, the shop offers fun dives and various certification courses in both open-water and cave/cavern diving. Divers can take one- or two-tank reef dives (US$50/80), cavern dives (US$140-160), or buy dive packages. Fun dives don't include equipment rental (US$30/day, US$150/week). Open-water certification courses take 3-4 days and cost US$485, equipment and materials included.

Just down the beach, **Akumal Dive Center** (tel. 984/875-9025, U.S. tel. 719/359-9672, www.akumaldivecenter.com, 8am-5pm) offers the same dives and courses at comparable prices.

On Half Moon Bay, **Akumal Dive Adventures** (next to La Buena Vida restaurant, tel. 984/875-9157, toll-free U.S. tel. 877/425-8625, www.akumaldiveadventures.com, 8am-5pm daily) offers somewhat lower prices than the other shops, as well as dive and accommodation packages starting at three nights lodging and four reef dives for US$300/400 per person double/single occupancy. Rooms are at the affiliated Vista del Mar hotel.

Aventuras Akumal has excellent diving and snorkeling, with a calm bay and less traffic than Akumal proper. **Aquatech Dive Center** (Aquatech Villas DeRosa, tel. 984/875-9020, U.S. tel. 801/619-9050, www.cenotes.com) has many years of experience and offers a complete range of dives and courses, with special emphasis on cenote and cave diving. Reef dives run US$45/75 for one/two tanks, while cenote dives are US$75/140. Open-water certification as well as cavern and cave diving instruction are also available.

Snorkeling

Laguna Yal-Ku (9am-5:30pm daily, US$10 adult, US$6 child 4-12, free 3 and under, US$5 apiece for mask, fins, and life vest, US$2 locker) is a favorite among many snorkelers for its large area, calm water, and unique mix of fresh- and saltwater ecosystems.

The dive shops also offer **guided snorkel tours,** which typically last 60-90 minutes and cost around US$25 per person, including gear.

You can **rent snorkel gear** at any of Akumal's dive shops for around US$12 per day or US$60 per week and head out on your own in either Akumal Bay or Half Moon Bay; both have nice coral, plentiful fish, and a good chance of seeing sea turtles. Be alert for boats, especially in Akumal Bay.

Sailing

Akumal Dive Shop (on the beach, tel. 984/875-9032, www.akumaldiveshop.com, 8am-5pm daily) offers a popular Robinson Crusoe cruise: a five-hour excursion on a catamaran sailboat, with stops for fishing and snorkeling (US$95 pp including lunch and equipment). Or try the two-hour Sunset/Moonrise Cruise, which doesn't include fishing and snorkeling, but offers beautiful evening views of the bay (US$45 pp).

Sportfishing

Akumal's dive shops also offer fishing tours year-round. The price, duration, and group size vary considerably based on the season, what kind of fishing you want to do, and the type of boat that's available. That said, expect to pay US$100-200 for a basic two- to three-hour tour with 2-6 anglers; you can usually extend the tour for an additional fee. Fishing is excellent year-round, but April-August are when sailfish and marlin are most prevalent.

Spas and Gyms

Yoga en Akumal (town arch, 2nd Fl., cell. tel. 984/745-3488 or 984/876-2652, www. akumalyoga.com) offers a variety of classes for all experience levels, including Hatha, Vinyasa Flow, and Kundalini, in a breezy studio inside the arch at the entrance to town. Sessions are led by one of four certified instructors; they cost US$15 per class, US$50 for six classes, or US$85 for an unlimited two-week pass; check online for the monthly schedule.

ACCOMMODATIONS

Akumal draws a number of long-term visitors and has a large number of fully equipped condos and villas, in addition to ordinary hotels. There's no hostel, but backpackers might be able snag a dorm room at CEA.

In Town

Centro Ecológico Akumal (CEA, next to Akumal Dive Shop, tel. 984/875-9095, www. ceakumal.org, 9am-1pm and 2pm-6pm Mon.-Fri.) has several large comfortable dorms—most even have air-conditioning—and a well-outfitted communal kitchen. CEA's volunteers have priority for the rooms, and they are usually full, but if not, they're available to walk-ins for US$25 per night (BYO linens).

Hotel Akumal Caribe (reception in the arches at the entrance to town, tel. 984/206-3500, toll-free U.S. tel. 800/351-1622, toll-free Can. tel. 800/343-1440, www.hotelakumalcaribe.com, US$89-134 s/d bungalow, US$169-185 s/d with a/c, US$174 s/d with a/c and kitchenette) is the oldest hotel in town, and it shows. Bungalows and hotel rooms are comfortable enough but, in their decor, they're throwbacks to the 1980s. If you can live with that, you'll enjoy the central location, the ocean views (from the hotel rooms only), the well-kept pool, and, of course, the palm-tree-laden beach. Continental breakfast is included in the rate, too.

On the eastern end of town, **Las Casitas Akumal** (tel. 984/875-9071, toll-free U.S./Can. tel. 800/525-8625, www.lascasitasakumal.com) has 18 airy condominiums, each with two bedrooms, two baths, living room, fully equipped kitchen, and private patio. Some have two floors and space for six people, and most feature bright, colorful Mexican artwork. All have ocean views and direct access to a semiprivate section of the beach. High-season rates average US$295-335 per night, with a seven-night minimum.

Half Moon Bay

Vista del Mar (tel. 984/875-9060, toll-free U.S. tel. 888/425-8625, www.akumalinfo.com, US$90-110 s/d, US$160-250 condo) has 16 spacious condos (studio to three-bedroom) plus 15 smallish hotel rooms, all overlooking a lovely stretch of beach. Condos have long balconies or porches, fully equipped kitchens, separate living and dining rooms, and master bedrooms with king-size beds. Colorful Mexican decor complements modern amenities like flat-screen TVs, mini air conditioners, in-room safes, Wi-Fi, and (in some) whirlpool tubs. Hotel rooms are comfortable but may feel cramped for longer stays. All units have daily maid service and share a well-tended beach with lounge chairs and *palapa* shades.

Hacienda de la Tortuga (tel. 984/875-9068, www.haciendatortuga.com, US$150 one-bedroom apartment, US$200 two-bedroom apartment) has just 16 rooms and cultivates a quiet, relaxed atmosphere geared toward couples. Roomy one-bedroom and two-bedroom condos all have huge ocean-view windows, plus a living room, kitchen, king-size bed(s), and air-conditioning in the bedrooms. Each is uniquely decorated, many with fine Mexican artwork and homey touches like a well-stocked bookcase. There's a small pool just steps from the beach, and a well-regarded Mexican restaurant.

La Joya (Half Moon Bay, U.S. toll-free tel. 877/489-6600, www.i-akumal.com/condominiums, US$115-200) is a great little condominium complex with seven units on three floors, ranging from studio to four-bedroom. The condos are individually owned so they vary in decor and amenities, but all share a high level of comfort and charm, not to mention a lovely beach (with excellent snorkeling), a small newly installed pool, and stellar views from the rooftop terrace. Parking, daily maid service, 24-hour security, on-site management office, and nearby convenience store are all added bonuses.

Aventuras Akumal

Aquatech Villas DeRosa (tel. 984/875-9020, U.S. tel. 801/619-9050, www.cenotes.com, US$80 s/d, US$110-200 condo) offers hotel rooms with garden and pool views, and spacious one-, two-, and three-bedroom condominiums with ocean views and private balconies. All units have air-conditioning, cable TV, Wi-Fi, and stereos, and condos have fully equipped kitchens as well. The bedrooms are a bit dark, but you're literally steps from a glorious white-sand beach lapped by azure water. The resort boasts a full-service dive shop, with

a special emphasis on cenote diving; dive/accommodation packages are available.

Smaller and cozier than the DeRosa, **Villa Las Brisas** (tel. 984/875-9263, www.aventuras-akumal.com, US$45-85 s/d, US$55-90 studio, US$90-150 one-bedroom condo, US$115-230 two-bedroom condo) has just three units, two of which can be combined to make a two-bedroom condo. All are spacious, spotless, and meticulously furnished, down to a stocked spice rack in the kitchen. The condos have large terraces with hammocks and stunning views; the smaller units have balconies that overlook a tidy garden. With comfortable beds, modern Mexican-style furnishings, and space to stretch out, it's easy to feel at home here; families are welcome. Beach chairs and umbrellas are free, while snorkel gear is available for rent. There's a simple mini-mart at the entrance (8am-4pm Mon.-Sat.), but you'll have to go to Akumal for additional shopping and services. There is free Wi-Fi but no air-conditioning.

Rental Properties

The majority of rooms for rent in Akumal are in privately owned homes and condos, especially along Half Moon Bay. Most are managed and rented by one of various property management companies; browse the listings of several agencies to get the best selection. Some reliable agencies include **Caribbean Fantasy** (www.caribbfan.com, toll-free U.S. tel. 800/523-6618), **Akumal Villas** (www.akumalvillas.com, toll-free U.S. tel. 866/535-1324), **Akumal Rentals** (www.akumal-rentals.com, U.S. tel. 815/642-4580), and **Loco Gringo** (www.locogringo.com, no phone).

FOOD
In Town

Lol-Ha Restaurant (Hotel Akumal Caribe, tel. 984/875-9014, www.hotelakumalcaribe.com, 7:30am-11am and 6:30pm-10pm daily, closed Oct. to mid-Nov., US$12-35) is Akumal's finest restaurant, with a beautiful wood and stucco dining room topped with a high *palapa* roof that opens onto a pleasant veranda.

Expect excellent seafood and Mexican and American specialties, including prime USDA steaks, grilled ahi tuna, and flambé specials prepared tableside. During high season, enjoy flamenco performances on Wednesday, and a Latin strings and percussion trio on Thursday; additional events are posted at the restaurant, and a small per-person cover charge is usually added to the bill. Reservations are highly recommended.

Next door, **Lol-Ha Beach Bar** (noon-9pm daily, US$8-14) serves the best hamburgers on the beach, and tasty tacos, too (the *tacos de cochinita* are particularly good). Three 32-inch TVs always have a sporting event on, whether Monday Night Football, March Madness, or the Kentucky Derby; hundreds of people turn out for the annual Super Bowl and Academy Awards parties (proceeds of which go to local community groups). Kids will love the adjacent game room with air hockey and foosball.

For a fresh, healthy meal, try **Imelda Ecococina** (no phone, 8am-9pm daily, US$3-6), next to Centro Ecológico Akumal. Breakfast options include eggs, omelets, pancakes, and French toast. For lunch, the *comida corrida* comes with a choice of main plate and a side dish or two. On Monday and Friday, the restaurant hosts a popular Maya buffet (7pm, US$20) followed by *cumbia* tunes and dancing.

In Plaza Ukana, ⟨ **Turtle Bay Café & Bakery** (tel. 984/875-9138, www.turtlebay-cafe.com, 7am-9pm Mon.-Sat., 7am-4pm Sun., US$5-20) offers creative comfort food like crab cakes, seafood-stuffed chiles rellenos, and "Black and Bleu" salad. For breakfast, try the famous sticky buns and eggs Benedict. Enjoy your meal surrounded by palm trees, either in the outdoor *palapa*-roofed dining room or on the porch of the main building. Free Wi-Fi is available.

For fresh seafood, check out **La Cueva del Pescador** (Plaza Ukana, tel. 984/875-9205, noon-9pm daily, US$5-25). Sink your teeth into fish kabobs, shrimp prepared nine different ways (e.g., grilled, à la tequila, with curry salsa, and so on), and lobster—most caught the

day you order it. The bar is especially popular on weekends.

For groceries, the best prices are across from the Akumal turnoff on Highway 307 in **Super Express Mar Caribe** (Av. Gonzalo Guerrero, 7am-11pm daily); look for the store about 100 meters (328 feet) west of the highway. Otherwise, just outside the arch, **Super Chomak** and **Supermercado El Pueblito** (both 7:30am-9pm daily) charge an arm and a leg for canned and dried food, soups and pastas, fresh and packaged meat, booze, and basics like sunscreen and bug repellent. All the markets also sell fresh fruit and veggies, but you may find a better selection at the **farmers market** held Wednesday and Saturday in Plaza Ukana.

Half Moon Bay

A fantastic flying serpent skeleton greets diners at **La Buena Vida** (Vista del Mar, tel. 984/875-9061, http://labuenavidarestaurant.com, 11am-11pm daily, US$6-27), where clients enjoy the varied menu—from hamburgers to shrimp ceviche—under *palapa*-shaded tables on the beach. If you've already had lunch, consider just stopping in for a drink at the swing-lined bar; happy hour runs 5pm-7pm.

⟨ **La Lunita** (Hacienda de la Tortuga, tel. 984/875-9070, www.lalunita-akumal.com, 11am-11pm daily, US$8-25) is an intimate bistro serving gourmet Mexican and international dishes, both small plates or full entrées. Seafood is king here, though there are plenty of options for vegetarians and serious meat eaters. With only a handful of tables, some overlooking the Caribbean, La Lunita is a perfect place for a romantic dinner—just be sure to make reservations.

INFORMATION AND SERVICES
Tourist Information

Akumal doesn't have an official tourist office, but it's a small town, and you can probably find what you're looking for by asking the first person you see. If that fails, the folks at **Centro Ecológico Akumal** (CEA, next to Akumal Dive Shop, tel. 984/875-9095, www.ceakumal.org,

9am-1pm and 2pm-6pm Mon.-Fri.) are friendly and well informed, and most speak English.

Emergency Services

Across the highway, **Akumal Medical Center** (Av. Gonzalo Guerrero, tel. 984/875-9090, 984/806-4616, or 984/876-2250, 8am-4pm Mon.-Sat., on call 24/7) is the medical office of longtime Akumal provider Dr. Néstor Mendoza Gutiérrez. He also has a small office facing Plaza Ukana. Pharmacy, ambulance, and house calls are available.

The **police** can be reached by calling 060 from any public phone.

Money

There is no bank in town, but there are **ATMs** inside Akumal's small supermarkets, near the town arch: **Super Chomak** and **Supermercado El Pueblito** (both 7:30am-9pm daily). They are sometimes out of cash, however, so plan accordingly.

Media and Communications

The **post office** (9:30am-3pm Tues. and Thurs.) is inside the Centro Ecológico Akumal, in the center of town.

Many hotels offer Wi-Fi to guests, as does **Turtle Bay Café & Bakery** (tel. 984/875-9138, www.turtlebaycafe.com, 7am-9pm Mon.-Sat., 7am-4pm Sun.) in Plaza Ukana.

Laundry

Lavandería Mulgrew (7am-noon and 5pm-7pm Mon.-Sat.) charges US$1.75 per kilo (2.2 pounds) and provides same-day service if you drop off your load before 8:30am (2-kilo/4.4-pound minimum). Look for it next to Supermercado El Pueblito, near the town arch.

GETTING THERE AND AROUND

The turnoff to Akumal is between kilometers 254 and 255 on the main highway. For

© GARY CHANDLER

Believe it or not, the Riviera Maya still has long stretches of untouched beach, including gorgeous Playa Xcacel.

Aventuras Akumal, the access road is just south of the main Akumal entrance; look for the sign to Hotel Villas DeRosa, as the community itself isn't well signed.

Bus and *Combi*

Combis and second-class buses stop at the Akumal turnoff, but it's a kilometer (0.6 mile) walk into town. Likewise, you can manage the center area by foot, but walking to and from Half Moon Bay can be long, hot, and dusty. Consider hiring a cab, which are often parked just outside the town arches.

Combis and second-class buses also stop at the Aventuras Akumal entrance; it's only about 500 meters (0.3 mile) into the community from there.

Car

If you drive into town, there is a **public parking lot** (7am-4pm daily, US$1.75/hour) in front of Plaza Ukana. Some shops and restaurants can validate your parking—be sure to bring your receipt. Parking is free after hours.

Taxi

Taxis gather near the Super Chomak grocery store at the entrance of Akumal, just outside of the arches. A ride from town to Laguna Yal-Ku costs US$5.

◖ PLAYA XCACEL

For all the breakneck construction along the Riviera Maya, much of the coastline remains virtually untouched, including some gorgeous stretches of white-sand beach. **Playa Xcacel** (Hwy. 307 Km. 247.5, 9am-6pm daily, US$2) is one of those, a gently curving band of thick white sand, with only a small parking lot, restrooms, and changing area, and popular with local residents. Xcacel's pristine state is thanks in part to the fact that sea turtles nest here, and development is restricted by federal law. Along the inland edge of the beach are scores of wood blades with dates on them, marking where and when sea turtles laid eggs; needless to say, do not move the markers or disturb the nests! A small freshwater cenote is located down a slippery path, about 350 meters (0.2 mile) south of the main entrance. The turnoff to Playa Xcacel is easy to miss, but it's located 11 kilometers (7 miles) north of Tulum, just south of Chemuyil community.

Tankah Tres and Soliman Bay

Tucked innocuously between Akumal and Tulum, Tankah Tres and Soliman Bay see only a fraction of the tourist traffic that its better-known neighbors do. But that's just the way visitors to this little stretch of coastline prefer it, enjoying excellent snorkeling, diving, and pretty beaches, with a sense of isolation that's hard to find in these parts. The area has three small bays, and the scattered hotels, villas, and private homes along their shores were once connected by a U-shaped access road. But development cut the *U* in half; the southern entrance is still marked Tankah Tres, while the northern entrance has a sign for Soliman Bay.

SIGHTS AND BEACHES

Playa Tankah

The handful of hotels here have nice beachfronts along three sandy bays. If you aren't staying at one of the hotels, **Casa Cenote** (1.5 kilometers/0.9 mile from the turnoff, tel. 521/984-6996, www.casacenote.com) allows nonguests to enjoy the hotel beach and lounge chairs if they order something at the restaurant.

Cenote Manatí

Across from Casa Cenote (and sometimes called by the same name), **Cenote Manatí** (1.5 kilometers/0.9 mile from the turnoff, no phone, sunrise-sunset, US$2) is a series of

© LIZA PRADO

Tankah Tres and Soliman Bay are quiet getaways with just a handful of hotels and rental properties.

THE RIVIERA MAYA

interconnected cenotes and lagoons extending from the road well inland. (An underground channel drains into the ocean.) The crystal-clear water, winding channels, and tangle of rocks, trees, and freshwater plants along the edges and bottom all make for terrific snorkeling. Look for schools of tiny fish near the surface and some bigger ones farther down.

ACCOMMODATIONS

Tankah Inn (southern entrance, 1.1 kilometers/0.6 mile from the turnoff, cell. tel. 984/100-0703, U.S. tel. 918/582-3743, www.tankah.com, US$111 s/d with a/c) has five spacious rooms with murals of Maya temples. Each room has a private terrace and ocean views; all feature minifridges, drinking water, and remote-controlled air-conditioning. A breezy common room has sweeping views of the Caribbean—comfy chairs and tables, lots of board games, and an honor bar make this a popular place to hang out. The beach, with its lounge chairs and hammocks, is a tempting

alternative. À la carte breakfast is included, as is use of the kayaks, snorkel gear, and Wi-Fi.

The first hotel on this bay, **Casa Cenote** (southern entrance, 1.5 kilometers/0.9 mile from the turnoff, tel. 521/984-6996, www.casacenote.com, US$125 s/d with shared bath, US$175 s/d with a/c) remains an area favorite. Large beachfront rooms have air-conditioning, one or two large beds, Wi-Fi, and fine ocean views. Decor is tasteful but low-key, with a large stucco relief of a Maya god in each room. There also are "eco accommodations"—very basic bungalows with shared bathroom and outdoor kitchen—that are too pricey considering how rustic they are. The hotel has a lovely beachfront pool, and Cenote Manatí is just across the street; guests can use the hotel's kayaks and snorkeling gear as well. Breakfast is included. A large five-bedroom house also is available for rent nearby.

In the process of being renovated when we passed through, **Blue Sky Hotel** (southern entrance, 1.7 kilometers/1 mile from the turnoff,

U.S. tel. 306/972-4283, www.blueskymexico.com, US$130-325 s/d with a/c) offers six breezy units occupying two matching towers, with views of the Caribbean that improve with each level. A nice pool faces the beach, where there are plenty of toys—kayaks, boogie boards, and snorkel gear—for guests to use. The shoreline and shallows can be quite rocky, which accounts for the excellent snorkeling but can be off-putting to some; in any case, bring water shoes.

Slice of Paradise (southern entrance, 2 kilometers/1.2 miles from the turnoff, www.sliceofparadise.com, US$2,000/week house, US$150 casita, US$125 *cabaña*) lives up to its name with a spacious house, smaller "casita," and two simple *cabañas,* for rent by the day or week. The house has a full-size kitchen, separate sitting and dining areas, and dramatic bay windows facing the beach. The casita also has kitchen and bath; both the house and casita have window-unit air conditioners. The two *palapa*-roofed *cabañas* are fan cooled, one with en suite bathroom, the other not. Decor is simple and tasteful throughout, and there's Wi-Fi and daily maid service.

A gorgeous boutique hotel, **◖ Jashita Hotel** (northern entrance, 1.2 kilometers/0.7 mile from the turnoff, tel. 984/139-5131, www.jashitahotel.com, US$210 s/d with a/c, US$440-1,800 suite) sits on the curving Soliman Bay. It's an intimate place with elegant rooms that have marble floors, fine hardwoods, basin sinks, rainfall showerheads—some even have private plunge pools. The common areas are just as opulent without being snooty; if anything, the fine art and high-end furnishings make you feel like you're staying at a very wealthy friend's home. There's also a great pool, a gourmet restaurant, and a breathtaking beach. Use of kayaks and snorkel gear is included in the rate, as is breakfast. There's a minimum three-night stay; five-night minimum December 20-January 10.

FOOD

The restaurant at **Casa Cenote** (1.5 kilometers/0.9 mile from the turnoff, tel. 521/984-6996, www.casacenote.com, 8am-9pm daily, US$7-18) has a breezy patio dining area just steps from the ocean. You can order beach food such as quesadillas or a guacamole plate, or something heftier—the seafood is always tasty and fresh. Every Sunday at noon, the hotel hosts an awesome Texas-style barbecue (US$12.50) that is popular with expats up and down the Riviera Maya.

The **◖ Blue Sky Hotel** (southern entrance, 1.7 kilometers/1 mile from the turnoff, U.S. tel. 306/972-4283, www.blueskymexico.com, 7:30am-10:30pm Tues.-Sun., 3pm-10:30pm Mon., US$7-24) specializes in Italian food, prepared to order, with simple but beautiful presentation. The pizza is famously good, handmade with fresh ingredients and baked in a custom brick oven. But appetizers like ceviche and mains like grilled calamari with vegetables are also worth sampling—you'll just have to come back more than once! With only a handful of tables, it's ideal for an intimate dinner.

INFORMATION AND SERVICES

There are no formal services here, because it's not really a formal town. Head to Tulum for ATMs, medical services, Internet, groceries, and more.

GETTING THERE AND AROUND

The turnoff to the southern portion of Tankah Tres is between kilometers 237 and 238 on the main highway, and marked with a large road sign. Driving south from Cancún, you'll have to overshoot the entrance a short distance until a break in the median (at Dreams Tulum Resort and Spa) allows you to make a U-turn and return to the turnoff; this access road makes a beeline for the shore, then turns abruptly to the left, hugging the beach and passing the listed hotels and sights. The access road to the northern section is a bit farther and is marked with a large sign for Lalo's Restaurant, which is actually on the west side of the highway. If you don't have a car, you can ask a *combi* to drop you at either turnoff, but it will not enter Tankah Tres or Soliman Bay itself.

TULUM AND SOUTHERN QUINTANA ROO

Tulum has long been favored by travelers who cringe at the splashy resorts and package tourism found in Cancún (and increasingly the Riviera Maya). In that sense, Tulum is a fitting bridge between Quintana Roo's booming northern section and its far-less-traveled south. Tulum has so far managed to avoid the impulse to fill the coast with ever-bigger resorts; prices have

Highlights

LOOK FOR ◖ TO FIND RECOMMENDED SIGHTS, ACTIVITIES, DINING, AND LODGING.

◖ **Tulum's Southern Beaches:** Mile after mile of powdery white sand, tranquil turquoise water, cozy bungalows peeking out from behind softly bending palm trees: These are the beaches you've been dreaming of and the reason you came to the Caribbean in the first place (page 193).

◖ **Cenotes near Tulum:** Sure the ocean reefs are gorgeous, but don't miss a chance to explore these eerie and unforgettable limestone caverns, bristling with stalagmites and stalactites, and filled with the crystalline water of the world's longest underground river system (page 193).

◖ **Bahía de la Ascensión:** A huge protected expanse of calm ocean flats and tangled mangrove forests make this a world-class destination for bird-watchers and anglers. Take an all-day tour from Tulum or sit back and stay awhile at a homey lodge or bed-and-breakfast in Punta Allen (page 210).

◖ **Banco Chinchorro:** A punishing two-hour boat ride across the open sea is rewarded with spectacular diving on one of the world's largest coral atolls. And now you can stay the night, doubling your diving pleasure (page 226).

◖ **Fuerte San Felipe Bacalar:** Housed in a stout star-shaped fort, this small-town museum

has fascinating and innovative displays on piracy and the Caste War. It overlooks beautiful Laguna Bacalar, which the Maya called Lake of Seven Colors (page 232).

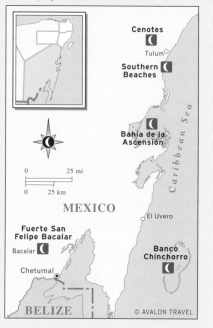

certainly gone up, but there are still no mega-developments here, or even power lines for that matter. Its beaches and *cabañas* remain as idyllic as ever.

If Tulum is the anti-Cancún, you might call southern Quintana Roo the non-Cancún. Though fairly close in distance, it's worlds apart by any other measure. Immediately south of Tulum is the massive Sian Ka'an Biosphere Reserve, one of the Yucatán's largest and richest preserves, whose bays, lagoons, mangrove stands, and inland forests support a vast array of plants and animals, from

dolphins to jaguars; there's even a large Maya ruin and several smaller temples. Beyond Sian Ka'an is the "Costa Maya," a fancy term for the sparsely populated stretch of coast reaching down to the Belize border; the largest towns are Mahahual and Xcalak, with numerous small bed-and-breakfasts and seaside hotels in both (and a highly incongruous cruise ship port in Mahahual). Most of the beaches aren't postcard perfect like Tulum's, but the isolation—not to mention the far-less-expensive lodging—are hard to match. Inland and farther south is the multicolored Laguna Bacalar and several

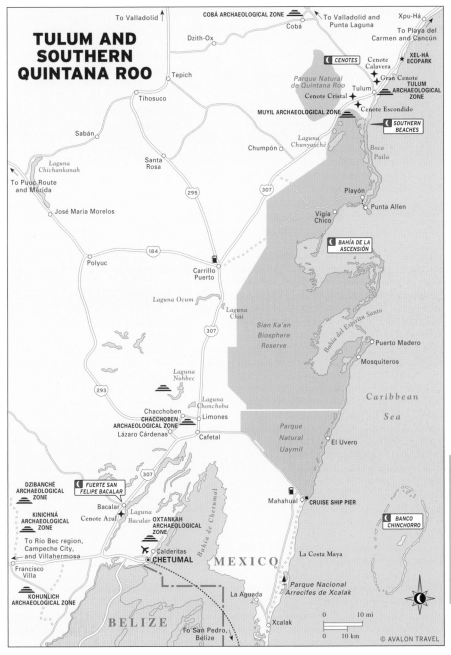

TULUM AND SOUTHERN QUINTANA ROO

To Valladolid

COBÁ ARCHAEOLOGICAL ZONE

Cobá

To Valladolid and Punta Laguna

Xpu-Há

To Playa del Carmen and Cancún

Dzith-Ox

XEL-HÁ ECOPARK

CENOTES

Cenote Calavera

Tepich

Parque Natural de Quintana Roo

Gran Cenote

TULUM ARCHAEOLOGICAL ZONE

Tulum

Tihosuco

Cenote Cristal

MUYIL ARCHAEOLOGICAL ZONE

Cenote Escondido

SOUTHERN BEACHES

Sabán

Laguna Chunyaxché

Chumpón

Boca Paila

Laguna Chichankanah

Santa Rosa

To Puuc Route and Mérida

295

307

Playón

Punta Allen

José Maria Morelos

Vigía Chico

184

BAHÍA DE LA ASCENSIÓN

Polyuc

Carrillo Puerto

Laguna Ocum

Laguna Chai

Sian Ka'an Biosphere Reserve

Bahía del Espíritu Santo

Puerto Madero

307

Mosquiteros

Laguna Nohbec

293

Caribbean Sea

Laguna Chonchoba

Chacchoben

CHACCHOBEN ARCHAEOLOGICAL ZONE

Limones

Lázaro Cárdenas

Cafetal

Parque Natural Uaymil

El Uvero

307

DZIBANCHÉ ARCHAEOLOGICAL ZONE

FUERTE SAN FELIPE BACALAR

Mahahual

CRUISE SHIP PIER

BANCO CHINCHORRO

KINICHNÁ ARCHAEOLOGICAL ZONE

Bacalar

Cenote Azul

Laguna Bacalar

OXTANKAH ARCHAEOLOGICAL ZONE

Bahía de Chetumal

To Río Bec region, Campeche City, and Villahermosa

Calderitas

CHETUMAL

MEXICO

La Costa Maya

Francisco Villa

Parque Nacional Arrecifes de Xcalak

KOHUNLICH ARCHAEOLOGICAL ZONE

La Aguada

BELIZE

To San Pedro, Belize

Xcalak

0   10 mi

0   10 km

© AVALON TRAVEL

significant but all-but-forgotten Maya ruins. Chetumal, the state capital, isn't much of a destination itself but has some unexpectedly appealing areas nearby, and is the gateway to Belize.

PLANNING YOUR TIME

Tulum is the first stop, of course, and for many people their main destination. From Tulum you can take day trips or short overnighters to Sian Ka'an reserve and Cobá archaeological site, both fascinating. To venture any farther south you'll probably want a rental car, as bus service grows infrequent. Mahahual and Xcalak are certainly worth savoring; despite their isolation, there's plenty to do in both, including snorkeling, diving, kayaking, fishing, and, of course, just relaxing. Laguna Bacalar is worth a day or possibly two, to take a boat trip on the Caribbean-like water, swim in Cenote Azul, and visit the surprisingly good history museum in town. Chetumal is a logical stopover for those headed west toward the Río Bec region or crossing into Belize, and it has an interesting Maya museum.

Tulum

Tulum is the subject of a thousand postcards, and justly so. It's hard to know if the name is more closely associated with the ancient Maya ruins—perched dramatically on a cliff overlooking the Caribbean—or the idyllic beaches and oceanfront *cabañas* that have long been the jewel of the Riviera Maya. What's certain is that Tulum manages to capture both the ancient mystery and modern allure of Mexico's Riviera Maya.

Tulum has definitely grown and changed, with more changes on the way. The beach used to be a haven for backpackers and bohemians, with simple *cabañas* facing beautiful untouched beaches. The beaches are still beautiful, but the prices have long since gone through the *palapa* roof, catering more to urban escapists and upscale yoga groups. It's still a lovely place to stay, no matter who you are, just not as cheap as it used to be.

One consequence of the spike in prices on the beach is that the inland village of Tulum (aka Tulum Pueblo) has perked up significantly. Long a dumpy roadside town, it now has a growing number of hotels, B&Bs, and recommendable restaurants catering to independent travelers who have been priced out of the beachfront hotels. To be sure, a beachside *cabaña* will always be the most appealing place to stay in Tulum—and there are a handful of bargains still to be had—but staying in town is no longer the huge step down that it once was.

ORIENTATION

The name Tulum is used for three separate areas, which can be confusing. The first is Tulum archaeological zone, the scenic and popular Maya ruins. This is the first part of Tulum you encounter as you drive south from Cancún. A kilometer and a half (1 mile) farther south (and well inland) is the town of Tulum, known as Tulum Pueblo, where you'll find the bus terminal, supermarket, and numerous restaurants, hotels, Internet cafés, and other shops. The third area is Tulum's beachfront hotel zone, or Zona Hotelera. Located due east of Tulum Pueblo, the Zona Hotelera extends for almost 10 kilometers (6 miles) from the Maya ruins to the entrance of the Sian Ka'an Biosphere Reserve, with fantastic beaches and bungalow-style hotels virtually the entire way. There's a walking path, but no road, connecting the Tulum ruins to the upper end of Tulum's Zona Hotelera.

TULUM ARCHAEOLOGICAL ZONE

The Maya ruins of **Tulum** (8am-5pm daily, US$4.75) are one of Mexico's most scenic archaeological sites, built atop a 12-meter

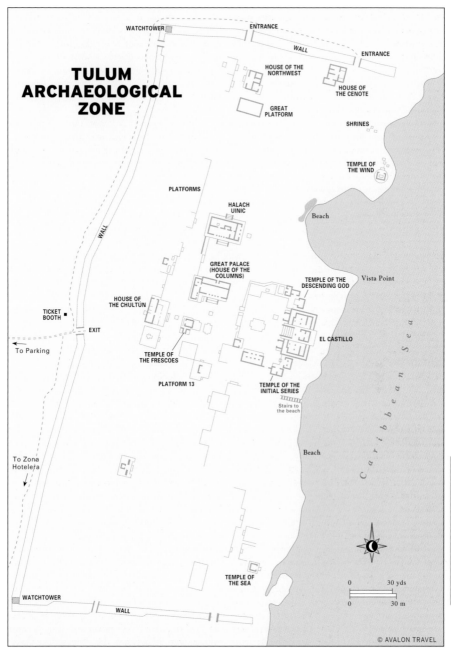

TULUM
ARCHAEOLOGICAL
ZONE

WATCHTOWER

ENTRANCE

WALL

ENTRANCE

HOUSE OF THE
NORTHWEST

HOUSE OF
THE CENOTE

GREAT
PLATFORM

SHRINES

TEMPLE OF
THE WIND

PLATFORMS

HALACH
UINIC

Beach

GREAT PALACE
(HOUSE OF THE
COLUMNS)

TEMPLE OF THE
DESCENDING GOD

Vista Point

HOUSE OF
THE CHULTÚN

TICKET
BOOTH

EXIT

To Parking

TEMPLE OF
THE FRESCOES

EL CASTILLO

PLATFORM 13

TEMPLE OF THE
INITIAL SERIES

Stairs to
the beach

To Zona
Hotelera

Beach

WALL

WATCHTOWER

WALL

TEMPLE OF
THE SEA

Caribbean Sea

0   30 yds
0   30 m

© AVALON TRAVEL

(40-foot) cliff rising abruptly from turquoise Caribbean waters. The structures don't compare in grandeur to those of Cobá, Uxmal, or elsewhere, but are interesting and significant nevertheless.

Tulum is the single most frequently visited Maya ruin in the Yucatán Peninsula, receiving thousands of visitors every day, most on package tours from nearby resorts. (In fact, it's second only to Teotihuacán, near Mexico City, as the country's most-visited archaeological site.) For that reason, the first and most important piece of advice for independent travelers regarding Tulum is to **arrive early.** It used to be that the tour bus madness didn't begin until 11am, but it creeps earlier and earlier every year. Still, if you're there right at 8am, you'll have the ruins mostly to yourself for an hour or so—which is about all you need for this small site—before the hordes descend. Guides can be hired at the entrance for around US$35 for 1-4 people. Bring your swimsuit if you fancy a morning swim: This is the only Maya ruin with a great little beach right inside the archaeological zone.

History

Tulum was part of a series of Maya forts and trading outposts established along the Caribbean coast from the Gulf of Mexico as far south as present-day Honduras. Its original name was Zamá-Xamanzamá or simply Zamá (derived from *zamal*, or dawn) but was later called Tulum, Yucatec Maya for fortification or city wall, in reference to the thick stone barrier that encloses the city's main structures. Measuring 380 by 165 meters (1,250 by 540 feet), it's the largest fortified Maya site on the Quintana Roo coast (though small compared to most inland ruins).

Tulum's enviable patch of seashore was settled as early as 300 BC, but it remained little more than a village for most of its existence, overshadowed by the Maya city of Tankah a few kilometers to the north. Tulum gained prominence between the 12th and 16th centuries (the Late Post-Classic era), when mostly non-Maya immigrants repopulated the Yucatan

Peninsula following the general Maya collapse several centuries prior. Tulum's strategic location and convenient beach landing made it a natural hub for traders, who plied the coast in massive canoes measuring up to 16 meters (52 feet) long, laden with honey, salt, wax, animal skins, vanilla, obsidian, amber, and other products.

It was during this Post-Classic boom period that most of Tulum's main structures were built. Although influenced by Mayapán (the reigning power at the time) and Central Mexican city-states, from which many of Tulum's new residents had emigrated, Tulum's structures mostly exemplify "east coast architecture," defined by austere designs with relatively little ornamentation and a predominantly horizontal orientation (compared to high-reaching pyramids elsewhere). Ironically, construction in these later eras tended to be rather shoddy, thanks in part to improvements in stucco coverings that meant the quality of underlying masonry was not as precise. Today, with the stucco eroded away, Tulum's temples appear more decayed than structures at other sites, even those built hundreds of years prior.

The Spanish got their first view of Tulum, and of mainland indigenous society, on May 7, 1518, when Juan de Grijalva's expedition along the Quintana Roo coast sailed past the then brightly colored fortress. The chaplain of the fleet famously described the city as "a village so large that Seville would not have appeared larger or better." Tulum remained an important city and port until the mid-1500s, when European-borne diseases decimated its population. The once-grand city was effectively abandoned and, for the next three centuries, slowly consumed by coastal vegetation. In 1840, Spanish explorers referred to an ancient walled city known as Tulum, the first recorded use of its current name; two years later the famous American/English team of John Lloyd Stephens and Frederick Catherwood visited Tulum, giving the world its first detailed description and illustrations of the dramatic seaside site. During the Caste

© LIZA PRADO

Archaeologists aren't really sure what purpose these miniature structures (dubbed the "Shrines") at Tulum's Temple of the Wind served.

War, Tulum was occupied by members of the Talking Cross cult, including the followers of a Maya priestess known as the Queen of Tulum.

House of the Cenote

The path from the ticket booth follows Tulum's wall around the northwest corner to two low corbel arch entryways. Using the second entrance (closest to the ocean), you'll first see the Casa del Cenote. The two-room structure, with a third chamber added later, is less impressive than the gaping maw of its namesake cenote. The water is not drinkable, thanks to saltwater intrusion, but that may not have been the case a half millennium ago; it's unlikely Tulum could have grown to its size and prominence without a major water source, not only for its own residents but passing traders as well. Cenotes were also considered apertures to Xibalba, or the underworld, and an elaborate tomb discovered in the floor of the House of the Cenote suggests it may have had a ceremonial function as well.

Temple of the Wind

Following the path, the next major structure is the Temple of the Wind, perched regally atop a rocky outcrop overlooking a picturesque sandy cove. If it looks familiar, that's because it appears on innumerable postcards, magazine photos, and tourist brochures. (The view is even better from a vista point behind El Castillo, and of course from the ocean.) The name derives from the unique circular base upon which the structure is built: In Central Mexican cosmology, the circle is associated with the god of the wind, and its presence here (and at other ruins, like San Gervasio on Isla Cozumel) is evidence of the strong influence that Central Mexican migrants/invaders had on Post-Classic Maya societies.

Temple of the Descending God

One of Tulum's more curious structures is the Temple of the Descending God, named for the upside-down winged figure above its doorway. Exactly who or what the figure represents is

TULUM AND QUINTANA ROO

disputed among archaeologists—theories include Venus, the setting sun, the god of rain, even the god of bees (as honey was one of the coastal Maya's most widely traded products). Whatever the answer, it was clearly a deeply revered (or feared) deity, as the same image appears on several of Tulum's buildings, including the upper temple of Tulum's main pyramid. The Temple of the Descending God also is notable for its cartoonish off-kilter position, most likely the result of poor construction.

El Castillo

Tulum's largest and most imposing structure is The Castle, a 12-meter-high (40-foot) pyramid constructed on a rocky bluff of roughly the same height. Like many Maya structures, El Castillo was built in multiple phases. The first iteration was a low broad platform, still visible today, topped by a long palace fronted by a phalanx of stout columns. The second phase consisted of simply filling in the center portion of the original palace to create a base for a new and loftier temple on top. In the process, the builders created a vaulted passageway and inner chamber, in which a series of intriguing frescoes were housed; unfortunately, you're not allowed to climb onto the platform to see them. The upper temple (also off-limits) displays Central Mexican influence, including snakelike columns similar to those found at Chichén Itzá and grimacing Toltec masks on the corners. Above the center door is an image of the Descending God. Archaeologists believe a stone block at the top of the stairs may have been used for sacrifices.

Temple of the Frescoes

Though quite small, the Temple of the Frescoes is considered one of Tulum's most archaeologically significant structures. The name owes to the fading but remarkably detailed paintings on the structure's inner walls. In shades of blue, gray, and black, they depict various deities, including Chaac (the god of rain) and Ixchel (the goddess of the moon and fertility), and a profusion of symbolic imagery, including corn and flowers. On the temple's two facades are carved

figures with elaborate headdresses and yet another image of the Descending God. The large grim-faced masks on the temple's corners are believed to represent Izamná, the Maya creator god.

Halach Uinic and the Great Palace

In front of El Castillo are the remains of two palatial structures: the House of the Halach Uinic and the Great Palace (also known as the House of the Columns). Halach Uinic is a Yucatec Maya term for king or ruler, and this structure seems to have been an elaborate shrine dedicated to Tulum's enigmatic Descending God. The building is severely deteriorated, but what remains suggests its facade was highly ornamented, perhaps even painted blue and red. Next door is the Great Palace, which likely served as residential quarters for Tulum's royal court.

Practicalities

Tulum's massive parking lot and strip-mall-like visitors complex ought to clue you in to the number of tourists that pass through here every day. (Did we mention to get here early?) You'll find a small museum and bookshop amid innumerable souvenir shops and fast-food restaurants. (If this is your first visit to a Maya ruin, don't be turned off by all the hubbub. Tulum is unique for its excessive and obnoxious commercialization; most sites have just a ticket booth and restrooms.)

The actual entrance and ticket booth are about one kilometer (0.6 mile) from the visitors center; it's a flat mild walk, but there are also **trolleys** that ferry guests back and forth for US$2.25 per person round-trip (kids under 10 ride free).

Getting There

The Tulum archaeological zone is a kilometer (0.6 mile) north of Tulum Pueblo on Highway 307. There are two entrances; the one farther south is newer and better, leading directly to the main parking lot (parking US$4). Arriving by bus or *combi,* be sure to ask the driver to let you off at *las ruínas* (the ruins) as opposed to the town. To return, flag down a bus or *combi* on the highway.

BEACHES AND CENOTES
Northern Beaches
The road from Tulum Pueblo hits the coast near the upper end of the Zona Hotelera, which stretches from the archaeological zone down to the entrance of Sian Ka'an reserve, almost exactly 10 kilometers (6 miles). The area north of the Tulum/Zona Hotelera junction has two easy-to-reach beach areas that are ideal for people staying in town.

Playa El Paraíso (Carr. Tulum-Punta Allen, 2 kilometers/1.2 miles north of junction, cell. tel. 984/113-7089, www.elparaisotulum.com, 8am-6pm daily, beach bar 8pm-midnight Thurs.-Sat.) is a popular beach club on a scenic beach of the same name. Once little more than a bar and some hammocks, the beach club has grown popular with tour groups and has morphed into a bustling expanse of lounge chairs, beach beds, and umbrellas (US$2-20/day), with waiters weaving between them. There's a full restaurant and beach bar, and the nearby water sports center offers snorkeling, diving, kiteboarding, and more. It's busy but still scenic and relaxing.

Directly north of Playa El Paraíso is **Playa Mar Caribe,** named after the rustic bungalows that have long fronted this portion of beach. Broad and unspoiled, this is a great place to come to lay out your towel on the soft white sand, which you share with a picturesque array of moored fishing boats. There are no services here, so be sure to bring snacks and plenty of water. (In a pinch, there's a restaurant at the neighboring beach club.)

(Southern Beaches
Tulum's very best beaches—thick white sand, turquoise-blue water, gently bending palm trees—are toward the southern end of the Zona Hotelera. Not surprisingly, Tulum's finest hotels are in the same area, and there are no official public access points. That said, hotels rarely raise an eyebrow at the occasional nonguest cutting through to reach the beach. You can also grab breakfast or lunch at one of the hotel restaurants and cut down to the beach afterward; in some cases, you can even use the lounge chairs.

Aimed at a mellow upscale crowd, **Ana y José Beach Club** (Carr. Tulum-Punta Allen, 2.4 kilometers/1.5 miles south of junction, no phone, www.anayjosebeachclub.com, 10am-6pm daily, free) is located about a kilometer north of the resort of the same name and is open to guests and nonguests alike. An airy sand-floored dining area serves mostly seafood, including ceviche, shrimp cocktail, and grilled fish, at decent prices and has a full bar. Chaise lounges and four-poster beach beds (US$5-15/day) are arranged a bit too close together, but they are comfy and relaxing nonetheless. Monday and Tuesday are the least crowded.

(Cenotes
Once a modest roadside operation, **Hidden Worlds** (Hwy. 307 Km. 115, toll-free Mex. tel. 800/681-6755, toll-free U.S. tel. 888/339-8001, www.hiddenworlds.com, 9am-sunset daily, last tour leaves at 2pm) is now a full-blown package tourist attraction, and part of the international Rainforest Adventures company. It remains a great introduction to underground snorkeling or diving, with a gorgeous on-site cenote system, frequent departures, and a staff that's accustomed to first-timers. A basic snorkeling tour (1 cenote, 1.5 hours) runs US$35, while one-tank dives are US$135; both including gear. The ever-growing list of nondiving attractions, including ziplines and rappelling, plus combo tours like "Ultimate Adventure + CoCoBongo," make this a fun destination for the whole family but detract somewhat from the underwater options.

Dos Ojos (Hwy. 307 Km. 117, tel. 984/877-8535, www.cenotedosojos.com, 8am-5pm daily) is located just north of Hidden Worlds but is far less commercialized. Dos Ojos, or Two Eyes, is a reference to twin caverns that are the largest openings—but far from the

© LIZA PRADO

one of Tulum's utterly perfect southern beaches

only ones—into the labyrinthine river system that runs beneath the ground here. You can snorkel on your own (US$10), but you'll see a lot more on a guided snorkeling tour (US$40 pp, no reservations required); be sure to ask to visit the Bat Cave. After the tour, you're free to keep snorkeling on your own; in fact, there are hammocks and benches, so you can bring food and drinks and make a day of it. Diving trips (US$130 for 2 tanks, maximum 4 divers per guide) should be arranged in advance. It's two kilometers (1.2 miles) from the entrance to the cenotes, so a rental car is handy. Discounts are available if you have your own gear.

Other favorite cenotes include **Zazil Ha, Car Wash/Aktun Ha, Gran Cenote,** and **Calavera Cenote** (all west of Tulum on the road to Cobá); **Cristal** and **Escondido** (Hwy. 307 just south of Tulum); **Casa Cenote** (at Tankah Tres); **Cenote Azul** and **Cristalina** (Hwy. 307 across from Xpu-Há); and **Chac Mol** (Hwy. 307, 2 kilometers/1.2 miles north of Xpu-Há). All can be visited on a tour or by

yourself, and most have snorkel gear for rent (US$6-8). Most are on private or *ejido* (collective) land and charge admission fees, usually US$3.50-6 for snorkelers and US$8.50 for divers. If you take a tour, ask if admission fees are included in the rate. Most cenotes are open 8am-5pm daily.

TOURS OF SIAN KA'AN BIOSPHERE RESERVE

CESiaK (Hwy. 307 just south of the Tulum ruins turnoff, tel. 984/871-2499, www.cesiak. org, 8am-2pm and 4pm-8pm daily) is a longstanding nonprofit group offering excellent tours of the Sian Ka'an Biosphere, a 1.3-million-acre reserve of coastal and mangrove forests and wetlands, with pristine coral reefs and a huge variety of flora and fauna. The most popular is the "Canal Tour," a six-hour excursion (US$78 pp) that includes taking a motorboat tour of the several lagoons, including stops to see a small Maya ruin and float down a mangrove canal. The late afternoon "Canal & Birdwatching" tour (US$78 pp)

© LIZA PRADO

Despite being deep underground, most of the Riviera Maya's popular cenotes are quite accessible, with stairways and interior lighting.

includes a boat tour of three bird-rich lagoons and a stop at the aptly named San Miguel Bird Island, or you can go by kayak (US$50, 3 hours). Most tours include hotel pickup, lunch or dinner, and a bilingual guide.

Community Tours Sian Ka'an (Calle Osiris Sur near Calle Sol Ote, tel. 984/871-2202 or cell. tel. 984/114-0750, www.siankaantours. org, 7am-9pm daily) is an excellent community-run agency offering a variety of Sian Ka'an tours, such as the Muyil route (US$99 pp, 7 hours), which begins with a visit to Muyil archaeological zone, then a boat tour of Muyil and Chunyaxche lagoons, including a chance to jump in and float down a long mangrove-edged canal; "Mayaking" in Sian Ka'an (US$45pp, 3 hours), a bird- and animal-spotting tour by kayak through the lagoons and mangroves; and a "Chicle" tour (US$99, 6 hours), where you learn about the practice of tapping *chicle* (gum) trees, from Maya times to today, followed by a swim in the lagoon.

ENTERTAINMENT AND SHOPPING
Entertainment

In the Zona Hotelera, the lounge bar at **La Zebra** (Carr. Tulum-Punta Allen, 4.8 kilometers/3 miles south of junction, cell. tel. 984/115-4726, www.lazebratulum.com) serves up shots and mixed drinks, including its signature Zebra margarita, made with pineapple and ginger and served on the rocks. On Sunday, it hosts a salsa party from 8pm to midnight, with a free dance class at 6pm. Dinner reservations are recommended if you want to feast on pulled-pork tacos between sets.

Papaya Playa Project (Carr. Tulum-Punta Allen, 1.5 kilometers/1 mile south of junction, cell. tel. 984/116-3774, www.papayaplayaproject) has a regular lineup of live musical acts, plus full-moon parties, bongo drum sessions, and an overall counterculture vibe. Saturdays are the main night, but look for schedules online or around town for upcoming events. Papaya Playa is actually a rustic-chic resort, hence all the *cabañas,* but is better known (and better liked, really) as a place to party. Most shows begin around 10pm; cover is US$5-10.

The upscale boutique resort **Mezzanine** (Carr. Tulum-Punta Allen, 1.3 kilometers/0.8 mile north of junction, cell. tel. 984/113-1596, www.mezzaninetulum.com) is known as the go-to bar on Friday nights, with cool cocktails and a hip vibe.

In Tulum Pueblo, **El Curandero** (Av. Tulum at Calle Beta, no phone, www.curanderotulum. com, 7pm-3am Mon.-Tues. and Thurs.-Sat.) is one of several local bars cut from the same cloth: small, mood lit, with great music and a relaxed vibe. Hookahs have become a popular feature in bars in the Riviera Maya, including Tulum. El Curandero has live music weekdays (except Wednesday), electronica on Saturday, and movies on Thursday.

Waye'Rest-Bar (Av. Tulum btwn Calles Beta and Osiris) and **Pepero** (Av. Tulum btwn Calles Jupiter and Acuario) are alternatives.

Shopping

Mixik Artesanía (Av. Tulum btwn Calles Alfa and Jupiter, tel. 984/871-2136, 9am-9pm Mon.-Sat.) has a large selection of quality folk art, from green copper suns to carved wooden angels and masks. Cool T-shirts, jewelry, cards, and more also are sold. There's a sister shop of the same name in the Zona Hotelera.

Casa Hernández (Av. Tulum at Calle Centauro, no phone, 9am-5pm daily except Thurs.) specializes in handcrafted pottery and ceramics, mostly from Puebla. Items range from mugs and picture frames to finely painted plates and dinner sets.

SPORTS AND RECREATION
Scuba Diving

The reef here is superb, but Tulum's diving claim to fame is the huge and easily accessible network of freshwater cenotes, caverns, and caves, offering truly one-of-a-kind dive environments. Divers with open-water certification can dive in cenotes (little or no overhead) and caverns (no more than 30 feet deep or 130 feet from an air pocket) without additional

training. Full-cave diving requires advanced certification, which is also available at many of Tulum's shops. If you haven't dived in a while, definitely warm up with some open-water dives before doing a cenote or cavern trip. Buoyancy control is especially important in such environments because of the roof above and the sediment below, and is complicated by the fact that it's freshwater instead of saltwater, and entails gear you may not be accustomed to, namely thick wetsuits and a flashlight.

Prices for cenotes and caverns are fairly uniform from shop to shop: around US$75-110 for one tank or US$95-130 for two. Be sure to ask whether gear and admission to the cenotes are included. Shops also offer multidive packages, cave and cavern certification courses, and hotel packages if you'll be staying awhile. As always, choose a shop and guide you feel comfortable with, not necessarily the least-expensive one.

If you plan on doing as much cave and cavern diving as possible, **Xibalba Dive Center & Hotel** (Calle Andrómeda btwn Calles Libra and Geminis, tel. 984/871-2953, www.xibalbahotel.com, 9am-7pm daily) not only has an excellent record for safety and professionalism, but now has an on-site hotel with comfortable rooms, a small swimming pool, and space to dry, store, and repair gear. Good lodging and diving packages are available. Xibalba also fills its own tanks, and offers free Nitrox to experienced clients. The shop's name, aptly enough, comes from the Yucatec Maya word for the underworld.

Koox Dive Center (Av. Tulum btwn Calles Beta and Osiris, cell. tel. 984/118-7031, www. kooxdiving.com, 9am-sunset daily) shares a shop with a popular kiteboarding outfit, and is another reliable option for diving and snorkeling, on the reef and in cenotes.

Mot Mot Diving (Av. Tulum at Calle Beta, cell. tel. 984/151-4718, www.motmotdiving. com, 9am-9pm daily) is recommended by several hotel owners.

Cenote Dive Center (Calle Centauro at Calle Andrómeda, tel. 984/876-3285, www. cenotedive.com, 8am-4pm Sun.-Fri.) offers a large variety of tours and courses, in Tulum and beyond.

In the Zona Hotelera, **Mexi-Divers** (Carr. Tulum-Punta Allen Km. 5, tel. 984/807-8805, www.mexidivers.com, 8:30am-5pm daily) is located opposite Zamas Hotel in the Punta Piedra area and has regularly scheduled snorkeling and diving trips, in the ocean and nearby cenotes, at somewhat lower prices.

Dos Ojos (tel. 984/877-8535, www.cenotedosojos.com, 8am-5pm daily) and **Hidden Worlds** (toll-free Mex. tel. 800/681-6755, toll-free U.S. tel. 888/339-8001, www.hiddenworlds.com, 9am-sunset daily, last tour leaves at 2pm) are located north of town and also offer excellent diving tours.

Snorkeling

Like divers, snorkelers have an embarrassment of riches in Tulum, with great reef snorkeling and easy access to the eerie beauty of the area's many cenotes. **Dive shops in Tulum** offer snorkel trips of both sorts; prices vary considerably so be sure to ask which and how many reefs or cenotes you'll visit, for how long, and what's included (gear, entrance fees, transport, snacks, etc.). Reef trips cost US$25-40 visiting 1-3 different spots, while cenote trips run US$45-70; snorkel gear can also be rented. North of Tulum, **Hidden Worlds** (toll-free Mex. tel. 800/681-6755, toll-free U.S. tel. 888/339-8001, www.hiddenworlds.com, 9am-sunset daily, last tour leaves at 2pm) and **Dos Ojos** (tel. 984/877-8535, www.cenotedosojos.com, 8am-5pm daily) both offer excellent cenote snorkeling tours for US$35-40; Hidden Worlds has a lot of extras, like rappelling and ziplines, while Dos Ojos allows you to snorkel on your own—all day if you like—after the tour is over.

Kiteboarding

Extreme Control (Av. Tulum btwn Calles Beta and Osiris, tel. 984/745-4555, www.extremecontrol.net, 9am-sunset daily) is Tulum's longest-operating kiteboarding outfit, offering courses and rentals for all experience levels and in various languages. Most classes are held at Playa El Paraíso Beach Club, north of the junction, where it also has an info kiosk. Private classes are US$72 per hour, or US$216-432 for three- to six-hour introductory packages, including equipment; group classes are somewhat less.

Morph Kiteboarding (cell. tel. 984/114-9524, www.morphkiteboarding.com) offers classes by IKO-certified instructors to all levels of kiteboarders. Rates are for private classes, though group lessons can be arranged as well: US$225, US$395, and US$420 for three-, five-, and six-hour courses, respectively. Rates include hotel pickup and transportation to the nearest kiting beach.

Ocean Pro Kite (Akiin Beach Club, Carr. Tulum-Punta Allen Km. 9.5, cell. tel. 984/119-0328, www.oceanprokite.com) is another option.

Stand-Up Paddling

Stand-up paddling, or "SUPing," has exploded in popularity, a challenging but relatively easy sport to master, and especially well-suited to the calm clear waters found in much of the Riviera Maya. You can see a surprising amount of sealife doing SUP instead of kayaking, thanks simply to the improved vantage point.

Ocean Pro Kite (Akiin Beach Club, Carr. Tulum-Punta Allen Km. 9.5, tel. 984/876-3263 or cell. tel. 984/119-0328, www.oceanprokite.com) offers SUP lessons for all levels, starting with safety and theory on the beach, graduating to kneeling paddling, then standing and catching waves. Private classes are US$60 per hour or US$120 half day, while groups of two or three start at US$40 per person per hour. Gear, guide, transport, and refreshments are all included.

Extreme Control (Av. Tulum btwn Calles Beta and Osiris, tel. 984/745-4555, www.extremecontrol.net, 9am-sunset daily) also offers SUPing lessons (US$70 private, US$50 pp 2 pax, US$35 pp 3+ pax; 2 hours) plus tours, rentals, and transport to and from Tulum, Akumal, and Tankah. Its office in town is convenient for information and booking.

Ecoparks

Built around a huge natural inlet, **Xel-Há** (Hwy. 307, 9 kilometers/5.6 miles north of Tulum, cell. tel. 984/105-6981, www.xel-ha. com, 8:30am-6pm daily, US$79 adult all-inclusive, US$119 adult with round-trip transportation, child under 12 half off, child under 5 free) is all about being in and around the water. Activities include snorkeling, snuba, tubing, and interactive programs with dolphins, manatees, and stingrays. Although it doesn't compare to snorkeling on the reef, there's a fair number of fish darting about, and it makes for a fun, easy intro for children and beginners. Check the website for online deals and combo packages with sister resorts Xcaret and Xplor.

Bicycling

In Tulum town, **Iguana Bike Shop** (Av. Satélite near Calle Andrómeda, tel. 984/871-2357 or cell. tel. 984/119-0836, www.iguanabike. com, 9am-7pm Mon.-Sat.) offers mountain bike tours to snorkeling sites at various cenotes

© GARY CHANDLER

Tulum is known for its whimsy and artfulness, including murals like this one.

and beaches, as well as turtle nesting grounds on Xcacel beach. Prices vary depending on the tour; they typically last four hours and are limited to six cyclists.

Spas

Overlooking the beach at Copal hotel, **Maya Spa Wellness Center** (Carr. Tulum-Punta Allen Km. 5, toll-free Mex. tel. 800/681-9537, www.maya-spa.com, 8am-8pm daily) offers a variety of massages, facials, and body wraps in a gorgeous setting. Massages run US$100 to US$150 (60-80 minutes), while other treatments average US$60 (1 hour).

Located at the Ana y José hotel, **Om... Spa** (Carr. Tulum-Punta Allen Km. 7, tel. 984/871-2477, ext. 202, www.anayjose.com, 9am-5pm daily) is a full-service spa set in a chic beachfront setting. Choose from a menu of massages (US$80-100) and body treatments (US$60-100).

Yoga

Surrounded by lush vegetation, **Yoga Shala Tulum** (Carr. Tulum-Punta Allen Km. 4.4, cell. tel. 984/137-3016, www.yogashalatulum.com, 7am-6pm Mon.-Sat., 4:30pm-6pm Sun.) offers a wide range of yoga instruction in its gorgeous open-air studio. Classes cost US$15 each or US$50 per week for unlimited classes. There also is an affordable hotel on-site. Look for it on the inland side of the Zona Hotelera road.

Maya Spa Wellness Center (Carr. Tulum-Punta Allen Km. 5, toll-free Mex. tel. 800/681-9537, www.maya-spa.com, 8am-8pm daily) also offers yoga sessions.

ACCOMMODATIONS

Chances are you've come to Tulum to stay in one of the famous beachside bungalow-type hotels. There are many to choose from, each slightly different but most sharing a laid-back atmosphere and terrific beaches. However, some travelers are surprised by just how rustic some accommodations are, even those charging hundreds of dollars per night. The root of the matter is that there are no power lines or freshwater wells serving the beach. Virtually all accommodations have salty water in the showers and sinks. Most have fans, but not all, and electricity may be limited to nighttime hours only. Air-conditioning is available in only a handful of places. At the same time, some hotels use generators to power their restaurants and reception, so it's worth asking for a room away from the generator; nothing is a bigger killjoy than a diesel motor pounding outside your window when the point of coming here was to enjoy the peace and quiet.

If staying on the beach is out of your budget (join the club!), staying in town is a perfectly good alternative. The options have improved significantly, with a crop of new bed-and-breakfasts and boutique hotels to go along with longtime hostels and budget digs. The beach is just a short drive or bike ride away, and prices for food, Internet, and laundry are much lower.

Zona Hotelera
UNDER US$100

A private home turned yoga hotel, **Yoga Shala Tulum** (Carr. Tulum-Punta Allen Km. 4.4, cell. tel. 984/137-3016, www.yogashalatulum.com, US$49/69 s/d with shared bath, US$79/89 s/d) offers simple but comfortable rooms on a jungly plot on the inland side of the Zona Hotelera. Rooms have whitewashed walls, polished cement floors, and good beds and linens, with a bit of boho flair, too. Outside is an impressive open-air yoga studio with a high *palapa* roof and gorgeous wood floors.

Ahau Tulum (Carr. Tulum-Punta Allen Km. 4.4, cell. tel. 984/167-1154 or 984/144-3348, www.ahautulum.com, US$29-99 s/d) is not exclusively a budget place—it's got rooms that go for over US$400—but its guesthouse units (with shared bathrooms) and stick-built "Bali Huts" are among the cheapest digs on the beach. Gaps in the walls and bathrooms that never get truly clean are the price you pay to be on the sand for this cheap—a bargain for boho beachhounds.

US$100-200

Although sharing a bathroom for $100 doesn't seem quite right, **Coco Tulum** (Carr. Tulum-Punta Allen Km. 7, cell. tel. 984/157-4830, www.cocotulum.com, US$79-98 s/d with shared bath, US$125-195 s/d) does the basics with style. Tidy *palapa*-roofed bungalows have cement floors, comfy beds, hanging bookshelfs, fans, and sleek black exteriors. The shared bathrooms are actually quite nice, with modern basin sinks, rainshower heads, hot water, and thrice-daily cleaning. And if sharing a bathroom really is beyond the pale, they've got a tower with three deluxe rooms, each with private bathroom, fan, and stellar views. Wind- and solar-powered electricity is available 24 hours.

Accommodations at the lovely and well-liked **Cabañas La Luna** (Carr. Tulum-Punta Allen Km. 6.5, U.S. tel. 818/631-9824, Mex. cell. tel. 984/146-7737 [urgent matters only], www.cabanaslaluna.com, US$160-300 s/d, US$550 two- and four-bedroom villas) range from cozy beachfront bungalows to spacious split-level villas, but share essential details like comfortable mattresses, high ceilings, fans and 24-hour electricity, and bright artful decor. The beach is stunning, of course, and the property is big enough for a sense of isolation, yet within walking distance of shops and restaurants in Punta Piedra. Service is excellent.

Tita Tulum (Carr. Tulum-Punta Allen Km. 8, tel. 984/877-8513, www.titatulum.com, US$160-190 s/d) has a lovely beachfront and low-key atmosphere—a great option for families and travelers who prefer modest comforts and a lower rate (especially off-season) over boutique eco-chic embellishments. Ten guest rooms form a semicircle around a sandy palm-fringed lot; they're a bit worn around the edges but have polished cement floors, clean bathrooms, and indoor and outdoor sitting areas, plus fans, Wi-Fi, and 24-hour electricity. Tita is a charming and attentive proprietor, and prepares authentic Mexican dishes in the hotel's small restaurant.

Posada Lamar (Carr. Tulum-Punta Allen Km. 6, cell. tel. 984/106-3682, www.posadalamar.com, US$125-195 s/d) has eight comfortable and artful bungalows, with salvaged-wood detailing and rich colors and fabrics. There

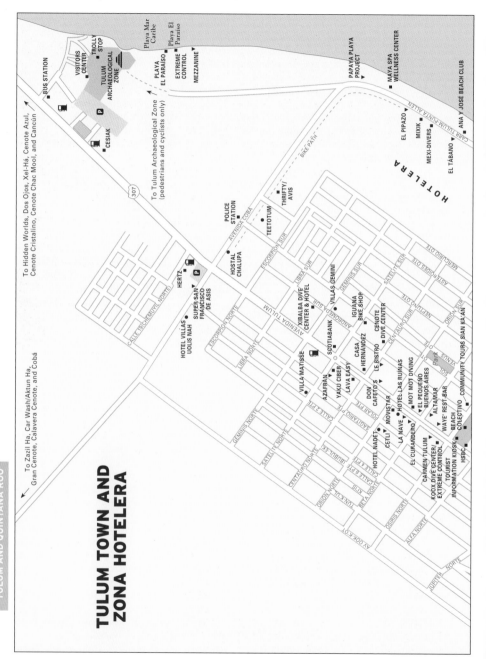

TULUM TOWN AND ZONA HOTELERA

To Zazil Ha, Car Wash/Aktun Ha, Gran Cenote, Calavera Cenote, and Cobá

To Hidden Worlds, Dos Ojos, Xel-Há, Cenote Azul, Cenote Cristalino, Cenote Chac Mool, and Cancún

307

BUS STATION

VISITORS CENTER

TROLLY STOP

TULUM ARCHAEOLOGICAL ZONE

CESIAK

Playa Mar Caribe

Playa El Paraiso

PLAYA EL PARAISO

EXTREME CONTROL

MEZZANINE

PAPAYA PLAYA PROJECT

MAYA SPA WELLNESS CENTER

To Tulum Archaeological Zone (pedestrians and cyclists only)

CARR. TULUM–PUNTA ALLEN

EL PIPAZO

MIXIK

MEXI-DIVERS

EL TABANO

EL PIPAZO

ANA Y JOSE BEACH CLUB

HOTELERA

BIKE PATH

POLICE STATION

AVENIDA COBA

THRIFTY/ AVIS

TEETOTUM

ESCORPION SUR

HOSTAL CHALUPA

HERTZ

SUPER SAN FRANCISCO DE ASIS

HOTEL VILLAS UOLIS NAH

CALLE 'B' CHEMUVIL NORTE

ESCORPION NORTE

LIBRA NORTE

LIBRA SUR

AVENIDA TULUM

ANDROMEDA SUR

XIBALBA DIVE CENTER & HOTEL

VILLAS GEMINI

IGUANA BIKE SHOP

CENOTE DIVE CENTER

GEMINIS SUR

SCOTIABANK

CASA HERNANDEZ

LE BISTRO

VILLA MATISSE

AZAFRAN

YAKU CIBER

LAVA EASY

DON CAFETO'S

MOVISTAR

LA NAVE

HOTEL LAS RUINAS

MOT MOT DIVING

EL PEQUEÑO BUENOS AIRES

ALTAMAR

'WAVE' REST-BAR

BEACH COLECTIVO

COMMUNITY TOURS SIAN KA'AN

SATELITE SUR

CENTAURO SUR

NEPTUNO OTE

ORION OTE

SOLIS

Park

Park

CETLI

HOTEL NADE

EL CURANDERO

CARMEN TULUM

KOOX DIVE CENTER/ EXTREME CONTROL

TOURIST INFORMATION KIOSK

HSBC

GEMINIS NORTE

SATELITE NORTE

CENTAURO NORTE

SOL DE AR PTE

SAGITARIO PTE

CALLE 'A' PTE

CALLE 4 PTE

CALLE 6 PTE

CALLE 8 PTE

BETA NORTE

KUIS

TUNK'UL OL

OSIRIS NORTE

AV COOK K'OT

ALFA NORTE

JUPITER NORTE

MERCURIO OTE

ASTR. POLOS OTE

NEPTUNO OTE

ORION OTE

SONS

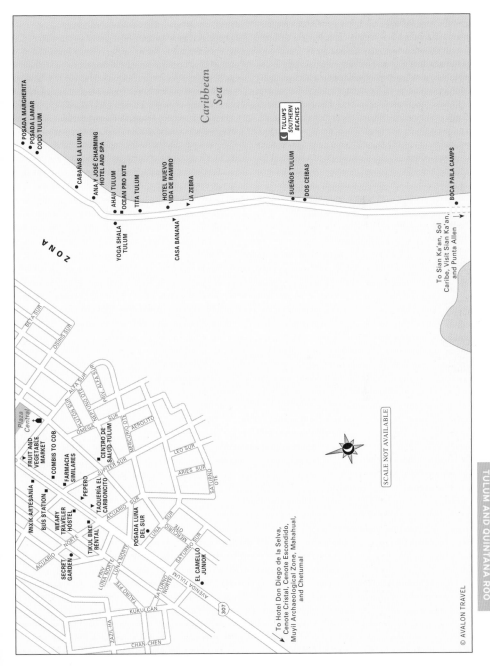

Caribbean Sea

TULUM'S SOUTHERN BEACHES

ZONA

POSADA MARGHERITA
POSADA LAMAR
COCO TULUM

CABAÑAS LA LUNA

ANA Y JOSE CHARMING HOTEL AND SPA

AHAU TULUM
OCEAN PRO KITE
TITA TULUM

HOTEL NUEVO VIDA DE RAMIRO
LA ZEBRA

YOGA SHALA TULUM

CASA BANANA

SUEÑOS TULUM
DOS CEIBAS

BOCA PAILA CAMPS

To Sian Ka'an, Sol Caribe, Visit Sian Ka'an, and Punta Allen

BETA SUR

OSIRIS SUR

ALFA SUR

PRIV. ALFA SUR

PLUTON SUR

NEPTUNO OTE

Plaza Central

FRUIT AND VEGETABLE MARKET

COMBIS TO COB

OMEGA

OTE

CENTRO DE SALUD TULUM

MERCURIO SUR

AEROLITO

LEO SUR

SCALE NOT AVAILABLE

FARMACIA SIMILARES

ARIES SUR

SATURNO OTE

MIxIK ARTESANIA

BUS STATION

PEPERO

TAQUERIA EL CARBONCITO

JUPITER SUR

AQUARIO SUR

WEARY TRAVELER HOSTEL

POSADA LUNA DEL SUR

LUNA SUR

MERCURIO OTE

SATURNO SUR

SECRET GARDEN

TIKUL BIKE RENTAL

AQUARIO NORTE

PRIV. LUNA NORTE

LUNA NORTE

SATURNO NORTE

EL CAMELLO JUNIOR

TAURO PTE

AVENIDA TULUM

307

To Hotel Don Diego de la Selva, Cenote Cristal, Cenote Escondido, Muyil Archaeological Zone, Mahahual, and Chetumal

KUKULCAN

ZAZIL-HA

CHAN-CHEN

© AVALON TRAVEL

are no fans or air-conditioning, and electricity (solar powered) is available only at night; fortunately the sea breezes keep the units cool (and the bugs at bay) most nights. The bungalows are a bit too close together, diminishing privacy, especially since you often need the windows and doors open, but the beach here is clean and beautiful, with plenty of chairs, beds, and *palapas*. Continental breakfast is included, served every morning on your private terrace.

Dos Ceibas (Carr. Tulum-Punta Allen Km. 10, tel. 984/877-6024, www.dosceibas.com, US$80-170 s/d) has eight comfortable, if a bit garish, bungalows on a beautiful stretch of beach. Bungalows range from a top-floor honeymoon unit to a "bargain" bungalow with a detached bathroom (and near enough the road to hear passing cars). Most have polished cement floors, brightly painted walls, and firm beds with mosquito nets hanging from the *palapa* roof; all but the two breezy oceanfront rooms and budget rear unit have ceiling fans (electricity available at night only).

OVER US$200

Nestled in a wonderfully jungly plot, ❰ **Hotel Nueva Vida de Ramiro** (Carr. Tulum-Punta Allen Km. 8.5, tel. 984/877-8512, www.tulumnv.com, US$105-345 s/d) has a large number (and variety) of accommodations, from spacious suites with pillow-top mattresses and gorgeous ocean views to simple thatch-roof bungalows, including some with kitchenette, and even an adults-only area. (The oldest rooms can be dark, however, and aren't a great value, despite being cheaper.) There's 24-hour clean power, but no air-conditioning, just fans and sea breezes. The beach here is glorious, and the hotel's restaurant, Casa Banana, is located across the street and well-recommended for tasty, affordable meals.

Artful, spirit-minded decor is nothing new in Tulum, but ❰ **Sueños Tulum** (Carr. Tulum-Punta Allen Km. 8.5, tel. 984/876-2152 or cell. tel. 984/115-4338, www.suenostulum.com, US$220-285 s/d) takes the theme further than most. Each of the hotel's 12 suites is decorated according to an essential force—Earth, Rain,

Moon, etc.—and there's Maya imagery inside and out. All have ceiling fans, most rooms have ocean views, and two are reserved for families. A small clean pool is an added bonus, even with beaches as gorgeous as these. Located at the far southern end of the hotel zone, Sueños is quiet and isolated, even by Tulum's standards.

Beachy and hip, **Posada Margherita** (Carr. Tulum-Punta Allen Km. 4.5, tel. 984/801-8493, www.posadamargherita.com, US$208 s/d) has just eight rooms, all boasting stone-inlaid showers, private patio or terrace, and intriguing art from around the world. The beach here is lovely, and the hotel has a restaurant and lounge area just steps from the sand. Posada Margherita runs on solar energy, which means 24 hours of silent electricity. And the restaurant here is not to be missed; it's pricey but one of the best in Tulum.

Ana y José Charming Hotel and Spa (Carr. Tulum-Punta Allen Km. 7, tel. 998/889-6022 reservations or 984/871-2476 reception, www.anayjose.com, US$390-620 s/d) was one of the first resorts in Tulum to offer air-conditioning, a swimming pool, and hotel-style rooms. Though sacrilege to some—and now they're adding TVs!—Ana y José has long been a favorite of those who love Tulum's beaches and isolation, but not so much the beach bungalow, mosquito-net, eco-chic thing. Rooms vary from comfortable doubles, to romantic ocean-view suites, to large family apartments, most with niceties like marble floors, basin sinks, and flower petals on the bed. The inflated prices are for air-conditioning. The beach and spa are lovely, of course, and Ana y José is popular for weddings.

In Town
UNDER US$50

A stylish hostel with a laid-back vibe, ❰ **Hostal Chalupa** (Av. Cobá near Av. Tulum, cell. tel. 984/871-2116, www.chalupatulum.com.mx, US$17 s dorm with a/c, US$21 d dorm with a/c, US$42/50 d/q with a/c) offers air-conditioned dorms with en suite bathrooms and good mattresses; private rooms are similar in look and comfort and sleep up to four. There's an inviting pool on the ground floor and a large rooftop solarium; movies are shown most nights at 8pm. The community kitchen is vegetarian-only. It's located just outside town, on the road toward the beach; bikes are available for rent (US$4.25/day).

Villa Matisse (Av. Satélite at Calle Sagitario, tel. 984/871-2636, shuvinito@yahoo.com, US$50 s/d) has six simple, comfortable rooms, a pleasant garden and reading area (with book exchange), and a community kitchen. The rooms are spotless, and the grounds and common areas are equally well maintained; the multilingual owner sets out coffee and small snacks in the morning and often supplies rooms with fresh flowers. There's no air-conditioning, but rooms have fans and good cross ventilation. Use of the hotel's bikes is included in the rate.

Hotel Las Ruínas (Av. Tulum btwn Calles Orion and Beta, cell. tel. 984/125-5506, US$50 s/d) won't win any awards for marketing (The Ruins Hotel?) but it does just fine as a budget option for non-hostellers. Rooms are plain and a bit dark, but reasonably clean and comfortable, with air-conditioning and TVs. No Wi-Fi, but there's an Internet café at the corner. The hotel is run by a friendly family who live on-site.

US$50-100

Tucked into a quiet residential street, **(☾ Secret Garden** (Calle Sagitario near Calle Acuario, tel. 984/804-3697, www.secretgardentulum.com, US$50-60 s/d with a/c, US$70 s/d with a/c and kitchenette, US$60-70 *palapa* bungalow with fan and kitchenette) offers stylish, comfortable rooms at affordable rates (guests over age 15 only). Units vary in size and layout (some with kitchenettes, some with lofts), but all have fashionable colors, artful stencils, and high-end linens. Rooms open onto a long, leafy central garden with hammocks and low couches, perfect for relaxing day or night. Service is outstanding; purified water, fruit, and baked goods are offered daily.

Hotel Don Diego de la Selva (Av. Tulum s/n, tel. 984/871-2233 or cell. tel. 984/114-9744, www.dtulum.com, US$55 s/d with fan, US$90

s/d with a/c) offers spacious rooms and bungalows with classy understated decor, comfortable beds, and large glass doors looking onto a shady rear garden. There's a large pool, and the hotel restaurant serves good French-Asian-Mexican cuisine; half-board options are available. The only catch is the location, about a kilometer (0.6 mile) south of the plaza. The hotel rents bikes, but most guests find a rental car indispensable. It's very popular with French travelers; wireless Internet and continental breakfast are included.

Set in a leafy garden on the road to Cobá, **Hotel Villas Uolis Nah** (Carr. Tulum-Cobá Km. 0.2, tel. 984/876-4965, www.uolisnah. com, US$63 s/d, US$80 s/d with a/c) has six simple studios with little touches like mosquito-net canopies, mosaic-tile bathrooms, and *palapa*-shaded terraces with hammocks. All units have fully equipped kitchens (even ovens), and one of Tulum's main supermarkets is just down the street. Continental breakfast, bike rental, and wireless Internet are included.

Hotel Nadet (Calle Orión at Calle Polar, 984/871-2114, www.hotelnadet.com, US$80-120 s/d with a/c) offers large, modern, reasonably priced rooms in a central location. While not luxurious, the rooms are quite nice, all with new linens, mini-split air conditioners, and well-equipped kitchenettes. Artful furnishings and decor lend a bit of color and class, and being a block off the main drag makes the hotel, which is operated by a friendly family, convenient but also quiet.

US$100-200

Rooms at **Posada Luna del Sur** (Calle Luna Sur 5 at Av. Tulum, tel. 984/871-2984, www. posadalunadelsur.com, US$99) are compact but tidy and pleasant, with whitewashed walls, comfortable beds (king or two doubles), and small terraces overlooking a leafy garden. Most have kitchenettes, though you may not use it much considering the tasty breakfasts and the many restaurant recommendations of the food-savvy owner-manager. The rooftop lounge is a great evening hangout, and service is excellent. The hotel is for ages 16 and over only.

A short distance from town on the road to the beach, **Teetotum** (Av. Cobá Sur s/n, cell. tel. 984/143-8956, www.teetotumhotel.com, US$125 s/d with a/c) has four sleek minimalist rooms—ceramic basin sinks, low bed stands—and artful decor throughout, including playful oversized murals in the dining room. All rooms have air-conditioning, Wi-Fi, and iPod docks, but no TV or telephone. Guests enjoy free continental breakfast and bike rentals, and a lovely plunge pool and rooftop sun beds, too. There's daily yoga, and various massages and other spa treatments are available on request. The restaurant serves a little of everything, from vegetable dumplings to seafood skewers, with an equally varied (and enticing) drink menu.

Villas Gemini (Calle Andrómeda at Calle Gemini, cell. tel. 984/116-6203, www.villas-geminis.com, US$110/140 one/two bedroom, rate for 4 pax, extra pax US$20) has spacious one- and two-bedroom condos with modern kitchens and private terraces, plus a small swimming pool and 24-hour security—an amazing deal considering they sleep 4-6 people. The owners and staff are attentive and capable, and there's maid service every three days. There's a large supermarket nearby, plus restaurants, bars, and dive shops. The property has cable TV and Wi-Fi, and bikes for rent.

FOOD
Zona Hotelera

E El Tábano (Carr. Tulum-Punta Allen, 2.2 kilometers/1.4 miles south of junction, cell. tel. 984/134-2706, 8am-11pm daily, US$8-22.50) is Spanish for horsefly, a good sign that this is no ordinary roadside eatery. Rough wood tables on a gravel lot belie a surprisingly nuanced menu, including watermelon gazpacho, pasta-less zucchini lasagna, and fresh fish with red pipian sauce. To drink, try the fresh lemonade or something off the wine list. It can be hot midday, and mosquitoey at dusk—bring repellent.

Fusion Thai is the specialty at **Mezzanine** (Carr. Tulum-Punta Allen, 1.3 kilometers/0.8 mile north of junction, cell. tel. 984/113-1596, www.mezzaninetulum.com, 8am-10pm daily,

US$10-25), one of Tulum's chicest hotels on the beach. Curries—red, green, or pineapple—and fried Thai tofu in peanut sauce are among the dishes served in a fashionable dining area or on a shaded outdoor patio, both with fine sea views. A full bar and cool music make this a place to linger.

La Zebra (Carr. Tulum-Punta Allen, 4.8 kilometers/3 miles south of junction, cell. tel. 984/115-4726, www.lazebratulum.com, 8am-10pm Mon.-Sat., 8am-midnight Sun., US$12-25) has a lovely beachfront patio and *palapa*-roofed dining area; at night, the long entry path is lit by lanterns. The menu is a bit plain—mostly standard fish and chicken dishes—but the Firestone Soup is a treat: seafood soup prepared at your table using a red-hot stone to cook the ingredients. On Sunday there's a barbecue and salsa party starting at 8pm (free dance classes at 6pm).

Posada Margherita (Carr. Tulum-Punta Allen, 2.4 kilometers/1.5 miles south of junction, tel. 984/801-8493, www.posadamargherita.com, 7:30am-10:30am and noon-9pm daily, US$8-30) specializes in gourmet Italian dishes, which are prepared with organic products and homemade pastas and breads. A huge tree-trunk plate of appetizers also is brought to each table (think olives, roasted red peppers, and artichoke hearts)—almost a meal in and of itself. Service is personalized to the point of having no menus—instead, the waiter typically pulls up an extra chair to discuss with you the dishes being prepared that night (ask for prices before ordering—many customers are shocked when the bill arrives). It's busy most nights, so you may have to wait to get a table.

Casa Banana (Carr. Tulum-Punta Allen, 4.7 kilometers/2.9 miles south of junction, tel. 984/877-8512, www.tulumnv.com, 7:30am-9:30pm daily, US$5-15) serves up tasty, well-priced Mexican and Caribbean dishes in a brightly painted patio dining area. Try the *motuleños,* a classic Yucatecan breakfast made with fried eggs, beans, cheese, salsa, and peas all atop a fried tortilla, or the *blaff,* white fish marinated in lime and herbs that will transport you directly to Martinique. Casa Banana is located on the inland side of the road, opposite (and part of) Hotel Nuevo Vida de Ramiro.

In Town

One of the best breakfast places in town, **《Azafrán** (Av. Satélite near Calle Polar, cell. tel. 984/129-6130, www.azafrantulum.com, 8am-3pm daily, US$4-9) serves up superb morning meals made with gourmet products: homemade bagels with prosciutto and Brie, crepes stuffed with an assortment of fresh fruits, *chaya* omelets, and pâté platters with freshly baked bread. Organic coffee is a must, as is the fresh-squeezed orange juice. The only bummer about this place is that there are only six tables—come early to beat the crowd.

Le Bistro (Calle Centauro near Av. Tulum, cell. tel. 984/133-4507, 9am-11pm daily, US$4-15) is a bustling café offering a full range of French delicacies—from freshly baked croissants to duck confit. Tables are set outdoors, either on the front porch or under umbrellas in the back courtyard; neither is very charming, but the food is so good, it's easy to overlook.

Don't let the nautical theme fool you: **La Nave** (Av. Tulum between Calles Beta and Osiris, tel. 984/871-2592, 7am-11pm Mon.-Sat., US$7-14) is more about thin crispy pizza than fish fry. Whether you go all out with a Brie and prosciutto pizza or stick with a classic margherita, you'll leave satisfied. Pasta dishes and hefty appetizers are excellent alternatives.

El Pequeño Buenos Aires (Av. Tulum btwn Calles Orion and Beta, tel. 984/871-2708, 11am-11pm daily, US$6-25) serves excellent cuts of beef, including a *parrillada Argentina,* which comes piled with various cuts, plus chicken and sausage. The menu also includes crepes, a few vegetarian dishes, and lunch specials.

For seafood, don't miss **《Altamar** (Calle Beta near Av. Tulum, cell. tel. 998/282-8299, www.altamartulum.com, 7pm-midnight daily, US$8-15), an upscale restaurant featuring regional dishes like *pan de cazón,* or whole fried fish, prepared using gourmet ingredients and presented with flair. Seating is in an open-air, classy dining room just off Avenida Tulum.

Cooking classes also are offered if you're looking to increase your culinary repertoire.

Cetli (Calle Polar Norte at Calle Orion Norte, cell. tel. 984/108-0681, 5pm-10pm Thurs.-Tues., US$10-20) serves up modern Mexican creations by Chef Claudia Pérez, a Mexico City transplant and a graduate of one of Mexico's top culinary schools. The menu is full of the unique and unexpected, from chicken and *chaya* roll in peanut mole to *agua de pepino con yerba buena* (mint cucumber water). Chef Pérez herself is a delight and often comes out to chat with diners. Reservations can be made via Facebook.

For home-style Mexican cooking, head to **Don Cafeto's** (Av. Tulum btwn Calles Centauro and Orion, tel. 984/871-2207, 7am-11pm daily, US$5-18), serving Mexican staples like mole and enchiladas, plus ceviche plates that are meals unto themselves. On a hot day, try a tall cold *chayagra,* an uplifting blend of pineapple juice, lime juice, cucumber, and *chaya* (similar to spinach).

Taquería El Carboncito (Av. Tulum btwn Calles Acuario and Jupiter; 6pm-2am daily except Tues., US$1-5) serves up hot tacos at plastic tables in the driveway of an auto shop that's closed for the night. That is, it's a great place for a cheap tasty meal, and popular with local families.

Many say Tulum's best seafood is at a low-key outdoor eatery just south of town called **El Camello Junior** (Av. Tulum at Av. Kukulkán, 10:30am-9pm daily except Wed., until 6pm Sun., US$6-12). You won't find any argument here: Ceviche, shrimp cocktail, and made-to-order fish dishes are served super fresh, super tasty, and in generous portions. It's a quick taxi ride or longish walk from town; don't be surprised if you have to wait a few minutes for a table to open up.

Groceries and Bakeries

The Zona Hotelera's largest market, **El Pipazo** (Punta Piedra, 9am-9pm daily) is one room filled with snack food, canned goods, water, liquor, and sunscreen.

For basics and then some, head to the **Super**

San Francisco de Asis (Av. Tulum at road to Cobá, 7am-10pm daily).

Tulum Pueblo has a great local **fruit and vegetable shop** (6am-9pm daily) on Avenida Tulum at Calle Alfa.

A classic Mexican bakery, **Carmen Tulum** (Av. Tulum near Calle Osiris, 6am-11pm daily, US$0.50-1.50) is a bustling shop offering everything from fresh rolls to chocolate-filled *cuernos* (croissants).

INFORMATION AND SERVICES
Tourist Information

A **tourist information kiosk** (no phone, 9am-5pm daily) is located on the central plaza, across from the HSBC bank. The chief attendant is quite knowledgeable, her teenage disciples less so. You often can glean useful information from the stacks of brochures there. The website **www.todotulum.com** also offers good information on current goings-on and offerings in Tulum.

Emergency Services

Tulum's modest local clinic, **Centro de Salud Tulum** (Calle Andrómeda btwn Calles Jupiter and Alfa, tel. 984/871-2050, 24 hours), is equipped to handle minor health problems, but for serious medical issues you should head to Playa del Carmen or Cancún. **Farmacia Similares** (Av. Tulum at Calle Jupiter Sur, tel. 984/871-2736) is open 8am-10pm Monday-Saturday, and 8am-9pm Sunday; it also has a doctor on staff for simple consultations 9am-9pm Monday-Saturday and 9am-3pm Sunday.

The **police** (toll-free tel. 066, 24 hours) share a large station with the fire department, about two kilometers (1.2 miles) from Tulum Pueblo on the road to the Zona Hotelera.

Money

HSBC (Av. Tulum at Calle Alfa next to city hall, 8am-7pm Mon.-Sat.) has a reliable ATM machine and will change foreign cash and AmEx travelers checks.

ScotiaBank (Av. Tulum at Calle Satélite, 8:30am-4pm Mon.-Fri.) has reliable ATMs.

Media and Communications

On the north end of town, **Yaku Ciber** (Av. Satélite near Av. Tulum, 8am-midnight daily except Sat., US$1.25/hour) has flat-screen computers and killer air-conditioning.

Movistar (Av. Tulum at Calle Orion, 9am-10pm daily, US$1/hour) has Skype-enabled computers plus direct-dial international calls (US$0.25-0.40/minute).

In the Zona Hotelera, most hotels offer free Wi-Fi in the reception or restaurant area for guests.

Laundry and Storage

Lava Easy (Av. Tulum btwn Av. Satélite and Calle Centauro, 8am-8pm Mon.-Sat.) charges US$1.25 per kilo (2.2 pounds), with a three-kilo (6.6-pound) minimum.

The **bus terminal** (Av. Tulum btwn Calles Alfa and Jupiter, tel. 984/871-2122, 24 hours) has luggage storage for US$0.50-1.20 per hour depending on the size of the bag.

GETTING THERE
Bus

Tulum's **bus terminal** (Av. Tulum btwn Calles Alfa and Jupiter, tel. 984/871-2122) is at the south end of town, a block from the main plaza.

Combi

Combis are white collective vans that zip between Tulum and Playa del Carmen all day, every day (US$3.50, 1 hour, 24 hours, every 10 minutes 5am-10pm). They leave more frequently than buses and are handier for intermediate stops, like Hidden Worlds, Dos Ojos, Akumal, and Xpu-Há. Flag them down anywhere on Avenida Tulum or Highway 307.

Combis also go to Cobá (US$4.25, 1 hour), stopping at cenotes along the way. They leave at the top of the hour from a stop on Avenida Tulum at Calle Alfa. You can also catch them at the intersection of Highway 307 and the Cobá/Zona Hotelera road.

Tukan Kin (tel. 984/871-3538, www.from-cancunairport.com) operates an **airport shuttle** from Tulum to Cancún airport

TULUM BUS SCHEDULE

Departures from the **bus terminal** (Av. Tulum btwn Calles Alfa and Jupiter, tel. 984/871-2122) include:

DESTINATION	PRICE	DURATION	SCHEDULE
Cancún	US$7-9	2-2.5 hrs	every 15-60 mins midnight-11:30pm
Carrillo Puerto	US$5-6.50	1-1.5 hrs	every 15-60 mins midnight-11:45pm
Chetumal	US$12.50-20	3.5 hrs	every 30-90 mins 12:30am-10:30pm
Chichén Itzá	US$8-12.50	2.5-3 hrs	7:15am, 8:30am, 9am, 2:30pm
Cobá	US$3.50-4	45-60 mins	every 30-60 mins 7:15am-11:15am and 3:30pm-7:15pm
Mahahual	US$13-21.50	3-3.5 hrs	10am and 5:50pm
Mérida	US$20-24.25	3.5-4 hrs	9 departures 1am-9:30pm
Palenque (Chiapas)	US$49-58	10.5-11 hrs	6:25pm, 7:15pm, 10:30pm
Playa del Carmen	US$3.15-5.50	1 hr	every 30-60 mins midnight-11:30pm
Valladolid	US$6-7.50	1.5-2hrs	every 30-90 mins 1:30am-7:30pm

(US$24 adult, US$12 child), with six designated pickup stops around Tulum town and door-to-door service from the Zona Hotelera. Service from the airport to Tulum also is available (US$29 adult, US$14.50 child). The trip takes just under two hours; advance reservations are required.

Car

Highway 307 passes right through the middle of Tulum Pueblo, where it is referred to as Avenida Tulum. Coming south from Cancún or Playa del Carmen, you'll first pass the entrance to Tulum archaeological site, on your left. A kilometer and a half later (1 mile) you'll reach a large intersection, where you can turn left (east) toward the beach and Zona Hotelera, or right (west) toward Cobá. Continuing straight ahead takes you into Tulum Pueblo, then onward to the Costa Maya.

GETTING AROUND

Bicycle

A bike can be very handy, especially for getting to or from the beach, or anywhere along the now-paved road through the Zona Hotelera. **Iguana Bike Shop** (Av. Satélite near Calle Andrómeda, tel. 984/871-2357 or cell. tel.

984/119-0836, www.iguanabike.com, 9am-7pm Mon.-Sat.) rents a variety of bikes, including beach cruisers (US$10 for 24 hours) and mountain bikes (US$13-15 for 24 hours), most in top condition. The owner also leads enjoyable tours to area cenotes and villages (which accounts for the shop sometimes being closed unexpectedly). Rates vary, but include a helmet, front and back lights, lock, and basket, as well as life and accident insurance. English is spoken. Attachable trailer-bikes for children are also available.

Tikul Bike Rental (Av. Tulum at Calle Acuario, cell. tel. 984/114-4657, 8am-10pm daily) rents bikes (US$6/day) and motorscooters (US$29/day), plus snorkel gear (USUS$4.25/day). Helmets are available for scooters only.

Beach Shuttle

There is a local *colectivo* (US$1-1.25) that goes from Tulum town to the arch at the southern end of the Zona Hotelera, and back again, starting at 6am. The last bus leaves the arch at 4pm. Catch it in front of the Palacio Municipal (Calle Osiris near Av. Tulum; departures at the top of the hour) or anywhere along Avenida Tulum or on the road to and along the beach.

The **Weary Traveler Hostel** (Av. Tulum near Calle Acuario, tel. 984/871-2390, www.wearytravelerhostel.com, US$1) operates a beach shuttle that goes north along the Zona Hotelera road. Its final stop is at Playa Maya and Don Cafeto restaurant near the Tulum ruins. Shuttles leave from the hostel at 7am, 9am, and 11:45am, returning at 12:15pm and 5pm.

Bus schedules do change, however, so always confirm the current departures.

Car

A car can be very useful in Tulum, especially in the Zona Hotelera, even if you don't plan on using it every day. Renting a car from the airport in Cancún is the easiest and most affordable option for most travelers, especially if you book online and in advance. In Tulum, agencies include:

- **Hertz** (Hwy. 307 at Carr. Tulum-Cobá, toll-free Mex. tel. 800/709-5000, www.hertz.com, 7am-10pm daily), located next to Super San Francisco supermarket.

- **Thrifty** (Av. Cobá Sur at Calle Sol Ote, tel. 987/869-2957, www.thrifty.com, 8am-2pm and 4pm-6pm daily).

- **Avis** (Av. Cobá Sur at Calle Sol Ote, cell. tel. 984/120-3972, toll-free Mex. tel. 800/288-8888, www.avis.com, 8am-8pm daily).

Taxi

Taxis are plentiful, and fares run about US$2 in town and US$6-10 to get to the Zona Hotelera (depending on where exactly you're going). In the Zona Hotelera, there is a taxi stand in Punta Piedra; rates are roughly the same within the Zona Hotelera or back into Tulum Pueblo. From either area, a ride to Tulum ruins costs about US$4.

Sian Ka'an Biosphere Reserve

Sian Ka'an is Yucatec Mayan for "where the sky is born," and it's not hard to see how the original inhabitants arrived at such a poetic name. The unkempt beaches, blue-green sea, bird-filled wetlands and islets, and humble accommodations are manna for bird-watchers, artists, snorkelers, and kayakers. But most visitors come here for the fishing. Sian Ka'an is one of the best fly-fishing spots in the world, with all three Grand Slam catches: bonefish, tarpon, and permit.

The reserve was created in 1986, designated a UNESCO World Heritage Site in 1987, and expanded in 1994. It now encompasses around 1.3 million acres of coastal and mangrove forests and wetlands, and some 113 kilometers (70 miles) of pristine coral reefs just offshore. A huge variety of flora and fauna thrive in the reserve, including four species of mangrove, many medicinal plants, and about 300 species of birds, including toucans, parrots, frigate birds, herons, and egrets. Monkeys, foxes, crocodiles, and boa constrictors also populate the reserve and are spotted by locals and visitors with some regularity. Manatees and jaguars are the reserve's largest animals but also the most reclusive: You need sharp eyes and a great deal of luck to spot either one. More than 20 Maya ruins have been found in the reserve, though most are unexcavated.

Spending a few days in Sian Ka'an is the best way to really appreciate its beauty and pace. Hotels and tour operators there can arrange fishing, bird-watching, and other tours, all with experienced local guides. But if time is short, a number of tour operators in Tulum offer day trips into the reserve as well.

SIGHTS
Muyil Archaeological Zone
The most accessible Maya site within the Sian Ka'an reserve is **Muyil** (Hwy. 307, 25 kilometers/15.5 miles south of Tulum, 8am-5pm daily, US$3), on the western edge of the park. Also

known as Chunyaxché, it is one of the oldest archaeological sites in the Maya world, dating back to 300 BC and occupied continuously through the conquest. It's believed to have been primarily a seaport, perched on a limestone shelf near the edge of Laguna Muyil; it is connected to the Caribbean via a canal system that was constructed by ancient Maya traders and still exists today.

Only a small portion of the city has been excavated, so it makes for a relatively quick visit. There are six main structures ranging from two-meter-high (6.6-foot) platforms to the impressive **Castillo**. At 17 meters (56 feet), it is one of the tallest structures on the peninsula's Caribbean coast. The Castillo is topped with a unique solid round masonry turret from which the waters of the Caribbean Sea can be seen. Unfortunately, climbing to the top is prohibited.

A *sacbé* (raised stone road) runs about a half kilometer (0.3 mile) from the center of the site to the edge of the **Laguna Muyil**. Part of this *sacbé* is on private property, however, so if you want to access the lagoon from the ruins—you also can get to it by car—there is an additional charge of US$3.50 per person. Along the way, there is a lookout tower with views over Sian Ka'an to the Caribbean.

Once you arrive at the water's edge, it's possible to take a **boat tour** (US$45 pp) that crosses both Muyil and Chunyaxché Lagoons, which are connected by a canal that was carved by the ancient Maya in order to reach the ocean. It's a pleasant way to enjoy the water, and you'll also get a view of several otherwise inaccessible ruins along the lagoons' edges and through the mangroves, with the final stop being **Xlapak ruins,** a small site thought to have been a trading post. If arriving by car, look for signs to Muyil Lagoon on Highway 307, just south of the similarly named archaeological site. More thorough tours of this part of Sian Ka'an can be booked in Tulum.

TULUM AND QUINTANA ROO

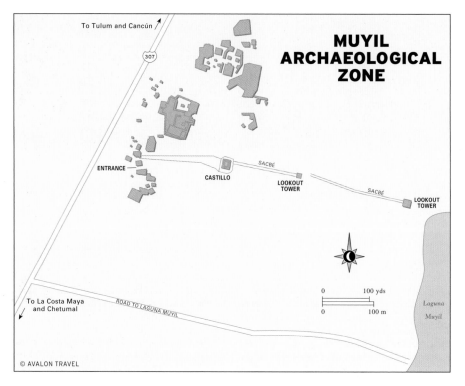

To Tulum and Cancún

307

MUYIL ARCHAEOLOGICAL ZONE

ENTRANCE

CASTILLO

SACBÉ

LOOKOUT TOWER

SACBÉ

LOOKOUT TOWER

To La Costa Maya and Chetumal

ROAD TO LAGUNA MUYIL

0   100 yds

0   100 m

Laguna Muyil

© AVALON TRAVEL

❮ Bahía de la Ascensión

Ascension Bay covers about 20 square kilometers (12.4 square miles), and its shallow flats and tangled mangrove islands teem with bonefish, tarpon, and huge permit—some of the biggest ever caught, in fact. It is a fly fisher's dream come true, and it has been attracting anglers from around the world since the mid-1980s. Don't fly-fish? No worries: The spin fishing is also fantastic, while the offshore reef yields plenty of grouper, barracuda, dorado, tuna, sailfish, and marlin.

SPORTS AND RECREATION

Sportfishing

Sportfishing is world-class in and around Sian Ka'an—it's hard to go wrong in the flats and mangrove islands, or with the Caribbean lapping at its shores. All the hotels listed in this section arrange fishing tours, and most

specialize in it, using their own boats and guides. If you prefer to go with an independent operator, recommended outfits include **Pesca Maya** (7 kilometers/4.3 miles north of Punta Allen, tel. 998/848-2496, toll-free U.S. tel. 888/894-5642, www.pescamaya.com, 8am-7pm daily); the **Palometa Club** (Punta Allen, north of the central plaza, toll-free U.S. tel. 888/824-5420, www.palometaclub.com, 8am-6pm daily); and **Club Grand Slam** (near the entrance to Punta Allen, cell. tel. 984/139-2930, www.grandslamfishinglodge.com).

Weeklong fly-fishing trips range US$2,750-3,750 per person, in shared room and shared boat, depending largely on the style and comforts afforded by the lodge. Most packages include airport transfer, daily guided fishing, meals, and admission to the reserve, but it's always a good idea to confirm this before booking. For private room or private boat, expect to

a stately pyramid at Muyil archaeological zone, just inside the Sian Ka'an Biosphere Reserve

©LIZA PRADO

pay an additional US$100-200 per day; shorter trips are available, but may incur extra transportation costs to and from the airport. Fishing day trips can be arranged through most hotels; rates start at around US$400 for a private full-day tour, including lunch and admission and license fees. Variations like renting gear, adding people, and half-day options can also be arranged.

Bird-Watching

Sian Ka'an is also an excellent place for bird-watching. Trips to Bird Island and other spots afford a look at various species of water birds, including male frigates showing off their big red balloon-like chests in the winter. Tours often combine bird-watching with snorkeling and walking around one or more bay islands. Hotels in Punta Allen and along the coastal road can arrange tours, as can outfits in Tulum. Prices are typically per boat, so don't be shy to approach other travelers in town about forming a group.

In Punta Allen, **Punta Allen Coop** (no phone, 6:30am-2pm daily) is a local cooperative that offers bird-watching tours (US$120-145, 2-3 hours, up to 6 pax); look for their two-story wooden shack along the main road near the entrance to town. Other operators to consider include **CESiaK** (Hwy. 307 just south of the Tulum ruins turnoff, tel. 984/871-2499, www.cesiak.org, 9am-2pm and 4pm-8pm daily); **Community Tours Sian Ka'an** (Tulum, Calle Osiris Sur near Calle Sol Ote, tel. 984/871-2202, www.siankaantours.org, 7am-9pm daily); and, if your budget permits, **Visit Sian Ka'an** (Sian Ka'an Biosphere Reserve, Carr. Tulum-Punta Allen Km. 15.8, cell. tel. 984/141-4245, www.visitsiankaan.com), which offers customized private tours.

Kayaking

The tangled mangrove forests, interconnected lagoons, and scenic bays make Sian Ka'an ideal for kayaking. **CESiaK** (Hwy. 307 just south of the Tulum ruins turnoff, tel. 984/871-2499, www.cesiak.org, 9am-2pm and 4pm-8pm daily) offers kayak tours (US$50, 3 hours) and

SPORT- AND GAME FISHING

Cozumel and the Riviera Maya are well known for trolling and deep-sea fishing, while Ascension Bay and the Costa Maya have terrific fly-fishing. Although you can hook into just about any fish at any time of the year, below is information on the peak and extended seasons for a number of top target species. Those fish not listed – tuna, barracuda, yellowtail, snapper, grouper, and bonefish – are prevalent year-round.

SPORTFISHING

Fish	Peak Season	Extended Season	Description
Sailfish	Mar.-June	Jan.-Sept.	Top target species, with a dramatic dorsal fin and a high-flying fighting style.
Blue Marlin	Apr.-Aug.	Mar.-Sept.	Largest Atlantic billfish, up to 500 pounds locally, but much larger elsewhere.
White Marlin	May-July	Mar.-Aug.	Smaller than the blue marlin, but still challenging.
Wahoo	Nov.-Jan.	June-Feb.	Lightning fast, with torpedo-like shape and distinctive blue stripes.
Dorado	May-July	Feb.-Aug.	Hard fighter with shimmery green, gold, and blue coloration; aka dolphin or mahimahi.

FLAT-WATER FISHING

Fish	Peak Season	Extended Season	Description
Tarpon	Mar.-Aug.	Feb.-Oct.	Big hungry tarpon migrate along the coast in summer months.
Snook	July-Aug.	June-Dec.	Popular trophy fish, grows locally up to 30 pounds.
Permit	Mar.-Sept.	year-round	March and April see schools of permit, with some 20-pound individuals.

rentals for do-it-yourself exploration (US$25/35 s/d, 3 hours). **Community Tours Sian Ka'an** (Tulum, Calle Osiris Sur near Calle Sol Ote, tel. 984/871-2202, www.siankaantours.org, 7am-9pm daily) is another good option.

ACCOMMODATIONS

Punta Allen is the only town on the peninsula and has the most options for lodging, food, tours, and other services. Along the long unpaved road leading there is a smattering of lodges and private homes, amid miles and miles of deserted coastline. **Note:** The town of Punta Allen often switches off the electricity grid at midnight—and hotels outside of town are entirely off the grid—so air-conditioning and TV are not functional unless the establishment has a generator. (Fans work as long as the hotel has solar or wind power.) If you're staying in a room with kitchen facilities, keep the fridge shut as much as possible to conserve the cold.

Toward Punta Allen

Just four kilometers (2.5 miles) from Tulum, **Boca Paila Camps** (tel. 984/871-2499, www. cesiak.org, US$65-80 s/d with shared bathrooms) has spacious "tent cabins"—heavy-duty canvas tents set on platforms—with real beds, tasteful decor, and terraces with views of the Caribbean or lagoon. All share bathrooms with rainwater showers, compost toilets, and 24-hour lighting. The cabins themselves don't have electricity, but candles and battery-powered lamps are provided. There's a restaurant in the main building, where guided kayaking, bird-watching, and fly-fishing tours also can be arranged.

Eight kilometers (5 miles) north of Punta Allen, **❰ Sol Caribe** (cell. tel. 984/139-3839, www.solcaribe-mexico.com, US$185 s/d, US$175-250 *cabaña*, US$100/40 extra per adult/child all-inclusive) offers modern rooms and *cabañas* set on a breezy palm-tree-laden beach. All feature en suite bathrooms with

© LIZA PRADO

TULUM AND QUINTANA ROO

Boca Paila Camps, just inside the Sian Ka'an Biosphere Reserve, offers terrific views from deluxe "tent cabins."

tropical woods, terraces with hammocks, 24-hour electricity (fan only), and gorgeous views of the ocean—a true hidden getaway of the Riviera Maya. There's a full-service restaurant on-site, too.

For more luxury that you'd rightly expect in a remote natural reserve, **Grand Slam Fishing Lodge** (near the entrance to town, cell. tel. 984/139-2930, toll-free U.S. tel. 855/473-5400, www.grandslamfishinglodge.com, US$45-55 s/d with a/c) has gigantic guest rooms in two-story villas, each with one or two king-size beds, fully-stocked minibars, marble bathrooms, and satellite service on large flat-screen TVs, plus 24-hour electricity for air-conditioning and Wi-Fi. The grounds include a tidy beach and aboveground pool, both with drink service, and a spacious restaurant-lounge. Guides and boats are first-rate.

Punta Allen

Casa de Ascensión (near the entrance to town, tel. 984/801-0034, www.casadeascensionhotel.com, US$41-50 s/d with a/c) is a small hotel with three brightly painted rooms, each with quiet air-conditioning, hot-water bathrooms, and Wi-Fi (two also have satellite TV). The owner, a longtime expat, lives on-site and provides attentive service, including breakfast to order in the hotel's 2nd-floor restaurant and recommendations for area tours.

Facing the central plaza, **Posada Sirena** (tel. 984/877-8521, www.casasirena.com, US$38-75 s/d) offers simple Robinson Crusoe-style rooms. Most are quite spacious, sleeping 6-8 people, and all have private bathrooms, fully equipped kitchens, and plenty of screened windows to let in the ocean breeze. Area excursions, including fly-fishing, snorkeling, and bird-watching, can be arranged on-site.

The accommodations at ⦅ **Serenidad Shardon** (road to the lighthouse, cell. tel. 984/107-4155, www.shardon.com, US$8.50-17 pp camping, US$150 s/d, US$200 s/d with kitchen, US$250 two-bedroom apartment for up to 5 guests, US$350 beach house for up to 10 guests) vary from oceanfront *cabañas* to a large beach house; all have basic furnishings

but are clean and well equipped. You also can camp using your own gear, or rent deluxe tents with real beds, electric lighting, and fans; access to hot showers and a full kitchen is included, too.

A dedicated fishing lodge, **The Palometa Club** (north of the central plaza, toll-free U.S. tel. 888/824-5420, www.palometaclub.com) has just six rooms in a two-story structure facing the beach. Each has tile floors, a private bathroom, and two double beds. Meals are served family-style, with cocktails and snacks (including fresh-made ceviche) available at the club's outdoor bar, après fishing. The Palometa is designed for serious anglers, with a fly-tying study, one-to-one guiding, and an emphasis on landing permits (*palometa* in Spanish, hence the name). Non-anglers are welcome if accompanying a fishing guest. The all-inclusive seven-night/six-day rate is US$3,650 per person (non-anglers US$2,000 per person). Rates are for shared room and boat; for private room, add US$100/night; for private boat, add US$200/day. Shorter packages are available but may include additional airport transfer fees.

FOOD

Punta Allen isn't a foodie's village, but it does have a handful of eateries, all specializing in fresh seafood. A few mini-marts and a tortilleria round things out a bit, especially if you're planning on staying more than a couple of days.

Restaurants

With a gorgeous view of the Caribbean, **Muelle Viejo** (just south of the central plaza, no phone, 11am-10pm Mon.-Sat., US$6-14) serves up fresh seafood dishes and cold beers—perfect for a long lazy lunch.

Taco Loco (just north of the central plaza, no phone, 8am-10pm Mon.-Sat., US$3-8) is a locals' joint with good, cheap eats.

The hotel restaurant at **Casa de Ascensión** (tel. 984/801-0034, www.casadeascensionhotel.com, 8am-10pm daily, US$4-17) offers a wide variety of Mexican dishes, pizza and pasta, and (of course) seafood. Seating is outdoors, under a large *palapa*. It's located two blocks from the beach, near the entrance to town.

Groceries

There are three **mini-marts** in town: on the north end (near the road to the lagoon-side dock), south end (two blocks west of Cuzan Guesthouse), and near the central plaza (one block west). Each sells basic foodstuffs and snacks, though you may have to visit all three to find what you're looking for. If you plan to cook a lot, stock up on supplies in Tulum.

INFORMATION AND SERVICES

Don't expect much in the way of services in Sian Ka'an—if there is something you can't do without, definitely bring it with you. There are **no banking services,** and few of the hotels or tour operators accept credit cards. There is one **Internet café** (9am-9pm Mon.-Fri., 9am-2pm Sat., US$1/hour), located inside a mini-mart near the southwest corner of the central plaza; many hotels have Wi-Fi. Cell phones typically don't work in Sian Ka'an, but there are **public telephones** in town. Punta Allen also has a modest **medical clinic**—look for it on the main road as you enter town. There is **no laundry,** but most hotels will provide the service.

GETTING THERE

Many of the hotels include airport pickup/drop-off, which is convenient and helps you avoid paying for a week's car rental when you plan on fishing all day. That said, a car is useful if you'd like to do some exploring on your own.

Bus

Public transport to and from Punta Allen is unpredictable at best—build some flexibility into your plans in case of missed (or missing) connections.

A privately run **Tulum-Punta Allen shuttle** (cell. tel. 984/115-5580, US$21, 3 hours) leaves Tulum at 2pm most days. You can catch it at the taxi station on Avenida Tulum between Calles Centauro and Orion, or anywhere along the Zona Hotelera road; advance reservations

© LIZA PRADO

the road to Punta Allen, in the heart of Sian Ka'an Biosphere Reserve

The Caste War

On July 18, 1847, a military commander in Valladolid learned of an armed plot to overthrow the government that was being planned by two indigenous men—Miguel Antonio Ay and Cecilio Chí. Ay was arrested and executed. Chí managed to escape punishment and on July 30, 1847, led a small band of armed men into the town of Tepich. Several officials and Euro-Mexican families were killed. The military responded with overwhelming force, burning villages, poisoning wells, and killing scores of people, including many women, children, and elderly. The massacre—and the longstanding oppression of indigenous people at its root—sparked spontaneous uprisings across the peninsula, which quickly developed into a massive, coordinated indigenous rebellion known as the Caste War.

Indigenous troops tore through colonial cities, killing and capturing scores of non-Maya. In some cases, the Maya turned the tables on their former masters, forcing them into slave labor, including building the church in present-day Carrillo Puerto's central plaza. Valladolid was evacuated in 1848 and left abandoned for nearly a year, and by 1849, the peninsula's indigenous people were close to expelling the colonial elite. However, as they were preparing their final assaults on Mérida and Campeche City, the rainy season came early, presenting the Maya soldiers with a bitter choice between victory and (were they to miss the planting season) likely famine. The men turned their backs on a hard-fought and near-certain victory to return to their fields to plant corn.

Mexican troops immediately took advantage of the lull, and the Maya never regained the upper hand. For the next 13 years, captured indigenous soldiers (and increasingly *any* indigenous person) were sold to slave brokers and shipped to Cuba. Many Maya eventually fled into the forests and jungles of southern Quintana Roo. The fighting was rekindled when a wooden cross in the town of Chan Santa Cruz (today, Carrillo Puerto) was said to be channeling the voice of God, urging the Maya to keep fighting. The war ended, however, when troops took control of Chan Santa Cruz in 1901. An official surrender was signed in 1936.

are required. To return, the same shuttle leaves Punta Allen for Tulum at 5am.

You also can get to Punta Allen from Carrillo Puerto, a slightly cheaper but much longer and more taxing trip. State-run *combis* leave from the market in Carrillo Puerto (a block from the main traffic circle) for a bone-jarring four-hour trip down a private road to the small settlement of Playón (US$10, 10am and 3pm daily), where water taxis wait to ferry passengers across the lagoon to Punta Allen (US$2.50 pp, 15 minutes). The *combi* back to Carrillo Puerto leaves Playón at 6am.

Car

To get to Punta Allen by car, head south along the coast through (and past) Tulum's Zona Hotelera. About eight kilometers (5 miles) from the Tulum/Zona Hotelera junction is *el arco* (the arch), marking the reserve boundary where you register and pay a US$4 per person park fee. From there it's 56 kilometers (35 miles) by dirt road to Punta Allen. The road is much improved from years past, and an ordinary car can make it in 2-3 hours. It can be much more difficult after a heavy rain, however. Be sure to fill the tank in Tulum—there is no gas station along the way or in Punta Allen, though some locals sell gas from their homes.

CARRILLO PUERTO

Highway 307 from Tulum to Chetumal passes through Carrillo Puerto, a small city that holds little of interest to most travelers except an opportunity to fill up on gas. Historically, however, it played a central role in the formation of Quintana Roo and the entire peninsula.

History

Founded in 1850, the town of Chan Santa Cruz (present-day Carrillo Puerto) was the center of a pivotal movement during the Caste War. As the

CARRILLO PUERTO BUS SCHEDULE

Departures from the **bus terminal** (Calle 65 near central plaza, tel. 983/834-0815) include:

DESTINATION	PRICE	DURATION	SCHEDULE
Bacalar	US$5.25-7.50	1.5-2 hrs	every 45-60 mins 1:50am-11pm, or take any Chetumal bus
Cancún	US$11.75-16.25	3.5-4 hrs	every 30-90 mins 1:05am-11:45pm
Chetumal	US$6.5-10	2-2.5 hrs	8 departures 8:35am-11:45pm
Mahahual	US$8.25	2 hrs	7pm
Mérida (second-class)	US$18	6 hrs	15 departures 12:30am-8:45pm
Tulum	US$4.75-7.50	1-1.5 hrs	every 30-60 mins 5:30am-11:50pm
Valladolid	US$7	2.5 hrs	11:15pm

Maya lost ground in the war, two indigenous leaders enlisted a ventriloquist to introduce the *Cruz Parlante* (Talking Cross) in Chan Santa Cruz. The cross "spoke" to the battle-weary population, urging them to continue fighting, even issuing tactical orders and predicting victory in the long, bitter conflict. Thousands joined the sect of the cross, calling themselves Cruzob (a Spanish-Maya conflation meaning People of the Holy Cross). Some accounts portray the talking cross as little more than political theater for a simpleminded audience, while others say most Cruzob understood it as a ruse to instill motivation. Some people, of course, believe in the cross's divinity. Whatever the case, it reinvigorated the Maya soldiers, and Chan Santa Cruz remained the last redoubt of organized indigenous resistance, finally submitting to federal troops in 1901. Once residing in Carrillo Puerto's Santuario de la Cruz Parlante, the Talking Cross is today housed in a small sanctuary in the town of Tixacal.

The town's name was changed in 1934 in honor of a former governor of Quintana Roo, much revered by indigenous and working-class people for his progressive reforms, for which he was ultimately assassinated.

Sights

The **Santuario de la Cruz Parlante** (Calle 69 at Calle 60, no phone, irregular hours, free) is a sacred place where the Talking Cross and two smaller ones were originally housed (they now reside in the nearby town of Tixacal). Today, there are several crosses in their place, all dressed in *huipiles,* which is customary in the Yucatán. Shoes and hats must be removed before entering. Be sure to ask permission before snapping any photographs.

Carrillo Puerto's main church, the **Iglesia de Balam Nah** (facing the central plaza, no phone), was reportedly built by white slaves—mostly Spaniards and light-skinned Mexicans—who were captured during the

TULUM AND QUINTANA ROO

Caste War. It was constructed in 1858 to house the Talking Cross and its two companion crosses because the original sanctuary had become too small to accommodate its worshippers. Unfortunately, at the end of the Caste War, federal troops used the church as an army storeroom, desecrating it in the eyes of many Maya; this led to the transfer of the Talking Cross to the town of Tixacal.

Despite outward appearances, Maya nationalism is still very much alive, and its adherents are not blind of the sometimes invasive effects of mass tourism. Don't miss the beautifully painted **Central Plaza Mural**, next to the Casa de Cultura, that reads: *La zona Maya no es un museo etnográfico, es un pueblo en marcha* (The Maya region is not an ethnographic museum, it is a people on the move).

Accommodations

Owned and operated by one of the founding families of the city, **Hotel Esquivel** (Calle 63 btwn Calles 66 and 68, tel. 983/834-0344, US$35 s/d with fan, US$42 s/d with a/c, US$55 suite with a/c and kitchenette) offers 37 rooms in four buildings, each with private bathroom and cable TV. The main building has by far the best rooms—gleaming tile floors, simple furnishings, decent beds, and even some with balconies overlooking a pleasant park. The suite is in the large house across the street—once the family home, it's now dark and dilapidated, and desirable only for having a kitchen.

Food

Parrilla Galerías (Calle 65 s/n, tel. 983/834-0313, 5:30pm-midnight daily, US$3-10) opens right onto the central plaza and offers traditional Mexican fare and grilled meats. Come here for the tacos and the *parrillada,* a platter piled high with an assortment of meats, grilled onions, and tortillas.

El Faisán y el Venado (Av. Benito Juárez

at Calle 67, tel. 983/834-0043, 6am-10pm daily, US$5-8) is Carrillo Puerto's best-known restaurant, as much for its location and longevity than for any particular noteworthiness of its food. The menu is filled with reliable Yucatecan standards, including 8-10 variations of fish, chicken, and beef, plus soup and other sides.

Information and Services

The **tourist office** (Av. Benito Juárez at Av. Santiago Pacheco Cruz, tel. 983/267-1452) is open 8am-2pm and 6pm-9pm Monday-Friday.

The **Hospital General** (Calle 51 btwn Av. Benito Juárez and Calle 68, tel. 983/834-0092) is open 24 hours daily. Try **Farmacia Similares** (Av. Benito Juárez at Av. Lázaro Cárdenas, tel. 983/834-1407, 8am-10:30pm Mon.-Sat., 9am-10:30pm Sun.) for meds.

The **police department** (central plaza, tel. 983/834-0369, 24 hours) is located in the Palacio Municipal (city hall).

Next to the PEMEX station, **HSBC** (Av. Benito Juárez at Calle 69, 9am-6pm Mon.-Fri., 9am-3pm Sat.) has one 24-hour ATM.

The **post office** (Calle 69 btwn Calles 64 and 66) is open 9am-4pm weekdays. Facing the central plaza, **Balam Nah Internet** (8am-1am daily) charges US$1 per hour.

Getting There

Carrillo Puerto's **bus terminal** (tel. 983/834-0815) is just off the central plaza, with service to Mahahual, Chetumal, Cancún, Mérida, and elsewhere.

If traveling by car, **fill your gas tank** in Carrillo Puerto, especially if you're headed to Mahahual, Xcalak, Xpujil, or Ticul. There are other roadside gas stations ahead (and in Chetumal), but they get less and less reliable—having either no gas or no electricity to pump it—as the stretches of empty highway grow longer and longer.

La Costa Maya

The coastline south of Tulum loops and weaves like the tangled branches of the mangrove trees that blanket much of it. It is a mosaic of savannas, marshes, lagoons, scattered islands, and three huge bays: Bahía de la Ascensión, Bahía del Espiritu Santo, and Bahía de Chetumal. Where it's not covered by mangroves, the shore has sandy beaches and dunes, and just below the turquoise sea is one of the least-impacted sections of the great Mesoamerican Coral Reef. Dozens of Maya archaeological sites have been discovered here, but few excavated, and much remains unknown about pre-Hispanic life here. During the conquest, the snarled coastal forest proved an effective sanctuary for indigenous rebels and refugees fleeing Spanish control, not to mention a haven for pirates, British logwood cutters, and Belizean anglers.

In the 1990s, Quintana Roo officials launched an effort to develop the state's southern coast, which was still extremely isolated despite the breakneck development taking place in and around Cancún. (It has always been a famous fly-fishing area, however.) The first order of business was to construct a huge cruise ship port, which they did in the tiny fishing village of Mahahual. They also needed a catchy name, and came up with "la Costa Maya." The moniker generally applies to the coastal areas south of Tulum, particularly the Sian Ka'an Biosphere Reserve; the towns of Mahahual and Xcalak; Laguna Bacalar; and Chetumal, the state capital and by far the largest city in the area. Few locals use the term, of course.

It's hard not to be a little cynical about cruise liners coming to such a remote area, whose entire population could fit comfortably on a single ship. The town of Mahahual, nearest the port, is utterly transformed when cruise ships arrive, their passengers moseying about Mahahual, beer bottles in hand, the beaches packed with sun worshippers

serenaded by the sound of Jet Skis. Then again, it's doubtful the area would have paved roads, power lines, or telephone service if not for the income and demand generated by cruise ships. Driving down the old rutted coastal road to Xcalak (an even smaller town south of Mahahual) used to take a half day or more; today, a two-lane paved road has cut the trip to under an hour. The state government has vowed to control development by limiting hotel size and density, monitoring construction methods, and protecting the mangroves and coral reef. Small ecofriendly bed-and-breakfasts have thrived, not surprisingly, and more and more independent travelers are drawn to the Costa Maya for its quiet isolation and pristine natural beauty.

MAHAHUAL

Mahahual is a place of two faces: cruise ship days, when the town's one road is packed with day-trippers looking to buy T-shirts and throw back a few beers; and non-cruise-ship days, when Mahahual is sleepy and laid-back, and the narrow white-sand beaches are free to walk for miles. Whether you stay here a night or a week, you're likely to see both, which is a good thing. You can be in a major party zone one day, and the next be the only snorkeler in town—all without changing hotels. If you seek long quiet days every day, though, definitely stay outside of town.

Whether or not there is a cruise ship in town, Mahahual is pretty easy to manage. Most of its hotels and services are located on, or just off, Avenida Mahahual (aka El Malecón), the three-kilometer (1.9-mile) pedestrian walkway that runs through town until it meets up with the coastal road heading south, the Carretera Antigua (literally, Old Highway). Just northwest of town, the tiny residential community of Las Casitas (aka Nuevo Mahahual) has additional restaurants, Internet, and laundry services.

Sports and Recreation

SCUBA DIVING

Mahahual has terrific diving on the coral reef just offshore, with dozens of sites a short boat ride away. It's also one of two jumping-off points for trips to Chinchorro Bank, the largest coral atoll in the Northern Hemisphere. The other departure point is Xcalak, south of Mahahual.

Don't be deterred by the slew of cruise shippers who crowd into **Dreamtime Dive Resort** (Av. Mahahual Km. 2.5, cell. tel. 983/124-0235, www.dreamtimediving.com, 9am-7pm daily)—the shop is an indie operation at heart and sends its students and "regular" guests on separate boats in groups of six divers or fewer. Fun dives cost US$50 for one tank, US$75 for two, and US$20 per day for rental equipment. Open-water, advanced, and other courses are also available.

Bucanero del Caribe (Av. Mahahual Km. 2, cell. tel. 983/120-5306, www.divemahahual.com, 9am-5pm daily) offers personalized service for independent travelers. Dive trips run US$55 for one tank, US$85 for two, including all equipment and a guide.

SNORKELING

You can rent snorkel gear for around US$5-10 a day from the dive shops or from the kiosks that pop up on cruise ship days. Swim or kayak out to the reef for a do-it-yourself experience, or join a guided tour, where you'll likely see more sealife, plus have extra safety and convenience. Mahahual's dive shops all offer guided snorkel trips for US$25-35 per person, including gear and about 90 minutes in the water.

TOURS

The Native Choice (Las Casitas, Av. Paseo del Puerto at Calle Chinchorro, tel. 998/869-3346, www.thenativechoice.com) is a small operation run by David Villagómez and Ivan Cohuo, both born and raised in the small village of Chacchoben and extremely knowledgeable about nearby ruins, Maya history, culture, and belief systems. Tours include visiting the archaeological sites of Chacchoben, Kohunlich,

© LIZA PRADO

a glimpse of Mahahual's beautiful waterfront

or Dzibanche (US$70-90 adult, US$60-85 child), a "Mayan Experience Tour," which includes touring Chacchoben ruins and a visit to a home in Chacchoben village (US$70 adult, US$65 child), plus a kayaking and hiking trip on and around Laguna Bacalar (US$55 adult, US$40 child). The tours are geared toward the cruise ship crowd, but hotel owners warmly recommend the outfit to independent travelers as well.

Accommodations

Many of Mahahual's lodgings, especially the ones with beachfront, are outside of the village itself, along the Carretera Antigua that hugs the coast south of town. The rest are in town, either on the Malecón or a stone's throw away.

IN TOWN

Under US$50: Set on a grassy lot facing the ocean, **Las Cabañas del Doctor** (Av. Mahahual Km. 2, tel. 983/832-2102, www.lascabanasdeldoctor.com, US$6.75 pp camping, US$33-45 *cabaña,* US$45-75 s/d, US$75 s/d with a/c) has

a good range of accommodations: camping on the beach with access to cold-water bathrooms (BYO gear); *cabañas—palapa*-roofed units with tile floors and fans; and hotel rooms, which are a step up in comfort and décor, plus they have private porches.

Kabañitas de Colores (Calle Almeja at Calle Huachinango, cell. tel. 983/137-4095, US$25 s, US$30 d) has a handful of brightly painted clapboard *cabañas.* There's not much to them: a bed, a fan, a bare bulb, a tiny cold-water bathroom. They're clean, though, and there's electricity 24/7. With the beach a stone's throw away, there's not much more you really need.

US$50-100: Posada Pachamama (Calle Huachinango btwn Calles Martillo and Coronado, cell. tel. 983/134-3049, www.posadapachamama.net, US$67-75 s/d with a/c) is a small hotel a block from the beach. Rooms are small but appealingly decorated with modern furnishings and stone-inlaid floors. All have air-conditioning and wireless Internet; the higher-priced rooms include Sky TV. Guests

TULUM AND QUINTANA ROO

also enjoy complimentary use of the beach club at Los 40 Cañones, just down the street.

With direct access to the beach and a rooftop bar with a spectacular view, **Hotel Caballo Blanco** (Malecón btwn Calles Martillo and Coronado, cell. tel. 983/126-0319, www.hotelelcaballoblanco.com, US$75-108 s/d with a/c) is a great place to land. Rooms are standard issue: modern and comfortable with air-conditioning, flat-screen TVs, and Wi-Fi. The only quirk? Murals of old-world villages in some of the rooms.

Luna de Plata (Av. Mahahual Km. 2, cell. tel. 983/125-3999, www.lunadeplata.info, US$67-92 s/d with a/c) is a restaurant-hotel offering a handful of rooms with tasteful decor. Hot water, quiet air-conditioning, and Wi-Fi cover the basic creature comforts. More expensive rooms have Sky TV, too. Town is an easy walk away, and there's a patch of beach and a dive shop in front.

OUTSIDE OF TOWN

US$50-100: Owned and operated by friendly Canadian expats, **◖ Balamku Inn on the Beach** (Carr. Antigua Km. 5.7, tel. 983/732-1004, www.balamku.com, US$85 s, US$95 d) offers artfully decorated rooms in a handful of *palapa*-roofed buildings. All run on solar power, wind turbines, and a nonpolluting wastewater system. Full breakfast is included, as is use of the hotel's kayaks, board games, and music and book library. Wi-Fi is available in all the rooms, too.

Kohunbeach (Carr. Antigua Km. 7, cell. tel. 983/700-2820, www.kohunbeach.blogspot.com, US$50 s/d) offers three spacious *cabañas* on the beach. Each has a queen bed, a foldout futon sofa, picture windows, and a mosaic-tile bathroom. All are solar powered. Kayaks and plenty of hammocks are available to guests, too. Continental breakfast is included and delivered to your porch.

Maya Luna (Carr. Antigua Km. 5.6, tel. 983/836-0905, www.hotelmayaluna.com, US$92 s/d) has four modern bungalows with 24-hour solar/wind power, rainwater showers, and *palapa*-shaded porches. Each has a private

rooftop terrace with views of the Caribbean in front and the jungle in back. A hearty and healthy breakfast also is included in the rate. A friendly dog and a handful of cats live—and roam about—the hotel grounds, too.

For a rustic getaway, **Kabah-na** (Carr. Antigua Km. 8.6, cell. tel. 983/116-6919, www.kabahna.com, US$67-75 s/d, US$84-100 s/d with kitchenette) has seven simple *cabañas*, each slightly different, sleeping 3-6 people. All have fans, *palapa* roof, and cold-water showers; those closest to the beach are a bit more polished. There's a decent restaurant on-site, and even a dive and tour guide offering personalized scuba, snorkeling, and other excursions. Guests can make free use of kayaks, snorkel gear, hammocks, and Wi-Fi.

Over US$100: With fully equipped kitchens, the studio apartments at **Margarita del Sol** (Carr. Antigua Km. 7, tel. 555/350-8522, toll-free U.S. tel. 877/473-1934, www.margaritadelsol.com, US$120 studio) are a great option if you want to save a bit on meals. The units themmezzanes are spacious and modern; each has an eating area, a private porch or terrace with an ocean view, and features like wireless Internet and DVD players (plus free access to a decent library of DVDs). Use of kayaks and snorkel gear is also included.

About 20 minutes south of town, **Almaplena Eco Resort and Beach Club** (Carr. Antigua Km. 12.5, cell. tel. 983/137-5070, www.almaplenabeachresort.com, US$140-160 s/d) is a small boutique resort with just eight rooms facing a gorgeous isolated stretch of beach. All have king-size beds, ceiling fans (no air-conditioning), cool stone floors, and tasteful decor. Suites are on the top floor and have private terraces, while standards share a wooden patio with direct access to the beach. Continental breakfast is included, and the on-site restaurant serves fine Italian and Mexican meals. The Italian owners provide friendly and attentive service.

About 21 kilometers (13 miles) north of Mahahual, **Mayan Beach Garden Inn** (Placer town, cell. tel. 983/130-8658, www.mayanbeachgarden.com, US$96-125 s/d, US$125 s/d with kitchenette, US$25 extra for a/c at night) has several rooms and one *cabaña,* all with whitewashed walls and Mexican-style decor, most with ocean views. A hearty breakfast is included in the rate, as are Wi-Fi and the use of kayaks. All-inclusive meal packages are also available. In the high season, there's a three-night minimum.

Food

IN TOWN

With a sand floor, plastic tables, and *palapa* roof, ◖ **100% Agave** (Calle Huachinango btwn Calles Sierra and Cherna, no phone, 8am-11pm Mon.-Sat., US$4-10) won't let you forget that you're at the beach—even if you're a block away. Serving up simple Mexican classics with monster-size drinks, this is a great place to check out the local scene. If it's packed, take a whole roasted chicken to go; it comes with tortillas, potatoes, and grilled onions (US$6).

An open-air eatery and beach club, **Nohoch Kay** (Big Fish in English, Malecón btwn Calles Liza and Cazón, no phone, 8am-7pm Mon.-Tues., 8am-10pm Wed.-Sun., US$5-12) serves up some of the best fish tacos in town. Thick pieces of fish—fried or grilled—are served with small tortillas, onion, cilantro, and plenty of lime. On cruise ship days, it gets overrun with clients, but otherwise it's a laid-back place to get a beachfront meal.

Ki'i Taco (Calle Huachinango at Calle Cherna, no phone, 11am-10pm Mon.-Sat., US$2-6) offers equally good fish tacos without the cruise ship scene. For a treat, order the garlic shrimp tacos.

Luna de Plata (Av. Mahahual Km. 2, cell. tel. 983/125-3999, www.lunadeplata.info, 11:30am-3:30pm and 6pm-midnight daily, US$8-30) serves well-prepared Italian dishes, from thin crispy pizzas to freshly made pasta with shrimp or lobster.

If you're cooking for yourself, consider buying fresh lobster from the local lobster fisherman's co-op, **Centro de Acopio de Langosta** (Calle Huachinango near Calle Almeja, no phone, 7am-7pm daily). At this roadside shack, you can take your pick of lobsters; they

generally sell for US$30 per kilo (2.2 pounds). Fresh conch also is sold here for about US$16 per kilo.

OUTSIDE OF TOWN

A longtime favorite, **Travel In'** (Carr. Antigua Km. 5.8, cell. tel. 983/110-9496, www.travel-in.com.mx, 5:30pm-9pm Tues.-Sat., US$5-20) is a great little restaurant a few kilometers down the coastal road. Pita bread is baked fresh every day—order it as an appetizer with an assortment of homemade dips. Daily seafood specials vary according to the day's catch, plus every Wednesday is tapas night. Open on Mondays from Christmas to Easter.

In Las Casitas, **Aroma** (Las Casitas, Av. Paseo del Puerto s/n, tel. 983/834-5740, 7am-midnight Mon.-Fri., 5pm-midnight Sun., US$4-14) is a cool corner bistro with an open kitchen. An international menu offers respite from standard Mexican fare, with items such as gazpacho, moussaka, and beef medallions in soy balsamic sauce. Wi-Fi is available, too.

Kitty-corner from Aroma, **Loco Ricky's** (Las Casitas, Av. Paseo del Puerto s/n, cell. tel. 983/105-3978, 11am-11pm Tues.-Sun., US$4-14) serves up classic American fare, including burgers, onion rings, and pizza. The bar has a large-screen TV for big games, and the staff makes everyone feel at home (or at least at their hometown sports bar).

For basic groceries, try **Minisuper Noé** (Las Casitas, Av. Paseo del Puerto near Calle Kohunlich, 8am-11pm daily).

Information and Services

Cruise ships have brought considerable modernization to this once-isolated fishing village, but services are still somewhat limited.

EMERGENCY SERVICES

The **Centro de Salud** (Calle Coronado btwn Calles Huachinango and Sardina, no phone, 8am-2:30pm daily, after 5pm emergencies only) offers basic health services. For serious health matters, head to Chetumal.

For meds, try **Pharmacy Mérida** (Calle Sardina btwn Calles Rubia and Sierra, cell.

tel. 983/132-1845, 7am-11pm Mon.-Fri., 9am-11pm Sat.-Sun.), the best-stocked pharmacy in town.

The **police department** (Calle Huachinango near Calle Martillo, toll-free Mex. tel. 066) is open 24 hours.

MONEY

There is no bank in town, but there are a handful of **ATMs**, all along El Malecón. At the time of research, however, none were affiliated with local banks, so withdrawal charges were hefty. Another option is to go to the gas station outside of town, where there's an **HSBC ATM** (though it often runs out of cash); alternatively, consider bringing enough money to get you through your stay.

MEDIA AND COMMUNICATIONS

In Mahahual proper, head to **V@mos** (Calle Cherna between El Malecón at Calle Huachinango, cell. tel. 983/106-4647, 9am-3pm and 7pm-9pm daily, US$1.75 per hour) for Internet service. If there's a long wait and you've got a car, head to Las Casitas, where **Mobius Internet** (9am-9pm Mon.-Sat.) charges US$3 per hour and offers international telephone service, too (US$0.30-0.60/minute calls to the United States and Europe). Most hotels and some restaurants offer wireless Internet as well.

LAUNDRY

Lavandería 4 Hermanos (Calle Huachinango near Calle Rubia, 7am-8pm daily) offers same-day laundry service for US$1.25 per kilo (2.2 pounds).

In Las Casitas, try **Qué Limpio** (Calle Chacchoben 24, 8am-6pm Mon.-Sat.), which charges US$1.25 per kilo (2.2 pounds). Service takes a day or two.

VOLUNTEER WORK

Global Vision International (www.gvi.co.uk) operates a popular volunteer-for-pay program just north of Mahahual, in partnership with Amigos de Sian Ka'an, a local nonprofit. GVI "expeditions," as they are called, last 4-12 weeks. Fees are reasonable considering how much diving is involved (including open-water scuba certification, if needed): US$3,052 for 4weeks, US$5,772 for 12 weeks, including room, board, and equipment, but not airfare. Advance registration is required, as the center is not designed to handle walk-ins. GVI also has programs in Sian Ka'an Biosphere Reserve as well as at the private inland reserve El Eden.

Getting There and Around

Just south of the grubby roadside town of Limones, a good paved road with signs to Mahahual breaks off Highway 307 and cuts through 58 kilometers (36 miles) of coastal forest and wetlands tangled with mangroves. It's a scenic stretch, whether in a car or on a bus, along which you can see occasionally egrets, herons, and other water birds.

Mahahual proper is very walkable—in fact, the main road that runs through town, El Malecón, is a three-kilometer (1.9-mile) pedestrian walkway. If you're staying outside of town, a car certainly comes in handy, but plenty of people manage without; dive shops and tour operators typically offer hotel pickup, and there are cabs and a local bus.

BICYCLE

Bike rentals are offered at **Costa Maya Tours** (Calle Cherna between El Malecón at Calle Huachinango, cell. tel. 983/106-4647, 9am-3pm and 7pm-9pm daily) for US$2.50 per hour, US$7.50 per half day, and US$12.50 per day. **Nacional Beach Club and Bungalows** (Calle Huachinango near Calle Coronado, tel. 983/834-5719) also rents bikes at similar rates.

BUS

Mahahual's bus terminal is a modest affair—an open-air lot near the entrance of town—but daily first-class service makes coming and going a breeze. Buses to Cancún (US$23, 5 hours) leave at 8:30am and 1pm daily, stopping at Carrillo Puerto (US$8.25, 2 hours), Tulum (US$14.50, 3 hours), Playa del Carmen (US$17, 3.5 hours), and Puerto Morelos (US$19, 4 hours) along the way. To Chetumal

(US$10, 2.5 hours) and Laguna Bacalar (US$7, 1.5 hours), buses depart at 7:30am and 6:30pm daily. All buses stop in Limones (US$7, 1.5 hours). The ticket booth is open a short time before and after scheduled departures only.

Note: Buses entering Mahahual stop in Las Casitas before arriving at the bus terminal; be sure you get off at the latter if you're headed to the beach or any of the hotels.

There also is occasional bus service to Xcalak (Mon.-Sat., US$3); buses pass through the center around 9am and drive down the coastal road, passing most of the hotels there before joining the main paved road into Xcalak. The bus heading back to town from Xcalak passes the outlying hotels around 3:30pm.

CAR AND TAXI

There is a PEMEX gas station (24 hours) on the main road to Mahahual, just east of the turn-off to Xcalak. It occasionally runs out of gas, so definitely fill your tank in Carrillo Puerto or Chetumal on your way here.

Note: There's often a military checkpoint set up just west of the turnoff to Xcalak, where officials conduct searches for illicit drugs and other contraband. As long as you or your passengers don't have anything illegal in the car, the longest you should be delayed is a couple of minutes.

Cabs abound in this town, especially on cruise ship days. In general, rates run US$1.25 per kilometer (0.6 mile).

AIRPORT

Mahahual has a small airport just outside of town. Well, it's more like a well-maintained airstrip with a nice shelter. At the time of research, it was only used by private or chartered planes.

XCALAK

The tiny fishing village of Xcalak lies just a short distance from the channel that marks the Mexico-Belize border, and a blessed long way from anything else. The town started out as a military outpost and didn't get its first real hotel until 1988. Villagers had to wait another decade to get a paved road; before that, the only way in or out of town was by boat or via 55 kilometers (34 miles) of rutted beach tracks. Electrical lines were installed in 2004 but only in the village proper, so many outlying areas (including most of the better hotels) still rely on solar and wind power, as well as generators. The town has no bank, no public phones, and no gas station. That is to say: perfect!

The area doesn't have much beach but makes up for it with world-class fly-fishing, great snorkeling and diving, and a healthy coral reef and lagoon. A growing contingent of expats, mostly American and Canadian, have built homes here, some for personal use, others for rent, others as small hotels. Large-scale tourism may be inevitable but still seems a long way off, and Xcalak remains a small and wonderfully laid-back place, perfect for those looking for some honest-to-goodness isolation.

Sights
PARQUE NACIONAL ARRECIFES DE XCALAK

Xcalak Reef National Park was established at the end of 2003, affording protection to the coastal ecosystem as well as Xcalak's nascent tourist economy. The park spans nearly 18,000 hectares (44,479 acres), from the Belize border to well north of town, and includes the reef—and everything else down to 100 meters (328 feet)—as well as the shoreline and numerous inland lagoons.

The main coral reef lies just 90-180 meters (100-200 yards) from shore, and the water is less than 1.5 meters (5 feet) deep almost the whole way out. Many snorkelers prefer the coral heads even closer to shore, which have plenty to see and less swell than the main reef. The shallow waters keep boat traffic to a minimum, and anglers are good about steering clear of snorkelers (you should still stay alert at all times, however).

Divers and snorkelers also can explore the reef at 20 or so official sites and many more unofficial ones. Most are a short distance from town, and shops typically return to port between tanks. **La Poza** is one of the more distinctive dives, drifting through a trench where

© LIZA PRADO

Kayaking is a great way to enjoy the Costa Maya.

hundreds, sometimes thousands, of tarpon congregate, varying in size from one-meter (3-foot) "juveniles" to two-meter (7-foot) behemoths.

A fee of US$5 per day technically applies to all divers and snorkelers (and kayakers and anglers) in the Parque Nacional Arrecifes de Xcalak; dive shops typically add it to their rates, while most hotels have a stack of wristband permits to sell to guests who want to snorkel right from shore.

BANCO CHINCHORRO

Chinchorro Bank is by some measurements the largest coral atoll in the Northern Hemisphere and a paradise for divers and snorkelers alike. About 48 kilometers (30 miles) northeast from Xcalak, Chinchorro is a marine reserve and is known for its spectacular coral formations, massive sponges, and abundant sealife. Scores of ships have foundered on the shallow reefs through the years, but (contrary to innumerable misreports) the wrecks cannot be dived. Not only are they protected as historical sites, but most are on the eastern side of the atoll, where the surf and currents are too strong for recreational diving. The famous **40 Cannons wreck,** in about three meters (10 feet) of water on the atoll's northwest side, is good for snorkeling but not diving, and thanks to looters there are far fewer than 40 cannons there. There are small government and fishermen's huts on one of the three cays, Cayo Centro; as of 2010, tourists are finally permitted to stay overnight, which means spectacular multiday diving and snorkeling opportunities.

Sports and Recreation
SCUBA DIVING AND SNORKELING

XTC Dive Center (north end of town, across bridge, no phone, www.xtcdivecenter.com, 9am-5pm daily) is a full-service dive shop that specializes in trips to Chinchorro Bank; its acronym officially stands for "Xcalak to Chinchorro," though the nearby ecstasy-inducing dives surely figured into the name. Trips to Chinchorro are US$199 per person for two tanks or US$149 per person for snorkelers, including lunch, drinks, and a hike on Cayo Centro, the main cay; multiday trips also are available. To get to Chinchorro, it's a 1.5- to 2-hour boat ride, which can be pretty punishing depending on conditions. Groups typically set out around 7am and return to port around 4:30 or 5pm. Dive shops usually require at least five divers or six snorkelers (or a combination of the two) and may not go for days at a time if the weather is bad (summer months are best). Closer to home, reef dives cost US$60 for one tank, US$90 for two; equipment costs extra. Snorkel tours run US$30-65 per person depending on how long and far you go; five-hour trips include jaunts into Chetumal Bay and Bird Island, which can be fascinating, especially in January and February when the birds are most plentiful. A 10 percent tax applies to most rates.

Costa de Cocos (3 kilometers/1.9 miles north of town, no phone, www.costadecocos.com) also offers diving, as does **Casa Carolina** (2.5 kilometers/1.6 miles north of town, U.S. tel. 610/616-3862, www.casacarolina.net). Prices at all three shops are comparable.

SPORTFISHING

Xcalak also boasts world-class sportfishing, with huge saltwater and brackish flats where hooking into the grand slam of fly-fishing—tarpon, bonefish, and permit—is by no means impossible. Add a snook, and you've got a super slam. Oceanside, tarpon and barracuda abound, in addition to grouper, snapper, and others. **Costa de Cocos** (3 kilometers/1.9 miles north of town, no phone, www.costadecocos.com) is the area's oldest fishing resort, with highly experienced guides and numerous magazine write-ups. Three- to seven-night packages include transfer to and from the airport, lodging, meals, open bar, and, of course, nonstop fly-fishing (US$1,830-4,105 s, US$1,420-3,095 d). **Hotel Tierra Maya** (2.1 kilometers/1.3 miles north of town, toll-free U.S. tel. 800/216-1902, www.tierramaya.net) also offers fly-fishing packages for 3-7 nights (US$1,370-3,605 s, US$770-2,099 d), though

they don't include all the perks that the Costa de Cocos packages do. The dive shops, as well as most hotels, also can arrange guided fishing tours.

Accommodations

Xcalak's most appealing accommodations are on the beach road heading north out of town. Few places accept credit cards on-site, but many have payment systems on their websites.

UNDER US$50

Xcalak Caribe (south of the lighthouse, no phone, www.xcalakcaribe.com, US$37.50 s/d) has large clean rooms, each with ceiling fan and private bathroom, just steps from the beach. The expat owners are friendly and attentive, and the restaurant here, specializing in Mediterranean-style seafood, is outstanding.

Right at the entrance of town, **Cabañas Tío Bon** (cell. tel. 983/836-6954, US$25 s/d) is a basic but reasonably clean option. Three wood cabins alongside the owner's home—you share a front gate—have tiny private bathrooms, fan, and 24-hour electricity. The plywood interior and lack of hot water will prevent any confusion between Uncle Bon's and the Westin.

US$50-100

Hotel Tierra Maya (2.1 kilometers/1.3 miles north of town, toll-free U.S. tel. 800/216-1902, www.tierramaya.net, US$90-100 s/d, US$150 apartment) is a pleasant hotel with ample rooms decorated with simple furnishings and colorful Mexican rugs. All have private terraces or balconies with views of the Caribbean. Continental breakfast is included in the rate and served in the hotel's excellent beachfront restaurant. Fly-fishing and dive packages are also available.

Xcalak's first hotel and oldest fishing and diving lodge, **Costa de Cocos** (3 kilometers/1.9 miles north of town, no phone, www.costadecocos.com, US$78 s, US$90 d) eschews fluff and formality for a jocular laid-back atmosphere that's perfectly suited to its clientele.

TULUM AND QUINTANA ROO

Simple wood-paneled *cabañas* are comfortable enough, with tile floors and hot water, and surround a well-kept sandy lot. Travelers looking for "charming" won't find it here, and that seems to be just how it's preferred. Continental breakfast is included.

US$100-150

It's hard not to feel at home at ◖ **Sin Duda** (8 kilometers/5 miles north of town, U.S. tel. 415/868-9925, www.sinduda villas.com, US$84 s/d, US$110 studio, US$120 apartment), a gem of hotel with beautifully decorated rooms featuring Mexican folk art and breathtaking views. Evening often brings cocktail hour, when guests can join the friendly American hosts for margaritas in the cozy lounge that doubles as a common kitchen and library. A healthy continental breakfast, brought to your room, is included in the rate.

Four cheerful units with fully equipped kitchenettes make **Casa Carolina** (2.5 kilometers/1.6 miles north of town, U.S. tel. 610/616-3862, www.casacarolina.net, US$100 s/d) a great choice for indie travelers. Add ocean views from private balconies and a wide beach with palm trees, and it's a classic beach vacation. Co-owner Bob Villier is an experienced NAUI dive instructor and offers personalized certification classes plus diving and snorkeling trips. Continental breakfast, with divine homemade muffins, is included.

OVER US$150

Playa Sonrisa (6.9 kilometers/4.3 miles north of town, no phone, www.playasonrisa. com, US$135-175 s/d, US$175-225 suite) is a clothing-optional resort on a palm-tree-laden stretch of beach. Units are clean and comfortable, though they lack the charm that you'd expect for the rate. What you mostly pay for is the freedom to enjoy the Caribbean in the buff. A continental breakfast buffet is included in the rate, as is Wi-Fi. Geared at naturist couples, the hotel welcomes naturist families during the low season only. Day

passes are available to naturist couples, too (10am-sunset, US$20 pp).

Food

The ◖ **Leaky Palapa** (2 blocks north of the lighthouse, no phone, www.leakypalaparestaurant.com, hourly seatings 5:30pm-8:30pm Thurs.-Sun., Nov.-May only, US$16-23) is a gourmet restaurant with boho flair and a menu that changes according to the day's catch and market offerings. It is invariably delicious, though, with such dishes as homemade ravioli with *huitlacoche* (corn fungus), lobster, and squash flower cream as well as snapper on a bed of plantain mash with green coconut salsa. Reservations are required and only cash is accepted.

Locally run **Restaurant Toby** (center of town, across from volleyball court, cell. tel. 983/107-5426, 11am-10pm Mon.-Sat., US$5-10) is a popular seafood restaurant serving up, among other tasty dishes, heaping plates of ceviche, coconut shrimp, and fish soup. It's a friendly, low-key place perfect for a beer and a good meal after a day of diving or relaxing on the beach. Wi-Fi is available, too.

Xcalak Caribe (no phone, www.xcalak-caribe.com, 11am-3pm and 5:30pm-10pm Tues.-Sun., US$5-20) serves seaside standards like ceviche and garlic grilled fish, as well as Mediterranean specialties, like paella and Gallego-style octopus. Cocktails are served from a bar artfully fashioned from the hull of an old fishing boat. Restaurant options are slim in Xcalak, but the tasty dishes, friendly service, and casual atmosphere would make this a popular eatery anywhere. Look for the *palapa*-roofed building just south of the lighthouse, facing the beach.

The Maya Grill (Hotel Tierra Maya, 2.1 kilometers/1.3 miles north of town, toll-free U.S. tel. 800/216-1902, www.tierramaya.net, 5pm-9pm daily, US$12-22) is a beachfront hotel restaurant offering fresh ingredients in its Mexican-inspired meals. As expected, seafood is the focus, but chicken and meat dishes edge their way onto the menu, too. Dinners are pricey but hearty.

The restaurant at **Costa de Cocos** (3 kilometers/1.9 miles north of town, no phone, www.costadecocos.com, 7am-10pm daily, US$5-28) serves up burgers, steak, pizza, and all manner of tall tales—though with fishing as good as it is, many just happen to be true. The service is seriously lacking, but the schedule, reservations policy (none required), and full bar make it a reliable option.

A popular culinary event is the weekly chicken barbecue at **Maya Campground** (north end of town, across bridge, no phone, US$5), held every Wednesday afternoon. Come early to get the best of the bird, which is served with coleslaw and beans.

If you are cooking for yourself, a **grocery truck** passes through town and down the coastal road several times per week—ask at your hotel for the current schedule. It comes stocked with eggs, yogurt, grains, basic produce, fresh meats, and canned food. You also can buy a broom or two. In town, there are a handful of small **mini-marts** selling basic canned and dried foods. Most are open daily 9am-9pm.

Information and Services

Xcalak has **no bank, ATM, or currency-exchange office,** and only a few places take credit cards—plan accordingly!

There's a basic **health clinic** (no phone, 8am-noon and 2pm-6pm Mon.-Fri.) two blocks from the soccer field, near the entrance of town.

Most hotels have Wi-Fi; in a pinch many hotel owners will let you use their computers to send a quick email. For more time on the net, **San Jordy** (center of town, hours vary, US$4/hour) is a reliable Internet café. To make an international or domestic call, head to **Telecomm/Telégrafos** (near The Leaky Palapa, 9am-3pm Mon.-Fri.).

Getting There and Around

Bus service is somewhat erratic in Xcalak.

Theoretically, buses bound for Chetumal (with stops in Mahahual and Limones) leave twice daily, typically around 5am and 2pm (US$7, 4-5 hours), but it's not unusual for one or both departures to be delayed or canceled. Upon arrival, your hotel may send a car to pick you up; otherwise a taxi from town is about US$10.

Most travelers come in a rental car, which certainly simplifies life here. The closest gas station is on the main road to Mahahual, near the turnoff for Xcalak. However, it occasionally runs out of gas, so you should fill up on Highway 307 as well—Carrillo Puerto is a good spot. In a pinch, a few Xcalak families sell gas from barrels in their front yards; ask your hotel owner for help locating them.

If your budget permits, there also is a well-maintained airstrip approximately 2 kilometers (1.2 miles) west of town. Despite rumors that commercial flights will begin using it regularly, at the time of research, it was only used sporadically by private or chartered planes.

CHACCHOBEN ARCHAEOLOGICAL ZONE

Chacchoben (8am-5pm daily, US$4) got its name from archaeologists who, after uncovering no inscription indicating what the city's original residents called it, named it after the Maya village to which the land pertained. The meaning of that name is also lost, even to local villagers, though the accepted translation is Place of Red Corn. The area may have been settled as early as 1000 BC, and most of the building activity probably took place AD 200-700, the Classic period.

Visiting the Ruins

Entering the site, a short path leads first to **Temple 24,** a squat pyramid that is the primary structure of a small enclosed area called **Plaza B.** Across that plaza—and the larger Gran Plaza beyond it—is a massive

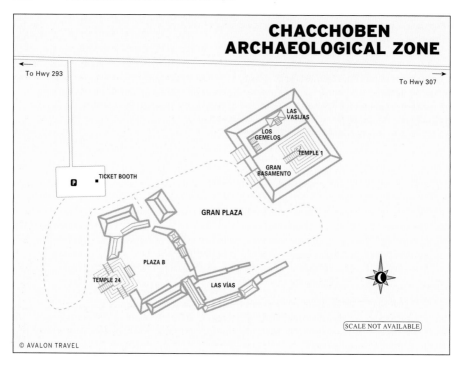

CHACCHOBEN
ARCHAEOLOGICAL ZONE

To Hwy 293

To Hwy 307

LAS VASIJAS

LOS GEMELOS

TEMPLE 1

GRAN BASAMENTO

TICKET BOOTH

P

GRAN PLAZA

PLAZA B

TEMPLE 24

LAS VÍAS

SCALE NOT AVAILABLE

© AVALON TRAVEL

raised platform, the **Gran Basamento,** with the site's largest pyramid, **Temple 1,** atop it; this pyramid is believed to have served astronomical and religious purposes. Also on the platform, two smaller structures, dubbed **Las Vasijas** and **Los Gemelos,** were likely used for ceremonial functions. The site has some well-preserved stucco and paint, and for that reason none of the pyramids can be climbed. Though it can get crowded when there's a cruise ship at Mahahual, Chacchoben has an appealingly remote feel, nestled in the forest with towering mahogany and banyan trees, and paths dotted with bromeliads.

Practicalities

Chacchoben is located about 70 kilometers (43 miles) north of Mahahual and 4 kilometers (2.5 miles) west of Limones. By **car,** take Highway 307 and turn west at the sign to Chacchoben ruins and like-named town, about 3 kilometers (1.9 miles) down a well-paved road. Alternatively, take a **bus** to Limones and then a **cab** (US$5) to the ruins.

Laguna Bacalar

Almost 50 kilometers (31 miles) long, Laguna Bacalar is the second-largest lake in Mexico and certainly among the most beautiful. Well, it's not technically a lake: A series of waterways do eventually lead to the ocean, making Bacalar a lagoon, but it is fed by natural springs, making the water on the western shore, where the hotels and town are, 100 percent *agua dulce* (fresh water).

The Maya name for the lagoon translates as Lake of Seven Colors. It is an apt description, as you will see on any sunny day. The lagoon's sandy bottom and crystalline water turn shallow areas a brilliant turquoise, which fades to deep blue in the center. If you didn't know better, you'd think it was the Caribbean.

The hub of the Laguna Bacalar region is the town of Bacalar. Located on the west side of

© LIZA PRADO

Fuerte San Felipe Bacalar is a restored fort with an excellent museum inside.

the lake, it won't win any prizes for charm, but it does have a terrific museum, one of the best hotels around, a handful of decent restaurants, and, of course, gorgeous views of the lagoon.

SIGHTS AND EVENTS
◖ Fuerte San Felipe Bacalar

The mid-18th-century **Fuerte San Felipe Bacalar** (central plaza, no phone, Av. 3 at Calle 20, 9am-7pm Tues.-Thurs. and Sun., 8am-8pm Fri.-Sat., US$5) was built by the Spanish for protection against English pirates and Maya that regularly raided the area. In fact, attacks proved so frequent—and successful—that the fort was captured in 1858 by Maya during the Caste War. It was not returned to Mexican officials until 1901. Today, the star-shaped stone edifice has been restored to its former glory: drawbridge, cannons, moat, and all. The fort also houses the excellent **Museo del Fuerte de San Felipe Bacalar,** a modern museum with exhibits on the history of the area, including details on the pirates who regularly attacked these shores.

Cenote Azul

As good or better than Laguna Bacalar for swimming, **Cenote Azul** (Hwy. 307 Km. 15) is two kilometers (1.2 miles) south of town. It's the widest cenote in Mexico, some 300 meters (984 feet) across at its widest, and 150 meters (492 feet) deep, with crystalline blue water. A rope stretches clear across, so even less-conditioned swimmers can make it to the far side. A large, breezy **restaurant** (tel. 983/834-2038, 7:30am-8pm daily, US$6-16) has the only entrance to the cenote, and doesn't charge admission if you order something.

Gilberto Silva Gallery

Gilberto Silva, an accomplished sculptor of Maya art, has a small **gallery and workshop** (Calle 26 btwn Calles 5 and 7, tel. 983/834-2657, hours vary) where some of his works are displayed and sold. Most are intricately carved limestone pieces, which are then cast in clay. Notably, his works have been displayed at the Museum of Natural History in New York City.

Fiesta de San Joaquín

Every July, the town of Bacalar celebrates San Joaquín, its patron saint. For nine consecutive days, different neighborhoods host festive celebrations, each trying to outdo the other for the year's best party. Visitors are welcome and should definitely join the fun—expect plenty of food, music, dancing, and performances of all sorts. Cockfights also are popular, and a three-day **hydroplane race** usually follows the festivities in early August.

SPORTS AND RECREATION
Ecotours

A friendly German couple founded **Active Nature** (Hotel Villas Ecotucán, Hwy. 307 Km. 27.3, cell. tel. 983/120-5742, www.activenaturebacalar.com) after fate and car trouble cut short their planned tour of the Americas and left them in lovely Laguna Bacalar. Tour options include kayaking through mangrove channels to hidden lagoons and freshwater beaches, sunset and moonlight outrigger canoe rides, biking to a great curassow breeding reserve and research center, and morning bird-watching walks. Prices range US$12.50-50 per person, including gear and often lunch and water; children under 10 are free, under 14 half off. Tours begin at Villas Ecotucán, whose guests get a 10 percent discount. Multiday kayak and paddle sailing tours are also available.

Páay bej Tours (Av. 5 btwn Calles 24 and 26, tel. 983/839-0830, www.bacalar-tours-paaybej.com) also offers kayaking tours of the lagoon and mangrove channels (US$37.50 pp), bike tours around the village with a visit to Fuerte San Felipe (US$17 pp), and guided tours of Chacchoben and other Maya ruins (US$37.50 pp, including transport and entrance fees). You can also rent bikes here (US$1.75/hour, US$8.50/day).

Kayaking

The **Club de Vela Bacalar** (Av. Costera at Calle 20, tel. 983/834-2478, 9am-6pm Mon.-Sat.) rents kayaks for US$8.50 per hour (single or double). **Active Nature** (Hotel Villas Ecotucán, Hwy. 307 Km. 27.3, cell. tel. 983/120-5742, www.activenaturebacalar.com) organizes kayaking tours, as does the local tour company, **Páay bej Tours** (Av. 5 btwn Calles 24 and 26, tel. 983/839-0830, www.bacalar-tours-paaybej.com).

Swimming

The **Balneario Ejidal de Bacalar** (Av. Costera near Calle 26, no phone, 7am-7pm, US$0.75) is a public swimming area complete with *palapas* for rent (US$3/day), bathrooms, and a restaurant (9am-7pm, US$3-10). Located just 250 meters (0.2 mile) from the central plaza, it's convenient and inexpensive place to enjoy the water.

The pier at the **Club de Vela Bacalar** (Av. Costera at Calle 20, tel. 983/834-2478, 9am-6pm Mon.-Sat.) is one of the best places to swim in town, with a long footbridge leading to a swimming dock, where the water is crystal clear and deep. Order something from the restaurant and stay as long as you want.

Other good swimming spots on Laguna Bacalar include **Rancho Encantado** (2 kilometers/1.2 miles north of town, tel. 983/839-7900, www.encantado.com) and **Hotel Laguna Bacalar** (Blvd. Costero 479, tel. 983/834-2206, www.hotellagunabacalar.com); plan on ordering something from the hotel restaurant to be able to use the waterfront.

Yoga and Spa

Nueva Gaia (Av. 3 near Calle 18, tel. 983/834-2963, www.gaia-maya.com, 8am-4pm Tues.-Sun.) offers various types of massage, from relaxation massage (US$48, 60 minutes) to hot stone massages (US$66, 80 minutes), in its holistic center near the central plaza.

ACCOMMODATIONS
In Town

One of the area's most charming and convenient accommodations, **⬛Casita Carolina** (Av. Costera btwn Calles 16 and 18, tel. 983/834-2334, www.casitacarolina.com, US$37.50-58.50 s/d, US$30-50 s/d with shared kitchen) offers lagoon-front units that open onto a large

© LIZA PRADO

Find utter tranquility at little-visited Laguna Bacalar.

grassy garden. Units are either stand-alone or occupy a converted home, but all have a private bathroom, a fan, and a homey feel. The friendly American owner lives on-site and is a wealth of information on area sights.

Hotelito Paraíso (Av. Costera at Calle 14, tel. 983/834-2787, www.hotelitoelparaiso.un-lugar.com, US$54 s/d with a/c) has 14 stark hotel rooms, with minifridge, cable TV, and Wi-Fi. All open onto a large grassy area that runs to the lakeshore; there's a *palapa* shade, plenty of chairs, and even a grill. Kayaks also are available for rent for US$4.50 per hour.

Outside of Town

Villas Ecotucán (Hwy. 307 Km. 27.3, cell. tel. 983/120-5743, www.villasecotucan.info, US$62.50-71 s/d) has five *palapa*-roofed *cabañas* and one suite, each spacious and simple, with a veranda to enjoy the view of the lake and surrounding tropical forest. Rates include two adults and two kids under 12, full breakfast for all, and use of the kayaks,

dock, and trails. Guided excursions—bike, kayak, sailboat, and on foot—also are available.

Rancho Encantado (Hwy. 307 Km. 24, tel. 983/839-7900, toll-free U.S. tel. 877/229-2046, www.encantado.com, US$120-142 s/d with fan, US$127-221 with a/c, breakfast included) has spacious *palapa*-roofed casitas and modern suites, both featuring Mexican tile floors, good beds, and views of either the lush garden or the lagoon. The prettiest spot here, however, is a pier that leads to a shady dock strung with hammocks—it's perfect for swimming and relaxing. Guests can receive massages and body treatments in a small kiosk built over the lake; a hot tub is nearby. The only downer here is the persistent hum of traffic from nearby Highway 307.

Built on a bluff just south of town, **Hotel Laguna Bacalar** (Blvd. Costero 479, tel. 983/834-2205, www.hotellagunabacalar.com, US$89 s/d with a/c) has spacious rooms, most with a balcony and dramatic views of the lagoon. The decor, once seriously kitschy, has been toned down to a bit of shell art. Stairs zigzag down to the water, where a pier, ladder, and a diving board make swimming in the lagoon easy. There's a small pool, too. Wi-Fi also is available for a nominal daily fee.

FOOD

For good cheap eats, **Cocina Orizaba** (Av. 7 btwn Calles 24 and 26, tel. 983/834-2069, 8am-6pm daily, US$3.50-10) serves a variety of classic Mexican dishes. The daily *comida corrida* (lunch special) includes an entrée, main dish, and drink.

On the main plaza, **Restaurante y Pizzeria Bertilla** (Av. 5 at Calle 20, cell. tel. 983/123-4567, 4pm-11pm Tues.-Sun., US$6-15) specializes in homemade pasta and pizza. Some traditional Mexican dishes are available, too.

El Carboncito (central plaza, Av. 5 near Calle 20, 7pm-11pm daily, US$2.50-6) is a popular *puesto* (food stand) that serves up grilled favorites like hot dogs, hamburgers, and tacos. If you want your meal to go, let the cook know it's *"para llevar."*

Groceries

Dunosusa (Calle 22 btwn Avs. 3 and 5, 7:30am-9pm Mon.-Sat., 8:30am-8pm Sun.) is a well-stocked supermarket on the central plaza.

INFORMATION AND SERVICES
Tourist Information

Bacalar does not have a tourist information office yet, but **www.bacalarmosaico. com** is a bilingual website offering useful information on the area's sights, activities, and businesses.

Emergency Services

The **Centro de Salud** (Av. 3 btwn Calles 22 and 24, tel. 983/834-2756, 24 hours) offers basic medical care; for serious matters, head to Chetumal. For meds, try **Farmacia San Joaquín** (Av. 7 btwn Calles 20 and 22, no phone, 8am-3pm and 6pm-9pm daily). The **police station** (Calle 20 near Av. 3, toll-free Mex. tel. 066, 24 hours) is located across from the Fuerte San Felipe Bacalar.

BACALAR BUS SCHEDULE

Departures from the **bus terminal** (Hwy. 307 near Calle 30, no phone) are almost all *de paso* (mid-route service), which means there's often a limited availability of seats. Destinations include:

DESTINATION	PRICE	DURATION	SCHEDULE
Cancún	US$17.50-23	5-6 hours	every 30-60 mins 5:45am-11:30pm
Carrillo Puerto	US$5.25-7.75	1.5-2 hours	take Cancún bus
Chetumal	US$2.50-3.50	50 mins	every 30-60 mins 6:05am-11:55pm
Mahahual	US$6.50	2 hours	6:15am and 8:15pm
Playa del Carmen	US$13.50-18.25	4-4.5 hours	take Cancún bus
Tulum	US$11-12	2.5-3 hours	take Cancún bus

Money

There is no bank in town, but there is a **Banorte ATM** on the west side of the central plaza. If you need other money services or the ATM has run out of cash, the closest bank is in Chetumal.

Media and Communications

The **post office** (Av. 3 near Calle 24, 8am-4:30pm Mon.-Fri., 8am-noon Sat.) is just east of the Fuerte San Felipe Bacalar. For email try the **no name Internet** (Av. 5 near Calle 24, 9am-10pm daily, US$1/hour), operated out of the living room of a private home. For telephone calls, your best bet is to use the **public phones** on the central plaza; Ladatel telephone cards can be purchased at the supermarket and at most corner stores.

Laundry

Lavandería Lolita (Av. 7 btwn Calles 24 and 26, tel. 983/834-2069, 9am-8pm daily) offers same-day service for US$1 per kilo (2.2 pounds). Pickup and delivery are available.

GETTING THERE AND AROUND

You can easily walk to all the sites of interest in Bacalar, with the exception of Cenote Azul. A taxi there from town costs around US$3; cabs typically wait for passengers around the central plaza and on Avenida 7 in front of Iglesia San Joaquín.

Bus

Bacalar's modest **bus terminal** (Hwy. 307 near Calle 30) is on the highway, about a 20-minute walk from the central plaza. The buses are almost exclusively *de paso* (midroute) service, which means there's often limited availability (i.e., as soon as you know your schedule, buy your ticket).

Combi

Combis and *taxi colectivos* (US$2-3, every 30 minutes) run between Bacalar and Chetumal daily. You can catch either in front of Iglesia San Joaquín (Calle 22 near Av. 7), one block up from the central plaza.

Chetumal

Chetumal is the capital of Quintana Roo and the gateway to Central America. It's not the prettiest of towns, and most travelers just pass through on their way to or from Belize or southern Campeche. However, Chetumal's modern Maya museum is one of the best you'll find in the region (albeit with few original pieces) and is well worth a visit. And if you're dying to see the Guatemalan ruins of Tikal, a shuttle from Chetumal can get you there in eight hours (cutting through Belize) and back again just as fast; a 90-minute boat ride also will take you to San Pedro, Belize, for a quick overnighter. The area around Chetumal is worth exploring, too, whether the bayside town of Calderitas or the intriguing and little-visited Maya ruins of Kohunlich, Dzibanché, Kinichná, and Oxtankah. North of town is Laguna

Bacalar, a beautiful multicolored lake with great swimming and kayaking.

SIGHTS
Museo de la Cultura Maya

One of the best museums in the region, the **Maya Culture Museum** (Av. de los Héroes at Calle Cristóbal Colón, tel. 983/832-6838, 9am-7pm Tues.-Sun., US$5) extends over three levels—the upper represents the world of gods, the middle the world of humans, and the lower Xibalba, the underworld. Each floor has impressive, well-designed exhibits describing Maya spiritual beliefs, agricultural practices, astronomy and counting, and more, all in English and Spanish. In fact, the only thing lacking is original artifacts. (The copies, however, are quite good.) The exhibition area past the ticket booth usually has good temporary

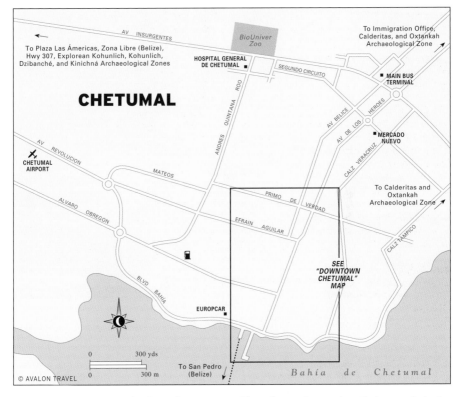

To Immigration Office, Calderitas, and Oxtankah Archaeological Zone →

AV INSURGENTES

BioUniver Zoo

To Plaza Las Ámericas, Zona Libre (Belize), Hwy 307, Explorean Kohunlich, Kohunlich, Dzibanché, and Kinichná Archaeological Zones

HOSPITAL GENERAL DE CHETUMAL ■

SEGUNDO CIRCUITO

■ MAIN BUS TERMINAL

CHETUMAL

ANDRES QUINTANA ROO

AV BELICE

DE LOS HEROES

AV DE LOS

■ MERCADO NUEVO

CALZ VERACRUZ

AV REVOLUCION

CHETUMAL AIRPORT

MATEOS

To Calderitas and Oxtankah Archaeological Zone →

ALVARO OBREGON

PRIMO DE VERDAD

EFRAIN AGUILAR

CALZ TAMPICO

SEE "DOWNTOWN CHETUMAL" MAP

BLVD BAHIA

EUROPCAR ■

0   300 yds
0   300 m

To San Pedro (Belize) ↓

© AVALON TRAVEL

Bahía   de   Chetumal

---

art shows, plus a cinema that hosts free screenings of independent films.

Monumento al Mestizo

Across from the Museo de la Cultura Maya is the **Monumento al Mestizo** (Av. de los Héroes s/n), a striking sculpture symbolizing the creation of a new race—the mestizo—through the union of the Spanish shipwrecked sailor Gonzalo Guerrero and Zazil Há, a Maya woman. Hernán Cortés offered to take Guerrero back to Spain, but Guerrero chose to stay in the Americas, wedding Zazil Há in a Maya marriage ritual. Note that the Maya symbol for the number zero as well as the cycle of life, the snail shell, provides the framework for the entire work of art.

Museo de la Ciudad

The **city museum** (Calle Héroes de Chapultepec btwn Avs. Juárez and de los Héroes, tel. 983/832-1350, 9am-7pm Tues.-Sat., 9am-2pm Sun., US$1) is small and well organized, and describes the political, economic, and cultural history of Chetumal, spanning the period from its founding in 1898 to the present day. Signage is in Spanish only.

El Malecón

Running six kilometers (3.7 miles) on the Boulevard Bahía, this breezy promenade makes for a fine bayfront stroll. Along it you'll find cafés, monuments, a lighthouse, government buildings, and, hopefully, a cooling breeze. Of particular note are two impressive **murals** found within the **Palacio Legislativo** (end of Av. Reforma, 9am-10pm Mon.-Fri.), a shell-shaped building that houses the State Congress. Created by local artist Elio Carmichael, one

TULUM AND QUINTANA ROO

© LIZA PRADO

The Museo de la Cultura Maya in Chetumal has fascinating displays on Maya sculpture, writing, mathematics, astronomy, and more.

mural outlines the state's history—from the creation of man to the devastating effects of Hurricane Janet in 1955—while the other depicts the law of the cosmos. Both are located in the reception area and are free for public viewing.

Maqueta Payo Obispo

The **Maqueta Payo Obispo** (Calle 22 de Enero near Av. Reforma, 9am-7pm Tues.-Sun., free) is a scale model of Chetumal as it looked in the 1930s, with brightly colored clapboard houses, grassy lots, and plenty of palm trees. It's a reproduction of a model made by longtime resident Luis Reinhardt McLiberty. Look for it in a glass-enclosed building across the street from the Palacio Legislativo, though glare on sunny days can make it hard to see the exhibit. A small history museum of the city also is on-site; signage is in Spanish only.

Trolley Tours

For a breezy overview of Chetumal's attractions, consider taking **Bule Buzz** (cell. tel. 983/120-5223, US$8 adult, US$5 child), a guided trolley tour of the city. Sites visited include the murals in the Palacio Legislativo, the sculptures along Boulevard Bahía, the Maqueta Payo Obispo, and the Museo de la Cultura Maya. The trolley leaves from the Monumento al Mestizo at noon and 3pm Tuesday-Saturday and 11am Sunday; admission to the Museo de la Cultura Maya also is included.

ENTERTAINMENT AND SHOPPING
Sunday on El Malecón

Every Sunday at 6pm, locals gather at the **Esplanada de la Bandera** (southern end of Av. de los Héroes) to enjoy city-sponsored events, typically performances by the municipal band or local musicians and singers. The events are

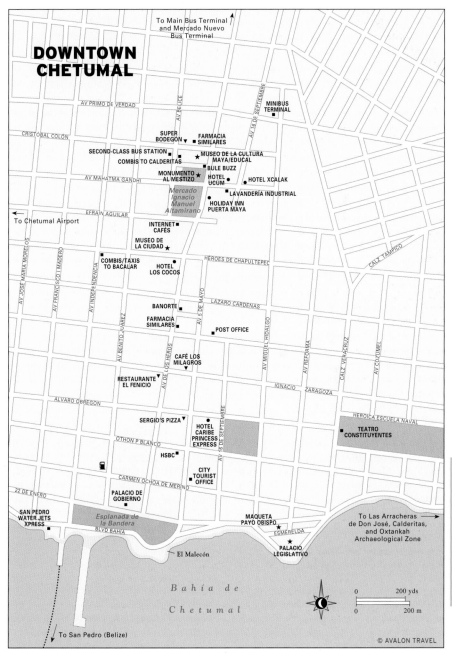

DOWNTOWN CHETUMAL

To Main Bus Terminal and Mercado Nuevo Bus Terminal

AV PRIMO DE VERDAD

AV BELICE

AV 16 DE SEPTIEMBRE

MINIBUS TERMINAL

CRISTOBAL COLON

SUPER BODEGON

FARMACIA SIMILARES

SECOND-CLASS BUS STATION

COMBIS TO CALDERITAS

MUSEO DE LA CULTURA MAYA/EDUCAL

BULE BUZZ

MONUMENTO AL MESTIZO

HOTEL UCUM

HOTEL XCALAK

AV MAHATMA GANDHI

Mercado Ignacio Manuel Altamirano

LAVANDERÍA INDUSTRIAL

HOLIDAY INN PUERTA MAYA

EFRAIN AGUILAR

To Chetumal Airport

INTERNET CAFÉS

MUSEO DE LA CIUDAD

AV JOSE MARIA MORELOS

AV FRANCISCO I MADERO

AV INDEPENDENCIA

COMBIS/TAXIS TO BACALAR

HOTEL LOS COCOS

HEROES DE CHAPULTEPEC

CALZ TAMPICO

AV BENITO JUAREZ

BANORTE

FARMACIA SIMILARES

AV 5 DE MAYO

LÁZARO CARDENAS

POST OFFICE

AV MIGUEL HIDALGO

AV REFORMA

CALZ VERACRUZ

AV COZUMEL

CAFÉ LOS MILAGROS

AV DE LOS HEROS

RESTAURANTE EL FENICIO

IGNACIO ZARAGOZA

ALVARO OBREGON

SERGIO'S PIZZA

HOTEL CARIBE PRINCESS EXPRESS

AV 16 DE SEPTIEMBRE

HEROICA ESCUELA NAVAL

TEATRO CONSTITUYENTES

OTHON P BLANCO

HSBC

CITY TOURIST OFFICE

CARMEN OCHOA DE MERINO

22 DE ENERO

PALACIO DE GOBIERNO

SAN PEDRO WATER JETS XPRESS

Esplanada de la Bandera

BLVD BAHIA

MAQUETA PAYO OBISPO

ESMERELDA

PALACIÓ LEGISLATIVO

To Las Arracheras de Don José, Calderitas, and Oxtankah Archaeological Zone

El Malecón

Bahía de

Chetumal

0   200 yds

0   200 m

To San Pedro (Belize)

© AVALON TRAVEL

free and family friendly, with vendors selling drinks and street food.

Cinema

If you're hankering to watch the latest Hollywood film, head to **Cinépolis** (Plaza Las Ámericas, Av. Insurgentes s/n, tel. 983/837-6043, www.cinepolis.com, US$3-5), an 11-screen theater where most films are in English with Spanish subtitles.

Shopping

Educal (Av. de los Héroes at Calle Cristóbal Colón, cell. tel. 983/129-2832, www.educal.com.mx, 9am-7pm Tues.-Sat., 9am-2pm Sun.) is a good bookstore located inside the Museo de la Cultura Maya.

Mercado Ignacio Manuel Altamirano (Efraín Aguilar btwn Avs. Belice and de los Héroes, 8am-4pm daily) is a two-story building mostly selling everyday items, from clothing to kitchenware. For travelers, it's a good place to buy a pair of flip-flops, a travel clock, or kitschy souvenirs.

Plaza Las Ámericas (Av. Insurgentes s/n, 9am-10pm daily) is a classic shopping mall with clothing and shoe boutiques, a Chedraui supermarket, a megaplex movie theater, and all the typical amenities, like ATMs, food court, and public bathrooms.

The **Zona Libre** (Corozal Duty Free Zone, 9am-7pm daily) is an area jam-packed with stores selling products from around the world. It's located in Belize, and visitors can enter and leave the area without passports or paying taxes on their purchases, mostly household and personal items. (There's a US$1 entrance fee, however.)

ACCOMMODATIONS

Chetumal's status as the state capital and its location on the Belize border make it a busy town, and reservations are recommended.

Under US$50

◖**Hotel Xcalak** (Av. 16 de Septiembre at Av. Mahatma Gandhi, cell. tel. 983/129-1708, www.hotelxcalak.com.mx, US$38 s/d with a/c) is the best budget deal in town: modern rooms with tasteful decor, strong but quiet air-conditioning, SKY TV, and wireless Internet. The hotel restaurant also provides room service (though you've got to order in person). The hotel is located one block from the Museo de la Cultura Maya.

Next door, the aqua-colored **Hotel Ucúm** (Av. Mahatma Gandhi btwn Avs. 5 de Mayo and 16 de Septiembre, tel. 983/832-0711, www.hotelucumchetumal.com, US$18 s/d with fan, US$23 s/d with fan and cable TV, US$32 s/d with a/c and cable TV) has aging but clean rooms. Beds are hit or miss, unfortunately, and some rooms can be downright stuffy (ask for one on the top floor for the best breeze). There's a decent pool on-site with a separate wading area for kids. There's also a secure parking lot.

US$50-100

Hotel Caribe Princess Express (Av. Alvaro Obregón btwn Avs. 5 de Mayo and 16 de Septiembre, tel. 983/832-0900, toll-free Mex. tel. 866/337-7342, US$42 s with a/c, US$50 d with a/c, US$64 suite with a/c) has comfortable nondescript rooms with decent beds, cable TV, and powerful air-conditioning. There's Wi-Fi in the lobby and a self-serve breakfast (i.e., toast, cereal, fruits) every day. Ask for a room facing the interior of the building; the karaoke bar in front blasts music—and keeps the windows rattling—until late.

Hotel Los Cocos (Av. de los Héroes at Calle Héroes de Chapultepec, tel. 983/835-0430, toll-free Mex. tel. 800/719-5840, www.hotelloscocos.com.mx, US$76-152 s/d with a/c) has three categories of rooms, all pleasant with updated furnishings and modern amenities. The more expensive ones have flat-screen TVs, quiet air conditioning, and more stylish decor. They all open onto a lush garden, which has a small inviting pool area. The on-site restaurant is great for breakfast.

Over US$100

Holiday Inn Chetumal-Puerta Maya (Av. de los Héroes near Av. Mahatma Gandhi, tel. 983/835-0400, toll-free U.S. tel. 888/465-4329, www.holidayinn.com, US$100-132 s/d with a/c) is the nicest hotel in town, with marble floors, wood-beam ceilings, and high-end amenities. There's a gym on-site, as well as a well-maintained pool, which is surrounded by a tropical garden. Kids also stay for free. Be sure to check the website for reservations—there often are terrific deals.

Outside of Chetumal

On the road to the like-named ruins, ◖ **Explorean Kohunlich** (tel. 555/201-8350, toll-free Mex. tel. 800/504-5000, toll-free U.S. tel. 800/343-7821, www.theexplorean.com, US$320-640 suite), is a luxurious resort with 40 deluxe suites set on 30 hectares (74 acres) of tropical forest. Each has gleaming stone floors, high *palapa* ceilings, elegant furnishings, and privacy walls for sunbathing. Two suites also have plunge pools. The main building houses a fine restaurant (7:30am-10:30pm daily, US$12-24, open to nonguests), a full-service spa, and a lap pool that overlooks the jungle (you can see the ruins at Kohunlich from here). One excursion per day—rappelling in the jungle, kayaking through a crocodile reserve, or mountain biking through forgotten forests—is included. Transportation to and from Chetumal's airport also is thrown in.

FOOD

Restaurante El Fenicio (Av. de los Héroes at Calle Zaragoza, tel. 983/832-0026, 24 hours, US$4-10) is a local favorite, not only because it's open around-the-clock but also because of its tasty, reliable meals. Be sure to try the "make your own taco" dish, a platter stacked with chicken, chorizo, beef, and melted cheese, served with tortillas and all the fixings.

A buzzing little place, ◖ **Café Los Milagros** (Calle Ignacio Zaragoza near Av. 5 de Mayo, tel. 983/832-4433, 7:30am-9pm Mon.-Sat., 7:30am-1pm Sun., US$3-7) serves up strong coffee drinks and especially good breakfasts. The best seating is outdoors—snag a table where you can, as it can get crowded fast.

Located on the Malecón, **Las Arracheras**

de Don José (Blvd. Bahía at Calle Josefa Ortiz de Dominguez, tel. 983/832-8895, 6pm-1am daily, US$4-10) serves some of the best tacos in town. Try the *tacos de arrachera* (broiled skirt steak marinated in lemon and spices), which can only be improved when downed with a cold beer.

Sergio's Pizza (Av. 5 de Mayo at Av. Alvaro Obregón, tel. 983/832-0491, 7am-midnight daily, US$5-17) serves much more than pizza in its dimly lit dining room. The extensive menu covers the gamut of Italian and Mexican dishes—from meat lasagna to *molletes rancheros*. Meals are hearty, making it popular with families.

Super Bodegón (Calle Cristóbal Colón btwn Avs. Belice and de los Héroes, 5am-9pm Mon.-Sat., 5am-3pm Sun.) is a grocery store with an impressive selection of fresh fruits and veggies. Canned goods, dry foods, and basic toiletries are also sold.

INFORMATION AND SERVICES

Tourist Information

Near the waterfront, the **city tourist office** (Av. 5 de Mayo at Carmen Ochoa de Merino, tel. 983/835-0860, 8:30am-4:30pm Mon.-Fri.) has a decent selection of brochures and maps. There also is a **tourist information booth** in the main bus terminal (Av. Insurgentes at Av. de los Héroes, 9am-8pm daily).

Emergency Services

About two kilometers (1.2 miles) from the center of town, **Hospital General de Chetumal** (Avs. Andrés Quintana Roo at Juan José Isiordia, tel. 983/832-8194, 24 hours) is the city's main hospital. For meds, try **Farmacia Similares** (Av. de los Héroes near Calle Plutarco Elias, tel. 983/833-2232, 8am-9pm daily) or its **sister store** (Calle Cristóbal Colón btwn Avs. Belice and de los Héroes, tel. 983/833-2331), which is open 24 hours. The **police** can be reached by dialing toll-free 066.

Money

HSBC (Av. Othon Blanco btwn Av. 5 de Mayo

and Av. de los Héroes, 8am-7pm Mon.-Sat.) and **Banorte** (Av. de los Héroes btwn Lázaro Cárdenas and Plutarco Elias, 9am-4pm Mon.-Fri.) are both conveniently located downtown. There also is an ATM at the **bus station.**

Media and Communications

The **post office** (Av. Plutarco Elias Calles btwn Avs. 5 de Mayo and 16 de Septiembre, 8am-4pm Mon.-Fri., 9am-1pm Sat.) is just a block from the main drag. For Internet access, there is a string of **Internet cafés** across from the Mercado Ignacio Manuel Altamirano (Efraín Aguilar btwn Avs. Belice and de los Héroes); most charge US$1 per hour and are open 7am-midnight daily. At the main bus station, **Cafeteria El Kiosko** (8am-8pm daily) has a row of computers (US$1.50/ hour) and telephone service (US$0.50/minute worldwide).

Immigration

The **immigration office** (Calzada del Centenario 582, tel. 983/832-6353, 9am-1pm Mon.-Fri.) is located on the road to Calderitas; signage is hard to spot, so keep your eyes peeled for the building.

Laundry and Storage

Though catering primarily to hotels and restaurants, **Lavandería Industrial** (Av. Mahatma Ghandi near Av. 16 de Septiembre, no phone, 8am-8pm daily) charges US$1.25 per kilo (2.2 pounds) and also takes small loads. There is no signage, so listen for the huge dryers and look for huge piles of tablecloths—it's surprisingly easy to miss.

Conveniently located in the main bus station, **Lockers, Revistas y Novedades Laudy** (Av. Insurgentes at Av. de los Héroes, 8am-8pm daily) stores bags for US$0.50 per hour.

GETTING THERE AND AROUND

Chetumal is a relatively large city, but the parts most travelers are interested in are all within easy walking distance—mostly along Avenida

de los Héroes and El Malecón. The exception is the main bus terminal and Mercado Nuevo, both of which are 10-12 grubby blocks from the center. A cab to either terminal, or anywhere around downtown, costs US$2-3.

Air

The **Chetumal Airport** (CTM, tel. 983/832-6625) receives only a few flights each day. Airlines serving it include **Interjet** (toll-free Mex. tel. 800/011-2345, toll-free U.S. tel. 866/285-9525, www.interjet.com.mx) and the air taxi service **Avioquintana** (tel. 998/734-1975, www.avioquintana.com).

Bus

All first-class buses leave from the **main bus terminal** (Av. Insurgentes at Av. de los Héroes, tel. 983/832-5110, ext. 2404), though most second-class buses stop here on the way in or out of town.

The **second-class bus station** (Avs. Belice and Cristóbal Colón, tel. 983/832-0639) is located just west of the Museo de la Cultura Maya; tickets for first-class buses also can be purchased here if you want to buy your tickets in advance but don't want to make the trek to the main terminal.

Two other terminals—the **Minibus terminal** (Av. Primo de Verdad at Av. Miguel Hidalgo, no phone) and **Mercado Nuevo** (Av. de los Héroes and Circuito Segundo, no phone)—have service to Bacalar, the Zona Libre, and to Belize.

Combi

Combis and taxi colectivos (US$1.50-2, every 30 minutes) run between Chetumal and Bacalar daily. You can catch either on Avenida Independencia at Calle Héroes de Chapultepec.

Car

The highways in this area are now all paved and well maintained. Car rental agencies in town include **Continental Rent-a-Car** (Holiday Inn, Av. de los Héroes near Av. Mahatma Gandhi, tel. 983/832-2411, www.continentalcar.com.mx, 8am-8pm daily) and **Europcar** (Chetumal

CHETUMAL BUS SCHEDULE

Departures from Chetumal's **main bus terminal** (Av. Insurgentes at Av. de los Héroes, tel. 983/832-7806) are for first-class service, though some second-class buses stop here as well (tickets for either service can be purchased downtown, in the **second-class bus terminal** (Av. Belice at Av. Cristóbal Colón). Destinations from the main bus terminal include:

DESTINATION	PRICE	DURATION	SCHEDULE
Bacalar	US$2.50-3.50	50 mins	every 15-60 mins 5:30am-11:45pm
Campeche	US$28.25	6.5 hours	noon
Cancún	US$17-25.50	5.5-6.5 hours	every 30-90 mins 4am-12:30am
Mahahual	US$10	2.5 hours	5am and 7:30pm, or take Xcalak bus (second-class only)
Mérida	US$30.50	5.5-6 hours	7:30am, 1:30pm, 5pm, and 11:30pm
Palenque	US$23-33	6.5-7.5 hours	9:45pm, 9:50pm, 11pm
Playa del Carmen	US$16-21	4.5-5 hours	take any Cancún bus
Tulum	US$12.50-15	3.5-4 hours	take any Cancún bus
Xcalak	US$10	4-5 hours	6am and 4:30pm, or 5:40am and 4:10pm in Mercado Nuevo terminal
Xpujil	US$5.75-9	1.5-2 hours	every 45-90 mins 6:30am-11:59pm

Buses for **Corozal** (US$4.50, 1 hour), **Orangewalk** (US$6, 2 hours), and **Belize City** (US$9.50, 3 hours) leave the **Mercado Nuevo** (Av. de los Héroes at Circuito Segundo, no phone) 18 times daily 4:30am-6:30pm. Some pass the main ADO terminal en route.

Buses to the **Zona Libre** (US$2, 30 minutes) leave the **Minibus terminal** (Av. Primo de Verdad at Av. Miguel Hidalgo, no phone) every 15 minutes 6:30am-8pm.

Noor Hotel, Blvd. Bahía at Ave. José Maria, tel. 983/833-9959, www.europcar.com, 8am-8pm daily).

Taxi

Taxis can be flagged down easily in downtown Chetumal. Few are metered, so be sure to agree on a price before you set off toward your destination.

Water Taxi

San Pedro Water Jets Xpress (Blvd. Bahía near Av. Independencia, tel. 983/833-3201, www.sanpedrowatertaxi.com) offers direct service to Ambergris Caye, Belize. Trips take 90 minutes and leave at 3:30pm daily, returning the following day at 8am (US$40 one-way, US$75 round-trip). Transfers to Caye Caulker and Belize City are also available.

Around Chetumal

The area around Chetumal has a number of worthwhile attractions, all the better because so few travelers linger here.

CALDERITAS

Located just seven kilometers (4 miles) north of Chetumal, Calderitas is a bayside town known for its **seafood restaurants** (8am-6pm daily, US$4-10)—most along the waterfront across from the main plaza—and its **public beaches.** During the week it's a mellow scene, but on weekends locals descend upon the town for a day of R&R and some revelry, too.

Boat rides can be arranged at many of the bayside establishments to explore **Chetumal Bay** (US$150, up to 8 people) in search of manatees, which were once abundant in these waters, or to visit **Isla Tamalcab** (US$40, up to 8 people), an uninhabited island with white-sand beaches and good snorkeling, and home to spider monkeys and *tepescuintles* (pacas in English).

If you want to stay overnight, the best place in town is **Yax Há Resort** (Av. Yucatán 415, tel. 983/834-4127, www.yaxha-resort.com, US$8.50 pp camping, US$20-30 per RV, US$42-58 s/d with fan, US$125 s/d with a/c and kitchenette). Located on the waterfront, it offers everything from camp- and RV sites to

© LIZA PRADO

Spanish missionaries often had their churches built alongside or atop ancient Maya ruins, like this chapel and archway found at the Oxtankah ruins near Chetumal.

OXTANKAH ARCHAEOLOGICAL ZONE

FRANCISCAN CHAPEL

TICKET BOOTH/ MUSEUM

STRUCTURE IV

PLAZA DE LAS ABEJAS

STRUCTURE I

STRUCTURE X

STRUCTURE III

STRUCTURE IX

PLAZA DE LAS COLUMNAS

STRUCTURE VI

SCALE NOT AVAILABLE

© AVALON TRAVEL

bungalows. The bungalows themselves range from simple one-room units with a minifridge and microwave to two-bedroom units with fully equipped kitchens; all have porches with chairs that overlook the bay. There also is a pool on-site and a restaurant, too.

Getting There

Calderitas is a quick bus ride from downtown Chetumal. **Combis** leave from Avenida Cristóbal Colón, behind the Museo de la Cultura Maya, roughly every half hour 6am-9pm daily (US$0.50, 15 minutes). If you've got a **car,** head east out of Chetumal on Boulevard Bahía, which becomes the main drag in Calderitas. Alternatively (though less scenic), take Avenida Insurgentes east until you get to the turnoff, and follow the signs from there.

OXTANKAH ARCHAEOLOGICAL ZONE

Oxtankah (8am-5pm daily, US$4) is a small archaeological site whose name means Between Branches, so called by early archaeologists after the many trees growing amid, and on top of, the structures. Relatively little is known about Oxtankah—including its true name—but it probably arose during the Classic era, between AD 300 and 600, and was dedicated primarily to trade and salt production. At its height, the city extended to

TULUM AND QUINTANA ROO

the shores of Chetumal Bay and included the island of Tamalcab.

Oxtankah's principal structures were constructed in this period, suggesting it was a fairly robust city, but it was apparently abandoned around AD 600, for unknown reasons. The city was reoccupied by Maya settlers almost a thousand years later, in the 14th or 15th century, during which time a number of structures were expanded or enhanced. It was still occupied, mostly by modest earthen homes, when the first Spanish explorers arrived.

Some researchers have suggested the infamous Spaniard castaway Gonzalo Guerrero lived here; Guerrero was shipwrecked in this area in 1511 and adopted Maya ways, even marrying a chieftain's daughter. Their children are considered the New World's first mestizos, or mixed-race people.

In 1531, conquistador Alonso de Avila attempted to found a colonial city on the site, but he was driven out after two years of bitter conflict with local residents. He did manage to have a Franciscan chapel built, the skeleton of which remains, including an impressive eight-meter-tall (26-foot) arch.

Today, most of the excavated structures in Oxtankah surround two plazas: **Abejas** (Bees) plaza, the city's main ceremonial and elite residential center, and the somewhat smaller **Columnas** (Columns) plaza, whose large palace probably served an administrative function. Architecturally, the structures are more closely related to those of the Petén region (present-day Guatemala) than to Yucatecan ones, suggesting a close relationship with that area. There's a small **museum** on-site; signage is in Spanish only.

Getting There

Oxtankah is located seven kilometers (4 miles) north of Calderitas, about one kilometer (0.6 mile) off the bayside road. There's no public transportation to the site; a **cab** from Calderitas costs US$3 each way; one from Chetumal will run about US$18 round-trip, including wait time.

KOHUNLICH ARCHAEOLOGICAL ZONE

Swallowed by the jungle over the centuries, **Kohunlich** (8am-5pm daily, US$4) was first discovered in 1912 by American explorer Raymond Merwin, but it was not until the 1960s that excavation of the site began in earnest. Today, the ruins are in harmony with the surrounding vegetation; wandering through it, you'll be rewarded with more than 200 structures, stelae, and uncovered mounds that have trees growing out of them and moss spreading over their stones—a beautiful sight. Most date to the Late Preclassic (AD 100-200) through the Classic (AD 600-900) periods.

Kohunlich's most famous and compelling structure is the **Temple of the Masks.** Constructed in AD 500, it features six two-meter-tall (6.6-foot) stucco masks, believed to be representations of the Maya sun god, with star-incised eyes, mustaches, and nose plugs. Intriguingly, each is slightly different, leading some to speculate that they also represent successive members of the ruling dynasty; it would not have been unusual for the city's elite to draw an overt connection between themselves and a high god.

Southwest of the Temple of the Masks is **27 Escalones,** the largest and most impressive residential area in Kohunlich. Built on a cliff with a spectacular bird's-eye view of the jungle, it is one of the largest palaces in the Maya world, reached by climbing its namesake 27 steps. As you walk through the site, keep an eye out for *aguadas* (cisterns) that once were part of a complex system of Kohunlich's reservoirs.

Getting There

Kohunlich is located about 60 kilometers (37 miles) west of Chetumal. By **car,** take Highway 186 west and turn south (left) at the sign to Kohunlich. An 8.5-kilometer (5.3-mile) paved road leads straight to the site. There is no public transportation to the site.

DZIBANCHÉ AND KINICHNÁ ARCHAEOLOGICAL ZONES

If the crowds at Chichén Itzá and Tulum get you down, these picturesque twin ruins may

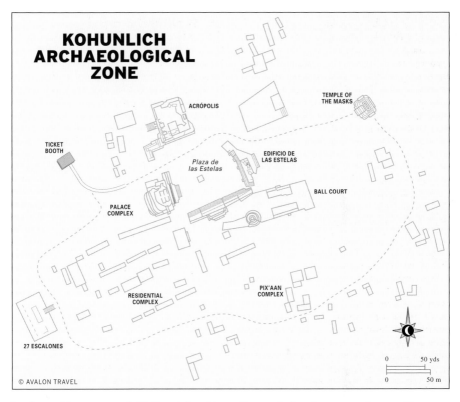

KOHUNLICH ARCHAEOLOGICAL ZONE

ACRÓPOLIS

TEMPLE OF THE MASKS

TICKET BOOTH

EDIFICIO DE LAS ESTELAS

Plaza de las Estelas

BALL COURT

PALACE COMPLEX

RESIDENTIAL COMPLEX

PIX'AAN COMPLEX

27 ESCALONES

© AVALON TRAVEL

0   50 yds

0   50 m

be the antidote you need. Dzibanché and its smaller neighbor, Kinichná, see very few visitors—it's not uncommon to have them to yourself, in fact—and feature modest-size temples in varying states of restoration. (A great many structures aren't excavated at all, but even they—abrupt tree-covered mounds—hold a certain mystery and appeal.)

Dzibanché

The larger of the two sites, Dzibanché is Yucatec Maya for Etched in Wood, a name created by archaeologists in reference to a wood lintel inscribed with hieroglyphics that was found in one of the primary temples. A date on the lintel reads AD 618, and the site seems to have flourished between AD 300 and AD 800. Archaeologists believe this area was occupied by a sprawling, widely

dispersed city that covered some 40 square kilometers (25 square miles).

The site has three main plazas, each higher than the next. Dzibanché's namesake lintel is still in the temple atop **Structure VI,** also called the Building of the Lintels, facing one of the plazas. Unfortunately, climbing Structure VI is no longer allowed, but it's just one of several large pyramids here, the rest of which you can clamber up. The largest is **Structure II,** with an ornate temple at its summit where archaeologists found a tomb of a high-ranking leader (judging from the rich offering found with his remains). The steep stairways and lofty upper temples here are reminiscent of Tikal and other temples in the Petén area of present-day Guatemala, suggesting a strong connection between the two regions.

TULUM AND QUINTANA ROO

Kinichná

Kinichná (House of the Sun) has just one structure, but it's a biggie: a massive pyramid whose summit affords a great view of the surrounding countryside. The structure has three distinct levels, each built in a different era over the course of around 400 years. As you climb up, it's fascinating to observe how the craftsmanship and artistry changed—generally for the better—over the centuries. At the top is a stucco image of the sun god, hence the site's name. As in Structure II in Dzibanché, archaeologists uncovered a tomb here, this one containing the remains of two people and a cache of fine jade jewelry and figurines.

Practicalities

Dzibanché and Kinichná are open 8am-5pm daily; admission is US$4 and valid for both archaeological zones. There is no public transportation to or from the area, and precious little local traffic, so a **car** (or tour van) is essential. To get here, look for the turnoff 50 kilometers (31 miles) west of Chetumal on Highway 186, before reaching the town of Francisco Villa; from there it's 15 kilometers (9 miles) north down a bumpy dirt road. You'll reach Kinichná first, then Dzibanché about 2 kilometers (1.2 miles) later.

INLAND ARCHAEOLOGICAL ZONES

If you can drag yourself away from the beaches at Cancún or Tulum, or the diving on Isla Cozumel, a short trip inland will bring you to three of the Yucatán Peninsula's most intriguing ancient ruins–Chichén Itzá, Ek' Balam, and Cobá. Each is quite different from the other, and together they form an excellent introduction to Maya archaeology and architecture. Venturing inland also will

© LIZA PRADO

Highlights

LOOK FOR ◖ TO FIND RECOMMENDED SIGHTS, ACTIVITIES, DINING, AND LODGING.

◖ **Chichén Itzá Archaeological Zone:** Voted one of the New Seven Wonders of the World, the Yucatán's most famous ruin is all about hyperbole: the iconic star-aligned pyramid, the gigantic Maya ball court, even the crush of bikini-clad day-trippers from Cancún—be sure to arrive early (page 252).

◖ **Iglesia y Ex-Convento San Bernardino de Siena:** Located in a quiet corner of Valladolid, this elegant church has a spacious esplanade and beautiful interior, a small museum, plus a natural cenote inside the convent walls (page 263).

◖ **Ek' Balam Archaeological Zone:** A stunning stucco frieze with angel-like figures and a huge "monster mouth" is the highlight of this small, serene site near Valladolid. A nearby cenote makes for a cool après-ruins swim (page 271).

◖ **Cobá Archaeological Zone:** Just an hour from Tulum are the terrific jungle-cloaked ruins of Cobá, where you can climb the Yucatán's second-highest pyramid and rent bikes to get from temple to temple. Arrive early to enjoy the rich birdlife, then hit the nearby cenotes or monkey reserve for a great all-day outing (page 275).

◖ **Cenotes near Cobá:** A visit to Cobá just got better, with the opening of three impressive

cenotes a short distance from the ruins. Each is unique, but all are massive caverns, with stalactites above and easy-to-use stairs descending to the cool shimmering water below (page 281).

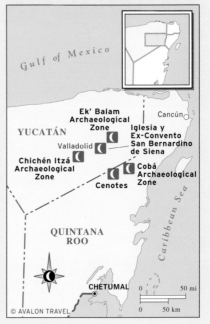

give you an opportunity to sneak a peek at how ordinary Yucatecans, including modern-day Maya, live today.

Chichén Itzá (200 kilometers/124 miles from Cancún) is one of the most famous ruins in the Maya world, with a massive four-sided pyramid and the largest Maya ball court ever built. Just two hours from Cancún, it's inundated with tour groups; get there early to beat the crowds.

Even closer to the coast, but far less visited, is the small ruin of Ek' Balam (175 kilometers/109 miles from Cancún), boasting a

beautiful stucco frieze partway up a massive pyramid. The frieze features winged priests and a gaping monster mouth that are so well preserved they look like they could be modern-day plaster art. A kilometer (0.6 mile) away, a cenote provides a welcome respite from the heat.

Less than an hour from Tulum—and a great alternative to the overcrowded ruins there—is the ancient city of Cobá (42 kilometers/26 miles from Tulum), home of the second-tallest known Maya pyramid. Unlike many other ruins, Cobá is ensconced in a thick tropical

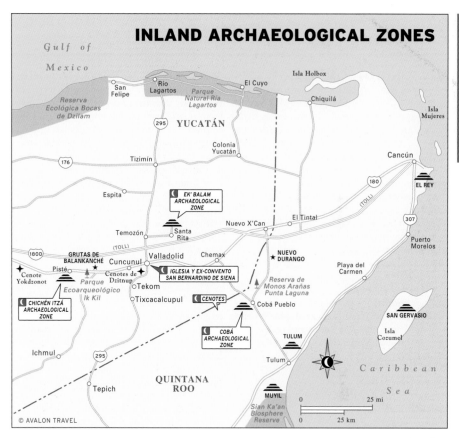

INLAND ARCHAEOLOGICAL ZONES

forest that teems with birdlife, including parrots and toucans.

PLANNING YOUR TIME

Chichén Itzá, Ek' Balam, and Cobá can each be reached as a day trip from Cancún or Tulum. You can visit all three in two or three days, staying overnight at hotels near the sites, or in Valladolid, an attractive and centrally located colonial town.

All the sites can be reached by bus or taxi, especially Chichén Itzá and Cobá. But if you plan on visiting more than one site, a rental car may make your trip easier and more rewarding. You won't be tied to a bus schedule, and you'll be able to beat the crowds by getting to the sites bright and early. There also are numerous organized tours to Chichén Itzá from Cancún (though fewer to Cobá and Ek' Balam). While certainly convenient, many travelers find the large groups off-putting.

Chichén Itzá

Chichén Itzá is one of the finest archaeological sites in the northern part of the peninsula, and in all of Mesoamerica. It is also one of the most visited. Located just two hours from both Cancún and Mérida, the site is inundated by tour groups, many of them bikini-clad day-trippers on loan from the pool at their all-inclusive. That fact should not dissuade independent travelers from visiting—crowded or not, Chichén Itzá is a truly magnificent ruin and a must-see on any archaeology tour of the Yucatán. That said, you can make the most of your visit by arriving right when the gates open, so you can see the big stuff first and be exploring the outer areas by the time the tour buses start to roll in.

Pisté is a one-road town that is strangely underdeveloped considering it is just two kilometers (1.2 miles) from such an important and heavily visited site. The hotels and restaurants here are unremarkable, and there's not much to do or see in town.

◖ CHICHÉN ITZÁ ARCHAEOLOGICAL ZONE

Chichén Itzá (8am-5pm daily, US$14.75 including sound and light show) is a monumental archaeological site, remarkable for both its size and scope. The ruins include impressive palaces, temples, and altars, as well as the largest-known ball court in the Maya world. One of the most widely recognized (and heavily visited) ruins in the world, it was declared a World Heritage Site by UNESCO in 1988 and one of the New Seven Wonders of the World in 2007. In 2012, INAH (Instituto Nacional de Antropología e Historia) partnered with Google to photograph—by bicycle—the site for Google Street View maps.

History

What we call Chichén Itzá surely had another name when it was founded. The name means Mouth of the Well of the Itzá, but the Itzá, an illiterate and semi-nomadic group of uncertain origin, didn't arrive here until the 12th century. Before the Itzá, the area was controlled—or at least greatly influenced—by Toltec migrants who arrived from central Mexico around AD 1000. Most of Chichén's most notable structures, including its famous four-sided pyramid, and images like the reclining *chac-mool*, bear a striking resemblance to structures and images found at Tula, the ancient Toltec capital, in the state of Hidalgo. Before the Toltecs, the area was populated by Maya, evidenced by the Puuc- and Chenes-style design of the earliest structures here, such as the Nunnery and Casa Colorada.

The three major influences—Maya, Toltec, and Itzá—are indisputable, but the exact chronology and circumstances of those groups' interaction (or lack thereof) is one of the most hotly contested issues in Maya archaeology. Part of the difficulty in understanding Chichén Itzá more fully is that its occupants created very few stelae and left few Long Count dates on their monuments. In this way Chichén Itzá is different from virtually every other ancient city in the Yucatán. It's ironic, actually, that Chichén Itzá is the most widely recognized "Maya" ruin considering it was so deeply influenced by non-Maya cultures, and its history and architecture are so atypical of the region.

Chichén Itzá's influence ebbed and flowed over its many centuries of existence and occupation. It first peaked in the mid-9th century, or Late Classic period, when it eclipsed Cobá as the dominant power in the northern Yucatán region. The effects of a widespread collapse of Maya cities to the south (like Calakmul, Tikal, and Palenque) reached Chichén Itzá in the late 900s, and it too collapsed abruptly. The city rose again under Toltec and later Itzá influence, but went into its final decline after an internal dispute led to the rise of Mayapán, which would come to control much of the Yucatán Peninsula. Chichén Itzá was all but abandoned

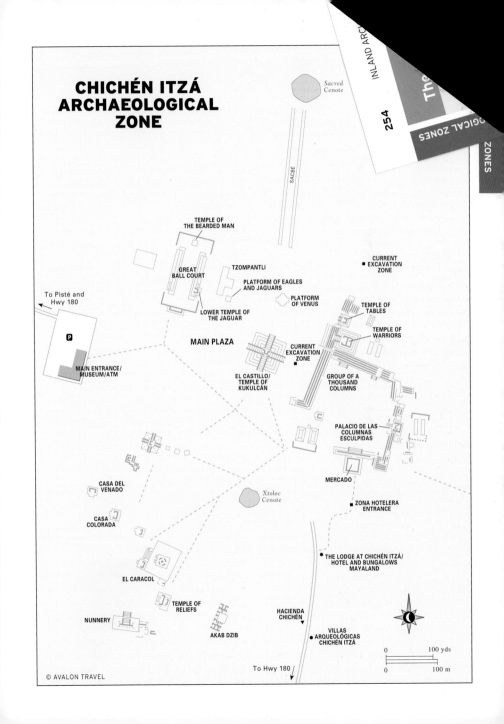

CHICHÉN ITZÁ ARCHAEOLOGICAL ZONE

Sacred Cenote

SACBÉ

TEMPLE OF THE BEARDED MAN

CURRENT EXCAVATION ZONE

GREAT BALL COURT

TZOMPANTLI

PLATFORM OF EAGLES AND JAGUARS

PLATFORM OF VENUS

TEMPLE OF TABLES

To Pisté and Hwy 180

LOWER TEMPLE OF THE JAGUAR

TEMPLE OF WARRIORS

P

MAIN PLAZA

CURRENT EXCAVATION ZONE

MAIN ENTRANCE/ MUSEUM/ATM

EL CASTILLO/ TEMPLE OF KUKULCÁN

GROUP OF A THOUSAND COLUMNS

PALACIO DE LAS COLUMNAS ESCULPIDAS

CASA DEL VENADO

Xtoloc Cenote

MERCADO

CASA COLORADA

ZONA HOTELERA ENTRANCE

THE LODGE AT CHICHÉN ITZÁ/ HOTEL AND BUNGALOWS MAYALAND

EL CARACOL

TEMPLE OF RELIEFS

NUNNERY

HACIENDA CHICHÉN

VILLAS ARQUEOLÓGICAS CHICHÉN ITZÁ

AKAB DZIB

To Hwy 180

0   100 yds

0   100 m

© AVALON TRAVEL

Maya Collapse

Something went terribly wrong for the Maya between the years AD 800 and 900. Hundreds of Classic Maya cities were abandoned, monarchies disappeared, and the population fell by millions, mainly due to death and plummeting birthrates. The collapse was widespread, but was most dramatic in the Southern Lowlands, a swath of tropical forest stretching from the Gulf of Mexico to Honduras and including once-glorious cities such as Palenque, Tikal, and Copán. (Archaeologists first suspected a collapse after noticing a sudden drop-off in inscriptions; it has been confirmed through excavations of peasant dwellings from before and after that period.)

There are many theories for the collapse, varying from climate change and epidemic diseases to foreign invasion and peasant revolt. In his carefully argued book *The Fall of the Ancient Maya* (Thames and Hudson, 2002), archaeologist and professor of anthropology at Pennsylvania State University David Webster suggests it was a series of conditions, rather than a single event, that led to the collapse.

To a certain degree, it was the very success of Maya cities during the Classic era that set the stage for their demise. Webster points to a population boom just before the collapse, which would have left agricultural lands dangerously depleted just as demand spiked. Classic-era farming techniques were ill-suited to meet the challenge; in particular, the lack of draft animals kept productivity low, meaning Maya farmers could not generate large surpluses of corn and other food. (Even if they could, stor-age was difficult given the hot, humid climate.) The lack of animals also limited how far away farmers could cultivate land and still be able to transport their crops to the city center; as a result, available land was overused. As Webster puts it, "too many farmers [growing] too many crops on too much of the landscape left the Classic Maya world acutely vulnerable to an environmental catastrophe, such as drought or crop disease."

Certain kingdoms reached their tipping point before others (prompting some to launch 11th-hour military campaigns against weakened rivals), but few escaped the wave of malnutrition, disease, lower birthrates, and outright starvation that seems to have swept across the Maya world in the 9th century. Kings and nobility would have faced increasing unrest and insurrection—after all, their legitimacy was based on their ability to induce the gods to bestow rain, fertility, and prosperity—further destabilizing the social structure and food supply.

The collapse was not universal, of course, and the fall of lowland powers gave other city-states an opportunity to expand and gain influence. But the Maya world was dramatically and permanently changed by it; the grand cities built by the Classic Maya were abandoned to the jungle, most never to be reoccupied, and, as Webster notes, "Cortés and his little army almost starved in 1525 while crossing a wilderness that had supported millions of people seven centuries earlier."

by the early 1200s, though it remained an important religious pilgrimage site even after the arrival of the Spanish.

El Castillo/Temple of Kukulcán

The most dramatic structure in Chichén Itzá is El Castillo (The Castle), also known as the Temple of Kukulcán. At 24 meters (79 feet), it's the tallest structure on the site, and certainly the most recognizable. Dating to around AD 850, El Castillo was built according to strict astronomical guidelines. There are nine levels, which, divided by the central staircase, make for 18 platforms, the number of months in the Maya calendar. Each of the four sides has 91 steps, which, added together along with the platform on top, total 365—one for each day of the year. And there are 52 inset panels on each face of the structure, equal to the number of years in each cycle of the Calendar Round.

On the spring and autumn equinoxes (March 21 and September 22), the afternoon sun lights up a bright zigzag strip on the outside wall of the north staircase as well as the giant

© LIZA PRADO

El Castillo, Chichén Itzá's famous main pyramid, as seen from the nearby Group of a Thousand Columns

serpent heads at the base, giving the appearance of a serpent slithering down the steps. Chichén Itzá is mobbed during those periods, especially by spiritual-minded folks seeking communion with the ancient Maya. The effect also occurs in the days just before and after the equinox, and there are significantly fewer people blocking the view.

Climbing El Castillo used to be a given for any visit to Chichén Itzá, and the views from its top level are breathtaking. However, an elderly tourist died in 2005 after tumbling from near the top of the pyramid to the ground. The accident, combined with longtime warnings from archaeologists that the structure was being irreparably eroded by the hundreds of thousands of visitors who climbed it yearly, prompted officials to close it off. Pyramids at other sites have been restricted as well, and it's looking more and more like a standard policy at Maya archaeological zones.

Deep inside El Castillo and accessed by way of a steep, narrow staircase are several

chambers; inside one is a red-painted, jade-studded bench in the figure of a jaguar, which may have served as a throne of sorts. You used to be able to climb the stairs to see the chambers and throne—a fascinating, albeit humid and highly claustrophobic affair—but access was closed at the same time climbing the pyramid was prohibited.

Great Ball Court

Chichén Itzá's famous Great Ball Court is the largest ball court in Mesoamerica by a wide margin. The playing field is 135 meters (443 feet) by 65 meters (213 feet), with two parallel walls 8 meters high (26 feet) and scoring rings in impossibly high perches in the center. The players would've had to hit a 12-pound rubber ball through the rings using only their elbows, wrists, and hips (they wore heavy padding). The game likely lasted for hours; at the game's end, the captain of one team—or even the whole team—was apparently sacrificed, possibly by decapitation. There's disagreement about *which* team got the axe, however. Some say it was the losers—otherwise the game's best players would constantly be wiped out. Some argue that it was the winners, and that being sacrificed would have been the ultimate honor. Of course, it's likely the game varied from city to city and evolved over the many centuries it was played. Along the walls, reliefs depict the ball game and sacrifices.

On the outside of the ball court, the **Lower Temple of the Jaguar** has incredibly fine relief carvings depicting the Maya creation myth. An upper temple is off-limits to visitors, but is decorated with a variety of carvings and remnants of what were likely colorful murals.

The Platforms

As you make your way from the ball court to the Temple of Warriors, you'll pass the gruesome **Tzompantli** (Wall of Skulls). A low T-shaped platform, it is decorated on all sides with row upon row of carved skulls, most with eyes staring out of the large sockets. Among the skulls are images of warriors holding the heads of decapitated victims, skeletons intertwined with snakes, and eagles eating human hearts (a common image in Toltec design, further evidence of their presence here). It is presumed that ceremonies performed on this platform culminated in a sacrificial death for the victim, the head then left on display, perhaps with others already in place. It's estimated that the platform was built AD 1050-1200. Nearby, the **Platform of Venus** and **Platform of Eagles and Jaguars** are smaller square structures, each with low stairways on all four sides, which were likely used for ritualistic music and dancing.

Sacred Cenote

This natural well is 300 meters (984 feet) north of the main structures, along the remains of a *sacbé* (raised stone road) constructed during the Classic period. Almost 60 meters (197 feet) in diameter and 30 meters (98.4 feet) down to the surface of the water, it was a place for sacrifices, mostly to Chaac, the god of rain, who was believed to live in its depths. The cenote has been dredged and scoured by divers numerous times, beginning as early as 1900, and the remains of scores of victims, mostly children and young adults, have been recovered, as well as innumerable jade and stone artifacts. (Most are now displayed at the Museo Nacional de Antropología in Mexico City.) On the edge of the cenote is a ruined sweat bath, probably used for purification rituals before sacrificial ceremonies. The name Chichén Itzá (Mouth of the Well of the Itzá) is surely derived from this deeply sacred cenote, and it remained an important Maya pilgrimage site well into the Spanish conquest.

Temple of Warriors and Group of a Thousand Columns

The Temple of Warriors is where some of the distinctive reclining *chac-mool* figures are found. However, its name comes from the rectangular monoliths in front, which are carved on all sides with images of warriors. (Some are also prisoners, their hands tied behind their backs.) This temple is also closed to entry, and it can be hard to appreciate the fading images from the rope perimeter. You may be able to get a closer look from the temple's south side, where you can easily make out the figures' expressions and dress (though access is sometimes blocked there as well). The south side is impressive for its facade, too, where a series of well-preserved human and animal figures adorn the lower portion, while above, human faces emerge from serpents' mouths, framed by eagle profiles, with masks of Chaac, the hook-nosed god of rain, on the corners.

The aptly named Group of a Thousand Columns is adjacent to the Temple of Warriors. It's perfectly aligned cylindrical columns likely held up a grand roof structure.

Across the plaza, the **Palacio de las Columnas Esculpidas** (Palace of Sculptured Columns) also has cylindrical columns, but with intricate carvings, suggesting this was the ceremonial center of this portion of the complex. Continuing through the trees, you'll reach the **Mercado** (market). The name is purely speculative, though it's easy to imagine a breezy bustling market here, protected from the sun under a wood and *palapa* roof built atop the structure's remarkably high columns.

Osario, El Caracol, and the Nunnery

From the market, bear left (away from El Castillo, just visible through the trees) until you meet the path leading to the site's southern entrance. You'll pass the **Osario** (ossuary), also known as the Tomb of the High Priest. Like a miniature version of El Castillo, the pyramid at one time had four stairways on each side and a temple at the crest. From the top platform, a vertical passageway leads into a chamber where seven tombs were discovered, along with numerous copper and jade artifacts indicating the deceased were of special importance (and hence the temple's name). Continuing on, you'll pass two more large structures, **Casa del Venado** (House of the Deer) and **Casa Colorada** (Red House).

The highlight of this portion of Chichén Itzá is **El Caracol** (The Snail Shell), also known as the Observatory, and perhaps the most graceful structure at Chichén Itzá. A two-tiered circular structure is set atop a broad rectangular platform, with window slits facing south and west, and another aligned according to the path of the moon during the spring equinoxes. Ancient astronomers used structures like this one to track celestial events and patterns—the orbits of the Moon and Venus, and the coming of solar and lunar eclipses, for example—with uncanny accuracy.

Beyond El Caracol is the **Nunnery,** so-named by Spanish explorers who thought it looked like convents back home. Judging from its size, location, and many rooms, the Nunnery was probably an administrative palace. Its exuberant facades show strong Chenes influence, another example of the blending of styles in Chichén Itzá.

Sound and Light Show

Though it was closed for retooling at the time of research, the site puts on a nightly high-tech sound and light show at 7pm in the winter (Oct.-Apr.) and at 8pm in the summer (May-Sept.). The fee to enter is included in the general admission; if you'd like to see the show the night before you visit the ruins, buy a US$10 partial entrance—*not* the show-only ticket—and keep your stub for credit the next morning. (Just tell the ticket seller your plan, and you'll get the right ticket. If you're only interested in the show and want to skip the ruins, the price is US$6.) The sound and light show is presented in Spanish, but for an additional US$3.25 you can rent headphones with translations in English, French, German, and Italian.

Practicalities

The grounds are open 8am-5pm daily. Admission is US$14.75 per person, plus US$3.75 to enter with a video camera; parking is US$1.80. The fee includes entrance to the ruins and the sound and light show, but there is no discount if you don't go to the latter.

Guides can be hired at the entrance according to fixed and clearly marked prices: US$42 for a two-hour tour in Spanish, US$50 in English, French, Italian, or German. Prices are per group, which can include up to eight people. Tips are customary and not included in the price. The visitors center has restrooms, an ATM, free luggage storage, a café, a bookstore, a gift shop, and an information center.

GRUTAS DE BALANKANCHÉ

Six kilometers (3.7 miles) east of Chichén Itzá, the **Balankanché Caves** (9am-5pm daily, US$8.50, child under 9 free) are a disappointment. The 1959 excavation of the caves by *National Geographic* archaeologist Dr. E. Wyllys Andrews uncovered numerous artifacts and ceremonial sites, giving researchers a better understanding of ancient Maya cosmology, especially related to the notion of *Xibalba* (the underworld). Nowadays, the caves are basically a tourist trap—a wide path meandering 500 meters (0.3 mile) down a tunnel with urns and other artifacts supposedly set up in their original locations. Wires and electric lights illuminate the path, but the recorded narration does nothing of the sort—it's so garbled you can hardly understand it, no matter what language it's in.

Entry times are fixed according to language: Spanish hourly 9am-4pm; English at 11am, 1pm, and 3pm; and French at 10am. A minimum of six visitors are needed for the tour to depart.

PARQUE ECOARQUEOLÓGICO IK KIL

Three kilometers (1.9 miles) east of Pisté, the centerpiece of the **Ik Kil Eco-Archaeological Park** (Carr. Mérida-Cancún Km. 122, tel. 985/851-0002, cenote_ikkil@hotmail.com, 8am-6pm daily Apr.-Oct., 8am-5pm daily Nov.-Mar., US$6 adult, US$3 child) is the immense, perfectly round **Cenote Sagrado Azul**, with a partial stone roof. Although the cenote is real, the alterations to its natural state—supported walls, a set of stairs leading you in, a waterfall—make it feel pretty artificial. While not representative of the typical cenote experience, this is a good option if you are traveling with small children and need a spot to cool off. Lockers are available for US$2.50. The cenote and on-site restaurant (breakfast US$6.25, lunch buffet US$12.50) get packed with tour groups 12:30pm-2:30pm; try visiting outside those times for a mellower experience. Better yet, stay at one of the on-site bungalows (US$104 s/d with a/c).

ACCOMMODATIONS

A handful of upscale hotels make up the small Zona Hotelera on the east side of Chichén Itzá, complete with its own entrance to the ruins. Nearby, in the town of Pisté, there are also a few budget and mid-range options. Be sure to reserve early during the spring and fall equinoxes. All the options below (except Ik Kil) have Wi-Fi available, though often in the reception area only. Book rooms online for the lowest rates.

US$25-50

On the eastern end of Pisté toward the ruins, **Pirámide Inn** (Calle 15 No. 30, tel. 985/851-0115, www.chichen.com, US$42 s/d) is a low,

sprawling hotel with large rooms that are clean though a bit dark. The decor is distinctly 1970s den, with some rooms sporting bubblegum paint jobs and lacquered brick walls. The air conditioners appear to be from the same era, and can be loud. Cement seating frames a pool in a pleasant fruit tree garden. Backpackers can **camp** or **rent a hammock** here (US$4-8 pp) with access to the pool and cleanish shared bathrooms.

Posada Olalde (Calle 6 at Calle 17, tel. 985/851-0086, US$21/29 s/d with fan) is the best budget option in town. Seven simple rooms are brightly painted, with a long shared porch facing a leafy courtyard. The hotel also has four pressed-earth bungalows, which sound nice but have saggy beds, bad light, and a dank feel—better to stick with the rooms. The dirt access road is easy to miss—look for it just west of (and on the opposite side of the street from) the OXXO mini-mart. There's street parking only.

Posada Chac-Mool (Calle 15 s/n, tel. 985/851-0270, US$25 d with fan, US$33 with a/c) has basic hot-water rooms with thin towels, loose-fill pillows, and beds in various age brackets. Still, it does have Wi-Fi and parking, and management will bargain if it's slow.

US$50-100

Affiliated with Best Western, **Hotel Chichén** (Calle 15 s/n, tel. 985/851-0022, US$71-112 s/d with a/c) is the nicest hotel in downtown Pisté, featuring king or two queen bed rooms with comfortable furnishings, large modern bathrooms, and simple Mexican decor. The less-expensive rooms face the street and can be noisy, while the top-floor ones are larger and overlook the hotel's attractive garden and pool area. There's a guest computer, plus a cavernous restaurant (7am-11pm daily) that's often packed with tour groups.

The **Hotel Dolores Alba Chichén** (Carr. Mérida-Cancún Km. 122, tel. 985/858-1555, www.doloresalba.com, US$54-58 s/d with a/c) is one of the best deals in the area, especially given its choice location three kilometers (1.9 miles) east of the ruins, one

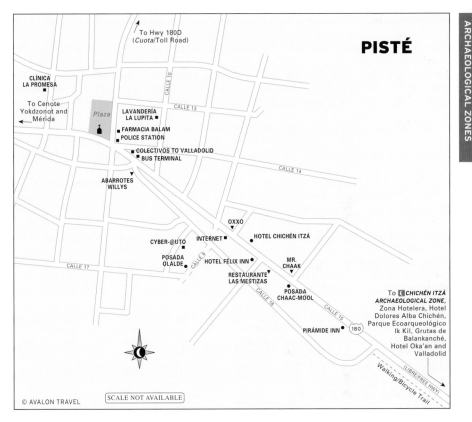

To Hwy 180D
(*Cuota*/Toll Road)

PISTÉ

CLÍNICA
LA PROMESA ■

CALLE 10

To Cenote
Yokdzonot and
Mérida ←

Plaza

LAVANDERÍA ■
LA LUPITA ■

CALLE 13

■ FARMACIA BALAM
■ POLICE STATION

■ COLECTIVOS TO VALLADOLID
■ BUS TERMINAL

CALLE 14

▼ ABARROTES
WILLYS

OXXO
▼

INTERNET ■
CYBER-@UTO ■

● HOTEL CHICHÉN ITZÁ

POSADA
OLALDE ●

CALLE 8

HOTEL FÉLIX INN ●

MR.
CHAAK ▼

CALLE 17

RESTAURANTE ▼
LAS MESTIZAS

CALLE 16

● POSADA
CHAAC-MOOL

CALLE 15

PIRÁMIDE INN ●   180

To ◖ *CHICHÉN ITZÁ*
ARCHAEOLOGICAL ZONE,
Zona Hotelera, Hotel
Dolores Alba Chichén,
Parque Ecoarqueológico
Ik Kil, Grutas de
Balankanché,
Hotel Oka'an and
Valladolid

Walking/Bicycle Trail
(LIBRE/FREE HWY)

© AVALON TRAVEL

SCALE NOT AVAILABLE

kilometer (0.6 mile) from the Balankanché Caves, and across the street from the Parque Ecoarqueológico Ik Kil. Rooms are spotless and smallish, with good beds and simple tile work on the walls to spiff up the decor, and tour groups are situated in an area separate from independent travelers. The hotel has a pleasant outdoor restaurant (7am-10pm daily, US$5-10) and two large swimming pools—the one in back has a mostly natural stone bottom, with holes and channels reminiscent of an ocean reef, which is perfect for kids with active imaginations. Other amenities include continental breakfast and a computer for rent in reception. The hotel also provides free shuttle service to the ruins during the day (though not back); it's US$1.70

per person round-trip for an evening shuttle to the sound and light show.

The **Hotel Fenix Inn** (Calle 15 btwn Calles 2 and 4, tel. 985/851-0033, US$54-63 s/d with a/c) features six rooms that open onto a lush garden with an aboveground pool and a *palapa*-roofed restaurant. Though overpriced, the rooms have nice wood furnishings from Michoacán, newish TVs, and silent air-conditioning. Still, reception seems to be permanently MIA, and it's a bit dark and dreary here in the evenings.

US$100-150

Set in a lush forest, ◖**Parque Ecoarqueológico Ik Kil** (Carr. Mérida-Cancún Km. 122, tel. 985/858-1525, US$104 s/d with a/c) offers 14 modern and ultra-comfortable bungalows. All are spacious and have whirlpool tubs and comfortable beds, and a handful sport pull-out sofas. Silent air-conditioning and a private porch make it all the better. Guests get unlimited use of the on-site cenote, including after hours. It's a fantastic value, especially for those traveling with kids.

Villas Arqueológicas Chichén Itzá (Zona Hotelera, Carr. Mérida-Valladolid Km. 120, tel. 985/851-0187, toll-free Mex. tel. 800/557-7755, www.villasarqueologicas.com.mx, US$104 s/d with a/c, US$154 suite with a/c) is a pleasant two-story hotel with a mellow ambience. Boxy but nice rooms are set around a lush courtyard with an inviting L-shaped pool. A library/TV room with comfy couches and a variety of reading material—from romance novels to archaeology books—also faces the courtyard. A decent restaurant and a tennis court (with nighttime lighting and racquets to borrow) are on-site too. Very tall folks should note that alcove walls bracket the ends of the beds.

A new holistic retreat center with two dozen rooms in a forest setting, **Hotel Oka'an** (Carr. Mérida-Cancún Km. 122, cell. tel. 985/105-8402, www.hotelokaan.com, US$115-200 s/d with a/c, US$240-280 suite with a/c) beckons with a full spa, yoga workshops, and the occasional spiritual ceremony. Ample standard rooms have balconies with hammocks, and corner units have an extra set of picture windows letting in more light. Larger and more luxurious bungalows have decorative stone butterflies and turtles detailing the floors and earthy contemporary architecture, plus private terraces. Continental breakfast is served in a draped open-air restaurant (8am-10pm daily, US$7.50-10), offering regional, international, and vegetarian options. For post-ruin lounging, an infinity pool cascades into smaller shaded basins, but don't miss the killer view from the *mirador* terrace—Chichén Itzá's El Castillo pops up over the (arduously manicured) treeline. Look for the road marquis just west of the Hotel Dolores Alba and continue 1.5 kilometers (0.9 mile) on an unpaved road; it's a US$8 taxi ride from Pisté.

Over US$150

Once the headquarters for the Carnegie Institute's Chichén Itzá expedition, the **Hacienda Chichén Resort** (Zona Hotelera, Carr. Mérida-Valladolid Km. 120, tel. 999/920-8407, toll-free U.S. tel. 877/631-4005, www.haciendachichen.com, US$169-265 with a/c) is now a tranquil hotel set in a lush tropical garden. Newer units are quite comfortable, with tile floors, exposed beam ceilings, and wood furnishings. Many of the older units occupy the original cottages used by archaeologists who conducted their first excavations of Chichén Itzá—very cool in theory, though the cinder-block walls and pervasive mustiness diminish the charm. Still, the latter are usually booked solid. Be sure to wander the grounds with an eye for the original hacienda (blocks from the ruins are incorporated into the main building) and narrow-gauge railroad tracks that were used to transport artifacts from Chichén Itzá. A pool, full-service spa (7:30am-9:30pm daily), and a fine dining room are also nice.

The Lodge at Chichén Itzá (Zona Hotelera, Carr. Mérida-Valladolid Km. 120, tel. 998/887-9162, toll-free Mex. tel. 800/719-5495, toll-free U.S. tel. 800/235-4079, www.mayaland.com, US$175-433 s/d with a/c) is part of the larger Mayaland resort, which is literally at the rear entrance to the ruins; guests and nonguests must pass through the resort (and two of its gift shops) to get to the ticket booth. The grounds are gorgeous: 100 acres of tamed tropical jungle featuring walking and horseback riding trails, a full-service spa, three restaurants, and three pools. The lodges *palapa*-roofed bungalows are pleasant (if somewhat dated), with stained-glass windows, hardwood furniture, and terraces with rocking chairs. Lodge accommodations are typically reserved for independent travelers, and their location—including a separate access road and parking lot—is fairly removed from Mayaland proper, where groups are handled. Still, you're bound to encounter various loud flocks of day-trippers during your stay, especially in the reception area or restaurant, which diminishes the charm for some.

FOOD

Eating options are pretty limited in Pisté but improve somewhat if you have a car and can get to and from the large hotels.

℃ Restaurante Las Mestizas (Calle 15 s/n, tel. 985/851-0069, 7:30am-10:30pm daily, US$4-12) is the best place to eat in Pisté, with an airy, colonial-style interior and tasty, good-sized portions. The food is classic Yucatecan fare, from *panuchos* to *pollo pibil.* Service is exceptional.

Excellent for a hearty breakfast before exploring the ruins, the shady garden deck at **℃ Mr. Chaak** (Calle 15 s/n, tel. 985/851-0081, 7am-10pm daily, US$6-7) hits the spot with a nice choice of *chilaquiles,* eggs, and French toast or waffles, served up with strong espresso drinks and frappés. Focaccia sandwiches and light Yucatecan fare round out the menu, which uses fresh herbs grown on-site and patisserie bread delivered from Mérida. Free Wi-Fi is available.

Set in a 16th-century hacienda, the **℃ Hacienda Chichén Resort's restaurant** (Zona Hotelera, tel. 999/920-8407, 7am-10pm daily, US$14-25) is a soothing place to eat after a long day at the ruins. The menu is varied—Yucatecan specialties, pastas, sandwiches—and on the occasional evening, a trio plays regional music. Some of the produce is grown in its beautiful organic garden.

If you can stand the tour groups, the lunch buffet at **Hotel and Bungalows Mayaland** (Zona Hotelera, Carr. Mérida-Valladolid Km. 120, tel. 985/851-0100, noon-4:30pm daily, US$13) offers a variety of hot and cold dishes that will definitely fill you up. Live music, ballet *folklórico* shows, and outdoor seating are nice touches.

For groceries, **Abarrotes Willy's** (Calle 2 s/n, 7am-10pm daily) has the best selection and prices in town. Follow the pulsating music a block southeast of the plaza.

INFORMATION AND SERVICES

There is no tourist office in Pisté; hotel receptionists are sometimes helpful—depends who you get—as are other travelers. Pisté also doesn't have a bank, but there are three local ATMs: inside the OXXO market, across the street from OXXO, and in Chichén Itzá's visitors complex.

Emergency Services

The **police** have an office (tel. 985/851-0365) in the Palacio Municipal, facing the church. An officer is on duty 24 hours a day, and there's usually one waving through traffic near the plaza. **Clínica La Promesa** (Calle 14 btwn Calles 13 and 15, tel. 985/851-0005, 24 hours) is one of two clinics in town. For anything serious, you're better off going to Mérida or Cancún. **Farmacia Balam** (Calle 15 s/n, 985/851-0358, 7am-midnight daily) is just north of the Palacio Municipal.

Media and Communications

In the middle of town, across from the OXXO mini-mart, a **no-name Internet place** (Calle 15 s/n, 10am-10pm daily, US$0.80/hour) has a fast connection plus international telephone service (US$0.40/minute to U.S. and Canada, US$0.60/minute to Europe).

Off the road that parallels the main drag, and across from the cemetery, **Ciber-@uto** (Calle 4A, 9am-7pm daily, US$1/hour), is a combination Internet café-and-car-wash run out of a family home.

Laundry

Lavandería La Lupita (Calle 10 near Calle 13, 8am-8pm Mon.-Sat.) charges US$1.70 per kilo (2.2 pounds) to wash and dry clothes; they'll do same-day service if you drop your load off first thing in the morning.

GETTING THERE AND AROUND
Bus

Pisté's small **bus terminal** (8:30am-5:30pm daily, cash only) is just southeast of the Palacio Municipal, and about 2.5 kilometers (1.5 miles) from the entrance to Chichén Itzá. There is also a **ticket office** in the gift shop at the ruins (tel. 985/851-0377, 9am-5pm daily). (The visitors center at Chichén Itzá also has **free luggage storage,** which makes it easy to catch a bus right after visiting the ruins.)

All first-class departures leave from Chichén Itzá only. Second-class departure times listed here are for the terminal in Pisté. Second-class buses coming and going between 8am and 5:30pm stop at both the terminal and the parking lot at the ruins. If planning to catch a second-class bus at the ruins, keep in mind that buses headed toward Cancún stop at the ruins slightly after the listed times, while those bound for Mérida pass by slightly earlier. Most bus service to and from Pisté and Chichén Itzá is on Oriente, ADO's second-class line, but the few first-class buses are worth the extra cost.

- Cancún: One daily first-class bus (US$16, 3.5 hours) at 4:30pm; second-class buses (US$10, 4-4.5 hours) every 30-60 minutes 5:30am-11:30pm.

- Cobá: For the town and archaeological site (US$5, 2.5 hours), take the second-class Tulum bus at 7:30am; the first-class buses do not stop there.

- Mérida: First-class buses (US$9.50, 2 hours) leave at 2:20pm and 5:15pm; second-class buses (US$5.50, 2.5 hours) every 30-60 minutes 6am-11:30pm.

- Playa del Carmen: Second-class buses (US$11, 4 hours) from Pisté at 1pm and 7pm Friday, 1pm Saturday, and 7pm Sunday.

- Tulum: First-class buses (US$12, 2.5 hours) leave at 8:25am and 4:30pm; one second-class departure at 7:30am (US$6.25, 3.5 hours).

- Valladolid: First-class buses (US$5, 50 minutes) at 11:20am and 4:30pm; second-class service (US$2, 1 hour) every 30-60 minutes 5:30am-11:30pm.

White *colectivos* (US$2, 40 minutes) leave for Valladolid every 30 minutes 7am-6pm from in front of the bus terminal.

Car

Chichén Itzá lies adjacent to Highway 180, 40 kilometers (25 miles) west of Valladolid, 120 kilometers (75 miles) east of Mérida, and 200 kilometers (124 miles) west of Cancún. For drivers, the quickest way to get there is via the *cuota,* a large modern freeway extending from Cancún most of the way to Mérida, with a well-marked exit for Chichén Itzá and Pisté. There's a price for speed and convenience, though: The toll from Mérida is just US$7, but a whopping US$33 from Cancún. You can also take the old *carretera libre* (free highway) all or part of the way; it's in reasonably good condition but takes much longer, mainly because you pass through numerous small villages and seemingly innumerable *topes* (speed bumps).

Air

Aeropuerto Internacional Chichén Itzá is 16 kilometers (9.9 miles) east of Pisté, between the towns of Xcalacot and Kaua. Inaugurated in April 2000, it is one of the most modern airports in the country, with an 1,800-meter (5,900-foot) runway capable of receiving 747 jets. Although it initially received dozens of regular and charter flights, its license was suspended in 2001. Today it stands virtually empty, receiving only a smattering of charters, mostly from Cancún, Cozumel, and Chetumal, though rumors of restarting service crop up from time to time.

Valladolid

Valladolid draws tourists because of its mellow colonial atmosphere and its central location: 30 minutes from the archaeological zones of Chichén Itzá and Ek' Balam, an hour from the ruins at Cobá and the flamingo reserve in Río Lagartos, and two hours from Mérida, Cancún, and Tulum. It's an easy bus or car ride to any of these destinations, restaurants and hotels are reasonably priced, and you have the advantage of staying in a colonial Mexican town. If you're en route to one of the regional sites or simply want to have a small-city experience, consider spending a night here—you're sure to be happily surprised.

HISTORY

The site of several Maya revolts against the Spanish, Valladolid was conquered in 1543 by Francisco de Montejo, cousin of the like-named Spaniard who founded Mérida. It was once the Maya city of Zací. Montejo brutalized its inhabitants and crushed their temples, building large churches and homes in their place. It is perhaps not surprising, then, that the Caste War started in Valladolid, and that the city played an important role in the beginning of the Mexican Revolution. Today, Valladolid is a charming colonial town with a rich history and strong Maya presence.

ORIENTATION

Valladolid is easy to get around. It's laid out in a grid pattern with even-numbered streets running north to south, odd-numbered streets running east to west. The central plaza at the center of the city is bordered by Calles 39, 40, 41, and 42.

SIGHTS
◖ Iglesia y Ex-Convento San Bernardino de Siena

Located at the end of the Calzada de los Frailes, the **Iglesia y Ex-Convento San Bernardino de Siena** (Calle 41-A, tel. 985/856-2160, 7am-1pm and 5pm-8pm daily) is one of Valladolid's most attractive structures. Built by Franciscan missionaries between 1552 and 1560, the church is entered through a series of arches, and the facade, covered in a checkerboard-like stucco pattern, rises into a squat tower with turrets. Inside, there are original 16th-century frescoes, catacombs, and crypts. Annexed to it, the ex-monastery has rooms radiating from a center courtyard that features, uniquely, a cenote. Called Ziis-Há (Cold Water), the cenote helped the monks be self-reliant. In 2004, an INAH-funded exploration of the cenote resulted in the discovery of 164 rifles and one cannon. Although neither the age nor the origin of the arms has been disclosed, it is speculated that they date from the mid-1800s, when the monastery was used as a fortress during the Maya uprisings. Mass is held at 7am and 7pm Monday-Friday; 7am, 8:30am, and 7pm Saturday; and at 7am, 8am, 9am, 10am, 5pm, 6pm, 7pm, and 8:30pm on Sunday. Special permission is required to visit the monastery; call ahead or ask in the church office.

Casa de los Venados

If you have even a passing interest in Mexican folk art—or an infatuation with exquisite colonial buildings—make sure to schedule a post-breakfast visit to the **House of the Deer** (Calle 40 btwn Calles 41 and 43, 985/856-2289, www.casadelosvenados.com, 10am tour daily, US$5 donation requested). After an architectural award-winning, eight-year remodel of this early 17th-century house, the American couple who own it had so many visitors stopping by to see their extensive art collection that they now welcome visitors at 10am daily for tours of their mansion home and their incredible 3,000-piece collection—the largest Mexican folk art collection not owned by a museum. The pieces span John and Dorianne Venator's 50 years of seeking out and commissioning *catrinas,* clay sculptures, wood carvings, paintings, and other

VALLADOLID

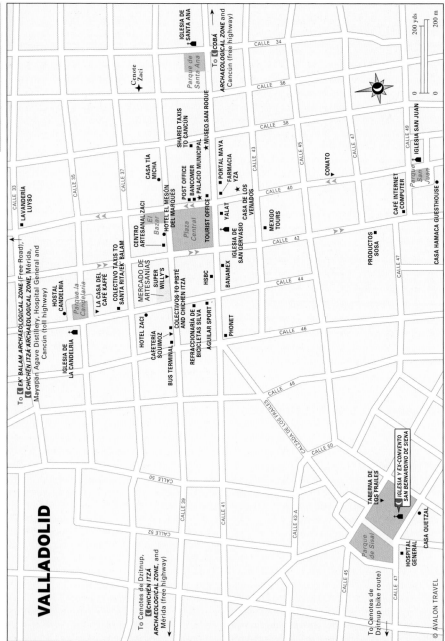

© AVALON TRAVEL

© LIZA PRADO

Valladolid's historic Iglesia de San Gervasio

churches in the Yucatán whose facade faces north instead of west.

Museo San Roque

A long, high-ceilinged room—this used to be a church—the **San Roque Museum** (Calle 41 btwn Calles 38 and 40, no phone, 9am-9pm Mon.-Fri., 8am-6pm Sat.-Sun., free) is a worthwhile stop, with history exhibits on Valladolid, many focusing on the Caste War and the beginning of the Mexican Revolution. Displays of local handicrafts are also notable. Signage is in Spanish only.

Palacio Municipal

On the 2nd floor of the **city hall** (7am-7pm daily, free) is a large balcony overlooking the central plaza, with four large paintings by local artist Manuel Lizama. The paintings depict events in Valladolid's history: pre-Hispanic communities, the city's founding, the Caste War, and the Mexican Revolution. It's not spectacular, but still something to see.

decorative objects created by some of the most talented contemporary artisans from across Mexico, and the work usually incorporates religious, indigenous, or cultural themes. The museum is a labor of love, with all donations benefiting a local volunteer-run medical clinic and the Lions Club.

Iglesia de San Gervasio

Overlooking the central plaza, the **San Gervasio Church** (Calle 41 at Calle 42, no phone) has a sober Franciscan style. It was originally built in 1545 but in 1705 was deemed profaned and ordered demolished by the local bishop as the result of a political rivalry that involved the storming of the church, the desanctifying of its altar, and the death of four politicians. (The incident is now known as *El Crimen de los Alcaldes,* or The Mayors' Crime.) The church was rebuilt a year later, but its orientation changed so that the new altar would not be in the same position as the prior—indeed, the Iglesia de San Gervasio is one of the only colonial-era

Cenote Zaci

Right in the middle of town, **Cenote Zaci** (Calle 36 btwn Calles 37 and 39, no phone, 8am-6pm daily, US$1.25 adult, US$0.80 child under 13) is a dark natural pool at the bottom of a huge cavern, with a bank of trees on one side and a path looping down from the entrance above. It's often pooh-poohed as inferior to cenotes at Dzitnup, but it's a perfectly peaceful and attractive spot, and a lot quicker and easier to get to. You may find leaves and pollen floating on the water's surface, but it's still great for swimming. To have the cenote to yourself, go midweek, or better yet right after closing time, entering through the restaurant (you can use their bathroom to change) instead of the main gates.

Mayapán Agave Distillery

Along Valladolid's northern ring road, two kilometers (1.2 miles) south of the Cancún toll highway, the artisanal **Mayapán Agave Distillery** (Libremiento Nte., tel. 985/856-1727, www.mayapan.mx, 7am-6pm Mon.-Fri.,

7am-1pm Sat., US$2.50) leads visitors on half-hour tours that take in its agave fields and warehouse-size facility, detailing the traditional steps used to ferment, mash by horse-drawn mill, and distill the agave plant into liquor. They can't call it tequila because it's not made in Jalisco, but your taste buds might not be so finicky. Tours conclude with three different tastings and a subtle nudge toward the gift shop. English tours are available.

Cenotes de Dzitnup

Four kilometers (2.5 miles) west of Valladolid on Highway 180 is the small community of Dzitnup, home to two appealing underground cenotes. Both make for a unique and refreshing swim—and on warm days you may find them somewhat crowded. Both share a ticket kiosk and a large parking lot. Many small *artesanía* stands sit at the entrance, and you'll be aggressively pursued by children offering to watch your car or sell you a postcard.

Although the two are across the street from each other, **Cenote Xkeken** (no phone, 8am-5pm daily, US$5.50 adult, US$2 under 17, video cameras US$2.50) has been open longer and is better known; many postcards and travel guides call it "Cenote Dzitnup." After a reasonably easy descent underground (in a few places you must bend over because of a low ceiling; there's a hanging rope to help), you'll come to a circular pond of clear, cool water. It's a pretty, albeit damp, place, with a high dome ceiling that has one small opening at the top letting in a ray of sun and dangling green vines. Often an errant bird can be seen swooping low over the water before heading to the sun and sky through the tiny opening. Stalactites and at least one large stalagmite adorn the ceiling and cenote floor.

At **Cenote Samula** (no phone, 8:30am-5pm daily, US$5.50 adult, US$2 under 17, video cameras US$2.50), tree roots dangle impressively from the cavern roof all the way down to the water. You enter through a narrow tunnel, which opens onto a set of stairs that zigzag down to the water. Fearless kids jump from the stairs into the clear turquoise water below.

Many people ride bikes here, following a paved path that runs parallel to the highway. A cab to the cenotes runs about US$5.

Tours

For small group **van tours** packing in local and regional attractions, **MexiGo Tours** (Calle 43 btwn Calles 40 and 42, tel. 985/856-0777, www.mexigotours.com) is highly recommended. Its "Flamingo" excursion (US$85 pp) visits Río Lagartos, Ek' Balam, and the cake-like 17th-century church in nearby Uayma; another popular outing visits Chichén Itzá and Izamal, with a stop for a dip at the dreamy Yokdzonot cenote (US$85). Both these tours include breakfast, lunch, and transportation, but not site entrance fees. There's a minimum of three people or it's an extra US$25 per person.

ENTERTAINMENT AND EVENTS

Taking the cue from Mérida's successful weekly celebrations, Sundays here now feature a year-round cultural event called **Domingo Vallisoletano.** From 10am until about 8:30pm, the city closes the streets around the central plaza for artisan expositions, *trova* balladeers, folkloric dancing, and programs for kids. The tourist office also leads free hour-long tours of the area around the plaza at 11am, 1pm, and 4pm, though you may want to confirm these times.

Every January 27-February 2, Valladolid celebrates its patron saint, La Virgen de la Candelaria, in the **Expo-Feria Valladolid.** It's a blowout outdoor festival, where you'll be sure to see bullfights, rodeos, musical entertainment, and lots of food stands selling local delicacies and heart-stopping goodies. Venues vary; ask at the tourist office or your hotel for details.

SHOPPING

A tranquil courtyard of workshops and stores, the **Centro Artesanal Zaci** (Calle 39 btwn Calles 40 and 42, 7am-10pm daily) showcases local Maya women who make and sell their *huipiles* and hand-stitched blouses on-site. For a wider number of offerings, the **Mercado de Artesanías** (Calle 39 at Calle 44, 8am-8pm Mon.-Sat., 8am-2pm Sun.) has a decent variety of *guayaberas,* embroidered *huipiles,* hammocks, and other popular handicrafts. The selection isn't very large—there are only about a dozen shops here—so be sure to bargain. If you're interested in high-end Mexican handicrafts and art, **Yalat** (Calle 41 btwn Calles 40 and 42, tel. 985/856-1969, 9am-8pm Mon.-Fri., 9am-7pm Sat.-Sun.) is worth a stop. It's pricey, but the quality and variety of the items sold is excellent.

A family-owned business still chugging away after more than 100 years, the unassuming shop of distiller **Productos Sosa** (Calle 42 btwn Calles 47 and 49, tel. 985/856-2142, 8:30am-1:30pm and 4pm-7:30pm Mon.-Fri., 8:30am-2:30pm Sat.) sells smooth sugar cane liquors infused with ingredients like mint or anise with honey.

ACCOMMODATIONS

Valladolid offers a good selection of simple and mid-range hotels. Most are convenient to the central plaza. All have free Wi-Fi and, except for the hostel, provide parking.

Under US$50

Cozy fan-cooled dormitories at **Hostel Candelaria** (Parque la Candelaria, Calle 35 btwn Calles 42 and 44, tel. 985/856-2267, www.hostelvalladolidyucatan.com, US$10 dorm, US$23-27 s/d with fan) have 10-14 beds sharing one bathroom, with a low-ceilinged women-only dorm and a roomier mixed dorm. What the dorms lack in space is more than made up for by a sprawling back garden thick with papaya trees and hibiscus, shading an al fresco kitchen and eating area and hammocks tucked in nooks with personal reading lights. Inside the colonial building, you'll find another kitchen, free computers, lockers—including some for charging electronics—and a TV room. Socialize with other travelers over the free continental breakfast, then rent a bicycle to tour the local cenotes.

Set around a grassy courtyard, **Hotel Zaci** (Calle 44 btwn Calles 37 and 39, tel. 985/856-2167, www.hotelzaci.com.mx, US$36-40 s with a/c, US$44-54 d with a/c) offers well-kempt ground-floor rooms with decorative details like stenciling and ironwork furnishings. The top two floors contain remodeled "premier" rooms, which boast flat-screen TVs and newer decor. But the difference between the two levels of rooms is pretty minimal—there's just better light on the upper floors. A small, clean pool is a nice plus.

US$50-100

Steps from the plaza yet still very quiet, the new five-room ◖ **Casa Tía Micha** (Calle 39 btwn Calles 38 and 40, 985/856-2957, www.casatiamicha.com, US$70-105 s/d with a/c) is run by the great-grandchildren of the former owner. Stately wooden doors, rainforest showerheads, wrought-iron or carved headboards, and vintage furniture can be found throughout, and one of the more luxurious upstairs rooms boasts a decadent Jacuzzi tub. A full breakfast is served in the tranquil fruit tree garden, near the old *pozo* (well).

A converted 17th-century home, **Hotel El Mesón del Marqués** (central plaza, Calle 39 btwn Calles 40 and 42, tel. 985/856-2073, www.mesondelmarques.com, US$61 s/d standard with a/c, US$75 s/d superior with a/c, US$116-196 s/d suite) boasts a free lobby computer, lush courtyards, a gurgling fountain, arches upon arches, and a verdant garden with an egg-shaped pool. Rooms are divided into three categories: standard, superior, and suite. The first two types are decorated similarly with heavy wood furniture, ironwork headboards, and brightly colored woven bedspreads—the main differences are that the standard is smaller, has old-school air conditioners, and clunky TVs. Suites have modern decor and amenities and updated bathrooms, and are spacious. Though the prices are a bit inflated, this is still one of the most comfortable places to stay in town.

Casa Quetzal (Calle 51 btwn Calles 50 and 52, tel. 985/856-4796, www.casa-quetzal.com, US$66-75 s/d) is a charming, well-run bed-and-breakfast a half block from the pretty San Bernardino de Siena church. Large, attractive, high-ceilinged rooms surround a pretty garden and swimming pool, while a community kitchen and lovely reading room—with high-quality Mexican artwork, especially from Oaxaca and Jalisco—lend a homey feel. All rooms have air-conditioning, cable TV, two double beds, and a hammock; ask for a room away from the street for less traffic noise. Free yoga classes take place in its dedicated salon twice daily. Breakfast gets good reviews, but is a bit pricey at US$8. The hotel is somewhat removed from the central plaza, but the 10-minute walk there—along Valladolid's iconic Calzada de los Frailes—is a pleasure itself.

US$100-150

⟨ Casa Hamaca Guesthouse (Parque San Juan, Calle 49 at Calle 40, tel. 985/856-5287, www.casahamaca.com, US$110-125 s/d with a/c, US$150 quad with a/c) has a convenient and peaceful location, facing a quiet church plaza about five blocks south of the main square. A lush garden and small pool add to the tranquility, and the guesthouse is spacious and bright. The eight rooms vary in size and decor: The Tree Suite has rattan furnishings, the Earth Suite has ochre highlights, and all rooms have dramatic hand-painted murals. A hearty breakfast is included, and massages, facials, Maya cleansings, and other treatments can be arranged. With advance notice the proprietor can also help set up rewarding volunteer opportunities or Spanish classes. Casa Hamaca is wheelchair accessible, and rates dip about US$20 in low season.

FOOD

Located next to the bus station, **⟨ Cafetería Squimoz** (Calle 39 near Calle 46, tel. 985/856-4156, 7am-11pm Mon.-Sat., 8am-4pm Sun., US$3.75-7.50) is well worth a stop even if you're not on your way out of town. Big breakfasts and sandwiches are the specialties, though the coffee drinks and to-die-for milkshakes shouldn't be overlooked. If you've got a sweet tooth, try the homemade flan.

Adjacent to the Iglesia y Ex-Convento San Bernardino de Siena, the low lighting, attentive service, and open-air *palapa* dining room at **Taberna de los Frailes** (Calle 49 at Calle 41A, tel. 985/856-0689, noon-11pm daily Nov.-Apr., 1pm-11pm May-Oct., US$7.50-12) set an elegant backdrop for a crowd-pleasing menu of creative Yucatecan mainstays, seafood cocktails, and a few vegetarian entrées like *chaya* tamales or risotto. Its upscale bar has some sofa seating and a terrace area shaded by a profuse canopy of passion fruit. The restaurant's proximity to the monastery cenote can draw the odd mosquito; ask the staff if you need repellent.

Bohemia is alive and well at **Conato** (Calle 40 btwn Calles 45 and 47, tel. 985/856-2586, 5:30pm-midnight Wed.-Mon., US$4.25-7), where religious iconography and images of Frida Kahlo clutter a dining room of family-style wooden tables set off by a colonial tile floor. Yucatecan-influenced chicken dishes, fresh salads, and serviceable pasta dishes have creative visual flourishes, and the govinda dessert crepes laced with cream and chocolate are almost too pretty to eat. Open until late, it's also a sociable place for drinks or coffee.

With tables on the lovely Parque Candelaria, **La Casa del Café Kaffé** (Calle 35 at Calle 44, tel. 985/856-2879, 9am-1pm and 7pm-10:30pm daily, US$2-3.50) is a fantastic place to get breakfast or a late-night snack. It's owned and run by a welcoming Chilean couple, and the menu features empanadas, quesadillas, sandwiches, fruit shakes, and a nice variety of coffee drinks. If you don't see what you crave on the menu, be sure to ask for it—meals often are made to order.

A gorgeous place to enjoy a meal, the restaurant at the **Hotel El Mesón del Marqués** (Calle 39 btwn Calles 40 and 42, tel. 985/856-2073, 7am-11pm daily, US$7.50-12.50) has an interior courtyard with a colonial-style fountain and masses of fuchsia-colored bougainvillea draped over the balconies. The menu is predominantly Yucatecan, though there are a variety of international options. Good choices include scrambled eggs with *chaya, sopa de lima,* and *poc-chuc.*

El Bazar (parque central, Calle 39 at Calle 40, US$1.25-5) is a local food court with a dozen or so inexpensive eateries selling mostly premade Yucatecan specialties. Hours are variable, but all are open for breakfast and lunch. Food is hit or miss—take a look at the offerings and decide which looks the freshest. (If anything, avoid the tamales.) Better yet, order something off the menu that hasn't been sitting around, like scrambled eggs or *salbutes.*

For groceries, **Super Willy's** (Calle 39 btwn Calles 42 and 44, 7am-10pm daily) has a decent selection of fresh and canned foods.

INFORMATION AND SERVICES
Tourist Information
Try your best at prying some useful information from Valladolid's **tourist office** (Palacio Municipal, Calle 40 at Calle 41, tel. 985/856-2529, ext. 114, 9am-9pm daily). At the very least, you should be able to get a map or two, and English is spoken.

Emergency Services
If you need medical assistance, the modern new **Hospital General** (Av. Chan Yokdzonot, tel. 985/856-2883, 24 hours) is located 4.5 kilometers (2.8 miles) south of the *cuota* highway; for meds only, **Farmacia Yza** (Calle 41 near Calle 40, tel. 985/856-4018), just off the central plaza, is open 24 hours. The **police** (Parque Bacalar, Calle 41 s/n, 24 hours) can be reached at 985/856-2100 or toll-free at 066.

Money
On or near the central plaza, **HSBC** (Calle 41 btwn Calles 42 and 44, 9am-5pm Mon.-Fri., 9am-3pm Sat.), **Banamex** (Calle 41 btwn Calles 42 and 44, 9am-4pm Mon.-Fri.), and **Bancomer** (Calle 40 btwn Calles 39 and 41, 8:30am-4pm Mon.-Fri.) all have ATMs.

Media and Communications
A tiny **post office** (Calle 40 btwn Calles 39 and 41, 8am-4:30pm Mon.-Fri., 8am-1pm Sat.) sits on the central plaza. There's free Wi-Fi in the central plaza, and we assume that the signal's strongest where the laptop-toting teens congregate in front of the Palacio Municipal. For computer access, try **Café Internet Computer** (Calle 49 at Calle 42, 8am-11pm daily, US$0.75/hour) or **Phonet** (Calle 46 at Calle 41, 7am-midnight daily, US$0.70/hour), which also offers long-distance telephone service (US$0.50/minute to the United States and Canada, US$0.70/minute to the rest of the world).

Laundry
The bustling **Lavandería Luyso** (Calle 40 at Calle 33, 8am-8pm Mon.-Sat., 8am-3pm Sun.) charges US$0.80 per kilo (2.2 pounds) and offers next-day service only.

GETTING THERE AND AROUND
Bus
Valladolid's **bus terminal** (Calle 39 at Calle 46, tel. 985/856-3448) is an easy walk from the central plaza, or if you have a lot of bags, a cheap taxi ride.

Taxi
Taxis are relatively easy to flag down, especially around the central plaza, and typically cost US$1.50-2 around town.

Colectivos (shared vans) to Pisté and Chichén Itzá (US$2, 40 minutes) depart approximately every 30 minutes from Calle 39 near the ADO bus terminal, and those for Mérida (US$11, 2.5 hours) leave from the terminal. Shared taxis for Cancún (US$10, 2.5 hours) congregate at Calle 38 between Calles 39 and 41.

Car
If you arrive from the toll highway (*cuota*), you'll enter town via Calle 42 (and return on Calle 40). It's a sobering US$20 toll driving in from Cancún, US$12 from Mérida (Kantunil), and US$5 to Chichén Itzá. In the center, eastbound Calle 41 and westbound Calle 39 access the free highway (*libre*).

VALLADOLID BUS SCHEDULE

Departures from Valladolid's **bus station** (Calle 39 at Calle 46, tel. 985/856-3448) include:

DESTINATION	PRICE	DURATION	SCHEDULE
Campeche	US$23.50	4.5 hours	1:35pm
Cancún	US$7.50-12	3 hours	every 30-60 mins 6am-10:30pm
Chetumal	US$14	5 hours	5:30am, 7:30am, 2:30pm, and 8:30pm
Chichén Itzá	US$2-5	50 minutes	every 30-60 mins 6am-10:30pm
Chiquilá	US$7.50	3 hours	2:45am
Cobá	US$2.75	1 hour	8:30am, 9:30am, 2:45pm, and 5:15pm
Izamal	US$4.30	1.5 hours	12:50pm
Mérida	US$7.50-12.50	2.5 hours	every 30-60 mins 5:45am-9:15pm
Playa del Carmen	US$8.50-12	3 hours	8:30am, 9:30am, 10:05am, 12:05pm, 1:05pm, 2:45pm, 3:05pm, 5:15pm, 5:30pm, and 8:05pm
Tizimín	US$1.90	1 hours	every 30-75 mins 5:30am-9:15pm
Tulum	US$5.50-7	2 hours	9 departures 8:30am-8:05pm

To rent a car in town, **Portal Maya** (Calle 41 btwn Calles 38 and 40, tel. 985/856-2513, www.portalmayatours.com.mx) is your lone option; it also organizes tours.

Bicycle

Bikes can be rented at both **Refraccionaría de Bicicletas Silva** (Calle 44 btwn Calles 39 and 41, tel. 985/856-3667, 9am-6pm daily) and neighboring **Aguilar Sport** (Calle 44 No. 195 btwn Calles 39 and 41, tel. 985/856-2125, 8am-2pm and 4pm-7pm daily) for US$0.80 per hour or US$5 per day, and from **Hostel Candelaria** (Parque la Candelaria, Calle 35 btwn Calles 42 and 44, tel. 985/856-2267) for US$1.25 per hour or US$7 per day.

Ek' Balam

Ek' Balam, Maya for Black Jaguar, is a unique and fascinating archaeological site whose significance has only recently been revealed and appreciated. Serious restoration of Ek' Balam didn't begin until the mid-1990s, and it was then that an incredibly well-preserved stucco frieze was discovered, hidden under an innocuous stone facade near the top of the site's main pyramid. The discovery rocketed Ek' Balam into preeminence, first among Maya scholars and more slowly among travelers in the Yucatán, once the frieze was excavated and opened to the public. Much remains a mystery about Ek' Balam, but archaeologists believe it was founded around 300 BC and became an important commercial center, its influence peaking in AD 700-1100.

Ek' Balam sees a fraction of the tourists that visit other Maya sites, despite being just 30 kilometers (19 miles) north of Valladolid and in close proximity to both Cancún and Mérida. Though the one-lane access road is riddled with potholes, the ruins and the adjacent cenote are an easy jaunt from Valladolid. Ek' Balam is small enough that even an hour is enough to appreciate its treasures, and it's a tranquil place that doesn't get besieged by mammoth tour groups.

The **village** of Ek' Balam is two kilometers (1.2 miles) from the ruins, with two good options for accommodations and food; for more options and other traveler services, head to Valladolid.

◖ EK' BALAM ARCHAEOLOGICAL ZONE

Entering **Ek' Balam** (8am-5pm daily, US$8), you'll pass through a low thick wall and an elegant corbeled arch. Walls are rare in Maya cities, and were most commonly used for defense, as in the cases of Becán and Tulum. Ek' Balam's low thick walls would not have slowed marauding rivals, however, and so they most likely served to enforce social divisions,

with some areas off-limits (but not out of view!) to all but the elite. They may also have been decorative—the city possessed great aesthetic flair, as the entry arch and the famous stucco frieze demonstrate.

Acrópolis and El Trono

The highlight of Ek' Balam is an artful and remarkably pristine stucco frieze known as **El Trono** (The Throne), located under a protective *palapa* roof two-thirds of the way up Ek' Balam's main pyramid, the **Acrópolis.** A steep stairway leads up the center of the pyramid, and a platform to the left of the stairs provides visitors a close-up view of El Trono.

About 85 percent of El Trono is the original stucco. Often structures like this would have been painted blue or red, but not so here. In fact, shortly after it was built, El Trono was sealed behind a stone wall 50-60 centimeters (19-24 inches) thick. It remained there untouched until the 1990s, when restoration workers accidentally—and fortuitously—dislodged one of the protective stones, revealing the hidden chamber beneath.

The tall, winged figures immediately catch your eye, as they appear so much like angels. In fact, they are high priests. Notice that one is deformed—his left arm is longer than the right, and has only four fingers. The Maya considered birth defects to be a sign of divinity, and the priest depicted here may have risen to his position precisely because of his deformation.

Directly over the door is a seated figure (unfortunately, the head is missing). This represents Ukit Kan Le'k Tok', one of Ek' Balam's former rulers, described in inscriptions as the "king of kings," and the person for whom El Trono was built and dedicated. A tomb was discovered in the chamber behind the frieze, containing thousands of jade, gold, obsidian, and ceramic artifacts left as offerings to this

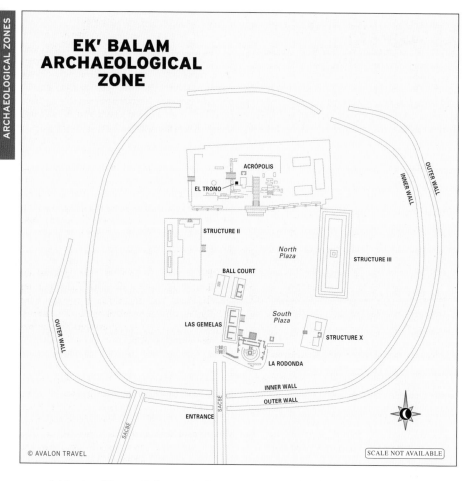

EK' BALAM
ARCHAEOLOGICAL
ZONE

ACRÓPOLIS

EL TRONO

OUTER WALL

INNER WALL

STRUCTURE II

North
Plaza

STRUCTURE III

BALL COURT

OUTER WALL

South
Plaza

LAS GEMELAS

STRUCTURE X

LA RODONDA

INNER WALL

OUTER WALL

SACBE

ENTRANCE

SACBE

© AVALON TRAVEL

SCALE NOT AVAILABLE

powerful leader. The small face at the king-figure's navel represents a rival whom he defeated in war.

Viewed as a whole, the frieze is unmistakably a Chenes-style monster mouth: a huge stylized mask in which the doorway represents the gaping mouth of a high god. The pointed upper and lower teeth are easy to spot, as are the spiral eyes. Monster mouths are never mundane, but this one is especially elaborate: Notice how two beautifully crafted figures straddle the lower eyelids, while hoisting the upper lids with their shoulders. At least five more figures, plus lattice

patterns and other designs, adorn the rest of the mask.

Before heading down, climb the rest of the way to the top of the Acrópolis for a panoramic vista. At 32 meters (105 feet) high and 158 meters (515 feet) wide, the Acrópolis is bigger than Chichén Itzá's main pyramid, and in fact is one of the largest Maya pyramids ever built, a detail that's often overlooked amid the excitement surrounding El Trono. The scene from atop is memorable; with the exception of the odd telephone and radio tower, and the site's visitors center, the view of the broad Yucatecan

© LIZA PRADO

Ek' Balam's remarkable stucco frieze, known as El Trono (The Throne)

(The Twins), known as Structure 17. As the plaque indicates, these identical structures are perhaps the best example of Ek' Balam's particular architectural style. Having perfected the use of stucco, Ek' Balam's builders did not concern themselves with precise masonry, as the stones would be covered in a thick stucco cap. However, stucco proved much less resilient to erosion, and centuries later the structures here appear shabbier than even much older ones, like in Campeche's Río Bec region, where stucco was less common and stone blocks were more carefully cut and fitted. Recent excavations have focused on these two buildings, where intriguing freehand marks and paintings—perhaps akin to graffiti today—have been discovered.

Practicalities

Ek' Balam is open 8am-5pm daily; general admission is US$8, use of video US$4. Guides can be hired at the entrance to the ruins (US$50, 1-1.5 hours, available in Spanish or English). French- and Italian-speaking guides are sometimes available.

landscape is probably not all that different than the one Maya priests and kings enjoyed from this very same vantage point more than a thousand years ago.

South Plaza

Descending the pyramid, you can see that Ek' Balam is a fairly small site, with two mid-size plazas (north and south), a ball court in the middle, and its main structures crowded together.

On the south side of the south plaza stands **La Rodonda,** or the Oval Palace. A squat mid-size structure, La Rodonda has an eclectic array of overlapping lines and curves, stairs, and terraces. It underwent numerous iterations, as did virtually all Maya temples, but the result here was especially eclectic. Archaeologists suspect La Rodonda was used for astronomical observations, and the discovery of several richly adorned tombs suggest it had a ceremonial purpose as well.

Flanking La Redonda are **Las Gemelas**

CENOTE X'CANCHÉ

A short distance from the Ek' Balam archaeological site, **Cenote X'Canché** (cell. tel. 985/100-9915, www.ekbalam.com.mx, 8am-4pm daily, US$4) is an excellent community-run ecotourism project, and a must-do add-on to a ruins visit. From Ek' Balam's parking area, a dirt road winds 1.5 kilometers (0.9 mile) through low dense forest to the cenote, which is 14 meters (46 feet) deep and nearly circular, with sheer walls and tree roots descending picturesquely to cool, clean water. A wooden staircase leads to the water's edge, great for swimming. It's a pleasant shaded walk in, though many visitors rent bikes (US$6 for 3 hours) or take advantage of the on-site bike taxis (US$4 pp round-trip). Facilities include restrooms, shower and changing areas, a restaurant, *palapa*-shaded hammocks for reading and hanging out, and comfortable overnight accommodations. Rappelling from the cenote edge or ziplining across it can each be arranged

© BETH KOHN

Near the ruins of Ek' Balam, Cenote X'Canché makes for a splendid swim.

for an additional fee (US$8-30, half price child under 12); there's also an admission package (US$25) that includes both those activities plus bicycle rental.

ACCOMMODATIONS

In the Maya village near the ruins, **⬛ Genesis Retreat Ek' Balam** (cell. tel. 985/101-0277 or 985/100-4805, www.genesisretreat.com, US$50-70 s/d, US$80 family unit) has nine rooms and *cabañas* set on a leafy enclosed property with a natural bio-filtered pool in the middle. Three units share a large clean bathroom, the others have private bathrooms, one has air-conditioning, and all are different in style and decor. One of the favorites, the Birdhouse, has screen windows on all sides and a small balcony overlooking the pool and garden. There's real environmental commitment at work here: Recycled materials were used in construction, its 101-hectare (250-acre) organic farm provides most of the produce for its meals, and there's a solar hot-water system and extensive

greywater reuse on the property. The hard-working Canadian owner offers tours of the village and local artisan workshops (US$15 pp, minimum 4 people), and is involved in a number of educational projects around town. Be aware that a number of friendly pooches lounge about the property—fine if you like dogs, but not everyone's thing—and that the property closes during September. Morning pastries and coffee are included, and full breakfasts and dinner are available. There's Internet access, and skilled work/lodging exchanges (2-week minimum) are negotiable.

Dolcemente Ek' Balam (cell. tel. 985/106-8083, www.fincacasaazul.com.mx/ekbalam.htm, US$50/71 d/t, US$62 s/d with a/c) doesn't compete with Genesis for Zen or eco-ambience; it's simply a nice comfortable hotel. Spacious rooms have tile floors, okay beds, private hot-water bathrooms, and fans (except for two rooms with air-conditioning). Upstairs units have higher ceilings and better ventilation—making them worth requesting—and all look onto the hotel's peaceful garden.

Recently completed, **Cenote X'Canché** (cell. tel. 985/100-9915, www.ekbalam.com.mx, US$38 s/d/t) rents three well-built and solar-powered *palapa cabañas* near the cenote, each with queen bed and a hammock (plus mosquito nets). The windows have good screens, and there's hot water and a fan. A three-course lunch or dinner at its restaurant costs US$8; breakfast is US$7.

FOOD

All the accommodations above have restaurants. Genesis Retreat Ek' Balam's restaurant **Chaya's Natural Restaurant** (cell. tel. 985/101-0277 or 985/100-4805, www.genesisretreat.com, US$8.50-12) serves breakfast and dinner to its guests, but is open to the public for lunch. Terrific vegetarian and vegan meals are prepared with organic produce grown on the owner's nearby farm.

Dolcemente Ek' Balam (cell. tel. 985/106-8083, www.fincacasaazul.com.mx/ekbalam.htm, noon-11pm Tues.-Sun., US$7.50-12) specializes in Italian food, including fresh handmade ravioli, fettuccini, and other pasta. Its products are also 100 percent natural and organic, and meals are served in a large, tasteful dining room.

GETTING THERE AND AROUND
Car
From Valladolid, drive north on Highway 295 toward Tizimín for about 17 kilometers (10.5 miles), past the town of Temozón, to a well-marked right-hand turnoff to Ek' Balam. From there, drive another 11 kilometers (6.8 miles) to an intersection: Turn left to reach the village and accommodations, or continue straight to reach the archaeological site.

Taxi
Colectivo (shared) taxis from Valladolid to the village of Ek' Balam leave from a stop on Calle 44 between Calles 35 and 37 (US$3); mornings have the most frequent departures. Otherwise, a private taxi costs about US$13 for up to four people. If you're planning on visiting the ruins only, you can often negotiate with the driver to wait there for a couple of hours and bring you back for around US$25.

Cobá

The Maya ruins of Cobá make an excellent complement—or even alternative—to the memorable but vastly overcrowded ruins at Tulum. Cobá doesn't have Tulum's stunning Caribbean view and beach, but its structures are much larger and more ornate—in fact, Cobá's main pyramid is the second tallest in the Yucatán Peninsula, and it's one of few you are still allowed to climb. The ruins are also surrounded by lakes and thick forest, making it a great place to see birds, butterflies, and tropical flora.

◖ COBÁ ARCHAEOLOGICAL ZONE
Cobá (8am-5pm daily, US$4) is especially notable for the complex system of *sacbeob,* or raised stone causeways, that connected to other cities, near and far. (The term *sacbeob*—whose singular form is *sacbé*—means white roads.) Dozens of such roads crisscross the Yucatán Peninsula, but Cobá has more than any other city, underscoring its status as a commercial, political, and military hub. One road extends in an almost perfectly straight line from the base of Cobá's principal pyramid to the town of Yaxuna, more than 100 kilometers (62 miles) away—no small feat considering a typical *sacbé* was 1-2 meters (3.3-6.6 feet) high and about 4.5 meters (15 feet) wide, and covered in white mortar. In Cobá, some roads were even bigger—10 meters (32.8 feet) across. In fact, archaeologists have uncovered a massive stone cylinder believed to have been used to flatten the broad roadbeds.

History
Cobá was settled as early as 100 BC around a collection of small lagoons; it's a logical and privileged location, as the Yucatán Peninsula is virtually devoid of rivers, lakes, or any other aboveground water. Cobá developed into an important trading hub, and in its early existence had a particularly close connection with the Petén region of present-day Guatemala. That relationship would later fade as Cobá grew more intertwined with coastal cities like Tulum, but Petén influence is obvious in Cobá's high steep structures, which are reminiscent of those in Tikal. At its peak, around AD 600-800, Cobá was the largest urban center in the northern lowlands, with some 40,000 residents and over 6,000 structures spread over 50 square kilometers (31 square miles). The city controlled most of the northeastern portion of the Yucatán Peninsula during the same period before being toppled by the Itzás of Chichén Itzá following a protracted war in

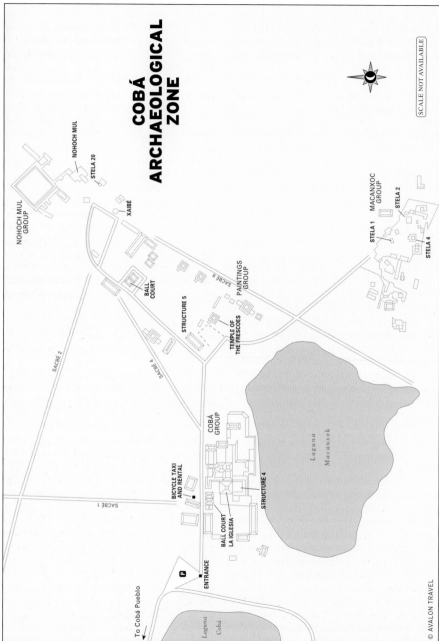

COBÁ ARCHAEOLOGICAL ZONE

SCALE NOT AVAILABLE

NOHOCH MUL GROUP

NOHOCH MUL

STELA 20

XAIBÉ

MACANXOC GROUP

STELA 1

STELA 2

STELA 4

BALL COURT

SACBE 8

PAINTINGS GROUP

STRUCTURE 5

TEMPLE OF THE FRESCOES

SACBE 2

SACBE 4

COBÁ GROUP

Laguna Macanxoc

BICYCLE TAXI AND RENTAL

SACBE 1

BALL COURT

LA IGLESIA

STRUCTURE 4

ENTRANCE

To Cobá Pueblo

Laguna Cobá

© AVALON TRAVEL

the mid-800s. Following a widespread Maya collapse—of which the fall of Cobá was not the cause, though perhaps an early warning sign—the great city was all but abandoned, save as a pilgrimage and ceremonial site for the ascendant Itzás. It was briefly reinhabited in the 12th century, when a few new structures were added, but had been abandoned again, and covered in a blanket of vegetation, by the time of the Spanish conquest.

Cobá Group

Passing through the entry gate, the first group of ruins you encounter is the Cobá Group, a collection of over 50 structures and the oldest part of the ancient city. Many of Cobá's *sacbeob* initiate here. Its primary structure, **La Iglesia** (The Church), rises 22.5 meters (74 feet) from a low platform, making it Cobá's second-highest pyramid. The structure consists of nine platforms stacked atop one another and notable for their round corners. Built in numerous phases beginning in the Early Classic era, La Iglesia is far more reminiscent of Tikal and other Petén-area structures than it is of the long palaces and elaborate facades typical of Puuc and Chenes sites. Visitors are no longer allowed to climb the Iglesia pyramid due to the poor state of its stairs, but it is crowned with a small temple where archaeologists discovered a cache of jade figurines, ceramic vases, pearls, and conch shells.

The Cobá Group also includes one of the city's two **ball courts,** and a large acropolis-like complex with wide stairs leading to raised patios. At one time these patios were connected, forming a long gallery of rooms that likely served as an administrative center. The best-preserved structure in this complex, **Structure 4,** has a long vaulted passageway beneath its main staircase; the precise purpose of this passageway is unclear, but it's a common feature in Cobá and affords a close look at how a so-called Maya Arch is constructed.

The Cobá Group is directly opposite the stand where you can rent bicycles or hire bike taxis. Many travelers leave it for the end of their visit, after they've turned in their bikes.

Nohoch Mul Group

From the Cobá Group, the path winds nearly two kilometers (1.2 miles) through dense forest to Cobá's other main group, Nohoch Mul. The name is Yucatec Maya for Big Mound—the group's namesake pyramid rises an impressive 42 meters (138 feet) above the forest floor, the equivalent of 12 stories. (It was long believed to be the Yucatán Peninsula's tallest structure until the main pyramid at Calakmul in Campeche was determined to be some 10 meters higher.) Like La Iglesia in the Cobá Group, Nohoch Mul is composed of several platforms with rounded corners. A long central staircase climbs steeply from the forest floor to the pyramid's lofty peak. A small temple at the top bears a fairly well-preserved carving of the Descending God, an upside-down figure that figures prominently at Tulum but whose identity and significance is still unclear. (Theories vary widely, from Venus to the God of Bees.)

Nohoch Mul is one of few Maya pyramids

The view from atop Cobá's highest pyramid, Nohoch Mul, is spectacular, but be sure to watch your step!

that visitors are still allowed to climb, and the view from the top is impressive—a flat green forest spreading almost uninterrupted in every direction. A rope running down the stairs makes going up and down easier.

Where the path hits Nohoch Mul is **Stela 20,** positioned on the steps of a minor structure, beneath a protective *palapa* roof. It is one of Cobá's best-preserved stelae, depicting a figure in an elaborate costume and headdress, holding a large ornate scepter in his arms—both signifying that he is an *ahau,* or high lord or ruler. The figure, as yet unidentified, is standing on the backs of two slaves or captives, with another two bound and kneeling at his feet. Stela 20 is also notable for the date inscribed on it—November 30, 780—the latest Long Count date yet found in Cobá.

Xaibé and the Ball Court
Between the Cobá and Nohoch Mul Groups are several smaller but still significant structures. Closest to Nohoch Mul is a curiously conical structure that archaeologists have dubbed **Xaibé,** a Yucatec Maya word for crossroads. The name owes to the fact that it's near the intersection of four major *sacbeob,* and for the same reason, archaeologists believe it may have served as a watchtower. That said, its unique design and imposing size suggest a grander purpose. Round structures are fairly rare in Maya architecture, and most are thought to be astronomical observatories; there's no evidence Xaibé served that function, however, particularly since it lacks any sort of upper platform or temple. Be aware that the walking path does not pass Xaibé—you have to take the longer bike path to reach it.

A short distance from Xaibé is the second of Cobá's **ball courts.** Both courts have imagery of death and sacrifice, though they are more pronounced here: a skull inscribed on a stone in the center of the court, a decapitated jaguar on a disc at the end, and symbols of Venus (which represented death and war) inscribed on the two scoring rings. This ball court also had a huge plaque implanted on one of its slopes,

with over 70 glyphs and dated AD 465; the plaque in place today is a replica, but the original is under a *palapa* covering at one end of the court, allowing visitors to examine it more closely.

Paintings Group
The Paintings Group is a collection of five platforms encircling a large plaza. The temples here were among the last to be constructed in Cobá and pertain to the latest period of occupation, roughly AD 1100-1450. The group's name comes from paintings that once lined the walls, though very little color is visible now, unfortunately. Traces of blue and red can be seen in the upper room of the **Temple of the Frescoes,** the group's largest structure, but you aren't allowed to climb up to get a closer look.

Although centrally located, the Paintings Group is easy to miss on your way between the more outlying pyramids and groups. Look for a sign for **Structure 5,** where you can leave your bike (if you have one) and walk into the group's main area.

Macanxoc Group
From the Paintings Group, the path continues southeasterly for about a kilometer (0.6 mile) to the Macanxoc Group. Numerous stelae have been found here, indicating it was a place of great ceremonial significance. The most famous of these monuments is **Stela 1,** aka the Macanxoc Stela. It depicts a scene from the Maya creation myth—"the hearth stone appears"—along with a Long Count date referring to a cycle ending the equivalent of 41.9 billion, billion, billion years in the future. It is the most distant Long Count date known to have been conceived and recorded by the ancient Maya. Stela 1 also has reference to December 21, 2012, when the Maya Long Count completed its first Great Cycle, equivalent to 5,125 years. Despite widespread reports to the contrary, there is no known evidence, at Cobá or anywhere, that the Maya believed (much less predicted) that the world would end on that date.

Deciphering the Glyphs

For years, scholars could not agree whether the fantastic inscriptions found on Maya stelae, codices, and temple walls were anything more than complex records of numbers and dates. Many thought the text was not "real writing," as it did not appear to reproduce spoken language. Even those who believed the writing to be more meaningful despaired at ever reading it.

Mayanist and scholar Michael D. Coe's *Breaking the Maya Code* (Thames and Hudson, 1992) is a fascinating account of the decipherment of Maya hieroglyphics. Coe describes how, in 1952, reclusive Russian scholar Yuri Valentinovich Knorosov made a crucial breakthrough by showing that Maya writing did in fact convey spoken words. Using a rough alphabet recorded by Fray Diego de Landa (the 16th-century bishop who, ironically, is best known for having destroyed numerous Maya texts), Knorosov showed that ancient texts contain common Yucatec Maya words such as *cutz* (turkey) and *tzul* (dog). Interestingly, Knorosov conducted his research from reproductions only, having never held a Maya artifact or visited an ancient temple. (When he did finally visit Tikal in 1990, Coe says Knorosov wasn't very impressed.)

But Knorosov's findings were met with staunch resistance by some of the field's most influential scholars, which delayed progress for decades. By the mid-1980s, however, decipherment picked up speed; one of many standouts from that era is David Stuart, the son of Maya experts, who went to Cobá with his parents at age eight and passed the time copying glyphs and learning Yucatec Maya words from local playmates. As a high school student he served as chief epigrapher on a groundbreaking exploration in Belize, and at age 18 he received a US$128,000 MacArthur Fellowship (aka "Genius Award") to, as he told Michael Coe, "play around with the glyphs" full-time.

Researchers now know that Maya writing is like most other hieroglyphic systems. What appears at first to be a single glyph can have up to four parts, and the same word can be expressed in pictorial, phonetic, or hybrid form. Depending on context, one symbol can have either a pictorial or phonetic role; likewise, a particular sound can be represented in more than one way. The word *cacao* is spelled phonetically as "ca-ca-u" but is written with a picture of a fish (*ca*) and a comb-like symbol (also *ca*, according to Landa) and followed by -u. One of David Stuart's great insights was that for all its complexity, much of Maya glyphic writing is "just repetitive."

But how do scholars know what the symbols are meant to sound like in the first place? Some come from the Landa alphabet, others are suggested by the pictures that accompany many texts, still others from patterns derived by linguistic analyses of contemporary Maya languages. In some cases, it is simply a hunch that, after applying it to a number of texts, turns out to be right. If this seems like somewhat shaky scientific ground, it is–but not without a means of being proved. The cacao decipherment was confirmed when the same glyph was found on a jar with cacao residue still inside.

Hundreds of glyphs have been deciphered, and most of the known Maya texts can be reliably translated. The effort has lent invaluable insight into Maya civilization, especially dynastic successions and religious beliefs. Some archaeologists lament, not unreasonably, that high-profile glyphic studies divert attention from research into the lives of everyday ancient Maya, who after all far outnumbered the nobility but are not at all represented in the inscriptions. That said, it's impossible not to marvel at how one of the world's great ancient civilizations is revealed in the whorls and creases of fading stone pictures.

Flora and Fauna

The name Cobá (Water Stirred by the Wind in Maya) is surely a reference to the group of shallow lagoons here (Cobá, Macanxoc, Xkanha, and Sacakal). The archaeological site and the surrounding wetlands and forest are rich with birdlife—herons, egrets, motmot, parrots, and the occasional toucan are not uncommon. Arrive early to see the most birds—at the very least you'll get an earful of their varied songs and cries. Later, as the temperature climbs, you'll start to see myriad colorful butterflies, including the large, deep-blue morphidae and the bright yellow-orange barred sulphur.

If you look on the ground, you'll almost certainly see long lines of leaf-cutter ants. One column carries freshly cut leaves to the burrow, and the other marches in the opposite direction, empty-jawed, returning for more. The vegetation decays in their nests, and the fungus that grows on the compost is an important staple of the ants' diet—a few scientists even claim that this makes leaf-cutter ants the world's second species of agriculturists. Only particular types of leaves will do, and the columns can be up to a kilometer (0.6 mile) long.

Practicalities

Cobá's main groups are quite spread apart, and visiting all of them adds up to several kilometers. Fortunately, you can rent a bicycle (US$3) or hire a *triciclo* (US$9 for 1 hour, US$15 for 2 hours) at a large stand a short distance past the entryway, opposite the Cobá Group. Whether you walk or ride, don't forget a water bottle, comfortable shoes, bug repellent, sunscreen, and a hat. Watch for signs and stay on the designated trails. Guide service is available—prices are not fixed but average US$52 per group (1.5 hours, up to 6 people). Parking at Cobá is US$4.

Cobá is not nearly as crowded as Tulum (and is much larger), but it's still a good idea to arrive as early as possible to beat the ever-growing crowds.

COBÁ PUEBLO

It's fair to say that the town of Cobá, a rather desultory little roadside community, has never regained the population or stature that it had as a Maya capital more than 1,000 years ago. Most travelers visit Cobá as a day trip from Tulum or Valladolid, or on a package tour from resorts on the coast. There are two decent hotels in town, used mostly by those who want to appreciate Cobá's rich birdlife, which means being at the gate right when the site opens at 8am; if you're lucky, the gatekeeper may even let you in early.

Sights

Cobá Pueblo itself doesn't have much in the way of sights—besides the ruins, of course—but a number of small eco-attractions have cropped up, all a short distance from town.

RESERVA DE MONOS ARAÑAS PUNTA LAGUNA

The **Punta Laguna Spider Monkey Reserve** (cell. tel. 985/107-9182, 7:30am-5:30pm daily, US$5) is a protected patch of forest that's home to various families of boisterous spider monkeys, as well as smaller groups of howler monkeys and numerous bird species. A short path winds through the reserve, passing a small unexcavated Maya ruin and a large lagoon where you can rent canoes (US$8.50). There's also a zipline and a place to rappel into a cenote, but it's typically reserved for large groups. Your best chance of spotting monkeys is by going in late afternoon, and by hiring one of the guides near the entrance (US$10 pp, minimum 2 people). The reserve (whose official name is Otoch Ma'ax Yetel Kooh, Yucatec Maya for House of the Spider Monkey and Puma) is operated by a local cooperative, whose members live in the nearby village and serve as guides; most speak at least some English. Be sure to wear good walking shoes and bring plenty of bug repellent. The reserve is located 18 kilometers (11 miles) north of Cobá, on the road toward Nuevo X'can.

Tropical Monkeys

The Yucatán is home to three types of monkeys: spider, howler, and black howler. Intelligent and endearing, these creatures are prime targets for the pet trade. They have been so hunted that today all three are in danger of extinction. Experts estimate that for every tropical monkey sold, three die during transportation and distribution. In an effort to protect these creatures, the Mexican government has prohibited their capture or trade. As you wander through the ruins of **Cobá** or through the **Punta Laguna Spider Monkey Reserve,** keep your ears perked and your eyes peeled. You're sure to see—or, at least, hear—them. Spider and howler monkeys are most active at sunrise and sundown; consider arriving early or staying late to increase your chances of spotting a few.

© LIZA PRADO

Howler monkeys are common in regional nature reserves.

CENOTES

If you've got a car, a cluster of three well-maintained and well-run cenotes (no phone, 8am-5pm daily) are a great addition to a day spent at Cobá. **Choo-Ha, Tamcach-Ha,** and **Multun-Ha** are southwest of Cobá and are operated jointly (US$5/7/10 for 1/2/3 cenotes); a fourth cenote called **Nohoch-Ha** is a bit farther and requires a separate entrance fee (US$2). Each is slightly different—one has a high roof and platform for jumping, another is wide and low—but

all are impressive enclosed chambers bristling with stalactites, filled with cool crystalline water that's heaven on a hot day. Cement or wooden stairways lead down to pools; showers and changing areas are available at Choo-Ha. To get there, continue past the Cobá ruins on the road to Tepich and follow the signs.

Accommodations

There are just two recommendable hotels in Cobá Pueblo; if both are booked, consider heading to Tulum or Valladolid, each about 45 minutes away by car or bus.

The low-key **Hotel Sac Be** (Calle Principal, tel. 984/206-7140 or cell. tel. 984/135-3097, US$29 s/d with fan, US$37.50 s/d with a/c) has friendly service and spotless rooms with one or two beds, televisions, old-school air conditioners, and a small desk. All have private bathrooms and open onto a long outdoor corridor. Guests get 10 percent off at the hotel restaurant (which is the small one right above the mini-mart reception area; the much larger attached restaurant has a different owner).

Somewhat overpriced but the only midrange option in town, **Villas Arqueológicas Cobá** (facing Laguna Cobá, tel. 984/206-7000, toll-free Mex. tel. 800/557-7755, www.villasarqueologicas.com.mx, US$92 s/d with a/c) started out as a Club Med, believe it or not, but has since become an independent hotel. Rooms are oddly pod-like, sort of what staying in the space station must be like. They open onto a wide corridor that in turn surrounds a large, pleasant pool. The hotel restaurant serves good but overpriced meals. Units have air-conditioning—which helps with mustiness—but no TV; free Wi-Fi in the lobby area only.

Food

With a large raised patio overlooking the lagoon, **La Pirámide** (Calle Principal at Laguna Cobá, no phone, 7:30am-9pm daily, US$6-15) is a nice place for lunch après-ruins or beer and snacks in the evening. The restaurant receives a number of tour groups, and it often has a buffet set up (US$12.50); otherwise the menu has grilled fish, chicken, and meat dishes as well as typical Mexican fare.

A few doors down and just before the entrance to Villas Arqueológicas, **Nicte Ha** (facing Laguna Cobá, tel. 984/206-7025, 8am-7pm daily, US$3-8) is a small place serving tacos, enchiladas, and various pork dishes.

The restaurant at **Villas Arqueológicas Cobá** (facing Laguna Cobá, tel. 984/206-7000, toll-free Mex. tel. 800/557-7755, www.villasarqueologicas.com.mx, 7:30am-10pm daily, US$6-16) is comfortable and quiet,

and has a decent selection of pasta, seafood, and Yucatecan dishes. It's pleasant, though a bit pricey.

Across the street from the church, **Abarrotes Neftali** (Calle Principal s/n, 7am-11pm daily) is a mini-mart that sells canned goods, bread, and some fresh produce.

Information and Services

Cobá has neither an official tourist office nor a health clinic. There also are no banks or ATMs—the nearest banking and medical services are in Tulum and Valladolid.

Facing the lagoon, **Farmacia El Porvenir** (Calle Principal s/n, no phone, 9am-1pm and 2pm-9pm Mon.-Sat.) is a small shop selling basic medicines and toiletries.

The **police station** (toll-free tel. 066) is halfway down the main drag, before you hit the lagoon.

Getting There and Around

You can easily walk to any of the listed hotels, restaurants, and services in town; the archaeological site is a five-minute walk down the main road, alongside the lagoon.

BUS

A tiny bus station operates out of El Bocadito restaurant (Calle Principal). For the coast, the lone first-class bus departs Cobá at 3:10pm, with stops in Tulum (US$4, 1 hour), Playa del Carmen (US$7.75, 2.5 hours), and Cancún (US$12.25, 3.5 hours). Second-class buses to the same destinations cost a bit less but take longer; departures are at 9:30am, 10:30am, 1:30pm, 3:30pm, 4pm, and 6pm.

There are just two first-class buses headed inland, leaving Cobá at 10am and 7:45pm for Valladolid (US$3.25-5.50, 1 hour), with first-class connections to Chichén Itzá and Mérida available there. Second-class bus departures for the same route (US$2.75 to Valladolid, US$5.25 to Chichén Itzá, US$10.75 to Mérida) are at 8am, 9:30am, 11am, noon, 1pm, and 7pm; note that the 8:30am, 11am, and noon buses go to Valladolid only, with connections available there.

CAR

Getting to Cobá is easiest by car. No matter what direction you're coming from, the roads are smooth and scenic, cutting through pretty farmland and small towns. Keep your speed down, however, as there are innumerable *topes* (speed bumps) and occasional people and animals along the shoulder. Buses ply the same routes, but somewhat infrequently.

Three different roads lead to Cobá; none are named or marked, so they are known by the towns on either end. There are no formal services along any of the roads, save a gas station in the town of Chemax.

The Cobá-Tulum road (45 kilometers/28 miles) is the busiest, cutting southeast to Tulum and the coastal highway (Hwy. 307).

The other two roads connect to Highway 180, the main highway between Cancún and Chichén Itzá. The Cobá-Nuevo X'Can road (47 kilometers/29 miles) angles northeast, connecting with Highway 180 about 80 kilometers (50 miles) outside Cancún and passing places like the Punta Laguna monkey reserve along the way. The Cobá-Chemax road (30 kilometers/19 miles) angles northwest to the town of Chemax; from there it's another 20 kilometers (12.4 miles) to Valladolid and Highway 180, connecting to the highway about 40 kilometers (25 miles) from Chichén Itzá.

All three roads, plus the short access road to Cobá, intersect at a large roundabout just north of Cobá village. Pay close attention to which road you want to avoid a long detour.

BACKGROUND

The Land

The history of Cancún, Cozumel, and really, the entire Yucatán Peninsula is deeply intertwined with its unique geology and ecology. From the ancient Maya to modern-day tourism, the land and its resources have shaped the course of Yucatecan events. And the Yucatán, in turn, has helped shape the course of Mexican history, from being the stage upon which the early Spanish conquest was conducted to helping rescue a moribund Mexican economy in the 1980s. An understanding of the Yucatán Peninsula's land, ecology, culture, and politics is vital to understanding the region today.

GEOGRAPHY

The Yucatán Peninsula spans some 113,000 square kilometers (70,215 square miles) in southeastern Mexico, and is made up of three states: Yucatán, Campeche, and Quintana Roo. It has more than 1,600 kilometers (994 miles) of shoreline, with the Caribbean Sea to the east and the Gulf of Mexico to the north and west. To the southwest are the Mexican states of Tabasco and Chiapas, and directly south are the countries of Belize and Guatemala.

Geologically, the Yucatán Peninsula is a flat shelf of limestone, a porous rock that acts like

a huge sponge. Rainfall is absorbed into the ground and delivered to natural stone-lined sinks and underground rivers. The result is that the Yucatán has virtually no surface water, neither rivers nor lakes. It also has very few hills. The geology changes as you move south, and the first sizable river—the Río Hondo—forms a natural boundary between Belize and Mexico.

The Coast

The northern and western coasts are bordered by the emerald waters of the Gulf of Mexico. Just inland, the land is dotted with lagoons, sandbars, and swamps. The east coast is edged by the turquoise Caribbean, and the glorious islands of Isla Cozumel, Isla Mujeres, and Isla Contoy lie just offshore. Along the coast runs the Mesoamerican Reef, the second-longest coral reef in the world.

Cenotes

Over the course of millennia, water that seeped below the Yucatán's porous limestone shelf eroded a vast network of underground rivers and caves. When a cave's ceiling wears thin, it may eventually cave in, exposing the water below. The Maya called such sinkholes *dzo'not*, which Spanish explorers recorded as *cenotes*. Most cenotes are extremely deep, and interconnected by way of underground channels. A cenote's surface may be near ground level, but more often it is much farther down, as much as 90 meters (295 feet) below ground level. In those cases, the Maya gathered water by carving stairs into the slick limestone walls or by hanging long ladders into abysmal hollows that led to underground lakes.

CLIMATE

The weather in the Yucatán falls into a rainy season (May-October) and a dry season (November-April). Travelers to the region in the dry season will experience warm days, occasional brief storms called *nortes,* and plenty of tourists. In the rainy season, expect spectacular storms and hot, muggy days. The region is infamous for its heat and humidity in May and June, which hovers around 90°F *and* 90 percent humidity.

Hurricane season runs July-November, with most activity occurring mid-August to mid-October. Cloudy conditions and scattered showers are common during this period, occasionally developing into tropical storms. Hurricanes are still relatively rare, but their effects are wide-reaching—even if a storm isn't predicted to hit the Yucatán, it may send plenty of heavy rain and surf that direction. If a hurricane *is* bearing down, don't try to tough it out; cut short your trip or head inland immediately.

ENVIRONMENTAL ISSUES

Hurricanes

Evidence that global warming may cause an increase in the number and/or intensity of Atlantic hurricanes has serious implications for the Yucatán Peninsula, already known to be within Hurricane Alley. The region has weathered countless storms, but something was different about Hurricanes Wilma (2005) and Dean (2007)—both storms broke records for intensity and caused major structural damage, but they also reshaped the shoreline in a way not seen before. Cancún's beaches were especially hard hit, the sand stripped away in many places to expose the hardened limestone beneath. Elsewhere, unusually thick deposits of sand on the coral reef and inland mangroves wiped out large portions of both important ecosystems.

Overdevelopment

Runaway construction along the Riviera Maya has a host of interconnected environmental impacts, some well known, others poorly understood (and surely many that have yet to be identified). An obvious impact is the destruction of mangrove swamps, which extend along much of the coast a short distance inland from the beach. Well-known for supporting wildlife, mangroves also help buffer the effects of hurricane-related surge and currents, and are an important source of nutrients for coral and other sealife, as water from the wetlands drains

conch shells, bleached white by the brilliant Riviera Maya sun

© LIZA PRADO

into the ocean. Although protected by federal law, mangroves have been a primary victim of massive development projects.

Mangroves are emblematic of a more general characteristic of the Riviera Maya: highly porous earth and a weblike underground watershed. Contamination is extremely difficult to clean up or even contain, as it spreads quickly in multiple directions via underground currents, including into the ocean. This is damaging not only to the environment but also to local communities—and the resorts themselves—which draw drinking water from the same system.

And those local communities are growing even faster than the resorts—by some estimates, resorts require an average of five employees for every guest room. Multiply that by the number of resorts operating and being built, and it's no surprise that the region's population is booming. In that sense, development is doubly dangerous: increasing the risk of contamination while simultaneously spurring demand for the very resource it most threatens.

Deforestation

Among the top concerns of environmentalists in Mexico is deforestation, which has accelerated with Mexico's burgeoning population. Slash-and-burn farming is still widely practiced in remote areas, with or without regulation. In an effort to protect the land, environmentalists are searching for alternative sources of income for locals. One is to train them to become guides by teaching them about the flora and fauna of the region as well as how to speak English. While not solving the problem, it does place an economic value on the forest itself and provides an incentive for preserving it.

Another focus is the plight of the palm tree. The palm is an important part of the cultural and practical lifestyle of the indigenous people of Quintana Roo—it is used for thatch roofing and to construct lobster traps. However, the palms used—*Thrinax radiata* and *Coccothrinax readii*—are becoming increasingly rare. Amigos de Sian Ka'an together with the World Wildlife Fund are studying the palms' growth patterns and rates; they are anticipating a management plan that will encourage future growth. Other environmental projects include limiting commercial fishing, halting tourist development where it endangers the ecology, and studying the lobster industry and its future. A number of other worthwhile projects are still waiting in line.

Flora and Fauna

Quintana Roo's forests are home to mangroves, bamboo, and swamp cypresses. Ferns, vines, and flowers creep from tree to tree and create a dense growth. The southern part of the Yucatán Peninsula, with its classic tropical rainforest, hosts tall mahoganies, *campeche zapote,* and *kapok*—all covered with wild jungle vines. On topmost limbs, orchids and air ferns reach for the sun.

Many animals found nowhere else in Mexico inhabit the Yucatán Peninsula's expansive flatlands and thick jungles. Spotting them can be difficult, though with patience and a skilled guide, not impossible.

TREES
Palms
A wide variety of palm trees and their relatives grow on the peninsula—tall, short, fruited, and even oil-producing varieties. Though similar, palms have distinct characteristics:

- Queen palms are often used for landscaping and bear a sweet fruit.

- Thatch palms are called *chit* by Maya, who use the fronds extensively for roof thatch.

- Coconut palms—the ones often seen on the beach—produce oil, food, drink, and shelter and are valued by locals as a nutritious food source and cash crop.

- Royal palms are tall with smooth trunks.

- Henequen is a cousin to the palm tree; from its fiber come twine, rope, matting, and other products. Because of its abundance, new uses for it are constantly sought.

Fruit Trees
Quintana Roo grows sweet and sour oranges, limes, and grapefruit. Avocado is abundant and the papaya tree is practically a weed. The *mamey* tree grows full and tall (15-20 meters/49-65 feet), providing not only welcome shade but also an avocado-shaped fruit, brown on the outside with a vivid, salmon-pink flesh that tastes like a sweet yam. The *guaya* is another unusual fruit tree and a member of the lychee nut family. This rangy evergreen thrives on sea air and is commonly seen along the coast. Its small, green, leathery pods grow in clumps like grapes and contain a sweet, yellowish, jellylike flesh—tasty! The calabash tree provides gourds used for containers by Maya.

Other Trees
The ceiba (also called *kapok*) is a sacred tree for the Maya. Considered the link between the underworld, the material world, and the heavens, this huge tree is revered and left undisturbed—even if it sprouts in the middle of a fertile cornfield.

When visiting in the summer, you can't miss the beautiful *framboyanes* (royal poinciana). When in bloom, its wide-spreading branches become covered in clusters of brilliant orange-red flowers. These trees often line sidewalks and plazas, and when clustered together present a dazzling show.

FLOWERS
While wandering through jungle regions, you'll see numerous flowering plants. Here in their natural environment, these plants thrive in a way unknown to windowsills at home: Crotons exhibit wild colors, pothos grow 30-centimeter (11.8-inch) leaves, the philodendron splits every

leaf in gargantuan glory, and common morning glory creeps and climbs effortlessly over bushes and trees. You'll also be introduced to less well-known residents of this semi-tropical world: the exotic white and red ginger, plumeria (sometimes called frangipani) with its wonderful fragrance and myriad colors, and hibiscus and bougainvillea, which bloom in an array of bright hues.

Orchids

Orchids can be found on the highest limbs of the tallest trees, especially in the state of Quintana Roo. Of the 71 species reported in the Yucatán Peninsula, 80 percent are epiphytic, attached to host trees and deriving moisture and nutrients from the air and rain. Orchids grow in myriad sizes and shapes: tiny buttons spanning the length of a half-meter-long (two-foot) branch, large-petaled blossoms with ruffled edges, or intense tiger-striped miniatures.

MAMMALS
Nine-Banded Armadillos

The size of a small dog and sporting a thick coat of armor, this peculiar creature gets its name from the nine bands (or external "joints") that circle its midsection and give the little tank some flexibility. The armadillo's keen sense of smell can detect insects and grubs—its primary food source—up to 15 centimeters (6 inches) underground, and its sharp claws make digging for them easy. An armadillo also digs underground burrows, into which it may carry a full bushel of grass to make its nest, where it will sleep through the hot day and emerge at night. Unlike armadillos that roll up into a tight ball when threatened, this species will race to its burrow, arch its back, and wedge in so that it cannot be pulled out. The Yucatán Peninsula is a favored habitat for its scant rainfall; too much rain floods the burrow and can drown young armadillos.

Giant Anteaters

A cousin of the armadillo, this extraordinary animal measures two meters (6.6 feet) from the tip of its tubular snout to the end of its bushy tail. Its coarse coat is colored shades of brown-gray; the hindquarters are darker in tone, while a contrasting wedge-shaped pattern of black and white decorates the throat and shoulders. Characterized by an elongated head, long tubular mouth, and extended tongue (but no teeth), it can weigh up to 39 kilograms (86 pounds). The anteater walks on the knuckles of its paws, allowing its claws to remain tucked under while it looks for food.

Giant anteaters are found in forests and swampy areas in Mexico and throughout Central and South America. It is mainly diurnal in areas where there are few people but nocturnal in densely populated places. Its razor-sharp claws allow it to rip open the leathery mud walls of termite and ant nests, the contents of which are a main food source. After opening the nest, the anteater rapidly flicks its viscous tongue in and out of its small mouth opening. Few ants escape.

Tapirs

South American tapirs are found from the southern part of Mexico to southern Brazil. A stout-bodied animal, it has short legs and a tail, small eyes, and rounded ears. The nose and upper lip extend into a short but very mobile proboscis. Tapirs usually live near streams or rivers, which they use for daily bathing and as an escape from predators, especially jaguars and humans. Shy and placid, these nocturnal animals have a definite home range, wearing a path between the jungle and their feeding area. If attacked, the tapir lowers its head and blindly crashes off through the forest; they've been known to collide with trees and knock themselves out in their chaotic attempt to flee.

Peccaries

Next to deer, peccaries are the most widely hunted game on the Yucatán Peninsula. Two species of peccaries are found here: the collared javelina peccary and the white-lipped peccary. The feisty collared javelina stands 50 centimeters (20 inches) at the shoulder and can be one meter (3.3 feet) long, weighing as much as 30 kilograms (66 pounds). It is black and white with a narrow, semicircular collar of white hair on the shoulders. The name javelina (which means spear in Spanish) comes from the two tusks that protrude from its mouth. A related species, the white-lipped peccary, is reddish brown to black and has an area of white around its mouth. Larger than the javelina, it can grow to 105 centimeters (41 inches) long, and is found deep in tropical rainforests living in herds of 100 or more. Peccaries often are compared to the wild pigs found in Europe, but in fact they belong to entirely different families.

Felines

Seven species of cats are found in North America, four in the tropics. One of them—the jaguar—is heavy chested with sturdy, muscled forelegs. It has small, rounded ears and its tail is relatively short. Its color varies from tan and white to pure black. The male can weigh 65-115 kilograms (143-254 pounds), females 45-85 kilograms (99-187 pounds). The largest of the cats on the peninsula, the jaguar is about the same size as a leopard. Other cats found here are the ocelot and puma. In tropical forests of the past, the large cats were the only predators capable of controlling the populations of hoofed game such as deer, peccaries, and tapirs. If hunting is poor and times are tough, the jaguar will go into rivers and scoop up fish with its large paws. The river is also one of the jaguar's favorite spots for hunting tapirs, when the latter come to drink.

Monkeys

The jungles of Mexico are home to three species of monkeys: spider, howler, and black howler. Intelligent and endearing, these creatures are prime targets for the pet trade. They have been so hunted, in fact, that today all three are in danger of extinction. Experts estimate that for every monkey sold, three die during transportation and distribution. In an effort to protect these creatures, the Mexican government has prohibited their capture or trade. As you wander through the ruins of Calakmul or Cobá, keep your ears perked and your eyes peeled. You're sure to see—or at least hear—a few monkeys.

Tropical monkeys are most active at sunrise and sundown; if possible, consider waking early or staying late to increase your chances of spotting a few. Other places to see spider and howler monkeys are the Punta Laguna spider monkey reserve and Yaxchilán archaeological site.

SEALIFE
Coral Reefs

The spectacular coral reefs that grace the peninsula's east coast are made up of millions of tiny carnivorous organisms called polyps. Individual polyps can be less than a centimeter (0.4 inch) long or up to 15 centimeters (6 inches) in diameter. Related to the jellyfish and sea anemone, coral polyps capture prey with tiny tentacles that deliver a deadly sting.

Reef-building polyps have limestone exoskeletons, which they create by extracting calcium from the seawater. Reefs are formed as generation after generation of polyps attach themselves to and atop each other. Different species attach in different ways, resulting in the many shapes and sizes of ocean reefs: delicate lace, trees with reaching branches, pleated mushrooms, stovepipes, petaled flowers, fans, domes, heads of cabbage, and stalks of broccoli. Though made up of individual polyps, coral structures function like a single organism, sharing nutrients through a central gastrovascular system. Even in ideal conditions, most coral grows no more than five centimeters (two inches) per year.

Reefs are divided into three types: barrier, atoll, and fringing. A barrier reef runs parallel to the coast, with long stretches separated by narrow channels. The Mesoamerican Reef extends 250 kilometers (155 miles) from the tip of Isla Mujeres to Sapodilla Cay in the Gulf of Honduras—only the Great Barrier Reef in Australia is longer. An atoll typically forms around the crater of a submerged volcano. The polyps begin building their colonies along the lip of the crater, forming a circular coral island with a lagoon in the center. The Chinchorro

Bank, off the southern coast of Quintana Roo, is the largest coral atoll in the northern hemisphere, measuring 48 kilometers long and 14 kilometers wide (30 miles by 9 miles). A fringing reef is coral living on a shallow shelf that extends outward from shore into the sea.

Fish

The Yucatán's barrier reef is home to myriad fish species, including parrot fish, candy bass, moray eels, spotted scorpion fish, turquoise angelfish, fairy basslets, flame fish, and gargantuan manta rays. Several species of shark also thrive in the waters off Quintana Roo, though they're not considered a serious threat to swimmers and divers. Sport fish—sailfish, marlin, and bluefin tuna—also inhabit the outer Caribbean waters.

Inland, anglers will find hard-fighting bonefish and pompano in the area's lagoons, and snorkelers and divers will find several species of blind fish in the crystal-clear waters of cenotes. These fish live out their existence in dark underground rivers and lakes and have no use for eyes.

Sea Turtles

Tens of thousands of sea turtles of various species once nested on the coastal beaches of Quintana Roo. As the coast became populated, turtles were severely overhunted for their eggs, meat, and shell, and their numbers began to fall. Hotel and resort developments have hastened the decline, as there are fewer and fewer patches of untrammeled sand in which turtles can dig nests and lay their eggs. The Mexican government and various ecological organizations are trying hard to save the dwindling turtle population. Turtle eggs are dug up and reburied in sand on safe beaches; or when the hatchlings break through their shells, they are brought to a beach and allowed to rush toward the sea in hopes of imprinting a sense of belonging there so that they will later return to the spot. In some cases the hatchlings are scooped up and placed in tanks to grow larger before being released into the open sea. The government is also enforcing tough penalties for people who take turtle eggs or capture, kill, or sell these creatures once they hatch.

Manatees

The manatee—sometimes called the sea cow—is a gentle, inquisitive giant. They are closely related to dugongs, and more distantly to elephants, aardvarks, and hyraxes. Newborns weigh 30-35 kilograms (66-77 lbs.), while adults can measure four meters (13 feet) in length and weigh nearly 1,600 kilograms (3,500 lbs.). Shaped like an Idaho potato, manatees have coarse pinkish-gray skin, tiny sunken eyes, a flattened tail and flipper-like forelimbs (including toenails), and prehensile lips covered in sensitive whiskers. The manatee is the only aquatic mammal that's completely vegetarian, eating an astounding 10 percent of its body weight every day in aquatic grass and vegetation; it's unique among all mammals for constantly growing new teeth to replace those worn down by its voracious feeding.

Large numbers of them once roamed the shallow inlets, bays, and estuaries of the Caribbean; their images are frequently seen in the art of the ancient Maya, who hunted them for food. Today, though posing no threat to humans or other animals, and ecologically important for their ability to clear waterways of oxygen-choking vegetation, manatees are endangered in the Yucatán and elsewhere. The population has been reduced by the encroachment of people in their habitats along the river ways and shorelines. Ever-growing numbers of motorboats also inflict deadly gashes on these surface-feeding creatures. Nowadays it is very rare to spot one; the most sightings are reported in Punta Allen and Bahía de la Ascensión.

BIRDS

Since a major part of the Yucatán Peninsula is still undeveloped and covered with trees and brush, it isn't surprising to find exotic, rarely seen birds across the landscape. The Mexican government is beginning to realize the great value in this and is making efforts to protect nesting grounds. In addition to the growing number of nature reserves, some of the best

©LIZA PRADO

Manatees are extremely hard to spot in the wild, but can be seen in some ecoparks where they have been rescued.

bird-watching locales are the archaeological zones. At dawn and dusk, when most of the visitors are absent, the trees that surround the ancient structures come alive with birdsong. Of all the ruins, Cobá—with its marsh-rimmed lakes, nearby cornfields, and relatively tall, humid forest—is a particularly good site for bird-watching. One of the more impressive birds to look for here is the keel-billed toucan, often seen perched high on a bare limb in the early hours of the morning. Others include *chachalacas* (held in reverence by the Maya), screeching parrots, and, occasionally, the ocellated turkey.

Flamingos

The wetlands along the Yucatán's northern coast are shallow and murky and bordered in many places by thick mangrove forests. The water content is unusually high in salt and other minerals—the ancient Maya gathered salt here, and several salt factories still operate. A formidable habitat for most creatures,

it's ideal for *Phoenicopterus ruber ruber*—the American flamingo, the largest and pinkest of the world's five flamingo species. Nearly 30,000 of the peculiar birds nest here, feeding on algae and other tiny organisms that thrive in the salty water. Flamingos are actually born white, but they turn pink from the carotene in the algae they eat.

For years, flamingos only nested around Río Lagartos, near the peninsula's northeastern tip. But in 1988, Hurricane Gilbert destroyed their nesting grounds—not to mention the town of Río Lagartos—and forced the birds to relocate. They are now found all along the north coast, including at three major feeding and reproduction grounds: Río Lagartos, Celestún, and Uaymitún.

The best way to observe flamingos is on a boat tour at sunrise, when the birds are most active, turning their heads upside down and dragging their beaks along the bottom of the shallow water to suck in the mud that contains their food. (In the morning, you should see

© LIZA PRADO

The Yucatán Peninsula is home to tens of thousands of American flamingos, the largest and pinkest of the world's five flamingo species.

dozens of other birds too, such as storks, herons, and kingfishers.) If you go in the spring, you may see the male flamingos performing their strange mating dance—craning their necks, clucking loudly, and generally strutting their stuff.

All three sites have flamingos year-round, but you'll see the highest numbers at Río Lagartos in the spring and summer and at Celestún in the winter. Uaymitún has a pretty steady population but has no boat tours—instead you observe the birds through binoculars from a raised platform. No matter when you go, make as little noise as possible and ask your guide to keep his distance. Flamingos are nervous and easily spooked into flying away en masse. While the exodus would no doubt be an impressive sight, it may cause the birds to abandon the site altogether.

Quetzals

Though the ancient Maya made abundant use of the dazzling quetzal feathers for ceremonial costumes and headdresses, they hunted other fowl for food; nevertheless, the quetzal is the only known bird from the pre-Columbian era and is now almost extinct. Today, they are still found (though rarely) in the high cloud forests of Chiapas and Central America, where they thrive on the constant moisture.

Estuaries

The Yucatán's countless estuaries, or *rías,* play host to hundreds of bird species; a boat ride into one of them will give you an opportunity to see American flamingos, a variety of wintering ducks from North America, blue-winged teals, northern shovelers, and lesser scaups. You'll also see a variety of wading birds feeding in the shallow waters, including numerous types of heron, snowy egret, and, in the summer, white ibis. There are 14 species of birds endemic to the Yucatán Peninsula, including the ocellated turkey, Yucatán whippoorwill, Yucatán flycatcher, orange oriole, black catbird, and the yellow-lored parrot. Río Lagartos and Celestún are the best-known and most-visited estuaries, but those in Sian Ka'an Biosphere Reserve, Isla Holbox, and Xcalak are also vibrant and accessible.

REPTILES

Although reptiles thrive in Yucatán's warm, sunny environment, humans are their worst enemy. In the past, some species were greatly reduced in number—hunted for their unusual skin. Although hunting them is now illegal, black marketers still take their toll on the species.

Caymans

The cayman is a member of the crocodilian order. Its habits and appearance are similar to those of crocodiles, with the main difference being in its underskin: The cayman's skin is reinforced with bony plates on the belly, making it useless for the leather market. (Alligators and crocodiles, with smooth belly skin and sides, have been hunted almost to extinction in some parts of the world because of the value of their skin.)

Several species of cayman frequent the brackish inlet waters near the estuaries of Río Lagartos (literally, River of Lizards). A large cayman can be 2.5 meters (8.2 feet) long and very dark gray-green and broad-snouted with eyelids that look swollen and wrinkled. Some cayman species have eyelids that look like a pair of blunt horns. They are quicker than alligators and have longer, sharper teeth. Skilled hunters, cayman are quick in water and on land, and will attack a person if cornered. The best advice is to give caymans a wide berth if spotted.

Iguanas

This group of American lizards—Iguanidae family—includes various large plant-eaters seen frequently in Quintana Roo. Iguanas grow to be one meter (3.3 feet) long and have a blunt head and long flat tail. Bands of black and gray circle its body, and a serrated column reaches down the middle of its back almost to the tail. The young iguana is bright

emerald-green and often supplements its diet by eating insects and larvae.

The lizard's forelimbs hold the front half of its body up off the ground while its two back limbs are kept relaxed and splayed alongside its hindquarters. When the iguana is frightened, however, its hind legs do everything they're supposed to, and the iguana crashes quickly (though clumsily) into the brush searching for its burrow and safety. This reptile is not aggressive—it mostly enjoys basking in the bright sunshine along the Caribbean—but if cornered it will bite and use its tail in self-defense.

From centuries past, recorded references attest to the iguana's medicinal value, which partly explains the active trade of live iguana in the marketplaces. Iguana stew is believed to cure or relieve various human ailments.

Other Lizards

You'll see a great variety of other lizards on the peninsula; some are brightly striped in various shades of green and yellow, others are earth-toned and blend in with the gray and beige limestone that dots the landscape. Skinny as wisps of thread running on hind legs, or chunky and waddling with armor-like skin, the range is endless and fascinating.

Be sure to look for the black anole, which changes colors to match its environment, either when danger is imminent or as subterfuge to fool the insects on which it feeds. At mating time, the male anole puffs out its bright-red throat-fan so that all female lizards will see it.

Coral Snakes

Two species of coral snakes, which are related to the cobra, are found in the southern part of the Yucatán Peninsula. They have prominent rings around their bodies in the same sequence of red, black, yellow, or white and grow to 1-1.5 meters (3.3-4.9 feet). Their bodies are slender, with no pronounced distinction between the head and neck.

Coral snakes spend the day in mossy clumps under rocks or logs, emerging only at night. Though the bite of a coral snake can kill within 24 hours, chances of the average tourist being bitten by a coral (or any other) snake are slim.

Tropical Rattlesnakes
The tropical rattlesnake (*cascabel* in Spanish) is the deadliest and most treacherous species of rattler. It differs slightly from other species by having vividly contrasting neckbands. It grows 2-2.5 meters (6.6-8.2 feet) long and is found mainly in the higher and drier areas of the tropics. Contrary to popular myth, this serpent doesn't always rattle a warning of its impending strike.

INSECTS AND ARACHNIDS
Air-breathing invertebrates are unavoidable in any tropical locale. Some are annoying (gnats and no-see-ums), some are dangerous (black widows, bird spiders, and scorpions), and others can cause pain when they bite (red ants); but many are beautiful (butterflies and moths) and *all* are fascinating.

Butterflies and Moths
The Yucatán has an incredible abundance of beautiful moths and butterflies, some 40,000 species in all. Hikers might see the magnificent blue morpho, orange-barred sulphur, copperhead, cloudless sulphur, malachite, admiral, calico, ruddy dagger-wing, tropical buckeye, and emperor. The famous monarch is also a visitor during its annual migration from Florida. It usually makes a stopover on Quintana Roo's east coast on its way south to the Central American mountains where it spends the winter. The huge black witch moth—males can have a wingspan of seven inches—is sometimes mistaken for bats—is called *mariposa de la muerte* ("butterfly of death" in Spanish) or *ma ha na* (Yucatec Maya for "enter the home"), stemming from a common belief that if the moth enters the home of a sick person, that person will soon die.

Spiders and Scorpions
The Yucatán has some scary-looking spiders and scorpions (*arañas* and *alacranes*), but none is particularly dangerous. The Yucatán rust rump tarantula is surely the most striking, a hairy medium-size tarantula with long legs and a distinctive orange or rust-colored rear. Like most tarantulas, they are nocturnal and fairly timid, with females spending much of their time in burrows in the ground, and males roaming around incessantly looking for them. Its bite is harmless, but that doesn't mean you should handle one: When threatened, tarantulas can shake off a cloud of tiny hairs, which are highly irritating if inhaled.

The Yucatán's long black scorpions—up to 10 centimeters (4 inches)!—have a painful sting that can cause swelling, and for some people shortness of breath, but is not deadly. Like tarantulas, scorpions avoid human contact and are therefore rare to see; that said, it's always a good idea to shake out shoes and beach towels before using them, just in case.

Bees
The Yucatán's most famous bee—of numerous species found here—is the aptly named Yucatán bee, also known as the Maya bee. The small stingless insect produces a particularly sweet honey that was prized by the ancient Maya, and was one of the most widely traded commodities in the Maya world. (Some researchers say the Descending God figure at Tulum and other archaeological sites is the god of bees.) The ancient Maya were expert beekeepers, a tradition that lives on today, albeit much reduced thanks in part to the availability of cheap standard honey. Yucatán honey (harvested using more modern methods) is still sold in Mexico and abroad, mostly online and in organic and specialty stores.

History

ACROSS THE BERING LAND BRIDGE

People and animals from Asia crossed the Bering land bridge into North America in the Pleistocene epoch about 50,000 years ago, when sea levels were much lower. As early as 10,000 BC, Ice Age humans hunted woolly mammoth and other large animals roaming the cool, moist landscape of central Mexico. The earliest traces of humans in the Yucatán Peninsula are obsidian spear points and stone tools dating to 9,000 BC. The Loltún caves in the state of Yucatán contained a cache of mammoth bones, which are thought to have been dragged there by a roving band of hunters. As the region dried out and large game disappeared in the next millennia, tools of a more settled way of life appeared, such as grinding stones for preparing seeds and plant fibers.

ANCIENT CIVILIZATION

Between 7,000 and 2,000 BC, society evolved from hunting and gathering to farming; corn, squash, and beans were independently cultivated in widely separated areas in Mexico. Archaeologists believe that the earliest people who we can call Maya, or proto-Maya, inhabited the Pacific coast of Chiapas and Guatemala. These tribes lived in villages that held more than 1,000 inhabitants apiece; beautiful painted and incised ceramic jars for food storage have been found from this region and time period. After 1,000 BC this way of life spread south to the highlands site of Kaminaljuyú (now part of Guatemala City) and, through the next millennium, to the rest of the Maya world. Meanwhile, in what are now the Mexican states of Veracruz and Tabasco, another culture, the Olmecs, was developing what is now considered Mesoamerica's first civilization. Its influence was felt throughout Mexico and Central America. Archaeologists believe that before the Olmecs disappeared around 300 BC, they contributed two crucial cultural advances to the Maya: the Long Count calendar and the hieroglyphic writing system.

LATE PRECLASSIC PERIOD

During the Late Preclassic era (300 BC-AD 250), the Pacific coastal plain saw the rise of a Maya culture in Izapa near Tapachula, Chiapas. The Izapans worshipped gods that were precursors of the Classic Maya pantheon and commemorated religious and historical events in bas-relief carvings that emphasized costume and finery.

During the same period, the northern Guatemalan highlands were booming with construction; this was the heyday of Kaminaljuyú, which grew to enormous size, with more than 120 temple-mounds and numerous stelae. The earliest calendar inscription that researchers are able to read comes from a monument found at El Baúl to the southwest of Kaminaljuyú; it has been translated as AD 36.

In the Petén jungle region just north of the highlands, the dominant culture was the Chicanel, whose hallmarks are elaborate temple-pyramids lined with enormous stucco god-masks (as in Kohunlich). The recently excavated Petén sites of Nakbé and El Mirador are the most spectacular Chicanel cities yet found. El Mirador contains a 70-meter-tall (230-foot) temple-pyramid complex that is the tallest ancient structure in Mesoamerica. Despite the obvious prosperity of this region, there is almost no evidence of Long Count dates or writing systems in either the Petén jungle or the Yucatán Peninsula just to the north.

EARLY CLASSIC PERIOD

The great efflorescence of the southern Maya world stopped at the end of the Early Classic period (AD 250-600). Kaminaljuyú and other cities were abandoned; researchers believe that the area was invaded by Teotihuacano warriors extending the reach of their Valley of Mexico-based empire. On the Yucatán Peninsula, there

Stephens and Catherwood

The Maya ruins of the Yucatán Peninsula were all but unknown in the United States and Europe until well into the 19th century. Although Spanish explorers and colonizers had occupied the peninsula for more than two centuries, conflicts with local Maya and Catholic antipathy for all things pagan probably account for the Spaniards' lack of research or even apparent interest. To be fair, the immensity of the task was surely daunting–by the time the Spanish reached the Yucatán in the early 1500s, the majority of sites had been abandoned for at least 300 years, and in some cases double or triple that. Many were piles of rubble, and those still standing were mostly covered in vegetation. Just getting to the sites was a task in itself.

And so it was an American and an Englishman–diplomat John Lloyd Stephens and artist-architect Frederick Catherwood–who brought the Maya world to worldwide attention. Between 1839 and 1841, they conducted two major explorations of the Maya region, including present-day Yucatán, Chiapas, and Central America, visiting a total of 44 ruins. Stephens kept a detailed account of their travels, making many observations on the nature of Maya civilization that proved remarkably prescient. He correctly surmised that Maya writing contained detailed dynastic and historical accounts, and rejected the prevailing notion that Mesoamerican civilizations were descended from Egyptian or other Old World societies, declaring the mysterious ruins "a spectacle of a people skilled in architecture, sculpture, and possessing the culture and refinement attendant upon those, not derived from the Old World, but originating and growing here without models or masters like the plants and fruits of the soil, indigenous." Meanwhile, Catherwood made incredibly precise drawings of numerous structures, monuments, hieroglyphs, and scenes of peasant life. (Though they've been widely reprinted, you can see a rare collection of original Catherwood prints in Mérida, at the highly recommended museum-gallery Casa Catherwood.)

Stephens and Catherwood published their work in two volumes, both of which were instant sensations in the United States and Europe, awakening immense interest in ancient Maya civilization. Their books now are condensed into a single, very readable volume, *Incidents of Travel in Yucatán* (Hard Press, 2007), available in English and in many bookstores in the Yucatán. It is a fascinating read, not only for the historical value but also as a backdrop for your own travels through the Yucatán.

is evidence of Teotihuacano occupation at the Río Bec site of Becán and at Acanceh near Mérida. You can see Teotihuacano-style costumes and gods in carvings at the great Petén city of Tikal and at Copán in Honduras. By AD 600, the Teotihuacano empire had collapsed, and the stage was set for the Classic Maya eras.

LATE CLASSIC PERIOD

The Maya heartland of the Late Classic period (AD 600-900) extended from Copán in Honduras through Tikal in Guatemala and ended at Palenque in Chiapas. The development of these city-states, which also included Yaxchilán and Bonampak, almost always followed the same pattern. Early in this era, a new and vigorous breed of rulers founded a series of dynasties bent on deifying themselves and their ancestors. All the arts and sciences of the Maya world, from architecture to astronomy, were focused on this goal. The Long Count calendar and the hieroglyphic writing system were the most crucial tools in this effort, as the rulers needed to recount the stories of their dynasties and of their own glorious careers.

During the Late Classic era, painting, sculpture, and carving reached their climax; objects such as Lord Pakal's sarcophagus lid from Palenque are now recognized as among the finest pieces of world art. Royal monuments stood at the center of large and bustling cities. Cobá and Dzibilchaltún each probably contained 50,000 inhabitants, and there was vigorous intercity trade. Each Classic city-state reached its apogee at a different time; the southern cities peaked first, with the northern Puuc region cities following close behind.

By AD 925, nearly all of the city-states had collapsed and were left in a state of near-abandonment. The Classic Maya decline is one of the great enigmas of Mesoamerican archaeology. There are a myriad of theories—disease, invasion, peasant revolt—but many researchers now believe the collapse was caused by a combination of factors, including overpopulation, environmental degradation, and a series of devastating droughts. With the abandonment of the cities, the cultural advances disappeared as well. The last Long Count date was recorded in AD 909, and many religious customs and beliefs were never seen again.

EARLY POSTCLASSIC PERIOD

After the Puuc region was abandoned—almost certainly because of a foreign invasion—the center of Maya power moved east to Chichén. During this Early Postclassic era (AD 925-1200), the Toltec influence took hold, marking the end of the most artistic era and the birth of a new militaristic society built around a blend of ceremonialism, civic and social organization, and conquest. Chichén was the great power of northern Yucatán. Competing city-states either submitted to its warriors or, like the Puuc cities and Cobá, were destroyed.

LATE POSTCLASSIC PERIOD

After Chichén's fall in AD 1224—probably due to an invasion—a heretofore lowly tribe calling themselves the Itzá became the Late Postclassic (AD 1200-1530) masters of Yucatecan power politics. Kukulcán II of Chichén founded Mayapán in AD 1263-1283. After his death and the abandonment of Chichén, an aggressive Itzá lineage named the Cocom seized power and used Mayapán as a base to take over northern Yucatán. They succeeded through wars using Tabascan mercenaries and intermarrying with other powerful lineages. Foreign lineage heads were forced to live in Mayapán where they could easily be controlled. At its height, the city covered 6.5 square kilometers (4 square miles) within a defensive wall that contained more than 15,000 inhabitants. Architecturally, Mayapán leaves much to be desired; the city plan was haphazard, and its greatest monument was a sloppy, smaller copy of Chichén's Pyramid of Kukulcán.

The Cocom ruled for 250 years until AD 1441-1461, when an upstart Uxmal-based lineage named the Xiu rebelled and slaughtered the Cocom. Mayapán was abandoned and Yucatán's city-states were weakened in a series of bloody intramural wars that left them hopelessly divided when the conquistadors arrived. By the time of that conquest, culture was once again being imported from outside the Maya world. Putún Maya seafaring traders brought new styles of art and religious beliefs back from their trips to central Mexico. Their influence can be seen in the Mixtec-style frescoes at Tulum on the Quintana Roo coast.

SPANISH ARRIVAL AND CONQUEST

After Columbus's arrival in the New World, other adventurers traveling the same seas soon found the Yucatán Peninsula. In 1519, 34-year-old Hernán Cortés set out from Cuba—against the wishes of the Spanish governor—with 11

Early Civilizations and Maya Timeline

- **Paleoindian:** before 7000 BC
- **Archaic:** 7000-2500 BC
- **Early Preclassic:** 2500-1000 BC
- **Middle Preclassic:** 1000-400 BC
- **Late Preclassic:** 400 BC-AD 250
- **Early Classic:** AD 250-600
- **Late Classic:** AD 600-800
- **Terminal Classic:** AD 800-1000
- **Early Postclassic:** AD 1000-1250
- **Late Postclassic:** AD 1250-1519

Fray Diego de Landa

Just north of Oxkutzcab, the town of Maní has a quiet, peaceful atmosphere that belies a wrenching history. It was here, in 1562, that Friar Diego de Landa conducted a now-infamous *auto de fé*, in which he burned at least two dozen irreplaceable Maya codices and thousands of painted vases and other items, because he deemed them works of the devil. He accused numerous Maya religious leaders and laypeople of idolatry, and ordered them tortured, publicly humiliated, and imprisoned. The act was outrageous, even by Spanish colonial standards, and Landa was shipped back to Spain to face the Council of the Indies, the colonial authority, for conducting an illegal inquisition. He was eventually absolved—a panel of inspectors found he had broken no laws—but not before Landa came to regret his act, at least somewhat. Confined to a convent awaiting judgment, he set about writing down all he could remember about the Maya.

It was no minor undertaking: Landa spoke Yucatec Maya fluently, and had lived, traveled, and preached throughout the Yucatán for 13 years before his expulsion. In all, Landa spent close to a decade completing *An Account of the Things of Yucatán*. He returned to Mérida in 1571 as the newly appointed bishop of Yucatán, and died there in 1579. Landa's manuscript was largely forgotten until being rediscovered in 1863. Among other things, the manuscript contains a crude alphabet (or more precisely, a syllabary), which has proved invaluable to the modern-day decoding of the Maya hieroglyphics. Ironically, the very man who destroyed so much of the Maya's written history also provided the key for future researchers to unlock what remained.

ships, 120 sailors, and 550 soldiers to search for slaves, a lucrative business. His search began on the Yucatán coast but eventually encompassed most of present-day Mexico. However, it took many decades and many lives for Spanish conquistadors to quell the Maya's resistance and cunning, despite a major advantage in military technology, including horses, gunpowder, and metal swords and armor. Francisco de Montejo, who took part in Cortés's earlier expedition into central Mexico, spent 1528-1535 trying to conquer the Yucatán, first from the east at Tulum and later from the west near Campeche and Tabasco, but was driven out each time. Montejo's son, also named Francisco de Montejo "El Mozo" (The Younger), took up the effort and eventually founded the city of Mérida in 1542 and Campeche in 1546. From those strongholds, the Spanish conquest slowly spread across the peninsula.

Economic and religious oppression were central to the conquest, too. The Xiu indigenous group proved an important ally to the Spanish after its leader converted to Christianity. And in 1562, a friar named Diego de Landa, upon learning his converts still practiced certain Maya ceremonies, became enraged and ordered the torture and imprisonment of numerous Maya spiritual leaders. He also gathered all the religious artifacts and Maya texts—which he said contained "superstitions and the devil's lies"—and had them burned. It was a staggering loss—at least 27 codices—and one that Landa later seemed to regret and attempted to reconcile by writing a detailed record of Maya customs, mathematics, and writing.

The Caste War

By the 1840s, the brutalized and subjugated Maya organized a revolt against Euro-Mexican colonizers. Called the Caste War, this savage war saw Maya taking revenge on every white man, woman, and child by means of murder and rape. European survivors made their way to the last Spanish strongholds of Mérida and Campeche. The governments of the two cities appealed for help to Spain, France, and the United States. No one answered the call. It was soon apparent that the remaining two cities would be wiped out.

© LIZA PRADO

The banner on this mural, located in the Plaza Central of Carrillo Puerto, reads "The Maya region is not an ethnographic museum, it is a people on the move."

But just as Mérida's leaders were preparing to evacuate the city, the Maya abruptly picked up their weapons and left. The reason was an unusually early appearance of flying ants, a sign of coming rain and to the Maya an all-important signal to begin planting corn. Despite the suffering visited upon them over three centuries of Spanish conquest, the Maya warriors, who were also farmers, simply could not risk missing the planting season. They turned their backs on certain victory and returned to their villages to tend their fields.

The unexpected reprieve allowed time for thousands of troops to arrive from Cuba, Mexico City, and the United States, and vengeance was merciless. Maya were killed indiscriminately. Some were taken prisoner and sold to Cuba as slaves; others left their villages and hid in the jungles—in some cases, for decades. Between 1846 and 1850, the population of the Yucatán Peninsula was reduced from 500,000 to 300,000. Quintana Roo along the Caribbean coast was considered a dangerous no-man's-land for almost another 100 years.

Growing Maya Power

Many Maya Indians escaped slaughter during the Caste War by fleeing to the isolated coastal forests of present-day Quintana Roo. A large number regrouped under the cult of the "Talking Cross"—an actual wooden cross that, with the help of a priest and a ventriloquist, spoke to the beleaguered indigenous fighters, urging them to continue fighting. Followers called themselves *Cruzob* (People of the Cross) and made a stronghold in the town of Chan Santa Cruz, today Carrillo Puerto. Research (and common sense) suggests the Maya knew full well that a human voice was responsible for the "talking," but that many believed it was inspired by God.

Close to the border with British Honduras (now Belize), the leaders of Chan Santa Cruz began selling timber to the British and were given weapons in return. Simultaneously (roughly 1855-1857), internal strife weakened the relations between Campeche and Mérida, and their mutual defense as well. Maya leaders took advantage of the conflict and attacked Fort Bacalar, eventually gaining control of the entire southern Caribbean coast.

Up until that time, indigenous soldiers simply killed the people they captured, but starting in 1858 they took lessons from the colonials and began to keep whites for slave labor. Women were put to work doing household chores and some became concubines, while men were forced to work the fields and build new constructions. (The main church in Carrillo Puerto was built largely by white slaves.)

For the next 40 years, the Maya people and soldiers based in and around Chan Santa Cruz kept the east coast of the Yucatán for themselves, and a shaky truce with the Mexican government endured. The native people were economically independent, self-governing, and, with no roads in or out of the region, almost totally isolated. They were not at war as long as everyone left them alone.

The Last Stand

Only when President Porfirio Díaz took power in 1877 did the Mexican federal government begin to think seriously about the Yucatán Peninsula. Through the years, Quintana Roo's isolation and the strength of the Maya in their treacherous jungle had foiled repeated efforts by Mexican soldiers to capture the region. The army's expeditions were infrequent, but it rankled Díaz that a relatively small and modestly armed Maya force had been able to keep the Mexican army at bay for so long. An assault in 1901, under the command of General Ignacio Bravo, broke the government's losing streak. The general captured a village, laid railroad tracks, and built a walled fort. Supplies arriving by rail kept the fort stocked, but the indigenous defenders responded by holding the fort under siege for an entire year. Reinforcements finally came from the capital and the Maya were forced to retreat, first from the fort and then from many of their villages and strongholds. A period of

brutal Mexican occupation followed, lasting until 1915, yet Maya partisans still didn't give up. They conducted guerrilla raids from the tangled coastal forest until the Mexican army, frustrated and demoralized, pulled out and returned Quintana Roo to the Maya.

Beginning in 1917 and lasting to 1920, however, influenza and smallpox swept through the Maya-held territories, killing hundreds of thousands of Maya. In 1920, with the last of their army severely diminished and foreign gum-tappers creeping into former Maya territories, indigenous leaders entered into a negotiated settlement with the Mexican federal government. The final treaties were signed in 1936, erasing the last vestiges of Maya national sovereignty in the region.

LAND REFORMS

Beginning in 1875, international demand for twine and rope made from henequen, a type of agave cactus that thrives in northern Yucatán, brought prosperity to Mérida, the state capital. Beautiful mansions were built by entrepreneurs who led the good life, sending their children to school in Europe and cruising with their wives to New Orleans in search of new luxuries and entertainment. Port towns were developed on the Gulf coast, and a two-kilometer (1.2-mile) wharf in Progreso was built to accommodate the large ships that came for sisal (hemp from the henequen plant).

The only thing that didn't change was the lifestyle of indigenous people, who provided most of the labor on colonial haciendas. Henequen plants have incredibly hard, sharp spines and at certain times emit a horrendous stench. Maya workers labored long, hard hours, living in constant debt to the hacienda store.

Prosperity helped bring the Yucatán to the attention of the world. But in 1908, an American journalist named John Kenneth Turner stirred things up when he documented the difficult lives of the indigenous plantation workers and the accompanying opulence enjoyed by the owners. The report set a series of reforms into motion. Carrillo Puerto, the first socialist governor of Mérida, helped native workers set up a labor union, educational center, and political club that served to organize and focus resistance to the powerful hacienda system. Carrillo made numerous agrarian reforms, including decreeing that abandoned haciendas could be appropriated by the government. With his power and popularity growing, conservatives saw only one way to stop him. In 1923, Carrillo Puerto was assassinated.

By then, though, the Mexican Revolution had been won and reforms were being made throughout the country, including redistribution of land and mandatory education. Mexico entered its golden years, a 40-year period of sustained and substantial growth dubbed The Mexican Miracle, all the more miraculous because it took place in defiance of the worldwide Great Depression. In the late 1930s, President Lázaro Cárdenas undertook a massive nationalization program, claiming the major electricity, oil, and other companies for the state, and created state-run companies like PEMEX, the oil conglomerate still in existence today. In the Yucatán, Cárdenas usurped large parts of hacienda lands—as much as half of the Yucatán's total arable land, by some accounts, most dedicated to the growing of henequen—and redistributed it to poor farmers.

THE PRI YEARS
The economic prosperity allowed the ruling Institutional Revolutionary Party (PRI) to consolidate power, and before long it held every major office in the federal government, and most state governments as well. The Mexican Miracle had not ameliorated all social inequalities—and in fact had exacerbated some—but the PRI grew increasingly intolerant of dissent. Deeply corrupt, the party—and by extension the state—resorted to brutal and increasingly blatant repression to silence detractors. The most notorious example was the gunning down of scores of student demonstrators—some say up to 250—by security forces in 1968 in Mexico City's Tlatelolco Plaza. The massacre took place at night; by morning the plaza was cleared of bodies and scrubbed of

blood, and the government simply denied that it ever happened.

The oil crisis that struck the United States in the early 1970s was at first a boon for Mexico, whose coffers were filled with money from pricey oil exports. But a failure to diversify the economy left Mexico vulnerable; as oil prices stabilized, the peso began to devalue. It had fallen as much as 500 percent by 1982, prompting then-president López Portillo to nationalize Mexico's banks. Foreign investment quickly dried up, and the 1980s were dubbed La Década Perdida (The Lost Decade) for Mexico and much of Latin America, a time of severe economic stagnation and crisis. In September 1985, a magnitude-8.1 earthquake struck Mexico City, killing 9,000 people and leaving 100,000 more homeless. It seemed Mexico had hit its nadir.

Yet it was during this same period that Cancún began to take off as a major vacation destination, drawing tourism and much-needed foreign dollars into the Mexican economy. The crises were not over—the implementation of the North American Free Trade Agreement (NAFTA) in 1994 was met simultaneously by a massive devaluation of the peso and an armed uprising by a peasant army called the Zapatistas in the state of Chiapas—but Mexico's economy regained some of its footing. A series of electoral reforms implemented in the late 1980s and through the 1990s paved the way for the historic 2000 presidential election, in which an opposition candidate—former Coca-Cola executive Vicente Fox of the right-of-center Partido de Acción Nacional (PAN)—defeated the PRI, ending the latter's 70-year reign of power. Fox was succeeded in 2006 by another PAN member, Felipe Calderón Hinojosa, in an election in which the PRI finished a distant third.

President Calderón campaigned on a promise to expand Mexico's job market and encourage foreign investment, including for new tourism projects in the Yucatán and elsewhere. But it was another pledge—to break up the drug trade and the cartels that controlled it—that consumed his entire presidency and plunged parts of Mexico into a spasm of violence unlike any since the revolution.

THE DRUG WARS

"The Drug War," as it is generally called, has its roots in the insatiable demand for drugs in the United States. For decades, cocaine, heroin, and other drugs from South America made their way to the United States mainly through the Caribbean on speedboats and small planes. But as that route was choked off by the U.S. Coast Guard and others, Mexico became an increasingly important conduit. (Drug production also has grown within Mexico itself, especially of marijuana and methamphetamines.) Mexican drug cartels have long operated within defined territories—the Gulf cartel, the Sinaloa cartel, the Juárez cartel, etc.—and did so largely with impunity, thanks to corruption in the police and PRI-controlled local governments. But if corruption encouraged the illicit trade, it also helped keep violence to a minimum; the cartels kept to themselves, and politicians and police turned a blind eye.

In 2006, encouraged by the United States, Calderón dispatched the Mexican military to various northern cities to break up the cartels and their distribution networks. They achieved some initial success—and continued to do so—but the broader effect was to disrupt the balance of power between the cartels, which began vying for valuable routes and territories. Violence erupted with shocking speed and ferocity, with shoot-outs among rival gangs and a gruesome cycle of attacks and reprisals, including decapitations and torture. As many as 60,000 people have died in the conflict, including more than 24,000 in 2011 alone. While most of the victims have been cartel members, more than 2,000 police, prosecutors, journalists, and even children have been killed, and another 20,000 people remain missing. It's notable that not only does American drug consumption account for most of the cartels' revenue, but virtually all the guns used in the drug war were smuggled there from the United States.

No wonder travelers are giving Mexico a second thought. The stories are scary, to be sure, but certain details help paint a different picture. Ninety percent of the deaths are of gang members, and another 7 percent are police and military. And the vast majority of the violence occurs in a few northern and central states, well removed from the Yucatán Peninsula. In fact, the region is one of the safest in Mexico, and tourism there has actually increased the last few years, despite rumors to the contrary. Travel to Cancún, Cozumel, and the Riviera Maya is extremely safe, especially if you steer well clear of drugs and weapons (which is a good policy even without a crisis going on).

MEXICO TODAY

In the summer of 2012, Mexico's national soccer team won its first Olympic gold medal, defeating heavily favored Brazil at the London games. It was a small blessing perhaps, in the scheme of things, but one that seemed to lift the country's collective spirit. Later that year, Mexicans elected Enrique Peña Nieto, the PRI candidate, as president. Without turning his back on drug cartel violence, Peña Nieto has focused on addressing drug abuse, unemployment, and corruption on a local level. The U.S. presidential election in 2012 gave Mexico a respite from the glare of international media attention, and tourism has bounced back stronger than ever. Mexico itself seems poised to do the same.

Government and Economy

GOVERNMENT

Mexico enjoys a constitutional democracy modeled after that of the United States, including a president (who serves one six-year term), a two-house legislature, and a judiciary branch. For 66 years (until the year 2000), Mexico was controlled by one party, the so-called moderate Partido Revolucionario Institucional (PRI). A few cities and states elected candidates from the main opposition parties—the conservative Partido de Acción Nacional (PAN) and leftist Partido de la Revolución Democrática (PRD)—but the presidency and most of the important government positions were passed from one hand-picked PRI candidate to the next, amid rampant electoral fraud.

Indeed, fraud and corruption have been ugly mainstays of Mexican government for generations. In the 1988 presidential election, PRI candidate Carlos Salinas Gortari officially garnered 51 percent of the vote, a dubious result judging from polls leading up to the election, and rendered laughable after a mysterious "breakdown" in the election tallying system delayed the results for several days.

Salinas Gortari ended his term under the same heavy clouds of corruption and fraud that ushered him in, accused of having stolen millions of dollars from the federal government during his term. That said, Salinas pushed through changes such as increasing the number of Senate seats and reorganizing the federal electoral commission that helped usher in freer and fairer elections. He also oversaw the adoption of NAFTA in 1993, which has sped up Mexico's manufacturing industry but seriously damaged other sectors, especially small farmers, many of whom are indigenous.

The 1994 presidential election was marred by the assassination in Tijuana of the PRI candidate Luis Donaldo Colosio, the country's first major political assassination since 1928. Colosio's campaign manager, technocrat Ernesto Zedillo, was nominated to fill the candidacy and eventually elected. Zedillo continued with reforms, and in 2000, for the first time in almost seven decades, the opposition candidate officially won. PAN candidate Vicente Fox, a businessman and former Coca-Cola executive from Guanajuato, took the reins, promising continued electoral reforms, a stronger private sector, and closer relations with the United States. He knew U.S. president-elect George W. Bush personally, having worked with him on border issues during Bush's term as governor of Texas. Progress was being made until the terrorist attacks of September 11, 2001, pushed Mexico far down on the U.S. administration's priority list. With Mexico serving a term on the U.N. Security Council, Fox came under intense pressure from the United States to support an invasion of Iraq. He ultimately refused—Mexican people were overwhelmingly opposed to the idea—but it cost Fox dearly in his relationship with Bush. The reforms he once seemed so ideally poised to achieve were largely incomplete by the time Fox's term ended.

The presidential elections of 2006 were bitterly contested and created—or exposed—a deep schism in the country. The eventual winner was PAN candidate Felipe Calderón Hinojosa, a former secretary of energy under Fox. His main opponent, Andrés Manuel López Obrador, is a former mayor of Mexico City and member of the left-leaning PRD. Though fraught with accusations and low blows, the campaign also was a classic clash of ideals, with Calderón advocating increased foreign investment and free trade, and López Obrador assailing the neo-liberal model and calling for government action to reduce poverty and strengthen social services. Both men claimed victory after election day; when Calderón was declared the winner, López Obrador alleged widespread fraud and called for a total recount. His supporters blocked major thoroughfares throughout the country for weeks. The Mexican Electoral Commission did a selective recount and affirmed a Calderón victory; the official figures set the margin at under 244,000 votes out of 41 million cast, a difference of just 0.5 percent. Calderón's inauguration was further marred by legislators fistfighting in the chamber and the new president shouting his oath over jeers and general ruckus.

Calderón was confronted with a number of thorny problems upon inauguration, including a protest in Oaxaca that had turned violent, and spiraling corn prices that in turn drove up the cost of tortillas, the most basic of Mexican foods. While addressing those and other issues, he pressed forward with promised law-and-order reforms, raising police officers' wages and dispatching the Mexican military to staunch rampant gang- and drug-related crime in cities like Tijuana and Juárez. The latter sparked an all-out war between cartels, police, and the military.

In 2012, Mexicans elected Enrique Peña Nieto, the PRI candidate, as president. The results may be less a sign that Mexicans have forgiven the PRI its misdeeds of the not-so-distant past, rather that they're simply exhausted by the violence that's taken place under the PAN (whose candidate finished a distant third). Without conceding the fight to the cartels, Peña Nieto has quietly shifted the federal government's focus to addressing drug abuse, unemployment, and corruption on a local level.

ECONOMY
Oil
The leading industry on the Yucatán Peninsula is oil. Produced by the nationally owned PEMEX, the oil industry is booming along the Gulf coast from Campeche south into the state of Tabasco. Most of the oil is shipped at OPEC prices to Canada, Israel, France, Japan, and the United States. Rich in natural gas, Mexico sends the United States 10 percent of its total output. Two-thirds of Mexico's export revenue comes from fossil fuels. As a result, peninsula cities are beginning to show signs of financial health.

Fishing
Yucatecan fisheries also are abundant along the Gulf coast. At one time fishing was not much more than a family business, but today fleets of large purse seiners with their adjacent processing plants can be seen on the Gulf of Mexico. With the renewed interest in preserving fishing grounds for the future, the industry could continue to thrive for many years.

Tourism
Until the 1970s, Quintana Roo's economy amounted to very little. For a few years the chicle boom brought a flurry of activity up and down the state—it was shipped from the harbor of Isla Cozumel. Native and hardwood trees have always been in demand; coconuts and fishing were the only other natural resources that added to the economy—but neither on a large scale.

With the development of an offshore sandbar—Cancún—into a multimillion-dollar resort, tourism became the region's number-one moneymaker. The development of the Riviera Maya (extending from Cancún to Tulum)—and now, the Costa Maya (south of Sian Ka'an to the border of Belize)—only guaranteed the continued success of the economy. New roads now give access to previously unknown beaches and Maya structures. Extra attention is going to archaeological zones ignored for hundreds of years. All but the smallest have restrooms, ticket offices, gift shops, and food shops.

People and Culture

DEMOGRAPHICS

Today, 75-80 percent of the Mexican population is estimated to be mestizo (a combination of the indigenous and Spanish-Caucasian races). Only 10-15 percent are considered to be indigenous peoples. For comparison, as recently as 1870, the indigenous made up more than 50 percent of the population. While there are important native communities throughout Mexico, the majority of the country's indigenous peoples live in the Yucatán Peninsula, Oaxaca, and Chiapas.

RELIGION

The vast majority of Mexicans are Roman Catholic, especially in the generally conservative Yucatán Peninsula. However, a vigorous evangelical movement gains more and more converts every year.

LANGUAGE

The farther you go from a city, the less Spanish you'll hear and the more dialects of indigenous languages you'll encounter. The government estimates that of the 10 million indigenous people in the country, about 25 percent do not speak Spanish. Of the original 125 native languages, 70 are still spoken, 20 of which are classified as Maya languages, including Tzeltal, Tzotzil, Chol, and Yucatec.

Although education was made compulsory for children in 1917, this law was not enforced in the Yucatán Peninsula until recently. Today, schools throughout the peninsula use Spanish-language books, even though many children do not speak the language. In some of the rural schools, bilingual teachers are recruited to help children make the transition.

Papel Picado

© GARY CHANDLER

papel picado hanging in the community gathering place in El Cedral, Cozumel

Mexicans are famous for their celebrations—whether it's to honor a patron saint or to celebrate a neighbor's birthday, partying is part of the culture. Typically, fiestas feature great music, lots of food, fireworks, and brightly colored decorations, often including *papel picado* (literally, diced paper).

Papel picado is tissue paper cut or stamped with a design that reflects the occasion in some way: a manger scene at Christmas, church bells for a wedding, skeletons in swooping hats for Day of the Dead. Once cut, row upon row of *papel picado* is strung across city streets, in front of churches, or in people's backyards. It typically stays up until wind or rain leaves just a thin cord and a few bits of torn paper as a reminder of the celebration that was.

Regional Holidays and Celebrations

- Jan. 1: **New Year's Day**
- Jan. 6: **Día de los Reyes Magos:** Three Kings Day–Christmas gifts exchanged
- Feb. 2: **Virgen de la Candelaria:** Religious candlelight processions light up several towns
- Feb./Mar.: **Carnaval:** Seven-day celebration before Ash Wednesday; celebrated big on Isla Cozumel
- Mar. 21: **Birthday of Benito Juárez:** President of Mexico for five terms; born in 1806
- Mar. 21: **Vernal Equinox in Chichén Itzá:** A phenomenon of light and shadow displays a serpent slithering down the steps of El Castillo
- Apr. 19: **Festival de San Telmo:** Culmination of a two-week festival celebrating the patron saint of fishermen; celebrated on Isla Holbox
- May 1: **Día del Trabajador:** Labor Day
- May 3: **Day of the Holy Cross:** Dance of

- the Pigs' Head performed in Carrillo Puerto and El Cedral
- May 5: **Cinco de Mayo:** Commemoration of the Mexican army's 1862 defeat of the French at the Battle of Puebla
- Sept. 16: **Independence Day:** Celebrated on the night of the 15th
- Sept. 29: **Fiesta de San Miguel Arcángel:** Celebration of Isla Cozumel's patron saint
- Oct. 12: **Día de la Raza:** Indigenous Peoples Day; celebrated instead of Columbus Day
- Nov. 1-2: **All Souls' Day and Day of the Dead:** Church ceremonies and graveside celebrations in honor of the deceased
- Nov. 20: **Día de la Revolución:** Celebration of the beginning of the Mexican Revolution in 1910
- Dec. 12: **Virgen de Guadalupe:** Religious celebration in honor of Mexico's patron saint
- Dec. 25: **Christmas:** Celebrated on the night of the 24th

ART

Mexico has an incredibly rich colonial and folk-art tradition. While not considered art to the people who make and use it, traditional indigenous clothing is beautiful, and travelers and collectors are increasingly able to buy it in local shops and markets. Prices for these items can be high, for the simple fact that they are hand-woven and can literally take months to complete. Mérida is an especially good place to purchase pottery, carving, and textiles from around the Yucatán and beyond.

HOLIDAYS AND FESTIVALS

Mexicans take celebrations and holidays seriously—of their country, their saints, and their families. You'll be hard-pressed to find a two-week period when something or someone isn't being celebrated. On major

holidays—Christmas, New Year's Eve, and Easter—be prepared for crowds at the beaches and ruins. Be sure to book your hotel and buy your airline and bus tickets well in advance; during holidays, the travel industry is saturated with Mexican travelers.

In addition to officially recognized holidays, villages and cities hold numerous festivals and celebrations: for patron saints, birthdays of officials, a good crop, a birth of a child. You name it, it's probably been celebrated. Festivals typically take place in and around the central plaza of a town with dancing, live music, colorful decorations, and fireworks. Temporary food booths are set up around the plaza and typically sell tamales (both sweet and meat), *buñuelos* (sweet rolls), tacos, *churros* (fried dough dusted with sugar), *carne asada* (barbecued meat), and plenty of regional drinks.

ESSENTIALS

Getting There

For centuries, getting to the Yucatán Peninsula required a major sea voyage to one of the few ports on the Gulf of Mexico, only to be followed by harrowing and uncertain land treks limited to mule trains and narrow paths through the tangled jungle. Today, the peninsula is easily accessible. Visitors arrive every day via modern airports, a network of good highways, excellent bus service, or by cruise ship. From just about anywhere in the world, the Yucatán is only hours away.

AIR

The main international airports on the Yucatán Peninsula are in Cancún and Mérida. The Cancún airport is by far the busiest, with dozens of daily domestic and international flights. There are smaller airports in **Cozumel and Chetumal,** and another reportedly being built in **Tulum,** though it remains far from completion. There also is an airport near **Chichén Itzá,** but currently it only receives chartered flights. In addition, there are small airports in **Mahahual** and **Isla Holbox** for private planes and air taxis.

Most travelers use the Cancún airport—it's well located for those vacationing in the Caribbean as well as for those traveling inland. Fares typically are cheaper to Cancún than to any other airport in the region.

© LIZA PRADO

Navigating the Cancún Airport

Some travelers find Cancun's airport somewhat daunting to navigate. The key is to not get drawn into any of the many sales pitches you'll encounter. Leaving the plane, simply follow the crowd, queueing first for immigration, then retrieving your luggage, then queueing again for customs, where you're asked to press a button: Green means go, red means stop and have your bags searched. Once through customs, you'll enter a large busy foyer packed with vendor booths, salespeople and tourist office folks, ranging from peppy to pushy, virtually all of whom you can ignore or politely rebuff. If you're renting a car, look for the booth of the company you've reserved with and let the attendant know you've arrived; he or she will direct you to a shuttle to take you to the rental center. If you need a taxi, look for one of three "Yellow Transfers" booths, the official airport taxi service. To catch a bus, walk out of the terminal—ignoring the hagglers and taxi drivers clustered in front—and look for large ADO buses parked a few steps to your right; you can buy your ticket at the mobile desk set up there. If your resort has arranged transport for you, look for a driver outside the terminal with your name or the name of the resort on a sign. None of the options requires much walking so you don't really need a porter; if you do use one, a couple dollars per bag is the customary tip.

Travelers who are planning to spend their entire time inland often choose to fly to Mérida instead—the city itself is an important destination, and it's close to many of the area's key sights and archaeological ruins.

Similarly, many travelers who only will be visiting Isla Cozumel fly directly there—it's often more expensive than landing in Cancún but avoids the time and hassle of traveling from the mainland to the island (more time to dive and to enjoy the island!).

There also are airports in Campeche City and Chetumal, which are typically used for domestic travel. However, for travelers planning to spend most of their time in Campeche, they may be more convenient.

Departure Tax
There is a US$48 departure tax to fly out of Mexico—most airlines incorporate the tax into their tickets, but it's worth setting aside some cash just in case.

BUS
The Yucatán's main interstate bus hubs are Mérida and Cancún, with service to and from Mexico City, Veracruz, Oaxaca, and other major destinations in the country. There also are buses between Chetumal and cities in Belize and Guatemala.

CAR
Foreigners driving into Mexico are required to show a valid driver's license, title, registration, and proof of insurance for their vehicle. Mexican authorities do not recognize foreign-issued insurance; Mexican vehicle insurance is available at most border towns 24 hours a day, and several companies also sell policies over the Internet. Do not cross the border with your car until you have obtained the proper papers.

CRUISE SHIP
Increasing numbers of cruise ships stop along Mexico's Caribbean coast every year, some carrying as many as 5,000 people. Many sail out of Miami and Fort Lauderdale, stopping at Key West before continuing to Punta Venado (Riviera Maya), Isla Cozumel, and Mahahual.

Prices are competitive, and ships vary in services, amenities, activities, and entertainment. Pools, restaurants, nightclubs, and cinemas are commonplace. Fitness centers and shops also make ship life convenient. To hone in on the type of cruise you'd like to go on, research options on the Internet, in the travel section of your local newspaper, and by contacting your travel agent.

If your budget is tight, consider traveling standby. Ships want to sail full and are willing to cut their prices—sometimes up to 50 percent—to do so. Airfare usually is not included. **Note:** Once you're on the standby list, you likely will have no choice of cabin location or size.

NEIGHBORING COUNTRIES

Cancún is an important international hub, not only for tourists from North America and Europe but also for regional flights to Central America and the Caribbean. In southern Quintana Roo, Chetumal is the gateway to Belize, and there's a direct bus to Flores, Guatemala. Most travel to Guatemala, however, is through Chiapas, from the towns of Palenque and San Cristóbal de las Casas.

Travel agencies can book tours to Belize, Guatemala, and Cuba, though it's relatively easy to arrange a trip yourself. Most travelers do not need prearranged visas to enter either Belize or Guatemala, but they may have to pay an entrance fee at the airport or border. Call the respective consulates for additional information.

Getting Around

AIR

Although budget airlines like Interjet are starting to appear on the Mexican airline scene, flying domestically is still relatively expensive, and the Yucatán is no exception. Once you factor in the check-in process, security, and baggage claim, there are very few flights within the region that make sense travel-wise, unless your time is incredibly tight. And if that is the case, you may as well see what you can do by car or bus and start planning a return trip.

BUS

Mexico's bus and public transportation system is one of the best in Latin America, if not the Western Hemisphere. In the Yucatán Peninsula, ADO and its affiliate bus lines practically have a monopoly, but that has not made bus travel any less efficient or less affordable. Dozens of buses cover every major route many times per day, and even smaller towns have frequent and reliable service.

Buses come in three main categories:

First Class: Known as *primera clase* or sometimes *ejecutivo,* first class is the most common and the one travelers use most often. Buses have reclining seats and TVs where movies are played on long trips. First-class buses make some intermediate stops but only in large towns. The main first-class lines in the Yucatán are ADO.

Deluxe Class: Usually called *lujo* (luxury), deluxe class is a step up; they often are slightly faster since they're typically nonstop. The main deluxe line is ADO-GL, which costs 10-25 percent more than regular ADO. ADO-GL buses have nicer seats and better televisions (and even more recent movies!). Sometimes there are even free bottles of water in a cooler at the back. Even nicer are ADO-Platino buses, which often charge twice as much as regular ADO. Platino offers cushy, extra-wide seats (only three across instead of four), headphones, and sometimes a light meal like a sandwich and soda.

Second Class: *Segunda clase,* or second class, is significantly slower and less comfortable than first class, and they're not all that much cheaper. Whenever possible, pay the dollar or two extra for first class. Second-class buses are handy in that you can flag them down anywhere on the roadside, but that is also precisely the reason they're so slow. In smaller towns, second class may be the only service available, and it's fine for shorter trips. The main second-class lines in the Yucatán are Mayab, Oriente, Noreste, and ATS.

© LIZA PRADO

Buses, taxis, rental cars, and good old-fashioned walking: you'll use them all while exploring the Riviera Maya.

For overnight trips, definitely take first-class or deluxe. Not only will you be much more comfortable, second-class buses are sometimes targeted by roadside thieves since they drive on secondary roads and stop frequently.

Wherever bus service is thin, you can count on there being frequent **colectivos** or **combis**—vans or minibuses—that cover local routes. They can be flagged down anywhere along the road.

FERRY

Ferries are used to get to and from the region's most visited islands, including Isla Mujeres (reached from Cancún), Isla Cozumel (reached from Playa del Carmen), and Isla Holbox (reached from Chiquilá). Service is safe, reliable, frequent, and affordable.

CAR

As great as Mexico's bus system is, a car is the best way to tour the Yucatán Peninsula. Most of the sights—ruins, deserted beaches, haciendas, caves, cenotes, wildlife—are well outside of the region's cities, down long access roads, or on the way from one town to the next. Having a car also saves you the time and effort of walking or the cost of cabbing to all those "missing links"; it also allows you to enjoy the sights for as much or as little time as you choose.

If you're here for a short time—a week or less—and want to sightsee, definitely get a car for the simple reason that you'll have the option of seeing and doing twice as much. If renting for your entire vacation isn't feasible moneywise, consider renting in choice locations: a couple of days in Mérida to see the Puuc Route, a few in Campeche to see the Río Bec archaeological zones, and a couple of days to explore the less-accessible parts of Quintana Roo. You also may want a car for a day in Cozumel to check out the island. Cars aren't necessary to visit Cancún, Isla Mujeres, or Playa del Carmen.

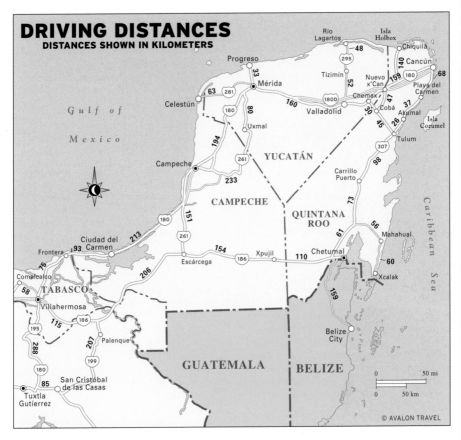

DRIVING DISTANCES
DISTANCES SHOWN IN KILOMETERS

Car Rental

The best rates (and best vehicles) are typically found online with the major international rental chains like Hertz, Thrifty, Budget, and Avis. That said, there are many local agencies in cities like Mérida and Cancún, however, and they occasionally have good walk-in deals.

- It's best to book on the car rental company's own website rather than a travel website. The prices are virtually the same, and if there are any problems, the rental office can't blame it on the other website.

- Ask your credit card company if your card

provides free collision (liability) insurance on rental cars abroad. (Most do.) Unlike ordinary insurance, you'll have to pay any charges upfront and then file for reimbursement once you return. The coverage is usually better, though, with zero deductible and coverage even on dirt roads. Remember you have to actually use the card to pay for the rental in order to get the benefit!

- Car rental agencies make most of their money off the insurance, not the vehicle. That's why they push so hard for you to buy coverage. They'll warn you that with credit card insurance you'll have to pay 100 percent

Driving in Mexico

Having a car can make exploring the Yucatán Peninsula quicker and easier, and there are many places you can only reach with your own wheels. Here are some tips to make your driving experience a bit smoother:

Off the highways, the biggest hazard are *topes* (speed bumps). They are common on all roads and highways, save the toll roads. They vary in size, but many are big and burly, and hitting them at even a slow speed can do a number on you, your passengers, and your car. As soon as you see a sign announcing an upcoming town or village, be ready to slow down.

Narrow one-way streets are common in many cities in the Yucatán. Fortunately, the **stop signs** in those areas usually have smaller plaques (beneath the big red one) indicating direction and right of way. A **black rectangle** means you have the right of way, a **red one** means you don't.

If you break down or run out of gas on a main road during daylight hours, stay with your car. **Los Ángeles Verdes** (The Green Angels, toll-free Mex. tel. 078 or 800/903-9200), a government-sponsored tow-truck and repair service, cruise these roads on the lookout for drivers in trouble. They carry a CB radio, gas, and small parts, and are prepared to fix tires. If you have a cell phone—or happen to be near a pay phone—call your car rental agency first; the Ángeles Verdes are a great backup.

of any damages upfront; this is true, but it will be reimbursed when you file a claim back home. They may require you to authorize a larger "hold" on your card, as much as US$5000, for potential damages. This is no big deal—it's not an actual charge—but that amount will be unavailable for other purchases. Consider bringing two or more credit cards, especially if your credit limit is low.

• Third-party insurance is required by law, and rental agencies are technically required to provide it. Lately, however, rental agencies say third-party coverage is free for anyone who also purchases collision insurance. But if you decline their collision insurance (because you get it through your credit card), suddenly there's a charge for third-party coverage. Credit cards typically do not offer third-party coverage, so you end up having to pay it. It's less expensive than collision insurance, but still a bummer to pay.

Before driving off, the attendant will review the car for existing damage—definitely accompany him or her on this part and don't be shy about pointing out every nick, scratch, and ding. Other things to confirm before driving off include:

• There is a spare tire (preferably a full-size, not temporary, one) and a working jack and tire iron.

• All doors lock and unlock, including the trunk.

• The headlights, brake lights, and turn signals work.

• All the windows roll up and down properly.

• The proper—and current—car registration is in the car. In some cases, your car rental contract serves as the registration.

• The amount of gas in the tank—you'll have to return it with the same amount.

• There is a 24-hour telephone number for the rental agency in case of an emergency.

Highways and Road Conditions

Driving in the Yucatán isn't as nerve-wracking as you might think. The highways are in excellent condition, and even secondary roads are well maintained. There are a few dirt and sand roads—mostly along the Costa Maya, in the Sian Ka'an Biosphere Reserve, and to some of the lesser-visited archaeological sites in Campeche. If anything, frequent—and sometimes unexpected—*topes* (speed bumps) in small towns are the biggest driving hazard.

The main highways in the region are Highway 307, which runs the length of Mexico's Caribbean coast; Highway 180, the thoroughfare that links Cancún, Mérida, and Campeche City; and Highway 186, which crosses the southern portion of the Yucatán Peninsula and leads travelers to Campeche's Río Bec region and Comalcalco in Tabasco.

In the entire region, there are only two toll roads, both sections of Highway 180: between Mérida and Cancún (a whopping US$33) and between Campeche City and the town of Champotón (US$5.50). Although far from cheap, they can save a significant amount of time driving, and are safer for driving at night. Secondary roads are free and pass through picturesque countryside and indigenous villages;

Taxi Scam

Beware of any taxi driver who tries to convince you that the hotel you're going to is closed, roach infested, flooded, burned down, has no running water, was destroyed by a hurricane (add your disaster of choice). As sincere as the driver might seem, he is more often than not retaliating against hotels that refuse to pay a finder's fee. Taxi drivers in Cancún and throughout the Riviera Maya earn significant commissions—as much as US$10 per person *per night*—for bringing guests to certain establishments. Some hotels refuse to pay the fee, and taxi drivers, in turn, try to take their clients to "cooperative" hotels instead. Don't fall for it. You may have to be firm, but insist that your driver take you to the hotel of your choice. Your best option is to call ahead for a room reservation, which also serves to confirm that the hotel actually is open and operational.

they are slower and have more obstacles like pedestrians, bicycles, and speed bumps, but can be a rewarding way to go.

Driving Scams

Most travelers have heard horror stories about Mexican police and worry about being taken for all their money or trundled off to jail without reason. While it is true that there is corruption among the police, they don't target tourists; foreigners are, after all, the economic lifeblood of the region—the police don't want to scare them away.

As long as you are a careful and defensive driver, it is very unlikely you'll have any interaction with the police. Most travelers who are pulled over actually have done something wrong—speeding, running a stop sign, turning on red. In those situations, remain calm and polite. If you have an explanation, definitely give it; it is not uncommon to discuss a given situation with an officer. Who knows, you may even convince him you're right—it's happened to us!

Of greater concern are gas station attendants. Full service is the norm here—you pull up, tell the person how much you want, and he or she does the rest. A common scam is for one attendant to distract you with questions about wiper fluid or gas additives while another starts the pump at 50 or 100 pesos. Before you answer any questions, be sure the attendant resets, or "zeroes," the pump before starting to pump.

HITCHHIKING

Hitchhiking is not recommended for either men or women. That said, it sometimes can be hard to know what is a private vehicle and what is a *colectivo* (shared van). If there's no bus terminal nearby, your best bet is to look for locals who are waiting for public transportation and see which vans they take. If you have no choice but to hitch a ride, opt for a pickup truck, where you can sit in the back.

TOURS

Regional travel agents and tour operators offer a vast range of organized trips. You pay extra, of course, but all arrangements and reservations are made for you: from guides and transportation to hotels and meals. Special-interest trips also are common—archaeological tours, hacienda and convent routes, bird-watching and dive trips. Ask around and surf the Internet—you'll find a world of organized adventure.

Visas and Officialdom

PASSPORTS
Gone are the days you could zip down to Mexico with just your driver's license and birth certificate. Since January 2007, all U.S. citizens returning from Mexico (and elsewhere) by air, land, or sea are required to have a passport. Canadians may travel to Mexico without a passport; they simply need an official photo ID and proof of citizenship, such as an original birth certificate. All other nationalities must have a valid passport.

VISAS AND TOURIST CARDS
Citizens of most countries, including the United States, Canada, and members of the E.U., do not need to obtain a visa to enter Mexico. All foreigners, however, are issued a white tourist card when they enter, with the number of days that they are permitted to stay in the country written at the bottom, typically 30-60 days. If you plan to stay for more than a month, politely ask the official to give you the amount of time you need; the maximum stay is 180 days.

Hold onto your tourist card! It must be returned to immigration officials when you leave Mexico. If you lose it, you'll be fined and may not be permitted to leave the country (much less the immigration office) until you pay.

To extend your stay up to 180 days, head to the nearest immigration office a week *before* your tourist card expires. Be sure to bring it along with your passport. There, you'll fill out several forms, go to a bank to pay the US$25 processing fee, make photocopies of all the paperwork (including your passport, entry stamp, tourist card, and credit card), and then return to the office to get the extension. For every extra 30 days requested, foreigners must prove that they have US$1,000 available, either in cash or travelers checks, or simply by showing a current credit card. The process can take anywhere from a couple of hours to a week, depending on the office.

CUSTOMS
Plants and fresh foods are not allowed into Mexico and there are special limits on alcohol, tobacco, and electronic products. Archaeological artifacts, certain antiques, and colonial art cannot be exported from Mexico without special permission.

Above all, do not attempt to bring marijuana or any other narcotic in or out of Mexico. Jail is one place your trusty guidebook won't come in handy.

Returning home, you will be required to declare all items you bought in Mexico. Citizens of the United States are allowed to reenter with US$800 worth of purchases duty-free; the figure for other travelers varies by country.

CONSULATES
The consulates in Cancún and Mérida handle passport issues (replacing a lost one, adding pages, etc.) and can help their citizens if they are in a serious or emergency situation, including hospitalization, assault, arrest, lawsuits, or death. They usually do not help resolve common disputes—with tour operators or hotels, for example.

Foreign consulates and consular agencies in the region include:

AUSTRIA
Cancún: Av. Tulum at Calle Pecari, tel. 998/884-5431, claudiaemx@yahoo.com.mx, 9am-2pm Monday-Friday

Mérida: Av. Colón Norte 501-C, tel. 999/925-6386, bulnesa@prodigy.net.mx, 9:30am-1pm and 5pm-8pm Monday-Friday

BELGIUM
Cancún: Plaza Tropical, Av. Tulum 192, Local 59, tel. 998/892-2512, www.diplomatie.be, 10am-2pm Monday-Friday

BELIZE
Chetumal: Calle Ramon F. Iturbe No. 476, tel. 983/832-5764, conbelizeqroo@gmail.com, 9am-1pm Monday-Friday
Mérida: Calle 53 between Calles 56 and 58, tel. 999/928-6152, consbelize@dutton.com.mx, 9am-1pm Monday-Friday

CANADA
Cancún: Plaza Caracol, Blvd. Kukulcán Km. 8.5, Local 330, tel. 998/883-3360, www.canada.org.mx, 9am-5pm Monday-Friday

CUBA
Cancún: Pecari 17, tel. 998/884-3423, www.cubadiplomatica.cu/mexico, 9am-1pm Monday-Friday
Mérida: Calle 1-D between Calles 42 and 44, tel. 999/944-4216, www.cubadiplomatica.cu/mexico, 8:30am-1:30pm Monday-Friday

DENMARK
Cancún: Omni Hotel, Blvd. Kukulcán Km. 16.5, tel. 998/881-0600, apresidencia@grupocancun.net, 9am-1pm Monday-Friday

FINLAND
Cancún: Edificio Popolnah, Av. Nader 28-1, tel. 998/884-1600, notariacancun@prodigy.net.mx, 9am-2pm and 5pm-8pm Monday-Friday
Mérida: Calle 86-B No. 595-B, tel. 999/984-0399

FRANCE
Mérida: Calle 60 btwn Calles 41 and 43, tel. 999/930-1500, consuladofrancia@sipse.com.mx, 9am-5pm Monday-Friday

GERMANY
Cancún: Calle Punta Conocó 36, tel. 998/884-5333, konsul_d@yahoo.com.mx, 9am-noon Monday-Friday
Mérida: Calle 49 between Calles 30 and 32, tel. 999/944-3252, konsulat@jerommel.de, 9am-noon Monday-Friday

GUATEMALA
Cancún: Edificio Barcelona, Av. Nader 148, 998/884-8296, 9am-1pm Monday-Friday
Chetumal: Avenida Héroes de Chapultepec 356, tel. 983/832-3045, 9am-1pm Monday-Friday

IRELAND
Cancún: Av. Cobá 15, tel. 998/112-5436, consul@gruporoyale.com, 9am-1pm Monday-Friday

ITALY
Cancún: Parque Las Palapas, Alcatraces 39, tel. 998/884-1261, conitaca@prodigy.net.mx, 9am-2pm Monday-Friday

NETHERLANDS
Cancún: Pabellón Caribe, Av. Nichupté MZ 2, SM 19, tel. 998/884-8672, nlconsulcancun@prodigy.net.mx, 9am-1pm Monday-Friday
Mérida: Calle 64 btwn Calles 47 and 49, tel. 999/924-3122, pixan2003@prodigy.net.mx, 8am-5pm Monday-Friday

NORWAY
Cancún: Calle Venado 30, tel. 998/887-4412, 9am-1pm Monday-Friday

SPAIN
Cancún: Edificio Oasis, Blvd. Kukulcán at Calle Cenzontle, tel. 998/848-9918, consules@oasishotel.com.mx, 10am-1pm Monday-Friday
Mérida: Calle 8 btwn Calles 5 and 7, tel. 999/948-0181, 10am-1pm Monday-Friday

SWEDEN
Cancún: Omni Hotel, Blvd. Kukulcán Km. 16.5, tel. 998/881-0600, katiavara@

omnicancun.com.mx, tel. 998/881-0600, 9am-6pm Monday-Friday

SWITZERLAND
Cancún: above Rolandi's restaurant, Av. Cobá 12, tel. 998/884-8446, 9am-2pm Monday-Friday

UNITED KINGDOM
Cancún: The Royal Sands Resort, Blvd. Kukulcán Km. 13.5, tel. 998/881-0100, http://ukinmexico.fco.gov.uk/en, 9am-3pm Monday-Friday

UNITED STATES
Cancún: Torre La Europea, Blvd. Kukulcán Km. 13, tel. 998/883-0272, cancunagency@gmail.com, 8am-1pm Monday-Friday, appointment required for some services
Isla Cozumel: Plaza Villamar, central plaza, tel. 987/872-4574, usgov@cozumel.net, noon-2pm Monday-Friday
Mérida: Calle 60 No. 338-K btwn Calles 29 and 31, tel. 999/942-5700, www.merida.usconsulate.gov, 7:30am-4:30pm Monday-Friday, appointment required for some services
Playa del Carmen: The Palapa, Calle 1 btwn Avs. 15 and 20, tel. 984/873-0303, playausca@gmail.com, 9am-1pm Monday-Friday

UNDERAGE TRAVELERS
In the United States, anyone under 18 traveling internationally without *both* parents or legal guardians must present a signed, notarized letter from the parent(s) or guardian(s) granting the minor permission to leave the country. This requirement is aimed at preventing international abductions, but it causes frequent and major disruptions for vacationers.

Accommodations and Food

ACCOMMODATIONS
Lodging in Cancún, Cozumel, and the surrounding area truly runs the gamut: campgrounds, hostels, small hotels, bed-and-breakfasts, boutique hotels, large modern hotels, and all-inclusive resorts. There are a handful of fishing lodges in places like Sian Ka'an reserve.

Taxes on your hotel bill, referred to generally as I.V.A. (value-added tax; pronounced EE-va in Spanish), are usually 12 percent but can be as high as 17-22 percent. Be sure to ask if the rate you're quoted includes taxes (*¿Incluye impuestos?*); in many cases, especially at smaller hotels, the taxes are applied only if you pay by credit card.

You may be required to make a deposit in order to reserve a room, especially in popular areas during high season. However, in Mexico credit cards cannot be charged without a physical signature, so they aren't much help as a deposit. Many hotels utilize PayPal or a similar service; those that do not will give you the name of their bank and account number, and you must stop by a branch and make the deposit with the teller. Be sure to get a receipt, and notify the hotel after making the deposit.

Cancellation policies tend to be rather unforgiving, especially during high season; you may be required to give a month or more advance notice to receive even a partial refund. Trip insurance is a good idea if your plans are less than concrete.

FOOD
Considered among the most distinct cuisines of the country, Yucatecan food reflects the influences of its Maya, European, and Caribbean heritage. Some of the most popular menu items include:

Cochinita Pibil: pork that has been marinated in achiote, Seville orange juice, peppercorn, garlic, cumin, salt, and pepper, wrapped in banana leaves, and baked. It's typically served on weekends.

Dzoto-bichay: tamales made of *chaya* (a leafy

vegetable similar to spinach) and eggs. It comes smothered in tomato sauce.

Empanizado: slices of pork or chicken that has been breaded and fried, often served with salad, rice, and beans.

Panucho: handmade tortilla stuffed with re-fried beans and covered with shredded turkey, pickled onion, and slices of avocado. Like a *salbute* plus!

Papadzules: hard-boiled eggs chopped and rolled into a corn tortilla, smothered in a creamy pumpkin-seed sauce.

Poc-Chuc: slices of pork that have been marinated in Seville orange juice and coated with a tangy sauce. Pickled onions are added on the side.

Salbute: handmade tortilla covered with shredded turkey, pickled onion, and slices of avocado.

Sopa de Lima: turkey-stock soup prepared with shredded turkey or chicken, fried tortilla strips, and juice from *lima,* a lime-like citrus fruit.

Conduct and Customs

CLOTHING

Perhaps the single most-abused social custom in Mexico is the use of shorts. Mexicans rarely wear them outside the home or off the beach, while many foreign travelers seem to have packed nothing but. There is a bit more flexibility in beach areas, but it's worth getting in the habit of wearing long pants or skirts whenever going to dinner, attending performances, and especially when entering churches and government offices, where shorts and tank tops are inappropriate.

© LIZA PRADO

Artists of all kinds can be found demonstrating their skills and plying their wares in the plazas of Cozumel and elsewhere.

Topless and nude sunbathing are not customary on Mexican beaches, and are rarely practiced in Cancún and other areas frequented by Americans and Canadians. However, on beaches popular with Europeans, especially Playa del Carmen and Tulum, it is more commonplace. Wherever you are, take a look around to help decide whether baring some or all is appropriate.

PHOTOGRAPHING LOCALS

No one enjoys having a stranger take his or her picture for no good reason, and indigenous people are no different. The best policy is simply not to take these photographs unless you've first asked the person's permission and he or she

has agreed. **Tip:** If the potential subject of your photo is a vendor, buy something and *then* ask if you can take a photo—you're more likely to get a positive response.

GREETINGS

Even a small amount of Spanish can go a long way in showing respect and consideration for people you encounter. Make a point of learning basic greetings like *buenos días* (good morning) and *buenas tardes* (good afternoon) and using them in passing, or as preface to a conversation; it is considered somewhat impolite to launch into a discussion without greeting the other person first.

Tips for Travelers

WHAT TO TAKE

Essentials for the Yucatán include sunscreen, sunglasses, and a billed hat. If you wear contacts or glasses, bring a replacement set. A good pair of shoes—or at least Teva-style sandals—are vital for exploring Maya ruins safely, and insect repellent definitely can come in handy. If you lose or forget something, Cancún, Cozumel, Playa del Carmen, Mérida, and Campeche all have huge supermarkets, including Walmart.

OPPORTUNITIES FOR STUDY AND EMPLOYMENT

While it may never approach neighboring Guatemala for the sheer number of Spanish schools, the Yucatán Peninsula has a variety of options for travelers who want to learn the language. Cancún, Isla Mujeres, Playa del Carmen, Mérida, and Campeche City all have schools or private instruction available. All are also well positioned to maximize travelers' enjoyment of the area's richness, whether its beaches, Maya ruins, or colonial cities.

ACCESS FOR TRAVELERS WITH DISABILITIES

Mexico has made many improvements for the blind and people in wheelchairs—many large

stores and tourist centers have ramps or elevators. A growing number of hotels also have rooms designed for guests with disabilities, and museums occasionally create exhibits with, for example, replicas of Maya artifacts or folk art that visually impaired travelers can hold and touch. (None were currently on display at the time of research, however.) That said, Mexico is still a hard place to navigate if you have a disability. Smaller towns are the most problematic, as their sidewalks can be narrow, and even some main streets are not paved. Definitely ask for help—for what Mexico lacks in infrastructure, its people often make up for in graciousness.

TRAVELING WITH CHILDREN

The Yucatán Peninsula is a great place to take kids, whether youngsters or teenagers. The variety of activities and relative ease of transportation help keep everyone happy and engaged. Cancún and the Riviera Maya are especially family friendly, with several different ecoparks and water parks, miles of beaches, and (if all else fails) plenty of malls with movie theaters, arcades, bowling, mini-golf, aquariums, and more. Perhaps best of all, Mexico is a country where family is paramount, so kids—even fussy ones—are welcome just about everywhere.

WOMEN TRAVELING ALONE
Solo women should expect a certain amount of unwanted attention, mostly in the form of whistles and catcalls. It typically happens as they walk down the street and sometimes comes from the most unlikely sources—we saw a man dressed as a clown turn mid-balloon animal to whistle at a woman walking by. Two or more women walking together attract much less unwanted attention, and a woman and man walking together will get none at all (at least of this sort—street vendors are a different story). While annoying and often unnerving, this sort of attention is almost always completely benign, and ignoring it is definitely the best response. Making eye contact or snapping a smart retort only will inspire more attention. Occasionally men will hustle alongside a woman and try to strike up a conversation—if you don't want to engage, a brief *no, gracias* should make that clear. To minimize unwanted attention, avoid revealing clothing, such as tight jeans, low-cut shirts, or bikini tops, as street wear. Carrying a notebook—or creating the appearance of working—also helps.

SENIOR TRAVELERS
Seniors should feel very welcome and safe visiting the Yucatán. Mexico is a country that affords great respect to *personas de la tercera edad* (literally, "people of the third age"), and especially in the tradition-minded Yucatán Peninsula. But as anywhere, older travelers should take certain precautions. The Yucatán, especially Mérida and the surrounding area, is known to be extremely hot and humid, especially May-July. Seniors should take extra care to stay cool and hydrated. Exploring the Maya ruins also can be hot, not to mention exhausting. Bring water and snacks, especially to smaller sites where they may not be commonly sold. Travelers with balance or mobility concerns should think twice about climbing any of the pyramids or other structures. They can be deceptively treacherous, with steps that are steep, uneven, and slick.

Cancún, Playa del Carmen, and Mérida all have state-of-the-art hospitals, staffed by skilled doctors, nurses, and technicians, many of whom speak English. Most prescription medications are available in Mexico, often at discount prices. However, pharmacists are woefully under-trained, and you should always double-check the active ingredients and dosage of any pills you buy here.

GAY AND LESBIAN TRAVELERS
While openly gay women are still rare in Mexico, gay men are increasingly visible in large cities and certain tourist areas. Mérida has a fairly large gay community, of which a number of expat hotel and guesthouse owners are a prominent part. Cancún and Playa del Carmen both have a visible gay presence and a number of gay-friendly venues. Nevertheless, many locals—even in large cities—are not accustomed to open displays of homosexuality and may react openly and negatively. Many hotel attendants also simply don't understand that two travel companions of the same gender may prefer one bed—in some cases they will outright refuse to grant the request. Some couples find it easier to book a room with two queen-size beds and just sleep in one.

TRAVELING WITH IMPORTANT DOCUMENTS
Scan and/or make copies of your passport, tourist card, and airline tickets. Whether you're traveling solo or with others, leave a copy with someone you trust at home. Store another copy online (i.e., your email account) and if you have a travel companion, give a copy to him or her. Be sure to carry a *copy* of your passport and tourist card in your purse or wallet and leave the originals in the hotel safe or locked in your bag; they're a lot more likely to be lost or stolen on the street than taken by hotel staff. When you move from place to place, carry your passport and important documents in a travel pouch, always under your clothing. Write down your credit card and ATM numbers and the 24-hour service numbers and keep those in a safe place.

Health and Safety

SUNBURN

Common sense is the most important factor in avoiding sunburn. Use waterproof and sweatproof sunscreen with a high SPF. Reapply regularly—even the most heavy-duty waterproof sunscreen washes off faster than it claims to on the bottle (or gets rubbed off when you use your towel to dry off). Be extra careful to protect parts of your body that aren't normally exposed to the sun—a good way to cover every inch is to apply sunscreen *before* you get dressed—and give your skin a break from direct sun every few hours. Remember that redness from a sunburn takes several hours to appear—that is, you can be sunburned long before you *look* sunburned.

If you get sunburned, treat it like any other burn by running cool water over it for as long and as often as you can. Do not expose your skin to more sun. Re-burning the skin can result in painful blisters that can easily become infected. There are a number of products designed to relieve sunburns, most with aloe extracts. Finally, be sure to drink plenty of water to keep your skin hydrated.

HEAT EXHAUSTION AND HEAT STROKE

The symptoms of heat exhaustion are cool moist skin, profuse sweating, headache, fatigue, and drowsiness. It is associated with dehydration and commonly happens during or after a strenuous day in the sun, such as while visiting ruins. You should get out of the sun, remove any tight or restrictive clothing, and sip a sports drink such as Gatorade. Cool compresses and raising your feet and legs helps too.

Heat exhaustion is not the same as heat stroke, which is distinguished by a high body temperature, a rapid pulse, and sometimes delirium or even unconsciousness. It is an extremely serious, potentially fatal condition, and victims should be taken to the hospital immediately. In the meantime, wrap the victim in wet sheets, massage the arms and legs to increase circulation, and do not administer large amounts of liquids. Never give liquids if the victim is unconscious.

DIARRHEA

Diarrhea is not an illness in itself, but your body's attempt to get rid of something bad in a hurry; that something can be any one of a number of strains of bacteria, parasites, or amoebae that are often passed from contaminated water. No fun, it is usually accompanied by cramping, dehydration, fever, and of course, frequent trips to the bathroom.

If you get diarrhea, it should pass in a day or two. Anti-diarrheals such as Lomotil and Imodium A-D will plug you up but don't cure you—use them only if you can't be near a bathroom. The malaise you feel from diarrhea typically is from dehydration, not the actual infection, so be sure to drink plenty of fluids—a sports drink such as Gatorade is best. If it's especially bad, ask at your hotel for the nearest *laboratorio* (laboratory or clinic), where the staff can analyze a stool sample for around US$5 and tell you if you have a parasitic infection or a virus. If it's a common infection, the lab technician will tell you what medicine to take. Be aware that medicines for stomach infection are seriously potent, killing not only the bad stuff but the good stuff as well; they'll cure you but leave you vulnerable to another infection. Avoid alcohol and spicy foods for several days afterward.

A few tips for avoiding stomach problems include:

• Only drink bottled water. Avoid using tap water even for brushing your teeth.

• Avoid raw fruits or vegetables that you haven't disinfected and cut yourself. Lettuce is particularly dangerous since water is easily trapped in the leaves. Also, as tasty as they look, avoid the bags of sliced fruit sold from street carts.

- Order your meat dishes well done, even if it's an upscale restaurant. If you've been to a market, you'll see that meat is handled very differently here.

INSECTS

Insects are not of particular concern in the Yucatán, certainly not as they are in other parts of the tropics. Mosquitoes are common, but are not known to carry malaria. Dengue fever, also transmitted by mosquitoes, is present but still here. Some remote beaches, like Isla Holbox and the Costa Maya, may have sand flies or horseflies, but they have been all but eliminated in the more touristed areas. Certain destinations are more likely to be buggy, like forested archaeological zones and coastal bird-watching areas, and travelers should bring and use insect repellent there, if only for extra comfort.

CRIME

The Yucatán Peninsula is generally quite safe, and few travelers report problems with crime of any kind. Cancún is the one area where particular care should be taken, however. You may find illicit drugs relatively easy to obtain, but bear in mind that drug crimes are prosecuted vigorously in Mexico (especially ones involving foreigners), and your country's embassy can do very little to help. Sexual assault and rape have been reported by women at nightclubs, sometimes after having been slipped a "date rape" drug. While the clubs are raucous and sexually charged by definition, women should be especially alert to the people around them and wary of accepting drinks from strangers. In all areas, commonsense precautions are always recommended, such as taking a taxi at night instead of walking (especially if you've been drinking) and avoiding flashing your money and valuables, or leaving them unattended on the beach or elsewhere. Utilize the safety deposit box in your hotel room, if one is available; if you rent a car, get one with a trunk so your bags will not be visible through the window.

Information and Services

MONEY
Currency and Exchange Rates
Mexico's official currency is the peso, divided into 100 centavos. It is typically designated with the symbol $, but you may also see MN$ (*moneda nacional,* or national currency). We've listed virtually all prices in their U.S. dollar equivalent, but occasionally use M$ to indicate the price is in Mexican pesos.

U.S. dollars and E.U. euros are accepted in a few highly touristed locations like the Zona Hotelera in Cancún and the shopping districts of Cozumel and Playa del Carmen. However, you'll want and need pesos everywhere else, as most shopkeepers appreciate visitors paying in the local currency.

At the time of research, US$1 was equal to M$12, slightly less for Canadian dollars, and M$16.25 for euros.

ATMs
Almost every town in the Yucatán Peninsula has an ATM, and they are without question the easiest, fastest, and best way to manage your money. Be aware that you may be charged a transaction fee by the ATM (US$1-3 typically) as well as your home bank (as much as US$5). It's worth asking your bank if it partners with a Mexican bank, and whether transaction fees are lower if you use that bank's cash machines.

Travelers Checks
With the spread of ATMs, travelers checks have stopped being convenient for most travel, especially in a country as developed as Mexico. If you do bring them, you will have to exchange them at a bank or a *casa de cambio* (exchange booth).

Credit Cards
Visa and MasterCard are accepted at all large hotels and many medium and small ones, upscale restaurants, main bus terminals, travel agencies, and many shops throughout Mexico. American Express is accepted much less frequently. Some merchants tack on a 5-10 percent surcharge for any credit card purchase—ask before you pay.

Cash
It's a good idea to bring a small amount of U.S. cash, on the off chance that your ATM or credit cards suddenly stop working; a US$200 reserve should be more than enough for a two-week visit. Stow it away with your other important documents, to be used only if necessary.

Tax
A 12 percent value-added tax (*IVA* in Spanish) applies to hotel rates, restaurant and bar tabs, and gift purchases. When checking in or making reservations at a hotel, ask if tax has already been added. In some cases, the tax is 17 percent.

Bargaining
Bargaining is common and expected in street and artisans' markets, but try not to be too aggressive. Some tourists derive immense and almost irrational pride from haggling over every last cent, and then turn around and spend several times that amount on beer or snacks. The fact is, most bargaining comes down to the difference of a few dollars or even less, and earning those extra dollars is a much bigger deal for most artisans than spending them is to most tourists.

Tipping
While tipping is always a choice, it is a key supplement to many workers' paychecks. In fact, for some—like baggers at the grocery store—the tip is the *only* pay they receive. And while dollars and euros are appreciated, pesos are preferred. **Note:** Foreign coins can't be changed to pesos, so are useless to workers. Average gratuities in the region include:

© LIZA PRADO

A little haggling is okay, but avoid going overboard.

- Archaeological zone guides: 10-15 percent if you're satisfied with the service; for informal guides (typically boys who show you around the site), US$1-2 is customary.

- Gas station attendants: around US$0.50 if your windshield has been cleaned, tires have been filled, or the oil and water have been checked; no tip is expected for simply pumping gas.

- Grocery store baggers: US$0.25-0.50.

- Housekeepers: US$1-2 per day; either left daily or as a lump sum at the end of your stay.

- Porters: about US$1 per bag.

- Taxi drivers: Tipping is not customary.

- Tour guides: 10-15 percent; don't forget the driver—US$1-2 is typical.

- Waiters: 10-15 percent; make sure the gratuity is not already included in the bill.

COMMUNICATIONS AND MEDIA

Postal Service

Mailing letters and postcards from Mexico is neither cheap nor necessarily reliable. Delivery times vary greatly, and letters get "lost" somewhat more than postcards. Letters (under 20 grams) and postcards cost US$1 to the United States and Canada, US$1.20 to Europe and South America, and US$1.35 to the rest of the world. Visit the Correos de México website (www.correosdemexico.com.mx) for pricing on larger packages and other services.

Telephone

Ladatel—Mexico's national phone company—maintains good public phones all over the peninsula and country. Plastic phone cards with little chips in them are sold at most mini-marts and supermarkets in 30-, 50-, 100-, and 200-peso denominations. Ask for a *tarjeta* Ladatel—they

Useful Telephone Numbers

TRAVELER ASSISTANCE
- Emergencies: 060 or 066
- Ángeles Verdes (Green Angels): 078 or 800/903-9200
- Directory Assistance: 044

LONG-DISTANCE DIRECT DIALING
- Domestic long-distance: 01 + area code + number

- International long-distance (United States only): 001 + area code + number
- International long-distance (rest of the world): 00 + country code + area code + number

LONG-DISTANCE COLLECT CALLS
- Domestic long-distance operator: 02
- International long-distance operator (English-speaking): 09

---

are the size and stiffness of a credit card, as opposed to the thin cards used for cell phones. Insert the card into the phone, and the amount on the card is displayed on the screen. Rates and dialing instructions (in Spanish and English) are inside the phone cabin. At the time of research, rates were roughly US$0.10 per minute for local calls, US$0.40 per minute for national calls, and US$0.50 per minute for calls to the United States and Canada.

A number of Internet cafés offer inexpensive **Web-based phone service,** especially in the larger cities where broadband connections are fastest. Rates tend to be significantly lower than those of Ladatel, and you don't have to worry about your card running out.

Beware of phones offering "free" collect or credit card calls; far from being free, their rates are outrageous.

If you've got an unlocked GSM cell phone, you can purchase a local SIM card for around US$15, including US$5 credit, for use during your trip. Calls are expensive, but text messaging is relatively cheap, including to the United States; having two local phones/chips can be especially useful for couples or families traveling together.

To call a local Mexican cellular phone from within Mexico, dial 044 plus the area code and number. If you're calling a Mexican cellular phone that's registered out of the area you're calling from, use the 045 prefix instead.

If you're calling a Mexican mobile phone from outside Mexico, add a 1 between the country code and the area code, and do not use the 044 or 045 prefixes. Be aware that calling a cell phone within Mexico can be very pricey, regardless of where you're calling from.

Internet Access
Internet cafés can be found in virtually every town in the Yucatán Peninsula. Most charge around US$1 per hour, though prices can be much higher in malls and heavily touristed areas. Most places also will burn digital photos onto a CD or DVD—they typically sell blank discs, but travelers should bring their own USB cable.

Wireless Internet is also becoming popular at all levels of hotels; if you need to stay connected while you're on the road, and you're willing to travel with a laptop or tablet, it's easy—and free—to access the Internet.

Newspapers
The most popular daily newspapers in the Yucatán Peninsula are *El Diario de Yucatán, Novedades Quintana Roo,* and *Tribuna de Campeche.* The main national newspapers are also readily available, including *Reforma, La Prensa,* and *La Jornada.* For news in English, you'll find the *Miami Herald Cancún Edition* in Cancún and occasionally in Playa del Carmen and Isla Cozumel.

Cell Phone Calls

MEXICAN LANDLINE TO MEXICAN CELL PHONE:

- Within the same area code: 044 + 3-digit area code + 7-digit phone number
- Different area code: 045 + 3-digit area code + 7-digit phone number

MEXICAN CELL PHONE TO MEXICAN CELL PHONE:

- Within the same area code: 7-digit number only

- Different area code: 3-digit area code + 7-digit number

INTERNATIONAL LANDLINE/CELL PHONE TO A MEXICAN CELL PHONE:

- From U.S. or Canada: 011 + 52 + 1 + 3-digit area code + 7-digit number
- From other countries: international access code + 52 + 1 + 3-digit area code + 7-digit number

Radio and Television

Most large hotels and a number of midsize and small ones have cable or satellite TV, which usually includes CNN (though sometimes in Spanish only), MTV, and other U.S. channels. AM and FM radio options are surprisingly bland—you're more likely to find a good *rock en español* station in California than you are in the Yucatán.

MAPS AND TOURIST INFORMATION
Maps

A husband-and-wife team creates outstanding and exhaustively detailed maps of Cancún, Playa del Carmen, Isla Cozumel, Isla Mujeres, and inland archaeological zones, sold at their website www.cancunmap.com. They're as much guidebooks as maps, with virtually every building and business identified, many with short personal reviews, plus useful information like taxi rates, driving distances, ferry schedules, and more. Maps cost around US$10 and often come with a couple of smaller secondary maps.

Dante produces reasonably reliable maps of the entire Yucatán Peninsula; it also operates a chain of excellent bookstores in Mérida and at various archaeological sites.

Most local tourist offices distribute maps to tourists free of charge, though quality varies considerably. Car rental agencies often have maps, and many hotels create maps for their guests of nearby restaurants and sights.

Tourist Offices

Most cities in the Yucatán have a tourist office, and some have two or more. Some tourist offices are staffed with friendly and knowledgeable people and have a good sense of what tourists are looking for. At others, you'll seriously wonder how the people there were hired. It is certainly worth stopping in if you have a question—you may well get it answered, but don't be surprised if you don't.

Photography and Video

Digital cameras are as ubiquitous in Mexico as they are everywhere else, but memory sticks and other paraphernalia can be prohibitively expensive; bring a spare chip in case your primary one gets lost or damaged. If your chip's capacity is relatively small, and you're not bringing your laptop along, pack a couple of blank DVDs and a USB cable to download and burn photos, which you can do at most Internet cafés.

Video is another great way to capture the color and movement of the Yucatán. Be aware that all archaeological sites charge an additional US$3.75 to bring in a video camera; tripods often are prohibited.

WEIGHTS AND MEASURES
Measurements

Mexico uses the metric system, so distances are in kilometers, weights are in kilograms, gasoline is sold by the liter, and temperatures are given in Celsius. See the chart at the back of this book for conversions from the imperial system.

Time Zone

The Yucatán Peninsula is in U.S. Central Standard Time. Daylight Savings Time is recognized April-October.

Electricity

Mexico uses the 60-cycle, 110-volt AC current common in the United States. Bring a surge protector if you plan to plug in a laptop.

RESOURCES

Spanish Glossary

The form of Spanish spoken in the Yucatán Peninsula is quite clear and understandable, and far less clipped or colloquial than in other countries. That's good news for anyone new to the language, and hoping to use their trip to learn more.

abarrotería: small grocery store

alcalde: mayor or municipal judge

alfarería: pottery

alfarero, alfarera: potter

amigo, amiga: friend

andador: walkway or strolling path

antojitos: Mexican snacks, such as huaraches, flautas, and quesadillas

artesanías: handicrafts, as distinguished from **artesano, artesana,** the person who makes handicrafts

audiencia: one of the royal executive-judicial panels sent to rule areas of Latin America during the 16th century

ayuntamiento: either the town council or the building where it meets

bienes raíces: literally "good roots," but popularly, real estate

boleto: ticket, boarding pass

bucear, buzo: to scuba dive, scuba diver

caballero: gentleman

cabecera: head town of a municipal district, or headquarters in general

cabrón: a bastard; sometimes used affectionately

cacique: chief or boss

calesa: early 1800s-style horse-drawn carriage; also called *calandria*

camionera central: central bus station; alternatively, *terminal camionera*

campesino: country person; farm worker

canasta: basket

cárcel: jail

casa de huéspedes: guesthouse, often operated in a family home

caudillo: dictator or political chief

charro, charra: cowboy, cowgirl

churrigueresque: Spanish baroque architectural style incorporated into many Mexican colonial churches, named after José Churriguera (1665-1725)

cofradía: Catholic fraternal service association, either male or female, mainly in charge of financing and organizing religious festivals

colectivo: a shared public taxi or minibus that picks up and drops off passengers along a designated route; alternatively, *combi*

colegio: preparatory school

colonia: city neighborhood or subdivision; similar to *fraccionamiento* or *barrio*

combi: a shared public minibus; alternatively, *colectivo*

comedor: small restaurant

correo: post office

criollo: person of all-Spanish descent born in the New World

cuadra: city block

Cuaresma: Lent

cuota: literally "toll," commonly refers to a toll highway

curandero, curandera: indigenous medicine man or woman

dama: lady

Domingo de Ramos: Palm Sunday

Don, Doña: title of respect, generally used for an older man or woman

ejido: a constitutional, government-sponsored form of community, with shared land ownership and cooperative decision-making

encomienda: colonial award of tribute from a designated indigenous district

farmacia: pharmacy or drugstore

finca: farm

fraccionamiento: city sector or subdivision; similar to *colonia* or *barrio*

gasolinera: gasoline station

gringo: term referring to North American caucasians, sometimes derogatorily, sometimes not

grito: impassioned cry; *El Grito* commonly refers to Mexican Independence Day celebrations, from Hidalgo's *Grito de Dolores*

hacienda: large landed estate; also the government treasury

impuestos, I.V.A. (pronounced EE-va): taxes, value-added tax

indígena: indigenous person; commonly, but incorrectly, an indian (*indio*)

jardín: garden or small park

jejenes: "no-see-um" biting gnats

judiciales: the federal or state police, best known to motorists for their highway checkpoint inspections; alternatively, *federales*

lancha: small motorboat; alternatively, *panga*

larga distancia: long-distance telephone service, or the *caseta* (booth) where it's provided

licenciado: academic degree (abbr. Lic.) approximately equivalent to a bachelor's degree

lonchería: small lunch counter, usually serving juices, sandwiches, and *antojitos* (Mexican snacks)

machismo; macho: exaggerated sense of maleness; person who holds such a sense of himself

mescal: alcoholic beverage distilled from the fermented hearts of maguey (century plant)

mestizo: person of mixed European/indigenous descent

milpa: native farm plot, usually of corn, squash, and/or beans

mordida: slang for bribe; literally, "little bite"

palapa: thatched-roof structure, often open air

panga: small motorboat; alternatively, *lancha*

parque central: town plaza or central square; alternatively, *zócalo*

PEMEX: government gasoline station, acronym for "Petróleos Mexicanos," Mexico's national oil corporation

peninsulares: the Spanish-born ruling colonial elite

petate: a mat, traditionally woven of palm leaf

plan: political manifesto, usually by a leader or group consolidating or seeking power

plaza: shopping mall

policía: municipal police, alternatively *preventativa*

Porfiriato: the 34-year (1876-1910) ruling period of president-dictator Porfirio Díaz

pozole: popular stew of hominy in broth, usually topped by shredded pork, cabbage, and diced onion

presidencia municipal: the headquarters, like a U.S. city or county hall, of a Mexican *municipio*, a county-like local governmental unit

propina: tip, as at a restaurant or hotel; alternatively, *servicio*

pueblo: town or people

puta: whore

quinta: a villa or country house

retorno: highway turnaround

Semana Santa: literally Holy Week, the week before Easter, a popular travel period for Mexicans

temporada: season, as in *temporada alta/baja* (high/low season)

tenate: soft, pliable basket, without handle, woven of palm leaf

terminal camionera: central bus station; alternatively, *camionera central*

vecindad: neighborhood, alternatively *barrio*

zócalo: town plaza or central square; alternatively, *parque central*

ABBREVIATIONS

Av.: *avenida* (avenue)

Blvd.: *bulevar* (boulevard)

Calz.: *calzada* (thoroughfare, main road)

Carr.: *carretera* (highway)

Col.: *colonia* (subdivision)

Nte.: *norte* (north)

Ote.: *oriente* (east)

Pte.: *poniente* (west)

s/n: *sin número* (no street number)

Yucatec Maya Glossary

The Maya language family includes 30 distinct languages, together spoken by nearly six million people in Mexico, Guatemala, and Belize. Yucatec Maya is spoken by around 800,000 people, and is the most commonly spoken Maya language in the Yucatán Peninsula (and second overall, after K'iche in Guatemala). Most ancient glyphs were written in early forms of Yucatec Maya or another Maya language, Ch'ol.

MAYA GODS AND CEREMONIES

Acanum: protective deity of hunters
Ahau Can: serpent lord and highest priest
Ahau Chamehes: deity of medicine
Ah Cantzicnal: aquatic deity
Ah Chuy Kak: god of violent death and sacrifice
Ahcit Dzamalcum: protective god of fishermen
Ah Cup Cacap: god of the underworld who denies air
Ah Itzám: the water witch
Ah kines: priests that consult the oracles and preside over ceremonies and sacrifices
Ahpua: god of fishing
Ah Puch: god of death
Ak'Al: sacred marsh where water abounds
Bacaboob: supporters of the sky and guardians of the cardinal points, who form a single god, Ah Cantzicnal Becabs
Bolontiku: the nine lords of the night
Chaac: god of rain and agriculture
Chac Bolay Can: butcher serpent living in the underworld
Chaces: priests' assistants in agricultural and other ceremonies
Cihuateteo: women who become goddesses through death in childbirth
Cit Chac Coh: god of war
Hetzmek: ceremony when the child is first carried astride the hip
Hobnil Bacab: bee god, protector of beekeepers
Holcanes: warriors charged with obtaining slaves for sacrifice

Hunab Ku: giver of life, builder of the universe, and father of Itzámna
Ik: god of the wind
Itzámna: lord of the skies, creator of the beginning, god of time
Ixchel: goddess of birth, fertility, and medicine; credited with inventing spinning
Ixtab: goddess of the cord and of suicide by hanging
Kinich: face of the sun
Kukulcán: quetzal-serpent, plumed serpent
Metnal: the underworld, place of the dead
Nacom: warrior chief
Noh Ek: Venus
Pakat: god of violent death
Zec: spirit lords of beehives

FOOD AND DRINK

alche: inebriating drink, sweetened with honey and used for ceremonies and offerings
ic: chili
itz: sweet potato
kabaxbuul: heaviest meal of the day, eaten at dusk and containing cooked black beans
kah: pinole flour
kayem: ground maize
macal: a root
muxubbak: tamale
on: avocado
op: plum
p'ac: tomatoes
put: papaya
tzamna: black bean
uah: tortillas
za: maize drink

ANIMALS

acehpek: dog used for deer hunting
ah maax cal: prattling monkey
ah maycuy: chestnut deer
ah sac dziu: white thrush
ah xixteel ul: rugged land conch
bil: hairless dog reared for food
cutz: wild turkey

cutzha: duck
hoh: crow
icim: owl
jaleb: hairless dog
keh: deer
kitam: wild boar
muan: evil bird related to death
que: parrot
thul: rabbit
tzo: domestic turkey
utiu: coyote

MUSIC AND FESTIVALS

ah paxboob: musicians
bexelac: turtle shell used as percussion instrument
chohom: dance performed in ceremonies related to fishing
chul: flute
hom: trumpet
kayab: percussion instrument fashioned from turtle shell
Oc na: festival where old idols of a temple are broken and replaced with new ones
okot uil: dance performed during the Pocan ceremony
Pacum chac: festival in honor of the war gods
tunkul: drum
zacatan: drum made from a hollowed tree trunk; one opening is covered with hide

ELEMENTS OF TIME

baktun: 144,000-day Maya calendar
chumuc akab: midnight
chumuc kin: midday
emelkin: sunset
haab: solar calendar of 360 days plus five extra days of misfortune, which complete the final month
kaz akab: dusk
kin: the sun, the day, the unity of time
potakab: time before dawn
yalhalcab: dawn

NUMBERS

hun: one
ca: two
ox: three
can: four
ho: five

uac: six
uuc: seven
uacax: eight
bolon: nine
lahun: ten
buluc: eleven
lahca: twelve
oxlahum: thirteen
canlahum: fourteen
holahun: fifteen
uaclahun: sixteen
uuclahun: seventeen
uacaclahun: eighteen
bolontahun: nineteen
hunkal: twenty

PLANTS AND TREES

ha: cacao seed
kan ak: plant that produces a yellow dye
ki: sisal
kiixpaxhkum: chayote
kikche: tree trunk that is used to make canoes
kuche: red cedar tree
k'uxub: annatto tree
piim: fiber of the cotton tree
taman: cotton plant
tauch: black zapote tree
tazon te: moss

MISCELLANEOUS WORDS

ah kay kin bak: meat-seller
chaltun: water cistern
cha te: black vegetable dye
chi te: eugenia, plant for dyeing
ch'oh: indigo
ek: dye
hadzab: wooden swords
halach uinic: leader
mayacimil: smallpox epidemic
palapa: traditional Maya structure constructed without nails or tools
pic: underskirt
ploms: rich people
suyen: square blanket
xanab: sandals
xicul: sleeveless jacket decorated with feathers
xul: stake with a pointed, fire-hardened tip
yuntun: slings

Spanish Phrasebook

Whether you speak a little or a lot, using your Spanish will surely make your vacation a lot more fun. You'll soon see that Mexicans truly appreciate your efforts and your willingness to speak their language.

Spanish commonly uses 30 letters–the familiar English 26, plus four straightforward additions: ch, ll, ñ, and rr.

PRONUNCIATION

Once you learn them, Spanish pronunciation rules–in contrast to English and other languages–generally don't change. Spanish vowels generally sound softer than in English. (*Note:* The capitalized syllables that follow receive stronger accents.)

Vowels

a like ah, as in "hah": *agua* AH-gooah (water), *pan* PAHN (bread), and *casa* CAH-sah (house)

e like eh, as in "hem": *mesa* MEH-sah (table), *tela* TEH-lah (cloth), and *de* DEH (of, from)

i like ee, as in "need": *diez* dee-EHZ (ten), *comida* ko-MEE-dah (meal), and *fin* FEEN (end)

o like oh, as in "go": *peso* PEH-soh (weight), *ocho* OH-choh (eight), and *poco* POH-koh (a bit)

u like oo, as in "cool": *uno* OO-noh (one), *cuarto* KOOAHR-toh (room), and *usted* oos-TEHD (you); when it follows a "q" the **u** is silent: *quiero* ki-EH-ro (I want); when it follows an "h" or has an umlaut, it's pronounced like "w": *huevo* WEH-vo (egg)

Consonants

b, d, f, k, l, m, n, p, q, s, t, v, w, x, y, z, and ch pronounced almost as in English; **h** is silent

c like k, as in "keep": *cuarto* KOOAR-toh (room), *Tepic* tay-PEEK (capital of Nayarit state); when it precedes "e" or "i," pro-nounce **c** like s, as in "sit": *cerveza* sehr-VEH-sah (beer), *encima* ehn-SEE-mah (atop)

g like g, as in "gift" when it precedes "a," "o," "u," or a consonant: *gato* GAH-toh (cat), *hago* AH-goh (I do, make); otherwise, pro-nounce **g** like h, as in "hat": *giro* HEE-roh (money order), *gente* HEN-tay (people)

j like h, as in "has": *Jueves* HOOEH-vehs (Thursday), *mejor* meh-HOR (better)

ll like y, as in "yes": *toalla* toh-AH-yah (towel), *ellos* EH-yohs (they, them)

ñ like ny, as in "canyon": *año* AH-nyo (year), *señor* SEH-nyor (mister, sir)

r is lightly trilled: *pero* PEH-roh (but), *tres* TREHS (three), *cuatro* KOOAH-troh (four)

rr like a Spanish r, but with much more em-phasis and trill: *burro* (donkey), *carretera* (highway), *ferrocarril* (railroad)

Note: The single exception to the above is the pronunciation of **y** when it's being used as the Spanish word for "and," as in *Eva y Leo*. In such case, pronounce it like the English ee, as in "keep": Eva "ee" Leo (Eva and Leo).

Accent

The rule for accent, the relative stress given to syllables within a given word, is straightforward. If a word ends in a vowel, an "n," or an "s," ac-cent the next-to-last syllable; if not, accent the last syllable.

Pronounce *gracias* GRAH-seeahs (thank you), *orden* OHR-dehn (order), and *carretera* kah-reh-TEH-rah (highway) with the stress on the next-to-last syllable.

Otherwise, accent the last syllable: *venir* vay-NEER (to come), *ferrocarril* feh-roh-cah-REEL (railroad), and *edad* eh-DAHD (age).

Exceptions to the accent rule are always marked with an accent sign: (á, é, í, ó, or ú), such as *teléfono* teh-LEH-foh-noh (telephone), *jabón* hah-BON (soap), and *rápido* RAH-pee-doh (rapid).

BASIC AND COURTEOUS EXPRESSIONS

Most Spanish-speakers consider formalities important. Whenever approaching anyone, try to say the appropriate salutation—good morning, good evening, etc. Standing alone, the greeting *hola* (hello) can sound brusque.

Hello. *Hola.*
Good morning. *Buenos días.*
Good afternoon. *Buenas tardes.*
Good evening. *Buenas noches.*
How are you? *¿Cómo está Usted?*
Very well, thank you. *Muy bien, gracias.*
Okay; good. *Bien.*
Not okay; bad. *No muy bien; mal.*
So-so. *Más o menos.*
And you? *¿Y usted?*
Thank you. *Gracias.*
Thank you very much. *Muchas gracias.*
You're very kind. *Muy amable.*
You're welcome. *De nada.*
Good-bye. *Adios.*
See you later. *Hasta luego.*
please *por favor*
yes *sí*
no *no*
I don't know. *No sé.*
Just a moment, please. *Un momento, por favor.*
Excuse me, please (when you're trying to get attention). *Disculpe* or *Con permiso.*
Excuse me (when you've made a mistake). *Lo siento.*
Pleased to meet you. *Mucho gusto.*
Do you speak English? *¿Habla Usted inglés?*
Is English spoken here? *¿Se habla inglés?*
I don't speak Spanish well. *No hablo bien el español.*
I don't understand. *No entiendo.*
How do you say... in Spanish? *¿Cómo se dice... en español?*
What is your name? *¿Cómo se llama Usted?*
My name is... *Me llamo...*
Would you like... *¿Quisiera Usted...*
Let's go to... *Vamos a...*

TERMS OF ADDRESS

When in doubt, use the formal *Usted* (you) as a form of address.

I *yo*
you (formal) *Usted*
you (familiar) *tu*
he/him *él*
she/her *ella*
we/us *nosotros*
you (plural) *ustedes*
they/them *ellos* (all males or mixed gender); *ellas* (all females)
mister, sir *señor*
missus, ma'am *señora*
miss, young lady *señorita*
wife *esposa*
husband *esposo*
friend *amigo* (male); *amiga* (female)
boyfriend; girlfriend *novio; novia*
son; daughter *hijo; hija*
brother; sister *hermano; hermana*
father; mother *padre; madre*
grandfather; grandmother *abuelo; abuela*

TRANSPORTATION

Where is...? *¿Dónde está...?*
How far is it to...? *¿A cuánto está...?*
from... to... *de... a...*
How many blocks? *¿Cuántas cuadras?*
Where (Which) is the way to...? *¿Dónde está el camino a...?*
the bus station *la terminal de autobuses*
the bus stop *la parada de autobuses*
Where is this bus going? *¿Adónde va este autobús?*
the taxi stand *la parada de taxis*
the train station *la estación de ferrocarril*
the boat *el barco* or *la lancha*
the airport *el aeropuerto*
I'd like a ticket to... *Quisiera un boleto a...*
first (second) class *primera (segunda) clase*
roundtrip *ida y vuelta*
reservation *reservación*
baggage *equipaje*
Stop here, please. *Pare aquí, por favor.*
the entrance *la entrada*
the exit *la salida*
the ticket office *la taquilla*

(**very**) **near; far** *(muy) cerca; lejos*
to; toward *a*
by; through *por*
from *de*
the right *la derecha*
the left *la izquierda*
straight ahead *derecho; directo*
in front *en frente*
beside *al lado*
behind *atrás*
the corner *la esquina*
the stoplight *el semáforo*
a turn *una vuelta*
here *aquí*
somewhere around here *por aquí*
right there *allí*
somewhere around there *por allá*
street; boulevard *calle; bulevar*
highway *carretera*
bridge *puente*
toll *cuota*
address *dirección*
north; south *norte; sur*
east; west *oriente (este); poniente (oeste)*

ACCOMMODATIONS
hotel *hotel*
Is there a room? *¿Hay cuarto?*
May I (may we) see it? *¿Podría (podríamos) verlo?*
What is the rate? *¿Cuál es la tarifa?*
Is that your best rate? *¿Es su mejor precio?*
Is there something cheaper? *¿Hay algo más económico?*
a single room *un cuarto sencillo*
a double room *un cuarto doble*
double bed *cama matrimonial*
twin bed *cama individual*
with private bath *con baño privado*
hot water *agua caliente*
shower *ducha; regadera*
towels *toallas*
soap *jabón*
toilet paper *papel higiénico*
blanket *cobija*
sheets *sábanas*
air-conditioned *aire acondicionado*
fan *abanico; ventilador*

key *llave*
manager *gerente*

FOOD
I'm hungry *Tengo hambre.*
I'm thirsty. *Tengo sed.*
menu *carta; menú*
order *orden*
glass *vaso*
fork *tenedor*
knife *cuchillo*
spoon *cuchara*
napkin *servilleta*
soft drink *refresco*
coffee *café*
tea *té*
drinking water *agua pura; agua potable*
carbonated water *agua mineral*
bottled uncarbonated water *agua sin gas*
beer *cerveza*
wine *vino*
milk *leche*
juice *jugo*
cream *crema*
sugar *azúcar*
cheese *queso*
snack *antojito; botana*
breakfast *desayuno*
lunch *almuerzo or comida*
daily lunch special *comida corrida*
dinner *cena*
the check *la cuenta*
eggs *huevos*
bread *pan*
salad *ensalada*
fruit *fruta*
mango *mango*
watermelon *sandía*
papaya *papaya*
banana *plátano*
apple *manzana*
orange *naranja*
lime *limón*
fish *pescado*
shellfish *mariscos*
shrimp *camarones*
meat (without) *(sin) carne*
chicken *pollo*

pork *puerco*
beef; steak *res; bistec*
bacon; ham *tocino; jamón*
fried *frito*
roasted *asado*
barbecue; barbecued *barbacoa; al carbón*
food to go *comida para llevar; para llevar*
delivery service *servicio a domicilio*

SHOPPING

money *dinero*
money-exchange bureau *casa de cambio*
I would like to exchange travelers checks. *Quisiera cambiar cheques de viajero.*
What is the exchange rate? *¿Cuál es el tipo de cambio?*
How much is the commission? *¿Cuánto cuesta la comisión?*
Do you accept credit cards? *¿Aceptan tarjetas de crédito?*
money order *giro*
How much does it cost? *¿Cuánto cuesta?*
What is your final price? *¿Cuál es su último precio?*
expensive *caro*
cheap *barato; económico*
more *más*
less *menos*
a little *un poco*
too much *demasiado*

HEALTH

Help me please. *Ayúdeme por favor.*
I am ill. *Estoy enfermo.*
Call a doctor. *Llame un doctor.*
Take me to... *Lléveme a...*
hospital *hospital; clinica medica*
drugstore *farmacia*
pain *dolor*
fever *fiebre*
headache *dolor de cabeza*
stomachache *dolor de estómago*
burn *quemadura*
cramp *calambre*
nausea *náusea*
vomiting *vomitar*
medicine *medicina*

antibiotic *antibiótico*
pill; tablet *pastilla*
aspirin *aspirina*
ointment; cream *pomada; crema*
bandage *venda*
cotton *algodón*
sanitary napkins *Kotex*
birth control pills *pastillas anticonceptivas*
contraceptive foam *espuma anticonceptiva*
condoms *preservativos; condones*
contact lenses *pupilentes*
glasses *lentes*
dental floss *hilo dental*
dentist *dentista*
toothbrush *cepillo de dientes*
toothpaste *pasta de dientes*
toothache *dolor de dientes*
delivery service *servicio a domicilio*

POST OFFICE AND COMMUNICATIONS

long-distance telephone *teléfono de larga distancia*
I would like to call... *Quisiera llamar a...*
collect *por cobrar*
person to person *persona a persona*
credit card *tarjeta de crédito*
post office *correo*
letter *carta*
stamp *estampilla, timbre*
postcard *tarjeta*
air mail *correo aereo*
registered *registrado*
money order *giro*
package; box *paquete; caja*
string; tape *cuerda; cinta*
Internet *internet*
Internet café *ciber café; ciber*
website *página web*
Web search *búsqueda*
link *enlace*
email *correo electrónico*
Skype *Skype*
Facebook *face*

AT THE BORDER

border *frontera*
customs *aduana*

immigration *migración*
tourist card *tarjeta de turista*
inspection *inspección; revisión*
passport *pasaporte*
profession *profesión*
marital status *estado civil*
single *soltero*
married; divorced *casado; divorciado*
widowed *viudado* (male); *viudada* (female)
insurance *seguro*
title *título*
driver's license *licencia de manejar*

AT THE GAS STATION
gas station *gasolinera*
gasoline *gasolina*
unleaded *sin plomo*
fill it up, please *lleno, por favor*
tire *llanta*
tire repair shop *vulcanizadora*
air *aire*
water *agua*
oil; oil change *aceite; cambio de aceite*
grease *grasa*
My... doesn't work. *Mi... no sirve.*
battery *batería*
radiator *radiador*
alternator *alternador*
generator *generador*
tow truck *grúa*
repair shop *taller mecánico*
tune-up *afinación*
auto parts store *refaccionería*

VERBS
In Spanish, verbs employ mostly predictable forms and come in three classes, which end in *ar*, *er*, and *ir*. Note that the first-person (*yo*) verb form is often irregular.

to buy *comprar*
I buy, you (he, she, it) buys *compro, compra*
we buy, you (they) buy *compramos, compran*

to eat *comer*
I eat, you (he, she, it) eats *como, come*
we eat, you (they) eat *comemos, comen*

to climb *subir*
I climb, you (he, she, it) climbs *subo, sube*
we climb, you (they) climb *subimos, suben*

Here are more (with irregularities indicated):

to do or make *hacer* (regular except for *hago*, I do or make)
to go *ir* (very irregular: *voy, va, vamos, van*)
to go (walk) *andar*
to love *amar*
to work *trabajar*
to want *desear, querer*
to need *necesitar*
to read *leer*
to write *escribir*
to repair *reparar*
to stop *parar*
to get off (the bus) *bajar*
to arrive *llegar*
to stay (remain) *quedar*
to stay (lodge) *hospedar*
to leave *salir* (regular except for *salgo*, I leave)
to look at *mirar*
to look for *buscar*
to give *dar* (regular except for *doy*, I give)
to carry *llevar*
to have *tener* (irregular but important: *tengo, tiene, tenemos, tienen*)
to come *venir* (similarly irregular: *vengo, viene, venimos, vienen*)

Spanish has two forms of "to be":

to be *estar* (regular except for *estoy*, I am)
to be *ser* (very irregular: *soy, es, somos, son*)

Use *estar* when speaking of location or a temporary state of being: "I am at home." *"Estoy en casa."* "I'm sick." *"Estoy enfermo."* Use *ser* for a permanent state of being: "I am a doctor." *"Soy doctora."*

NUMBERS
zero *cero*
one *uno*

two *dos*
three *tres*
four *cuatro*
five *cinco*
six *seis*
seven *siete*
eight *ocho*
nine *nueve*
10 *diez*
11 *once*
12 *doce*
13 *trece*
14 *catorce*
15 *quince*
16 *dieciseis*
17 *diecisiete*
18 *dieciocho*
19 *diecinueve*
20 *veinte*
21 *veintiuno*
30 *treinta*
40 *cuarenta*
50 *cincuenta*
60 *sesenta*
70 *setenta*
80 *ochenta*
90 *noventa*
100 *cien*
101 *cientiuno*
200 *doscientos*
500 *quinientos*
1,000 *mil*
10,000 *diez mil*
100,000 *cien mil*
1,000,000 *millón*
one half *medio*
one third *un tercio*
one fourth *un cuarto*

TIME

What time is it? *¿Qué hora es?*
It's one o'clock. *Es la una.*
It's three in the afternoon. *Son las tres de la tarde.*
It's 4am *Son las cuatro de la mañana.*
six-thirty *seis y media*
a quarter till eleven *un cuarto para las once*
a quarter past five *las cinco y cuarto*
an hour *una hora*

DAYS AND MONTHS

Monday *lunes*
Tuesday *martes*
Wednesday *miércoles*
Thursday *jueves*
Friday *viernes*
Saturday *sábado*
Sunday *domingo*
today *hoy*
tomorrow *mañana*
yesterday *ayer*
January *enero*
February *febrero*
March *marzo*
April *abril*
May *mayo*
June *junio*
July *julio*
August *agosto*
September *septiembre*
October *octubre*
November *noviembre*
December *diciembre*
a week *una semana*
a month *un mes*
after *después*
before *antes*

Suggested Reading

The following titles provide insight into the Yucatán Peninsula and the Maya people. A few of these books are more easily obtained in Mexico, but all of them will cost less in the United States. Most are nonfiction, though several are fiction and great to throw into your carry-on for a good read on the plane, or for when you're in a Yucatecan mood. Happy reading!

Beletsky, Les. *Travellers' Wildlife Guides: Southern Mexico*. Northampton, MA: Interlink Books, 2006. A perfect companion guide if you plan on bird-watching, diving/snorkeling, hiking, or canoeing your way through your vacation. Excellent illustrations.

Coe, Andrew. *Archaeological Mexico: A Traveler's Guide to Ancient Cities and Sacred Sites*. Emeryville, CA: Avalon Travel Publishing, 2001.

Coe, Michael D. *Breaking the Maya Code*. New York: Thames and Hudson, 1999. A fascinating account of how epigraphers, linguists, and archaeologists succeeded in deciphering Maya hieroglyphics.

Coe, Michael D. *The Maya*. New York: Thames and Hudson, 2005. A well-illustrated, easy-to-read volume on the Maya people.

Cortés, Hernán. *Five Letters*. New York: Gordon Press, 1977. Cortés's letters to the king of Spain, telling of his accomplishments and justifying his actions in the New World.

Davies, Nigel. *The Ancient Kingdoms of Mexico*. New York: Penguin Books, 1991. An excellent study of the preconquest of the indigenous peoples of Mexico.

De Landa, Bishop Diego. *Yucatán Before and After the Conquest*. New York: Dover Publications, 2012. This book, translated by William Gates from the original 1566 volume, has served as the basis for much of the research that has taken place since.

Díaz del Castillo, Bernal. *The Conquest of New Spain*. New York: Penguin Books, 1963. History straight from the adventurer's reminiscences, translated by J. M. Cohen.

Fehrenbach, T. R. *Fire and Blood: A History of Mexico*. New York: Collier Books, 1995. Over 3,000 years of Mexican history, related in a way that will keep you reading.

Ferguson, William M. *Maya Ruins of Mexico in Color*. Norman, OK: University of Oklahoma Press, 1985. Good reading before you go, but too bulky to carry along. Oversized with excellent drawings and illustrations of the archaeological structures of the Maya.

Franz, Carl, and Lorena Havens. *The People's Guide to Mexico*. Berkeley, CA: Avalon Travel, 2012. A humorous guide filled with witty anecdotes and helpful general information for visitors to Mexico. Don't expect any specific city information, just nuts-and-bolts hints for traveling south of the border.

Greene, Graham. *The Power and the Glory*. New York: Penguin Books, 2003. A novel that takes place in the 1920s about a priest and the antichurch movement that gripped the country.

Heffern, Richard. *Secrets of the Mind-Altering Plants of Mexico*. New York: Pyramid Books, 1974. A fascinating study of many substances, from ancient ritual hallucinogens to today's medicines that are found in Mexico.

Maya: Divine Kings of the Rain Forest. Cologne: Könemann, 2006. A beautifully compiled book of essays, photographs, and sketches relating to the Maya, past and present. Too heavy to take on the road but an excellent read.

McNay Brumfield, James. *A Tourist in the Yucatán.* Watsonville, CA: Tres Picos Press, 2004. A decent thriller that takes place in the Yucatán Peninsula; good for the beach or a long bus ride.

Meyer, Michael, and William Sherman. *The Course of Mexican History.* New York: Oxford University Press, 2006. A concise one-volume history of Mexico.

Nelson, Ralph. *Popul Vuh: The Great Mythological Book of the Ancient Maya.* Boston: Houghton Mifflin, 1974. An easy-to-read translation of myths handed down orally by the Quiche Maya, family to family, until written down after the Spanish conquest.

Perry, Richard, and Rosalind Perry. *Maya Missions: Exploring Colonial Yucatán.* Santa Barbara, CA: Espadaña Press, 2002. Detailed and informative guide, including excellent hand-drawn illustrations, about numerous colonial missions and structures in the Yucatán Peninsula.

Sodi, Demetrio M. (in collaboration with Adela Fernández). *The Mayas.* Mexico City: Panama Editorial S.A., 1987. This small book presents a fictionalized account of life among the Maya before the conquest. Easy reading for anyone who enjoys fantasizing about what life *might* have been like before recorded history in the Yucatán.

Stephens, John L. *Incidents of Travel in Central America, Chiapas, and Yucatán.* 2 vols. New York: Cosimo Classics, 2008. Good companions to refer to when traveling in the area. Stephens and illustrator Frederick Catherwood rediscovered many of the Maya ruins on their treks that took place in the mid-1800s. Easy reading.

Thompson, J. Eric. *Maya Archaeologist.* Norman, OK: University of Oklahoma Press, 1963. Thompson, a noted Maya scholar, traveled and worked at many of the Maya ruins in the 1930s.

Thompson, J. Eric. *The Rise and Fall of the Maya Civilization.* Norman, OK: University of Oklahoma Press, 1973. One man's story of the Maya. Excellent reading.

Webster, David. *The Fall of the Ancient Maya.* New York: Thames and Hudson, 2002. A careful and thorough examination of the possible causes of one of archaeology's great unsolved mysteries—the collapse of the Classic Maya in the 8th century.

Werner, David. *Where There Is No Doctor.* Palo Alto, CA: The Hesperian Foundation, 1992. This is an invaluable medical aid to anyone traveling not only to isolated parts of Mexico but to any place in the world where there's not a doctor.

Wolf, Eric. *Sons of the Shaking Earth.* Chicago: University of Chicago Press, 1962. An anthropological study of the indigenous and mestizo people of Mexico and Guatemala.

Wright, Ronald. *Time Among the Maya.* New York: Grove Press, 2000. A narrative that takes the reader through the Maya country of today, with historical comments that help put the puzzle together.

Internet Resources

www.almalibrebooks.com
Bookstore website that's packed with information about Puerto Morelos; also has listings for short- and long-term rentals.

www.bacalarmosaico.com
Laguna Bacalar's online resource for tourists and locals—a mishmash of information, in a good way.

www.backyardnature.net/yucatan
Notes and observations by an experienced naturalist about the major plants and animal species in the northern Yucatán Peninsula.

www.cancunmap.com
An excellent source of detailed maps of the Riviera Maya and some inland archaeological zones.

www.cancuntips.com.mx
The online version of Cancún's main tourist magazine, with tons of listings, travel tips, and tourist resources.

www.colonial-mexico.com
Photos and text on colonial Mexico by Richard and Rosalind Perry, authors of the *Maya Missions* handbook.

www.cozumelinsider.com
Good website covering Cozumel, including current tourist information and issues important to locals.

www.islamujeres.gob.mx
Official website of the island of Isla Mujeres, including information for tourists.

www.islamujeres.info
Excellent resource for the goings-on about Isla Mujeres, including activities, ferry schedules,

and even a message board with participation by longtime expats.

www.locogringo.com
Website with extensive business listings for the Riviera Maya.

www.mapapocketcancun.com
Online resource for Cancun's restaurants, including menus, reviews, and discount coupons.

www.mesoweb.com
Website relating to Mesoamerican cultures, including detailed reports and photos of past and current archaeological digs.

www.mostlymaya.com
Eclectic but informative website on various Maya topics; especially useful for info on Maya languages.

www.playa.info
An established website with lots of travel planning information to Playa and the Riviera Maya. It also has a popular forum for asking questions and sharing tips.

www.puertoaventuras.com
Good website with updated information about Puerto Aventuras.

www.qroo.gob.mx
Official website of Quintana Roo state, including information for tourists.

www.thisiscozumel.com
Excellent website for Cozumel, including up-to-date tourist information.

www.todotulum.com
Great resource for Tulum—everything from nightlife to real estate.

www.travelyucatan.com

Detailed information and practical advice about traveling to and around the Yucatán Peninsula.

www.visitmahahual.com

Website with information on activities, hotels, and restaurants in Mahahual.

Index

List of Maps

Acknowledgments

From Gary Chandler and Liza Prado

Our sincere thanks, first, to the hundreds of everyday residents of Cancún, Cozumel, and the Riviera Maya—from bus drivers to hotel workers to passersby—whose help and patience were essential to researching this book. We're also grateful for the tips and information we received from travelers and expatriates along the way, and from those who contacted us with suggestions and comments.

Thank you to coauthor and guidebook veteran Beth Kohn, for contributing to the Inland Archaeological Zones chapter. When we realized we needed help with the section, Beth was the first person we thought of.

On the road, special thanks go to Steven at Casa Sirena, and Hillary and Jill at Casa El Pío, both in Isla Mujeres; to Eliane at Tamarindo B&B in Cozumel; and to Gibrán Rodriguez at Mallorca Hotel & Suites in Cancún, for their invaluable help and generosity.

We are fortunate to have such excellent editorial and production support from everyone at Moon Handbooks. Thanks to Grace Fujimoto for sending us off and to Kathryn Ettinger for her sharp editing. Many thanks as well to Lucie Ericksen and the graphics department, and to Kat Bennett and the cartography department, for making this book look so great, inside and out.

Finally, we're extremely grateful for the support and encouragement we enjoy from friends and family. Thank you especially to Mom and Dad Prado for their help on the ground in Mexico and back home in Colorado, to Grandpa Joe and Grandma Elyse for seeing us down the home stretch, and to Koko—teacher, friend, and babysitter extraordinaire. And of course our life is immeasurably richer for having Eva and Leo in it: There's nothing like having kids to reopen your eyes to the world around you.

From Beth Kohn

Thank you to Denis Larsen at Casa Hamaca Guesthouse in Valladolid, Lee Christie of Genesis Retreat Ek' Balam, and the state tourism office in Mérida.

www.moon.com

DESTINATIONS | EXPLORE | MAPS | BOOKS

MOON.COM is ready to help plan your next trip! Filled with fresh trip ideas and strategies, interviews, informative travel tips, and a printable map library, Moon.com is all you need to get out and explore the world—or even places in your own backyard. While at Moon.com, sign up for our monthly email newsletter for updates on new guidebook releases, giveaway alerts, and expert advice from our on-the-go Moon authors. When you travel with Moon, expect an experience that is uncommon and truly unique.

KEEP UP WITH MOON: f 🐦 📌

MAP SYMBOLS

═══ Expressway	【 Highlight	✈ Airport	⚓ Golf Course
─── Primary Road	○ City/Town	✈ Airfield	🅿 Parking Area
─── Secondary Road	◉ State Capital	▲ Mountain	🔺 Archaeological Site
─ ─ ─ Unpaved Road	✹ National Capital	✦ Unique Natural Feature	♦ Church
- - - - Trail	★ Point of Interest		🟥 Gas Station
·········· Ferry	• Accommodation	🌴 Waterfall	🐬 Dive Site
━·━·━ Railroad	▾ Restaurant/Bar	⚑ Park	🌿 Mangrove
═══ Pedestrian Walkway	■ Other Location	ⓣ Trailhead	〰 Reef
▭▭▭ Stairs	▲ Campground	🕯 Lighthouse	〰 Swamp

CONVERSION TABLES

°C = (°F - 32) / 1.8
°F = (°C x 1.8) + 32
1 inch = 2.54 centimeters (cm)
1 foot = 0.304 meters (m)
1 yard = 0.914 meters
1 mile = 1.6093 kilometers (km)
1 km = 0.6214 miles
1 fathom = 1.8288 m
1 chain = 20.1168 m
1 furlong = 201.168 m
1 acre = 0.4047 hectares
1 sq km = 100 hectares
1 sq mile = 2.59 square km
1 ounce = 28.35 grams
1 pound = 0.4536 kilograms
1 short ton = 0.90718 metric ton
1 short ton = 2,000 pounds
1 long ton = 1.016 metric tons
1 long ton = 2,240 pounds
1 metric ton = 1,000 kilograms
1 quart = 0.94635 liters
1 US gallon = 3.7854 liters
1 Imperial gallon = 4.5459 liters
1 nautical mile = 1.852 km

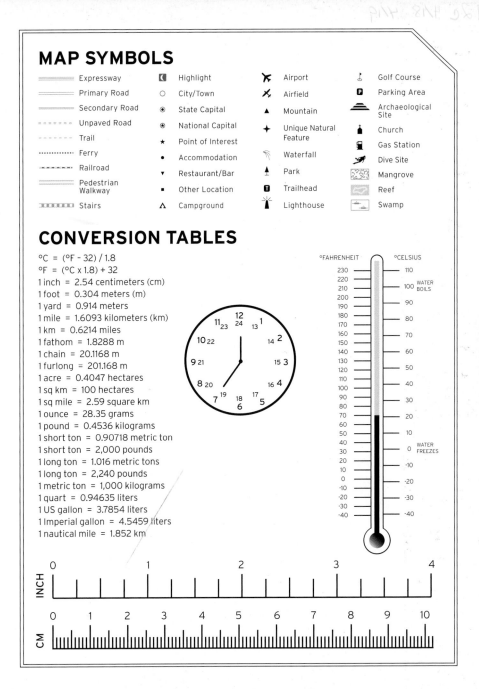

'12c 4/18 4/19

MOON CANCÚN & COZUMEL
Avalon Travel
a member of the Perseus Books Group
1700 Fourth Street
Berkeley, CA 94710, USA
www.moon.com

Editor and Series Manager: Kathryn Ettinger
Copy Editor: Ann Seifert
Graphics Coordinator: Lucie Ericksen
Production Coordinator: Lucie Ericksen
Cover Designer: Lucie Ericksen
Map Editor: Kat Bennett
Cartographers: Chris Henrick, Kat Bennett, Kaitlin Jaffe
Indexer: Greg Jewett

ISBN-13: 978-1-61238-615-7
ISSN: 1556-5122

Printing History
1st Edition – 1990
11th Edition – December 2013
5 4 3 2 1

Text © 2013 by Gary Chandler & Liza Prado.
Maps © 2013 by Avalon Travel.
All rights reserved.

Some photos and illustrations are used by permission and are the property of the original copyright owners.

Front cover photo: Playa del Carmen © Ian Dagnall/ Alamy

Title page photo: iguana in a tree © Liza Prado
Other front matter photos: pages 8, 9, 11 bottom-right, 14 left, 18, 22 right, 25-30: © Liza Prado; pages 10, 12, 13 bottom-left, 14 right, 17, 19 right, 22 left, 23: © Gary Chandler; page 20 © Jeff Wang/ iStock.com; pages 11 top and bottom-left, 13 top and bottom-right, 19 left: © H.W. Prado

Printed in China by RR Donnelley

All recommendations, including those for sights, activities, hotels, restaurants, and shops, are based on each author's individual judgment. We do not accept payment for inclusion in our travel guides, and our authors don't accept free goods or services in exchange for positive coverage.

KEEPING CURRENT

If you have a favorite gem you'd like to see included in
that needs updating, clarification, or correction, plea
ments via email to feedback@moon.com, or use the address above.